International Organization:
Theories and Institutions

International Organization:
Theories and Institutions

J. Samuel Barkin

INTERNATIONAL ORGANIZATION: THEORIES AND INSTITUTIONS

First published in 2006 by
PALGRAVE MACMILLAN™
175 Fifth Avenue, New York, N.Y. 10010 and
Houndmills, Basingstoke, Hampshire, England RG21 6XS.
Companies and representatives throughout the world.

PALGRAVE MACMILLAN is the global academic imprint of the Palgrave Macmillan division of St. Martin's Press, LLC and of Palgrave Macmillan Ltd. Macmillan® is a registered trademark in the United States, United Kingdom and other countries. Palgrave is a registered trademark in the European Union and other countries.

ISBN 1-4039-7248-6 hardback
ISBN 1-4039-7250-8 paperback

Library of Congress Cataloging-in-Publication Data

Barkin, J. Samuel, 1965-
    International organization : theories and institutions / J. Samuel Barkin
        p. cm.
    Includes bibliographical references and index.
    ISBN 1-4039-7248-6—ISBN 1-4039-7250-8 (pbk.)
        1. International organization. 2. International agencies. I. Title.
JZ1308.B37 2006
341.2—dc22   2005051247

A catalogue record for this book is available from the British Library.

Design by Macmillan India Ltd.

First edition: March 2006

10 9 8 7 6 5 4 3 2 1

Printed in the United States of America.

Transferred to digital printing in 2007.

Contents

List of Acronyms

ACCOBAMS	Agreement on the Conservation of Cetaceans of the Black Sea, Mediterranean Sea and Contiguous Atlantic Area
ADB (AfDB)	African Development Bank
ADB (AsDB)	Asian Development Bank
AFNOR	Association française de normalization
ANSI	American National Standards Institute
AU	The African Union
BIRPI	United International Bureaux for the Protection of Intellectual Property
CCAMLR	Convention for the Conservation of Antarctic Marine Living Resources
COE	Council of Europe
CSCE	Conference on Security and Co-operation in Europe
DPKO	United Nations Department of Peacekeeping Operations
DSM	Dispute Settlement Mechanism
EBRD	European Bank for Reconstruction and Development
ECOSOC	United Nations Economic and Social Council
ECOWAS	Economic Community of West African States
ECSC	European Coal and Steel Community
EEC	European Economic Community
EU	European Union
FAA	Federal Aviation Administration
FAO	Food and Agriculture Organization
G-77	Group of 77
GA	United Nations General Assembly
GATS	General Agreement on Trade in Services
GATT	General Agreement on Tariffs and Trade
GDP	Gross domestic product
GEF	Global Environment Facility
GSTP	Global System of Trade Preferences Among Developing Countries
IADB	Inter-American Development Bank
IASB	International Accounting Standards Board
IATA	International Air Transport Association

IBRD	International Bank for Reconstruction and Development
ICANN	Internet Corporation for Assigned Names and Numbers
ICAO	International Civil Aviation Organization
ICC	International Criminal Court
ICJ	International Court of Justice
ICPO	International Criminal Police Organization (also INTERPOL)
ICRC	International Committee of the Red Cross
ICSID	International Centre for the Settlement of Investment Disputes
ICTR	International Criminal Tribunal for Rwanda
ICTY	International Criminal Tribunal for the Former Yugoslavia
IDA	International Development Association
IFC	International Finance Corporation
IFI	International financial institution
ILO	International Labour Organization
IMF	International Monetary Fund
IMO	International Maritime Organization
INTELSAT	International Telecommunications Satellite Organization (currently ITSO)
INTERPOL	International Criminal Police Organization (also ICPO)
IO	International organization
IOC	International Olympic Committee
IPCC	Intergovernmental Panel on Climate Change
ISO	International Organization for Standardization
ITO	International Trade Organization
ITSO	International Telecommunications Satellite Organization (formerly INTELSAT)
IUCN	World Conservation Union
IWC	International Whaling Commission
MAI	Multilateral Agreement on Investment
MDG	UN Millennium Development Goals
NAFO	Northwest Atlantic Fisheries Organization
NATO	North Atlantic Treaty Organization
NGO	Non-governmental organization
NIEO	New International Economic Order
OAS	Organization of American States
OAU	Organization of African Unity
OECD	Organization for Economic Co-operation and Development
OEEC	Organization for European Economic Co-operation
OSCE	Organization for Security and Co-operation in Europe
PD	Prisoners' dilemma
SADC	Southern African Development Community
SARS	Severe Acute Respiratory Syndrome
SC	United Nations Security Council
SPS	Agreement on Sanitary and Phytosanitary Measures
TBT	Agreement on Technical Barriers to Trade
TNC	Transnational corporation

TRIMs	Agreement on Trade-Related Investment Measures
UDHR	Universal Declaration of Human Rights
UN	United Nations
UNCTAD	United Nations Conference on Trade and Development
UNDAF	United Nations Development Assistance Framework
UNDP	United Nations Development Programme
UNEP	United Nations Environment Programme
UNESCO	United Nations Educational, Scientific, and Cultural Organization
UNFCCC	United Nations Framework Convention on Climate Change
UNFICYP	United Nations Peacekeeping Force in Cyprus
UNHCHR	Office of the United Nations High Commissioner for Human Rights
UNHCR	Office of the United Nations High Commissioner for Refugees
UNICEF	United Nations Children's Fund
UNMIK	United Nations Interim Administration Mission in Kosovo
UNODC	United Nations Office on Drugs and Crime
UNRWA	United Nations Relief and Works Agency for Palestinian Refugees in the Near East
UPU	Universal Postal Union
USSR	Union of Soviet Socialist Republics
WFP	World Food Programme
WHO	World Health Organization
WIPO	World Intellectual Property Organization
WMO	World Meteorological Organization
WTO	World Trade Organization

Preface

This is not a book about international organizations (IOs). Nor is it a book about global governance. It is a book about IO theory, and about the use of this theory to understand international relations. It does not attempt to systematically review the world of IOs or to comprehensively describe the UN or any other particular organization. Its goal is to review IO theory, and to use particular IOs illustratively, to suggest ways in which the theories discussed can help us understand the role of IOs in international politics. Similarly, because its focus is exclusively on IO theory and the application of that theory to IOs, it does not attempt to deal with other aspects of global governance, such as the role of non-governmental organizations (NGOs) and global civil society in international relations.

This book is written as a primer for upper-level undergraduate students and for graduate students, either for courses on IOs or for the IO component of courses on international relations theory. It is designed either as a supplement to textbooks on IOs, or as an introduction to primary sources on IO theory (or both). In particular, the goal of the book is to show students of IOs the analytic tools available to them to understand what IOs are designed to do, how they work, what effects they have, and how to design them better. It goes beyond simple questions of whether IOs matter, and looks at the ways in which the different analytical tools developed within the rubric of IO theory are useful for answering different questions about the role of IOs in international politics.

The book is intended to fill what I see as a gap in books on IOs and IO theory: a gap between introductory textbooks and primary sources of theory. There are a number of books that do a good job of presenting the UN system from a bureaucratic, organizational, or historical perspective, but they are largely atheoretical. There are a number of introductory textbooks that present IOs in a theoretical context, but this context is based on a distinction between realism and liberalism that does not do justice to the breadth and nuance of IO theory. Primary sources for IO theory provide this breadth and nuance, but they generally relate theory to very specific questions or organizations. Putting these sources together to arrive at a big picture of IO theory can be a challenge for students. This book is designed to provide a concise bridge among these other categories of readings.

Books, even when authored alone, are always collaborative projects, and in the process of writing this one I have accumulated some debts of thanks. I would like to thank Beth DeSombre for comments on several versions of this manuscript, and much else besides, and Chip Hauss and Craig Murphy for their support for the project. The publication and editorial staff at Palgrave are excellent people to work with. Thanks are due to the Political Science Department of the University of Florida for its support of this project. Several generations of students in INR 3502 and INR 6507 (the course number for *International Organization* at the under-graduate and graduate levels, respectively, at the University of Florida) contributed (intentionally or not) to my thinking about how to teach about IO and IOs. Finally, thanks are due to Jessica Peet, who compiled the index for the volume.

Introduction: The State and International Organizations

The traditional literature in international relations begins with, and focuses on, states. From a political perspective, states have power, both military and economic, that other institutions or individuals do not. From a legal perspective, states are sovereign. In international law, states are recognized as actors; other institutions (or, for that matter, individuals) are not. And yet, international organizations (IOs) are attracting increasing attention, both positive and negative. They are also increasingly becoming a focus of study by political scientists. This book is an introduction to the study of IOs in the field of international relations. It looks at the different ways in which IOs are studied, and then applies these different modes of study to a variety of specific case studies.

Do IOs matter? What are their effects on international relations? Where do they fit into the international relations literature? How should we study them? These are the primary questions underlying this book. First, though, there is the matter of definition. "International organizations" are understood in this book to be inclusive intergovernmental organizations. Intergovernmental organizations, as opposed to nongovernmental organizations (NGOs) and corporations, are organizations that are created by agreement among states rather than by private individuals. Amnesty International, Greenpeace, and the General Motors Corporation all operate across national boundaries, but they were not created by governments. These NGOs and transnational corporations (TNCs) are integral parts of the international political system, but they are not IOs. The United Nations (UN), the Northwest Atlantic Fisheries Organization (NAFO), and the World Bank, however, were all created by treaties signed by states and are thus intergovernmental institutions. This book is about the latter group.[1]

Inclusive organizations are those that all interested parties can join, whereas exclusive organizations are those designed specifically to exclude some countries. The most common example of an exclusive intergovernmental organization is the military alliance. Military alliances are exclusive because some countries are inevitably kept out of them; that is the point of alliances. They are organizations designed to protect those in the alliance from those outside it. As such, military alliances, such as the North Atlantic Treaty Organization (NATO), are not covered in depth in this book. In contrast, even though the UN deals with security issues, it is an inclusive organization because all states can join it. Rather than defending states in the UN from those outside it, the UN is designed to protect its members from other members who break the rules. It should be noted here that regional organizations can be inclusive even if only members of the region can join, as long as the organization is focused inward and is not intended to work against those outside the region. An organization such as the European Union (EU) is in a middle ground between inclusive and exclusive organizations; in principle, all the countries of Europe can become members, but only after extensive negotiation with, and approval by, existing members.

Restricting the discussion to inclusive intergovernmental organizations may seem at first to be too restrictive, but doing so still leaves us with tens of thousands of organizations to look at and allows us to focus on the specific attributes of those organizations as a class. And these organizations cover a wide scope, in a number of ways. They can have anywhere from 2 to 200 member states (the UN, at the time of writing, has 191 members). They can have budgets anywhere from the tens of thousands of dollars per year to the billions. Some employ one staff member, others have thousands of people on the payroll. Some are relatively anonymous, with only people who work within the same arcane issue-area having heard of them; others, such as the UN or the World Bank, are household names. Finally, IOs cover a huge range of issue-areas. Some deal with issues of peace and security, others with human rights or international economic or environmental issues, and yet others with the coordination of international aviation or broadcast standards. In fact, there are few areas of contemporary life in which there are no IOs creating rules, monitoring behavior, or promoting cooperation.

How can we study these institutions? How do we know what they are accomplishing and whether they are working? This book begins to address these questions by looking at four distinctions to be found in the theoretical literature on IOs. These distinctions are reflected by the titles of Chapters 1 through 4: the distinction between sovereignty and globalization, between power and interdependence, between regimes and institutions, and between efficiency and ideas. The rest of the book is devoted to applying these distinctions, these sets of theoretical concepts, to a set of specific cases. Chapters 5 through 11 focus on particular IOs within each issue-area that are either representative or particularly central. The IOs discussed in the second half of the book are meant to be illustrative examples; these chapters do not provide comprehensive surveys of the organizations active in each issue-area. The EU is not covered in any of these chapters, both because it is in so many ways an outlier, different from other IOs, and because there is an extensive literature on the EU that is separate from the literature on IOs, one that is too large to cover comprehensively in one volume along with the general literature on IOs.

The first of the distinctions around which the first half of this book is organized is between sovereignty and globalization. Sovereignty is the starting point in traditional international relations theory, which sees world politics as a struggle for power among sovereign states. In the past decade, however, globalization has become a buzzword both for those applauding and for those opposing trends toward policy convergence among states. Is globalization undermining the sovereign state system? If so, what role do IOs play in the process? International organizations can be seen as the agents through which states are promoting the forces of globalization, or they can be seen as the agents that states are using to protect themselves from the broader forces of globalization. If the former, they are helping to undermine the traditional state system. If the latter, they are helping to support it. Chapter 1 looks at the theoretical relationship between IOs and globalization.

The second distinction follows from the first, and is the distinction between power and interdependence. Globalization results from, among other things, changes in technology, communications, and economics that make states more interdependent. In other words, the policy options of states are becoming increasingly constrained by the policy choices made by other states. Many analysts of IOs argue that they are the most effective ways for states to deal with interdependence. In other words, that they are vehicles through which states cooperate to promote the best outcomes for everyone in an interdependent world. Others argue, however, that IOs are not neutral agents of cooperation, but that they represent the interests of particular states and are mechanisms through which powerful states control less-powerful ones. Chapter 2 examines both arguments.

The third distinction is less about the place of IOs in the world, and more about how we can study them. This is the distinction between regimes and institutions. The regimes literature studies the effects of IOs on other actors in international relations, particularly states. It looks at IOs as if they were black boxes, and examines the inputs into and outputs from these boxes. The institutions literature looks within the organizations themselves, and asks how the structure of the organization as an institution, and the people within it, affect what the IO does. In other words, the regime approach looks at the effects of IOs on other actors, whereas the institutional approach looks at the organization itself as an actor. Chapter 3 looks at these two different approaches, and asks what sort of information can be had from which sort of analysis.

The fourth and final distinction relates to what it is that IOs actually accomplish. This distinction can best be represented as one between efficiency and ideas. Some analysts of IOs focus on their role in making relations among states as efficient as possible. They do this by submitting IOs to what is essentially an economic style of analysis. Other analysts focus on how IOs affect the way that states, national decision-makers, and global populations more broadly think. In other words, they examine the effects of IOs on norms of behavior in international politics. This calls for a more sociological mode of analysis. International organizations clearly affect both the efficiency of relations among states and the ideas underlying those relations, but the distinction is important in terms of *how* we study the effects of IOs. Chapter 4 discusses the methodologies of both approaches.

Chapter 5, on the UN system, provides necessary background information rather than being a comparative case study per se. Chapters 6 through 11 examine particular organizations and issue-areas through the lenses of theories of international organization. Chapter 6 looks at issues of peace and security, focusing on the concept of collective security and on the organizations involved in the collective security system. These include the Security Council and Secretariat of the UN, and regional collective security organizations such as the Organization for Security and Co-operation in Europe (OSCE) and the Organization of American States (OAS).

Chapter 7 focuses on issues of human rights and humanitarian aid. The institutions used as examples include the Office of the United Nations High Commissioner for Human Rights (UNHCHR), the Council of Europe (COE), the Office of the United Nations High Commissioner for Refugees (UNHCR), and the World Food Programme (WFP). Chapter 8 deals with the international political economy. It focuses on a comparison of the International Monetary Fund (IMF) and World Trade Organization (WTO), and discusses in less detail organizations such as the World Intellectual Property Organization (WIPO) and the Organization for Economic Co-operation and Development (OECD). Chapter 9 focuses on international development issues, using as examples the World Bank, the United Nations Development Programme (UNDP), and the United Nations Conference on Trade and Development (UNCTAD).

Chapter 10 is organized around a discussion of IOs that deal with some of the more mundane aspects of international life, but on which life in the modern world has come to depend. These are often referred to as functional organizations, and the examples discussed in this chapter include the International Civil Aviation Organization (ICAO), the Universal Postal Union (UPU), and the World Health Organization (WHO). Chapter 11 looks at some organizations that lie at the border of our definition of intergovernmental institutions. These organizations are either hybrids of IOs and NGOs, or are NGOs that play some official role in the international system. The examples discussed in the chapter include the International Organization for Standardization (ISO), the World Conservation Union (IUCN), the International Criminal Police Organization (ICPO, or Interpol), the International Telecommunications Satellite Organization (ITSO, formerly INTELSAT), the International Committee of the Red Cross (ICRC), and the International Olympic Committee (IOC). Finally, Chapter 12 revisits the basic questions underlying this book: Do international institutions matter, and how do we study them?

1

Sovereignty and Globalization

This chapter starts with the distinction between sovereignty and globalization as a way of getting at the big picture of international governance. What is the place of international organizations (IOs) in world politics? International organizations, defined here as inclusive intergovernmental organizations, are a relatively new phenomenon in international relations. They first appeared on the scene a little more than a century ago, in a modern state system that had already been around for more than 200 years. Before the advent of inclusive IOs there had been military alliances, exclusive intergovernmental organizations, among sovereign states. Predating the state system altogether were important international non-state actors such as the Catholic Church and the Holy Roman Empire. But these actors were not intergovernmental—they were not created by states, but rather existed independently of them.

The first organizations created by treaties among states designed specifically to deal with problems that a number of states faced in common appeared in the nineteenth century. At first they were designed to address very specific issues of an economic and technical nature, such as creating clear rules for navigation on the Rhine River, delivering international mail, or managing the Pacific fur seal fishery in a sustainable manner.[1] While these very focused organizations grew slowly in number, they were followed in the wake of World War I (1914–1918) by new organizations with broader remits. The best known of these organizations was the League of Nations, created to help its member nations to maintain international peace and security, and avoid a repeat of the horrors of the war. But other organizations with relatively broad mandates were created as well, such as the International Labour Organization (ILO), the charter of which allows the organization to deal with international labor issues, broadly defined.[2]

The ILO still exists, and still does roughly the same job envisioned by its creators. The League of Nations does not—it failed to prevent the World War II and failed to survive it. In the aftermath of the war, the League was replaced by an even more ambitious organization, the UN. A primary goal of the UN, as stated in its Charter, is to deal with the same sorts of issues of international peace and security that the League was supposed to deal with.[3] But the UN system brings under its umbrella a broad range of organizations that run the gamut of international issues.[4] Since

World War II, the number of IOs has proliferated, slowly at first, and more quickly in the past few decades. According to the Union of International Associations, the number of intergovernmental organizations crossed 1,000 in the early 1980s, and by the early twenty-first century, there were more than 5,000.[5]

Does this proliferation of IOs fundamentally change the way in which international politics works? International relations scholarship has traditionally regarded the sovereign state as the central institution in international politics. Recently, particularly in the past ten years, the concept of globalization has begun to appear in the international relations literature. A key implication of globalization is that the state is losing its autonomy as the central locus of decision-making in international relations. The debate between those who see the sovereign state as the key institution in world politics and those who see the process of globalization as displacing states is a good place to start the discussion of the role of IOs in international relations.

Sovereignty

When we think about international relations, we think primarily about the system of sovereign states. There are two key parts to such a system, what we might call internal sovereignty and external sovereignty. Internal sovereignty refers to autonomy, the ability of the state to make and enforce its own rules domestically. External sovereignty refers to the recognition of the state by other states, the acceptance of the state by the international community.[6] States do not necessarily have equal levels of both kinds of sovereignty. Taiwan, for example, has a level of internal sovereignty that is equivalent to that of many other industrialized countries. But it does not have full external sovereignty, and as a result cannot participate in many UN activities that lead to the creation of international rules. The Democratic Republic of the Congo, by contrast, has full external sovereignty, and can thus participate more fully in international activities. But it has limited internal sovereignty, because it has no control over what happens in much of its territory.[7]

The sovereign state system has not always been the central organizing feature of international relations. Empires, rather than sovereign states, wrote much of the political history of ancient civilizations, and the feudal era in Europe featured overlapping and territorially indistinct patterns of political authority. The genesis of the current system of states has often been dated back to 1648, when the Peace of Westphalia ended the Thirty Years War by diminishing the political role of many tiers of the feudal nobility. While this is a simplification of history, much of the system of sovereign states as we know it emerged in seventeenth-century Europe.[8]

One important feature of sovereignty, however, changed fundamentally in the nineteenth century. In the seventeenth and eighteenth centuries, princes were sovereign. From the perspective of the international community, a country was the property of its ruler, and representatives of the country represented the interests of the ruler, rather than of the population. Beginning in the nineteenth century, and even more so in the twentieth, citizens became sovereign. Rulers became representative of their populations, rather than the other way around.[9] In the twentieth century, even dictators usually claimed to be ruling in the interests of the people, rather than for their own gain. This meant that although countries still warred with their neighbors to increase their territory, they also became more likely to cooperate with their neighbors to maximize the welfare of their citizens. This helps to explain the genesis of intergovernmental cooperation through IOs in the nineteenth century.

Globalization

But is this cooperation, and the increased prevalence of IOs that results from it, undermining sovereignty? The most popular set of arguments that it is can be called the globalization approach.[10] This approach begins with the observation that a set of transnational forces, ranging from mobile investment capital to global environmental degradation, is limiting the ability of states to make independent policy decisions. There are two effects of these forces. The first is an increasing tendency to act multilaterally rather than unilaterally—in other words, to create and act through IOs.[11] The other effect is to mold policy to fit the dictates of international economic forces.[12] A combination of these effects can be seen in many issue-areas. In international trade issues, for example, many states participate in the World Trade Organization (WTO) for fear of being ignored by international investors and transnational corporations (TNCs) if they do not.

Globalization can undermine both internal and external sovereignty. It can undermine internal sovereignty by diminishing state autonomy. The more practical decision-making power is transferred from governments to both IOs and non-governmental actors, the less ability states have to meaningfully make policy decisions. This can affect some states more than others. The United States, for example, has much more input into the making and changing of WTO rules than, say, Singapore, even though Singapore, being much more of a trading nation than the United States, is affected more by the rules. Critics of globalization also hold it responsible for what is called a regulatory "race to the bottom," in which governments compete to get rid of labor and environmental regulations in order to attract investment by internationally mobile capital.[13] Countries can avoid this phenomenon, goes the argument, but only at great economic cost.

Globalization can undermine external sovereignty by loosening the monopoly of the sovereign state system on international political activity. This argument suggests that the more decision-making autonomy that IOs get, the more scope private actors such as NGOs have to participate in international policy-making, and the weaker the traditional state system becomes. Furthermore, the more that IOs are looked to as the arbiters of regulation internationally, the more TNCs may be able to avoid being subject to national regulations, further weakening the state system. Of those who see IOs as helping to undermine state autonomy, some see it as a good thing, others as a bad thing. Some human rights and environmental activists, for example, see internationalization as the only effective check on regulatory races to the bottom.[14] Others see IOs as contributing to the problem by forcing on countries international rules pertaining to issues such as trade, which are not sensitive to local conditions or problems.[15]

These sorts of arguments are not new. In the early days of the Cold War, proponents of world government saw it as the best way to avoid perhaps the ultimate transnational problem, large-scale nuclear war.[16] Opponents of world government saw it as akin to losing the Cold War, as a means of selling out our values to a global lowest common denominator. The language of the debate has changed from world government to globalization, and the idea of a centralized world government has given way to one of a more diffuse form of global governance, but the basic issues being debated have not changed fundamentally. But are those who believe that globalization is undermining sovereignty right?

Realism, Internationalism, and Universalism

One organizational framework that might help us to address this question is provided by Hedley Bull in *The Anarchical Society: A Study of Order in World Politics*.[17] Bull speaks of three traditions of thought in understanding the problem of international order: the realist tradition, the internationalist tradition, and the universalist tradition. The realist tradition sees states in a situation of anarchy, with little to constrain them except the power of other states. The internationalist tradition sees international relations as taking place within a society of states: states are the primary actors, but they are bound by this society's rules of behavior. The universalist tradition looks not to international politics, understood as politics among states, but to a global politics, which represents people directly as individuals rather than through states. Each of these three traditions takes a very different view of IOs, and each view can be instructive in helping us to understand the role of these organizations in international relations.

Realism looks to the role of IOs in international relations with some skepticism. For realists, the ultimate arbiter of outcomes in international relations is power. Outcomes can be expected to favor those with the most power, or those who bring their power to bear most effectively. And for realists, in the contemporary world, states are the organizations with the most power. States control most of the planet's military power, have an ability to tax that is not shared by any other institution, and are the issuers of the world's currencies.[18] International organizations share none of these features. Having no independent military capability, they depend on states to enforce their rules. Having no ability to tax, they depend on states to fund them. Having no territory, they depend on states to host them. As such, IOs can only really succeed when backed by powerful states. For realists, then, it makes little sense to focus attention on IOs, because IOs reflect the existing balance of power and the interests of powerful states. As such, it makes more sense to understand IOs as tools in the power struggles of states, than as independent actors or independent effects.[19]

The internationalist tradition has roots in the study of international law rather than in the study of power politics. It sees states in international society as somewhat analogous to people in domestic society. Domestic society works because most people follow most of its rules most of the time. Similarly, analysts of the internationalist tradition argue that most states follow most international law most of the time.[20] At any given point in time, the argument goes, there are generally accepted rules about how states should relate to each other, and we cannot understand international politics without looking at those rules. Even during times of war, when we would expect international society to be at its weakest, states usually follow certain rules of acceptable conduct. They do not necessarily do this out of altruism, in the same way that people in domestic society do not necessarily follow laws out of altruism. Rather, they recognize that they all benefit from a society that is rule-governed, and are therefore willing to accept rules if those rules bind others as well. From this perspective, IOs become the expressions of the rules that govern international society. Whether or not IOs have an independent effect as actors in international relations depends on whether they create the rules, or simply oversee rules created by agreement among states. But in either case, IOs are important because they regulate relations among states. It is important to note here, though, that from this perspective, states are still seen as the primary actors in international relations.

The universalist tradition differs fundamentally from both the realist and internationalist traditions in that it is not state-centric. Whereas the internationalist tradition sees states as constrained by the norms of a society of states, the universalist tradition sees states as increasingly irrelevant in the face of a developing global society, a society of people rather than of states. This tradition shares with the internationalist tradition the presupposition that domestic society works as much because its population accepts its rules as because the state enforces them. The difference is that the internationalist tradition applies this by analogy to states, whereas the universalist tradition applies it to people globally.[21] The greater the extent to which global civil society comes to be governed by a set of rules and behavioral norms shared across different peoples and cultures, the greater the extent to which it is this civil society, rather than the society of states, that guides global politics. In this tradition, IOs are more important as expressions of, and creators of, global civil society than they are as regulators of relations among states.[22] Accordingly, IOs should be studied as partial replacements for states rather than as mediators among states.

Approaching the sovereignty/globalization debate from the perspective of these three traditions, we get three different answers to what is happening. The pure realist answer to the question of the future of sovereignty is that the sovereign state system is continuing much the same as always. States remain the locus of power in the international system. Therefore, external sovereignty can be expected to remain as strong as ever, because states, the organizations with the power, have an interest in keeping it that way. In this view, states' degree of internal sovereignty is also not changing. Larger states are not losing autonomy to IOs, because those same large states are creating the rules of those organizations. Smaller, weaker states, it is true, do lack autonomy in the face of some IOs, but these states were always subject to a similar degree to the preferences of the larger, more powerful states.[23]

The pure universalist answer to the question of the future of sovereignty is that globalization is undermining it. The greater the extent to which IOs make rules that reflect global civil society, the less autonomy states have to make rules domestically that are incongruent with international norms. By the same logic, globalization also undermines external sovereignty, as IOs, NGOs, and other representatives of global civil society begin to replace states as the legitimate representatives of the global citizenry.[24]

The internationalist answer to the future of sovereignty in the face of globalization depends on whether one is asking about internal or external sovereignty. The internationalist tradition agrees with the universalist that globalization is eroding internal sovereignty, the autonomy of states to make rules domestically as they see fit. As international society, as represented by IOs, becomes stronger, states are increasingly bound to make rules collectively rather than individually. For example, as states participate increasingly in international trade, they gain a greater stake in trade rules that everyone shares, because trade would be hurt by the absence of such rules. This leaves states with less autonomy to make rules that conflict with those embodied in IOs. At the same time, however, the internationalist tradition agrees with the realist that the sovereign state system remains strong in the face of globalization. Rules are being made by states collectively rather than individually, but they are still being made by states.

This increasing tendency of states to make rules collectively is often labeled multilateralism and is the basis of a school of analysis located within the internationalist tradition. Unilateralism refers to a state acting alone, bilateralism to two states acting together. Multilateralism refers to a system in which it is expected that states will act as a group, through negotiation and IOs. The multilateralist school of analysis argues that multilateralism has, in the past half century or so, become the expected way of doing business internationally.[25] States, multilateralists argue, still sometimes act alone, but this has become the exception rather than the rule. As such, multilateralism is a concept that will reappear regularly throughout this book.

Multilateralism can be seen as a form of globalization. In fact, antiglobalization protestors often point to multilateral organizations, such as the WTO and the IMF, as undermining national autonomy, the ability of countries to make trade and monetary policy to suit local conditions.[26] In other words, antiglobalization protestors are often opposed to some of the ways in which multilateralism undermines internal sovereignty. But it is also possible to argue that the state system as a whole, and with it external sovereignty, is actually made stronger when IOs are responsible for international decision-making. Multilateralism, and internationalist logic more generally, sees states, as opposed to other political actors or other potential representatives of global civil society, as the key decision-makers and policy-makers in global politics. To the extent that only states have votes in IOs and that only states participate in multilateral decision-making, multilateralism reinforces the role of the state. In other words, rather than undermining sovereignty, the multilateralist system is creating a new kind of sovereignty.

A good example of the tension between the internationalist and the universalist impulses in the creation of IOs can be found in the European Union (EU). The EU is an IO whose members share a common market for international trade and common legislation on a wide variety of issues ranging from social policy to environmental policy. The EU also has its own legal institutions and is developing its own foreign policy and military capability. This makes the EU the most wide-ranging and comprehensive IO. It has twenty-five members from throughout Europe, including ten countries from central and eastern Europe and the Mediterranean that became members in May of 2004.

There are three central bodies that participate in making EU policy and legislation. The first is the European Commission, which is a bureaucracy made up of commissioners who come from all the member countries, but who are meant to represent the EU rather than the country that appointed them. The second is the European Parliament, which is made up of members directly elected by the populations of the member countries. Conversely, the third body, the Council of Ministers, is made up of national politicians whose job is to represent their countries in making EU policy. The Commission and the Parliament can be seen as exercises in universalism. They are pan-European bodies that are supposed to both represent and develop a pan-European political consciousness. The Council, on the other hand, is more straightforwardly internationalist. It is an intergovernmental body in which participants representing individual countries act in the name of member governments to promote the national interest of those countries. The evolution of the EU, and its current politics, reflects this institutional compromise between a universalist EU and an internationalist EU. Either way, members of the EU have given up broad swathes of their decision-making autonomy—they are committed to enact regulations decided upon at the EU level. But individual states remain much more important actors in the Council, where they are directly involved in decision-making, than they are in the Commission and Parliament, where they are not.[27]

Globalization and Democracy

There are two ways to look at the realist, internationalist, and universalist traditions. One way is as descriptions of what is actually happening in the world of IOs. Each tradition allows us to look at an institution from a different perspective and thereby learn different things about it. Looking, for example, at the WTO, an internationalist lens allows us to observe the ways in which states are cooperating for their collective benefit. A realist lens allows us to observe the ways in which the more powerful states can achieve rules closer to their interests than to the interests of weaker states. A universalist lens allows us to observe the ways in which the WTO as an organization, and the idea of a rules-based trade system as a norm, are replacing states as the locus of real decision-making in issues of international trade. The balance among these three perspectives may well differ from organization to organization. Some IOs, for example, might offer greater scope for power politics than others, and some might engage in more universalist, rather than intergovernmental, decision-making than others. But we can address this balance empirically, by studying individual IOs and what they do. This balance will be discussed in more detail in the next chapter.

The other way to look at the three traditions is normatively. Looked at this way, each tradition describes not the way in which IOs *do* work, but the way in which they *should* work. Realists believe that the state should represent the interests of its citizens rather than pursue a global common good. Universalists often see direct global governance, rather than a competitive state system, as an ultimate goal. And to internationalists, a society of states regulated by IOs combines the best of both the realist and the universalist traditions.

Whether or not any one of these traditions provides a more accurate description of contemporary international politics than the other two is open to empirical argument. But these traditions can also be used normatively, as sources of moral arguments about what international politics should look like. One illustrative line of moral argumentation concerns the relationship between IOs and democracy. The effects of IOs on democratic governance are important parts of both the anti- and proglobalization arguments, and a different perspective on these effects is offered by each of the three traditions. None of these perspectives is inherently more or less right than the others, and all provide perspectives worth considering.

Realism

There is a tendency to see the realist tradition as amoral, as simply a practical acceptance of the reality of power politics. But there is a democratic argument to be made for retaining state autonomy in matters of decision-making. Allowing nation-states to make their own rules allows different cultures to govern themselves as they see fit. Autonomy also fosters competition among states for better governance. (World government, its critics might argue, is no more than a lowest common denominator, and encounters little pressure to improve.)[28] Under the heading of the realist tradition here could be included nationalists, both cultural and economic, who feel that the role of the state is to represent the interests of its citizens and of its culture. If the state defers to a global good while other states pursue their own interests, then the state, and its citizens, lose.

There are three key empirical arguments against this realist perspective on the morality and democratic legitimacy of power politics. The first is that because of power disparities among states, only the interests of those who happen to live in powerful states determine international outcomes. Realism thus looks very different from the perspective of the United States than it does from the perspective of the Central African Republic. The second is that as the issues facing states are increasingly global in nature, global rather than national solutions are needed. Attempts to deal with issues such as climate change, air traffic control, or the international financial architecture through purely national policy are futile. The third argument against the realist perspective that state decision-making autonomy is preferable to collective decision-making is that competition among states can do much more harm than good. Competition can lead to stable balances of power, and it can lead to policy innovation. But it can also lead to hostility and war, in a way that multilateral or universalist cooperation are unlikely to.[29]

Internationalism

The moral claim made in this context by proponents of an internationalist perspective is that a multilateralist state system is more democratic than a competitive state system. Because multilateralism is a process in which all concerned states can participate, both the more powerful ones and the weaker ones, it allows all peoples to be represented in the making of international rules. In IOs such as the UN General Assembly (GA), this equal representation is formalized by a one-country, one-vote system. To the extent that the trend internationally is for more states to become democratic, the link between representative government at the domestic level and representative government at the international level is even stronger. International organizations then become representative bodies of states, which are themselves representative bodies of citizens. As is the case with domestic legislatures, decisions are made by elected representatives of the people.

This internationalist perspective is itself, however, open to criticism. Where internationalists see democratic representation, some critics see decision-making behind closed doors by an international elite. Others see the process of negotiation leading up to the creation of IOs and the modification of their rules as an exercise in the finding of lowest common denominators that often please no one. Universalists see negotiations among states as favoring existing national elites, and as freezing out the institutions of international civil society, such as NGOs. Antiglobalization protestors at meetings of the WTO or of the international financial institutions (IFIs, primarily the IMF and World Bank) indeed attack these multilateral negotiating forums from both perspectives: economic nationalists argue that these IOs need tighter rules or no rules, while universalists demand more direct participation for NGOs that represent human rights or environmental issues.

Universalism

Universalists argue that it is only through the direct representation of global civil society that international relations can become more democratic. As such, any effort to improve direct representation by separating IOs from direct control by member states is a positive development. At present, the two most common ways of ensuring that this happens are increasing the autonomy of IOs and increasing NGO participation in them.

But both independent IO decision-making and NGO participation can also be criticized as antidemocratic. Nongovernmental organizations may well be expressions of global civil society, but they are not elected, and they represent the interests of their members, not of the population at large. Critics of NGO participation in IOs also point out that NGO membership is disproportionately biased toward middle-class, white citizens of Western states. In this sense, NGOs can be criticized as being neocolonial, as a mechanism for reintroducing rule by the West over the South through nonmilitary means.[30] Independent IO decision-making can similarly be criticized as being neocolonial, because the secretariats of IOs tend to be made up of "professionals," people trained in Western techniques for managing their issue-areas.[31] Even if they are acting from the best of intentions, they may focus on what they think they should do rather than what the population at large wants them to do.

Conclusion

Most of this book looks at IOs at the micro level, at the workings of particular IOs and their effects within their issue-areas. This chapter, focusing on the sovereignty/globalization distinction, looks at the macro level, at the effects of IOs in general, and individual IOs in particular, on patterns of global governance in general. Of the four distinctions discussed in the introduction, that between sovereignty and globalization is the only one that focuses broadly on the effects of IOs on governance patterns, rather than on governance outcomes within particular issue-areas. This broad focus provides both an opportunity and a potential pitfall. The pitfall is getting stuck at the general level. This can be seen in some discussions about globalization: arguments that globalization is good or bad miss the complexity of the issue. The distinction between sovereignty and globalization is nonetheless both a good starting point for discussions of IOs, and something worth keeping in mind when looking at IOs at the micro level. In particular, it is worth asking, as one looks at the effectiveness of an IO in dealing with a particular issue-area, does this present a good model of the way the world should be governed?

2
—

Power and Interdependence

Another of the distinctions that provide the theoretical focus for this book is that between power and interdependence. This distinction is related to that between sovereignty and globalization. The realist tradition assumes that power is the ultimate arbiter of outcomes in international relations. Both the internationalist and the universalist traditions take interdependence as a basic assumption. Dependence refers to a situation in which a state cannot effectively make and enforce policy on its own, but can do so only in cooperation with another country or countries. Interdependence is when these other countries, in turn, also find themselves dependent on the first country. A key part of the concept of interdependence, then, is reciprocity.[1] The internationalist response to interdependence is cooperation among states. The universalist response is the replacement of states by centralization of decision-making.

One interpretation of the internationalist tradition would be that with multilateral cooperation in decision-making, cooperation would replace power as the focus of international politics. The debate between the pure cooperation position and the pure power position has often taken place using the language of absolute and relative gains.[2] Absolute gains are gains that states make compared with what would have been the case otherwise. For example, if a bilateral free trade agreement increases gross economic output of the two countries that have signed it by 3 percent over what would have been the case without the agreement, and both countries share in that increase equally, then both countries would have absolute gains of 3 percent in their GDPs. Relative gains are gains that a state makes in comparison with its rivals. For example, if two rival states increase their military force levels by 3 percent each, neither will have made a relative gain, because their force levels would have stayed the same relative to each other. If, however, one state's force level stays the same and that of its rival increases by one division, the first state's relative force level would have declined by a division, even though its absolute force level stayed the same.

If one state makes a gain of 4 percent and the other a gain of 2 percent, both states would have gained in absolute terms, but in relative terms, one state would have gained and the other would have lost. Whether a state in this situation perceives itself as gaining or losing depends on how that state defines its interests. Realists, who tend to see issues of security as paramount, argue that in measures of military capabilities only relative gains matter, because military capabilities are measured against the capabilities of other states. Economists, for whom trade issues are paramount, usually focus on absolute gains, because what matters to them is the ability of individuals to consume. Therefore, they focus on the amount available to individuals with international cooperation compared with the amount available to the same individuals without cooperation.[3]

Despite the relative/absolute gains debate, most students of international organizations (IOs) would agree that states care about both. In multilateral negotiations, states generally care about both a good overall outcome and an outcome that reflects their own particular national interests, although the balance between the two can vary.[4] States that participate in trade negotiations, for example, are likely to care both that the agreement maximizes global economic output and that they benefit individually as much as possible from the increase in output. In other words, both interdependence and power matter. The question for students of IOs then becomes, How do we study and contrast these two phenomena?

The phrase "power and interdependence" is familiar to most students of international relations theory from a book of the same title by Robert Keohane and Joseph Nye, first published in 1977.[5] Keohane and Nye argue that the traditional focus by students of power politics on force in international affairs is becoming obsolete. In some parts of the world, such as India and Pakistan, military power still matters. But, argue Keohane and Nye, in other parts of the world, such as the United States and Canada, the military balance is largely irrelevant, because neither country considers the use of force to settle bilateral disputes. They call the pattern of international relations in these latter parts of the world "complex interdependence."[6]

Complex interdependence has three key characteristics. As already mentioned, one of these characteristics is that military force plays a minor role in settling disputes. A second characteristic is that states have multiple channels of communication with each other. In essence, this means that national bureaucracies negotiate directly with each other. For example, if the United States and Canada are negotiating a fisheries agreement, it will probably be negotiated between officials of the National Marine Fisheries Service and the Department of Fisheries and Oceans, rather than by the Secretary of State and the Foreign Minister. On other issues, other sets of bureaucrats in different bureaucratic hierarchies negotiate with each other, often without much central coordination. The third characteristic is that there is no clear hierarchy of issues. In a traditional realist world, national security issues matter more than other issues. In a complex interdependent world, states do not clearly prioritize issues. A diverse array of issue-areas, ranging from security to trade, finance, the environment, human rights, telecommunications policy, and health policy may find their way onto the international agenda, but states do not clearly prioritize among them.

This complex interdependent world is similar to the globalized world, with cooperation among states, envisioned by internationalists, as discussed in Chapter 1. States generally deal with global issues multilaterally, without clearly prioritizing some issues over others, and with a focus on finding the best technical solutions rather than on political gain. Keohane and Nye do not conclude from this, however, that power has become irrelevant. Military power continues to be important in those parts of the world that are less involved in complex interdependent multilateralism. And even in the core of the complex interdependent world, power remains relevant. The difference is that power in a multilateralist world no longer comes primarily from the threat of military force, because such threats are rarely credible. Rather, in these contexts, power comes from asymmetries in interdependence.[7]

In a dependent relationship, State A depends on State B, but State B does not depend on State A. This should give State B power over State A, because State B can threaten to terminate their relationship. Should the relationship be terminated, it would hurt State A much more than State B. As an example, during the oil crisis of 1973–1974, many Western states depended on Persian Gulf states for petroleum, but the Gulf states did not depend on Western states for anything as critical in the short term. This gave the Gulf states (after an embargo of a few months, to show that their threat of terminating the relationship was credible) the power to dictate oil prices to Western states and contract terms to Western oil companies.[8]

In a perfectly interdependent relationship, State A and State B depend on each other equally. As such, neither state can credibly threaten to terminate or impede their relationship, because everyone knows that this would be equally costly to both states. This means that neither state can gain an advantage in bargaining power from the level of dependence of the other. To continue with the example used above, in the 1980s, most Western countries reduced their dependence on petroleum from the Persian Gulf by improving their energy efficiency and by finding other sources of supply. At the same time, many of the states in the Gulf became more dependent on the West for trade, services, and security. These trends reduced asymmetries in dependence to the point where the Gulf states could no longer credibly expect that the threat of an embargo would allow them to dictate prices.

Perfectly interdependent relationships, however, are not the norm in international relations, even in a complex interdependent world. In between pure dependence and perfect interdependence, there are asymmetries in interdependence. This is when all countries depend on each other, but some more than others. For example, both the United States and Singapore would suffer if the WTO, and with it, multilateral rules on international trade, collapsed. But the Singaporean economy is much more dependent on trade than the U.S. economy, so Singapore would suffer proportionally more.[9] Singapore's greater dependence on trade gives the United States greater bargaining power than Singapore in negotiations on WTO rules. As a general rule, the greater the asymmetry of interdependence, the greater the relative power of the less-dependent country.

Keohane and Nye look at these issues from a primarily internationalist perspective. A complex interdependent world is one in which states are still the primary agents of governance internationally, but in which they approach this governance multilaterally rather than unilaterally. From this perspective, the primary question of the role of power in the study of IOs is how state power manifests itself in the creation and management of IOs. From a universalist perspective, the question is different. A universalist would look less at the power of states as it affects IOs than at the power of IOs themselves and at the relationship between their power and the power of states.

Power in IOs

Beginning with the internationalist perspective, there are a number of sources of state power and a number of ways in which the power of particular states can be expressed in the creation and management of IOs. Power can be expressed in negotiations, in the setting of agendas, and in the creation of institutional bureaucracies and procedures. Sources of power include asymmetries of interdependence among countries, asymmetrical dependence of IOs on particular countries, structural power, and ideology.

The most straightforward expression of state power in the creation of IOs and multilateral rules is negotiating power. When an issue comes up, and State A favors one outcome and State B another, and in the end State B accedes to the preferred outcome of State A, then State A can be said to have greater negotiating power than State B. In practice, it can be a little more difficult to identify negotiating power. State A might have made a concession on some other issue, or State B might simply have cared less about this particular issue than State A. But on the whole, it is clear that some states, such as the United States, have more overall negotiating power in multilateral forums than others, such as Monaco or Burundi.[10]

Negotiating power can be thought of as the direct use of power by a state in managing an IO. But there is also what has been called the "second face of power,"[11] that is, the ability to set the agenda. Negotiating power looks at who gets their way on an issue that comes up for discussion. The second face of power looks at who gets to set the negotiating agenda in the first place, or, who gets to decide what gets talked about and what does not. Agenda-setting power can be more difficult to study than negotiating power, because it involves looking at what does not happen, rather than at what does. In other words, it involves asking about the things that did not make it onto an IO's agenda, which is an inherently more open-ended question than looking at the outcomes of issues that did make it onto the agenda.

As an example of agenda-setting power, consider the negotiations leading up to the Kyoto Protocol to the United Nations Framework Convention on Climate Change (UNFCCC). The negotiations were based on the idea that each state would cut back greenhouse gas emissions a certain amount from their existing emission levels. As a result, the states that polluted the most before the negotiations can continue to pollute the most under the terms of the Protocol. This approach can be seen as favoring states that came into the negotiations as particularly heavy polluters, and as penalizing both countries that were more environmentally responsible in the past and countries that were too poor to have polluted much at that point. Other pollution baselines, such as one based on national population, are conceivable, but were not on the negotiating agenda. Does this mean that none of the states were interested in talking about this possibility, or that some states had an interest in keeping this possibility off the agenda and had the power to do so? Arriving at an answer requires looking in considerable detail at the prenegotiation process, the process through which the agenda was decided.[12]

One can also speak of a third face of power, the power to shape the way people think about issues.[13] Take, for example, the preference shown by the United States since the 1980s for the use of market mechanisms in dealing with pollution issues. As a result of this, many IOs have included market mechanisms in their issue-areas, even though the United States has made no active effort to put them on the agenda. Joseph Nye, while discussing U.S. foreign policy, calls this "soft power."[14] The third face of power is thus the ability to set general terms of discourse. The third face of power is even more difficult to identify empirically than the second. Do IOs use market mechanisms more than they used to because of U.S. power, or because market mechanisms have worked well in the past? It can be very difficult to tell.

The final entry on the list of ways in which states can express power with respect to IOs is through the creation of institutional bureaucracies and procedures. This can be called institutional power. It refers to the ability of particular states to put their own people into positions of power in IO bureaucracies, and the ability of particular states to affect the structures of those bureaucracies in ways that suit their interests. This can vary from institution to institution. For example, the President of the World Bank and the Managing Director of the IMF are always an American and a European, respectively, but since 1982, the Secretary-General of the UN has been from a developing country. This reflects the different levels of relative institutional power of the North and South in these two institutions.

There are thus a variety of ways in which state power can be expressed in the creation and management of IOs. But what is the source of this power? The answer that Keohane and Nye provide us with is asymmetries of interdependence.[15] When one country needs an IO less than another, it will have relatively more power in creating and managing it. In the case of the World Bank, for example, some countries primarily put money into the organization, and others primarily borrow from it. The borrowers, for the most part, need the organization more than the investors. This means that investors are more willing to walk away from the organization than the borrowers, which gives the investors bargaining leverage with respect to the borrowers, a leverage that in effect gives them relative power within the organization. This allows the investors to maintain, and freeze borrowers from, direct control of the World Bank.

Asymmetries of interdependence can be less straightforward. Sometimes, wealthier countries need an agreement more, or faster, than poorer ones, which undermines their negotiating power.[16] In negotiations over geosynchronous satellite spots, for example, countries that had no ability to build or launch such satellites received concessions from those that did, because the latter needed an agreement relatively quickly, and the former did not.[17] In environmental negotiations, states that are recipients of other states' pollution need the biggest polluters to participate in IOs in order for those IOs to usefully address the problem. This gives big polluters, or even potential big polluters, negotiating power, because the recipients of pollution are asymmetrically dependent on them to solve the problem.[18] Asymmetries of interdependence, in short, need to be established on a case-by-case basis, and are not always obvious.

Asymmetries of interdependence not only affect states in their relationships with each other and with IOs, but also affect IOs in their relationships with states. For example, when the United States started withholding dues in an attempt to force the UN to reform its administration and budgeting, the UN reacted by undertaking reforms in an attempt to appease the United States and get it to pay its dues.[19] Had Nauru withheld its dues for the same reason, it is unlikely that the UN would have reacted at all. This difference is probably caused by relative levels of UN financial dependence—it receives 22 percent of its budget from the United States, and 0.001 percent of its budget from Nauru.[20] The UN's financial dependence on the United States has given the latter substantial power to force change in the UN.

An additional source of power for some states with respect to others in the forum of IOs is structural. This refers to elements in the structure of particular IOs that confer power to particular states or groups of states at the expense of others. These structural elements can be constitutional, enshrined in the treaty that gave rise to the organization. They can also stem from such factors as personnel or location.

There are several constitutional elements of an IO that can confer relative power to some states rather than others. One of the most straightforward of these elements is voting structure. A majority of IOs work on a one-country, one-vote basis. But not all do. In the UN, for example, each country has the same one vote in the General Assembly (GA) and most of its subsidiary bodies. But in the Security Council, five specific countries have a special voting category that allows them to singlehandedly veto resolutions, an ability not shared by the other ten members of the Security Council. [21] Structurally, this veto power gives those five states significantly more power than the non-veto states in the central security organ of the contemporary multilateral system. Most countries have no vote at all in the Council at any given point in time, and many have never had the opportunity to serve on the Council at all.

There are other examples of IOs that do not have a one-country, one-vote rule. Both the World Bank and the IMF, for example, have voting structures based on what is called historical subscription. This means that a country's proportion of the total vote in those institutions is equal to the proportion of capital that the country has put into the organization over its history. In practice, in the IMF, the United States has more than 17 percent of the vote, and Japan and Germany each have more than 6 percent. Several dozen countries, meanwhile, have less than 0.1 percent of the vote.[22] There are some IOs in which the European Union (EU), rather than its constituent countries, is a member, meaning that it gets one vote rather than the twenty-five it would get if its constituent countries voted separately.[23]

Even the one-country, one-vote rule is not power-neutral. China, with more than 1.2 billion people, gets the same one vote as Palau, with fewer than 100,000 people. This has the effect of empowering less-populous countries. And within one-country, one-vote systems, different levels of majority are needed for a vote to carry. Sometimes, a simple majority suffices, as is the case with most GA resolutions. At other times, a two-thirds or three-quarters majority, or even consensus, is needed. For example, decisions by the GA on "important issues," including the admission of new members and the apportioning of budgetary dues, require a two-thirds majority.[24] The Convention for the Conservation of Antarctic Marine Living Resources (CCAMLR) requires consensus for "matters of substance," but simple majorities for other matters.[25] The higher the voting threshold, the greater the power of individual disaffected countries to block agreement. Simple majority systems empower the median state, the country with the average opinion, because that country is needed to carry a majority either way. Consensus systems empower those states whose preferences are farthest from average, because they have the ability to hold up agreement until they are appeased.

As well as voting rules, other constitutional elements of international relations such as problem definition and bureaucratic structure can convey structural power to specific states. The effects of these constitutional elements on relative state power are often less clear than those of voting structure, but they are real nonetheless. Both problem definition and bureaucratic structure play a role in influencing the way in which an IO is set up to deal with a particular issue. The closer problem definition is to a country's own interest in that issue, the more empowered that country is likely to be by the IO. Bureaucratic structure often follows from problem definition, reinforcing the effect.

Take two examples, fisheries and narcotics. The Northwest Atlantic Fisheries Organization (NAFO) was created by the countries that account for most of the fishing in the international waters of the northwest Atlantic, with a mandate to maximize long-term potential fishing yields of individual species. The structure of NAFO includes a scientific committee, the job of which is to provide scientific estimates of how much of each species fished commercially in the region can be fished in any given year without depleting the breeding stock and undermining the long-term viability of the fishery. This problem definition and bureaucratic structure has the effect of favoring the interests of coastal states (primarily Canada and Greenland) over noncoastal states with long-range fleets that fish in the region. It does so because the coastal states tend to be more interested in long-term viability of the stock, which is an issue best determined scientifically, whereas countries with long-range fleets tend to be more interested in maximizing returns in the medium term, which is a less technical and more political issue.[26]

In the case of narcotics, IOs that are involved in international narcotics issues, such as the United Nations Office on Drugs and Crime (UNODC), tend to focus on the production and export of narcotics rather than on the importation and consumption of narcotics.[27] This problem definition tends to favor major consumer countries, such as the United States, over major producer countries, such as Colombia. A problem definition that focuses on production and export puts the onus on producing and exporting countries to change their behavior, but does not require of importing and consuming countries a similar change in behavior. In short, the problem is defined internationally as being the fault of the exporters rather than the importers, and there is more pressure on the former to combat production than on the latter to combat consumption.

In addition to constitutional elements, matters such as location and personnel can also influence the distribution of national power in international institutions. It is no accident, for example, that both the IMF and the World Bank are headquartered in Washington, DC.[28] The location of the GA and Security Council in New York may also empower the United States.[29] It is not clear whether the location of other IOs, particularly those with a primarily technical rather than political function, matters. For example, it is unlikely that Canada gains any political advantage at all from hosting the ICAO in Montreal. Geneva served as a second home for the UN and as the headquarters for a range of UN subsidiary organizations for over half a century before Switzerland even joined the UN in 2002. Kenya may gain some slight political advantage from hosting the United Nations Environment Programme (UNEP) in Nairobi, but no more than that. Kenya did, however, gain significant international prestige from being the first developing country to host the secretariat of a major IO. A headquarters in Nairobi, however, can be a mixed blessing from the perspective of the effectiveness of the organization. It makes UNEP a less appealing draw for experts, and keeps it farther from the centers of the multilateral system than would be the case if its secretariat were located in Geneva.

Personnel issues are often more the result of relative national power than its cause. For example, South Africa holds the presidency of the Security Organ of the Southern African Development Community (SADC) more than any other member country. But this is a reflection of, rather than any real source of, the central role that South Africa plays in southern African security issues. Personnel issues can matter in IO bureaucracies below the top level as well. Many positions throughout IO bureaucracies require "professional" qualifications and university degrees. A much higher proportion of citizens of developed countries than developing countries have these sorts of qualifications, meaning that a disproportionate number of the middle managers of IOs are often from developed countries. Furthermore, many of the managers from developing countries received their qualifications from universities in developed countries. Even if IO bureaucrats do not consciously represent the interests of their home countries or regions in their professional capacities, they can nonetheless imbue their organizations with values and mindsets that were learned in or reflect the interests of the developed rather than developing world.[30]

This observation leads to the final category of sources of relative national power in the creation and management of IOs: ideology. The notion that the ideology underlying IOs can empower some states over others is more contentious than the notion that different voting structures can be differentially empowering. Ideology is a form of the third face of power; its effects can be very difficult to measure. But it is an issue worth taking seriously, for both research design and empirical reasons. In terms of research design, the difficulty of measurement should not determine what social scientists do and do not study. Empirically, IOs are often charged by their detractors with ideologically empowering some states over others. If students of IOs are to weigh these charges, they must be able to determine whether there is any substance to them.

Examples of these sorts of charges come from across the ideological spectrum. During the latter half of the Cold War, the UN as a whole, along with particular organizations within it, such as the GA and UNESCO (the United Nations Educational, Scientific, and Cultural Organization), was deemed by many U.S. politicians to be too sympathetic to socialism, thus empowering the Soviet Bloc in the Cold War.[31] This charge contributed to the U.S. withdrawal from UNESCO, and to the gradual decline of American enthusiasm for the UN from its peak in the early post–World War II era.[32] Meanwhile, both critics of IOs from developing countries and critics of globalization from developed countries have charged that much of the IO system, particularly those institutions dealing with economic issues, favors neoliberal economics and capitalism. This has the effect, they say, of empowering the West—since the IOs focus on Western ways of doing business, they legitimize neoliberal economics and delegitimize other forms of economic organization.[33] These criticisms will be discussed in more detail in Chapters 8 and 9.

These charges merit examination, both on their own merits and because, if they are believed, they can undermine the potential of IOs to offer cooperative solutions to global issues. Other charges of ideological empowerment are more straightforward. The IO system, for example, as well as several particular IOs, defines and promotes human rights in a way that is more compatible with Anglo-American tradition than with other cultural traditions. This empowers Western countries, where these rights tend to be respected, at the expense of those countries where non-rights-based traditions predominate. This is so because the bias of the IO system toward human rights legitimizes Western countries' use of human rights as a political weapon. Many readers will find this perfectly reasonable on the grounds that human rights are ideologically progressive (although cultural relativists may well disagree). It nonetheless remains the case, however, that human rights norms, as adopted by the IO community, have an effect on relative state power.

The Power of IOs

So far, the discussion of the relative effects of IOs on state power has been from an internationalist perspective, on the basis of the assumption that the primary role of IOs is to mediate among states. From a universalist perspective, the next step is to ask, Do IOs themselves have power? There is no question that IOs, as a whole, are asymmetrically dependent on states. They are created by states, depend on them for their funding, and can be terminated by states. But this does not necessarily mean that IOs are entirely dependent on states. This leaves a question: To what extent do IOs, as actors in international relations, have power distinct from the power of the states that support them?

International organizations do not have the traditional sine qua non of power in international relations, military force.[34] Some IOs, however, have some policing and juridical powers. They can, for example, employ independent means for monitoring whether or not states are complying with international rules, although it is more often the case that they rely on states for this information. It is more frequent that IOs have the power to adjudicate. Examples of organizations with this power include the International Court of Justice (ICJ) and the Dispute Settlement Mechanism (DSM) of the WTO. But realists might respond that IOs can play judicial roles in the absence of independent enforcement capabilities, not because they have independent power, but because they are backed by the power of states. Universalists might argue in response, however, that to the extent that these judicial bodies adjudicate agreements and create authoritative interpretations of international law, they do, in effect, have the power to affect international law, and international norms of behavior, in ways that states cannot precisely control.[35]

There are two primary sources of independent power for IOs: moral authority and information. Moral authority is the power of an IO to legitimately speak as the official international voice with respect to its issue-area in order to get both people and states to pay attention to it, even when it does not have material resources. Moral authority in turn provides two routes through which IOs are empowered.[36] The first is the ability to shame.[37] Most states accept principles of multilateralism, and IOs represent sets of rules and procedures that the member states have already explicitly agreed to. Because of this, states do not want to be seen, either by other states or by their own populations, as breaking IO rules any more than necessary. During the 1990s, for example, Guatemala and Honduras improved their human rights records significantly. This change of behavior was partly in response to the activities of human rights IOs, which had no powers of enforcement per se, but did have significant powers of international embarrassment.[38] In the late 1990s, Canada changed the development standards for its national parks under pressure from the World Conservation Union (IUCN). The IUCN had no powers of enforcement, but the Canadian government found the charge of environmental irresponsibility, coming from the IO that oversees the system of international natural heritage sites, to be an unacceptable embarrassment to a domestic population that thinks of itself as relatively environmentally responsible.[39]

The other way in which IOs can use moral authority as a source of power is through political entrepreneurship. Political entrepreneurship is the use of structures of governance by individuals or organizations to advance particular political positions or to put particular issues on the political agenda. Leaders of IOs, in their official capacities, speak with the authority of their organizations and can use that authority to put things onto the international agenda that might not otherwise be there. For example, when the Secretary-General of the UN (at the time of writing, Kofi Annan) makes a major pronouncement, it almost as a matter of course gets widely reported in news media throughout the world. There are few other people who can claim this sort of automatic media exposure. Similarly, the World Health Organization (WHO) declared a focus on mental health for World Health Day 2001.[40] This had the effect of putting mental health issues on the domestic healthcare agendas of countries where these issues might otherwise not have been discussed.

Along with moral authority, the other primary source of independent IO power in international politics is control over, and ability to create, information. One way in which IOs exercise this control is through the agency of what some scholars call "epistemic communities." Peter Haas, who popularized the phrase in the context of IO theory, defines an epistemic community as "a network of professionals with recognized expertise and competence in a particular domain and an authoritative claim to policy-relevant knowledge within that domain or issue-area."[41] In other words, an epistemic community can be said to exist when all of the technical experts on an issue agree. Particular IOs can come to represent epistemic communities. For example, when all of the scientists dealing with the issue of pollution in the Mediterranean Sea agree on a particular plan of action, it can be very difficult for states in the Mediterranean basin to disagree with that plan.[42] Similarly, the Intergovernmental Panel on Climate Change (IPCC) is a more or less conscious attempt by the World Meteorological Organization (WMO) and UNEP to create an epistemic community on the subject of climate change. This is starting to work: fewer and fewer governments now attempt to argue that global climate change is not happening, in part because the epistemic community of the IPCC is making such arguments less and less credible.

Along with epistemic communities, IOs can create standards that affect the ways in which both governments and countries do business. A concrete example of such standards can be found in the International Civil Aviation Organization (ICAO). Because all current international commercial airline flights use ICAO standards, any attempt to change international civil aviation standards has to go through the ICAO. Otherwise, the change would either be pointless (because no one would subscribe to it), or it would require both creating a new organization and luring a critical mass of countries away from the ICAO, which would be a major political challenge. This gives the ICAO a pivotal position in all discussions of international civil aviation standards. A different sort of example is provided by the creation, under the auspices of the UN, of the concept of sustainable development. Once the concept became generally accepted within the UN, it began to find its way into the constitutional documents of other IOs as well. Gradually, it became the accepted concept within which international discussions of issues that affect both environment and development were discussed. The UN, by creating the idea of sustainable development as a standard, has thus created a language within which a whole range of issues is discussed.[43]

Conclusion

Does interdependence generate a more cooperative international relations, or are IOs simply a new forum for traditional power politics? The answer, of course, lies somewhere between these two categorical statements. But what the interrelationships are between IOs and power in international relations is a question to which the answer is likely to vary across different issue-areas and different IOs. Unfortunately, there is no clear way to measure power. Sometimes we can get at questions of power by looking at negotiations, at other times by looking at outcomes, and at still other times by looking at institutional structures. The one key thing to take from this chapter is to remember to look, and to remember to look beyond the obvious, at all of the potential sources and forms of power.

3

Regimes and Institutions

What do we look at when we study international organizations (IOs)? There are two general approaches to this question in the field of IO theory: the regime approach and the institutional approach. Regimes, as used in this context, refer to the behavioral effects of IOs on other actors, principally on states. They have been defined as "sets of principles, norms, rules, and decision-making procedures around which actor expectations converge in a given issue-area."[1] This definition will be unpacked below. For the moment, the key element of the regime approach is the focus on actor expectations; the definition does not even mention IOs per se. In contrast, the institutional approach looks at what happens within particular IOs, rather than at the effects of IOs on other actors.

An analogy can be made here to an approach to the study of political institutions more generally called the "black box" approach. Some approaches to the study of politics look at political institutions as if they were black boxes, where we can see what goes in and what comes out, but not what happens within the box itself.[2] A pluralist approach to the study of national politics, for example, looks at the pressures on government from various domestic political groups (the inputs), and the resultant government policy (the output).[3] It does not, however, look at what happens within the government to turn pressures into policy. Rather, it usually assumes some sort of decision rule. Other approaches, conversely, focus on what happens within the "black box" of government, on, perhaps, the relationship between the executive and legislative branches or on the mechanics of party politics. Regime analysis is a black-box approach to the study of IOs. Institutional analysis looks inside the black box. In addition to discussing the theoretical implications of these two approaches, this chapter will focus primarily on the mechanics of the institutional approach. The mechanics of the regime approach will be discussed in more detail in Chapter 4.

Institutional Approaches

Many of the earliest studies of IOs fit into a category that has been called formal institutional analysis.[4] This approach looks at the formal structure, organization, and bureaucratic hierarchy of IOs. The starting point for this sort of analysis is the organization's charter, which is in turn usually the text of an international treaty. The charter specifies when and why an IO will come into being, what it is called, and which countries (or other actors) can be members. It also specifies what the bureaucratic structure of the organization will be, and what powers it will have. It often discusses decision-making procedures within the organization, and its voting structure. Finally, it indicates how the organization will be financed, often provides a process for countries to leave the IO, and sometimes, though infrequently, provides a mechanism for the organization to be terminated once its function has been fulfilled.[5]

Formal institutional analysis is an important starting point for institutional research into IOs. The previous chapter discussed the importance of such things as voting structure to questions of relative power in IOs. One cannot, for example, understand the politics of the UN Security Council without understanding the mechanics of the veto power of the five permanent members. Similarly, one cannot understand the lending patterns of the IMF and World Bank without knowing about the strong voting position of the United States and its allies. International organizations that work on a unanimity or consensus basis, such as the Convention for the Conservation of Antarctic Marine Living Resources (CCAMLR),[6] generate different patterns of cooperation than those that work on a majority vote basis.

Understanding the bureaucratic structure of an IO is similarly important in understanding what the organization can and cannot do. This involves looking at the size, composition, and components of the structure of a given organization.[7] The issue of size is a relatively straightforward one. A bureaucracy with a thousand full-time employees will operate differently from a bureaucracy with two. For example, the IMF, with a staff of roughly 2,700 people, can track, research, publish extensive reports on, and make policy toward the economies of over one hundred countries simultaneously.[8] In contrast, the Agreement on the Conservation of Cetaceans of the Black Sea, Mediterranean Sea and Contiguous Atlantic Area (ACCOBAMS), headquartered in Monaco, has only a handful of staff, and is thus far more limited than the IMF, both in the range of activities it can monitor and in the depth in which it can report on them.[9]

When looking at the composition of an IO's bureaucracy, a key distinction to keep in mind is the difference between administrative employees and political appointees. Most IOs have both an administrative and a political element. Administrative employees work for the organization itself, and their primary loyalty is presumably to the organization and its goals. Political appointees work with the IO, but work for their home governments, with which their primary loyalty is supposed to lie. For example, a specialist on the economy of a particular country at the IMF will be an administrative employee of the IMF. Irrespective of the country the analyst came from, she or he is employed by, paid by, and ultimately answerable to the IMF as an institution. A member of the Board of Governors of the IMF, on the other hand, will be an appointee of a particular member country, and will be expected to represent the interests of that country in the making of IMF policy. As a general rule, the bodies that act as the equivalents of legislatures for IOs and make broad policy (such as general assemblies) are composed of political appointees, whereas executive bodies, the bureaucracies that implement the policies, are staffed with administrative employees. The relative balance of power between these two groups, however, can vary from organization to organization. An organization with a strong secretariat can influence policy-making, whereas when the secretariat is relatively weak member states can end up micro-managing implementation.[10]

Different IOs can also have different components in their bureaucratic structure. Almost all IOs will have some sort of secretariat, which is the central administrative organ of the organization. These, as has already been mentioned, can vary greatly in size and scope. Some IOs will piggyback on the secretariats of larger IOs rather than create a wholly new bureaucratic structure. This can save resources when an IO is starting up, and allows smaller IOs to use their limited budgets and resources more efficiently. A good example of this sort of setup is the United Nations Environment Programme (UNEP), which provides secretariat functions for at least ten different treaty organizations, ranging from the Montreal Protocol on Substances that Deplete the Ozone Layer to the Convention on Migratory Species of Wild Animals.[11]

Beyond the strictly administrative functions of the secretariat, IOs can have bodies that deal with scientific research, technical standards, adjudicating disputes, and interactions with member countries. These bodies can be either subsidiary to or separate from the secretariat. Many IOs that deal with environmental issues, for example, have separate scientific bodies. These bodies are tasked with developing programs of research into the relevant environmental phenomena that are separate from the research undertaken by national research communities. There are two reasons for an IO to have this sort of research capability. The first is to provide research in areas where such research does not already exist. The Intergovernmental Panel on Climate Change (IPCC), for example, was authorized by the UN General Assembly (GA) explicitly to provide the sort of overview of climate science and the issue of climate change that did not exist at the time. The IPCC issues reports every five years that remain significantly more extensive than any other overviews available on the issue.[12]

The second reason that some IOs have separate research capabilities is to create a body of scientific expertise that is seen by the member-states of the organization as being politically neutral, and thus independent of the interests of other states. This allows states to have a common body of accepted facts on which to base discussion of rules and national obligations. For example, in many IOs that deal with international fisheries issues, states often suspect the scientific reports of other states of being designed to maximize those states' fisheries quotas, rather than to accurately portray the health of fish stocks. An independent scientific council associated with the IO can allay those fears and generate a body of estimates of stock health that all participants will be willing to use as a basis for negotiating quotas. It is often through these scientific bodies, whether designed to provide impartial research or create new knowledge, that IOs develop the epistemic communities discussed in the previous chapter.[13]

Bodies that deal with technical standards are similar to scientific committees, except that they focus on setting specific technical standards rather than on independent research. For example, the secretariat of the International Civil Aviation

Organization (ICAO) includes the Air Navigation Bureau and the Air Transportation Bureau. These bureaus employ technical experts on the subject of air navigation and civilian air transportation, who then propose international standards for the airline industry. These standards are then accepted or rejected by the ICAO Council, the governing body made up of member country political appointees. Technical bodies tend mainly to employ people with specific professional expertise in the relevant issue-areas. These also often work with representatives both of national standard-setting bodies, and of the relevant industries. The technical bureaus of the ICAO would thus create new standards in consultation both with national airline regulators (such as the Federal Aviation Administration [FAA] in the United States) and representatives of both the airline industry and the major manufacturers of commercial jets.[14]

Another category of administrative function to be found in many IOs is juridical, or legal. This function can consist of offering legal advice and adjudicating the settlement of disputes among states. Many IOs have a legal department or bureau that provides advice both to the secretariat and to member states on legal issues related to the IO's remit. To continue with the example from the last paragraph, the ICAO secretariat includes a legal bureau, the job of which is to provide advice "to the Secretary General and through him to the various bodies of the Organization and to ICAO Member States on constitutional, administrative and procedural matters, on problems of international law, air law, commercial law, labour law and related matters."[15]

There is one IO that deals almost exclusively with adjudication: the International Court of Justice (ICJ). There are also a few bodies that deal with the enforcement of international law with respect to individuals, such as the special tribunals set up to deal with war crimes in the former Yugoslavia and Rwanda, and the International Criminal Court (ICC).[16] Many treaties call for the creation of ad hoc panels to settle specific disputes relating to their rules. A few IOs have full-time dispute settlement bodies as part of their organizational structure. The best known example is the WTO's Dispute Settlement Mechanism (DSM), which adjudicates trade disputes among WTO member states. Judges from a variety of member states who are generally accepted as experts in international trade law preside at hearings at which states are represented by their lawyers. International adjudicative bodies such as the DSM, whether permanent or ad hoc, tend to behave very much like domestic courts.

The final major category of administrative function to be found in the secretariats of many IOs is what might be called direct implementation. Many IOs, particularly those that deal with development and humanitarian issues, have employees on the ground in member countries, either assisting governments or undertaking activities that governments might normally undertake. Not all IOs that deal with humanitarian issues do all of their own direct implementation. Many subcontract with NGOs for some or all of this work. But for many IOs, direct implementation is their primary *raison d'être*.

A good example of this latter sort of IO is the Office of the United Nations High Commissioner for Refugees (UNHCR). The UNHCR secretariat fulfills all of the standard administrative functions of bureaucracies, and plays an active role in publicizing refugee issues, lobbying for the rights of refugees, monitoring member country behavior with respect to refugees, and fund-raising. But the bulk of its efforts are aimed at giving direct relief to refugees on the ground, through 120 regional offices and direct representation in crisis areas and at refugee camps. The UNHCR works in concert with more than 500 NGOs, so it does engage in some subcontracting of its efforts. But it does much of the work itself, as suggested by its in-house staff of more than 5,000 employees, 84 percent of whom work in the field rather than at the head office in Geneva.[17]

Several other IOs focus on direct implementation. Many of these, like the UNHCR, are UN agencies, including the United Nations Children's Fund (UNICEF) and the United Nations Relief and Works Agency (UNRWA). For other IOs, such as the World Health Organization (WHO) and the Food and Agriculture Organization (FAO), direct implementation is a major but not predominant function. Some IOs that focus on implementing specific projects in member countries, such as UNICEF, the World Bank, and the United Nations Development Programme (UNDP), maintain representation in many countries, but implement projects primarily through grants to governments and NGOs, rather than through in-house staff.

Many IOs that one might not normally think of as dealing with direct implementation do in fact have administrative components that focus on this task. To return to an example used above, the ICAO has a Technical Cooperation Bureau that sends experts to assist developing countries in improving their civil aviation technical standards. The Bureau's job is to provide expertise, rather than funding. Funding for the Bureau's programs comes either from other IOs, such as the UNDP, or from the governments being assisted.[18] Other IOs have different approaches to direct implementation. The International Maritime Organization (IMO), for example, runs the World Maritime University in Mälmo, Sweden, which offers courses and degrees on issues and techniques related to maritime and shipping safety.[19]

A final administrative function, noted above with respect to the UNHCR, is fund-raising. International organizations are generally thought of as being funded by member states, and this is usually the case to a significant degree. The constitutional documents of most IOs specify either the funding mechanism or rules for arriving at a funding mechanism for the IO. Assessments are sometimes based on a flat rate per country, but more often require that larger and wealthier countries pay more. For example, the structure of UN dues is based on the concept of ability to pay. This results in the United States paying 22 percent of the UN's basic budget, and several small, poor countries paying the minimum level of dues, 0.001 percent.[20] Many IOs set their dues structure based on the UN structure.

But not all funding for IOs comes from mandatory dues from member states. Many IOs raise funds, both voluntary funds from member states and donations from private individuals. The largest single pledge by a private individual to an IO was $1 billion, by Ted Turner to the UN.[21] There are a number of IOs that depend on a constant stream of smaller donations in order to maintain their programs. The UNHCR, for example, has a Donor Relations and Resource Mobilization Service in the Division of Communication and Information in its Secretariat.[22] UNICEF runs a network of thirty-seven national committees, each of which is registered as an NGO in a developed country, to raise funds for it. These national committees contribute roughly a third of UNICEF's annual budget of just over $1 billion.[23]

Neofunctionalism

Formal institutional analysis is based on the premise that we can learn about what an IO does from the way it is set up, and the way in which it is organized at any given point in time. This is certainly a good, perhaps even a necessary, starting point in understanding IOs. It is, however, static: it can paint for us a picture of where an IO is at a particular point in time, but cannot tell us anything about how and when an organization will change. And IOs do change. Sometimes, they disappear when their function has become obsolete. But they can grow and acquire new roles. What started off as the European Coal and Steel Community (ECSC), a relatively narrow and limited organization, has become the European Union (EU), an organization that affects almost all aspects of life in its member states. The IMF was designed to oversee a system of fixed exchange rates. That system collapsed in the early 1970s, and yet the IMF still exists, having found new roles for itself.

The inability of formal institutional analysis to deal with functional change in IOs led, in the 1950s, to the development of an approach to the study of IOs known as functionalism. This approach suggested that as the problems facing both states and IOs were becoming more international, the scope for global governance was expanding. This meant that the functions of IOs had to continuously expand to keep apace. Functionalists saw IOs themselves as important drivers of this process, by identifying new areas where international governance was needed and by proposing ways of dealing with these new demands. This approach developed to a large extent with reference to the process of European integration through the European Economic Community (EEC), although one of the seminal works of the functionalist approach focused on the ILO. [24]

The functionalist approach focused on technical demands for international governance. The ICAO provides a good example of this process: as international civil air transport expanded, the complexity of the rules needed to keep the industry operating smoothly grew as well. This change generated a technical need for greater international cooperation, and helps to explain the gradual expansion of the ICAO. The increased technical need also had the effect of empowering the ICAO as an agenda setter in its area of expertise, allowing it an active role in moving the process of functional integration forward.

By the 1960s, it was becoming clear, however, that much of the increase in international cooperation through IOs was political rather than purely technical.[25] The UNHCR, for example, grew much faster than the number of refugees in the world in the second half of the twentieth century. The UNHCR's growth, then, could not have been fueled exclusively by the technical demands imposed by a greater refugee population. It was fueled as well (perhaps primarily) by an increasing political consensus among states that they had an ethical responsibility to ameliorate the plight of refugees. This consensus was helped along to a significant degree by the UNHCR itself, by both its successes in helping refugees and its lobbying on their behalf.

A variant of functionalism, called neofunctionalism, developed in the 1960s to account for political as well as technical demands for increased global governance.[26]

A neofunctionalist approach, then, looks at the political, as well as technical, processes of integration of governance functions globally. As an approach to the study of IOs that developed largely in tandem with the EEC, neofunctionalism looks more at the evolution of governance patterns within an existing institutional and organizational structure, rather than at the creation of new forms of organization.[27] It would, for example, look at why the WHO declared a focus on mental health for World Health Day in 2001, thus putting an issue that had existed longer than the organization on the global health agenda. No new institution was created, but political leadership made a global issue out of something that had previously been entirely within the purview of national governments.

The political leadership that leads to neofunctionalist integration can come either from states or from IOs. Neofunctionalism thus spans the distinction made at the beginning of this chapter between institutional approaches and regime approaches. To the extent that the political leadership comes from states, or, for that matter, from any actors other than IOs, neofunctionalism is a precursor of regime approaches.[28] The evolution in IO theory from neofunctionalism to regime theory is discussed in the next section. To the extent that the political leadership comes from within IOs, neofunctionalism takes an institutionalist perspective. It looks at the way IOs, as actors, are changing global governance. It has the advantage over formal institutional approaches that it directly addresses the issue of change, be it change of structure, change of mission, change of scope, or change of scale, in IOs. It has the advantage over earlier functionalist approaches that it can cope with the broad array of issue-areas in international governance that are political rather than purely technical. In other words, it allows us to ask why IOs push some issues rather than others onto the international agenda.

Neoinstitutionalism

Neofunctionalism served to bring politics back into the study of IOs, in a way that classical functionalism or formal institutionalism did not allow for. But it shares one major limitation of its two predecessors. It can address the question of what IOs do, but not of how well they do it. It can look at the place an IO holds on the international agenda, and the way in which it changes that agenda, but it cannot really look at the overall effect that the organization has on world politics. By the 1980s, this common limitation of institutionalist approaches led to a focus within the IO theory community on regime approaches, which is discussed in the following section.[29]

By the late 1990s, however, some students of IOs began to feel that the pendulum had swung too far in the direction of regime analysis.[30] Since regime analysis black-boxes IOs as institutions, it cannot address the effects of what goes on inside those boxes on international politics. If IOs in fact operate as they are designed, and work efficiently to deal with the problems they are designed to deal with, then treating them as opaque black boxes should not be a problem. But this assumes both that IOs are efficient organizations that deal with the problems they are designed to deal with, and that they have little independent power separate from states to redefine their missions and their internal organization. A rejuvenation of institutionalist approaches was driven by the observation that these assumptions were not entirely reasonable.[31]

But both formal institutionalism and neofunctionalism are also limited in the extent to which they can capture the politics internal to IOs, and the political power of IOs. Formal institutionalism looks at how IOs are designed on paper. This is a necessary step in understanding the internal politics of IOs, but not a sufficient step, because organizations do not always function in the way they are designed and laid out. Formal institutionalism can also capture the power resources that IOs are formally given in their constitutional documents, but not those that they develop informally. Neofunctionalism, meanwhile, recognizes both that IOs have significant agenda-setting power in international politics, and that IOs have some autonomy in deciding how to affect those agendas. But neofunctionalism is nonetheless limited by the assumptions that IOs set agendas to further international governance in the issue-areas that they were designed to deal with, and that they will ultimately act to represent the broader interests of the states that created them.[32]

A response to these limitations is neoinstitutionalism, also called sociological institutionalism.[33] Rather than taking as a starting point the structure and purpose of an organization as defined by outside actors, neoinstitutionalism looks at the actual organizational dynamics within institutions.[34] It borrows from fields outside of international relations theory, such as the study of bureaucratic politics in political science and the study of institutions in sociology, that look at the way bureaucracies behave and at the effects of these broader patterns of behavior.[35]

As applied to IOs, this means looking at bureaucratic and institutional rules and politics within the IOs, rather than at constitutional documents or the demands of the issue-area. This can be done in a number of ways. Historical institutionalism looks at the ways in which norms and procedures within particular institutions have developed over time. This approach tends to understand institutional histories as path-dependent, limiting the extent to which the analyst can generalize across institutions. Functional institutionalism focuses on the rules and procedures within organizations, and looks at how these rules and procedures shape the behavior both of the organization and of the people within it.[36] Analysts using this approach to the neoinstitutionalist study of IOs have often concluded that IOs exhibit a strong tendency to be as committed to their own internal rules and procedures as they are to their formal mission, and a tendency to be committed to their own survival as institutions.

There are two ways to look at an IO's commitment to its own rules and procedures. The first is as an empowering mechanism. States create IOs to serve a particular purpose, and create their structure to further that purpose. But it is the IOs themselves, once they have been created, that create their own norms and operating procedures over time. To the extent that they are committed to these procedures, and to the extent to which the IO makes a difference in international politics, the creation and maintenance of procedures allows the IO to dictate how things will be done within its issue-area. When combined with effective claims by IOs to both impartiality (they serve the international community, rather than the interests of particular states) and expertise, this functional autonomy allows IOs to operate as independent actors with considerable freedom of action.

The IMF is a good example of this process. This organization is limited in what it can do by its charter and by its member states. Within these limitations, it is supposed "to promote international monetary cooperation, exchange stability, and orderly exchange arrangements; to foster economic growth and high levels of employment; and to provide temporary financial assistance to countries to help ease balance of payments adjustment."[37] One of the main ways in which it does this is to lend money on condition that the borrower state adopt certain policies. But the organization has considerable leeway in deciding which conditions to impose. There is little oversight of the conditions imposed on certain loans, which are determined within the bureaucratic structure of the IMF, and which can have a major effect on the economic health of individual countries. Understanding which conditions are to be imposed requires looking in some detail at rules, procedures, and politics internal to the IMF.

The second way to look at an IO's commitment to its own rules and procedures is as a "pathology."[38] A pathology in this context is when the bureaucratic empowering mechanisms discussed above lead to organizational dysfunction. This can mean behavior that is at odds with the organization's mission, which is internally contradictory, or which simply does not make sense.[39] An example of such a pathology can be found in the World Bank. The staff in the World Bank's bureaucracy who are in charge of making loans to developing countries are judged by the volume of loans that they make. They are not judged by whether the project for which the money was loaned is ultimately a success. This gives them an incentive to approve loans that are of dubious development value in order to maximize their loan portfolio and increase their profile within the World Bank bureaucracy.[40]

Another example of organizational pathology can be found at the UNHCR. The High Commission's Protection Division, located primarily at the organization's headquarters in Geneva, is the UNHCR's legal arm. It is responsible for protecting the rights of refugees under international law, and tends to approach this mission in a narrow legalistic sense. The regional bureaus, on the other hand, are more interested in the ultimate causes of refugee flows. This can lead to internal dispute within the organization on issues such as the repatriation of refugees. The Protection Division will concern itself primarily with the individual rights of refugees, including the right not to be repatriated without consent. The regional office, on the other hand, may well be more concerned with figuring out what course of action will stop the flow of refugees in the first place, whether or not that course of action is in strict compliance either with international law or with the official institutional norms of the UNHCR.[41]

More broadly, an organization as large and as wide-ranging as the UN will inevitably find itself in situations where different parts of the organization are trying to do incompatible things. In late 2001, for example, some parts of the UN sympathized with the bombing of Afghanistan,[42] while other parts were attempting to engage in supplying humanitarian aid. This resulted in an unclear message as to where the UN stood, and what role it played, with respect to governance in Afghanistan.

A final observation of neoinstitutionalist analysis is that bureaucracies will often have a great commitment at minimum to their own self-preservation and at maximum to institutional growth. For example, the system of fixed international exchange rates, known as the Bretton Woods system, fell apart in the early 1970s. The organization designed to manage the system, the IMF, might have been expected to go out of business as a result, and perhaps be replaced by a new IO designed to meet the needs of the system of floating exchange rates that replaced the Bretton Woods system. But the IMF did not go out of business. Instead, it created a new role for itself based on the concept of conditionality, a role that was never really envisioned for it.[43] Several IOs, not least among them the UN and the EU, are constantly expanding the range of issues over which they have authority. Most new IOs these days are created by existing organizations, rather than by states; in other words, IOs are not only expanding, but are also reproducing.[44] A neofunctionalist may ascribe this to the demands of global governance in an increasingly globalized world. A neoinstitutionalist would want to find out if it was the result of institutional pathologies. Only empirical research could resolve this dispute.

A relatively new attempt to bridge the gap between traditional institutionalism (in which IOs do what they are designed to do) and neoinstitutionalism (in which IOs do what is in their institutional interest) has been through the use of the principal–agent model. This model, developed in microeconomics and brought into the study of IOs relatively recently, sees states (principals) as creating IOs (agents) to undertake specific tasks for them. As long as the agents undertake those tasks reasonably well, the principals will leave them alone, because extensive oversight is expensive. But when the behavior of the agents strays too far from the goals of the principals, the principals must act to rein the agents in. This theoretical approach can be useful for explaining both why states give IOs some autonomy, and when states will act to limit that autonomy. The principal–agent model has been applied to analyses of the EU and the World Bank, among other IOs.[45]

Regime Analysis

While institutional analysis was the predominant approach used for studying IOs in the 1950s and 1960s, and has been making something of a comeback recently, the predominant approach for studying IOs in the 1980s and 1990s was regime analysis. Arguably, it is still the predominant approach.

The key difference between a regime approach and an institutional approach lies in whom the different approaches look to as actors. Institutionalists look to the IOs themselves as actors, and ask what it is that the organizations do. Regime analysts, on the other hand, look to other actors, primarily states, as the source of outcomes in international politics, and ask what effects the various principles, norms, rules, and decision-making procedures associated with IOs have on the expectations and behaviors of states. Institutionalists study IOs by looking at what happens within the organizations. Regime analysts study IOs by looking at the behavior of states and at the effects of the norms and rules that the organizations embody on that behavior.

Regime analysis, as suggested above, arose out of a frustration with the limitations of institutional analysis. Primary among these limitations is the inability of institutional analysis to address the bigger picture of the effect of IOs on patterns of behavior in international relations more broadly. It can tell us what IOs do, but not what difference they make. Regime analysis provides a corrective to this by allowing us to question both where IOs come from and how effective they are.

Some students of IO theory have suggested that regime theory is an evolutionary development from early formal institutionalism, through neofunctionalism.[46] But it is perhaps more useful to think of a pendulum, with institutionalist analysis at one end and regime analysis at the other. A broad understanding of the role of IOs in international relations requires both approaches: it requires that we understand both how IOs work and what effects they have on other actors in international politics. The pendulum occasionally swings too far in one direction, but after a while, the gravitational pull toward understanding IOs pulls it back into balance. Unfortunately, it often then gets pulled too far, and swings out of balance in the other direction. This is what happened in the 1980s, when the balance swung in the direction of regime theory. It remains to be seen whether the pendulum is currently being pulled back into equilibrium by neoinstitutionalism, or whether it will overcompensate and put regime analysis out of fashion for a while.

There are a few observations worth mentioning at this point about the definition of regimes. The first is that they are issue-area specific: the systems for repatriating refugees or for allocating national fishing quotas are regimes, the international system as a whole is not. The second is that regime analysis specifies a range of things to look at, such as principles, norms and rules, and decision-making procedures. This covers the gamut from the very general (principles) to the very specific (decision-making procedures), and from the explicit (rules) to the implicit (norms). Different schools of thought within regime theory tend to focus on different parts of this definition. In particular, there is a rationalist approach to regime theory that focuses mostly on rules and procedures and asks how we can make regimes as efficient as possible in solving the problems they are created to solve. There is also what has been called a reflectivist approach,[47] which focuses on principles and norms. Proponents of this approach tend to ask questions about the effects of IOs on the ways in which actors in international politics think and on the ideas that drive international relations. This tension between efficiency and ideas is the fourth distinction around which the theoretical section of this book is constructed, and provides the focus of Chapter 4.

4

Efficiency and Ideas

The tension between efficiency and ideas, between rationalist and reflectivist methodologies, affects both the institutional and regime approaches to the study of international organizations (IOs). But the effects of this tension are most evident in the latter, which, as we have already noted, looks not at IOs themselves, but at their effects on the patterns of international politics more broadly. The regime approach first caught on in the early 1980s, and has since then remained the predominant framework in political science for studying IOs. Both the rationalist (often called neoliberal institutionalist) approach and the reflectivist (often called constructivist) approach can trace their lineage back to the early days of the literature on regimes.[1]

Rationalism and Transparency

The rationalist approach to the study of international regimes is essentially an attempt to apply some of the concepts and tools of economics to the study of IOs. It looks at states the way most economists look at people—as unitary, rational, utility-maximizing actors. Unitary in this context means that states have an identifiable national interest and a single identifiable voice, rather than being a collection of individual decision-makers and domestic interest groups. Rational and utility-maximizing mean that states make cost–benefit calculations of the behavioral options open to them and make decisions on the basis of what will maximize their interests. Rationalists recognize that these assumptions are gross simplifications of the way state decision-making works, but argue that they are useful approximations of the way that international politics works.

   The starting point for the rationalist analysis of international regimes is what has been called the rational cooperation literature.[2] This literature begins with the premise of the collective action problem, a situation where everyone would be better off if everyone cooperates, but each actor has an individual incentive to free ride and have everyone else cooperate. The classic example of a collective action problem is union membership.[3] All individual workers want the benefits that collective bargaining can give but would just as soon avoid paying union dues as their individual dues will have very little impact on how good a job the union can do in contract negotiations. An international example of this problem is the case of free trade. Economists tell us that all countries in aggregate will be best off if they all adopt free trade policies. But individual countries can benefit by judicious use of tariffs as long as other countries remain free traders. The problem, though, is that if all countries choose tariffs (as they may if given a choice), everyone is worse off.[4]

A collective action problem with two participants is often called a prisoners' dilemma (PD). This dilemma is often used in international relations theory as a metaphor for collective action problems more broadly. In a PD situation, the first choice of each actor is to cheat while the other cooperates, the second choice is to cooperate while other actors cooperate as well, the third choice is to cheat while other actors cheat as well, and the least preferred outcome for each actor is to co-operate while the other actor cheats. In this situation, the best collective outcome is for the actors to cooperate. But each actor individually has a strategic incentive to cheat, because each actor does better cheating than cooperating regardless of what the other actor does, if each actor cannot affect the actions of the other. In a perfect world, the two states would cooperate, but left to their own devices, they will probably cheat. Each state will thus get the third rather than second choice. One way in which they can get from the third choice to the second is to sign a con-tract that commits them both to mutual cooperation.[5]

Why do people enter into long-term contracts that constrain their behavior in the future? Economic theory tells us that the market is the most efficient way of allocating resources. Long-term contracts have the effect of taking goods and serv-ices off the market by committing them to a single buyer or seller for some time in the future. The economic rationale for doing this is a concept known as market fail-ure. Markets are only completely efficient when they work perfectly, which they can only do in theory. In practice, there are always market imperfections, and the more imperfect markets are, the less efficient they are. There are three kinds of market imperfections: imperfect information, transaction costs, and imperfect property rights. Contracts are a way of dealing with these imperfections.

Imperfect information is when one or both of the parties to a transaction do not know enough to be fully informed about what they are doing. This is the reason, for example, that we are willing to pay more for a doctor's opinion about our health than for the opinion of someone with no medical training. We do not have enough information to make a fully informed decision about our health, and are willing to pay someone with the appropriate qualifications a premium to help us do so.

Transaction costs are the costs of doing business. When we walk to the store to pick up some milk, for example, the transaction costs include the time spent walk-ing to the store. This is why we usually buy enough milk to last awhile, even at the risk of some of it going bad, rather than going to the store for fresh milk every day. One of the reasons most employment contracts are only renegotiated every year or more is that it would be hopelessly inefficient to negotiate salary terms with employers before starting work each day: the transaction costs, the time spent nego-tiating, would be too high.

Property rights specify who owns what and who is responsible for what costs. For example, it would be hard to sell a piece of polluted land if no one knew who was responsible for cleaning up the pollution. People are generally not willing to invest as much in property for which they do not hold clear title as they are when they do, because without clear title the investor cannot know the extent to which he or she will benefit from the investment. This need for clear property rights provides the explanation for a wide range of government activity, from basic criminal law to specific regulations on issues such as pollution standards. For economists, in fact, it is a basic role of government to create as perfect a market structure as possible domestically by creating a legal and physical infrastructure that maximizes the clarity of property rights and information flows and minimizes transaction costs.[6]

Rationalists have applied these insights to the study of international regimes. Having assumed that states are rational unitary actors, rationalists then go on to look at international relations as a sort of marketplace. States transact in this marketplace for policies rather than for goods and services, but the rationalist's starting point is that the logic of the marketplace operates nonetheless. In this view, treaties and agreements among states are like contracts among people and corporations.[7] People enter into contracts in order to maximize their interests in whatever situation they find themselves. States sign treaties and agreements for the same reason.

The seminal works in the rationalist approach to the study of international regimes have focused on the demand for regimes: When will states want to form regimes, and for what purposes?[8] The answer these analyses gave was that states will want to create regimes when faced with collective action problems that result from highly imperfect markets in the international political marketplace. When states are unable to maximize their interests because of poor international flows of information, high transaction costs in international politics, and inadequately defined international property rights, they will attempt to create regimes to improve information flows, reduce transaction costs, and specify property rights. These goals are sometimes lumped together under the broader heading of the "transparency" function of international regimes.[9]

A regime can improve the international flow of information in a number of ways. It can create new information, act as a repository for existing information, or create standards that improve the comparability of different sources of information. The scientific bodies often created by multilateral environmental agreements are an example of the first category. Examples of the second category include the Intergovernmental Panel on Climate Change (IPCC), which is tasked with providing an overview of existing science on the subject of climate change,[10] and the International Whaling Commission (IWC), which requires that member states submit the statistics that they generate to the IWC so that all of the available statistics can be found together in one place.[11] Examples of the third category (creating standards that improve comparability) include the IMF, which creates standards for reporting national accounts statistics so that these statistics will be comparable across states, and the International Organization for Standardization (ISO), which creates product standards that companies are free to adopt or not, as they choose.[12]

A regime can reduce transaction costs by providing a forum for discussing issues, by creating standard rules and procedures for dealing with issues, and by creating administrative structures. A good example of a regime that has implemented these strategies is the UN Security Council. The logic behind the Council is that when threats to international security occur, an authoritative international body should discuss them. But to set up such a body each time there is a new threat to international security would take weeks or even months, when the response time required is often measured in hours. The Security Council is thus in part an exercise in reducing transaction costs. It is the accepted forum for discussing threats to international security, so when such a threat occurs, states do not have to waste time figuring out where to discuss it. Furthermore, the members of the Council have representatives in residence, so they can get to a meeting in a matter of hours, rather than days. It has standard rules of procedure, so that state representatives can get straight to the business at hand rather than having to discuss how to proceed. And it has an administrative structure to deal with things such as record-keeping, translation, etcetera, so that the representatives can get directly to the point without having to worry about these functions.[13] The same logic can apply to most international regimes, and the more often the parties to a regime need to deal with new issues, the greater the need to reduce transaction costs.

A regime can specify property rights by creating specific rules that demarcate who owns what and who is responsible for what, and by enforcing them, or at least adjudicating disputes relating to them. The term "property rights" as used here should be understood broadly, to mean any rule that affects who has the right to benefit from an economic good. It refers to the right to be compensated for exposure to an economic "bad," such as pollution, caused by others. The WTO, which is almost entirely about the specification of property rights, provides an example of this function. Most WTO rules are about what countries are and are not allowed to do with their borders with respect to trade. A basic rule of the WTO is that a country must treat foreign goods the same way it treats domestic goods.[14] This gives countries the right to have their goods treated fairly by the countries that import them. The general acceptance of this right should then encourage countries to participate more fully in international trade. The WTO also has a Dispute Settlement Mechanism (DSM), which is in effect an international trade court that adjudicates disputes and sets clear rules as to what countries are allowed to do in retaliation (punishment) for breaches in the rules. The WTO, in short, is designed to increase international trade by specifying and enforcing national property rights with respect to international trade issues.

This example does not mean, however, that specifying property rights is only useful for IOs that focus on economic issues. It can help promote international cooperation in a variety of issue-areas. In the issue-area of international security, for example, the most basic rule that the Security Council is supposed to enforce is the prohibition against invading the territory of another state. This rule defines a property right—states have the right to their territorial integrity unless they fail to meet specific conditions of behavior set by international law. In the area of international environmental management, fisheries agreements often specify precise quotas of particular fish species for national fleets. This is also a property right, because ships from a given country have the right to fish up to the quota, and no more. Property rights in this context should be understood broadly as including any rule about who can do what with respect to anything that countries might want to own or control.

Rationalism and Efficiency

From the rationalist perspective, states will create regimes and will agree to be bound by the rules of those regimes in order to minimize market imperfections in the international political marketplace. Looked at another way, this is the same thing as saying that states create regimes to maximize the efficiency of their inter-actions with each other. The rationalist approach can explain the creation of a wide range of international regimes in a variety of issue-areas where states focus on min-imizing costs and maximizing benefits, such as international security, economic cooperation, and even human rights.

The rationalist regime literature, as we have seen, began with a focus on the demand for regimes. But the concept of efficiency, which is a fundamental part of this approach, allows analysts to do other things as well. Efficiency gives us both a goal to keep in mind when designing regimes and a tool for evaluating how suc-cessful the regimes are. The questions to keep in mind with respect to both of these tasks are, Does this regime make states better off than they were without it? and Can it be designed, or redesigned, to make them better off still?

In the case of economic regimes, the answer to these questions is sometimes rel-atively straightforward, at other times less so. Trade economists, for example, can create estimates of the extent to which a specific trade agreement is beneficial. The World Bank, for example, estimated in 2001 that the results of a new round of trade talks could add $2.8 trillion to the global economy by 2015.[15] The effect of the IMF's activities in response to the Asian economic crisis of 1997, however, is harder to assess, because we do not know what would have happened without the IMF.

Similarly, in the case of environmental regimes, the answer can often be specified quite precisely. International environmental regimes are usually created to deal with situations where environmental problems are happening at a larger scale than can be contained effectively within the borders of individual states. Regulation by indi-vidual states would therefore lead to suboptimal management—either overuse or underprotection—of environmental resources. The effects of regimes on the man-agement of these resources can often be measured fairly accurately.[16] For example, many fish species on the high seas are overfished because no single country is in a position to impose quotas on the amount fished, as they might do were the fish within national waters. This results in a classic collective action problem, where the incentives for individual countries match those of a PD game. The efficiency of an international fisheries regime can be measured by looking at how well its quota sys-tem works compared with a system under the control of an individual state.

In the case of regimes in issue-areas such as human rights or international secu-rity, the efficiency of regimes can be harder to measure, because we know less about what would be happening without the regimes. For example, most people who look at security issues agree that the UN Security Council works better than the League of Nations at improving international security. But it is very hard to know how much difference this makes, because the international contexts of the 1920s and the early twenty-first century are so different. Even in the unlikely event that we could eliminate the Security Council for a year as a control experiment, it would be hard to tell how much difference its absence was making, because each security crisis is different.

The discussion to this point has looked at the question of regime efficiency inductively, by asking how much difference a regime has made once it has been created. But rationalist scholars of international regimes have also used their approach to study regimes deductively, by asking how what we know about market failure and efficiency can be applied to ensure the creation of better regimes. With respect to reducing transaction costs, this can be fairly straightforward, and involves creating forums for interaction, administrative structures, and sets of rules and procedures that make repeated interactions on the issue less costly. With respect to improving information flows and specifying property rights, it can be more complicated.

The literature on maximizing efficiency with respect to information flows and property rights has tended to focus on two issues, monitoring and enforcement. Monitoring is important both to improving information flows and to improving property rights. It is important to improving information flows because it generates information that states need in order to handle the issue-area in question effectively. In international fisheries agreements, for example, states cannot decide on reasonable quotas until they know who is fishing how much, how many fish are out there, and how quickly they can reproduce. Monitoring the behavior both of fishers and of fish thus generates information that is necessary to the proper functioning of the regime. But monitoring is also important to improving property rights, because in order to enforce property rights, participants must first know who is trying to breach the rights of other states. In both cases, monitoring is a necessary first step to enforcement, because enforcement requires knowledge of who is breaking the rules.

Successful monitoring can be hampered by inadequate technology and by excessive cost. Monitoring activity in support of the international whaling regime is hampered by the fact that we do not have the technology to track the movements of populations of whales at sea.[17] Many treaties require countries to report on domestic conditions, either economic or environmental. Examples of this include national accounts statistics gathered by the IMF, or information on atmospheric carbon emissions gathered for the United Nations Framework Convention on Climate Change (UNFCCC). Generating such reports is generally not an onerous burden for developed countries, which often gather these statistics for domestic purposes anyway. But many smaller, poorer countries do not have the resources, either fiscal or human, to collect these statistics effectively. The cost of self-monitoring in these cases, even given the best of intentions, can hamper the transparency of the regime.[18]

The greatest obstacle to successful monitoring, however, is the unwillingness of states to cede too much authority to representatives of international regimes. The various international regimes on nonconventional weapons (nuclear, biological, and chemical) provide good examples here. In order for these treaties to be fully enforceable, the regimes would have to allow for on-site monitoring both of weapons sites and of industrial sites, either by other states or by the treaty secretariat. The relevant treaties allow some of this, but the amount of on-site inspection to which countries will acquiesce is limited by their fears both of having military secrets compromised and of industrial espionage.

Often, the obstacles generated by inadequate technology, high costs, and sovereignty concerns work together. In international fisheries cooperation, for example, monitoring can be made more accurate by putting third-party observers on all boats that fish in international waters. But many states object to this on the grounds of both cost and sovereignty, with the result that monitoring cannot be carried out at an adequate level. One of the objections that the United States has to proposed amendments to the Biological Weapons Convention, for example, is that the monitoring is inadequate.[19] This inadequacy is due to a combination of sovereignty issues (not all states will allow sufficiently intrusive monitoring) and dual-use issues (it can be difficult, particularly at the early stages of research, to distinguish between the development of biotechnology for civilian uses and for military uses).

Technological innovation can help to overcome some of the problems in monitoring. Satellite tracking, for example, can accomplish much of the monitoring that used to require on-site or on-vessel inspection, at a fraction of the cost and without raising many of the sovereignty issues.[20] So new technologies are worth looking to for solutions to monitoring issues. They are not, however, a panacea; sometimes technological solutions can be found, but at other times they cannot. Figuring out the most effective point at which to regulate behavior can also make monitoring easier. For example, agreements to control pollution from ships at sea can work well when they focus on equipment standards, which can be inspected at any port. But they do not work as well when they focus on behavior standards, because ships usually violate the standards when they are in the middle of the ocean, where it is difficult to for them to be caught.[21] Careful thought to what sorts of regulations can most easily be monitored effectively will often yield regimes that are more effective.

Successful monitoring can by itself help to increase compliance with international regimes.[22] Countries are less likely to cheat on their obligations the more likely they are to be caught. This is true because states do not want to undermine either the agreements they have entered into (assuming that they felt the agreement to be beneficial in the first place) or their credibility as negotiating partners in the negotiation of future agreements. But in many cases, monitoring is only a first step toward getting countries to fully comply with their obligations to international regimes. An often-necessary second step is enforcement.

How do we punish states and force them to change their behavior when they cheat? There are four main avenues for enforcement of international regimes: juridical, political, economic, and (for want of a better term) ethical. The juridical avenue involves the use of international courts or tribunals. The political avenue allows individual states to enforce the regime through the traditional mechanisms of state power. The economic avenue builds incentives into agreements that make compliant behavior economically beneficial and noncompliant behavior costly. The ethical avenue uses shaming as a technique to embarrass states into complying with their international commitments. In practice, these four avenues of enforcement often overlap, but they are still useful theoretical concepts.

The juridical avenue is perhaps more an exercise in transparency than in enforcement per se. Political realists in fact often deride international law, the result of international juridical activity, as futile because it lacks direct enforcement powers. But the role that courts and tribunals play in maintaining the property rights of states in international interactions is nonetheless important, as it makes clear, in a forum seen to be impartial, who is in the right and who is in the wrong in any particular dispute. An example of an international regime focused on juridical enforcement is the International Court of Justice (ICJ). By the logic of realism, the ICJ should be irrelevant. But states continue to make use of it anyway.[23]

Much of the actual enforcing of international regimes is done by states rather than by international organizations, through diplomatic, military, or economic means. A good example here is the Security Council. This is a political, rather than juridical, body; the representatives to the Security Council who decide who is in the right and who is in the wrong with respect to a threat to international security are diplomats and politicians, not jurists. And when the Security Council makes a decision that requires enforcing, it does not have the ability to do the enforcing itself. For that, it relies on the military (and other) capabilities of its member countries. Forces may intervene in disputes under the banner of the UN, but the soldiers themselves are part of national armies.

Some regimes include facilities for distributing funds, which can be used as avenues of economic enforcement. Money can be withheld or increased in response to state compliance with the regime. A classic example of this approach to enforcement can be found in IMF conditionality. The regime of which the IMF is the institutional anchor requires states to engage in certain sorts of fiscal and macroeconomic behavior. The IMF makes adhering to these behaviors a condition for providing loans, and often gives loans in multiple segments (which in the financial world are called "tranches") in order to have something to withhold should states cease complying with the regime after they have got some money. Other research indicates that this sort of economic enforcement only works well when funds are withheld until after states have demonstrated regime-compliant behavior.[24]

An example of a combination of enforcement tools can be found in the WTO. Disputes concerning the international trade regime can be taken to a juridical body, the WTO's DSM, which decides whether states have violated the rules of the regime. If the juridical body finds that a state is in breach of the rules, it authorizes the complainant to take retaliatory action through its own trade policy. So there is a juridical element (the DSM), a political element (enforcement through state trade and tariff policy), and an economic element (WTO rules clearly specify the economic magnitude of allowable retaliation in any given case).[25]

Finally, there is ethical enforcement, or shaming. Sometimes states, as is often the case with people, are simply embarrassed when caught cheating. As was discussed in Chapter 2, this is a source of power for IOs. But it is not only IOs that can enforce a regime through shaming. Shaming can be done by states, by nongovernmental organizations (NGOs), or by other civil society actors, such as news media. Whatever the source, as long as it embarrasses governments sufficiently that they change their behavior in a way that brings them more in line with the regime, shaming has the effect of enforcing the regime. Unlike juridical, political, and economic enforcement, however, shaming does not fit well into a rationalist logic. It relies on decision-makers thinking in terms of the appropriateness of behaviors, rather than in terms of cost–benefit analysis. This logic of appropriateness has less to do with transparency than with legitimacy. And legitimacy, in turn, is something generally discussed in the literature from a reflectivist, rather than a rationalist, perspective.

Reflectivism and Legitimacy

Regimes are about the effects of IOs and international cooperation on state behavior. These effects can take two broad forms, regulative and constitutive. A regulative effect is one in which actors accept, and abide by, certain rules of the game. A constitutive effect is one that creates a new game for the actors to play. Rationalist methodologies focus exclusively on regulative effects. Reflectivist methodologies address both kinds of effects, but tend to emphasize the constitutive ones.[26]

Take, as a metaphor, a game of chess. In order to play chess, one must understand the regulative rules: knights can move only on the vertical and horizontal, bishops only on the diagonal, pawns only one square at a time, and so on. One could presumably change the regulative rules, if both players agreed, and still be playing chess, just a slightly different form of chess. There are also, however, constitutive rules that are often not clearly stated, but that are fundamental to the game. For example, you cannot dump the board if you are losing. If you make a habit of this, no one will play with you. This is a constitutive rule because the basic concept of chess does not work unless the players are willing to accept a loss when the regulative rules indicate that they have lost.

Analysts who look at regulative rules try to figure out how successful these rules are at making the game work smoothly and effectively. In professional sports, for example, the rule-making bodies often modify the rules, by changing the height of the pitcher's mound, the rules governing illegal defense, or the number of points given for a win relative to a tie. These rule-making bodies all agree on the ultimate goal—to make the sport as exciting as possible, for the purpose of attracting as many spectators as possible. The changes to the rules are intended to achieve that goal as efficiently as possible. Analysts who look at constitutive rules tend to ask why the relevant actors are playing a particular game in the first place. Why, for example, do people play football in the United States and rugby in Europe? What motivates people to play and watch team sports in the first place?

Two examples from the world of IOs might help to clarify this distinction. The first is from the international trade regime. This system abounds in regulative minutiae—the final document from the Uruguay round of negotiations, which created the WTO, ran to approximately 550 pages of regulative detail.[27] But all of this detail depends on the norm of nondiscrimination, the idea that countries treat all other countries equally. Nondiscrimination has regulative effects, but it is also a constitutive norm: if countries do not accept the basic principle, the entire system falls apart. Nondiscrimination is not the only principle available upon which one could base international trade,[28] but it is the one that the current system is built on. The entire superstructure of international trade rules requires that participating countries accept it.

A second example is from the rules of war. One of these rules is that a country is not allowed to target civilians in war.[29] This rule certainly has regulative effects; for example, it affected U.S. targeting choices in its air campaigns in Iraq in 2003, Afghanistan in 2001, and the former Yugoslavia in the 1990s. But it depends on the idea that belligerents, soldiers, are in principle different from civilians. When military efforts require support, funding, etcetera, from national communities, this distinction can be weak, both in practice and in principle. Why, for example, is a janitor working at a military base (and working there because it was the only job available) a legitimate target, while a journalist who is not in uniform but who argues loudly in favor of the war not a legitimate target? The answer is that this is a constitutive distinction that has been accepted by the international community. It is one of the ideas on which the rules are based, rather than being one of the rules.[30]

In the same way that the object of rationalist study in regime theory can be summed up as *transparency*, the object of reflectivist study can be summed up as *legitimacy*.[31] Most people obey most laws most of the time not because of specific calculations of interest or fear of punishment, but because they accept the law as legitimate.[32] For instance, most people do not resort to murder as a method of dispute settlement, because they accept the idea that murder is morally wrong. Constitutive rules help us to determine what constitutes legitimate behavior and what does not. For example, most moral systems see human life as having value in and of itself. This makes taking such a life, in the absence of a good reason for doing so (e.g., self-defense) illegitimate. Underpinning regulative law (no murder) with generally accepted constitutive rules (human life has moral value) makes the specific law more likely to be widely accepted. A regulative law that does not have accepted constitutive underpinnings can be much more difficult to enforce, as the United States discovered during prohibition.

The reflectivist approach to the study of international institutions, then, tends to focus on ideas about what constitutes legitimate behavior, by looking at both the regulative and constitutive elements of international regimes. Whereas the rationalist approach assumes that human behavior will be based on maximizing utility, the reflectivist approach assumes that people will pay attention to the appropriateness of behavior. Applied to the international level, this approach argues that states will want to behave in ways that are seen as appropriate, given accepted international norms. These norms, in other words, legitimate state behavior.

Arguably the most basic constitutive norm in contemporary international relations is the idea of sovereignty.[33] Sovereignty gives rights to states, primarily the right to noninterference by other states.[34] But sovereignty requires legitimacy, and legitimacy can only be granted by the international community, the community of states.[35] As an example, the Taliban were never recognized by the UN as the legitimate government of Afghanistan, even though they controlled most of the country. Diplomatically, this made it relatively easy for the United States to use force to remove the Taliban from power in 2001. The United States may well have done the same thing anyway, but one of the reasons that no other country even questioned U.S. interference in Afghanistan was that even though the international community recognized Afghanistan as a country, it did not recognize the Taliban as a legitimate government.

Another increasingly important norm in international politics is respect for human rights. This is a much newer constitutive norm than sovereignty; it did not really enter the international relations discourse until after World War II. There are several international organizations and international agreements that focus on human rights, which together can be thought of as the international human rights regime.[36] This regime is so strong that most of the world's countries have signed most of the agreements. Skeptics would argue, however, that these agreements have no teeth, that countries sign them in order to avoid international opprobrium, but that they do not go on to reform their human rights behavior, as required by the agreements.[37] Optimists say that on the whole, respect for human rights is increasing globally and that these agreements have played a role in bringing about this improvement.[38] How do we know who is right? How can we tell if a constitutive norm, an international regime understood reflectively, is working?

Reflectivism and Effectiveness

The question of the effectiveness of international regimes is more complicated from a reflectivist perspective than from a rationalist one. From the rationalist perspective, effectiveness can be reduced to efficiency, the extent to which the regime is efficient at changing the behavior of states and other actors in international relations. The rationalist approach focuses on regulative rules that clearly specify how actors are expected to behave, and those same rules can be used as a metric for effectiveness. States either follow them or they do not; the regime is either effective or not.

Approached from a reflectivist perspective, this same metric is less useful for measuring the effectiveness of a regime. This is the case for three reasons. First, the reflectivist approach tends to focus on patterns of behavior in general rather than on compliance specifically. A good analogy can be drawn here with speed limits. From a rationalist perspective, speed limits, as rules of behavior, are often failures; they are more often broken than obeyed. But from a more sociological perspective, they can be seen as successful, as they provide a baseline for behavior. People will generally drive at a different speed on a road with a 30 mph limit than on a road with a 70 mph limit. People may not be strictly obeying the rule, but the rule is still affecting their behavior. Similarly, states often cheat at the margins of their obligations under the WTO system. From a rationalist perspective, this suggests a weak regime with inadequate enforcement. From a reflectivist perspective, however, the fact that the international trade regime provides the behavioral baseline of expectations from which states cheat only at the margins suggests that the regime has been effective in establishing multilateralism, nondiscrimination, and other criteria as legitimate standards of behavior.

The second reason why adhesion to rules is less useful as a metric for determining regime effectiveness from a reflectivist perspective is that constitutive regimes do not always specify clear rules for behavior. For example, as previously suggested, a core constitutive regime in the contemporary practice of international relations is sovereignty. Some actors in world politics can be thought of, for a variety of reasons, as semisovereign.[39] One instance of such an actor is Taiwan, which although in many ways is like a normal state, is not considered by the international system to be fully sovereign. This status affects Taiwan in a variety of ways. It cannot join the UN. It can join the WTO, but as a "separate customs territory," not as a state.[40] The Taiwanese government gives generous aid to countries that allow it diplomatic representation, because such representation makes it seem more legitimately sovereign. None of this is governed by explicit rules, but the actions both of the Taiwanese government and of other governments toward Taiwan suggest that these fuzzy rules about sovereignty still matter.

The third reason why adherence to specific rules does not necessarily tell us about the effectiveness of a regime from a reflectivist perspective is that there is no clear hierarchy of norms. Norms of human rights, for example, often come into conflict with norms against interference in the affairs of other states. Sometimes one norm will predominate, sometimes the other, and sometimes there will be some sort of compromise. This does not make either norm more or less effective than the other, or one necessarily preeminent. The answer to questions of effectiveness in this context is provided by the degree to which each norm affects actor behavior overall.

So what does this tell us about the question that led into this section, whether or not the international human rights regime is effective? It tells us to look at human rights as a norm rather than as a rule, as a baseline for expectations of state behavior, and as a legitimator of sovereignty. There are a number of ways of going about doing this. We can compare the behavior of states in general, or of less rights-respecting states in particular, with their behavior in the past and see if overall patterns with respect to human rights have changed. This can tell us the extent to which respect for human rights has become the norm in world politics.

We can also look at instances in which human rights norms are clearly being broken and observe the responses both of the states breaking the norms and of other states. When a state does something that it knows to be illegitimate, and either has been or expects to be caught doing it, it often responds by justifying its behavior either as supported by a different norm, or as a justifiable exception. When looking at the behavior of states breaking a norm, then, a good indicator of regime strength is to look at the extent of the "yes, but … " response. For example, Russia often responded to criticism of the extent of its use of force in Chechnya by labeling the Chechens as terrorists. China has responded to criticisms that it lacks democracy at the national level by attempting to create democratic processes at the local level. To use a different norm as an example, since the end of the Cold War, the United States has been careful to nest all of its uses of force internationally (which break a general norm against the use of force) in multilateral settings, thus drawing legitimacy from the norms of multilateralism and collective security. This is true, for example, even of the case against Iraq in 2003. The weapons of mass destruction issue provided leverage in part because that issue could draw on a decade of Security Council resolutions.

The responses of other states are also good indicators of the strength of a regime. When other states protest a behavior, it suggests that the international community as a whole sees the behavior as illegitimate. This does not mean that states cannot engage in illegitimate behavior, but it does make such behavior costly. To use an example of an extreme breach of human rights norms, the Rwandan genocide suggested that the genocide regime was real, but weak. It was sufficiently effective that the perpetrators of the genocide were no longer accepted as legitimate participants in international politics. But it was not sufficiently effective to motivate states or the international community to do anything to stop the genocide while it was in progress.[41]

A third way of looking at the effectiveness of regimes, understood reflectively, is to look at patterns of discourse in international politics. The extent to which actors in international politics—both representatives of states and representatives of NGOs—speak about a norm, and speak in the terms of a norm, the more the norm is likely to serve as a baseline for expectations. This form of analysis begins with the assumption that language matters, that the terms we use to communicate with each other about an issue affect how we think about the issue.[42] If, for example, we find that the leaders of China speak often about human rights, when they did not twenty years ago, we can conclude that human rights norms are stronger than they used to be.

Conclusions

The rationalist and reflectivist approaches to the study of international regimes study different kinds of regime effects. The rationalist approach is best for studying issue-specific cooperation among states. It is useful for designing regimes that make such cooperation work efficiently. The reflectivist approach is best for studying conceptually how the international system, how international organization, works more broadly. It is useful for studying the general rules of the game, rather than specific regulations.

Regimes will have both rationalist and reflectivist effects. In some regimes, particularly the more functional ones, the rationalist effects may predominate. In other regimes the reflectivist effects may predominate. The international regime literature tends to divide the field into camps—you are either on one side or the other.[43] The rationalist/reflectivist distinction might be more usefully understood, however, as different methodologies appropriate for addressing different questions. A full understanding of any given regime, one that addresses both regulative and constitutive effects, requires that both approaches be used.

5

The United Nations and Its System

The first half of this book discusses theoretical approaches to the study of international organizations (IOs). The second half examines the role of IOs in particular issue-areas. This chapter acts as a bridge between the two halves by looking at the overall structure of IOs in the international system. A majority of multilateral IOs in today's world are related in some way or other to the UN, and therefore, the UN provides a good focal point for a discussion of the IO system as a whole. The UN is also the focus of many of the debates on the role of IOs in contemporary global governance, particularly those discussed in Chapters 1 and 2. This chapter will thus both lay out the institutional background for the issue-specific chapters to follow and show how some of the theoretical discussions in the study of IOs apply to the UN system.

The Structure of the UN

To speak simply of the UN can be misleading, because the term can refer to a number of different things. It can refer to a set of countries, to a specific set of institutional structures located in New York City, or to the entire set of institutional structures that come under the administrative purview of the UN headquarters. More broadly, it can refer to what is known as the "UN system," which encompasses a large group of IOs, many of which are not in any way within the administrative hierarchy of the UN headquarters. A good place to start any discussion of the UN, therefore, is with an explanation of how the various institutions that are a part of the UN system relate to one another.

At its most basic, the UN refers to a set of member countries (currently 191), a constitutional document (the Charter of the UN), and six basic organs: the General Assembly (GA), the Security Council, the Secretariat, the International Court of Justice (ICJ), the Economic and Social Council (ECOSOC), and the Trusteeship Council. These organs are directly mandated by the Charter. Many of the organs have in turn created subsidiary agencies (see the organizational chart of the UN, fig. 5.1). There are a number of autonomous agencies that are part of the UN system but these are not administratively subsidiary to the central organs of the UN.[1]

The United Nations system

PRINCIPAL ORGANS

| Trusteeship Council | Security Council | General Assembly | Economic and Social Council | International Court of Justice | Secretariat |

Subsidiary Bodies
Military Staff Committee
Standing Committee and ad hoc bodies
International Criminal Tribunal for the Former Yugoslavia
International Criminal Tribunal for Rwanda
UN Monitoring, Verification and Inspection Commission (Iraq)
United Nations Compensation Commission
Peacekeeping Operations and Missions

Subsidiary Bodies
Main committees
Other sessional committees
Standing committees and ad hoc bodies
Other subsidiary organs

Programmes and Funds
UNCTAD United Nations Conference on Trade and Development
  ITC International Trade Centre (UNCTAD/WTO)
UNDCP[1] United Nations Drug Control Programme
UNEP United Nations Environment Programme
UNICEF United Nations Children's Fund
UNDP United Nations Development Programme
  UNIFEM United Nations Development Fund for Women
  UNV United Nations Volunteers
  UNCDF United Nations Capital Development Fund
UNFPA United Nations Population Fund
UNHCR Office of the United Nations High Commissioner for Refugees
WFP World Food Programme
UNRWA[2] United Nations Relief and Works Agency for Palestine Refugees in the Near East
UN-HABITAT United Nations Human Settlements Programme (UNHSP)

Research and Training Institutes
UNICRI United Nations Interregional Crime and Justice Research Institute
UNITAR United Nations Institute for Training and Research
UNRISD United Nations Research Institute for Social Development
UNIDIR United Nations Institute for Disarmament Research
INSTRAW International Research and Training Institute for the Advancement of Women

Other UN Entities
OHCHR Office of the United Nations High Commissioner for Human Rights
UNOPS United Nations Office for Project Services
UNU United Nations University
UNSSC United Nations System Staff College
UNAIDS Joint United Nations Programme on HIV/AIDS

Functional Commissions
Commissions on:
Human Rights
Narcotic Drugs
Crime Prevention and Criminal Justice
Science and Technology for Development
Sustainable Development
Status of Women
Population and Development
Commission for Social Development
Statistical Commission

Regional Commissions
Economic Commission for Africa (ECA)
Economic Commission for Europe (ECE)
Economic Commission for Latin America and the Caribbean (ECLAC)
Economic and Social Commission for Asia and the Pacific (ESCAP)
Economic and Social Commission for Western Asia (ESCWA)

Other Bodies
Permanent Forum on Indigenous Issues (PFII)
United Nations Forum on Forests
Sessional and standing committees
Expert, ad hoc and related bodies

Related Organizations
WTO[a] World Trade Organization
IAEA[b] International Atomic Energy Agency
CTBTO Prep.Com[c] PrepCom for the Nuclear-Test-Ban-Treaty Organization
OPCW[c] Organization for the Prohibition of Chemical Weapons

Specialized Agencies[d]
ILO International Labour Organization
FAO Food and Agriculture Organization of the United Nations
UNESCO United Nations Educational, Scientific and Cultural Organization
WHO World Health Organization
World Bank Group
IBRD International Bank for Reconstruction and Development
IDA International Development Association
IFC International Finance Corporation
MIGA Multilateral Investment Guarantee Agency
ICSID International Centre for Settlement of Investment Disputes
IMF International Monetary Fund
ICAO International Civil Aviation Organization
IMO International Maritime Organization
ITU International Telecommunication Union
UPU Universal Postal Union
WMO World Meteorological Organization
WIPO World Intellectual Property Organization
IFAD International Fund for Agricultural Development
UNIDO United Nations Industrial Development Organization
WTO[e] World Tourism Organization

Departments and Offices
OSG Office of the Secretary-General
OIOS Office of Internal Oversight Services
OLA Office of Legal Affairs
DPA Department of Political Affairs
DDA Department for Disarmament Affairs
DPKO Department of Peace-keeping Operations
OCHA Office for the Coordination of Humanitarian Affairs
DESA Department of Economic and Social Affairs
DGACM Department for General Assembly and Conference Management
DPI Department of Public Information
DM Department of Management
OHRLLS Office of the High Representative for the Least Developed Countries, Landlocked Developing Countries and Small Island Developing States
UNSECOORD Office of the United Nations Security Coordinator
UNODC United Nations Office on Drugs and Crime
UNOG UN Office at Geneva
UNOV UN Office at Vienna
UNON UN Office at Nairobi

NOTES: Solid lines from a Principal Organ indicate a direct reporting relationship; dashes indicate a non-subsidiary relationship. [1] The UN Drug Control Programme is part of the UN Office on Drugs and Crime. [2] UNRWA and UNIDIR report only to the GA. [3] The World Trade Organization and World Tourism Organization use the same acronym. [4] IAEA reports to the Security Council and the General Assembly (GA). [5] The CTBTO Prep.Com and OPCW report to the GA. [6] Specialized agencies are autonomous organizations working with the UN and each other through the coordinating machinery of the ECOSOC at the intergovernmental level, and through the Chief Executives Board for coordination (CEB) at the inter-secretariat level.

Published by the UN Department of Public Information
DPI/2342—March 2004

Figure 5.1 An organizational chart of the United Nations system.

And finally, there are regional organizations designed to provide some of the functions of the central organs for regional issues. As with autonomous agencies, these regional organizations are generally not administratively subsidiary to the central organs, but are encouraged within the UN system as regional mini-UNs.

The subsidiary agencies, which are often thought of as major IOs in their own right, have in common that they have been created by, are in principle overseen by, and can be disbanded by their superior organizations. In other words, they are answerable to the central organs of the UN. They usually draw at least a portion of their budgets from UN funds as well. Apart from these similarities, subsidiary agencies can be quite different in focus, scope, and scale. Their foci run the gamut from international security (such as specific peacekeeping operations), to economics and development (e.g., the United Nations Conference on Trade and Development [UNCTAD] and the Regional Economic Commissions), to human rights and humanitarian intervention (including the United Nations High Commissioner for Refugees [UNHCHR] and United Nations High Commissioner for Human Rights [UNHCR]). Some are run from within the UN Secretariat (e.g., the Office of the UN Security Coordinator); others have their own secretariats, headquarters, and bureaucratic structures (such as the United Nations Children's Fund [UNICEF]). Some focus on research and monitoring, while others are active on the ground in implementing the goals of the UN. Some employ a handful of people, others employ thousands. Some are fairly actively overseen by the UN organ that created them, and others operate almost independently of the central UN bureaucracy.

The autonomous agencies (some of which predate the UN) and the regional organizations have much more tenuous administrative links with the UN proper. Autonomous agencies interact with and send reports to ECOSOC but are not answerable to it, and do not draw their funding from general UN funds. They have been brought into the UN system because they perform functions that are in keeping with the UN's general mission and with the UN's multilateral approach. But they would in all probability function in much the same way if all formal links with the UN proper were severed. Similarly, the UN is supportive of regional cooperation organizations as a sort of multilateralism of first resort for regional issues. This allows issues that are essentially of a regional nature to be dealt with in a way that is in keeping with that of the UN system, but without burdening the UN proper with issues that could be effectively dealt with in a more local forum.

Figure 5.1 is a schematic representation of the UN system. This is the UN's version of its organizational chart, and can be found online at http://www.un.org/aboutun/chart.html. The online version has links to the homepages of all of the organizations listed.

The UN, Sovereignty, and Power

This book started with questions about the effects of IOs on state sovereignty, and the extent to which IOs have power in contemporary international relations. To the extent that it is the central IO in the system, the UN would seem to be a good place to begin answering these questions. But the answers depend on what we mean by the UN—whether we are speaking of the central organs, these organs plus their associated subsidiary organizations, or the UN system as a whole. This is particularly true when asking questions about agency, that is, about IOs as actors. One can certainly speak of particular institutions and agencies within the UN, whether the UN Secretariat or a particular subsidiary agency, as a corporate actor, in the same way that international relations scholars often speak of states as if they were individuals. Ascribing agency to the UN more broadly, including all of the subsidiary agencies, is more problematic. While all of the particular institutions within the UN are technically administratively interrelated, the links, both authoritative and operational, are often quite tenuous. In other words, the extent to which any one individual or office speaks for the UN, broadly defined, is not clear. And finally, ascribing agency to the UN system is, in most cases, inappropriate. The autonomous and regional agencies are simply not part of the authority structure of the UN proper, let alone its administrative structure. As such, the UN proper cannot authoritatively speak for them.

The questions with which this book began concerned the relationships between sovereignty and globalization, between power and interdependence, and the place of IOs in these relationships. Applied to the UN, these questions can be phrased as follows: To what extent is the UN replacing states as the primary locus for international and global governance? How powerful is the UN becoming relative to states? The answer depends on whether one is looking at the UN as an actor or the UN as a system. Looking at the UN as an actor, it does indeed have some power, but certainly not power of the sort that might threaten either the sovereignty of the core states in the system or the centrality of the sovereign state system itself in global governance. Looking at the UN as a system, it has little direct power, but at the same time, it plays a fundamental role not in undermining but in redefining the sovereign state system.

Looking at the UN, even narrowly defined, as an actor is, as was suggested above, problematic. It makes more sense to locate agency in the specific organs of the UN, which is what the next section of this chapter will do. The organs taken together speak neither with the same voice nor with the same sort of authority. One can draw a loose analogy between the various organs of the UN and the components of domestic governments (e.g. the GA being analogous to a legislature, the Security Council to an executive, the Secretariat to a permanent bureaucracy, and the ICJ to a supreme court). This analogy suggests the possibility of the UN as a whole as representative of an international community that itself has agency. But this agency is at best diffuse, and the agency of the international community tends to be expressed with respect to particular issues through the appropriate international institution.

Given the difficulty of ascribing agency to the UN in general, rather than to specific organs and institutions within it, it is also difficult to speak of the UN as a whole as a locus of power, rather than speaking of the specific institutions within it as individual loci of power. This suggests that those people who view the UN as an actor and as a source of world government, rather than as a representative example of a mode of governance, are seriously overestimating its capabilities as an actor. This is true both of those who look forward to a UN-led world government and of those who fear it.[2] Those who hope for a UN-led world government think that the UN's various components cumulatively give it the potential to act as a global government.

But these components do not make the UN an actor in the way that well-functioning national governments are. To speak of, say, the U.S. government as an actor with respect to the international community, despite its checks and balances, can be both meaningful and useful: however fractious the process of making foreign policy, the policy can be put into practice in a coherent and relatively unified way. In other words, the U.S. government may not think like a unitary actor, but it can act as one. The same cannot be said of the components of the UN.

When looked at as a system rather than as an actor, the UN has a different impact on sovereignty and a different sort of power. The UN as a system can be seen as redefining the way in which states habitually interact with each other, the basic way in which the state system operates. In other words, the UN system has in important ways redefined sovereignty. This is not to say that it has necessarily weakened sovereignty as an institution. Rather, it has changed the content of the set of rules, the international regime that we understand by the term sovereignty. The UN system has created this change by normalizing and routinizing the practices associated with multilateralism, a pattern of state interaction focused on inclusive negotiation aimed at the creation of rule-based solutions to issues that have the potential to create international conflict. Multilateralism is now the expected norm of state behavior in a way that was not true half a century ago.[3] States still act unilaterally on occasion, but when they do they are often seen as acting inappropriately.

Multilateralism can be, and often is, seen as a form of globalization. It is a pattern of collectively making rules that apply to all participant countries. In this sense, it can be seen as undermining state sovereignty, because it does decrease the autonomy of states to make domestic rules and regulations as they see fit. But at the same time, multilateralism reifies sovereignty, because it is states, and only those states recognized as sovereign by the community of states, that participate in the creation of common rules. Thus, multilateralism, the modus operandi of the UN system, simultaneously promotes a form of globalization and reifies a form of sovereignty.

Does the UN system have power? The answer to this question depends on how one defines power. If one defines power in terms of agency, the ability of an actor to get something done or to change an outcome, then the answer is no. The UN as a system has little independent agency. If one defines power in terms of changes in outcomes, without requiring that it be the result of some conscious or active attempt to change outcomes, then the UN system does have some real power, through the regime of multilateralism. This regime has significant agenda-setting power and does help to define the way actors, both states and individuals, think about international politics and what constitutes appropriate political behavior in international relations. It has, in short, become habitual practice for states to think in terms of inclusive negotiation as a first resort when confronted with international issues, either political or technical. The regime of multilateralism also has some real power in constraining conscious state behavior. An example of this is the attempt by the Bush administration to work through the UN Security Council in dealing with Iraq. Acting multilaterally became a goal in itself (although not necessarily a primary goal), even though the United States was perfectly capable of acting non-multilaterally, and even when the administration in question was among the more skeptical of the practice of multilateralism. There are limits to the constraining power of the regime—the United States in the end took action without multilateral support. But the efforts made by the United States to gain this support suggest that the power is real.

The GA

Thus, the UN as a system has a significant amount of power, but a passive sort of power, a power without agency. To find agency in the UN, one must look at its specific institutions. The remainder of this chapter examines the central organs of the UN both as institutions and as regimes. This discussion will illustrate some of the theoretical debates discussed in earlier chapters and provide some background to the examination of the role of IOs in particular issue-areas to be undertaken in later chapters.

The first of these organs is the GA, which is, in a way, the core organ of the UN in that it is the only organ in which all member countries are represented all of the time. Its primary activities are to pass resolutions and to create subsidiary agencies to deal with particular issues. The resolutions are not binding; they are indicative of the majority opinion of the community of nations, but they are not considered to be international law, nor are they enforceable. The GA works on a one-country one-vote basis. Resolutions on most issues can be passed by majority vote, although "important questions,"[4] including, among other things, those relating to membership in the UN and to budgetary issues, require a two-thirds majority. The GA includes both the plenary body (the GA proper) and several permanent committees, each of which, like the plenary GA, includes all countries that are members of the UN. It is in these committees that much of the actual negotiating and crafting of resolutions is done. The GA elects a new president and seventeen vice presidents each year from among the members of the national delegations. It thus has no senior bureaucrats of its own; its senior management is drawn from within the ranks of the national delegations.

The GA is therefore best seen as a forum, as a regime, rather than as an institutional actor. It is a place for the community of states to discuss issues of common concern, and is a creature of those states rather than an independent actor on the international stage. It does not have an executive function, although many of its subsidiary organizations do. It does, however, have significant budgetary powers (although in practice, it is the staff of the Secretariat that proposes budgets, subject to the approval of the GA). The structure of the GA, with its emphasis on equal representation and majority voting, yields a voting majority for developing countries, particularly the Group of 77 (G-77), a caucus of third-world countries.[5] This gives the G-77 effective control over the distribution of much of the UN's budget. This control, however, only matters insofar as the countries with the biggest assessments of UN dues pay up. In practice, the largest donor countries, particularly the United States, have been able to restrain the growth of UN budgets, and force a decline in the size of the UN's bureaucracy, by threatening to (and, for much of the 1990s, actually proceeding to) withhold the payment of assessed dues. The GA, therefore, is in practice more democratic as a forum than as manager of the UN's budget.

From a regime perspective, it seems easy at first glance to dismiss the GA as a talking shop, where small countries with little power on the international stage vote on resolutions that in the end have little effect on outcomes in international politics. In fact, the report of a recent high-level panel sponsored by the Secretary-General criticized the GA for an "inability to reach closure on issues" and an "unwieldy and static agenda."[6] From a rationalist perspective, a talking shop has some minor benefits in terms of transparency. It reduces transaction costs by providing a permanent structure and set of rules for communication within the community of states, and it can improve flows of information by making it easier for states to communicate their preferences effectively to the community of states as a whole. But given that the results of GA debates rarely include specific rules of behavior or decision-making procedures, skeptics can argue that this improved transparency does not really translate into an increased efficiency of meaningful international cooperation.

This rationalist skepticism overlooks the role of the GA in facilitating the creation and oversight of its subsidiary bodies, in which role it may not be particularly efficient but is certainly more efficient than such creation and oversight would be absent the Assembly. More importantly, a rationalist examination of the GA can miss perhaps its most important function: legitimation. It may not be able to enforce its resolutions, but it nonetheless speaks with some real moral authority simply because it is the core democratic organ of the UN, and, to some extent, the voice of the community of nations.[7] The Assembly helps to legitimate broad principles such as the sovereign equality of nations and the cooperative settlement of disputes, and can also be used to legitimate positions on specific issues.

For example, the signatory states of the Antipersonnel Mine Ban Convention (also known as the Ottawa Convention)[8] faced a situation in which the world's major powers refused to join them, even though they constituted a large majority of the world's states. This threatened to make the convention pointless. The signatory states then made a conscious decision to launch the convention through a GA resolution, not a normal course of action with technical treaties. Clearly, they took this route in order to legitimize the campaign against antipersonnel landmines despite the refusal of some key major military powers to cooperate. This suggests that these states, the majority of the world's states, take the GA's legitimation role seriously.

The Security Council

The UN Security Council is both more specialized in its focus and more unusual in its design than the GA. The Security Council is designed to focus specifically on issues of international security, and is the body charged by the UN charter to authorize the use of force to maintain collective security. The question of collective security as such is discussed in the next chapter, but the design of the Security Council as an institution is discussed here.

The design of the Security Council is, at its core, a response to the failures of the collective security mechanisms of the League of Nations. From a regime perspective, the League's inefficiency at promoting transparency made it ineffective at contributing to collective security. The Security Council was designed specifically both to decrease the transaction costs inherent in the League model and to specify property rights much more clearly to promote more efficient cooperation.[9] The League failed, among other reasons, because its rules and decision-making procedures neither allowed for fast and detailed responses to threats to international security, nor clearly identified those responsible for enforcing the responses that had been agreed upon.

The Security Council was designed to overcome these shortcomings through the mechanisms of a limited membership and a clear connection between those states that made decisions about collective security and those charged with enforcing them. Membership in the Council is restricted to fifteen states.[10] The Council is permanently in session (unlike the GA), and the size of each national delegation is strictly limited. The effect of these organizational features is to limit transaction costs—the Council can debate an issue on very short notice, and the debate can proceed relatively efficiently because of the small number of states and people participating. The Security Council then has clear authority both to decide what issues constitute threats to international security and to mandate action—diplomatic, economic, and military—to combat those threats.

The Council's voting structure supports its ability to use this mandate effectively. A key problem with the League's attempts to deal with issues of collective security was a disjuncture between those who mandated action and those expected to actually undertake it. Action could be mandated by a group of small states that collectively constituted more than half of the membership, but that even collectively did not have any real enforcement capabilities. The Security Council was designed to overcome this problem by giving the major powers in the system permanent membership, a disproportionate share of the vote, and the ability to veto potential Council decisions. This improves the "property rights" of the enforcement system by giving those who will supply enforcement more direct and individual control over the assignment of enforcement. But the veto power innovation has not proved to be ideal. During the Cold War, Soviet and U.S. vetoes led to deadlock on the Council, resulting in a quarter century during which the Council did little.[11] The selection of veto powers has also become increasingly dissonant with actual distributions of power more than half a century after the end of World War II. But the innovation did nonetheless create an institution that is more effective, and certainly more long-lived, than the League.

Beyond efficiency, the Security Council is an effective legitimator in international politics, perhaps even more than the GA. One might have expected the disproportionate voice given to the major powers on the Council, in a UN that otherwise promotes the sovereign equality of states, to lead most other countries to view it as more representative of the international power structure than of international legitimacy. But this has not really turned out to be the case. The Security Council has an integral institutional role in determining the legitimacy of states, both through its authority to adjudicate questions of international security and its role in allowing countries to join the UN.[12] But the Security Council is also seen by much of the contemporary world as the only body that can legitimately authorize international violence. A good example of its role in political legitimation is the debate that preceded the invasion of Iraq in 2003. There was never any question that an invasion would be carried out overwhelmingly by U.S. forces. But much of the world was nonetheless willing to accept such an invasion only if the Security Council authorized it, despite a widespread recognition that such an authorization would in function be a matter of political horse-trading among the permanent members.

Having said this, and as the above comment about political horse-trading suggests, the Security Council is better viewed as a forum than as an actor. A number of features of its institutional structure militate against it functioning as an independent actor in international politics. It has no bureaucracy independent of its participating members. Its president is drawn from among the delegates representing its fifteen members, and the presidency rotates on a monthly basis,[13] suggesting that there is little vesting of interests in that office. And while the five permanent members lend a continuity to the Council, the ten rotating members are elected for two years only and cannot be immediately reelected, meaning that the continuity is only partial. The Council also has no independent powers of enforcement. It is dependent for these on the capabilities of UN member countries, so that even were it to develop an interest separate from those of its member states, it could not do anything to promote that interest independently of them.

Nevertheless, the structure of the Security Council clearly has empowering effects. Its legal and treaty structure as the organ of the UN charged with the authority to legitimize the use of force internationally, has clearly helped to make the international community into a reality to be taken into account by states making decisions relating to issues of international security. And the membership and voting structure has had the effect of empowering the five permanent members at the expense of the rest of the membership of the UN. In the contemporary world this is perhaps least true of the United States, which, as the world's predominant military power, is constrained by the legitimacy of the Security Council's authority as much as it is enabled by its veto on the Council. It is more true of the other four permanent members, who, through their veto power, have a greater individual say in matters of international security than their interests in the issue at hand, or their potential contribution to enforcement measures, may warrant. It can also give them a greater say than other countries that are more directly involved in an issue or that are in position to contribute more to enforcement. As an aside, this voting structure also has the incidental effect of disempowering the European Union (EU) in matters of international security. Because two EU members (the United Kingdom and France) are permanent members of the Security Council, but the EU as an institution is not represented there (unlike at many IOs dealing with economic issues), these two countries have a vested interest in acting as individuals with respect to issues that the SC deals with, rather than as members of the EU.

The Secretariat

The UN Secretariat, much more than any of the other five organs of the UN, can reasonably be seen as an independent actor in international politics. The Secretariat is the UN's central bureaucracy, and as such deals with the everyday details of managing a large organization. In this sense it provides the institutional support for the transparency and legitimation functions of the other UN organs. But it is also the only one of the organs that can speak with a strong and (somewhat) independent voice about international politics. It can do so largely through the office of the Secretary-General. The Secretary-General is charged in the UN Charter to "be the chief administrative officer of the Organization,"[14] but is not empowered to play an active role in international politics beyond bringing "to the attention of the Security Council any matter which in his opinion may threaten the maintenance of international peace and security."[15] The Secretary-General is also instructed by the Charter to remain politically neutral, to maintain an "international character."[16] Over the years, this combination of political neutrality and authority to raise issues on the international stage has increasingly given Secretaries-General a significant independent voice in international politics.

This voice is empowered by the moral authority of the UN system and by the position the UN, and the Secretariat, holds within that system. It is constrained, however, by the same factors. The UN charter gives the Secretary-General the ability to effectively put items on the Security Council's agenda. But perhaps more importantly, the moral authority of the UN gives the Secretary-General an effective bully pulpit from which to put issues on the international agenda, and an effective claim to neutrality from which to mediate in disputes. But in order to maintain this moral authority, the Secretary-General must remain within the bounds of the instructions of the Charter and must maintain a reputation both of internationalism and of political neutrality. In other words, the office empowers its occupant only insofar as he or she[17] acts in a manner in keeping (or generally perceived to be in keeping) with the office. Furthermore, since the Secretary-General has neither the ability to legislate nor the ability to enforce, the power and effective agency of the office depends on the ability to persuade. This in turn means that the effectiveness of any given Secretary-General as an independent actor in international politics depends greatly on political skill (and the skill levels of Secretaries-General has varied greatly).[18]

As an actor in international relations, the Secretary-General tends to play the role either of agenda-setter or of mediator. As agenda-setters, the Secretaries-General can use the authority of the position, and the access to the media that goes with that authority, to raise or promote certain issues on the international agenda, and to embarrass states into changing their behavior. This can be done through either public or private diplomacy. As mediators, the Secretaries-General have often used the office proactively to defuse escalating crises, and to monitor potentially escalatory situations. They do this personally in some cases, and in others appoint special representatives to mediate in or monitor a variety of places at the same time; the current Secretary-General, Kofi Annan, has several dozen Special Representatives, Personal Representatives, and Envoys throughout the world.[19] These act to a certain extent as a personal foreign service for the Secretariat.

In addition to the lack of legislative and enforcement powers, and the need to maintain the legitimacy of the office, the Secretary-General is also constrained as an independent actor in international politics by the need to administer the UN. This is a substantial task, involving a Secretariat staff of 8,900 people. Kofi Annan has in fact devoted quite a bit of effort toward administrative reform within the

Secretariat, an effort that is still underway.[20] Functionally, the need to successfully administer the UN also entails remaining on good terms with member countries in general, and major donor countries and permanent members of the Security Council in particular. It also entails restrained use of the Secretary-General's independent voice: A bully pulpit used too often dilutes its message, and too much activity on the part of the Secretariat would put strain on a limited budget. Secretaries-General tend also to be relatively moderate and centrist as a function of the way in which they are chosen. They are appointed by the GA on the recommendation of the Security Council. This means that they must first be approved by vote of the Security Council, without a veto being cast by any of the five permanent members, and then by two-thirds of the GA. In other words, they must be approved both by the Council veto powers and by the G-77, a process that generally leads to a compromise candidate.

ECOSOC, the ICJ, and the Trusteeship Council

The other three organs of the UN are dealt with here only briefly. The ICJ is a body designed to adjudicate disputes between countries and to interpret international law. Although those who view IOs as instruments of globalization might see the ICJ as such an instrument because its existence suggests an international law to which all states are subject, an equally strong, or perhaps stronger, argument can be made that the ICJ serves to reify the sovereign state and the international state system. This is the case both because only states have standing before the ICJ, and because acceptance of arbitration by the ICJ is voluntary. Only states have standing before the court because in international law, only states have legal personality; people do not. In effect this means that the ICJ is reifying the idea that states are the core actors in international relations. And states need only appear before the court when they agree to do so. In other words, the ICJ does not even infringe on national sovereignty to the point of requiring states to submit to international arbitration. Many state have committed themselves in advance to appearing before the ICJ when called upon to do so, a process called compulsory jurisdiction.[21] But many of these commitments are qualified: they do not apply in all circumstances, and states still retain the right to rescind their commitments. Discussion of the role of the ICJ beyond this observation is best done in a book on international law rather than a book on international institutions.[22]

The Trusteeship Council was created to oversee "the administration of territories whose peoples have not yet attained a full measure of self-government,"[23] the actual administration of which was to be undertaken by specific (usually colonial) states. The last territory that fell within the Council's mandate to become independent, Palau, did so in 1994, at which point it voted to suspend its activities indefinitely. In other words, even though the Trusteeship Council is officially still one of the UN's six central organs, it is for all practical purposes defunct. There has recently been discussion within the UN of eliminating the Council altogether.[24]

The final organ is the Economic and Social Council, commonly known as ECOSOC. The responsibilities of this body include information gathering, the drafting of treaties, and coordination of UN functions within economic and social issue-areas, broadly defined. ECOSOC consists of fifty-four members, elected by the GA for three-year terms. Despite this limited membership, it functions in many ways like a committee of the GA. It is the focal point for liaison with a wide array of subsidiary IOs and is the main point of contact and coordination with the affiliated specialized agencies (see the UN organizational chart, fig. 5.1). It has also created a number of commissions, both functional and regional, designed both as coordinative and as information-gathering bodies. Many treaties and conventions, including those leading to the creation of new IOs in economic and social issue-areas, are first discussed and drafted here.

In terms both of the forum/actor distinction and the regime/institution distinction, it is reasonable to think of ECOSOC as a more constrained version of the GA. It has little agency, and is better understood as a forum, yet the organizations and commissions subsidiary to it often do have agency and are capable of putting issues on the international agenda independently of the actions of states. Its power lies mainly in the ability to set agendas and bestow legitimacy, a power both less broad and less deep than that of the GA, but significant nonetheless. From a rationalist regime perspective, it has some success in improving information flows and decreasing transaction costs. From both a regime and an institutional perspective, it is subject to the same criticisms as the GA. The cumbersomeness of its procedures and the size and complexity of its organizational structure limit the effectiveness with which it can increase the efficiency of cooperation with respect to economic and social issues and legitimize new ways of thinking about and dealing with them.

6

Collective Security

The UN system is involved in the whole gamut of issue-areas in international politics. The second half of this book consists of chapters that focus on the role of specific international organizations (IOs) in these issue-areas. The first of these chapters looks at collective security. There are two reasons to begin with collective security. One is that in many ways it provides the core design function of the UN, the IO at the heart of the contemporary multilateral system. It is the issue that features most prominently in the UN Charter, and is probably still the function most closely associated with the UN in the popular imagination. The second reason is that many students of international relations are more skeptical of the role of IOs in the realm of security than in other issue-areas, and those analysts who question most pointedly whether IOs matter at all tend to focus their skepticism on security issues.[1] Security thus constitutes at the same time a central function of IOs and a hard-case test of whether or not they matter in international relations.

The core security mechanism of a multilateralist world is the system of collective security. This is a system in which all participant states agree to forswear the use of force in the settlement of disputes, and furthermore agree to act collectively against any state that chooses to initiate the use of force. Such collective action must be authorized by a multilateral mechanism, in other words, by an IO that is responsible for defining breaches of international security. Collective security can be contrasted with more traditional security alliances in that it is inclusive, while alliances are exclusive. In other words, alliances are usually formed against an outside enemy (whether current or potential), while a collective security organization aims to include all states and provide each with security against all of the others.

This is a difficult time to discuss IOs and collective security. In 2003, U.S. forces occupied Iraq without authorization from the UN Security Council, although the Security Council did legitimize a temporary occupation of the country after the fact. There was some discussion that this action could diminish the legitimacy of the Security Council (and of the UN more broadly) in the long term, and that it undermines such basic multilateralist concepts as collective security and respect for international law. Partly in response to these fears, the Secretary-General sponsored a high-level panel[2] to report on the role of the UN in collective security in the twenty-first century. The report suggested some significant reforms, as will be noted below. At the time of writing, it is not yet clear which of these reforms will be successfully implemented, but early indications are that they will be considerably watered down.[3]

While the crisis leading up to the war was a difficult time for the UN, it also highlighted the extent to which general populations, at least among industrialized countries, currently accept the Security Council as the arbiter of legitimacy in the use of force internationally. We do not know what effects this current crisis will have on the long-term workings and legitimacy of the Security Council, and of the UN more broadly, and we will in all likelihood not know for several years. The more dire predictions are probably overstated, as evidenced by the U.S. government's enthusiasm for using the Security Council to deal with issues ranging from Iran's nuclear program to crimes against humanity in Darfur, only two years after its failure to get the Council's approval for the war in Iraq.

This chapter begins with a general discussion of the concept of collective security and its development over time in the context of the UN and the Security Council. It then discusses the institutional features of some of the other IOs involved in international security issues, such as the UN Secretariat, the Department of Peacekeeping Operations (DPKO), and regional organizations such as the Organization for Security and Co-operation in Europe (OSCE). These organizations are then analyzed in the context of the four theoretical distinctions discussed in the earlier chapters of this book. This chapter, in other words, focuses on particular institutions in the context of theories of IO more generally. It does not provide a comprehensive discussion of international peacekeeping and peacemaking, or a full history of the development of these functions. One cannot do justice to such a discussion or in one short chapter, and these tasks have been performed well and at length elsewhere.[4]

The Security Council

That collective security is a core design feature of the UN is suggested by the Charter, the preamble of which begins with the words "We the peoples of the United Nations determined to save succeeding generations from the scourge of war," and the first article of which states that "The Purposes of the United Nations are: 1. To maintain international peace and security, and to that end: to take effective collective measures for the prevention and removal of threats to the peace, and for the suppression of acts of aggression and other breaches of the peace." The Charter provides two mechanisms for maintaining international peace and security, both of which focus on the Security Council as the institutional mechanism for carrying out this task. Chapter VI, entitled "Pacific Settlement of Disputes," allows the Security Council to involve itself in any dispute that it sees as a threat to the international peace, and to investigate, arbitrate, and recommend solutions. Chapter VII, "Action with Respect to Threats to the Peace, Breaches of the Peace, and Acts of Aggression," gives the Security Council the authority to define threats to and breaches of the peace, and to define the appropriate response of the international community, ranging from diplomatic pressure, to economic sanctions, to the use of force.[5]

In practice, the extent to which the Security Council has used these two mechanisms has varied over time. The use of both mechanisms was limited during the Cold War by the U.S.–Soviet confrontation. A result of the Cold War confrontation was that many, if not most, local conflicts took on geopolitical implications, as one side in the local conflict aligned itself with one side in the Cold War, and the other local side aligned with the other geopolitical pole. Since any kind of action by the Security Council required the agreement of both superpowers (for reasons discussed below), many disputes generated stalemate rather than action from the Council.

There were, nonetheless, several occasions on which the United States and the Soviet Union could agree on language for a Security Council resolution, either because neither cared particularly about the conflict in question, or because they agreed that a conflict was getting out of hand and represented a genuine threat to international stability. One of the best known of these resolutions, and a good example of a Chapter VI action, is Security Council Resolution 242, passed at the end of the Arab–Israeli war in 1967. This resolution called, among other things, for a cease-fire and withdrawal from territories occupied during the war. Even though the resolution had little effect on the course of the war, it did have both short-term and long-term effects. In the short term, the resolution provided the basis for a cease-fire that both sides could agree to without having to negotiate with each other directly. In the long-term, Resolution 242 still provides a starting point for most discussions of conflict resolution in that part of the world. The resolution thus provided both transparency and legitimacy in much the same way as was envisioned by the drafters of the UN Charter.

While the use of Chapter VI actions was constrained by the Cold War, the use of Chapter VII was, with one exception, eliminated entirely by the U.S.–Soviet confrontation. In the Korean War, the first major use of the UN system to authorize a collective use of force, it was the General Assembly (GA) rather than the Security Council that legitimated the use of force. The first large-scale military intervention authorized by the Security Council under Chapter VII, in the Belgian Congo in 1960, turned into a disaster for the UN, both politically and financially. UN forces spent four years in the Congo without a clear mandate, and the UN was not able to raise sufficient funds over and above its standard dues to cover the costs of the operation. The intervention went so badly that the Security Council did not authorize another full-scale Chapter VII intervention for another three decades. The next Chapter VII action was in response to Iraq's invasion of Kuwait in 1990. This action, made possible by the end of the Cold War, differed from the intervention in the Congo in that there was a clear and achievable mission (removing Iraqi forces from Kuwait), and sufficient force and funding available to achieve it.

Between the failure of the Congo intervention and the success in Kuwait, the Security Council created a new mechanism for promoting international peace and security, called peacekeeping. This is the activity for which the Security Council was known best for many years. Often referred to as "chapter six-and-a-half" (because it involves the use of military forces, but only with the consent of all of the parties to a conflict), peacekeeping missions use UN-sponsored forces as buffers between combatants to help secure cease-fires that the combatants have already agreed to.

Whereas Chapter VII is clearly talking about an enforcement mechanism, peace-keeping is really more of a transparency mechanism. It is a more limited tool, because it is only useful after the terms for cessation of hostilities have been agreed to, but it is a less contentious tool; because all parties agree to the presence of the peacekeepers, the Security Council does not have to choose one side of a dispute over the other. In other words, peacekeeping is a mechanism through which the Security Council can contribute to international peace and security without having to identify one particular party as responsible for breaching the international peace in the first place.

Peacekeeping, as a mission, was first created in response to the Suez Crisis in 1956. The crisis began when, in response to the nationalization of the Suez Canal by the government of Egypt, the United Kingdom and France invaded and occupied the area surrounding the Canal, supported by an attack by Israel on the Sinai peninsula. The idea of a UN-sponsored force to replace British, French, and Israeli forces in Egypt, with the consent of all parties, was suggested by Lester Pearson, the Canadian Foreign Minister (a suggestion for which he later won the Nobel Peace Prize). The concept of peacekeeping caught on, because it allowed the Security Council to play a less ambitious, less politically contentious, but still useful role in international dispute resolution at a time when the realities of the Cold War prevented full-fledged Chapter VII interventions. By the middle of 2004, the UN had listed sixteen ongoing peacekeeping operations, although some of these might be better described as state-building operations (see below). These missions employed close to 60,000 personnel, and cost close to $3 billion annually. The longest running current operation, the United Nations Peacekeeping Force in Cyprus (UNFICYP), has been in continuous operation since 1964.[6]

The second new mechanism for the promotion of international peace and security that has evolved in Security Council practice more recently is often referred to as state-building. This new mission, which the Security Council only really got involved in after the end of the Cold War, has UN forces oversee the administration of post-conflict areas and the building of local capacity for self-governance. State-building is thus a curative and preventive mechanism, rather than an enforcement mechanism per se. In helping areas that have been the sites of threats to international security to build viable self-governance structures, the hope is that they will not once again degenerate into security-threatening behavior. State-building missions have had considerable success in stabilizing several countries around the globe over the past decade, ranging from East Timor to Bosnia to Sierra Leone to Honduras. The missions have certainly not made any of these places model states, but conditions in all of them are significantly better than before the UN arrived, and probably much better than had the UN not arrived.

The recent willingness of the Security Council to involve itself in state-building also often blurs the conceptual boundaries between the maintenance of international peace and security on the one hand, and humanitarian assistance on the other. This willingness to undertake missions that have a clear humanitarian element to them mirrors a trend in the UN community more broadly: the trend toward focusing on human security as much as on international security (the former being a focus on the security of individuals, the latter being a focus on the security of states).

The creation of these two mechanisms (peacekeeping and state-building), which are not specified in the UN Charter, reflected the ambitions of the Security Council with respect to authorizing the use of force at two particular points in time. These ambitions have varied significantly since the creation of the UN. While the language of the UN Charter suggests grand ambitions for the role of the Security Council in the maintenance of international peace and security, the reality of the Cold War quickly limited that role. The end of the Cold War created new hope that the Security Council would play an activist role, an optimism that was reinforced by the success of the first major post–Cold War test of the Council in response to the Iraqi invasion of Kuwait in 1990. This new optimism allowed for the expansion of Security Council activities into the area of state-building, and it is this new optimism that is being brought into question as a result of the second war with Iraq in 2003—this time, without Security Council authorization.

The reason that the end of the Cold War had such an effect on the ambitions of the Security Council has to do with its voting structure, one of two institutional particularities that have a major impact on the way in which it operates. As noted in Chapter 2, the Council has what is basically a two-tier or two-class membership and voting structure. The Council has at any given time fifteen members. Of these, ten are elected on a rotating basis for two-year terms (five new members are elected each year) from among the membership of the UN, in a way that ensures that all regions of the world are represented. These temporary members have one standard vote each. The other five members are permanent. These are the United States, Russia, China, France, and the United Kingdom. The five permanent members have special votes, often referred to as vetoes. A resolution in the Security Council needs nine votes to pass, but a vote against it by any one of the permanent members, even if all other fourteen members vote in favor, prevents the resolution from being adopted.[7]

This veto power prevented the Security Council from playing an active role in international politics during the Cold War because the superpowers tended to have conflicting interests to at least some extent in most international conflicts, threatening a veto by either the United States or USSR.[8] The voting structure was designed to give the countries that would necessarily play the greatest role in maintaining international security, by virtue of their size and military capabilities, the greatest role in determining where force would be used. The goal in designing the system like this was to avoid the dynamics of the League of Nations between the two world wars, when the League would call for military action to combat threats to the peace, but no countries with significant military forces would actually be willing to contribute the necessary forces. Somewhat coincidentally, the five veto powers are also the five major nuclear powers, although China and France were veto powers for two decades before they became nuclear powers. In this context, it makes some sense that the five original permanent members are still holders of Security Council vetoes.

But there are other countries that argue that the balance of power has changed since the end of World War II, and that the structure of the Security Council should change in response. Japan, Germany, and India have all campaigned for permanent seats on the Security Council. Japan in fact announced not long ago that it was considering reductions in the funds it was willing to make available to the UN, and tied this explicitly to the fact that its attempts to get representation on the Security Council were getting nowhere.[9] At the same time, there is widespread support among the large majority of UN members who do not have permanent seats on the Security Council for the idea of expanding the number of countries on the Council, to achieve broader representation and a better balance between the traditional great powers and the rest of the world.[10] The Secretary-General's High-level Panel noted that "a decision on the enlargement of the Council ... is now a necessity."[11] The panel proposed two models for enlarging the Council, both of which would increase its total membership to twenty-four.[12] The 2005 World Summit, a meeting of world leaders hosted by the GA that was designed in part to deal with the reforms proposed by the Panel, supported in principle the idea of Security Council reform, but was unable to agree on any particular plan.[13]

But whether or not an expansion of the number of rotating members happens soon, any change in the veto mechanism is unlikely. The reason for this is simply that any change in the structure of the Security Council needs to be approved by the existing Council, meaning that any one of the five existing permanent members can veto any change. At minimum, the veto power means that none of the existing permanent members can be voted off without their consent. But it also means that it will be very difficult to expand the number of states with vetoes. Expansion would mean dilution of the institutional power accorded to the existing permanent members by their special powers, and that makes them resistant to change. One of the two models for expansion proposed by the Secretary-General's panel would get around this problem by creating a new class of six permanent members without vetoes (the other would create a new class of eight members elected for renewable four-year terms). But even a plan to expand the permanent membership without creating new vetoes could run into trouble with the existing veto powers.[14]

The second institutional peculiarity of the Security Council that has a major impact on the way in which it operates is that it does not have its own secretariat. Its secretariat functions are performed by the UN Secretariat. In other words, there are no senior bureaucrats who work for the Security Council as an organization— they work either for the Secretariat or for member governments. This undermines the extent to which the Security Council as an institution can be an independent actor in international politics, as well as a regime. Each new mission that the Security Council authorizes requires the creation of a new organization, a new institution designed specifically for the task at hand, with coordination among the missions being provided by the UN Secretariat.

For peacekeeping and traditional collective security missions, the personnel for the new institutions are drawn exclusively from forces seconded by national militaries. These forces retain their own command structures, so coordination across the different national components within individual missions can be problematic. In other words, personnel for these missions work for their home governments, and are on loan to the Security Council. For nation-building missions, personnel can be seconded both from member countries and from other UN IOs with relevant expertise. These sorts of missions also sometimes employ people directly.

Another category of institution created by Security Council resolutions is war crimes tribunals. At the time of writing, two such tribunals were active, covering war crimes and crimes against humanity committed in the conflicts in Rwanda and the former Yugoslavia.[15] These tribunals tend to employ the bulk of their staff directly. Because they are courts of law, it is important for reasons of judicial credibility that they be staffed by people committed to the court itself, rather than to member countries. So some of the mission-specific organizations subsidiary to the Security Council do employ their own staff directly, but the bulk of the personnel in these missions work for member governments, overwhelmingly so in missions that involve the use of military force.

The creation of new institutions for each Security Council mission has the advantage of flexibility—organizational structure can be arranged to suit each specific mission. It also has the advantage, from the perspective of member states, of maximizing state control over the use of military force by minimizing the operational discretion of the UN bureaucracy in such matters. The proliferation of mission-specific organizations, however, also has disadvantages. One is resource inefficiency, in that each new mission has to create its own bureaucratic structure. Another disadvantage is that each new mission must solicit donations of forces from member countries, which takes time and is not always as successful as it might be. A third disadvantage is that it makes coordination both across and within missions more difficult. Coordination across missions is more difficult because of the institutional peculiarities of the individual organizations and because there is little in the way of central bureaucratic capabilities to oversee communication among institutions. Coordination within missions is made more difficult because the proliferation of specific institutional structures undermines the orderly development of standardized procedures and expectations.

The Secretariat

There are two ways in which the UN Secretariat directly involves itself in the maintenance of international peace and security. The first, as suggested above, is by providing secretariat services to the Security Council and to specific institutions subsidiary to the Council. In a general sense, this is done through a wide variety of activities that the Secretariat performs as a matter of course, from financial management and the provision of legal services to basic housekeeping functions. The Secretary-General's High-level Panel has recommended the creation of a new administrative position, Deputy Secretary-General for Peace and Security, to help coordinate and bring more institutional coherence to these various activities.[16]

There is one department within the Secretariat devoted specifically to servicing international peacekeeping and peace-enforcing missions: the DPKO. The DPKO is responsible, among other things, for general administrative, logistic, and coordinative functions for Security Council missions. It is also responsible more broadly for training forces of member countries in peacekeeping operations, and for setting standards for behavior on these missions.[17] A relatively new part of the DPKO is the Situation Centre. This office was created in response to some serious operational problems caused by the structure of Security Council missions operating in the early 1990s. As noted above, the forces donated by various countries tend to maintain separate command structures, with coordination to be provided by the UN headquarters in New York. These forces also often operate under fairly restrictive rules and need authorization from headquarters to escalate levels of force in response to provocations from local forces. But until 1993 it was never clear who an on-site commander should call for coordination and authorization. One could call headquarters in need of urgent consultation and find no one there at that particular hour. The Situation Centre was created to ensure that there was always someone answering the telephone in New York, who could give on-site commanders an answer or at least get the Security Council to discuss an issue quickly.

The second way in which the Secretariat involves itself directly in issues of international peace and security is by the use of the good offices of the Secretary-General. Although not discussed in the UN Charter, this political role was one that Secretaries-General began to play almost immediately upon the creation of the UN. The role involves the Secretary-General, either in person or through an appointed representative, helping to solve disputes by providing neutral third-party intermediation, and by lending the prestige and moral authority of the Secretary-General's office to negotiating processes. The role that these good offices can play, however, is circumscribed by the fact that moral authority is generally the only kind of authority that the Secretary-General can bring to bear.[18] The Secretariat has neither any legal authority nor any recourse to economic or military incentives or threats to back up its involvement.

The Secretary-General currently has more than sixty Special Representatives, Special Envoys, and Special Advisors, assigned both to mediate particular conflicts and to monitor specific issues.[19] Many of these are associated with specific Security Council missions or subsidiary organizations of the UN, but many are not. In either case, these representatives report specifically to the Secretary-General. The fact that they have been a constant feature of the Secretary-General's office almost since the inception of the UN, and that Secretaries-General are willing to put their limited resources into maintaining so many of them, suggests that they do play some useful role in international politics and in the maintenance of international peace and security, despite the Secretary-General's lack of authority to impose solutions and agreements.

Regional Security Organizations

Chapter VIII of the UN Charter encourages the creation of "regional arrangements" (i.e., regional collective security organizations) to deal with security issues that can successfully be dealt with on a regional level. These arrangements allow the Security Council to focus its attention on broader threats to international peace and security. There are regional security organizations in many parts of the world that are explicitly designed to fit within Chapter VIII. A good example of such an organization is the Organization of American States (OAS). Some regions have two tiers of collective security organizations, to deal with both continental and subcontinental crises. The African Union (AU),[20] for example, is designed in part to deal with threats to peace and security in Africa in general, while the collective security arms of the

Southern African Development Community (SADC)[21] and the Economic Community of West African States (ECOWAS) are designed to deal with threats specifically within Southern and Western Africa, respectively.

A particularly interesting region in which to look at regional collective security arrangements is Europe, because there are a number of different kinds of regional security arrangements in operation there. The institutions that represent two of these arrangements, the OSCE and the North Atlantic Treaty Organization (NATO), are well enough funded to be able to take on significant security obligations. The OSCE fits explicitly within the realm of Chapter VIII. NATO, on the other hand, began as a traditional security alliance; it was designed to protect its members against an external threat (the Soviet Union), rather than internal threats. But when its primary mission became obsolete with the end of the Cold War, it transformed itself into a sort of hybrid traditional alliance/collective security organization. The OSCE has the bigger membership of the two organizations, with fifty-five members, including all of the countries of Europe and all fifteen of the countries of the former Soviet Union. NATO has twenty-six members and "partnership agreements" with another twenty countries.[22] The United States and Canada are members of both organizations.

The OSCE, as its name suggests, is a forum designed to increase the ability of member countries to enhance security cooperation in Europe. Of the various multilateral collective security organizations, the OSCE has perhaps the broadest definition of security, including human security, environmental security, and the promotion of democracy and good governance. It has a substantial secretariat, with a staff of over 400, and various associated political bodies (made up of state representatives), dealing with various issues related to its broad definition of security, such as minority and language rights. Unlike either the UN Security Council or the GA, it works on a consensus basis. It does not have the authority to call on member countries for enforcement measures, either economic or military, but does work with Security Council missions that have the authority to use force.

The OSCE evolved from the Conference on Security and Co-operation in Europe (CSCE). The earlier body was a forum for discourse among member states, an attempt to improve communication between East and West in Europe during the Cold War. The CSCE met only occasionally and did not have a permanent bureaucracy. As the Cold War wound down, member countries began to add functions, resources, and a permanent bureaucracy to the CSCE in an attempt to increase its capabilities. In 1994, these accretions had enlarged the institution sufficiently that it formally promoted itself from a "conference" to an "organization". The OSCE has retained the forum function of the CSCE, but has added to it a permanent secretariat that is able to monitor potential security threats in Europe, and provide advice and expertise in institution- and democracy-building to countries in need of it.

NATO is not, strictly speaking, a multilateral IO as defined in the first chapter of this book, although it is in the process of expanding its membership significantly. It is a special case, and as such will not be discussed in great detail here. But it does have capabilities not shared by other IOs. In particular, NATO has a military infrastructure and capabilities. The organization requires of its members that they impose certain common technical standards on their armed forces. This gives

NATO armies a high degree of interoperability–they can communicate with each other and provide technical and logistical support to each other to a much greater degree than is common among militaries of different countries. NATO also has some committed military assets, including command, transportation and information-gathering capabilities. These assets are still part of national military forces (more often than not part of the U.S. military) but are committed for use for NATO purposes. These institutional features give NATO the ability to coordinate uses of force by its member countries to a far greater degree than is the case for traditional collective security organizations such as the Security Council.

An interesting comparison of the roles of the Security Council, the OSCE, and NATO can be found in the international community's intervention in Bosnia in 1995 and Kosovo in 1999. In both cases, force was used by other countries (most of the force used in both cases was provided by U.S. air power), leading in effect to an international administration designed to build local governmental institutions to the point of viability. In both cases the OSCE was assigned responsibility for most of the institution-building and civil administration. In the case of Bosnia, the use of force was sponsored by NATO and approved after the fact by the Security Council. In the case of Kosovo, it was authorized from the outset by the Security Council. In Bosnia, NATO's use of force helped to convince the local combatants to sign a peace treaty that explicitly invited NATO forces into Bosnia to oversee implementation of the peace. This invitation suggested a mutual consent to the presence of outside forces, which is how NATO got around the absence of direct Security Council legitimation of its military presence in Bosnia.[23] In Kosovo, such an invitation was not necessary, because the Security Council authoritatively legitimized the presence of the foreign military forces. Although the role of the OSCE is similar in the two missions (both of which are ongoing as of 2005), because of their different histories, the OSCE Secretariat coordinates the mission in Bosnia, but in Kosovo it is subsidiary to the UN Secretariat, which is responsible for overall coordination there.

Collective Security and IO Theory

What do these various institutional specifics tell us about the role of IOs in collective security more generally? In order to address this question, the rest of this chapter looks at the four distinctions discussed in the preceding chapters, beginning with the distinction between efficiency and legitimacy. The institutions discussed in this chapter generally work to achieve both, but the balance between the two differs in different institutions. Of these IOs, the DKPO is most focused on efficiency, almost exclusively so. It is specifically designed to increase efficiency and transparency of peacekeeping and other Security Council-organized uses of armed forces by reducing the transaction costs of cooperating, and by increasing information flows among participant forces. It does play what might be called a background legitimating function through its involvement in training forces to be used for Security Council missions, thereby decreasing the chances that those forces will behave in the field in a way that undermines the legitimacy of Security Council missions more generally. But this stretches the interpretation of the legitimacy function, and the inability of the DPKO to punish misbehavior impedes any legitimating effect. If anything, recent revelations of misconduct by soldiers operating under UN auspices are having the effect of delegitimizing Security Council peacekeeping and peacebuilding operations.

Also nearer to the efficiency role of the spectrum is NATO, largely because it is not a multilateral collective security organization in the traditional sense. NATO's resources and capabilities allow it to play a much more substantial role in maximizing the efficiency of member countries' military activities. The OCSE plays a somewhat greater legitimating role, and is likely to be more widely accepted in the state-building role, both by the target country and by the international community, than single outside states or NGOs. An interesting indicator of the different levels of legitimacy accorded to NATO and the OSCE by the UN can be seen in Security Council Resolution 1031, the resolution discussed above that legitimated the agreement that ended the Bosnian war. It refers to the OSCE by name as a participant in the mandated state-building process, but it clearly avoided specifying NATO by name, even while legitimating a NATO peacekeeping force.[24]

At the other end of the spectrum is the good offices function of the Secretary-General. This function does have a minor efficiency-maximizing role, in that the Secretary-General or his appointees can successfully increase meaningful communication and exchange of information among the parties to a crisis. But there is no shortage of skilled third-party mediators. The major difference between the Secretary-General's mediation and other potential mediators is the prestige and legitimacy of the office and person of the Secretary-General.

The Security Council is the IO in which the efficiency and legitimacy roles are most closely integrated. It was clearly designed with efficiency in mind. The UN Charter specifically identifies it as the body with ultimate authority in deciding issues of international peace and security. This is a way of specifying property rights, particularly ways of deciding breaches of sovereign property associated with the use of force. The Council is permanently in session, members are required to have representatives available at all times, and emergency meetings can be called in a matter of hours, a rarity in IOs. This both decreases transaction costs and improves information flows, by making the debating forum available to members quickly and easily. The small size of the Council has a similar effect, making debate more efficient and decision-making smoother. And the two-tier voting structure is designed to make a clear link between those who are making decisions about the use of force, and those who will actually have to contribute the bulk of the force. This should increase transparency in the implementation of Council decisions. It should also, in the long run, increase the Council's credibility by decreasing the frequency with which it makes pronouncements that cannot be implemented.

Because most of the veto powers are also the traditional great (imperialist) powers, the Council's two-tier voting structure might also be expected to undermine the its legitimacy. The diplomatic crisis leading up to the war in Iraq in 2003, however, indicates that the legitimacy accorded to the Security Council, both by states and by populations at large, is surprisingly high. Before the war, the United States went to some lengths to try to get Security Council approval, and polls suggested that popular opinion in many countries would have been much more favorable to the war had the United States succeeded in getting such approval. After the war, the United States, although in military control of the country, nonetheless felt the need to seek Security Council approval of its postwar administration there.[25] Despite a decidedly mixed record in maintaining collective security over the years, the legitimacy function of the Security Council appears to be alive and well.

The next distinction is that between IOs as regimes and IOs as institutions. The most interesting comparison in this context is between the Security Council and the good offices of the Secretary-General. The Security Council is best looked at as a regime; its activities and procedures are dominated almost exclusively by representatives of member states. Since the Council has no independent bureaucracy, it is difficult for it to develop either an independent voice or bureaucratic pathologies, in the way organizations with their own secretariats do. The Secretary-General, on the other hand, acts to a large degree on his own decision-making authority. The good offices, in other words, operate at the discretion of the bureaucracy, rather than as part of a set of clear rules and procedures that states expect to be followed. Neither institution, of course, is an ideal type of the regime or the institutionalist model, but they are closer to the ideal types than are most IOs. Both NATO and the OSCE have more even mixes of regime and institutional dynamics. Both embody sets of rules and procedures that help to define actor expectations in the issue-area of European security. At the same time, both organizations have substantial bureaucracies that can and do develop institutional pathologies and that can put bureaucratic interests ahead of the defined interests of the organization. An example of this phenomenon can be found in the efforts of NATO headquarters to define a new mission for the organization after the end of the Cold War, in an attempt to keep it relevant.[26]

The third distinction is that between power and interdependence. One can certainly make the argument that interdependence is less pronounced in the issue-area of collective security than in many of the issue-areas discussed in the coming chapters. At the same time, however, the importance of interdependence is not negligible. Security crises in weak states can, and often do, destabilize nearby states and draw in members of the international community more broadly. But the role of power in security issues is clear. Most clear, perhaps, is the role of military power, without which a country can simply not participate meaningfully on the ground in the maintenance of international peace and security. But the structure of IOs conveys power to states as well. This is most clearly the case in the Security Council. The five states with vetoes are empowered to deal with security issues in a way that other countries are not. They have the ability to block any Security Council action against themselves and their allies, which may help to explain why they tend to use force abroad more often than most other countries. They also have a permanent voice on the Council, whereas other countries have at best only occasional and temporary voices. And they also have veto power over major structural and constitutional change in the UN, and over the appointment of senior UN personnel, including the Secretary-General.

The extent to which permanent membership on the Security Council empowers states is suggested by the extent to which several large countries, including Japan, Germany, and India, are willing to expend political capital to try to get a permanent seat, despite the obvious hurdles to doing so. But membership in other collective security IOs has the effect of empowering smaller states with fewer military resources. For example, because the OSCE operates on a consensus basis, it has the effect of giving small European countries with negligible military capabilities a real voice in those issues that the OSCE is active in. The voice is, for various reasons, not as great as that of countries with significant military capabilities, but it is in all probability greater than it would otherwise be.

The structure of the multilateral collective security system has the effect of empowering certain bureaucracies and individuals within the relevant IOs. This is most clearly the case with the Secretary-General, who is empowered to play a significant, if limited, role in international security issues by virtue of the office. The role is limited both because of the lack of material resources to back up the Secretary-General's diplomacy, and because if the Secretary-General overplays the role, it undermines the credibility both of the individual and of the office in future crises. Other individuals can be even more greatly empowered within more constrained contexts. The Secretary-General's representative in Kosovo, for example, is for the time being[27] de facto dictator of that region. On a more modest scale, though, members of the secretariats of a number of collective security organizations are empowered by the ability their positions give them to set (or at least affect) the agenda in issue-areas that can profoundly impact upon people's lives, such as state-building and military cooperation.

The last of the four distinctions is between sovereignty and globalization. This review of the institutions of collective security suggests that states' attachment to sovereignty and resistance to globalization are most pronounced with respect to issues of war. The focus on sovereignty becomes on the whole less pronounced the farther the issue gets from national security and the more it gets to be about human security. The Security Council, which can authorize the use of force, is made up almost entirely of representatives of sovereign states, with no one who directly represents the interests of global governance. The OSCE, on the other hand, which has no such authority, has much more leeway to act in the interests of good global governance, because its structure does not allow it to directly threaten the national security interests of member states. This conclusion will probably not surprise anyone. It does not mean, however, that in issues of war and national security, IOs are irrelevant. States are least willing to give up sovereignty in these issue-areas, but IOs nonetheless affect outcomes, by empowering some states at the expense of others, by legitimating some actions and delegitimating others, and by making international security cooperation more efficient when states choose to cooperate.

7

Human Rights and Humanitarian Aid

While the UN Charter clearly establishes collective security as the central goal of the UN, it accords human rights and humanitarian aid much less prominent roles. Nonetheless, over time both the protection of human rights and provision of humanitarian aid have become major roles of the UN system, and of regional international organizations (IOs) and international NGOs as well. This chapter compares the role of the UN system as protector of human rights with its role as provider of humanitarian aid. Even though the two roles would seem at first to have much in common as two parts of a broader human security agenda, the UN's role in the two issue-areas is very different.

In the field of human rights, the three focal organizational forms discussed in this chapter are the Office of the United Nations High Commissioner for Human Rights (UNHCHR), the Commission on Human Rights, and the various human rights committees. These will be contrasted with the role of the Council of Europe (COE) in protecting human rights in Europe. In the issue-area of humanitarian aid, the two IOs discussed here are the Office of the United Nations High Commissioner for Refugees (UNHCR) (not to be confused with UNHCHR) and the World Food Programme (WFP). The human rights organizations at first glance seem weak, often to the point of irrelevance, whereas the two humanitarian aid organizations seem robust and efficient. But in the end, an argument can be made that the human rights organizations can also be effective in helping to change how international politics works in the long term.

Human Rights

Although the phrase "human rights" does not appear in the UN Charter, it quickly became a significant focus of UN activities. An early result of this activity, and one that remains a seminal part of the international human rights discourse, is the Universal Declaration of Human Rights (UDHR) of 1948, which has been accepted by all members of the UN. There had been a few treaties prior to this date that are now classified as human rights treaties, such as the Convention to Suppress the Slave Trade and Slavery (1926) and the Convention Concerning Forced Labour

(1930), although these treaties did not actually use the phrase "human rights." But 1948 marked the beginning of a tradition of international human rights discourse that continues to this day. Along with the UDHR, 1948 saw as well the creation of the Convention on the Prevention and Punishment of Genocide and the Convention Concerning Freedom of Association.

The UDHR was followed by a variety of human rights treaties over the years, of which some refer explicitly to human rights while others do not. Some of these are regional treaties that are general statements of human rights, such as the European Convention on Human Rights and the American Convention on Human Rights. Others are agreements dealing with particular sorts of rights, such as civil and political rights, labor rights, and regional and minority language rights. Still others are aimed at eliminating certain kinds of behavior, such as torture, slavery, trafficking in people, racial discrimination, and the mistreatment of prisoners of war or civilians under foreign occupation. And there are many treaties designed to protect particular categories of people, such as women, children, refugees, migrants, and indigenous peoples.[1] A survey of these treaties, and of the various political histories and social commentaries and critiques that surround them, cannot be done effectively in the limited space of this chapter. In any case, such surveys have been done well elsewhere.[2]

Many of these more specific treaties mandated the creation of oversight committees, made up of human rights experts nominated and elected by signatory states.[3] The role of these committees is to field complaints against signatory countries, and to report both about individual country compliance and about general issues relating to their treaty.[4] They report to the General Assembly (GA), the Economic and Social Council (ECOSOC), and the Secretary-General, although they are officially subsidiary to the GA. While these committees are certainly useful monitoring mechanisms, they are quite limited in their abilities. They tend to have limited personnel (usually around ten people), often not working for them on a full-time basis, with limited institutional and financial support. And their output is limited to reports to other UN bodies. The committees themselves have no direct means of enforcement, and they cannot engage in the sorts of publicity campaigns against specific human rights violations that have often proved successful for human rights NGOs.

A more general body to oversee human rights issues was created by ECOSOC in the early days of the UN, and continues to operate as one of ECOSOC's functional commissions. This is the Commission on Human Rights. The Commission, like ECOSOC, is a political body, and the members of the Commission are representatives of member states. Fifty-three states are members of the Commission, elected by the membership of ECOSOC for three-year terms. The Commission has created and oversees a number of Working Groups and Special Rapporteurs to look into human rights abuses both with respect to specific issues and specific countries, which in turn report back to the Commission.[5]

Some analysts see the Commission as doing some good work, by creating transparency and legitimacy in the area of human rights in much the same way the committees do. Others, however, see the Commission as something of a farce, because it often includes as members some of the most egregious human rights violators. An example of such an irony was the election of Libya as President of the Commission for its 2003 session.[6] The recent Report of the Secretary-General's High-level Panel, referred to a number of times in previous chapters of this book, goes so far as to as to say that the Commission "has been undermined by eroding credibility and professionalism," and suggests a number of possible reforms.[7] The 2005 World Summit that was in part a response to the Panel's report did not discuss the Commission, but did recommend the creation of a UN Human Rights Council (the details of which had not been worked out at the time of writing) and the doubling of the UNHCHR's budget.

The plethora of specific human rights bodies within the UN system led to the creation of the UNHCHR in 1993. This office was created by a resolution of the GA, but it operates as part of the Secretariat.[8] Its job is to coordinate among and provide administrative infrastructure and support to the various UN human rights commissions and committees. It is also meant to support the activities of the High Commissioner, who is appointed by the Secretary-General, subject to the approval of GA. The High Commissioner is the public face of the UN on human rights issues, and is tasked with representing the Secretary-General on human rights issues and promoting the universal recognition of and respect for human rights.

In other words, the UNHCHR is designed to fulfill both efficiency and legitimacy functions, each of which is fairly distinct from the other. The efficiency function mostly involves coordination among existing bodies, to maximize information flows among them and from them to the Secretary-General and the public, and to minimize bureaucratic waste and duplication of effort in their operation. The legitimacy function is in ways similar to the good offices function of the Secretariat. By specifying who the UN's voice will be on human rights issues, the hope is that the moral authority of that voice can get things done even in the absence of formal authority or material resources. This design has clearly benefited from lessons learned from the problems of older UN human rights bodies, which were plagued by multiple voices and poor coordination. The UNHCHR is, however, limited by both the bodies it is supposed to coordinate and its own skill in representing the UN and promoting human rights issues. The UNHCHR does help to improve the efficiency of existing UN human rights bodies, but those bodies are themselves either sufficiently modest in resources, or sufficiently political in operation, or both, that even their increased level of efficiency does not necessarily translate into an effective UN human rights infrastructure.

The extent to which the Commissioner has moral authority, particularly in a relatively young office such as the UNHCHR, is affected by the competence of the Commissioner as public spokesperson. The results of the legitimizing role of the office in its first decade have been mixed. Many successful smaller-scale campaigns have been offset by the occasional large-scale public relations failure. Perhaps the greatest of these failures was the World Conference against Racism, held in Durban, South Africa, in 2001. The High Commissioner at the time, Mary Robinson, billed it in advance as "a conference of actions not just words."[9] In practice, it degenerated into unproductive debates about issues such as Zionism, compensation for slavery, and caste systems. It resulted in a Declaration that urged states to do hundreds of thing, but required them to do nothing, and suggested no mechanisms for monitoring, let alone enforcement.[10] It was, in other words, precisely the sort of very public, very political, and, ultimately, ineffective exercise that perhaps does most to undermine the image of the UN.

The UN is not the only organization that is active in the field of human rights. A plethora of NGOs are dedicated to this role, the best known of which is Amnesty International. The success of these NGOs, with Amnesty being the best example, has made them de facto fixtures in global governance and the international human rights discourse, and, in individual cases, has given them some real power in changing the behavior of states. Some national governments also report on human rights abuses internationally. Both the NGOs and these national governments tend to take the standards promulgated by IOs, and by international treaties, as their baselines, and embarrass governments by showing ways in which they fail to live up to standards they have committed themselves to.[11]

There are also some regional IOs that are involved in human rights issues, perhaps the most notable of which is the COE. This IO currently has forty-six members, which includes all of Europe except for Belarus (which has applied for membership) and the Holy See. Roughly half of its current membership has joined since the end of the Cold War. An integral part of the COE is the European Convention on Human Rights, and member states are legally bound by the terms of the Convention.[12] Countries are always legally bound by the treaties that they sign; this does not mean that they always comply with them. What makes this Convention, and the COE, different is the European Court of Human Rights. Residents of member states have the right to take their government to this Court if they feel that the government is not living up to its obligations under the Convention, and if they cannot get acceptable legal redress within their national court system. The Court has heard thousands of cases, and has often ruled against states. Perhaps more remarkably, the states have usually done what the Court has told them to, either by changing rules and procedures or by providing restitution to individuals, or both.[13]

In short, then, one could at first glance be highly critical of the extent to which IOs create meaningful behavioral change in human rights issues. The various UN bodies make some efforts at monitoring the human rights behavior of states and at embarrassing recalcitrant states into changing their behavior. But these efforts are limited by the material resources and the legitimacy that the UN brings to bear on the issue. States are willing to sign up to human rights treaties, but are not willing to give these treaties teeth. The result is human rights IOs that are enfeebled in their role as actors in international politics, and have little power. The biggest exception to this rule is the COE and its European Court of Human Rights, because of its close association with the European Union (EU) and because its human rights rules are coupled with significant resources in other issue-areas that member countries can draw on.

Having said this, the combined effects over the past six decades of the various international efforts, both intergovernmental and nongovernmental, at promoting human rights norms have been huge. One could argue that they have fundamentally changed the way international politics works.[14] A concept neither widely known nor accorded much importance at the beginning of the process has now become a major constraint on the behavior of states toward their own citizens. An example of the effect that human rights IOs can have in global politics can be found in the Helsinki Final Act. This was a human rights agreement signed by countries on both sides of the Cold War, including the United States and the Soviet Union, under the auspices of the Conference on Security and Co-operation in Europe (CSCE) (the forerunner organization to the Organization for Security and Co-operation in Europe [OSCE]). The Soviet side was willing to sign the agreement because they saw it as a toothless exercise in international propaganda. But when domestic opposition to the communist regimes in Eastern and Central Europe began to grow in the late 1980s, the Act served as a focal point for dissent, and may have played a significant role in the process of peaceful regime change at the end of the Cold War.[15]

States do, of course, still violate human rights. But they do it self-consciously and are, for the most part, embarrassed about it. Because of their higher level of consciousness on human rights issues, and the range of organizations devoted to monitoring these issues, states are much more loath than used to be the case to engage in habitual violations of rights. In other words, states still violate human rights, but on the whole they do it much less often than they used to. This suggests that the mechanisms of global governance have over time been fairly successful at legitimizing human rights norms internationally.

A final note on human rights and the UN system involves the International Criminal Court (ICC). This court came into being in 2002, its founding treaty having been ratified by the specified sixty states, and is empowered to try individuals for war crimes, genocide, and crimes against humanity.[16] It is thus fundamentally different from most international adjudicative bodies, which deal with states rather than individual people. It is meant to play, permanently and globally, the role that the International Criminal Tribunal for the Former Yugoslavia (ICTY) and its equivalent for Rwanda (ICTR) play for those specific conflicts.[17] The ICC has at the time of writing not yet tried anyone, but it has begun investigative proceedings with respect to six different situations, all of them in Central and East Africa, and has issued warrants for the arrest of five members of the Lord's Resistance Army, an armed group operating in northern Uganda.[18] The United States is not a member of the ICC: President Clinton signed the Court's Statute, but had little or no chance of getting it ratified. The current U.S. administration has generally been vehemently opposed to the ICC.[19] It did, however, recently abstain on, thus allowing the passage of, a Security Council resolution that referred to the ICC the cases of fifty-one people implicated in crimes against humanity in Darfur.[20] In sum, the ICC may well prove to play a major role in international human rights issues, but at this point, it is too early to tell either what or how big that role may be.

Humanitarian Aid

There is no clear dividing line among such activities as protecting human rights, providing humanitarian assistance, engaging in humanitarian intervention, and ensuring collective security broadly defined. Yet there is a clear subset of organizations within the UN system that focus primarily on emergency humanitarian assistance, defined as providing basic necessities of life to people who suddenly find themselves without access to food and shelter. Humanitarian aid, by this definition, can be distinguished from humanitarian intervention, because it always involves the consent of the local authorities and is not delivered using military capabilities. It can be distinguished from development assistance because it is designed to ameliorate a need in the short term, rather than to develop capabilities in the long term. The two foremost humanitarian aid IOs within the UN system are the UNHCR and the WFP (there are other IOs, such as UNICEF, that provide significant amounts of emergency aid, but this is not their primary activity).[21]

Humanitarian aid IOs tend to be far more robust institutionally than human rights IOs. Both the UNHCR and the WFP are large organizations, with employees numbering in the thousands, budgets in the billions of dollars, extensive networks of NGOs with which they work closely, and active fundraising programs. Their funding patterns are similar as well. Neither organization can count on income from general UN funds or from member dues. The WFP is funded entirely by voluntary donations, and the UNHCR gets roughly 98 percent of its funds from such donations.[22] The resulting need to keep donors convinced that their money is being well spent may well be a significant contributing factor to the focus of both organizations on providing services effectively and visibly to those in need. The same focus on the short-term provision of services, however, provides part of the logic for the criticism made of both organizations, that their focus on short-term aid can exacerbate long-term problems. This criticism is discussed in more detail below.

The office of the UNHCR was created by the GA in 1950 for reasons similar to those that lay behind the later creation of the UNCHR.[23] The UN was involved in refugee issues in an ad hoc and inefficient way, and the UNHCR was designed to make the UN's refugee program more efficient by coordinating the efforts of other various organizations. The High Commissioner reports to the Secretary-General, and is appointed by the Secretary-General subject to the approval of the GA. The organization is headquartered in Geneva.

The UNHCR deals with its remit not by coordinating the efforts of other IOs, but by centralizing the UN's refugee activities in one office.[24] It still engages in much coordination, because it subcontracts extensively to a wide network of NGOs, both international and local, to provide many services on the ground. But it does so as contractor, not as facilitator—it provides funds and directions, rather than information and advice. It also maintains a presence on the ground in much of the world, with field offices in 120 countries and a staff of roughly 5,000.[25] When faced with a new refugee crisis, such as the (at time of writing) current crisis in Darfur, in the Sudan, the UNHCR will publicize the crisis and attempt to raise funds to deal with it, and will either coordinate or manage directly the creation and sustenance of refugee camps in which refugees can find food, shelter, and basic medical care. The UNHCR cares for millions of people in such camps. The organization also provides legal assistance to refugees, and helps with resettlement when refugees attempt to return home.

The provision of basic necessities to refugees that have fled to countries that cannot or will not provide for them is not the UNHCR's only activity. It also monitors compliance with various treaties that deal with refugee issues, and acts as advocate for refugees and refugee issues in international politics, much in the same way that the UNHCHR is supposed to act as advocate internationally for human rights issues. The UNHCR helps to keep refugee issues on the international political agenda and visible to the international public, and works to raise funds for the Commission's activities. Despite efforts to raise funds privately, 97 percent of voluntary contributions come from states, to fund a budget that has remained in the range of US$1 billion recently. Of these, the largest single contributor is the United States, followed by Japan, the EU, the Netherlands, and Sweden.[26]

The WFP was created in 1963 by joint resolution of the GA and the Food and Agriculture Organization (FAO) to oversee the food-related humanitarian efforts of both organizations. It was designed from the outset as a functional organization, a primary provider of services, rather than a coordinator of the activities of other IOs. It reports to the secretariats of both the UN and the FAO, and its Executive Director is appointed by both in consultation, and subject to the approval of both the GA and the Director-General of the FAO. Because of its relationship with the FAO in Rome, it is headquartered there. Like the UNHCR, it subcontracts much of the logistics of its food distribution to NGOs. It does not play as active a role politically in international relations as the UNHCR, because there is little debate as to who constitutes starving people, and whether or not they should be left to starve. But it does play the same sort of role in trying to keep the issue of famine visible to the international public and to donor countries, and in publicizing specific cases of immediate need.

The WFP raises most of its funds for specific food emergencies rather than for general programmatic needs. Although a large majority of its funds are donated by member governments, it is increasing its efforts to raise funds from NGOs, corporations, and individuals as well (it is now possible to donate online at its website[27]). Despite this range of sources, however, and unusually for a UN-subsidiary IO, a majority of its funds consistently come from one source: the U.S. government.[28] The WFP prides itself on being the most administratively efficient of IOs; it claims that only 9 percent of its budget goes to administrative overhead, while more than 90 percent goes directly to its programs, which undertake the provision of food.[29] Not only is this an impressive ratio for an IO, it would be an impressive ratio for an NGO as well. This focus on efficiency in the administration of aid may well explain why the U.S. government, which has always been keener on promoting efficiency (in the business management sense) in the UN than most other countries, is such an enthusiastic contributor of funds.

Both the UNHCR and the WFP, then, are fairly efficient providers of humanitarian assistance. In 2003, for example, the WFP fed some 104 million people, and the UNHCR helped approximately 21.8 million people.[30] But both organizations have been criticized for the long-term effects of their short-term aid. The UNHCR has been criticized for creating and becoming the focus of what is essentially a refugee industry, committed to taking care of refugees in place. Many countries, particularly those that are home to the largest refugee flows, prefer that refugees be kept separate from domestic populations and be dealt with primarily by the international community. This results in often huge refugee camps, which are overseen by the UNHCR. The organization tries to promote voluntary repatriation of refugees from these camps to their original homes, but it is often the case that the situation on the ground does not permit this to happen for long stretches of time. The UNHCR's commitment to short-term aid in place and long-term repatriation means that some refugees remain in internationally sponsored camps for generations, without permanent communities or viable economies to sustain them. The international community can ignore them, and the host countries can isolate them, because the High Commission is there to prevent short-term humanitarian disasters. The humanitarian aid, in other words, often contributes to the degree to which refugee problems are allowed by the international community to fester in the long term.[31]

In the case of the WFP, it would seem at first that feeding starving people should be nonproblematic. But emergency food aid often has the effect of undermining the local agricultural infrastructure. When the WFP gives food away for free, people will be less willing to pay local farmers for the food that they grow. So the bad harvests that often lead to famines and thereby to international food aid, can also (because of this aid) lead to decreases in local prices for agricultural products. In other words, farmers not only grow less, they also face lower returns on what they do grow. At the same time, the sorts of logistics brought in by industrial-scale international emergency aid can overwhelm local transport and distribution infrastructures. The WFP, in other words, can have the paradoxical effect in the medium term of putting local farmers and local agricultural infrastructures out of business. Providing emergency aid in the short term can thus undermine the ability of a country to feed itself in the medium term. This effect is often referred to as the "aid trap."[32]

There are ways of getting around the aid trap. For example, emergency food aid could be coupled with aid to local farmers in the form of seed and equipment for the next planting season and harvest. But the WFP's resources are limited, and thus medium-term aid to farmers comes at the expense of short-term food aid. For an organization that depends entirely on voluntary donations, emergency food aid can be a more effective fundraising tool than medium-term farm aid. Furthermore, medium-term aid both creates different aid traps and takes the WFP outside of its remit and into conflict with that of one of its parent organizations, the FAO. Having said all of this, however, the emergency aid infrastructure maintained by organizations such as the WFP and the UNHCR clearly save many lives that otherwise could not be saved.

Human Rights, Humanitarian Aid, and IO Theory

In terms of institutional effectiveness narrowly defined, there is no question that, on the whole, the UN's humanitarian aid organizations are far more effective than its human rights organizations. The humanitarian aid organizations are bigger, better funded, and have greater reach and clearer operational goals. They are also, as far as IOs go, quite effective. They identify and publicize areas of need, they serve as effective focuses for humanitarian aid funding, and they manage to get basic necessities to millions of people in need of them, often in a timely fashion and in logistically difficult situations. They provide useful coordination to NGO humanitarian efforts, and represent an impressive storehouse of practical information and knowledge about the provision of emergency aid. Their legitimacy functions are less pronounced, but are important nonetheless, particularly in the case of the UNHCR, which is the UN's guardian of both the concept of and the rights of refugees.

The various human rights organizations are not particularly effective in this sense. They do fulfill some efficiency and transparency functions, such as monitoring state compliance with treaty commitments and specifying and defining various categories of rights. But they do not fulfill transparency functions particularly effectively; as a result, NGOs and states are often looked to as the more reliable monitors of human rights treaty compliance. They fulfill as well some legitimacy functions, but not nearly as well as one might expect of the human rights arms of an organization such as the UN. Because of their institutional structures and their frequent high levels of politicization, they are often not seen as credible legitimators of international human rights norms.

And yet, in the long run, the UN's efforts in the area of human rights have had as great an impact on overall patterns of global governance. The humanitarian aid IOs are effective in providing for the basic needs of refugees and famine and disaster victims in the short term, but they have not been particularly effective at eliminating the broader problems of refugee flows and of famines. The institutionalization of the discourse of human rights within the international community, on the other hand, has changed, in a real and fundamental way, the manner in which states think about their relationships with their own citizens. Practices that were common a century ago, such as slavery or torture, are accepted by all states now as illegitimate. They may still happen, but they happen on a far less widespread and systemic scale than used to be the case. So while organizations such as the UNHCHR or the Commission on Human Rights are rarely effective in the short term in ameliorating the suffering of particular individuals, over the longer term they represent a significant change in what is considered legitimate behavior internationally.

The relative institutional weakness of human rights IOs can be related to issues of sovereignty and power. Humanitarian aid does not threaten the sovereignty of states. Neither the UNHCR nor the WFP can operate in a state without that state's permission. Nor do the norms underlying humanitarian intervention particularly affect state autonomy, although norms relating to refugees do commit states to certain minimum standards of behavior toward them. Human rights norms, on the other hand, directly affect state sovereignty. Their whole point is to limit the autonomy of states by delegitimizing whole categories of behaviors by states toward their citizens. Therefore, robust IOs designed to deal with humanitarian aid are likely to be more acceptable to states concerned about maintaining norms of sovereignty than robust human rights IOs.

Issues of sovereignty are also implicated in the tension between the short-term missions of humanitarian aid IOs and their inability to deal with the longer-term issues surrounding these missions. Both the refugee trap, in the case of the UNHCR, and the aid trap, in the case of the WFP, involve contradictions inherent in the missions of these two organizations, the contradiction between the need in some cases for immediate humanitarian aid, and the broader and longer-term effects of that aid on the ability of affected communities to develop. When the WFP is responding to short-term need created by natural disasters, such as the tsunami that devastated much of South and Southeast Asia in December 2004, this contradiction is not really an issue. In such cases, the resources of humanitarian IOs can prove invaluable. But when humanitarian IOs respond to famines and refugee flows created by political negligence, incompetence, or malice, the contradiction can end up keeping bad governments in place for longer than would otherwise be the case.

From the perspective of the countries in which the aid is needed as a result of political rather than natural factors, emergency aid helps to isolate the effects of problems such as famine and refugee flows from their causes. If countries know that IOs will take care of refugees and of the victims of famine, governments need worry less about their roles in causing these problems in the first place. In the absence of effective international emergency aid, there would be more pressure on these governments to change policies that contribute to famines, or to either stop creating, or help in resettling refugees. Effective IOs prevent this sort of pressure, thus limiting a threat to the political autonomy of recipient states. Similarly, emergency aid is less likely to come with conditions than other forms of aid. From the perspective of donor countries, emergency aid creates the belief that something is being done, that people are being saved, without the need to look in any great detail at the workings of the international system that would be created by attempts to deal with the more fundamental long-term problems leading to famines and to refugee flows.

In terms of power, there are two ways to look at the relative weakness of human rights organizations. The first is to note that humanitarian aid issues are more likely to have cross-border effects than human rights issues. For example, wealthier states know that if they do not help to take care of refugees in areas where they first flee, they are more likely to have the refugees show up at their borders. And they know that they need the participation of the poorer states that the refugees usually get to first in order to prevent a greater influx into the wealthier states. To a certain extent the same argument can be made for human rights—countries that respect human rights are less likely to generate refugees and other cross-border effects that the West wants to avoid. But by and large, those countries committed to human rights domestically can ensure these rights at home regardless of what is happening in other states. So governments do not need to cooperate on human rights for reasons of interdependence. Since powerful states, often the states that care most about human rights, do not need the help of others to protect these rights at home, they can cooperate on their own terms with other states less respectful of human rights.

The second way to look at the relative weakness of human rights IOs in terms of power is through the lens of neocolonialism. One of the critiques heard most often from the global South about the international human rights regime is that these rights are expressions of Northern, particularly American and European, culture. Whereas humanitarian aid does not particularly threaten local cultural forms and local power structures, critics of the human rights regime argue that the imposition of human rights norms can threaten local cultural forms and undermine local governance structures.[33] To these critics, international human rights norms are being imposed on the rest of the world by the Northern governments and by Northern NGOs.

Either way, the countries most interested in promoting human rights norms internationally are generally the most economically developed. For them, the international politics of human rights can be undertaken most effectively by creating relatively weak IOs to allow for the direct bilateral application of power when appropriate. International organizations tend to empower weaker and poorer countries at the expense of stronger and richer ones, because of the legal equality, and often the equal voting power, of states. Since it is the economically and militarily most powerful states that are most interested in the status of human rights norms globally, they have an interest in minimizing the effects of IOs where other states are relatively empowered, and resorting to more bilateral or less formal kinds of relationships, where more traditional forms of power in international relations are less constrained.[34]

Money, Trade, and Multilateralism

One of the issue-areas in which IOs are both most active and most contentious is the international political economy. The three most prominent organizations in this issue-area, and three of the most prominent international organizations overall, are the IMF, the World Bank, and the WTO. The IMF and the World Bank are the world's two predominant multilateral lenders, so much so that they are often referred to in development parlance simply as "the multilaterals." The WTO dominates the international trading system to an extent that few IOs can claim in their issue-areas. The World Bank is discussed in some detail in the next chapter. The bulk of this chapter focuses primarily on a comparison of the IMF and the WTO.

The IMF and the WTO provide an interesting comparison because, beyond their centrality to the international political economy's system of multilateral governance and to debates on globalization, they are different in almost every way. They have different internal structures, different job descriptions, and different degrees of institutional power and agency. They also have very different outputs: primarily loans in the case of the IMF, and primarily rules in the case of the WTO. As a result, they play different roles with respect to such issues as sovereignty and globalization. This chapter first looks at the two institutions individually, and then compares their places in global governance. It also notes the role of some less-visible IOs in the governance of the international political economy.

The World Trade Organization

The WTO is a relatively recent IO, having come into existence in 1995. It does, however, incorporate the General Agreement on Tariffs and Trade (GATT), which dates from 1947. The GATT in turn was originally meant to be a part of an International Trade Organization (ITO). The ITO was the result of multilateral negotiations on the creation of a rule-based international trading system following World War II, and included, among other things, a set of rules for trade in manufactured goods (the GATT), and an authoritative arbitration body to settle trade disputes. The ITO never came into being. It was undermined, among other things, by the opposition of the U.S. Congress, which objected to two features of the proposed organization. The first was the arbitration body, which was seen as a threat to national sovereignty. The second was the provisions for the liberalization of trade in agricultural products, which threatened the system of agricultural supports created in the United States during the Great Depression and Dust Bowl era in the 1930s. The GATT proved less objectionable than the broader ITO, and was adopted as the basic set of rules for international trade among countries outside of the Soviet sphere of influence.[1]

The WTO, which resulted from the Uruguay round of international trade talks held between 1986 and 1993, recreates much of what had been part of the ITO, including a formal dispute settlement mechanism. It incorporates the GATT, the Dispute Settlement Mechanism (DSM), and the General Agreement on Trade in Services (GATS), as well as a host of subsidiary agreements that spell out more detailed rules in specific issue-areas.[2] These agreements are the core of the WTO system—they are the rules that are the *raison d'être* of the organization.

The basic rule in both cases is nondiscrimination, the idea that states that are members of the WTO should treat all other members equally. There are a number of exceptions to this rule for developing countries, countries with industries in distress, and regional trading organizations. But the basic principle is equal treatment. The principal function of the WTO is to encourage and oversee negotiations that reduce general tariff levels, bring new kinds of goods and services into the rules-governed trade system, and generate agreement on how individual countries will put the rules into effect. The WTO is therefore best seen as a forum for negotiations leading to more open and more specific international trade rules. The WTO, as an institution, is heavily weighted toward its legislative function, its rules and rule-making apparatus. Its judicial function, considerably strengthened in the transition from GATT to WTO in 1995, plays a less important, but still central, role. The executive function of the organization is minimal; because the system is designed to be rule-based and self-policing, there should be little need for an active executive.

Organizationally, there are two central components to the WTO: the decision-making structure and the Secretariat. Decisions about WTO rules are taken by member countries through a multilayered decision-making structure. At the top of this structure is the Ministerial Conference, a meeting of ministerial-level representatives of all member countries that must convene at least every alternate year. The most recent meetings (at the time of writing) were in Cancun, Mexico, in September of 2003; Doha, Qatar, in November of 2001; and Seattle, United States, in November of 1999—the meeting in Hong Kong in December of 2005 will take place after this book has gone to press. Subsidiary to the Conference is the General Council, a body that meets frequently at the WTO's headquarters in Geneva. All member countries are represented in the Council, usually by their permanent representatives to the WTO. Subsidiary to the General Council are some three dozen councils and committees that deal with specific trade-related issues and negotiate changes in the WTO's rules. All member countries are represented in all of these councils and committees.[3] The DSM is also technically subsidiary to the General Council,[4] although the actual panelists on specific dispute settlement panels are experts in trade law and are supposed to be politically impartial. They are chosen by the Director-General of the WTO in consultation with the parties to the particular dispute. Appeals to panel rulings are heard by a standing tribunal called the Appellate Body, which consists of seven independent jurists appointed for four-year terms.

The Secretariat consists of a Director-General, chosen by consensus by the membership,[5] and a Secretariat staff of approximately 550 people. They serve to provide technical and logistical support to the decision-making structure, mostly in the form of expertise on specific trade issues under negotiation in the various councils and committees. They also provide technical assistance and training in trade policy enforcement to countries that need it. The Secretariat performs little in the way of executive functions, simply because there are few executive functions to be performed within the structure of the WTO. The rules for trade that are the core of the regime are supposed to be monitored and enforced by member states, not by the WTO itself. This limits the role of the Director-General to administration of the bureaucracy and to political entrepreneurship, using the moral authority of the position to promote world trade and to cajole countries into negotiating in good faith.

A key feature of the WTO, and of the GATT process before 1995, is its voting structure. The basic voting rule is unanimity; the regime is strongly biased toward consensus rather than majoritarian control. Technically speaking, each new negotiating result leads to a formal change in the rules of the WTO and is thus not binding on any state that does not accept the change. Because a rule-based trading system requires that everyone be using the same rules, changes are only made when all participants accept them. But in practice, the unanimity rule is not quite so clear cut. One or two small countries could probably not obstruct acceptance of a new set of rules, because other countries could credibly threaten to simply leave them out of the trading system. The United States or the European Union (EU), on the other hand, could obstruct such acceptance, because a threat to run a global trading system without them is not credible.[6] Smaller, poorer countries often deal with this practical power imbalance by negotiating in blocs big enough to make credible threats of nonparticipation.

The result of the consensus structure of WTO negotiations is that they take a very long time. The Uruguay round of negotiations that led to the creation of the WTO took seven years; the Tokyo round of GATT negotiations before it took six. And this means full-time negotiations concurrently in a variety of committees, not just occasional plenary meetings. It also leads to very high levels of detail in the resultant documents: the list of national commitments under the Uruguay round filled some 22,500 pages, which mostly contained details about commitments to lower tariffs on a specific good with respect to a specific trading partner, or to change a particular regulatory policy to allow greater transparency or competition.[7] A new round of negotiations was launched at the Ministerial Conference in Doha in 2001. This round was supposed to be concluded by January 1, 2005, but at that date many major disagreements among member states had yet to be resolved. One of the major areas of current disagreement is the extent to which WTO rules should apply to agricultural products—the same issue that contributed to the demise of the ITO more than half a century ago.

The IMF

The IMF was one of two institutions created at the conference held at Bretton Woods, New Hampshire, in 1944, designed to recreate an international monetary system after the end of World War II. The other institution, the World Bank, was designed to fund specific projects to assist countries in postwar reconstruction and in development. The IMF was designed to assist in the maintenance of macroeconomic stability and of the fixed exchange rate system (known as the Bretton Woods system) by lending money to assist countries having balance-of-payments difficulties. The system of fixed exchange rates fell apart in the early 1970s, but the IMF continues to operate, and continues its focus on macroeconomic stability and on balance-of-payments difficulties.

The Fund and the Bank are often referred to together as the International Financial Institutions (IFIs). They are similar in many structural respects, and are collectively quite different from most other intergovernmental institutions. Much of what is said here about the structure of the IMF, therefore, also holds true for the World Bank. Many of the differences between the IFIs and other IOs can be explained by the fact that the IFIs are, in important ways, hybrids of the standard model of IOs and regular banks. They are like the standard model of IOs in that their members are states, and in that they are designed to address specific problems of international cooperation: in this case, the provision of infrastructural needs to the international monetary and financial systems. They are more like for-profit financial institutions, however, in their operation and governance. The most straightforward aspect of this observation is that they operate at a profit. They charge interest on their loans to member governments, and this interest is more than sufficient to cover both their operating costs and losses from loan defaults.[8] As a result, member governments do not need to contribute operating funds on an annual basis, as they must with most IOs. Rather, they are asked on a more occasional basis to contribute funds to the IFI's working capital.

The idea of working capital informs the IFI's voting structure, which is more like that of corporate shareholding than that of most IOs. There is no one-member, one-vote rule. Rather, the proportion of the total vote that each member country has is equal to the proportion of the organization's total working capital contributed by the country. In other words, the more shares you buy, the more control you get. In essence, this means that the big industrialized countries have not only *de facto* but also *de jure* control over the activities of the IFIs. In the IMF, this means that the United States alone has 17.14 percent of the vote, and that voting together, the United States, the EU, and Japan have a majority. Many decisions can be made by this simple majority of the vote, but other more fundamental decisions require 70 percent of the vote, and major changes to the structure of the IMF require 85 percent. The 70 percent threshold can be met by the twenty countries with the biggest votes. At the 85 percent threshold the United States can individually vote a measure down, but the all of the countries of Africa and Central and South America voting collectively cannot.[9]

This voting structure affects major decisions of the IFIs, but in both the IMF and the World Bank a considerable degree of authority over operations, including authority over most lending decisions, has been delegated to the managing director and the executive staff. The highest levels of management of the IFIs are their respective Boards of Governors, which are made up of the finance ministers or central bank directors of all of the member countries. These boards meet once a year at the IMF and World Bank's joint annual meeting in Washington. Day-to-day management rests in the hands of the twenty-four Executive Directors. The United States, Japan, Germany, France, the United Kingdom, China, Russia, and Saudi Arabia, as eight of the largest shareholders, each have their own Executive Director.[10] The other sixteen are elected by groupings of states, although the Director chosen is often from the country with the most votes in each group.[11] Reporting to the Executive Board is the Managing Director, whose position is equivalent to that of Secretary-General or Director-General. Although in principle the Managing Director is chosen by the membership of the IFIs as a whole, in practice it is an unofficial but generally accepted rule that the Managing Director of the World Bank will be an American, and that of the IMF will be a European.

The Managing Director of the IMF has a staff of approximately 2,650 people and an annual operating budget (which does not include the value of loans made) of roughly $740 million.[12] The staff is organized both regionally and functionally.[13] The total value of loans and credits by the IMF currently outstanding is $90 billion.[14] The IMF describes its three main activities as surveillance, financial assistance, and technical assistance. Surveillance means "maintain[ing] a dialogue with its member countries on the national and international repercussions of their economic and financial policies."[15] Financial assistance means the lending of money and the extension of credit lines. Technical assistance means in practice the lending of IMF economists to help countries improve the management of their fiscal and financial systems.

In practice, these three activities come together in what the IMF calls conditionality. This entails making loans to countries contingent on their governments' fulfillment of (or the promise to fulfill) a set of macroeconomic policy conditions, usually involving neoliberal reforms to national fiscal and regulatory policy. The reforms required by IMF conditionality usually include some combination of reducing budget deficits, increasing fiscal transparency, fighting corruption, opening markets, reforming domestic financial and banking structures, and privatizing government-held businesses.[16] These conditions are designed to make governments and economies more efficient, and to stabilize the country's currency. The conditions are often unpopular within recipient countries, however, because they often result in lower government spending, higher taxes, a less valuable currency (meaning that imports become more expensive), and weaker labor regulation. Economic theory suggests that these changes should be good for the economy in the medium term, but they inevitably create hardships for many individuals within the country in the short term.

Conditionality brings together all three of the IMF's central activities in that the surveillance identifies what the conditions should be, the technical assistance helps governments to implement the conditions when they cannot do so themselves, and the financial assistance provides the tool with which the IMF enforces conditions. The logic underlying conditionality is based on the fact that IMF loans are designed to help countries overcome macroeconomic instability. The assumption is that such instability is usually caused (at least in part) by macroeconomic policies, such as monetary and fiscal policies, that interfere with the operation of a market economy. Overcoming instability therefore requires a change in macroeconomic policy to get at the underlying cause of the instability, as well as funds to deal with the effects of the instability in the short term.[17]

And yet, it is for this practice of conditionality that the IMF is most commonly criticized, from both a principled and a practical point of view. The principled critique is that conditionality does not adequately respect national sovereignty, and does so in a neocolonial sort of way. The practice, in effect, means that the economists at the IMF, unelected employees of an intergovernmental organization, are telling national governments how to run their countries, often in ways that undermine the democratic legitimacy of those countries. Since it is only developing, usually postcolonial, countries that borrow from the IMF, and since it is the developed, often ex-colonial, countries that control it, this amounts to the old colonial powers regaining control of their former colonies at the expense of self-determination and (sometimes) democratic governance.

The practical critique of conditionality is that it quite often involves inappropriate conditions. Critics of the IMF charge that despite the Fund's claims that it takes local circumstances into account, the reality is that it imposes conditions based on economic theory to countries in a cookie-cutter fashion, conditions that are often grossly inappropriate to local circumstances. They also charge that the IMF is prone to subscribing to economic fashion: for example, they allege that it recommends currency boards to countries when the idea of currency boards is popular among development theorists, then changes its mind once countries have already committed themselves to putting the idea into effect.[18]

The WTO, IMF, Regimes, and Institutions

Do these two institutions, the WTO and the IMF, work as international regimes? From a rationalist perspective, the answer is a qualified yes. A core function of both institutions is transparency, and as such a good starting point in discussing their effectiveness as regimes is with a rationalist analysis of the extent to which they increase the efficiency of international cooperation. Both regimes do fulfill market-perfecting functions in their issue-areas, although their focuses are different. The WTO's primary function, from an efficiency perspective, is to improve property rights in the issue-area of international trade. The rules of the international trading system, the core of the WTO, are in effect specifications of property rights, and the DSM is a mechanism for clarifying and adjudicating these rights. The specification of these property rights is not perfect, but it is clearly better than what had gone before.[19] In this sense, the WTO, as a regime, has been remarkably successful. It has also had some success at decreasing transaction costs and at improving information flows, but this success has been more muted. Trade negotiations carried out under the WTO's auspices retain high transaction costs, in that they can last more than half a decade and employ thousands of people, although this process is probably more efficient than holding a large number of bilateral trade negotiations. The

WTO also collects and publishes trade statistics, but this often duplicates information available elsewhere. This more modest role in dealing with transaction costs and information flows, however, should not be taken as a serious criticism of the WTO, because its primary design function is the specification of property rights with respect to international trade.

Conversely, the emphasis of the IMF's market-perfecting activities is on increasing information flows and reducing transaction costs. The IMF increases information flows by doing research on the economic situation of various countries and publishing the information. It also develops standards for the reporting of national accounts (such as GDP) and balance-of-payments figures, increasing the comparability of these figures across countries, and thereby increasing the amount of comparative economic information available in the system as a whole. At the same time, the IMF reduces the transaction costs of international cooperation in macroeconomic management and lending by acting as a central authority for both. This decreases the degree to which countries have to coordinate anew with each other each time questions of macroeconomic management arise, or when the need for lending to countries in macroeconomic crisis makes itself apparent. Its relatively strong and independent executive gives the IMF the ability to reduce transaction costs by acting on its own initiative in many such cases. The absence of such executive powers probably hinders the WTO's capabilities in this regard. But in a world of sovereign states that are only legally bound by new rules when they choose to accept them, the consensus-building structure of the WTO allows it to authoritatively create new property rights more effectively than the IMF.

Both the executive independence and the transparency-building function of the IMF run into limits with respect to one of its particular roles: that of an international lender of last resort. The IMF lends money to bail out countries that are facing financial crises.[20] Last-resort lending is one of the few economic functions where perfectly specified property rights can be problematic. This is because of what is called moral hazard, the risk that if investors (or governments) know that they will be bailed out in crises, they will undertake riskier behavior, which in turn makes a crisis more likely. Furthermore, the large lines of credit often needed by countries in crisis mean that these loans can become political issues, decided upon by the Executive Directors rather than by the application of purely economic criteria by the IMF's professional staff.[21] As a result, the criteria for small and nonemergency loans by the Fund are far better specified than the criteria for large and emergency loans.

Both the IMF and the WTO also play important legitimizing roles in contemporary international politics. The IMF, along with the World Bank, legitimizes a certain model of development that to an important degree becomes the standard against which developing country policies are compared. This model is often referred to as the "Washington Consensus" because of the proximity of the two organizations to each other in Washington, DC. The model changes over time, but at any given point in time, it legitimizes a particular orthodoxy of development. The model is, however, somewhat weaker than it was in the mid-1990s; the IMF and World Bank do not agree on what it should contain to the extent that they did a decade ago, and the various financial crises of the late 1990s and early 2000s have dented its credibility. Similarly, the WTO has legitimized a model of international trade based on the idea that trade should be rule-based and nondiscriminatory. This model of trade may seem obvious to the early twenty-first century reader—this is a sign of the effectiveness of the WTO, and the GATT before it, at legitimizing these norms, which were quite exceptional when first proposed in the mid-twentieth century. Most of the criticism of the IMF and the WTO as regimes focuses on their legitimizing roles, rather than on their market-perfecting roles. Few would argue that they fail to increase the efficiency of cooperation. Rather, as is discussed below, critics are more prone to arguing that they are too efficient, because the content of the cooperation is flawed.

Looked at as institutions, the IMF and WTO are very different. Among other things, the IMF is simply a much larger organization, with a staff five times larger, and an operating budget (that is, excluding loans) more than six times larger, than the WTO. This means that the amount of research and analysis that the IMF can do is far greater, as is the breadth of expertise that it can bring to bear. The IMF is also in a much better position to act independently than the WTO, both because it has greater independent executive powers and because it has money to lend, with which to convince countries to take its advice. In other words, the IMF is more of an actor in international politics, the WTO more of a forum. What they have in common, though, is that they are staffed primarily by a particular kind of professional. In the IMF, this means professional economists, generally orthodox neoclassical economists. In the WTO, this means trade experts, trained both in the discipline of economics and that of trade law. Critics of both organizations often suggest a link between this personnel specialization and the flawed content of cooperation discussed above.

The International Economic Institutions and Their Critics

Both the WTO and the IMF have been, and continue to be, criticized not for failing to do what they do well, but for being too successful at doing the wrong thing. In particular, both organizations have been criticized for globalizing a model of economic policy, the Washington Consensus, both too hard and too far. This criticism has recently become much more visible, in a pattern first seen when some 50,000 protestors showed up at the WTO's biennial meeting in Seattle in November 1999, and seen frequently since then at all of the major meetings of the big three international economic institutions.[22] The thrust of this criticism has been twofold: that the policies that the international economic institutions have been promoting are flawed, and that the processes through which they are promoting them are undemocratic.

The first of these criticisms, that the policies that the international economic institutions have been promoting are flawed, has already been alluded to. These criticisms can take a range of forms, from criticism of specific sets of IMF loan conditions from people who are broadly sympathetic to market capitalism, to more fundamental criticisms of the role of these IOs in promoting market capitalism in general. The latter group often point, as noted above, to the training of the personnel in these organizations—that they hire only people who believe in their goals from the outset, and are therefore unable to examine those goals critically. Criticism of the WTO and IMF policies also often points to their focus on economic issues to the exclusion of other goals, such as maintaining labor or environmental standards, or empowering women.[23] The Seattle protestors represented a range of these criticisms, from labor activists who supported the status quo in general and wanted the status quo protected from further globalization, to environmental activists who objected to market capitalism and international trade in principle.

The second criticism, that international economic institutions such as the IMF and the WTO are undemocratic, is actually more germane to the subject of this book. The argument from this perspective is that in the IMF a bunch of unelected economists are dictating policy to elected governments, and in the WTO a bunch of unelected trade lawyers are dictating policy to the world as a whole. In essence, this is a critique of contemporary globalization, and an argument in favor of reinforcing national economic sovereignty. The WTO's response to this charge is that it is in fact very democratic; it claims that its consensus decision-making makes it even more democratic than majority-rule governance systems, as does the fact that new rules do not apply to countries until they explicitly accept them.[24] This answer refers, of course, to democracy among countries rather than among the global population at large. But those people are represented through their governments, and a majority of those governments in turn are democratically elected.

Another version of the charge that the WTO in particular is undemocratic is that the DSM is unrepresentative. Only countries party to a dispute have a right to be heard there, whereas individuals, and NGOs representing the interests of social, labor, environmental, or indigenous groups, are generally excluded. This seems, on the face of it, an odd criticism, because the DSM is intended as a court, a legal body, and not as a political body. In liberal democratic societies, including the United States, the role of courts is generally assumed to be the impartial adjudication of the law, and as such, courts are generally thought most effective when they are most insulated from political pressures. The critique that the DSM is unrepresentative, therefore, is based on the idea that international arbitration should not work in the way that domestic arbitration works, but should instead be a political activity. The implication is that the rule of law at the international level undermines, rather than reinforces, democracy. This critique is not really directed at the DSM in particular, but is a much broader indictment of the idea of globalization, and an argument in favor of stronger national sovereignty.

The IMF cannot claim to be a participatory democracy in the way that the WTO can. Its weighted voting structure is more suggestive of corporate governance than of political governance, and it has considerable executive powers in dealing with individual countries. The IMF has argued that it should not in fact be expected to be a democratic institution, for two reasons. The first is that a corporate governance structure is appropriate to its primary activity, lending money at interest. In other words, it is designed to make lending decisions based on economic rather than political criteria, and therefore requires an economic rather than political decision-making structure.[25] The second argument against democratizing the IMF is that many of its functions are the international equivalents of what central banks do for domestic economies. It is the current international fashion to depoliticize central banks as much as possible and to insulate them from electoral politics to allow them to focus on their primarily technical goals, such as stabilizing currency values and moderating business cycles. The same logic that argues that central banks should be insulated from political pressures should in principle hold true for the IMF as well.[26] And yet, the basic critique of the IMF remains, that it is an undemocratic institution dictating economic policy to sovereign governments, which are themselves often democratically legitimate.

Despite these responses by supporters of a corporate form of governance at the IMF, the Fund has in the past decade or so begun to look for ways to increase the participatory, if not democratic, legitimacy of its lending conditions. It has increased its institutional transparency and has begun to try to work with various NGOs and civil society groups, to try to make its lending conditions reflect points of view other than just those of the economists on the IMF's staff. At the same time, it has begun to use the term "program ownership" in tandem with conditionality. This implies an effort to work with governments to create lending programs and conditions that they approve of and support, rather than simply dictating conditions to governments.[27] Whether this change in language will lead to a significant change in the practice of conditionality remains to be seen. Even if it does, however, it will undoubtedly not affect the more fundamental critics of the role of the IMF.

Other International Economic Institutions

The focus of so much debate on the big three international economic institutions often distracts the casual observer from realizing that there are many other IOs that deal with economic issues as well. The line separating an international economic institution from an organization focusing on, say, development or technical co-operation, is unclear, and some of the organizations that straddle this line are discussed in other chapters. The rest of this chapter briefly discusses two particular organizations that focus primarily on issues of economic cooperation. These two IOs are the World Intellectual Property Organization (WIPO) and the Organization for Economic Co-operation and Development (OECD).

WIPO is an IO that oversees a system of twenty-three treaties dealing with issues relating to intellectual property, including patents and copyrights, and has a current membership of 179 countries. It is a specialized agency of the UN, affiliated with rather than subsidiary to the General Assembly (GA) and ECOSOC. While WIPO has existed with its current name and structure only since 1970, it is a direct linear descendent of one of the oldest IOs, the United International Bureaux for the Protection of Intellectual Property (or BIRPI, the acronym of its French name), created in 1893; BIRPI itself traces its roots back to 1883. WIPO's major challenges in the near future involve coping with the growth of the Internet and related technologies, and expanding international intellectual property rules to cover the new electronic economy.

WIPO's structure is fairly typical of IOs, with a legislative body made up of member states, and a Secretariat led by a Director-General. The Secretariat has a staff of just under 900 people and administers a budget of roughly a quarter of a billion dollars a year. Unusually for an IO, over 90 percent of this budget comes from service charges levied by WIPO on companies and individuals, mostly for use of its international patent registration system, rather than from membership dues.[28] The role of the Secretariat is to oversee the implementation of treaties, and as such it plays mostly a technical and informational role. But the Secretariat nonetheless does have some independent impact on international relations through the technical advice it gives, and through its efforts to promote intellectual property issues and foster international cooperation on these issues. In this sense, the WIPO Secretariat, as an actor, is comparable to the WTO Secretariat. Basic policy decisions are taken through the modification of existing treaties and the creation of new ones, meaning that states need not accept new rules that they do not agree with. As with the WTO, this promotes a tendency toward consensus decision-making. WIPO sees its task primarily as one of maximizing efficiency, by getting member countries to agree to a common definition of intellectual property rights. But it does play a role in legitimating internationally the idea that intellectual property rights should be strongly protected and enforced.[29]

The OECD is less typical of IOs in that while it is a multilateral organization, it is not part of the UN system, and has a limited membership of thirty countries, all of which are relatively wealthy. It is, in essence, the club of rich market democracies. The forerunner of the OECD, the Organization for European Economic Cooperation (OEEC), was created to oversee the distribution of Marshall Fund aid in the late 1940s. This aid was specifically tied to the creation and maintenance of democratic political and market-based economic systems in the recipient countries.[30] The membership of the OECD (which was created from the OEEC in 1961) has always been limited to market-oriented democracies. Unlike most multilateral organizations and UN-related organizations, it does not have a membership that is open to all countries; membership is by invitation only.

The OECD is best known for its research on international economic issues, particularly issues of concern to developed countries, and for its reports and statistics. This research is compiled by a staff of close to 2,000 at its headquarters in Paris. The organization also creates standards (nonbinding rules) in a variety of different realms of economic activity, such as guidelines for multinational corporations, and standards for competition policy and insurance industry oversight. The OECD has recently become more enthusiastic about promoting the negotiation of formal treaties under its auspices. It has had some successes in this regard, such as the recent Convention on Combating Bribery of Foreign Public Officials in International Business Transactions (1997). It has also had one notable and public failure, in its attempt to generate a Multilateral Agreement on Investment (MAI) in the late 1990s.[31] The MAI dissolved under a barrage of criticism from the antiglobalization movement within OECD member countries.

Organizations such as the WTO, WIPO, and the OECD overlap in terms of membership and often in terms of function. On some intellectual property rights issues, for example, negotiation could reasonably happen under the auspices of any one of the three organizations. If it took place under WIPO, then the issue would likely be discussed on its own and by most of the world's countries. If under the OECD, then it would still be discussed on its own, but only by industrialized countries.

And if under the WTO, then it would be discussed by most of the world's countries and in the context of a much broader negotiation. This range of possibilities allows countries trying to pursue a particular goal multilaterally to engage in what is called forum-shopping—to raise an issue in whatever forum is most likely to yield the result that the country in question is looking for.[32] This helps to explain why the MAI, for example, was pursued under the auspices of the OECD—the countries party to the negotiations were looking for a venue where rich countries could maintain control of the agenda.

These three organizations are, however, quite different from the IMF, for two reasons. The first is that the IMF has an existing source of funds, and does not need to be funded by its member countries every year. The second is that the IMF's primary output is money, in the form of loans, while that of the WTO, WIPO, and the OECD are rules and reports. These two differences combine to make the IMF more of an independent agent in international politics than the other three organizations, both because it is more independent from the states funding it and because it can threaten to withhold its loans from the states that need them. Rules and reports, once they are agreed to by most countries, exist for any country to make use of. But loans can be withheld from specific countries. This latter difference not only makes the IMF a more independent actor in international politics than most other IOs, but also a more powerful one.

9

Development

While the WTO and the IMF are the predominant international institutions in the issue-areas of international trade and monetary cooperation, respectively, there is no equivalently predominant institution in the issue-area of development. The role of international organizations (IOs) in development can be divided into three rough categories: development lending, development assistance, and development discourse. This chapter examines leading institutions in each of these three categories: the World Bank, the United Nations Development Programme (UNDP), and the United Nations Conference on Trade and Development (UNCTAD), respectively.

The World Bank and Development Lending

The World Bank is the world's premier development lending institution. Its job is to lend money to development projects in poorer countries. The Bank is, in many ways, a sister institution to the IMF. The two institutions are often referred to as the International Financial Institutions, or IFIs. Their genesis was at the same conference in Bretton Woods in 1944, and they have similar organizational structures. In particular, the World Bank shares with the IMF a corporate shareholding and management structure and an almost identical pattern of voting power. It is also a profit-making institution—most of its loans are at market rates, and it is one of the last creditors that countries would consider defaulting on. The Bank and the Fund often work in tandem with individual countries to create development plans, although, as is discussed below, this cooperation is not always seamless. As such, many of the criticisms of the IMF that were discussed in the previous chapter hold true for the World Bank as well, including the pattern of development that it promotes and legitimizes, and concerns about democratic governance.

There are also, however, a number of important differences between the Bank and the Fund. A key difference, of course, is that they perform different tasks. They both lend money to developing countries, but for different purposes. Whereas the Fund makes credit available to governments for general budgetary purposes, the Bank lends money to finance specific development projects. These are usually infrastructural projects, either in the form of the physical infrastructure needed for economic development, such as roads or electrical systems, or the human infrastructure that promotes economic development, such as better education. A government will come to the Bank with a project proposal (although Bank personnel often participate in preparing the proposal) that indicates how the project is economically viable. In other words, the projects that the Bank funds are supposed to generate economic returns sufficient to pay off the loan; they are supposed to be financially viable. For example, if a country wants to borrow money from the Bank to help fund a new school, the proposal needs to show that the increased productivity generated by the increase in employment will generate enough new revenue over the long term to pay for the cost of building and running the school.

Because of the difference in focus between the two institutions, the Fund tends to think in terms of macroeconomic stability, and the Bank in terms of microeconomic growth. This has led to the growth of different expertise within the two IOs, and a reputation on the part of the Bank for being less "orthodox," less focused on economic theory, and more willing to take social considerations in borrowing countries into account. Because the focus on microeconomic development means that the Bank needs to know about individual national economies in greater detail, it has also led to the evolution of a much bigger research bureaucracy: the permanent staff of the Bank, at 9,300 people, is more than three times the size of the Fund's staff.

A second difference between the IMF and the World Bank is that there is only one Fund, and no regional monetary funds.[1] There are, however, regional development banks, organizations that are structured like the World Bank and operate in the same basic manner, but focus their lending within a specific region. This does not mean, however, that all of the member countries are from the region. The United States, for example, is not only a member, it also has the largest share of the vote in all of the major regional development banks. The major Western European countries, Japan, and Canada are also members of all of the major regional development banks. These banks include the Asian Development Bank (ADB), the African Development Bank (also ADB),[2] the Inter-American Development Bank (IADB), and the European Bank for Reconstruction and Development (EBRD).[3] While the capital that each of the regional development banks can call on, and the amount that each lends, is far smaller than the equivalent figure for the World Bank, the regional banks collectively lend amounts similar to those lent by the World Bank. Nonetheless, they remain far less central to international development issues than the World Bank because of the more central role that the latter institution plays in the discourse on and legitimation of the Washington Consensus development model.

A third difference between the IMF and the World Bank is that the Bank is actually made up of a number of different components, each with separate tasks. The original component, and still the core of the institution, is the International Bank for Reconstruction and Development (IBRD), which is what people are in fact often referring to when they speak of the World Bank. This is the component that lends money to member governments for development projects, at a profit. The IBRD in 2002 lent roughly $11.5 billion. The International Development Association (IDA) provides loans to the poorest of countries at concessional rates (often charging no interest, but still requiring repayment of the capital, over a long term). The International Finance Corporation (IFC) makes loans to corporations in developing countries rather than governments. The IDA lent about $8 billion in 2002, and the IFC about $3.5 billion.[4] The other two components of the Bank are the Multilateral Investment Guarantee Agency (MIGA), which provides investment insurance to investors in developing countries in order to reduce risk premiums, and the International Centre for the Settlement of Investment Disputes (ICSID), an arbitration body.

The World Bank, as a regime, has been criticized from both efficiency and legitimacy perspectives. From the efficiency perspective, there have been some recent questions as to whether development banks are still necessary in a globalizing world in which there is free movement of capital and an increasing number of financial mechanisms that developing countries can use to raise capital on world markets. From this perspective, there may still be a need for the IDA (with its concessionary lending) and the ICSID (with its arbitration function), as well as for the World Bank's efforts at collecting and disseminating development information and coordinating development efforts in particular countries.[5] But from the perspective of neoclassical economics, the imperfections in the international market for development finance that were behind the creation of the Bank in the first place have largely disappeared, and creditworthy development projects should have no problem obtaining finance from private sources. The Bank's response to this observation is to stress that it is a development agency, not a bank. It lends money for projects that would have trouble finding private financing, and lends to countries at lower rates of interest, and for longer periods of time, than private lenders would. The Bank also notes that it provides a wide array of development services in addition to lending.

From a legitimacy perspective, the World Bank regime has been subjected to many of the same criticisms as the IMF. The details of the criticisms are marginally different because the Bank supports specific projects rather than macroeconomic adjustment, but the basic gist of the criticism is the same: that the Bank promotes a particular idea of development, one that many people find problematic. It does so through the mechanism of moral suasion, by using its position as the lead multilateral development lender and voice of the international community on development issues as a source of legitimate authority and as a bully pulpit. But it also does so institutionally, by causing the creation of bureaucracies in developing countries that are designed primarily to interact with the Bank (and the IMF). By creating government bureaucracies in developing countries that are by design concerned primarily with responding to the World Bank and IMF, the IFIs have the effect of legitimizing their models of development within the governments of the countries they lend to.[6]

One can certainly argue that the Bank's vision of development has beneficial aspects. For example, the shift in emphasis in the internationally accepted idea of what development means—from industrialization to poverty alleviation—in the 1960s and 1970s has been traced to the Bank.[7] But critics argue that the Bank remains too focused on physical infrastructure at the expense of social infrastructure, and that it is insufficiently sensitive to the social and environmental effects of the projects to which it lends.[8] At the extreme, this sort of criticism argues against development lending in general, inasmuch as it by definition promotes the development of a monetary economy at the expense of alternative economic forms, be they traditional or radical. Nonetheless, there are many critics who accept the principle of development lending, but argue that the Bank lends inappropriately.

The World Bank has, particularly in the past two decades, taken these criticisms to heart. It has changed its lending policies to reflect social and environmental concerns. It has modified the definition of development that it legitimizes to focus more on the development of human capital and infrastructure at the expense of physical infrastructure.[9] And it has put a variety of institutional mechanisms in place that are designed to ensure that social and environmental concerns are incorporated into specific lending projects.[10] For example, before the Bank lends money to fund a dam, it will conduct studies into how much environmental damage the dam will do, how many people the dam's reservoir will displace, and what the effect of the dam on any indigenous populations will be, among other things. The Bank is also becoming much less sympathetic to projects that focus on physical infrastructure, such as dams and highways, and more sympathetic to projects that fund human infrastructure, such as primary education and health care.[11]

Critics contend, however, that these changes are (at least to some extent) only cosmetic, that the basic institutional structure of the Bank does not allow it to reform itself effectively. The argument is that the basic task of the Bank is to lend money, and that employees are rewarded on the basis of how much money they lend and how much of that gets paid back. As attention to environmental and social side effects is a distraction from this goal, the lenders will attempt as much as possible to marginalize those in charge of social and environmental reviews. And loans to social infrastructure do not generate a clear cash flow that can be used for repayment.[12] The Bank is doing a better job of dealing with these issues than it used to, but the question remains, however, whether or not it is in fact doing a *good* job of dealing with these issues.

From the perspective of the study of IOs, the pattern of change in lending focus within the Bank is interesting not only because of its impact on development, but also as a case study of leadership and agency in IOs. In particular, a number of studies have asked how much difference changes of leadership at the Bank make to institutional norms and policy. These studies have tended to suggest that leaders can in fact make quite a difference, that the priorities of particular presidents of the Bank have had a real impact on Bank policies.[13] Since Bank policies in turn affect accepted models of development, this means both that the President has real institutional power in international politics and that the ability to choose the President of the Bank is a source of power for the country that makes this appointment (by tradition, the United States). The U.S. government recently announced (and the Bank's Board of Governors approved) the appointment of Paul Wolfowitz, until then U.S. Deputy Secretary of Defense and a noted neoconservative, as president. It remains to be seen what effect this appointment will have on Bank policy.

The UNDP and Development Assistance

Development assistance is used here to mean programs that transfer resources to developing countries (in other words, provide aid), as opposed to development lending, where resources are lent but repayment is expected.[14] The volume of money lent by the development lending institutions is an order of magnitude greater than what the multilateral development assistance institutions can spend. But this comparison understates the importance of the development assistance institutions, for three reasons. The first is that assistance does not increase the indebtedness of the recipient countries, and therefore does not feed into the cycle of debt that the lending institutions both contribute to and are called upon to alleviate. The second reason is that the development assistance institutions can fund programs that do not have a direct economic logic, or that do not yield a cash flow for repayment. In other words, they can fund many kinds of programs that the development lenders would not, such as the development of democratic institutions. And finally, the development assistance institutions are important actors in the development field because they are more like normal IOs than the development lenders. In particular, their policy-making bodies work on a one-country, one-vote basis, unlike the corporate voting structures of the IFIs. This gives them a greater legitimacy in the eyes of developing countries than the IFIs, which are seen by some to be Northern-dominated and neocolonial.

There are a variety of IOs that fit under the heading of development assistance institutions, and the distinction between these institutions and organizations that offer humanitarian aid is not always clear. Various UN-related organizations, such as the UNDP, the United Nations Children's Fund (UNICEF), the Food and Agriculture Organization (FAO), the World Food Programme (WFP), and the World Health Organization (WHO), as well as the World Bank and IMF, focus on their own specific issue-areas, but also try to coordinate their activities where they overlap, in a process that will be discussed at the end of this chapter. The organization that is most directly focused on development assistance per se is the UNDP. Its particular remit is to provide technical assistance to developing countries, primarily by providing and promoting technical expertise.

The UNDP is a subsidiary body to the UN General Assembly (GA) and the Economic and Social Council (ECOSOC). It was created in 1966 from the merger of already-existing technical assistance funds within the UN.[15] Its executive board consists of thirty-six countries elected for three-year terms from within ECOSOC. It has a relatively weak central secretariat; most of its bureaucratic structure is to be found in its regional offices and its 131 country offices. In other words, unlike many of the IOs examined to this point, its emphasis is on on-site implementation rather than centralized rule-setting or oversight. The central office, through the executive board, sets general funding priorities, which currently include democratic governance, poverty reduction, and HIV/AIDS.[16] But regional and country offices have a significant degree of latitude in implementing these priorities, in deciding which particular programs to fund in specific countries. UNDP country offices also often cooperate with the local offices of other IOs, such as the World Bank or UNICEF, and with an array of development NGOs, to provide funding.

The institutional history of the UNDP, as an amalgam of voluntary development funds rather than an IO created *de novo*, is reflected in its current funding structure. The organization does not have access to any of the UN's membership dues and does not charge any dues of its own. It is funded entirely by voluntary contributions from its members. These contributions yielded some $670 million in core resources in 2002.[17] The voluntary nature of the contributions means that they tend to come disproportionately from those countries that are favorably disposed toward the idea of multilateral development assistance. In 2002, for example, while the largest donor to the UNDP was the United States, and the second-largest Japan, the third-largest was Norway, a country of less than 5 million people. Looked at another way, the U.S. contribution amounted to 35¢ per person, the Japanese contribution to 68¢, and the Norwegian contribution to over $17. The Scandinavian countries as a group account for over a quarter of total UNDP core funds.[18]

Viewed as a regime, the UNDP has both efficiency-maximizing functions and legitimating functions. Its primary efficiency-maximizing function is to reduce the transaction costs of development aid. In maintaining offices in most developing countries for the purpose of technical assistance for development, it eliminates a need for donor countries to do so individually. In other words, it means that rather than having twenty or thirty technical assistance offices, one from each major donor country, in each developing country, there can be only one central office. This matters most to smaller donor countries, for whom maintaining such a variety of offices abroad would consume a large share of total aid available. The efficiency gain is less important for the largest donors, who are more likely to maintain their own networks of recipient country offices in parallel with the UNDP's network. This helps explain why smaller donor countries are so disproportionately represented among the UNDP's funders—their relative efficiency gain from providing development assistance through the UNDP is greater.

The UNDP as a regime also has legitimizing functions. At the most basic level, the organization legitimizes the idea of multilateral development assistance, such that all of the large industrialized countries, even those with extensive bilateral aid programs, donate some funds. The UNDP's role in determining what constitutes legitimate development programmatically is less clear. The organization's priorities are a good indicator of internationally accepted development priorities. Its inclusion of, for example, democratization and HIV/AIDS, neither of which would have been priorities a decade ago, indicates that these two issues have become a generally accepted part of the development agenda. But the UNDP's role in setting this agenda is unclear—is the organization driving the agenda, or simply responding to it? Answering this question would require detailed study of the politics within the organization, to determine whether its agenda is being set primarily at the political level or at the operational level.

As an institution, the UNDP is somewhat diffuse, with considerable decision-making autonomy devolved to the country offices. These offices can at times be quite important within their countries, particularly when governments are not functioning effectively or lack access to the expertise needed to govern. At the same time, the offices tend to be more focused on the governance needs of the particular country, and less on the development priorities of the central IO bureaucracy, than is true of World Bank local offices. This suggests that, institutionally, it may be more accurate to think of the country offices as relevant independent actors within specific developing countries than to think of the UNDP, as a whole, as a key actor in the international discourse and practice of development.

UNCTAD and Development Discourse

The third category of international institutions active in the issue-area of development comprises those that promote development discourse, institutions that serve primarily as forums for discussion. There are a variety of such institutions, including the regional and functional commissions that report to ECOSOC (see the organizational chart of the UN in chapter 5). The premier development discourse IO, however, is UNCTAD. Like the UNDP, UNCTAD was created by the GA in the mid-1960s (UNCTAD was in fact the earlier institution, created in 1964), has the same membership as the GA, and reports to ECOSOC. Beyond this common lineage, the two organizations are fundamentally different.

Unlike the UNDP's dispersed decision-making structure, most of UNCTAD's activities take place at its headquarters in Geneva. And unlike the UNDP's funding base of voluntary contributions, UNCTAD is financed primarily from the GA's regular budget. The two organizations both have programs to promote technical cooperation, but the programs themselves are fundamentally different. Whereas the UNDP's technical cooperation programs are focused on North–South cooperation and involve the creation of on-site expertise, UNCTAD's programs focus on South–South technical cooperation and involve the creation of guidelines and formats for cooperation through negotiation in Geneva, rather than the implementation of technical cooperation on the ground.[19]

UNCTAD grew out of the rapid increase in developing country membership in the UN in the early 1960s (thirty-two new members joined the UN between 1960 and 1964). Suddenly, the third world had a voting majority in the GA, and UNCTAD was one of the first institutional results of this development. It was created to assist developing countries with issues of trade and development, and was designed from the outset as an institutional counterweight to the Northern-dominated system of international trade and development. While all members of the UN are also members of UNCTAD, the organization was designed primarily as a forum for developing countries to discuss development issues. It has generally reflected the positions of developing countries, and has always been closely associated with the G-77.[20]

UNCTAD is perhaps best known as the forum of the New International Economic Order (NIEO), an attempt by developing countries to alter the international terms of trade in favor of exporters of primary products.[21] The idea of an NIEO has more or less died, and UNCTAD has accepted the basic premise that free markets are the main engines of international trade. But UNCTAD remains more focused on the prerogatives of the developing world in the international system (as opposed to development projects within countries) than other development organizations. It can do so in part because of its funding structure. Whereas the UNDP has to raise funds anew from volunteer donors every year, UNCTAD gets most of its funding from the regular UN budget. This has the effect of keeping its operations small—it has an annual budget of less than $70 million, and a total staff of some 400 people. This size constraint means that UNCTAD operates mainly as a forum, as a place where developing countries can set the agenda for discussions of issues of trade and development. Although UNCTAD does attempt to offer some technical assistance programs to countries dealing with the technical requirements of international trade, such as help with the bureaucratic processes of conforming to internationally accepted technical standards, these efforts are quite modest. But the resulting freedom from the need to raise funds from developed countries gives UNCTAD the political leeway to be more critical of market economics than other UN agencies.

As a regime, UNCTAD functions more in the realm of legitimacy than in the realm of efficiency-maximizing. In other words, it is primarily about political rather than technical cooperation. It does generate some efficiency gains, in the way that international forums do, by decreasing transaction costs of consensus-building and increasing information flows on relevant political positions among participants, as well as doing some of its own research on trade and development. But its main function is to act as a political counterweight to the formally Northern-dominated IFIs, and to other more democratic but still informally Northern-dominated economic IOs, such as the GATT, the WTO and, to a lesser extent, the UNDP. Its main function is to attempt to legitimate an alternative view of the trade–development nexus, or at least to provide a legitimate alternative voice to those of the big three international economic institutions. It is not clear that UNCTAD does so particularly effectively.

Development, Efficiency, and Legitimacy

As a whole, does the community of international institutions working in the field of development make a difference? This question can be addressed from two perspectives, that of efficiency and that of legitimacy. From an efficiency perspective, the question is not whether the activities of these IOs help development or improve the living conditions of people in developing countries. Rather, the appropriate questions are whether or not the resources committed to development IOs are used more efficiently than they would be if they were used for bilateral development aid, and whether or not the current institutional structure could be redesigned to use those resources yet more efficiently.

The efficiency gains of multilateral development assistance are, as was discussed above, greatest for wealthy but smaller donor countries, as these countries make greater proportional use of development IOs. Even for larger donors that maintain their own local development offices, however, multilateral coordination can lead to more efficient allocation of development resources by improving information flows about various projects and thus eliminating some program duplication. This gain is mitigated somewhat by the proliferation of multilateral development organizations. The UN is dealing with the efficiency costs of various IOs with overlapping remits by creating new, country-specific coordinating bodies.[22] These in turn improve information flows among specific national offices of development IOs, but at the expense of creating yet another layer of bureaucracy. In short, the international development organization community is aware of the problems in balancing regime efficiency (having a central location for information and decision-making) with institutional efficiency (keeping the size of specific bureaucracies under control). But it is a difficult balancing act.

Critics of the IFIs argue that many of their functions, with the possible exception of crisis lending, could be performed equally effectively by the private sector.

To the extent that they are right, the IFIs function more as vehicles for rich country power than as efficiency maximizers in the process of aiding development. In any case, the major donors to the IFIs are also those that, by virtue of being the biggest economies, would suffer the fewest efficiency losses in managing development lending bilaterally rather than multilaterally. Perhaps the greatest efficiency gains that the IFIs provide in this context are in the realm of property rights. They maintain a pool of capital that is committed to development lending, in a way that would make it very difficult even for the biggest donor countries to change. Thus, the developing world can expect that this pool will remain (conditionally) accessible to a greater degree than would be the case if the funds were controlled by separate national governments.

From the perspective of legitimacy, the success of the community of international development organizations is mixed. In their favor, it can be argued that they have had two beneficial effects. They have increased levels of development funding by legitimating minimum development funding levels. They have also affected definitions of what constitutes a legitimate development project, and therefore, what projects should be funded. In terms of levels of funding, UNCTAD got most developed countries to agree in principle that they should be giving annual development aid equal to 0.7 percent of their GDPs. More generally, the simple existence of the various development IOs and their constant calls for funding probably do increase overall levels of development funding, by embarrassing countries that fail to contribute. However, it is probably impossible to determine how much difference the development IO community has made to overall development funding levels. There is also some evidence that development IOs can expand existing definitions of legitimate development to include issues such as poverty alleviation, as discussed earlier.[23]

On the other hand, the success of the development IO community both at increasing funding levels for development and at legitimating particular understandings of development has been partial at best. UNCTAD did get developed countries to agree to the 0.7 percent funding level in principle. But only five countries, all of them small, met the target, and most developed countries remain well below half of it.[24] Furthermore, development assistance from most developed countries is well down compared with a decade ago,[25] although we do not know by how much funding levels might have fallen absent the IOs.

Similarly, while UNCTAD was active throughout the 1970s, promoting the NIEO, this activity ultimately had very little effect on the structure of international trade and commerce. In fact, the structure of the international trading system became more liberal at a time when the NIEO was arguing for greater checks on liberal international trade. Leaving UNCTAD aside as an outlier for the moment, the picture remains unclear. International organizations clearly have some independent effect on understandings of what constitutes legitimate development, even after allowing for the interests of their donor countries. But the question of what effects they will have is confused by the fact that the development IO community itself is not in agreement as to what should be considered legitimate. There is a growing rift on this issue (and on issues of institutional governance) between the IMF and the World Bank,[26] and the UNDP is critical of both of the development lending institutions for their patterns of governance and, by extension, for the outputs of that governance.[27] Presumably, the more these IOs snipe at each others' governance structures, the more likely they are to undermine the ability of the development IO community as a whole to effectively legitimize particular approaches to development.

On a final note, one of the most successful recent attempts at legitimating particular development goals has come not from a development IO, but from the GA. The UN Millennium Development Goals (MDG) originated in a GA Resolution entitled the "United Nations Millennium Declaration" in 2000.[28] The Declaration included some specific development goals, such as reducing the number of people living on less than one dollar a day by half by 2015. Because all UN member countries have signed on to the MDG, it represents an international consensus. And because the goals originated in a report by the Secretary-General, the UN bureaucracy is enthusiastic about them as well. As a result, many development IOs, including the World Bank, UNDP, and UNCTAD, have incorporated the MDG into their own development programs, as have many national development agencies.

10

The Technical Details

Chapters 6 through 9 looked at specific international organizations (IOs) as agents of international cooperation in issue-areas that have strong political components. The IOs themselves were designed in part to answer political questions, to decide in favor of one set of state preferences over others as a prior condition to cooperation. But there is a wide range of IOs, relatively small and narrowly focused, that are designed to deal with technical and functional, rather than political, cooperation. They are designed to take goals that all countries agree on—such as efficient international postal delivery, the safety of international civil aviation, and combating dread diseases—and allow them to cooperate on achieving those goals more effectively. All countries agree on goals such as international peace and development, but disagree about what exactly those goals mean and about the conditions under which they should be achieved. With a goal such as safe international civil aviation, there is likely to be less disagreement about both goal definition and the conditions of cooperation.

The organizations that deal with this type of technical and functional cooperation tend to get much less press than the more political IOs. And yet, they can be quite important in the everyday lives of a wide range of people. We assume that mail will get delivered internationally, and that airplanes will be able to communicate effectively with ground control overseas. International commerce, among other things, would be severely impacted were these services to stop functioning. Therefore, we should apply theories of international organization to better understand technical and functional IOs, and to make them work as effectively as possible. These IOs can also yield some useful observations about some of the broader questions in IO theory that are different from those suggested by the more political IOs.

In particular, the trajectory of cooperation managed by technical IOs speaks to the first of the theoretical distinctions discussed in the first half of this book: the distinction between sovereignty and globalization, between an internationalist model of global governance and a universalist one. One way of looking at this distinction is through the theoretical lens of functionalism, as discussed in Chapter 3. Functionalist theory argues that as increasing economic complexity drives demands for more international regulatory coordination, technical cooperation among countries will drive political integration. This theoretical approach fell out of vogue in the late 1960s as scholars recognized the limits of technological cooperation in the absence of political cooperation. But a major part of the antiglobalization critique of many IOs is that they are too technical, and not political enough; that rules that affect individuals the world over are made by narrowly focused technical experts and bureaucrats without sufficient popular input.

Three such technical organizations are the Universal Postal Union (UPU), the International Civil Aviation Organization (ICAO), and the World Health Organization (WHO). These three IOs represent a wide range both in terms of scale (size of bureaucracies and budgets) and in terms of issue-area of focus. The extent to which they represent examples of technical expertise driving international cooperation and, in particular, international political integration, should tell us something about the extent to which functionalist theory accurately describes contemporary international organization.

The UPU

The UPU is in many ways a prototypical functional IO. It claims to be the second-oldest multilateral IO, having been founded in 1874 (it was brought within the UN system in 1948).[1] It is specifically designed to increase transparency and reduce transaction costs in international postal delivery, goals shared by all of its members, and generally does not address politically contentious issues. Although its members are national governments, in practice, these governments are represented by national postal bureaucracies, which tend to be bureaucratically distinct from broader national executives and legislatures.

The UPU was created to replace a complicated system of bilateral postal agreements with a single, simpler, multilateral one. The original system was in fact quite simple: the member countries agreed that for all letters sent internationally, the postal service of the sending country would receive all of the stamp revenue, and that of the country to which the letter was sent would receive none. The logic underlying this system was that the number of letters sent by any given country should be roughly equal to the number received, so that the revenues across postal services should even out over time. By the 1960s, it had become clear that this was not the case; more letters were sent from rich to poor countries than from poor to rich. This meant, in essence, that the postal services of poorer countries were subsidizing those of richer countries. In 1969, in response to this situation, the UPU created, and continues to oversee, a system of "terminal dues."[2] This system in essence compensates postal services for international letters they deliver in excess of those that they send.

Whereas the core function of the UPU is managing a set of rules to create transparency in the delivery of mail internationally, in the past several decades the organization has branched out into other areas. It now focuses much of its energy on technical assistance to postal services in developing countries, and works on mechanisms to "promote stakeholder interaction and customer satisfaction,"[3] which means helping postal services to deliver mail, and serve other needs of their customers, more quickly and efficiently. It also coordinates efforts to create international standards for new technologies that relate to postal services, primarily the increased use of information technology, such as offering online services to customers and using bar-code technologies in mail sorting. On a more ideological note, the focus of the UPU's activities on these fronts is on helping postal services to transform themselves from traditional government bureaucracies to consumer-oriented service companies. This focus seems to reflect a general movement among member countries toward a neoliberal consensus on postal reform, and the desire of the postal services themselves not to get left behind in a rapidly globalizing industry.

The UPU is one of the most broad-based of IOs, with a membership of 189 countries (membership is open to all UN members, and to other countries by vote of two-thirds of existing members). Its governing body is the Universal Postal Congress, which meets every five years and at which all members are represented. The Congress elects two councils of forty members each, the Council of Administration and the Postal Operations Council, each representing the geographic diversity of the UPU. The UPU's secretariat, the International Bureau, coordinates its day-to-day activities and provides technical assistance. As well as working with the postal services of member countries, the International Bureau also coordinates its activities with those of other IOs when appropriate. For example, the UPU will coordinate with the United Nations Office on Drugs and Crime (UNODC) on issues relating to the shipment of drugs by mail, and with the ICAO on issues relating to international airmail coordination.

The UPU is one of the smaller of the UN-affiliated IOs. Its secretariat has a full-time staff of about 150 people and a budget of 35 million Swiss francs per year (about $25 million). The budget comes predominantly from membership dues, which are calculated in an interesting way. Members can essentially choose how much to pay when they join. Five countries—France, Germany, Great Britain, Japan, and the United States—have chosen to pay the maximum (just under $1.5 million a year), while forty countries have chosen to pay the minimum allowable, just under $15,000.[4]

As suggested above, the UPU can be understood quite well from a rationalist, efficiency-maximizing perspective. The organization's goal is quite straightforward—to make international postal service work more efficiently—and its activities mostly fit uncontentiously within this goal. It works primarily by reducing transaction costs, clarifying and standardizing rules, and bringing standards of postal services internationally up to the point where they can participate effectively in the system. The UPU has little effect in creating or legitimating new ideas. The exception to this rule is the recent bias noted above toward making postal services less like government bureaucracies and more like private companies. This bias probably reflects the interests of those countries that pay the largest share of the UPU's budget, rather than any internal bureaucratic interest. The organization also has little effect on national interests; states generally begin with an interest in efficient international postal services, and look to the UPU to facilitate them.

In many ways, then, the UPU fits the bill for functionalist theory. It is a forum for technical cooperation, with participation largely by experts in the field rather than by political appointees. It tends to be an efficiency-maximizer rather than a forum for political competition. And, by and large, it works. International mail delivery may not be perfect, but the mail generally gets through with little difficulty. If it sometimes takes a while to do so, it is more the fault of the national postal services than of the UPU. As the need for effective postal cooperation has expanded, so has the UPU; first, in response to the postal needs of new countries in the system and second (more recently), in response to advances in communications technologies. But in another sense, the UPU does not fulfill the promise of functionalist integration theory. This approach sees international cooperation not only as a solution to specific technical problems, but also as a driver of broader patterns of integration. Despite the increasing complexity of its issue-area and the increasing breadth of its technical abilities, it is difficult to see the UPU as a driver of integration, managerial or political, outside of its immediate issue-area.

The ICAO

The ICAO, which was created in 1944 to provide the same sort of transparency to the business of international civil aviation that the UPU provides to international mail delivery, would seem at first to be a similarly functionalist organization. In many ways it is. Its membership is almost the same size as the UPU's, with 188 members at last count. Administratively, it is a larger organization than the UPU, with a budget of roughly twice the size, reflecting the technical complexities of the aviation business. Some of the organizational details of the ICAO are discussed in Chapter 3, and need not be repeated here. The gist of that discussion is that the ICAO secretariat has within it several functional bureaus specializing in specific technical issues relating both to the safety and the commercial viability of international civil aviation. The primary output of these bureaus, and of the ICAO in general, is a set of agreed-upon rules and technical standards for civil airliners flying internationally. Secondarily, the ICAO also provides direct technical advisors to help poorer and smaller countries to implement these rules and standards.

As with all functional IOs, these parts of the secretariat make recommendations that are then submitted to the governing political element of the IO for approval. The ultimate governing element of the ICAO is the Assembly, which meets every three years and at which all member countries are represented. The Assembly elects a Council of thirty-six countries from among its members to represent both geographic diversity and "states of chief importance in air transport."[5] While the Assembly is responsible for setting the general direction and goals of the organization, the Council is the practical governing body, responsible for approving or rejecting the rules and standards recommended by the various parts of the Secretariat.

So far, the ICAO appears to be functionally similar to the UPU. They both exist to standardize procedures to make international cooperation in their issue-areas more efficient, and they both supplement their rule- and standard-setting functions with technical assistance to less-developed countries to help them meet and participate in international standards. But there are two differences in their operation that make the former a less purely technical organization than the latter. One difference is to be found within the bureaus of the Secretariat, and the other is to be found in the degree of political contentiousness of some of the issues facing both the Council and the Assembly.

The technical rule-making and standard-setting functions within the secretariats of both the UPU and the ICAO are similar, in that they involve technical experts in the field of postal management and civil aviation, respectively, making suggestions based both on their own expertise and on extensive consultation with and inputs from the industry that they regulate. But the two industries are very differently structured. The postal industry is mostly made up of government monopolies that are required to provide a universal service. It is in fact these monopolies that generally provide the representatives to the organization, removing most of the potential tension between the goals of the technical experts and the goals of the political representatives. The civil aviation industry, on the other hand, is made up of companies, many government-owned but many not, in a highly competitive industry. The ICAO works closely with the International Air Transport Association (IATA), the industry group of the airlines that operate internationally, as well as with representatives of both airport operators and pilots' unions. The technical recommendations of the ICAO's secretariat, therefore, are more likely than those of the UPU to represent industry interests that may not match the broader political interests of the organization's governing body.

The second difference between the ICAO and the UPU as functionalist IOs is to be found in the sorts of issues that confront the political governing bodies. Postal cooperation is simply less political than cooperation in civil aviation. Few issues in postal cooperation generate much in the way of value trade-offs or ideological disagreement. Even the recent trend in the UPU to focus on the professionalization of postal services is relatively noncontentious. Civil aviation, however, does involve more contentious issues. One of these is the question of who can fly where. There are complex laws about what airlines from one country can do in another country, and these laws are often governed by bilateral agreements between countries. A simple set of multilateral rules, or at least norms, would be more efficient. But such a major change in the rules would inevitably favor the airlines of some countries over those of others. This puts the Secretariat in the difficult position of on the one hand, trying to make the industry more efficient by rationalizing international civil aviation rules, but on the other hand, running the risk of alienating various elements of its membership.[6] In other words, the ICAO can improve efficiency when all countries benefit similarly, but is more constrained when some countries will benefit more than others.

Another trade-off that the ICAO is beginning to face is that between providing affordable international air travel and dealing with environmental damage, particularly climate change. Civil aviation contributes about 3.5 percent of the human-generated climate change effect, but international aviation is exempt from emissions quotas under the Kyoto Protocol to the United Nations Framework Convention on Climate Change (UNFCCC). The Kyoto Protocol calls specifically on the ICAO to regulate these emissions. Given the political contentiousness of the Kyoto Protocol, it seems likely that the ICAO faces some serious political hurdles in trying to regulate carbon emissions from international civil aviation among member countries that have very different positions on climate change.[7]

The WHO

The WHO was created in 1948 as the UN specialized agency for health. Unlike the UPU and ICAO, which were created as autonomous organizations and later brought into the UN system, the WHO was created explicitly as a UN agency from the outset. Its official mandate is to work toward the "attainment by all peoples of the highest possible level of health."[8] Within this broad remit, the organization has considerable latitude in defining its specific health goals and operational priorities at any given point in time. The WHO undertakes a wide range of activities, ranging from long-term health planning and coordination, to functional assistance in the provision of health services in developing countries, to the coordination of international responses to specific international health crisis, such as the SARS (Severe Acute Respiratory Syndrome) epidemic in 2003.[9]

Given the breadth of its mandate, one can question whether the WHO is a functional organization of a kind that can reasonably be compared with the two IOs discussed above. The WHO, as an organization, is an order of magnitude bigger than the UPU and ICAO, with a staff of some 3,500 people in the organization's headquarters in Geneva and in six regional offices. It has a budget of $400 million per year from mandatory assessments of its 192 member states, and raises almost twice that figure through voluntary contributions from governments.[10] As such, it is organizationally more like development agencies such as the United Nations Development Programme (UNDP) or the United Nations Children's Fund (UNICEF) than the smaller functional IOs.

On the other hand, the WHO does resemble the smaller functional IOs in terms of its focus on professional expertise. Its structure is designed to maximize the input of health care professionals into organizational policy, in order to encourage decision-making based on medical rather than political criteria. This emphasis can be seen almost up to the highest governing body of the organization, the World Health Assembly, which is composed of representatives of all of the member countries, as is the case with almost all IOs, and meets annually to set overall policy and to choose the organization's executive management. More immediate political governance, however, is provided by the Executive Board. As is the case with many IOs, the thirty-two members of the Executive Board are appointed by countries chosen by the Assembly. But countries cannot appoint whom they choose to the Board; they can only appoint people who are "technically qualified in the field of health,"[11] meaning that governance is provided by people with at least some background in and knowledge of this field.

Both the size of the WHO and the breadth of its mandate provide it with opportunities not available to the smaller functional IOs, but they also present it with difficulties that the smaller organizations do not share. Size gives the WHO the ability to be active in a wide range of activities, to have a strong global presence, and to have spare capacity on hand in case of new developments and global health crises. The scope of its remit gives it the flexibility to set its own agenda. In other words, the WHO is much more of an independent actor in world politics, with some real power within its issue-area, and capable of considerable activity on its own initiative. It has the ability to affect the global health agenda in much the same way that the

UNDP is able to affect the global development agenda. But the size of the WHO also gives it a bureaucracy that is larger and more unwieldy than that of the smaller functional IOs. The opportunities provided by the broad scope of its various activities also threaten it with loss of direction and focus in the absence of strong leadership within the organization.

Perhaps the WHO's greatest success has been the eradication of smallpox. The smallpox campaign was launched in 1967, and victory over the disease was declared in 1979. This campaign shows what the organization can accomplish when it combines a focus of its institutional capabilities with political will among its backers.[12] The WHO played four essential roles in the campaign. The first was as agenda-setter and publicist. It was central in getting various countries to agree to commit the resources necessary to eradicate smallpox, and in keeping them focused on that goal. The second role was as information coordinator. The WHO was responsible for keeping track of the science of combating smallpox, the spread of the disease, and who was doing what operationally, thus helping to prevent individual countries from wasting resources by duplicating the efforts of others or by using obsolete science. The third role was as provider of funding for smallpox eradiation programs in developing countries. And the final role that the WHO played in the smallpox campaign was to provide its own medical specialists to assist with the campaign in those countries where such outside help was needed most. These four roles are indicative of what the WHO does more broadly.

But the smallpox campaign, and the role of the WHO in the SARS epidemic, are also symptomatic of some of the criticisms of the WHO: that it focuses too much on infectious diseases at the expense of other threats to health, that it focuses too much on the diseases of the wealthy and on publicity-friendly campaigns, at the expense of less-glamorous health capacity-building.[13] The organization has also been criticized for institutional inertia and lack of direction following the success of the smallpox campaign. Recent reforms, particularly under the two most recent Directors-General, Drs. Gro Harlem Brundland and Jong-Wook Lee, have attempted to address all of these criticisms. In the past several years, the WHO's bureaucracy has become more transparent, and there has been a greater institutional emphasis on health capacity-building and on addressing the health concerns of developing countries.[14] But whether the reforms have gone far enough remains open to dispute.[15]

Another general criticism of the WHO is that is has not lived up to its broader institutional potential and to the goals invested in it by its founders.[16] Along with the executive functions that the organization performs, such as coordinating activities to combat specific diseases and building health-services capacity in developing countries, its constitution gives it substantial legislative prerogatives. For example, the World Health Assembly has the authority to adopt binding regulations with the approval of two-thirds of the membership (subject to individual country opt-outs), and to propose international conventions (treaties) on health issues. The Assembly has adopted only two regulations (the more recent one in 1951), and only just adopted its first convention, the Framework Convention on Tobacco Control, in 2003.[17]

In short, then, the WHO's record as a functional organization is mixed. It clearly does some good work, and it would be difficult to argue that the world is not at least a somewhat better place because of it.[18] But it does not seem to have lived up to the expectations of its founders to the extent that some other functional IOs have. In part, this is because of the nature of the issue-area: all the mail can in principle get through, but everyone cannot in principle always be healthy. But in part it is also because of its greater level of ambition, reflected in the greater size and scope of the organization. Since the WHO has much more leeway in determining what its specific program focuses will be, it is easier for the organization to lose focus. And since it has greater agency in determining its activities, it runs a greater risk of meeting political opposition in its choice of activities. As a functional organization, this leaves it in a dilemma. Either it can make contentious choices, in which case it becomes as much a political as a functional organization, or it can shy away from these choices, in which case it fails to live up to its functionalist potential.

Functionalism and Technical IOs

What does this comparison tell us about functional IOs, organizations that are designed to enhance cooperation within specific technical issue-areas? From a rationalist regime perspective, it tells us that they can work quite well. When the issue-area is well defined, functional IOs can increase transparency efficiently and relatively cheaply. When the issue-area is less well defined, technical cooperation can be hindered both by bureaucratic inertia and by political disagreement. In the language of game theory, the greater the element of prisoners' dilemma mixed in with a coordination game, the less smoothly will cooperation work.[19] This suggests that, from the perspective of efficiency-maximizing, functional IOs are best kept small, issue-specific, and as technical as possible.

From an institutional perspective, however, the result is more mixed. Larger and more diffuse organizations such as the WHO are more vulnerable to bureaucratic pathologies and inertia, but they are also more able to act meaningfully as international political players, to use their institutional position to push particular items onto the international agenda. In other words, there can be a trade-off between technical efficiency and political effectiveness. An interesting and topical example of this trade-off can be found in the debate about whether the United Nations Environment Programme (UNEP) should be replaced with a broader IO that is more comprehensive in dealing with international environmental issues. Those in favor of such a change argue that the resultant organization will be more politically effective, while those opposed argue that such an organization would be too unfocused and politically contentious, and therefore ineffective.[20]

From the perspective of functionalist theory, the role played by these technical IOs in driving international political integration is surprisingly small. The technical cooperation sponsored by the three organizations discussed in this chapter has grown both deeper and more complex in response to scientific, technological, and managerial developments. But the cooperation sponsored by them has tended to remain squarely within the bounds of the issue-areas that the IOs were designed to oversee. There have been exceptions to this pattern (the ICAO, for example, is the repository for a convention on the production of plastic explosives, and the WHO has been critical of Israeli policy with respect to the Palestinian Authority),[21] but these have been few and isolated. In fact, far from driving patterns of political integration, the functional IOs have tended to shy away from political issues in the absence of broad agreement among member states. In other words, they have tended to coordinate activity within their issue-areas at the level of the lowest common denominator of political consensus among their members.

This observation in turn suggests that technical cooperation is not driving any broader patterns of political integration. In other words, a technical or functionalist version of the universalist model of global governance is not threatening to supplant internationalist cooperation. Even when looking at the internationalist model, functionalism seems to have little impact in driving changes in patterns of global governance. With respect to the sorts of technical IOs discussed in this chapter, the political authorities of the traditional nation-states appear to retain a firm grasp on the evolution of the formal system of global governance through IOs.

11

The Fuzzy Borders of Intergovernmentalism

This is a book about multilateral intergovernmental institutions. The definition of this category of institutions, as discussed in the introduction, is relatively straightforward. It comprises institutions whose constituent members are states—either all states, or all states meeting certain criteria. Identifying institutions that meet this definition should not be particularly problematic, and in most cases it is not. But there are several institutions that, for a variety of reasons, do not fit neatly into the definition. In other words, there are some institutions that are clearly part of the international organization (IO) system, and are clearly involved in global governance, but are not traditional IOs. This chapter focuses on such organizations.

Sources of global governance can be divided into two broad categories: intergovernmental sources and nongovernmental sources. The latter category includes both networks of not-for-profit NGOs, sometimes referred to as global civil society, and industry and business groups. This book is primarily about intergovernmental sources. But the two categories of sources cannot always be neatly separated. This is true operationally, as has been discussed in earlier chapters. For example, IOs such as the United Nations High Commissioner for Refugees (UNHCR) subcontract many of their operational duties to NGOs, working with as many as 500 specific ones. Many IOs sponsor forums for NGOs, or have institutionalized mechanisms through which NGOs, as representatives of global civil society, can be heard directly rather than through state representatives. Other IOs, such as the International Civil Aviation Organization (ICAO) or the International Maritime Organization (IMO), work closely with industry groups to gather information about their issue-areas and to set standards.

But beyond these operational relationships, there are some hybrid IOs that involve both states and nongovernmental actors as primary participants. One of the classic works of functionalist theory, Ernst Haas' *Beyond the Nation-State*, looks at one such organization, the International Labour Organization (ILO).[1] This chapter will look at a number of other hybrid IOs. In some of these organizations, both states and non-state actors can be members. In some, the organization began as an

NGO and over time transmuted into an IO. Other organizations remain NGOs, but have been directly co-opted into playing a formal role in international politics and in the IO system. This chapter examines examples of all of these patterns. It looks briefly at six organizations: the International Criminal Police Organization (ICPO, or Interpol), the International Organization for Standardization (ISO), the International Telecommunications Satellite Organization (ITSO, formerly INTEL-SAT), the World Conservation Union (IUCN), the International Committee of the Red Cross (ICRC), and the International Olympic Committee (IOC).

The ICPO, or Interpol

Interpol is at present a relatively standard functional IO. It serves to coordinate efforts among national police forces to combat crime when either the crimes or the criminals cross international borders. It has the standard IO structure, with a General Assembly in which all member states (currently 182) are represented, an Executive Committee of thirteen members elected from among the member states, and a Secretariat, managed by a Secretary-General, with some 400 staff and a budget of about $30 million a year. The organization is funded by member dues, which are based on the national GDPs of member countries, and is headquartered in Lyon, France.

While Interpol is currently an IO, it did not start off that way. It started life as an NGO called the International Criminal Police Commission. It was created in 1923 by the initiative of the police chief of Vienna, who invited police officials from twenty countries to an International Police Conference. These police officials undertook to create the Commission under their own authority. They drafted the organization's constitution, which was accepted by a number of police organizations in various countries, but was never submitted to governments for ratification. Interpol's founding membership thus consisted of police departments, not governments. It gradually changed into an intergovernmental organization. It was granted UN consultative status in 1948, was upgraded from a commission to an organization in 1956, and was granted full IO status by Special Arrangement with the Economic and Social Council (ECOSOC) in 1971.[2] Technically speaking, it is still police organizations that are members, but only one such organization per country, "appointed by the competent governmental authority of that country."[3] In practice, this is no different from representation in traditional functional IOs, in which country representatives are functional experts chosen from the relevant national bureaucracy.

The main task of Interpol, as the functional IO in the issue-area of criminal policing, is increasing the efficiency of cooperation among police forces. Its General Assembly acts a forum for international discussion of policing issues, and passes resolutions on these issues. Its Secretariat, both on its own and in cooperation with police forces in member countries, studies and collects data on various key and emerging forms of international criminal activity and coordinates activities among these forces. One of the best known of Interpol functions is the issuing of "red notices," a type of international arrest warrant. These allow police forces in any member country to request the arrest and extradition of particular criminal suspects in all member countries. They make the process of finding criminals internationally much easier by creating a central clearing-house of suspects rather than requiring police forces to communicate with hundreds of individual police forces abroad. Red notices are currently being issued at a rate of about 1,200 per year.[4]

Interpol does not maintain any independent policing ability; it works entirely through member police forces. Perhaps the most important institutional innovation of the organization is the requirement that member countries identify National Central Bureaus, which are particular offices in member countries that are responsible for coordinating all interactions between domestic police forces on the one hand and the international policing community on the other. National Central Bureaus are sometimes part of national police forces (in Canada, for example, the Bureau is a part of the Royal Canadian Mounted Police), but are sometimes administratively separate bodies (in the United States, the Interpol–U.S. National Central Bureau is part of the Justice Department, but is separate from the FBI and other specific police organizations). This means that any time a police department needs to deal with a counterpart in another country, or with police forces abroad in general, it knows where to turn to bureaucratically.

The ISO

The ISO acts as an international coordinative body for various kinds of commercial standards. It oversees more than 13,000 international standards, which together fill almost half a million pages. These standards cover a vast array of topics, from the definition of units of measurement in the metric system, to definitions of screw, paper, and battery sizes, to postal codes, to the thickness of ATM cards. In other words, the ISO makes sure that an AA battery in one country is the same thing as an AA battery in other countries. Besides these sorts of specific standards, the ISO is also known for two sets of generic business principles: the ISO 9000 and ISO 14000 series. These are quality management and environmental management principles, respectively. When a company claims to be ISO 9000 or ISO 14000 compliant (these claims may occasionally be seen on company advertisements), it is claiming to subscribe to these general management principles. All of the ISO's standards are voluntary.[5]

In many ways, the ISO seems like an IO, but technically, it is an NGO. Its members are national standards organizations, and it was created by agreement among those organizations rather among governments per se. It was not created by treaty, and does not have the standing in international law that IOs have. The ISO has three categories of members. Along with full members, there are also correspondent members, representing countries that have not yet developed fully functional national standards organizations, and subscriber members, representing countries that are too small to have their own fully functional national standards organizations. Membership numbers for these three categories are 94, 37, and 15, respectively, for a total of 146 countries represented.[6]

Only one national standards organization per country can be a member of the ISO. Some of the national organizations are either part of their national governments' bureaucracies or are semiautonomous governmental corporations. For example, the

Standards Council of Canada (SCC) is a Crown Corporation, a semi-autonomous but wholly owned corporate subsidiary of the Canadian government. Other national organizations, however, are private. The Association française de Normalisation (AFNOR), the French body, is a private not-for-profit organization, loosely supervised by the Ministry of Industry. The American National Standards Institute (ANSI), AFNOR's equivalent in the United States, is also a private not-for-profit organization, which has as members various government agencies, industry and trade groups, and specific businesses. It is this variation in the governmental status of the member organizations that makes the ISO a true hybrid IO–NGO.

The ISO is also notable for the way in which it organizes its work. It has a headquarters in Geneva, with a staff of about 160 that acts in a primarily coordinative capacity. The specific standards are arrived at by a network of some 3,000 committees, subcommittees, and working groups. Each of these committees and groups deals with a specific type of standard, and includes representatives from government, industry, research institutes, consumer groups, and, where relevant, IOs. Standards are arrived at by consensus. The headquarters secretariat in Geneva, however, does not directly oversee and administer the work of these committees and groups. Rather, this work is farmed out to member organizations, of which thirty-six volunteer to do the secretariat work for particular committees and groups. In other words, ANSI will oversee some international standards, and AFNOR others. The ISO estimates that this system is the equivalent of the thirty-six organizations donating 500 people to the ISO, and saves the latter some $80 million a year. This sort of voluntary group-secretariat approach to institutional organization is unique to the ISO.

The ITSO, or INTELSAT

The ITSO is not an example merely of an interesting hybrid organizational structure, but an example of three different structures, the first lasting from 1964 to 1972, the second lasting from 1972 to 2001, and the third beginning in 2001 and currently ongoing. The ITSO, which until the second of these institutional changes was more generally known as INTELSAT, was created to overcome public goods problems in the provision of commercial telecommunications satellites. In the early 1960s, the United States, by far the world leader in telecommunications and satellite technologies at the time, wanted to ensure both common international standards and a global network of terrestrial base stations for its new technology. Other countries, primarily the United States' European allies, wanted to ensure both access to new satellites and the right to participate in the development of new technologies and telecommunications systems. The resulting compromise was INTELSAT.[7]

The ITSO started off as an intergovernmental commercial venture. It was intergovernmental in that the members were states. The organization was created in 1964 with nineteen member states, but this number grew rapidly, reaching seventy-five by the end of the decade. INTELSAT was commercial in that it was structured on a shareholder basis, like the Bretton Woods organizations, rather than on a one-country, one-vote basis, and was designed to be a commercially profitable entity that charged for use of its product. National contributions to INTELSAT's capital were based on the share of the satellites' capacity that each country expected to use.

On the basis of this formula, the United States started off with more than half of the votes in the organization; the next closest country was the United Kingdom, with just over 7 percent. U.S. dominance, in terms of ownership, use, and technology, was so pronounced that INTELSAT was more or less run by the American domestic communications satellite company, COMSAT.[8]

These arrangements had always been intended as temporary, and the original multilateral agreement had called for a renegotiation in five years. This process of renegotiation began in 1969 and yielded a new organizational structure in 1972. By this point, INTELSAT had launched four commercially successful communications satellites, and had some eighty-three members. Also by this point, the technologies involved had diffused to a much greater degree, and some countries other than the United States had developed the ability to build commercially viable communications satellites. The renegotiation of the governance of the ITSO was based on a recognition that the organization was fulfilling two functions, one commercial and the other political/governmental. In other words, the organization was both acting as a regulator, ensuring access to satellite telecommunications to all countries, and as a satellite operator.[9]

The results of the renegotiation were twofold. First, it capped U.S. dominance of the organization. Second, it separated the commercial and governance functions to a greater degree than had been the case earlier. A new organizational structure was mandated for the management of commercial operations, to separate INTELSAT from COMSAT. This new structure was to be overseen by national satellite communication or telecommunication bodies. It retained shareholder voting, but the U.S. vote was limited to 40 percent. At the same time, a new level of governance was created that was similar in structure to traditional IOs. This new aspect of the ITSO was to oversee the regulatory functions of the organization, and to make decisions that were of a political rather than commercial nature.[10]

This second organization scheme remained in place for almost thirty years. By the beginning of the new millennium, INTELSAT operated more than twenty satellites, at a substantial profit, which were used by more than 140 member countries. But the difficulties and inefficiencies of trying to operate a commercial venture with an IO governing structure were undermining INTELSAT's long-term competitiveness. In response, the members of the organization decided to privatize the commercial part of INTELSAT, and to retain the ITSO as a regulatory IO in charge of ensuring that the new private company fulfilled its public service commitments of providing access in a nondiscriminatory way to all of its member countries. As such, in 2001, INTELSAT became a private company registered in Bermuda, and was sold to a consortium of some 200 companies,[11] the largest single share being owned by Lockheed Martin, an American multinational corporation and a major player in the satellite telecommunication business. At the same time, the ITSO became a standard functional IO, with an organizational structure and voting rules resembling those of most typical functional IOs.[12]

The IUCN

The IUCN (it now refers to itself as the World Conservation Union, but its official name remains the International Union for the Conservation of Nature and Natural

Resources) is, in terms of its structure, perhaps the most hybrid of the organizations discussed in this chapter. It was created in 1948 to "encourage and assist societies throughout the world to conserve the integrity and diversity of nature."[13] It was designed to be open to all organizations interested in its mission, both governmental and nongovernmental, and remains open to both states and NGOs. The IUCN itself is formally an NGO, incorporated as such under Swiss law and headquartered near Geneva.

The IUCN has two primary membership categories: governmental and nongovernmental. In the governmental category, both states in general and specific governmental bureaucracies can join, as well as IOs and regional integration organizations such as the European Union (EU). In the nongovernmental category, NGOs, both national and international, can join. Membership dues differ both between and within the two categories, on the basis of the size of the country or NGO. For states, dues range from 6,623 to 421,871 Swiss francs (about $5,000 to about $300,000), while for NGOs they range from 381 to 18,300 Swiss francs (just under $300 to about $13,000).[14] All members, irrespective of category, can send a designated representative to be a full participant at the World Conservation Congress, the Union's highest decision-making and planning body, which meets once every three years. These triennial Congresses set general policy for the IUCN, pass resolutions, and elect the Council, the Union's primary governing body, in between Congresses. The voting structure of the Congresses is essentially bicameral; in order to pass a resolution or elect the Council, a motion requires a majority both of the governmental and the nongovernmental members.[15] In other words, major decisions must be approved by both the governmental and nongovernmental parts of the membership.

The Council, which consists of thirty-eight members, is unlike the equivalent body in IOs in that its members do not represent their home states or particular NGOs, but are supposed to serve the IUCN in a personal capacity (although, unlike the members of the IUCN's Secretariat, they are not employees of the Union, because they cannot be paid for service to the Council). Of the members, twenty-four represent regions of the world, six are the chairs of the Commissions, two are elected as President and Treasurer, one represents the host government (Switzerland), and five are selected by the Council "on the basis of diverse qualifications, interests and skills."[16] The Council, in turn, appoints the Secretariat, which fulfills standard secretariat functions.

The bulk of the work of the IUCN is done by its six commissions. These focus on education and communication; environmental, economic, and social policy; environmental law; ecosystem management; species survival; and protected areas. The commissions are networks of experts in the relevant fields, some 10,000 in all, who work for the IUCN on a volunteer basis. They are responsible for doing research and writing reports on issues within the purview of the respective commissions, and providing expert advice to governments, IOs, and NGOs. This research tends to result in databases, assessments, and guidelines. An example of an IUCN activity that involves all three outputs is its Red List, a comprehensive list of species threatened by extinction. The Red List creates guidelines for what counts as an endangered species, guidelines that are often incorporated into national endangered species lists as well as being used by the IUCN. The Union carries out assessments of specific species and regions to determine which species should be on the list. It also publishes a comprehensive list of endangered species globally (currently numbering 15,589)[17] that can be used as a database by anyone interested in the subject.

The major function of the Union is thus advisory and research-oriented, rather than regulatory. This function has both transparency effects, by creating and disseminating information, and legitimacy effects, by setting single international standards. The IUCN does, however, also fulfill some official functions within the international system, as mandated by some international treaties. For example, the IUCN is given an official advisory role in the text of the Convention Concerning the Protection of the World Cultural and Natural Heritage.[18]

The ICRC and the IOC

Both the ICRC and the IOC, unlike the organizations discussed above, are true NGOs. They are governed not by representatives of states or of national organizations, but by an autonomous and self-replicating membership. In other words, new members of both committees are chosen by the existing members. This method of governance does not necessarily make the ICRC and the IOC exceptional among NGOs. What does make the two committees exceptional is the formal role that they play in international and, more specifically, intergovernmental politics.

The ICRC's role in intergovernmental politics is the more formal of the two. The Committee is written into the Geneva Conventions on the rules of warfare as an official neutral party and as a guarantor of the rights and conditions of prisoners of war. States that have ratified the Geneva Conventions commit themselves to allowing the ICRC access to prisoners of war whom they hold, noncombatants in war zones, and protected persons in occupied territories. The ICRC in these situations, along with national Red Cross/Red Crescent societies in some cases, is supposed to act both to increase transparency by determining the conditions of treatment of prisoners of war and noncombatants, and to provide medical and humanitarian services. This is the only example of an NGO, over which states or other IOs have no administrative control, being identified exclusively and by name in an international treaty as the guarantor of that treaty.

There are also other ways in which the ICRC is different from other NGOs. Like IOs, but unlike most other NGOs, the ICRC has concluded headquarters agreements with the governments of most of the countries in which it operates. These agreements give the organization international legal standing and the same level of extraterritoriality enjoyed by IOs in those countries. The ICRC also draws almost all of its funding from national governments. In 2001, eighty-two governments (plus the EU) donated funds, ranging from a contribution of 225 million Swiss francs by the United States to one of 127 Swiss francs by Madagascar.[19]

The governance structure of the ICRC is based on the premise of Swiss neutrality. It is headquartered in Switzerland, where it was founded in 1863. It maintains operations in more than eighty countries with some 12,000 staff, 800 of whom work at the headquarters in Geneva. It is administratively separate from the national Red Cross and Red Crescent societies, and from the International Federation of

Red Cross and Red Crescent Societies. Unlike almost all of the other organizations discussed in this book, individuals, rather than states or NGOs, are members of the ICRC, and all of these members play an active role in the governance of the organization. All of the members (there can be between fifteen and twenty-five at any given time) must be Swiss citizens, on the assumption that Switzerland will be neutral in all interstate conflicts. New members are elected by the existing members. Members tend to be either academics, generally with a specialization in international law, or active members of the humanitarian aid community, or (frequently) both. Several of the current members worked for the ICRC extensively before they were invited to be members.[20]

The IOC is not a formal part of the multilateral international system in the way that the ICRC is. It is part of the system to the extent that the Olympic Games are an international event. The IOC has sole authority to decide where the Olympics will be held and owns all rights to the Games. When governments decide to boycott the Games, as happened in 1976, 1980, and 1984,[21] they are in effect saying that the Olympics are an important international event, one worthy of grand gestures by states. In other words, they are saying that the Games convey legitimacy within the state system. The IOC has the right to decide which countries the Olympics will legitimate.

The IOC is a much bigger committee than the ICRC. The IOC's rules call for a Committee of 115 members: 15 represent National Olympic Committees; 15 represent International Federations, the international governing bodies of specific sports; 15 are active Olympic athletes elected by their peers; and the remaining 70 need not be any of the above. Most members have had at least some experience in national Olympic committees. As is the case with the ICRC, new members are nominated and elected by existing members.[22] Although its committee is bigger than that of the ICRC, the IOC as an organization is much smaller, having only a very small professional secretariat (located in Lausanne, Switzerland). It provides some coordination for national Olympic committees and international federations of Olympic sports, but does not engage in any activities on the ground in the way that the ICRC does. The IOC raises its funds through the commercial marketing of the Olympics, and thus has no need to raise funds from governments. In fact, it raises sufficient funds from marketing to be able to help support both the national committees and the federations.[23]

The IOC recently changed many of its rules in response to allegations of corruption in the awarding of the 2002 Olympics to Salt Lake City. Among other things, it committed itself to publishing some financial information for the first time. On the whole, however, the IOC does not have a reputation either for transparency or for financial probity. The ICRC, on the other hand, prides itself on its reputation for both. It claims to be the first humanitarian organization to meet the rigorous criteria of the International Accounting Standards (see below).[24] The difference between degrees of transparency in the two organizations may well be related to funding sources. The IOC, owning as it does the rights to the Olympic Games, has a secure source of funds. The ICRC needs to make the case to governments every year to renew its funding. This means that the ICRC needs to convince donors that their money is being well spent, while the IOC does not.

Is There a Pattern to Hybrid Organizations?

The set of organizations discussed in this chapter is by no means exhaustive. There are several other hybrids, and new ones continue to be created. One of the oldest IOs, the ILO, is a hybrid: both states and national labor unions can be members. Two examples of recently created NGOs that have an authoritative role in international governance are the International Accounting Standards Board (IASB) and the Internet Corporation for Assigned Names and Numbers (ICANN). The IASB was created in 2001, replacing the earlier International Accounting Standards Committee, created in 1973. It is charged with creating a uniform set of international accounting standards, which governments may (and often do) write into their national law as national standards. It is an NGO registered in the United States but operates in the United Kingdom, with a self-perpetuating membership. ICANN is also an NGO registered in the United States, and is responsible for overseeing the system of names and addresses that allows the Internet and the World Wide Web to function. It was founded in 1998 to take over functions that had previously been performed by the U.S. government. Unlike many of the other NGOs discussed here, the Directors of ICANN are not self-perpetuating; they are selected by a number of relevant user groups, representing both geographical regions and functional constituencies.

Can any general conclusions be gleaned from this review of various kinds of hybrid IO–NGOs? Not really. There are few institutional and organizations commonalities across them. They fulfill both transparency and legitimacy functions in the international system. They tend to reflect either the demands of particular issue-areas or specific historical contexts. They have always been, and remain, a fairly small part of the system of multilateral global governance. And, although new hybrids continue to be created occasionally, the overall importance of their role does not seem to be increasing. Furthermore, as new hybrids are created, existing hybrids are sometimes dehybridized, and made into traditional IOs. Of the organizations discussed here, this happened with both Interpol and INTELSAT, and may well be in the process of happening with ICANN. Most of the other hybrids can retain their status because they create voluntary standards, and thus do not pose a threat to the authority of states or the multilateral system. The remaining NGOs, such as the ICRC and the IOC, are unusual enough that they can be looked at as exceptions to broader patterns of global governance.

12

Conclusions

Are international organizations (IOs), and other forces of globalization, replacing sovereign states as the central actors in global governance? No. Are IOs fundamentally changing the way in which international relations work? Yes. In figuring out how these two observations fit together, we find some of the most interesting aspects of the study of IOs.

The introduction to this book began by asking whether or not IOs matter. The answer in general is clearly yes: they matter in a variety of ways. They enable technical cooperation among states in a range of areas that are vital to modern societies and economies. They encourage dialogue and communication among states as a first response to disagreements, and they foster rules-based, rather than power-based, dispute settlement in a variety of functional realms. They act as agents for the international community in dealing with humanitarian issues that might otherwise go unaddressed. At a more general level, they are changing the basic expectations of states and foreign policy makers about how international relations work, by substituting a bilateral model with a multilateral one.

Nevertheless, the role of IOs should not be overstated. They have their limits, and expecting them to perform beyond those limits is bound to lead to disappointment. They can affect international relations by facilitating cooperation and by legitimating rules. But they do not have the traditional power resources of states; they cannot tax, and they do not have either independent means of force or the right to regulate actors authoritatively. In the end, they are beholden to the states that formed them and are constrained by the interests and preferences of those states. Such power as they do have can be co-opted by some states to promote their interests at the expense of others. In concluding a book that reviews the study of IOs, it is as important to point out their limits as it is to point out their successes. The rest of this chapter, therefore, addresses a more nuanced question than the one that the book started off with: Under what circumstances do IOs matter, and in what way? It also addresses a more practical and policy-oriented follow-up question: How can we make IOs work better?

Efficiency and Ideas

Theories of international organization suggest two primary ways in which IOs can improve cooperation among states: by improving the efficiency of cooperation among states that recognize cooperative interests and by making the perceived interests of states more cooperative. The earlier issue-specific chapters suggest that both of these pathways to cooperation do in fact occur in international relations, and with some frequency. These chapters also suggest some of the limitations of IOs.

Focusing on efficiency, on international regimes as maximizers of transparency in the international marketplace for cooperation, has some definite advantages. From the perspective of the theoretician and policymaker in the field of international organization, it has the advantage of clarity and specificity. Focusing on transaction costs, information flows, and property rights gives designers of IOs specific, and often quantifiable, measures of institutional performance and success; from the perspective of the student of international relations, it identifies a wide array of issue-areas in which IOs are, and can be, successful.

The focus on efficiency has also yielded several useful lessons about how to design new institutions and how to fix existing ones, lessons that by now have been widely recognized within the IO community. The need to minimize transaction costs, for example, means that IOs should create mechanisms for monitoring and enforcing agreements that require as little extra effort as possible on the part of states. The more the effort required, the more costly it is to ensure compliance with agreements, and therefore the less credible the agreements are. This observation means that, for example, incorporating a more thorough monitoring and enforcement mechanism into an agreement will not necessarily make the agreement work better if the mechanism is likely to be employed only sporadically because of cost or complexity.

Similarly, the need to maximize information flows means that IOs need to be designed both to gather as much credible information as possible and to disseminate that information as effectively as possible. Small investments in increasing information flows, such as the creation of the Situation Centre in the UN Secretariat's Department of Peacekeeping Operations (DPKO), can yield large improvements in cooperative efficiency. And the need to specify property rights means that the rules of cooperation overseen by IOs should be as clear as possible, as should be the process of mediating disagreements among states over the interpretation of those rules.

At the same time, a focus on efficiency in the study of international regimes has three clear limitations. The first is that it applies only to a circumscribed set of situations in international politics. The second is that it fails to fully describe what IOs actually do. And the third is that a focus on efficiency, which is value-neutral in the sense that it says nothing about what is being made more efficient, can be used to mask more traditional power relationships in international relations. This third limitation is discussed below, in the section on power and interdependence.

The first of the limitations is straightforward; rational regime theory only claims to be applicable in situations where states have overlapping interests *ex ante*. It also applies best in iterated situations, where states care more about long-term patterns of behavior than they do about the outcomes of individual interactions. This limitation makes the efficiency approach highly applicable in areas such as postal cooperation, where cooperative and long-term interests predominate, but makes it more problematic in areas such as security cooperation, where goals are more likely to diverge and where states are more likely to focus on outcomes of particular interactions than on long-term cooperative patterns. It also makes the approach problematic in issue-areas ranging from trade to the environment, where states are sometimes more concerned about the distribution of gains from cooperation than they are about the aggregate size of those gains.

The second of the limitations of the rationalist efficiency approach to studying international regimes is that it fails to capture much of what IOs do and much of what states want them to do. This is where the second approach to studying international regimes comes in: the reflectivist approach, focused on ideas and ideals. The reflectivist approach can explain a range of phenomena that the rationalist approach cannot, but at the expense of specificity. The causal links between how an IO is designed and, say, its ability to legitimate a particular idea are much less clear than the causal links between institutional design and efficiency. This creates difficulties both for the student of IOs, who cannot necessarily tell how much of a state's behavior can be attributed to the ideas generated by an IO, and for the policymaker, who has fewer clear guidelines in designing effective legitimating institutions than in designing effective efficiency-maximizing institutions.

Despite these difficulties, theories of international regimes that focus on ideas, such as the reflectivist approach, can illuminate some of the broader and more fundamental effects of IOs that the rationalist approach misses. In particular, they can illuminate both processes of change in international relations and the role of IOs in the basic rules of interaction of the state system. In other words, without applying the reflectivist approach we can determine much of the effect that an IO is having on international relations at any given point in time, but we cannot discover much about whether, or how, that organization is changing international relations. We can discover how states with compatible interests can cooperate better with rationalist theory, but we need reflectivist theory to discover how those states came to have compatible interests in the first place.

Regimes and Institutions

Both the rationalist and the reflectivist approaches to regime theory begin with the premise that IOs at best do good, and at worst do no harm. But neoinstitutionalist IO theory warns us that IOs are bureaucracies and can suffer from the same bureaucratic pathologies as other large organizations. In particular, they can evolve to work in the interests of the members of the bureaucracy rather than in the interests of those who created, and fund, the organization. International organizations are also, for the most part, specialist organizations. This specialization gives them the ability to focus on specific goals, but can also lead them to lose track of the bigger picture within which those goals are embedded.

The problem of bureaucratic pathologies can manifest itself in a number of ways, from nepotism and poor financial management to an operational focus on organizational growth at the expense of a focus on specific institutional goals. The best (although not perfect) solution to this problem is external oversight and a focus on institutional transparency and accountability. External oversight can come either from member states, which have the ability to withhold funding from IOs, or from NGOs, which have the ability to embarrass them. Institutional transparency refers to the ability of people from outside the organization to see inside it, to figure out what is being done and where the organization's resources are going. Accountability refers to any system in which the organization needs to account for its activities to an outside body, and report on the extent to which it is achieving its intended goals.

The UN Secretariat, for example, has for some two decades now been under pressure from some of its members (and in particular some of its biggest donor countries) to make itself more transparent and accountable. As a result, the Secretariat now sees transparency and accountability as important even without constant prompting by members. The withdrawal of the United States and the United Kingdom from the United Nations Educational, Scientific, and Cultural Organization (UNESCO) (as discussed in Chapter 2) is one extreme example of the sort of pressure member states can exert on IOs (both have since rejoined, their primary complaints having been addressed). In both the Secretariat and UNESCO, by all accounts, increased external scrutiny, leading to a greater focus on institutional transparency and accountability, has meant that the organizations actually work more effectively at achieving their institutional goals than they used to.

It should be noted, however, that the bureaucratic impulse to self-perpetuation and organizational growth is not necessarily a bad thing. It depends on the situation and on whether the impulse detracts from or contributes to the goals that member states have for the IO. For example, in the early 1970s, the IMF reoriented itself from overseeing the system of fixed exchange rates (the Bretton Woods system) that had just collapsed to acting (among other things) as a sort of credit-approval agency for developing countries. This change was, for the most part, generated from within the organization. But the change was accepted by the major donor countries because it served their interests at the time. The United Nations Environment Programme (UNEP) is another example of an IO whose responsibilities continue to grow and change. This organization regularly identifies new environmental issues that require international cooperation, thereby increasing its responsibilities and, over time, its capabilities. In an issue-area marked by high degrees of uncertainty, this ability to identify new needs for its services is a necessary part of UNEP's function.

The negative effect of institutional specialization—losing sight of the big picture—is a more difficult problem to address. It requires that someone be thinking in terms of the big picture, be thinking of unintended consequences. Good examples of this problem can be found in such issue-areas as development assistance and aid to refugees. In both cases, well-meaning aid can lead to the creation of long-term dependence on the IO, when the intended goal is precisely to reduce the dependence of the recipients in the long term. This problem is not one of accountability, because in the short term everyone benefits from the aid. It is rather a problem of disjuncture between short- and long-term goals. There are in fact no simple or straightforward solutions to this problem; it requires a careful balancing of the short- and long-term goals. Both development and refugee-assistance IOs are more conscious of this problem than used to be the case, which is a necessary prerequisite to drawing the balance between short- and long-term goals in a thoughtful way. But it is a problem that needs to be kept continuously in mind.

Power and Interdependence

These various observations about regimes and institutional theory are based on an assumption of interdependence. International organizations, in these theories, are designed to enhance international cooperation, and this cooperation is itself made necessary by the fact of interdependence among states and peoples. The logic is that since we are driven to cooperate because of the fact of increasing interdependence in a world of globalization and technological advancement, we may as well cooperate as effectively and efficiently as possible.

But, some critics say, this focus on interdependence masks much of what is really going on in IOs, because it does not address the way in which power is being used through and by IOs and the patterns of cooperation that they represent. The critics would note as well that this focus glosses over the relative powerlessness of more peripheral countries that are full participants in the system, but are unable to affect it in any major way. As the multilateralist system matures, and as both IOs and countries proliferate in the international system, it is worth looking at the way in which power relationships in the system are changing.

There are ways in which power in the multilateral system is becoming more diffuse. At an obvious institutional level, new IOs are no longer created with voting structures that are as biased toward the great powers as those of the IMF, the World Bank, or the Security Council. Even when new IOs are created that are not based on the one-country, one-vote principle, voting tends to be distributed in ways that ensure that both sides of the issue in question are represented. For example, the Multilateral Fund of the Montreal Protocol on Substances that Deplete the Ozone Layer requires majorities of both donor and recipient countries to carry a motion, and the International Tropical Timber Agreement requires a majority of both producer and consumer countries. In this sense, the creation of structural power favoring wealthier or more militarily powerful states over others in particular IOs is no longer accepted to the degree that it was half a century ago.

The same phenomenon can be seen in many international negotiations. In the Doha round of international trade negotiations, for example, developing countries threatened to veto a new agreement if their needs were not met in a way that had never happened before. In a range of environmental negotiations, including those dealing with ozone-depleting substances and climate change, developing countries have wielded the threat of nonparticipation in a way that has allowed them significant input into the form and content of the final agreement, and a more lenient set of obligations. In short, in a significant subset of issues about which states negotiate to create agreements and form IOs, developing countries have accreted considerably more negotiating power than was evident in the earlier days of the multilateral system. But this new negotiating power is inconsistent across issue-areas and is far from evenly distributed across developing countries. It is concentrated in a small group of big and influential developing countries, led by China and India. Smaller countries, and most of Africa, remain essentially powerless.

And it remains the case that the big, rich states are by far the most powerful in most international negotiations. In other words, for the most part, the states that are most powerful in IOs are those that would be most powerful without them. This is true not only of observable bargaining power, but perhaps even more so in the background conditions of international negotiations. In fact, in terms of background conditions it can be argued that the multilateral system is actually more unilateral than it has ever been. The system always operated in the tacit recognition of U.S. financial hegemony, which is less pronounced now than in the early days of the system but, arguably, still a meaningful condition. But it is the case now, to a far greater extent than it has ever been before, that the system operates in the tacit recognition of overwhelming U.S. military hegemony. This recognition in all likelihood does not have a great impact on many negotiations, those far removed from military issues. But in any issues related to international security, the UN's official core function, U.S. military hegemony is a fact that helps to set the agenda for discussion.

Critics of the IO system argue that even more than the "hard" power of military and financial capabilities, the West, and particularly the United States, sets the ideological agenda of the multilateral system. Even if the larger developing countries seem to be holding their own in negotiations, they can do so only within the context of discussions that fit into a neoliberal and neocolonial setting. This critique of the system can be made at the level of rational decision-making; third world leaders recognize the rules of the system, and try to do as well as they can within those rules. But the critique can also be made via the cooptation of elites, in which the West convinces elites in developing countries that neoliberalism is a good thing, even though it may in fact not be the best policy for their countries. This latter critique is inherently normative; it cannot be addressed on a purely empirical basis, because it depends on the analysts' determination of what the goals of developing countries should be.

Whatever one makes of the ideological critique of the multilateral system, the grip of neoliberalism over the system appears to be weaker in the early years of the twenty-first century than in the mid-1990s. The Washington Consensus is no longer a clear consensus, with the World Bank and the IMF no longer clearly on the same page in terms of policy recommendations: the credibility of both institutions was undermined by five years of financial crises in the developing world. At the same time, clear rifts have opened up between the United States and the European Union (EU) on a variety of trade issues, and the United States has undermined its multilateralist credentials in a variety of issue-areas, from climate change to the International Criminal Court (ICC) to international security. It remains to be seen what long-term effect this weakening of the ideological consensus underlying multilateralism will have on the international system.

A final note on power, interdependence, and international organization has to do with the power of IOs themselves. This power is constrained, but nonetheless real. Some IOs have the power to allocate financial and other material resources, but only within reasonably narrow parameters. Most IOs have access to only modest material resources, and when they have access to substantial resources, as in the case of the IFIs, the distribution of those resources is watched by donor states, which in turn have been known to interfere in the IFIs' lending decisions for political reasons. Most of the power that IOs have access to is not material; it is the power of moral authority. In some cases, this moral authority is accepted by third parties as authoritative; thus, the effect of IMF loans in securing the credit-worthiness of developing states, and the World Health Organization's ability to declare regions dangerous to travel for health reasons.

But it is important not to confuse the power of IOs with the power of member states. The Security Council, for example, has the moral authority to legitimize uses of force. However, it has essentially no military power of its own, and depends entirely on the material capabilities of its members to put its moral authority into material effect. The WTO as an IO has remarkably little power, serving predominantly as a forum for member states. Even its Dispute Settlement Mechanism (DSM), which can authorize states to punish other states for breaking trade rules, cannot enforce its rulings on its own. The power of other IOs, particularly those with lower political profiles or with stronger secretariats (or both), lies in their ability to set agendas and to cajole states and other actors, but this power is always severely limited in the face of active opposition by the larger, and richer, member states.

Paradoxically, critics both overestimate and underestimate the power of IOs. Political realists often dismiss IOs as being ineffectual. These critics have a point insofar as IOs ultimately depend on the consent and on the resources of their member states, and thus cannot replace states in the enforcement of rules or the maintenance of international peace and security. At the same time, however, saying that they are not ultimately the only actors in international relations does not mean that they do not matter at all. International organizations do affect the way states behave, do affect the international political agenda, and do succeed at improving cooperation and legitimizing behavior. Criticizing IOs for not being states is missing the point.

At the other extreme, critics of the UN system from the political far right and critics of the international economic institutions from the far left see IOs as potentially undermining state sovereignty. These fears are unfounded. International organizations do not have the power to impose trade rules on unwilling states, let alone invade the United States with black helicopters. They remain ultimately constrained by the states that created them, and therefore cannot undermine the sovereign state system without undermining their own authority and legitimacy. The organizations often come to represent rules that critics oppose, but these rules are nonetheless the result of negotiations and agreements among states. The place to look for the source of these rules, therefore, is with states themselves.

Sovereignty and Globalization

This observation brings us to the broadest of the four distinctions with which this book started, that between sovereignty and globalization. Chapter 1 discusses three traditions of looking at IOs: the realist, the internationalist, and the universalist. The evidence from Chapters 6 to 10 suggests that the international political system as it is currently constituted falls primarily within the internationalist tradition.

There is a trend toward globalization, toward the creation of rules and norms that affect all countries, which states are increasingly hard-pressed to ignore. And IOs play an active role in this trend. But they do so largely as agents of states, not as replacements for states.

There are certainly elements of contemporary global governance that are better described by the realist or universalist traditions. States still play power politics, only partially mediated by cooperative institutions. And there are universalist market and social forces that drive patterns of global governance that do not fall within the direct control of states operating either individually or in concert with each other. The UN system is increasingly attempting to access these universalist forces through the co-optation of NGOs (as representatives of global civil society) and through such initiatives as the "Global Compact," the co-optation of transnational corporations (as the operatives of the international market system).[1] But the evidence from this book suggests that the core of the contemporary international system is best described by the internationalist tradition.

The discussion of the internationalist tradition in Chapter 1 argues that the ideological basis for contemporary IOs is the norm of multilateralism. This norm suggests that IOs are agents of globalization, but of a particular form of globalization that changes rather than undermines sovereignty. In multilateralist globalization, states do lose much of their ability to act independently, to do what they want within their own borders. In return, they get to be the primary participants in the cooperative making of global rules. State sovereignty comes to be less about domestic autonomy and more about participatory decision making at the international level. The processes described in this book, which reveal a proliferation both of IOs and of issue-areas subject to multilateral rules, bear out the view of the internationalist tradition. This empirical support in turn leads to two questions.

The first, and most straightforward, question is this: To the extent that the internationalist tradition accurately explains how international politics works, how do we make the multilateral system work more effectively? At the level of organizational specifics, this question can be addressed by regime and institutional theory, as has been done above. At a broader, systemic level, it seems likely that the system would be at its most effective the more the participant states believe in it. From this perspective, the recent skepticism about multilateralism from the most powerful state in the system, which has traditionally been one of the system's greatest proponents, is worrying. How U.S. skepticism and, occasionally, nonparticipation will affect the system as a whole is unclear. It should be noted, however, that while the United States began the twenty-first century by indicating an unwillingness to play by multilateralist rules in a few specific issue-areas, it remains an active participant in most aspects of the system.

The second question is, To what extent do those who are ultimately affected by its rules—the world's people—see the multilateralist system as legitimate? The participants in the system are states, not individuals; thus, multilateralist politics risks leaving populations feeling disenfranchised. As noted in Chapter 1, the phenomenon of perceived disenfranchisement is most visible in the politics of the EU, and in the various protests against the role of the international economic institutions in globalization. The EU, over the past decade and more, has tried to deal with the problem by expanding the powers and the visibility of the European Parliament, the EU institution directly elected by EU citizens. This strategy, in terms of alleviating the perception of a democratic deficit, has had only limited success to this point.

Other IOs have less ability, in fact usually no ability, to create direct representation for citizens in their decision making. With most IOs this is not a problem—no one really cares about the representativeness of the Universal Postal Union (UPU) as long as its job gets done well. But with a few IOs, particularly the international economic institutions such as the WTO, IMF, and World Bank, it does seem to be a real problem. Oddly enough, it seems to be less of a problem with international security institutions such as the Security Council, perhaps because of a stronger assumption that issues of war and peace will be discussed among states rather than among populations. The international economic institutions, and other IOs working in the public eye, have to this point responded by trying to make their inner workings more transparent, and by trying to work more closely and intimately with NGOs as representatives of global civil society. These strategies, like the strategy of empowering the European Parliament, ameliorate the problem without getting to its core. The issue of direct representation of people in decision making at the multilateral level is going to remain one of the key obstacles facing the multilateralist international system in the foreseeable future.

Notes

Introduction: The State and International Organizations

1. Some IOs are created by other IOs rather than by states directly. These are often referred to as "emanations," and they still count as IOs because their members are sovereign states: even though they were created by other IOs, they are ultimately answerable to their member states. For a discussion of the frequency of emanations, see Cheryl Shanks, Harold Jacobson, and Jeffrey Kaplan, "Inertia and Change in the Constellation of International Governmental Organizations, 1981–1992," *International Organization* 50 (1996): 593–628.

Chapter 1   Sovereignty and Globalization

1. The Rhine Commission, which claims to be the first international organization, first met in 1816. Renamed the Central Commission for Navigation on the Rhine, it continues to fulfill the function for which it was originally designed. See La Commission Centrale Pour la Navigation du Rhin, "Background History," http://www.ccr-zkr.org/. On fur seal fishery cooperation, see the *Convention between the United States, Great Britain, Russia and Japan for the Preservation and Protection of Fur Seals* (1911), accessible online at http://fletcher.tufts.edu/multi/sealtreaty.html. International postal cooperation is discussed in Chapter 10.
2. International Labour Organization, Constitution (Geneva: ILO, 2001 [1919]).
3. The role of the UN in the maintenance of international peace and security is discussed in more detail in Chapter 6.
4. The UN's structure is discussed in detail in Chapter 5.
5. Union of International Organizations, *Yearbook of International Organizations, 2004–2005* (Munchen: K.G. Saur, 2004), 5:3.
6. On this distinction, see Janice Thomson, "State Sovereignty in International Relations: Bridging the Gap between Theory and Empirical Research," *International Studies Quarterly* 39 (1995): 213–234.
7. For a broader discussion of the practical limits of sovereignty in Africa, see Robert Jackson, *Quasi-States: Sovereignty, International Relations, and the Third World* (Cambridge: Cambridge University Press, 1990).
8. On Westphalia as metaphor versus Westphalia as history, see Stephen Krasner, "Westphalia and All That," in *Ideas and Foreign Policy: Beliefs, Institutions, and Political Change*, ed. Judith Goldstein and Robert Keohane (Ithaca, NY: Cornell University Press, 1993), pp. 235–264.
9. J. Samuel Barkin, "The Evolution of the Constitution of Sovereignty and the Emergence of Human Rights Norms," *Millennium* 27 (1998): 229–252.
10. For a good general introduction to the globalization literature, see Jan Aart Scholte, *Globalization: A Critical Introduction* (Houndmills, Hampshire: Palgrave, 2000).

11. On multilateralism, see John Gerard Ruggie, "Multilateralism: The Anatomy of an Institution," *International Organization* 46 (1992): 561–598.

12. For a discussion of the mechanics of this process, and an example of it in the realm of financial regulation, see Beth Simmons, "The International Politics of Harmonization: The Case of Capital Market Regulation," *International Organization* 55 (2001): 589–620.

13. For a discussion of regulatory races to the bottom, see H. Jeffrey Leonard, *Pollution and the Struggle for World Product: Multinational Corporations, Environment, and International Comparative Advantage* (Cambridge: Cambridge University Press, 1988) and Daniel Drezner, "Globalization and Policy Convergence," *International Studies Review* 3 (2001): 53–78. For a range of arguments against globalization, see Jerry Mander and Edward Goldsmith, eds., *The Case against the Global Economy: And for a Turn Toward the Local* (San Francisco: Sierra Club Books, 1996).

14. See, for example, Jennifer Clapp, "Africa, NGOs, and the International Toxic Waste Trade," *Journal of Environment and Development* 3 (1994): 17–46.

15. Examples of both arguments can be found in Kevin Gallagher and Jacob Werksman, eds., *The Earthscan Reader on International Trade & Sustainable Development* (London: Earthscan, 2002).

16. For a discussion of this literature in the context of disarmament, see Klaus Knorr, "Supranational Versus International Models for General and Complete Disarmamant," in *The Strategy of World Order*, vol. 4, *Disarmament and Economic Development*, ed. Richard Falk and Saul Mendlovitz (New York: World Law Fund, 1966), pp. 326–353.

17. Hedley Bull, *The Anarchical Society: A Study of Order in World Politics* (London: Macmillan, 1977).

18. The major exception to the rule that it is states that issue currencies is the Euro, issued by the European Central Bank, which is in turn related to (but not, institutionally, part of) the EU.

19. See, for example, Susan Strange, "*Cave, Hic Dragones:* A Critique of Regime Analysis," *International Organization* 36 (1982): pp. 479–496; John Mearsheimer, "The False Promise of International Institutions," *International Security* 19 (1994–1995): 5–49; and Lloyd Gruber, *Ruling the World: Power Politics and the Rise of Supranational Institutions* (Princeton, NJ: Princeton University Press, 2000).

20. See, for example, Louis Henkin, *How Nations Behave: Law and Foreign Policy*, 2nd ed. (New York: Columbia University Press, 1979).

21. Bull, *The Anarchical Society*, pp. 24–27.

22. See, for example, Margaret Keck and Kathryn Sikkink, *Activists Beyond Borders: Advocacy Networks in International Politics* (Ithaca, NY: Cornell University Press, 1998).

23. On "sovereignty" being more of a convenience for powerful states than being an absolute rule, see Stephen Krasner, *Sovereignty: Organized Hypocrisy* (Princeton, NJ: Princeton University Press, 1999).

24. See, for example, Paul Wapner, *Environmental Activism and World Civic Politics* (Albany: State University of New York Press, 1996).

25. Ruggie, "Multilateralism."

26. Mander and Goldsmith, *The Case Against the Global Economy*.

27. See, for example, Desmond Dinan, *Ever Closer Union: An Introduction to European Integration*, 2nd ed. (Boulder, CO: Lynne Rienner, 1999) and Andrew Moravcsik, *The Choice for Europe: Social Purpose and State Power from Messina to Maastricht* (Ithaca, NY: Cornell University Press, 1998).

28. This is the same argument made in favor of limiting federal policy-making in the United States, and allowing states to experiment with different approaches to public policy.

29. On the processes through which competitive behavior can lead to war, see Robert Jervis, *Perception and Misperception in International Politics* (Princeton, NJ: Princeton University Press, 1976).
30. See, for example, Shirin Sinnar, "Mixed Blessing: The Growing Influence of NGOs," *Harvard International Review* 18 (1995–1996): 54–57.
31. This criticism is discussed in more detail in Chapter 3.

Chapter 2   Power and Interdependence

1. See, for example, Robert O. Keohane, "Reciprocity in International Relations," *International Organization* 40 (1986): 1–27.
2. For different positions in the absolute/relative gains debate, see David Baldwin, ed., *Neorealism and Neoliberalism: The Contemporary Debate* (New York: Columbia University Press, 1993).
3. For an example of the trade economist viewpoint on international cooperation, see Jagdish Bhagwati, *In Defense of Globalization* (New York: Oxford University Press, 2004).
4. On the subject of the national interest, see Stephen Krasner, *Defending the National Interest: Raw Materials Investment and U.S. Foreign Policy* (Princeton, NJ: Princeton University Press, 1978) and Martha Finnemore, *National Interests in International Society* (Ithaca, NY: Cornell University Press, 1996).
5. Robert Keohane and Joseph Nye, *Power and Interdependence: World Politics in Transition* (Boston, MA: Little, Brown, 1977). It is now in its third (and substantially expanded) edition.
6. Ibid., pp. 23–37.
7. Ibid., p. 11.
8. For an example of a conscious effort to create asymmetrical dependence as a power resource, see Albert O. Hirschman, *National Power and the Structure of Foreign Trade* (Berkeley: University of California Press, 1945).
9. In 1999, trade in goods equaled 275 percent of Singapore's GDP, but slightly less than 20 percent of the United States'. Figures from World Bank, *World Development Indicators 2001* (Washington, DC: World Bank, 2001), p. 322.
10. For an argument that this difference in bargaining power has created a system of IOs that are strongly biased against developing countries, see Lloyd Gruber, *Ruling the World: Power Politics and the Rise of Supranational Institutions* (Princeton, NJ: Princeton University Press, 2000).
11. The term was coined by Peter Bachrach and Morton Baratz, "Two Faces of Power," *American Political Science Review* 56 (1962): 947–952.
12. This process has in many cases, however, become much easier than it was in the days before widespread use of the Web. Many documents on Kyoto's prenegotiation negotiations can be found on the UNFCCC's website, http://www.unfccc.org/. Other useful reports can be found in various issues of the *Earth Negotiation Bulletin*, available on the website of the International Institute for Sustainable Development (IISD), http://www.iisd.ca.
13. See, for example, Steven Lukes, *Power: A Radical View* (London: Macmillan, 1974). He speaks of a third dimension of power, rather than a third face.
14. Joseph Nye, *Bound to Lead: The Changing Nature of American Power* (New York: Basic Books, 1990).
15. Keohane and Nye, 1977.
16. For a discussion of why a more immediate need for cooperation undermines negotiating power, see J. Samuel Barkin, "Time Horizons and Multilateral Enforcement in International Cooperation," *International Studies Quarterly* 48 (2004): 363–382.

17. See Stephen Krasner, "Global Communications and National Power: Life on the Pareto Frontier," *World Politics* 43 (1991): 336–366.
18. J. Samuel Barkin and George Shambaugh, eds., *Anarchy and the Environment: The International Relations of Common Pool Resources* (Albany: State University of New York Press, 1999).
19. The UN has since internalized the norm of administrative efficiency, and stresses its efforts at reform. See, for example, the "Reform at the UN" website, at http://www.un.org/reform/index.html.
20. As of 2003. The complete set of country assessments can be found in General Assembly Resolution 55/5, *Scale of Assessments for the Apportionment of the Expenses of the United Nations* (New York: UN, 2001).
21. These countries are the United States, China, Russia, the United Kingdom, and France. A UN report has recently recommended changing the structure of the Security Council. Its recommendations are discussed in Chapter 6.
22. International Monetary Fund, *Annual Report 2001* (Washington, DC: IMF, 2001), Appendix VII.
23. One example is the Northwest Atlantic Fisheries Organization (NAFO), in which the EU is a member rather than its individual member countries. If the countries that constitute the EU were all members individually, they would have together half of the votes in NAFO (to complicate the issue, France and Denmark have separate membership to represent their territories in St. Pierre et Miquelon and Greenland, respectively, which are not part of the EU). In other organizations, such as the WTO, both the EU and its constituent countries are separate members.
24. United Nations, *Charter of the United Nations* (New York: UN, 1965), Article 18.
25. CCAMLR, "Rules of Procedure," *Basic Documents* (North Hobart, Australia: CCAMLR, 2004), Rule 4.
26. See J. Samuel Barkin and Elizabeth DeSombre, "Unilateralism and Multilateralism in International Fisheries Management," *Global Governance* 6 (2000): 339–360 and Elizabeth DeSombre and J. Samuel Barkin, "The Turbot War: Canada, Spain, and the Conflict over the North Atlantic Fishery," *PEW Case Studies in International Affairs*, Case Study #226 (Washington, DC: Institute for the Study of Diplomacy, 2000).
27. United Nations Office on Drugs and Crime, "About Us," http://www.unodc.org/unodc/about.html.
28. See Richard Gardner, *Sterling–Dollar Diplomacy in Current Perspective: The Origins and the Prospects of Our International Economic Order* (New York: Columbia University Press, 1980).
29. The GA first met in London, and the UN's site in New York was not chosen until a private citizen (albeit one of the world's richest people), John D. Rockefeller Jr., donated the money to buy the land.
30. See, for example, Jeffrey Chwieroth, "A Capital Idea: The Role of Neoliberalism in the Liberalization of Finance in Emerging Markets." (PhD thesis, University of California at Santa Barbara, 2003).
31. See, for example, Stephen Ryan, *The United Nations and International Politics* (New York: St. Martin's Press, 2000), pp. 90–91.
32. Ibid., p. 93.
33. For examples of these criticisms from both perspectives in the context of the interaction of the international trading system and environmental politics, see Gary P. Sampson and W. Bradnee Chambers, eds., *Trade, Environment, and the Millennium* (Tokyo: United Nations University Press, 1999).
34. Some organizations, such as the North Atlantic Treaty Organization (NATO), do have some military assets. But these assets, and the accompanying personnel, are ultimately working for and on loan from a national military force. The EU has discussed the

creation of an EU military force, but to the extent that this has actually happened, the forces involved are again national troops seconded by the EU.

35. For a discussion of different theoretical approaches to international law, see J. Craig Barker, *International Law and International Relations* (New York: Continuum, 2000).

36. On moral authority and power in International Relations, see Rodney Bruce Hall, "Moral Authority as a Power Resource," *International Organization* 51 (1997): 555–589.

37. See, for example, Abram Chayes and Antonia Handler Chayes, *The New Sovereignty: Compliance with International Regulatory Agreements* (Cambridge, MA: Harvard University Press, 1995).

38. Susan Burgerman, *Moral Victories: How Activists Provoke Multilateral Action* (Ithaca, NY: Cornell University Press, 2001).

39. See, for example, Darcy Henton, "Not so Picture Perfect," *Toronto Star*, June 4, 1998.

40. World Health Organization, *World Health Report 2001 – Mental Health: New Understanding, New Hope* (Geneva: WHO, 2001).

41. Peter Haas, "Introduction: Epistemic Communities and International Policy Coordination," *International Organization* 46 (1992): 3.

42. Peter Haas, *Saving the Mediterranean: The Politics of International Environmental Cooperation* (New York: Columbia University Press, 1990).

43. Steven Bernstein, *The Compromise of Liberal Environmentalism* (New York: Columbia University Press, 2001).

Chapter 3   Regimes and Institutions

1. Stephen Krasner, "Structural Causes and Regime Consequences: Regimes as Intervening Variables," in *International Regimes*, ed. Stephen Krasner (Ithaca, NY: Cornell University Press, 1983), p. 1.

2. For a discussion of the black-box model and its limitations with respect to domestic politics in the U.S., see Roger Hilsman, with Laura Gaughran and Patricia Weitsman, *The Politics of Policy-Making in Defense and Foreign Affairs: Conceptual Models and Bureaucratic Politics*, 3rd ed. (Englewood Cliffs, NJ: Prentice Hall, 1993).

3. An example of this approach is Robert Dahl, *Who Governs? Democracy and Power in an American City* (New Haven, CT: Yale University Press, 1961).

4. The history of IO theory presented here follows that provided in Friedrich Kratochwil and John Gerard Ruggie, "International Organization: A State of the Art on an Art of the State," *International Organization* 40 (1986): 753–775.

5. See, for example, Lawrence Susskind, *Environmental Diplomacy: Negotiating More Effective Global Agreements* (New York: Oxford University Press, 1994), pp. 28–29. He provides a list of the "elements of a typical global environmental convention," but these elements are in fact typical of most treaties that create IOs.

6. Christopher Joyner, "Managing Common-Pool Marine Living Resources: Lessons from the Southern Ocean Experience," in *Anarchy and the Environment: The International Relations of Common Pool Resources*, ed. Samuel Barkin and George Shambaugh (Albany: State University of New York Press, 1999), pp. 70–96.

7. See, for example, Robert Cox and Harold Jacobson, eds., *The Anatomy of Influence: Decision-Making in International Organization* (New Haven, CT: Yale University Press, 1973).

8. International Monetary Fund, "The IMF at a Glance: A Factsheet – February 2005," http://www.imf.org/external/np/exr/facts/glance.htm.

9. See, for example, "Monaco Agreement on the Conservation of Cetaceans in the Black Sea, Mediterranean Sea and Contiguous Atlantic Areas," *ACCOBAMS Bulletin #3* (Monaco: Interim ACCOBAMS Secretariat, 2000).

10. See, for example, Susskind, *Environmental Diplomacy*.

11. United Nations Environment Programme, *UNEP Annual Report 1999* (Nairobi: UNEP, 2000).

12. The most recent report, published in 2001 and running to 2,600 pages, is available in three volumes: Intergovernmental Panel on Climate Change, *Climate Change 2001: The Scientific Basis; Climate Change 2001: Impacts, Adaptation and& Vulnerability; Climate Change 2001: Mitigation* (Cambridge: Cambridge University Press, 2001).

13. For a more thorough discussion of the role of science and knowledge in international environmental cooperation, see Elizabeth DeSombre, *The Global Environment and World Politics* (London: Continuum, 2002), esp. ch. 4.

14. International Civil Aviation Organization, "Facts About the ICAO," available at http://www.icao.org/cgi/goto.pl?icao/en/download.htm.

15. International Civil Aviation Organization, "Legal Bureau," http://www.icao.int/icao/en/leb/.

16. The main distinction between the ICJ and the ICC is that the former adjudicates disputes between states, and the latter tries individuals for crimes. Another related distinction is that states can legally decline to accept the jurisdiction of the ICJ if they so choose, whereas individuals cannot decline to accept the jurisdiction of the ICC.

17. United Nations High Commission for Refugees, *Basic Information About the UNHCR* (Geneva: UNHCR, 2001).

18. International Civil Aviation Organization, "Technical Cooperation Bureau," http://www.icao.int/icao/en/tcb/.

19. Information on the World Maritime University can be found at its website, http://www.wmu.se/.

20. As of 2003. The complete set of country assessments can be found in General Assembly Resolution 55/5, *Scale of Assessments for the Apportionment of the Expenses of the United Nations* (New York: UN, 2001).

21. David Rohde, "Ted Turner Plans a $1 Billion Gift for U.N. Agencies." *New York Times,* September 19, 1997, A1.

22. United Nations High Commission for Refugees, "UNHCR Headquarters Structure," available at http://www.unhcr.ch/cgi-bin/texis/vtx/admin.

23. In the fiscal year 2000, they contributed $378 million out of a total income of $1,118 million. United Nations Children's Fund, *2001 UNICEF Annual Report* (New York: UNICEF, 2001), p. 33.

24. Ernst Haas, *Beyond the Nation-State: Functionalism and International Organization* (Stanford, CA: Stanford University Press, 1964).

25. See, for example, Ernst Haas, "Is There a Hole in the Whole? Knowledge, Technology, Interdependence, and the Construction of International Regimes," *International Organization* 29 (1975): 827–876.

26. Philippe Schmitter, "Three Neo-Functionalist Hypotheses about International Integration," *International Organization* 23 (1969): 161–166.

27. See, for example, Leon Lindberg and Stuart Scheingold, *Europe's Would-Be Polity: Patterns of Change in the European Community* (Englewood Cliffs, NJ: Prentice Hall, 1970).

28. See, for example, Stanley Hoffmann, "International Organization and the International System," *International Organization* 24 (1970): 389–413.

29. Kratochwil and Ruggie, "International Organization."

30. See, for example, Michael Barnett and Martha Finnemore, "The Power, Politics, and Pathologies of International Organizations," *International Organization* 53 (1999): 699–732.

31. Interestingly, one of the first voices in this trend was that of Ernst Haas, who had earlier been a pioneer both of functionalism and neofunctionalism. See Haas, *When Knowledge Is Power* (Berkeley: University of California Press, 1990).

32. On IOs as being in the general good, see Harold Jacobson, *Networks of Interdependence* (New York: Alfred A. Knopf, 1979).

33. Barnett and Finnemore, "Pathologies of International Organizations."

34. James March, *Decisions and Organizations* (Boston, MA: Basil Blackwell, 1988) and James March and Johan Olsen, *Rediscovering Institutions: The Organizational Basis of Politics* (New York: Free Press, 1989).

35. On bureaucratic politics see Graham Allison, *Essence of Decision: Explaining the Cuban Missile Crisis* (Boston, MA: Little, Brown, 1971); on sociological institutionalism see Paul DiMaggio and Walter Powell, "The Iron Cage Revisited: Institutional Isomorphism and Collective Rationality in Organizational Fields," *American Sociological Review* 48 (1983): 147–160.

36. James March and Johan Olsen, "The Institutional Dynamics of International Political Orders," *International Organization* 52 (1998): 943–969.

37. International Monetary Fund, "About the IMF," http://www.imf.org/external/about.htm. This statement is an abridgement of Article 1 of the *Articles of Agreement of the International Monetary Fund* (Washington: IMF, 1945).

38. Barnett and Finnemore, "Pathologies of International Organizations."

39. Ibid. This term has been applied to the same sort of behavior when undertaken by states as well, for example, James Fearon, "Rationalist Explanations for War," *International Organization* 49 (1995): 379–414.

40. See, *inter alia*, Bruce Rich, *Mortgaging the Earth: The World Bank, Environmental Impoverishment, and the Crisis of Development* (Boston, MA: Beacon Press, 1994).

41. Example taken from Barnett and Finnemore, "Pathologies of International Organizations." See also David Kennedy, "International Refugee Protection," *Human Rights Quarterly* 8 (1986): 1–9.

42. See, for example, United Nations Security Council Resolutions 1368 and 1373 (New York: UN, 2001).

43. Conditionality refers to a process in which the IMF sets policy conditions, usually involving policy liberalization, that developing countries must meet in order to gain access to IMF loans. This process is discussed in more detail in Chapter 8.

44. These IOs are called "emanations." Cheryl Shanks, Harold Jacobson, and Jeffrey Kaplan, "Inertia and Change in the Constellation of International Governmental Organizations, 1981–1992," *International Organization* 50 (1996): 593–628.

45. Mark A. Pollack, *The Engines of European Integration: Delegation, Agency, and Agenda Setting in the EU* (New York: Oxford University Press, 2003), and Daniel L. Nielson and Michael J. Tierney, "Delegation to International Organizations: Agency Theory and World Bank Environmental Reform," *International Organization* 57 (2003): 241–276.

46. See, for example, Kratochwil and Ruggie, "International Organization."

47. The term "reflectivism" was introduced into the IO discourse by Robert Keohane in "International Institutions: Two Approaches," *International Studies Quarterly* 32 (1988): 379–396.

Chapter 4   Efficiency and Ideas

1. See, for example, Stephen Krasner, ed., *International Regimes* (Ithaca, NY: Cornell University Press, 1983). The "rationalist" and "reflectivist" terminology is from Robert Keohane, "International Institutions: Two Approaches," *International Studies Quarterly* 32 (1988): 379–396. The term "neo-liberal institutionalism" was introduced by Joseph Grieco in "Anarchy and the Limits of Cooperation: A Realist Critique of the Newest Liberal Institutionalism," *International Organization* 42 (1988): 485–507. The term "constructivism" was introduced into the international relations discourse by Nicholas

Onuf in *World of Our Making: Rules and Rule in Social Theory and International Relations* (Columbia: University of South Carolina Press, 1989).

2. See, *inter alia*, Kenneth Oye, ed., *Cooperation under Anarchy* (Princeton, NJ: Princeton University Press, 1986), and James Fearon, "Bargaining, Enforcement, and International Cooperation," *International Organization* 52 (1998): 269–306.

3. The seminal work on collective action problems, which uses the union membership example, is Mancur Olson's *The Logic of Collective Action: Public Goods and the Theory of Groups* (Cambridge, MA: Harvard University Press, 1965).

4. Joanne Gowa, "Rational Hegemons, Excludable Goods, and Small Groups: An Epitaph for Hegemonic Stability Theory?" *World Politics* 41 (1989): 307–324.

5. On PD, and on the use of this sort of 2 × 2 game in the study of international relations more generally, see Glenn Snyder and Paul Diesing, *Conflict among Nations: Bargaining, Decision Making, and System Structure in International Crises* (Princeton, NJ: Princeton University Press, 1977).

6. Douglass North and Robert Paul Thomas, *The Rise of the Western World: A New Economic History* (Cambridge: Cambridge University Press, 1973), and Douglass North, *Structure and Change in Economic History* (New York: Norton, 1981) go so far as to claim that economic history as a whole can be written through the story of governments improving markets.

7. Keohane, *After Hegemony: Cooperation and Discord in the World Political Economy* (Princeton, NJ: Princeton University Press, 1984).

8. Keohane, "The Demand for International Regimes," *International Organization* 36 (1982): 325–356.

9. Friedrich Kratochwil and John Gerard Ruggie, "International Organization: A State of the Art on an Art of the State," *International Organization* 40 (1986): 753–775, and Ronald Mitchell, "Sources of Transparency: Information Systems in International Regimes," *International Studies Quarterly* 42 (1998): 109–130.

10. A discussion of the origin and task of the IPCC can be found on its website, http://www.ipcc.ch/.

11. They are then, in practice, often ignored. See, for example, William Aron, "Science and the IWC," in *Toward a Sustainable Whaling Regime,* ed. Robert Friedheim (Seattle: University of Washington Press, 2001), pp. 105–122.

12. Both the IMF and the ISO will be discussed in more detail below, in Chapters 8 and 11, respectively.

13. The administrative functions are provided by the Secretariat (the internal structure of the UN will be discussed in more detail in the next chapter). The rules and procedures of the Security Council are published as Chapter 1 of the *Repertoire of the Practice of the Security Council* (New York: UN, serial).

14. GATT, *General Agreement on Tariffs and Trade: Text of the General Agreement* (Geneva: GATT, 1994), Articles I and III.

15. Joseph Kahn, "Nations Back Freer Trade, Hoping to Aid Global Growth," *New York Times,* November 15, 2001, A12.

16. Oran Young, ed., The *Effectiveness of International Environmental Agreements* (Cambridge, MA: MIT Press, 1999), and Edward Miles, Arild Underdal, Steinar Andresen, Jorgen Wettestad, Tora Skodvin, and Elaine Carlin, *Environmental Regime Effectiveness* (Cambridge, MA: MIT Press, 2001).

17. For a complete discussion of the problems of the international whaling regime, see Robert Friedheim, ed., *Toward a Sustainable Whaling Regime* (Seattle: University of Washington Press, 2001).

18. Peter Haas, Robert Keohane, and Marc Levy, eds., *Institutions for the Earth: Sources of Effective International Environmental Protection* (Cambridge, MA: MIT Press, 1993).

19. Bureau of Arms Control, *Fact Sheet: The Biological Weapons Convention* (Washington, DC: US Department of State, released May 22, 2002), viewed at http://www.state.gov/t/ac/rls/fs/10401.htm.

20. See, for example, Elizabeth DeSombre and J. Samuel Barkin, "Turbot and Tempers in the North Atlantic," in *Conserving the Peace: Resources, Livelihoods, and Security*, ed. Richard Matthew, Mark Halle, and Jason Switzer (Winnipeg, MB: International Institute for Sustainable Development, 2002).

21. Ronald Mitchell, *Intentional Oil Pollution at Sea: Environmental Policy and Treaty Compliance* (Cambridge, MA: MIT Press, 1994).

22. On the debate about the relationship between regime compliance and regime effectiveness, see Abram Chayes and Antonia Handler Chayes, "On Compliance," *International Organization* 47 (1993): 175–205, and George Downs, David Rocke, and Peter Barsoom, "Is the Good News About Compliance Good News About Cooperation?" *International Organization* 50 (1996): 379–406.

23. For a discussion of international law and adjudication that both discusses and argues against the realist position, see Louis Henkin, *How Nations Behave: Law and Foreign Policy* (New York: Praeger, 1968).

24. Elizabeth DeSombre and Joanne Kauffman, "The Montreal Protocol Multilateral Fund: Partial Success Story," in *Institutions for Environmental Aid: Pitfalls and Promise*, ed. Robert Keohane and Marc Levy (Cambridge, MA: MIT Press, 1996).

25. GATT, *General Agreement on Tariffs and Trade*, Article XXIII.

26. For a more complete discussion of constitutive rules in international relations, see Alexander Wendt, *Social Theory of International Politics* (Cambridge, MA: Cambridge University Press, 1999).

27. WTO, "A Summary of the Final Act of the Uruguay Round," http://www.wto.org/english/docs_e/legal_e/ursum_e.htm.

28. For example, in the period between World Wars I and II the United States' approach to international trade was based on bilateral concessions, while British trade policy before World War I was based on unilateral free trade.

29. Convention (IV) Relative to the Protection of Civilian Persons in Time of War. *United Nations Treaty Series* No. 973, vol. 75, p. 287 (Geneva: UN, 1949).

30. For an argument that these ideas can be biased in favor of some actors in international relations at the expense of others, see Thomas W. Smith, "The New Law of War: Legitimizing Hi-Tech and Infrastructural Violence," *International Studies Quarterly* 46 (2002): 355–374.

31. The seminal work on the role of legitimacy in the study of international organizations is Inis Claude, Jr., "Collective Legitimization as a Political Function of the United Nations," *International Organization* 20 (1966): 367–379. See also Ian Hurd, "Legitimacy and Authority in International Politics," *International Organization* 53 (1999): 379–408.

32. On the relationship between law and legitimacy in international relations, see Judith Goldstein, Miles Kahler, Robert Keohane, and Anne-Marie Slaughter, eds., *Legalization and World Politics* (Cambridge, MA: MIT Press, 2001) and Henkin, *How Nations Behave*.

33. J. Samuel Barkin and Bruce Cronin, "The State and the Nation: Changing Norms and Rules of Sovereignty in International Relations," *International Organization* 48 (1994): 107–130, and Thomas Biersteker and Cynthia Weber, eds., *State Sovereignty as a Social Construct* (Cambridge, MA: Cambridge University Press, 1996).

34. Stephen Krasner, *Sovereignty: Organized Hypocrisy* (Princeton, NJ: Princeton University Press, 1999).

35. J. Samuel Barkin, "The Evolution of the Constitution of Sovereignty and the Emergence of Human Rights Norms," *Millennium* 27 (1998): 229–252.

36. For a discussion of the history and current state of international human rights agreements, see Jack Donnelly, *International Human Rights* (Boulder, CO: Westview, 1998).

37. See, for example, Rosemary Foot, *Rights Beyond Borders: The Global Community and the Struggle over Human Rights in China* (Oxford: Oxford University Press, 2000).

38. Thomas Risse, Stephen Ropp, and Kathryn Sikkink, eds., *The Power of Human Rights: International Norms and Domestic Change* (Cambridge: Cambridge University Press, 1999).

39. Robert Jackson, *Quasi-States: Sovereignty, International Relations, and the Third World* (Cambridge: Cambridge University Press, 1990).

40. World Trade Organization, "China to Join on 11 December, Chinese Taipei's Membership Also Approved," *Doha WTO Ministerial 2001: Summary of 11 November 2001,* http://www.wto.org/english/thewto_e/minist_e/min01_e/min01_11nov_e.htm.

41. See, for example, Michael N. Barnett, *Eyewitness to a Genocide: The United Nations and Rwanda* (Ithaca, NY: Cornell University Press, 2002).

42. Jennifer Milliken, "The Study of Discourse in International Relations: A Critique of Research and Methods," *European Journal of International Relations* 5 (1999): 225–254.

43. See, for example, Peter Katzenstein, Robert Keohane, and Stephen Krasner, eds., *Exploration and Contestation in the Study of World Politics* (Cambridge, MA: MIT Press, 1999).

Chapter 5   The United Nations and Its System

1. To complicate matters further, there are agencies jointly administered by subsidiary agencies and autonomous agencies. For example, the WFP is overseen jointly by ECOSOC and the FAO, and the Global Environment Facility (GEF) projects are managed jointly by the World Bank , UNEP, and the UNDP, the latter two of which are themselves subsidiary agencies to both the GA and ECOSOC.

2. For an extreme example of the latter, see Lim Keith, *Black Helicopters over America: Strikeforce for the New World Order* (Lilburn, GA: IllumiNet Press, 1994).

3. For a more thorough discussion of multilateralism, see John Gerrard Ruggie, ed., *Multilateralism Matters: The Theory and Praxis of an Institutional Form* (New York: Columbia University Press, 1993).

4. United Nations, Charter of the United Nations (New York: UN, 1965), Article 18 (2).

5. The caucus got its name because it had seventy-seven members when it was founded in 1964. It currently has 133 members. More information on the organization can be found at its website, www.g77.org.

6. The Secretary-General's High-level Panel on Threats, Challenges and Change, *A More Secure World: Our Shared Responsibility* (New York: UN, 2004), p. 78.

7. See, for example, Inis Claude Jr., "Collective Legitimation as a Political Function of the United Nations," *International Organization* 20 (1966): 367–379.

8. Officially, the "1997 Convention on the Prohibition of the Use, Stockpiling, Production and Transfer of Antipersonnel Mines and Their Destruction." The text can be found at International Campaign to Ban Landmines, "Text of the Mine Ban Treaty," http://www.icbl.org/treaty/text.

9. The designers of the Security Council did not use these terms, but the focus on these issues is implicit in the design of the institution.

10. The membership was originally eleven states, but was expanded in 1965 to allow for greater geographic representation as the process of decolonization increased numbers of states in much of the global South. As will be discussed in more detail in Chapter 6, there is currently some discussion of expanding the membership to twenty-four states.

11. See, for example, Inis Claude Jr., *Swords into Plowshares,* 4th ed. (New York: Random House, 1984), pp. 157–158.

12. Membership in the UN "will be effected by a decision of the GA upon the recommendation of the Security Council." This means in effect that more than a third of the UN's members need to oppose a state's admission in the GA, but one of the permanent members can effectively veto admission in the Security Council. UN Charter, Article 4 (2).

13. The system of rotation of Security Council presidents is alphabetic, so all members of the Council will serve as president at least once during their tenure on the Council.

14. UN Charter, Article 97.

15. UN Charter, Article 99. Gendered language in the original.

16. UN Charter, Article 100, paragraph 2. The entire staff of the Secretariat is similarly supposed to be politically neutral, in other words to work for the UN, not for member states.

17. Historically, thus far always a he.

18. For a political history of Secretaries-General, see Stephen Ryan, *The United Nations and International Politics* (New York: St. Martin's, 2000), especially ch. 3.

19. A complete list of these representatives can be found at http://www.un.org/News/ossg/srsg/.

20. See, for example, two reports of the Secretary-General, *Renewing the United Nations: A Programme for Reform* (New York: United Nations General Assembly A/51/950, 1997) and *Strengthening the United Nations: An Agenda for Further Change* (New York: United Nations General Assembly A/57/387, 2002).

21. A list of these countries, and the declarations by which they have committed themselves, can be found at http://www.icj-cij.org/icjwww/ibasicdocuments/ibasictext/ibasicdeclarations.htm.

22. See, for example, J. Craig Barker, *International Law and International Relations* (London: Continuum, 2000).

23. UN Charter, Article 73, chapeau.

24. See, for example, The Secretary-General's High-level Panel, *A More Secure World,* pp. 92–93, and "2005 World Summit Outcome," United Nations General Assembly Resolution A/60/L1 (New York: UN, 2005), Article 176. Formally eliminating the Trusteeship Council requires amending the UN Charter.

Chapter 6   Collective Security

1. See, for example, Robert Jervis, "Security Regimes," *International Organization* 36 (1982): 357–378 and John Mearsheimer, "The False Promise of International Institutions," *International Security* 19 (1994–1995): 5–49.

2. High-level in the sense that the panel members are political heavyweights, including former heads of state, foreign ministers, ambassadors to and for the UN, heads of major IOs, and a former U.S. national security advisor. For a complete list, see The Secretary-General's High-level Panel on Threats, Challenges and Change, *A More Secure World: Our Shared Responsibility* (New York: UN, 2004), pp. 117–118.

3. See, for example, "2005 World Summit Outcome," United Nations General Assembly Resolution A/60/L1 (New York: UN, 2005).

4. See, for example, Paul Diehl, *International Peacekeeping* (Baltimore, MD: Johns Hopkins University Press, 1994).

5. All of the quotations in this paragraph are from United Nations, *Charter of the United Nations* (New York: UN, 1965).

6. United Nations, "United Nations Peacekeeping Operations," United Nations Department of Public Information (DPI/1634/Rev. 39, August 2004).

7. The wording of the UN Charter suggests that a resolution needs all five permanent members to vote in favor if it is to pass. But in actual practice, abstentions by permanent members do not prevent a resolution from passing, only votes against it do. See the *UN Charter*, Article 27.

8. The USSR was an original permanent member of the Security Council. When the Soviet Union broke up in 1990, Russia adopted both the international prerogatives and the international responsibilities of the USSR, including the permanent seat.

9. See, for example, David Pilling, "Japan Urged to Cut Payments to UN," *Financial Times*, January 17, 2003.

10. See, for example, Kofi Annan, "Secretary-General's Address to the General Assembly, New York, 23 September 2003," accessed at http://www.un.org/apps/sg/sgstats.asp? nid=517.

11. The Secretary-General's High-level Panel, *A More Secure World*, p. 80.

12. Ibid., pp. 80–82.

13. "2005 World Summit Outcome," United Nations General Assembly Resolution A/60/L1 (New York: UN, 2005), Article 153.

14. See, for example, Joseph Kahn, "If 22 Million Chinese Prevail at U.N., Japan Won't," *New York Times*, April 1, 2005, Section A, p. 4.

15. Because of the creation of the International Criminal Court (ICC), which will be discussed briefly in the next chapter, these two tribunals are likely to be the last of their kind to operate under the auspices of the Security Council.

16. The Secretary-General's High-level Panel, *A More Secure World*, p. 91.

17. More information on the DPKO can be found at the organization's website, http://www.un.org/Depts/dpko/dpko/index.asp.

18. There are exceptions to this rule; for example, the Secretary-General's Special Representative for Kosovo is also head of the UN's Interim Administration Mission in Kosovo (UNMIK). But the Representative's authority over the mission comes from a Security Council resolution (resolution 1244), not from the Secretary-General.

19. Cf. Ch.5, fn. 19.

20. The AU was created in 2002, amalgamating the Organization of African Unity (OAU), an organization that dealt with regional collective security issues, and the African Economic Community.

21. Technically, the Organ on Politics, Defence and Security Co-operation of the SADC. See the Protocol on Politics, Defence and Security Co-operation to the Declaration and Treaty of SADC (2001), available online at http://www.sadc.int/index.php? action=a1001&page_id=protocols_politics.

22. A map of member and partner countries can be found at http://www.nato.int/icons/ map/b-worldmap.jpg.

23. The peace treaty did call on the Security Council to legitimize the peace treaty through a resolution, which it did. See "Security Council Resolution 1031 (1995) on implementation of the Peace Agreement for Bosnia and Herzegovina and the transfer of authority from the UN Protection Force to the multinational Implementation Force (IFOR)," United Nations Security Council S/RES/1031, December 15, 1995.

24. Security Council Resolution 1031. The OSCE is mentioned by name in Article 6. In Article 14, NATO is referred to as "the organization referred to in annex 1-A of the Peace Agreement," which is a rather unwieldy way of saying NATO.

25. This approval was forthcoming in "Security Council Resolution 1483," United Nations Security Council S/RES/1031, December 15, 1995.

26. On the various aspects of NATO's new mission, and its reorganization to achieve that mission, see NATO Office of Information and Press, *NATO Handbook* (Brussels: NATO, 2001).

27. At the time of writing.

Chapter 7   Human Rights and Humanitarian Aid

1. A fairly comprehensive list of these treaties can be found on the website of the Fletcher Multilaterals Project, a service of Tufts University's Fletcher School, at http://fletcher.tufts.edu/multi/humanRights.html.

2. For good general discussions of international human rights issues, see Jack Donnelly, *International Human Rights,* 2nd ed. (Boulder, CO: Westview Press, 1998) and David P. Forsythe, *Human Rights in International Relations* (Cambridge: Cambridge University Press, 2000).

3. See, for example, the *Convention against Torture and Other Cruel, Inhuman or Degrading Treatment or Punishment,* UN General Assembly RES 39/46 Annex (New York: UN, 1984), Articles 17 and 18, and the *International Convention on the Elimination of All Forms of Racial Discrimination,* 60 UNTS 195 (New York: UN, 1966), Article 8.

4. There are six of these bodies created by treaties covering economic, social and cultural rights, human rights, torture, racial discrimination, discrimination against women, and the rights of the child.

5. Office of the High Commissioner for Human Rights, "Commission on Human Rights," http://www.ohchr.org/english/bodies/chr/index.htm.

6. See, for example, Barry James, "Libya to Lead UN Human Rights Body; Tripoli Easily wins Vote US Demanded," *International Herald Tribune,* January 21, 2003, p. 1.

7. Including an expansion of the Commission from fifty-three members to all members of the UN, higher profile delegates, and more money. The Secretary-General's High-level Panel on Threats, Challenges and Change, *A More Secure World: Our Shared Responsibility* (New York: UN, 2004), p. 89 (quotation) and pp. 88–90 (recommendations).

8. United Nations General Assembly, *Resolution 48/141: High Commissioner for the Promotion and Protection of All Human Rights* (New York: UN, 1994).

9. Quoted in World Conference against Racism, "Basic Information: The World Conference against Racism, Racial Discrimination, Xenophobia and Related Intolerance," http://www.un.org/WCAR/e-kit/backgrounder1.htm.

10. See, for example, "Battling over Racism: The UN Racism Conference," *The Economist,* August 24, 2001. The *Durban Declaration and Programme of Action* can be found online at http://www.unhchr.ch/html/racism/02-documents-cnt.html.

11. On the role of NGO groups, or "advocacy networks," in the international politics of human rights, see Margaret E. Keck and Kathryn Sikkink, *Activists Beyond Borders: Advocacy Networks in International Politics* (Ithaca, NY: Cornell University Press, 1998).

12. The text of the *Convention for the Protection of Human Rights and Fundamental Freedoms* of the Council of Europe (the formal name for the European Convention on Human Rights), can be found at http://conventions.coe.int/treaty/en/Treaties/html/005.htm.

13. See, for example, European Court of Human Rights, "Subject Matter of Judgments delivered by the Court (Strassbourg: COE, 1999–2004)," http://www.echr.coe.int/Eng/Judgments.htm.

14. This argument is made in J. Samuel Barkin, "The Evolution of the Constitution of Sovereignty and the Emergence of Human Rights Norms," *Millennium* 27 (1998): 229–252.

15. See Daniel C. Thomas, *The Helsinki Effect: International Norms, Human Rights, and the Demise of Communism* (Princeton, NJ: Princeton University Press, 2001).

16. The ICC can try nationals of countries that have signed on to the Court, and people who have committed crimes within countries that have signed on to the Court. The ICC only has jurisdiction over crimes committed after the Court came into being. See the International Criminal Court, *Rome Statute of the International Criminal Court* (The Hague: ICC, 1998), Articles 11 and 12.

17. On the history of war crimes tribunals, see Gary Jonathan Bass, *Stay the Hand of Vengeance: The Politics of War-Crimes Tribunals* (Princeton, NJ: Princeton University Press, 2000).

18. The International Criminal Court, "Sitations and Cases," http://www.icc-cpi.int/cases.html.

19. For a brief statement on the U.S. government's position on the ICC, see United States Department of State, "Fact Sheet: The International Criminal Court," Office of War Crimes Issues, Washington, DC, May 6, 2002, available online at http://www.state.gov/s/wci/fs/2002/9978.htm.

20. United Nations Security Council, *Security Council Resolution 1593* (New York: UN, 2005).

21. The WFP does engage in what it calls development aid. This is still food aid, but it is targeted at long-term malnutrition rather than crisis starvation. In any case, this development aid accounted, as of 2001, for only 13 percent of expenditures. See World Food Programme, *WFP in Statistics – 2001* (Rome: WFP, 2003), table 1.

22. In a total budget of about $1.2 billion for 2003, the UNHCR was expecting $20 million from the UN regular budget. Office of the United Nations High Commissioner for Refugees, *Revised UNHCR Financial Requirements for 2003, In USD, April 25, 2003* (Geneva: UNHCR, 2003).

23. Even then, the idea was not a new one. The League of Nations had named a High Commissioner for Refugees in 1921.

24. The major exception to this rule is activities relating to Palestinian Refugees, which are undertaken by UNRWA, the United Nations Relief and Works Agency for Palestinian Refugees in the Near East.

25. United Nations High Commission for Refugees, *Basic Information About the UNHCR* (Geneva: UNHCR, 2001).

26. Figures for the breakdown of funding sources are for 2001, and are from "Contributions to 2001 UNHCR Programs (in United States Dollars): Situation as at 31 December 2001" (Geneva: UNHCR, 2002), available at www.unhcr.ch.

27. At the "Donate Online" link on the WFP's homepage at www.wfp.org. There is a similar "donor button" on the UNHCR's homepage at www.unhcr.ch.

28. Figures on amounts donated for the last several years can be found at "WFP Donors," http://www.wfp.org/appeals/Wfp_donors/index.asp?section=3&sub_section=4.

29. World Food Programme, "Frequently Asked Questions," viewed at http://www.wfp.org/aboutwfp/faq/.

30. The WFP figure is from "WFP in 2003: A Quick Glance" (Rome: WFP, 2003), viewed at http://www.wfp.org/aboutwfp/facts/2003/index.asp?section=1&sub_section=5. The UNHCR figure is from *Helping Refugees: An Introduction to UNHCR*, 2001 edition (Geneva: UNHCR, 2001). "Helped" can mean anything from providing food and shelter to providing legal advice.

31. This critique is made, among other places, in Michael Barnett and Martha Finnemore, "The Power, Politics, and Pathologies of International Organizations," *International Organization* 53 (1999): 699–732.

32. On the problems with food aid, see, *inter alia*, Edward Clay and Olav Stokke, eds., *Food Aid Reconsidered: Assessing the Impact on Third World Countries* (London: Frank Cass, 1991). For a more radical critique, see Michael Maren, *The Road to Hell: The Ravaging Effects of Foreign Aid and International Charity* (New York: Free Press, 1997).

33. See, for example, Adamantia Pollis, "Liberal, Socialist, and Third World Perspectives on Human Rights," in *Human Rights in the World Community*, ed. Richard Claude and Burns Weston, 2nd ed. (Philadelphia: University of Pennsylvania Press, 1992).

34. For an argument that the promotion of human rights internationally is in the United States' national interest, see William F. Schultz, *In Our Own Best Interest: How Defending Human Rights Benefits Us All* (Boston, MA: Beacon Press, 2001).

Chapter 8   Money, Trade, and Multilateralism

1. A good discussion of the negotiations that led to the creation of the GATT, as well as the IMF and World Bank, during and immediately after World War IIcan be found in Richard Gardner, *Sterling-Dollar Diplomacy: Anglo-American Collaboration in the Reconstruction of Multilateral Trade* (Oxford: Clarendon Press, 1956).

2. These include agreements on Sanitary and Phytosanitary Measures (SPS), Technical Barriers to Trade (TBT), and Trade-Related Investment Measures (TRIMs). A complete list of these agreements can be found at http://www.wto.org/english/docs_e/legal_e/legal_e.htm.

3. There are some exceptions to this rule, but these are either committees/councils that are strictly advisory in nature or that deal with rules that do not apply to all of the WTO's member countries. An example is the Committee on Trade in Civil Aircraft. A complete organizational chart of the WTO can be found at http://www.wto.org/english/thewto_e/whatis_e/tif_e/org2_e.htm.

4. Organizationally, it reports both to the General Council and to the Director-General.

5. This process worked smoothly in choosing the current Director-General, Pascal Lamy. In the previous attempt to choose a Director-General, developed and developing countries could not agree. The compromise reached was that the standard term would be split in half, the first half of which would be served by a New Zealander, Mike Moore, and the second half by a Thai, Supachai Panitchpakdi.

6. The member states of the EU have formally ceded control over tariff policy to the Union. As such, it is the EU that is the formal negotiating party at the WTO, rather than its member countries.

7. These commitments currently run to 30,000 pages (because existing members have made new commitments, and new members have joined the WTO), and can be found at http://www.wto.org/english/docs_e/legal_e/legal_e.htm.

8. In 2002, for example, the Fund ran a profit of about $450 million. See International Monetary Fund, *Annual Report 2002: Making the Global Economy Work for All* (Washington, DC: IMF, 2002), p. 156.

9. The current distribution of votes can be found at http://www.imf.org/external/np/sec/memdir/members.htm.

10. Italy and Canada are larger shareholders than Russia, and Italy is a larger shareholder than China, yet neither country has its own Executive Director.

11. For example, the Netherlands has 49 percent of the vote in its group, and the Director from this group is Dutch. The alternate is from the Ukraine, which holds the second largest bloc of votes in the group.

12. Figures are for fiscal year 2003, and are from International Monetary Fund, Office of Budget and Planning, *The FY 2004 Budget and the Medium-Term Framework* (Washington, DC: IMF, 2003), p. 6.

13. An organizational chart for the IMF can be found at http://www.imf.org/external/np/obp/orgcht.htm.

14. As of February, 2005. From IMF, "The IMF at a Glance: A Factsheet – February 2005," at http://www.imf.org/external/np/exr/facts/glance.htm. The IMF has its own internal accounting currency, the Special Drawing Right (SDR), but for convenience figures here are translated into US dollars.

15. IMF, "IMF Surveillance: A Factsheet – September 2004," http://www.imf.org/external/np/exr/facts/surv.htm.

16. Specific conditions agreed to between various countries and the IMF can be found at the "Country Information" gateway on the IMF's website, at http://www.imf.org/external/country/index.htm.

17. An explanation of conditionality by the IMF can be found in "IMF Conditionality: A Factsheet – April 2005," available at http://www.imf.org/external/np/exr/facts/conditio.htm.

18. For a general overview of criticisms of conditionality from the perspective of an international economist, see Joseph Stiglitz, *Globalization and Its Discontents* (New York: Norton, 2002).

19. Recall from Chapter 4 that in a perfect market, with perfectly specified property rights, the market will always produce the most efficient outcome, but different sets of property rights will result in different allocations of the wealth from that outcome. "Better" in this sense refers only to the efficiency of the outcome, and not to the appropriateness or fairness of the allocation of the benefits from this efficiency.

20. For a discussion of the role of international lender of last resort, see Charles Kindleberger, *Manias, Panics, and Crashes: A History of Financial Crises* (New York: Basic Books, 1978).

21. Criticism of the IMF on this point was particularly acute with respect to loans to Russia in the 1990s. See, for example, Zanny Minton Beddoes, "Why the IMF Needs Reform," *Foreign Affairs* 74 (May–June 1995): 123–133.

22. And seen as well at meetings of other related international regimes, particularly meetings of the G-8, an annual summit of the leaders of eight of the largest industrialized economies (the United States, Japan, Germany, France, the United Kingdom, Italy, Canada, and Russia).

23. See, for example, Stiglitz, *Globalization and Its Discontents.*

24. See World Trade Organization, *10 Common Misunderstandings About the WTO* (Geneva: WTO, 2002).

25. Although, as noted above, the IMF has indeed been criticized on occasion for making lending decisions on political criteria when these loans did not really make economic sense.

26. On both of these arguments, see Manuel Guitián, *The Unique Nature of the Responsibilities of the International Monetary Fund,* Pamphlet Series #46 (Washington, DC: IMF, 1992).

27. Leo Van Houtven, *Governance of the IMF: Decision-Making, Institutional Oversight, Transparency, and Accountability,* Pamphlet Series #53 (Washington, DC: International Monetary Fund, 2002).

28. Figures from World Intellectual Property Organization, *Annual Report 2001* (Geneva: WIPO, 2001).

29. More information on WIPO can be found at the organization's website, http://www.wipo.int.

30. For discussions of the Marshall Plan, see Michael Hogan, *The Marshall Plan: America, Britain, and the Reconstruction of Europe, 1947–1952* (Cambridge: Cambridge University Press, 1987) and Alan Milward, *The Reconstruction of Western Europe, 1945–51* (Berkeley: University of California Press, 1984).

31. This was not the OECD's first venture in this issue-area. It also sponsored the Convention on the Protection of Foreign Property in 1967.

32. See, for example, Kal Raustiala and David Victor, "The Regime Complex for Plant Genetic Resources," *International Organization* 58 (2004): 277–309.

Chapter 9 Development

1. A regional equivalent of the IMF for Asia was discussed in the wake of the East Asian financial crisis of 1997, but nothing came of the discussions.

2. The two acronyms are sometimes written as AsDB and AfDB in order to distinguish the institutions from each other.

3. The United States and Japan are tied at first place in the Asian Development Bank, with roughly 13 percent of the vote each (shares of the vote can be found at Asian Development Bank, "Members," http://www.adb.org/About/members.asp).

4. World Bank Group, *The World Bank Annual Report 2002*, vol. 1, *Year in Review* (Washington, DC: World Bank, 2002), pp. 8–9.

5. The best-known result of the World Bank's efforts to collect and disseminate information is its annual *World Development Reports*.

6. See, for example, Martha Finnemore, *National Interests in International Society* (Ithaca, NY: Cornell University Press, 1996).

7. Ibid.

8. On the Bank's efforts on the environment, see Tamar L. Gutner, *Banking on the Environment: Multilateral Development Banks and Their Environmental Performance in Central and Eastern Europe* (Cambridge, MA: MIT Press, 2002).

9. See, for example, World Bank, *10 Things You Never Knew About the World Bank* (Washington, DC: World Bank, 2002).

10. See, for example, World Bank, *Making Sustainable Commitments: An Environment Strategy for the World Bank* (Washington, DC: World Bank, 2001). On the mixed success of these efforts, see Gutner, *Banking on the Environment.*

11. An example of this change can be seen in the film *Our Friends at the Bank* (New York: First Run/Icarus Films, 1997), in which Ugandan officials tell Bank officials that they need money for roads, and the Bank officials respond that they prefer to loan money for education and social development programs.

12. For an example of this criticism from an environmental perspective, see Bruce Rich, *Mortgaging the Earth: The World Bank, Environmental Impoverishment, and the Crisis of Development* (Boston, MA: Beacon Press, 1994).

13. See, for example, Finnemore, *National Interests,* and Daniel Nielson and Michael Tierney, "Delegation to International Organizations: Agency Theory and World Bank Environmental Reform," *International Organization* 57 (2003): 241–276.

14. This terminology is not universally used—"development assistance" is sometimes used to cover both aid-granting institutions and the development lenders.

15. Specifically, the Technical Assistance Board and the United Nations Special Fund. For a history of this merger, see Ruben Mendez, "United Nations Development Programme," available from the United Nations Studies at Yale program, at http://www.yale.edu/unsy/UNDPhist.htm.

16. For a complete list of the UNDP's development priorities, see the United Nations Development Programme, "About UNDP: A World of Development Experience," http://www.undp.org/about/.

17. The UNDP lists its total resources for that year at $2.83 billion, including cofinancing, cost sharing, and income from trust funds. *United Nations Development Programme Annual Report 2003: A World of Development Experience* (New York: UNDP, 2003), p. 22. Co-financing means contribution from donor countries, and other organizations, to specific UNDP programs. Cost sharing means contributions from recipient countries to specific programs.

18. Ibid., p. 23.

19. For details of the various UNCTAD technical cooperation programs, see the "Technical Cooperation" section of UNCTAD's website at http://www.unctad.org.

20. The G-77 in fact grew out of the first UNCTAD meeting in 1964, and some G-77 projects, such as the Global System of Trade Preferences Among Developing Countries

(GSTP), are run through the UNCTAD Secretariat. Information on the GSTP can be found at its website, http://www.g77.org/gstp/index.htm.

21. For a discussion of the rise and fall of the NIEO, see Stephen Krasner, *Structural Conflict: The Third World against Global Liberalism* (Berkeley: University of California Press, 1985).

22. The primary process for doing this is through the United Nations Development Assistance Framework (UNDAF). For details about this program, see United Nations Development Assistance Framework, *UNDAF Guidelines* (New York: United Nations, 1999).

23. The multilateral development community has recently been coalescing around the idea of good governance, but it is not clear at this point to what extent this idea has been promoted independently by the IOs, and to what extent it reflects the policies of the major donor countries.

24. As of 2000. The five countries were Denmark, the Netherlands, Sweden, Norway, and Luxembourg. United Nations Development Programme, *Human Development Report 2002: Deepening Democracy in a Fragmented World* (New York: Oxford University Press, 2002), p. 202.

25. UNDP, *Human Development Report 2002*.

26. It may prove to be the case that the public aspect of this rift could be traced mostly to one figure, Joseph Stiglitz, during his tenure as Senior Vice President and Chief Economist at the World Bank, which he left in 2000. For his views, see his *Globalization and Its Discontents*. For a response from the IMF, see Kenneth Rogoff, "An Open Letter to Joseph Stiglitz," available at http://www.imf.org/external/np/vc/2002/070202.htm#1 (Dr. Rogoff is currently head of research at the IMF).

27. See, for example, United Nations Development Programme, "International Institutions Need Injection of Democracy," *Human Development Report 2002 News Release E-3*, July 24 (Manila: UNDP, 2002).

28. United Nations General Assembly, *Resolution 55/2: United Nations Millennium Declaration* (New York: UN, 2000).

Chapter 10   The Technical Details

1. Universal Postal Union, "UPU at a Glance," http://www.upu.int/about_us/en/glance.html.

2. Universal Postal Union, "Universal Postal Union: Frequently Asked Questions," http://www.upu.int/news_centre/en/faq.html.

3. UPU, "Frequently Asked Questions."

4. Specifically, 2 million Swiss francs and 20,000 Swiss francs, respectively.

5. International Civil Aviation Organization, "How It Works," http://www.icao.org/cgi/goto_m.pl?/icao/en/howworks.htm.

6. For a broader discussion of this topic, see Baldav Raj Nayar, "Regimes, Power, and International Aviation," *International Organization* 49 (1995): 139–170.

7. See, respectively, Article 2, paragraph 2 of the Kyoto Protocol to the United Nations Framework Convention on Climate Change, and International Civil Aviation Organization, *Council Resolution on Environmental Charges and Taxes* (Montreal: ICAO, 1996).

8. World Health Organization, *Constitution of the World Health Organization* (Geneva: WHO, 1994), Article 1.

9. For more information on the role of the WHO in the SARS outbreak, see the organization's SARS homepage, at http://www.who.int/csr/sars/en/index.html.

10. World Health Organization, *Financial Report and Audited Financial Statements for the Period 1 January 2000–31 December 2001 and Report of the External Auditor to the World Health Assembly* (Geneva: WHO, 2002).

11. *Constitution of the World Health Organization*, Article 24.

12. See, for example, F. Fenner, D. A. Henderson, I. Arita, Z. Jezek, and I. D. Ladnyi, *Smallpox and Its Eradication* (Geneva: WHO, 1988).

13. Eric Stein, "International Integration and Democracy: No Love at First Sight," *American Journal of International Law* 95 (2001): 498–499.

14. See, for example, World Health Organization, *Report of the Director-General, 2001* (Geneva: WHO, 2002).

15. Stein, "International Integration and Democracy."

16. Ibid., p. 497.

17. For more information on the Convention process, and on the WHO's Tobacco Free Initiative more broadly, see http://www.who.int/tobacco/en/.

18. The WHO's work on SARS, for example, in the end generated some quite good press. See, for example, Donald McNeil Jr. and Lawrence Altman, "As SARS Outbreak Took Shape, Health Agency Took Fast Action," *New York Times,* May 4, 2003, p. 1.

19. On the distinction between the coordination and PD game, see Duncan Snidal, "Coordination Versus Prisoners' Dilemma: Implications for International Cooperation and Regimes," *American Political Science Review* 79 (1985): 923–942.

20. On this debate, see Frank Biermann and Steffan Bauer, eds., *A World Environmental Organization: Solution or Threat for Effective International Environmental Governance?* (Aldershot: Ashgate, 2005). This volume discusses both sides of the debate.

21. See, respectively, *Convention on the Marking of Plastic Explosives for the Purpose of Detection,* accessible at http://untreaty.un.org/English/Terrorism/Conv10.pdf, and World Health Assembly Resolution WHA55.2, "Health Conditions of, and Assistance to, the Arab Population in the Occupied Arab Territories, Including Palestine," *Fifty-Fifth World Health Assembly,* Document WHA55/2002/REC/1 (Geneva: WHO, 2002).

Chapter 11   The Fuzzy Borders of Intergovernmentalism

1. Ernst Haas, *Beyond the Nation-State: Functionalism and International Organization* (Stanford: Stanford University Press, 1964).

2. For a more detailed version of this story, see Michael Fooner, *A Guide to Interpol: The International Criminal Police Organization in the United States* (Washington, D.C.: US Department of Justice, National Institute of Justice, 1985).

3. ICPO-Interpol, *Constitution* (Lyon: Interpol, 2004), Article 7.

4. Interpol, "Fact Sheet: Interpol's International Notices System," http://www.interpol.int/Public/ICPO/FactSheets/FS200105.asp.

5. Basic information about the ISO can be found through International Organization for Standardization, "Overview of the ISO System," http://www.iso.org/iso/en/aboutiso/introduction/index.html.

6. International Organization for Standardization, "ISO Members," http://www.iso.org/iso/en/ aboutiso/isomembers/index.html.

7. Steven Levy, "INTELSAT: Technology, Politics, and the Transformation of a Regime," *International Organization* 29 (1975): 655–680.

8. Jonathan Galloway, "Worldwide Corporations and International Integration: The Case of INTELSAT," *International Organization* 24 (1970): 503–519.

9. Levy, "INTELSAT."

10. Ibid.
11. Some of these investor companies are themselves government-owned, but are nonetheless investors in INTELSAT on a purely commercial basis.
12. "Privatization of INTELSAT," *American Journal of International Law* 95 (2001): 893–895.
13. World Conservation Union, *Statutes and Regulations* (Gland, Switzerland: IUCN, 2002), Article 2.
14. For NGOs dues depend on the organizations' operating expenditures. Figures are for dues for 2003, taken from World Conservation Union, *Membership Dues 2001–2005* (Gland, Switzerland: IUCN, 2001).
15. There are further complications in the voting structure within the categories; for example, national NGOs get one vote while international NGOs get two. For details see World Conservation Union, *Statutes and Regulations,* Articles 30–35.
16. World Conservation Union, *Statutes and Regulations,* Article 38.
17. The IUCN Species Survival Commission, *2004 IUCN Red List of Threatened Species: A Global Species Assessment,* ed. Jonathan E. M. Baillie, Craig Hilton-Taylor, and Simon N. Stuart (Cambridge: IUCN – World Conservation Union, 2004).
18. See, *inter alia,* Articles 8, 13, and 14 of the treaty, which can be found on the UNESCO website at http://whc.unesco.org/world_he.htm#debut.
19. At the time of writing, this translated into a U.S. contribution of $160 million, and a Madagascar contribution of $90, of a total ICRC budget of 830 million Swiss francs, or $590 million. International Committee of the Red Cross, *ICRC Annual Report 2001* (Geneva: ICRC, 2002), pp. 434–437.
20. François Bugnion, "The composition of the International Committee of the Red Cross," *International Review of the Red Cross* 307 (1995): 427–446.
21. In 1976, a majority of African countries boycotted the Olympics in Montreal to protest the participation of South African teams in some international competitions. In 1980, the United States led a boycott of the Olympics in Moscow to protest the Soviet invasion of Afghanistan. And in 1984, the USSR boycotted the Olympics in Los Angeles in retaliation for the 1980 boycott.
22. For a more detailed discussion of these rules, see International Olympic Committee, *Olympic Charter* (Lausanne: IOC, 2003).
23. International Olympic Committee, *2002 Marketing Fact File* (Lausanne: IOC, 2002).
24. International Committee of the Red Cross, "ICRC 2001 Financial Statements Meet International Accounting Standards—ICRC First Humanitarian Organization to Apply IAS," ICRC Press Release 02/45, August 16, 2002.

Chapter 12   Conclusions

1. Information on the UN Global Compact can be found at its website, http://www.unglobalcompact.org/.

References

Print Sources

Allison, Graham. *Essence of Decision: Explaining the Cuban Missile Crisis.* Boston, MA: Little, Brown, 1971.

Aron, William. "Science and the IWC." In *Toward a Sustainable Whaling Regime,* edited by Robert Friedheim, pp. 105–122. Seattle: University of Washington Press, 2001.

Bachrach, Peter, and Morton Baratz. "Two Faces of Power." *American Political Science Review* 56 (1962): 947–952.

Baldwin, David, ed. *Neorealism and Neoliberalism: The Contemporary Debate.* New York: Columbia University Press, 1993.

Barker, J. Craig. *International Law and International Relations.* New York: Continuum, 2000.

Barkin, J. Samuel. "The Evolution of the Constitution of Sovereignty and the Emergence of Human Rights Norms." *Millennium* 27 (1998): 229–252.

———. "Time Horizons and Multilateral Enforcement in International Cooperation." *International Studies Quarterly* 48 (2004): 363–382.

Barkin, J. Samuel, and Bruce Cronin. "The State and the Nation: Changing Norms and Rules of Sovereignty in International Relations." *International Organization* 48 (1994): 107–130.

Barkin, J. Samuel, and Elizabeth DeSombre. "Unilateralism and Multilateralism in International Fisheries Management." *Global Governance* 6 (2000): 339–360.

Barkin, J. Samuel, and George Shambaugh, eds. *Anarchy and the Environment: The International Relations of Common Pool Resources.* Albany: State University of New York Press, 1999.

Barnett, Michael. *Eyewitness to a Genocide: The United Nations and Rwanda.* Ithaca, NY: Cornell University Press, 2002.

Barnett, Michael, and Martha Finnemore. "The Power, Politics, and Pathologies of International Organizations." *International Organization* 53 (1999): 699–732.

Bass, Gary Jonathan. *Stay the Hand of Vengeance: The Politics of War-Crimes Tribunals.* Princeton, NJ: Princeton University Press, 2000.

"Battling over Racism: The UN Racism Conference." *The Economist,* August 24, 2001.

Beddoes, Zanny Minton. "Why the IMF Needs Reform." *Foreign Affairs* 74 (May–June 1995): 123–133.

Bernstein, Steven. *The Compromise of Liberal Environmentalism.* New York: Columbia University Press, 2001.

Bhagwati, Jagdish. *In Defense of Globalization.* New York: Oxford University Press, 2004.

Biermann, Frank, and Steffen Bauer. *A World Environmental Organization: Solution or Threat for Effective International Environmental Governance?* Aldershot: Ashgate, 2004.

Biersteker, Thomas, and Cynthia Weber, eds. *State Sovereignty as a Social Construct.* Cambridge: Cambridge University Press, 1996.

Bugnion, François. "The composition of the International Committee of the Red Cross." *International Review of the Red Cross* 307 (1995): 427–446.

Bull, Hedley. *The Anarchical Society: A Study of Order in World Politics*. London: Macmillan, 1977.

Burgerman, Susan. *Moral Victories: How Activists Provoke Multilateral Action*. Ithaca, NY: Cornell University Press, 2001.

Chayes, Abram, and Antonia Handler Chayes. "On Compliance." *International Organization* 47 (1993): 175–205.

———. *The New Sovereignty: Compliance with International Regulatory Agreements*. Cambridge, MA: Harvard University Press, 1995.

Chwieroth, Jeffrey. "A Capital Idea: The Role of Neoliberalism in the Liberalization of Finance in Emerging Markets." Santa Barbara: University of California at Santa Barbara PhD thesis, 2003.

Clapp, Jennifer. "Africa, NGOs, and the International Toxic Waste Trade." *Journal of Environment and Development* 3 (1994): 17–46.

Claude, Inis Jr. "Collective Legitimation as a Political Function of the United Nations." *International Organization* 20 (1966): 367–379.

———. *Swords into Plowshares*. 4th ed. New York: Random House, 1984.

Clay, Edward, and Olav Stokke, eds. *Food Aid Reconsidered: Assessing the Impact on Third World Countries*. London: Frank Cass, 1991.

Convention for the Conservation of Antarctic Marine Living Resources. *Basic Documents*. North Hobart, Australia: CCAMLR, 2004.

Cox, Robert, and Harold Jacobson, eds. *The Anatomy of Influence: Decision-Making in International Organization*. New Haven, CT: Yale University Press, 1973.

Dahl, Robert. *Who Governs? Democracy and Power in an American City*. New Haven, CT: Yale University Press, 1961.

DeSombre, Elizabeth. *The Global Environment and World Politics*. London: Continuum, 2002.

DeSombre, Elizabeth, and Joanne Kauffman. "The Montreal Protocol Multilateral Fund: Partial Success Story." In *Institutions for Environmental Aid: Pitfalls and Promise*, edited by Robert Keohane and Marc Levy. Cambridge, MA: MIT Press, 1996.

DeSombre, Elizabeth, and J. Samuel Barkin. "The Turbot War: Canada, Spain, and the Conflict over the North Atlantic Fishery." *PEW Case Studies in International Affairs*, Case Study #226. Washington, DC: Institute for the Study of Diplomacy, 2000.

———. "Turbot and Tempers in the North Atlantic." In *Conserving the Peace: Resources, Livelihoods, and Security*, edited by Richard Matthew, Mark Halle, and Jason Switzer. Winnipeg, MB: International Institute for Sustainable Development, 2002.

Diehl, Paul. *International Peacekeeping*. Baltimore: Johns Hopkins University Press, 1994.

DiMaggio, Paul, and Walter Powell. "The Iron Cage Revisited: Institutional Isomorphism and Collective Rationality in Organizational Fields." *American Sociological Review* 48 (1983): 147–160.

Dinan, Desmond. *Ever Closer Union: An Introduction to European Integration*. 2nd ed. Boulder, CO: Lynne Rienner, 1999.

Donnelly, Jack. *International Human Rights*. 2nd ed. Boulder, CO: Westview Press, 1998.

Downs, George, David Rocke, and Peter Barsoom. "Is the Good News About Compliance Good News About Cooperation?" *International Organization* 50 (1996): 379–406.

Drezner, Daniel. "Globalization and Policy Convergence." *International Studies Review* 3 (2001): 53–78.

Fearon, James. "Rationalist Explanations for War." *International Organization* 49 (1995): 379–414.

———. "Bargaining, Enforcement, and International Cooperation." *International Organization* 52 (1998): 269–306.

Fenner, F., D.A. Henderson, I. Arita, Z. Jezek, and I.D. Ladnyi. *Smallpox and Its Eradication.* Geneva: WHO, 1988.

Finnemore, Martha. *National Interests in International Society.* Ithaca, NY: Cornell University Press, 1996.

Fooner, Michael. *A Guide to Interpol: The International Criminal Police Organization in the United States.* Washington, DC: U.S. Department of Justice, National Institute of Justice, 1985.

Foot, Rosemary. *Rights Beyond Borders: The Global Community and the Struggle over Human Rights in China.* Oxford: Oxford University Press, 2000.

Forsythe, David, P. *Human Rights in International Relations.* Cambridge: Cambridge University Press, 2000.

Friedheim, Robert, ed. *Toward a Sustainable Whaling Regime.* Seattle: University of Washington Press, 2001.

Gallagher, Kevin, and Jacob Werksman, eds. *The Earthscan Reader on International Trade & Sustainable Development.* London: Earthscan, 2002.

Galloway, Jonathan. "Worldwide Corporations and International Integration: The Case of INTELSAT." *International Organization* 24 (1970): 503–519.

Gardner, Richard. *Sterling–Dollar Diplomacy: Anglo-American Collaboration in the Reconstruction of Multilateral Trade.* Oxford: Clarendon Press, 1956.

———. *Sterling–Dollar Diplomacy in Current Perspective: The Origins and the Prospects of Our International Economic Order.* New York: Columbia University Press, 1980.

General Agreement on Tariffs and Trade. *General Agreement on Tariffs and Trade: Text of the General Agreement.* Geneva: GATT, 1994.

Goldstein, Judith, Miles Kahler, Robert Keohane, and Anne-Marie Slaughter, eds. *Legalization and World Politics.* Cambridge, MA: MIT Press, 2001.

Gowa, Joanne. "Rational Hegemons, Excludable Goods, and Small Groups: An Epitaph for Hegemonic Stability Theory?" *World Politics* 41 (1989): 307–324.

Grieco, Joseph. "Anarchy and the Limits of Cooperation: A Realist Critique of the Newest Liberal Institutionalism." *International Organization* 42 (1988): 485–507.

Gruber, Lloyd. *Ruling the World: Power Politics and the Rise of Supranational Institutions.* Princeton, NJ: Princeton University Press, 2000.

Guitián, Manuel. *The Unique Nature of the Responsibilities of the International Monetary Fund.* Pamphlet Series #46. Washington, DC: IMF, 1992.

Gutner, Tamar L. *Banking on the Environment: Multilateral Development Banks and Their Environmental Performance in Central and Eastern Europe.* Cambridge, MA: MIT Press, 2002.

Haas, Ernst. *Beyond the Nation-State: Functionalism and International Organization.* Stanford: Stanford University Press, 1964.

———. "Is There a Hole in the Whole? Knowledge, Technology, Interdependence, and the Construction of International Regimes." *International Organization* 29 (1975): 827–876.

———. *When Knowledge Is Power.* Berkeley: University of California Press, 1990.

Haas, Peter. *Saving the Mediterranean: The Politics of International Environmental Cooperation.* New York: Columbia University Press, 1990.

———. "Introduction: Epistemic Communities and International Policy Coordination." *International Organization* 46 (1992): 1–35.

Haas, Peter, Robert Keohane, and Marc Levy, eds. *Institutions for the Earth: Sources of Effective International Environmental Protection.* Cambridge, MA: MIT Press, 1993.

Hall, Rodney Bruce. "Moral Authority as a Power Resource." *International Organization* 51 (1997): 555–589.

Henkin, Louis. *How Nations Behave: Law and Foreign Policy.* 2nd ed. New York: Columbia University Press, 1979.

Henton, Darcy. "Not so Picture Perfect." *Toronto Star,* June 4, 1998.

Hilsman, Roger, with Laura Gaughran and Patricia Weitsman. *The Politics of Policy-Making in Defense and Foreign Affairs: Conceptual Models and Bureaucratic Politics.* 3rd ed. Englewood Cliffs, NJ: Prentice Hall, 1993.

Hirschman, Albert O. *National Power and the Structure of Foreign Trade.* Berkeley: University of California Press, 1945.

Hoffmann, Stanley. "International Organization and the International System." *International Organization* 24 (1970): 389–413.

Hogan, Michael. *The Marshall Plan: America, Britain, and the Reconstruction of Europe, 1947–1952.* Cambridge: Cambridge University Press, 1987.

Hurd, Ian. "Legitimacy and Authority in International Politics." *International Organization* 53 (1999): 379–408.

Intergovernmental Panel on Climate Change. *Climate Change 2001: Impacts, Adaptation & Vulnerability.* Cambridge: Cambridge University Press, 2001.

———. *Climate Change 2001: Mitigation.* Cambridge: Cambridge University Press, 2001.

———. *Climate Change 2001: The Scientific Basis.* Cambridge: Cambridge University Press, 2001.

International Civil Aviation Organization. *Council Resolution on Environmental Charges and Taxes.* Montreal: ICAO, 1996.

International Committee of the Red Cross. *ICRC Annual Report 2001.* Geneva: ICRC, 2002.

———. "ICRC 2001 Financial Statements Meet International Accounting Standards – ICRC First Humanitarian Organization to Apply IAS." ICRC Press Release 02/45, August 16, 2002.

International Criminal Court. *Rome Statute of the International Criminal Court.* The Hague: ICC, 1998.

International Criminal Police Organization-Interpol. *Constitution.* Lyon: Interpol, 2004.

International Labour Organization. *Constitution.* Geneva: ILO, 2001 [1919].

International Monetary Fund. *Articles of Agreement of the International Monetary Fund.* Washington, DC: IMF, 1945.

———. *Annual Report 2001.* Washington, DC: IMF, 2001.

———. *Annual Report 2002: Making the Global Economy Work for All.* Washington, DC: IMF, 2002.

———. Office of Budget and Planning. *The FY 2004 Budget and the Medium-Term Framework.* Washington, DC: IMF, 2003.

International Olympic Committee. *2002 Marketing Fact File.* Lausanne: IOC, 2002.

———. *Olympic Charter.* Lausanne: IOC, 2003.

IUCN Species Survival Commission. *2004 IUCN Red List of Threatened Species: A Global Species Assessment,* edited by Jonathan E. M. Baillie, Craig Hilton-Taylor, and Simon N. Stuart. Cambridge: IUCN (The World Conservation Union), 2004.

Jackson, Robert. *Quasi-States: Sovereignty, International Relations, and the Third World.* Cambridge: Cambridge University Press, 1990.

Jacobson, Harold. *Networks of Interdependence.* New York: Alfred A. Knopf, 1979.

James, Barry. "Libya to Lead UN Human Rights Body; Tripoli Easily Wins Vote U.S. Demanded." *International Herald Tribune,* January 21, 2003, p. 1.

Jervis, Robert. *Perception and Misperception in International Politics.* Princeton, NJ: Princeton University Press, 1976.

———. "Security Regimes." *International Organization* 36 (1982): 357–378.

Joyner, Christopher. "Managing Common-Pool Marine Living Resources: Lessons from the Southern Ocean Experience." In *Anarchy and the Environment: The International Relations of Common Pool Resources,* edited by Samuel Barkin and George Shambaugh, pp. 70–96. Albany: State University of New York Press, 1999.

Kahn, Joseph. "Nations Back Freer Trade, Hoping to Aid Global Growth." *New York Times,* November 15, 2001, A12.

———. "If 22 Million Chinese Prevail at U.N., Japan Won't." *New York Times,* April 1, 2005, A4.

Katzenstein, Peter, Robert Keohane, and Stephen Krasner, eds. *Exploration and Contestation in the Study of World Politics.* Cambridge, MA: MIT Press, 1999.

Keck, Margaret, and Kathryn Sikkink. *Activists Beyond Borders: Advocacy Networks in International Politics.* Ithaca, NY: Cornell University Press, 1998.

Keith, Lim. *Black Helicopters over America: Strikeforce for the New World Order.* Lilburn, GA: IllumiNet Press, 1994.

Kennedy, David. "International Refugee Protection." *Human Rights Quarterly* 8 (1986): 1–9.

Keohane, Robert. "The Demand for International Regimes." *International Organization* 36 (1982): 325–356.

———. *After Hegemony: Cooperation and Discord in the World Political Economy.* Princeton, NJ: Princeton University Press, 1984.

———. "Reciprocity in International Relations." *International Organization* 40 (1986): 1–27.

———. "International Institutions: Two Approaches." *International Studies Quarterly* 32 (1988): 379–396.

Keohane, Robert, and Joseph Nye. *Power and Interdependence: World Politics in Transition.* Boston, MA: Little, Brown, 1977.

———. *Power and Interdependence.* 3rd ed. New York: Longman, 2001.

Kindleberger, Charles. *Manias, Panics, and Crashes: A History of Financial Crises.* New York: Basic Books, 1978.

Knorr, Klaus. "Supranational Versus International Models for General and Complete Disarmamant." In *The Strategy of World Order.* Vol. IV, *Disarmament and Economic Development,* edited by Richard Falk and Saul Mendlovitz. New York: World Law Fund, 1966, pp. 326–353.

Krasner, Stephen. *Defending the National Interest: Raw Materials Investment and U.S. Foreign Policy.* Princeton, NJ: Princeton University Press, 1978.

———, ed. *International Regimes.* Ithaca, NY: Cornell University Press, 1983.

———. "Structural Causes and Regime Consequences: Regimes as Intervening Variables." In *International Regimes,* edited by Stephen Krasner, pp. 1–21. Ithaca, NY: Cornell University Press, 1983.

———. *Structural Conflict: The Third World against Global Liberalism.* Berkeley: University of California Press, 1985.

———. "Global Communications and National Power: Life on the Pareto Frontier." *World Politics* 43 (1991): 336–366.

———. "Westphalia and All That." In *Ideas and Foreign Policy: Beliefs, Institutions, and Political Change,* edited by Judith Goldstein and Robert Keohane, pp. 235–264. Ithaca, NY: Cornell University Press, 1993.

———. *Sovereignty: Organized Hypocrisy.* Princeton, NJ: Princeton University Press, 1999.

Kratochwil, Friedrich, and John Gerard Ruggie. "International Organization: A State of the Art on an Art of the State." *International Organization* 40 (1986): 753–775.

Leonard, H. Jeffrey. *Pollution and the Struggle for World Product: Multinational Corporations, Environment, and International Comparative Advantage.* Cambridge: Cambridge University Press, 1988.

Levy, Steven. "INTELSAT: Technology, Politics, and the Transformation of a Regime." *International Organization* 29 (1975): 655–680.

Lindberg, Leon, and Stuart Scheingold. *Europe's Would-Be Polity: Patterns of Change in the European Community*. Englewood Cliffs, NJ: Prentice Hall, 1970.

Lukes, Steven. *Power: A Radical View*. London: Macmillan, 1974.

Mander, Jerry, and Edward Goldsmith, eds. *The Case against the Global Economy: And for a Turn Toward the Local*. San Francisco: Sierra Club Books, 1996.

March, James. *Decisions and Organizations*. Boston, MA: Basil Blackwell, 1988.

March, James, and Johan Olsen. *Rediscovering Institutions: The Organizational Basis of Politics*. New York: Free Press, 1989.

———. "The Institutional Dynamics of International Political Orders." *International Organization* 52 (1998): 943–969.

Maren, Michael. *The Road to Hell: The Ravaging Effects of Foreign Aid and International Charity*. New York: Free Press, 1997.

Mearsheimer, John. "The False Promise of International Institutions." *International Security* 19 (1994–95): 5–49.

McNeil, Donald, Jr., and Lawrence Altman. "As SARS Outbreak Took Shape, Health Agency Took Fast Action." *New York Times*, May 4, 2003, p. 1.

Miles, Edward, Arild Underdal, Steinar Andresen, Jorgen Wettestad, Tora Skodvin, and Elaine Carlin. *Environmental Regime Effectiveness*. Cambridge, MA: MIT Press, 2001.

Milliken, Jennifer. "The Study of Discourse in International Relations: A Critique of Research and Methods." *European Journal of International Relations* 5 (1999): 225–254.

Milward, Alan. *The Reconstruction of Western Europe, 1945–51*. Berkeley: University of California Press, 1984.

Mitchell, Ronald. *Intentional Oil Pollution at Sea: Environmental Policy and Treaty Compliance*. Cambridge, MA: MIT Press, 1994.

———. "Sources of Transparency: Information Systems in International Regimes." *International Studies Quarterly* 42 (1998): 109–130.

Monaco Agreement on the Conservation of Cetaceans in the Black Sea, Mediterranean Sea and Contiguous Atlantic Areas. *ACCOBAMS Bulletin #3*. Monaco: Interim ACCOBAMS Secretariat, 2000.

Moravcsik, Andrew. *The Choice for Europe: Social Purpose and State Power from Messina to Maastricht*. Ithaca, NY: Cornell University Press, 1998.

Najam, Adil. "The Case against a New International Environmental Organization." *Global Governance* 9 (2003): 367–384.

NATO Office of Information and Press. *NATO Handbook*. Brussels: NATO, 2001.

Nayar, Baldav Raj. "Regimes, Power, and International Aviation." *International Organization* 49 (1995): 139–170.

Nielson, Daniel L., and Michael J. Tierney. "Delegation to International Organizations: Agency Theory and World Bank Environmental Reform." *International Organization* 57 (2003): 241–276.

North, Douglass. *Structure and Change in Economic History*. New York: Norton, 1981.

North, Douglass, and Robert Paul Thomas. *The Rise of the Western World: A New Economic History*. Cambridge: Cambridge University Press, 1973.

Nye, Joseph. *Bound to Lead: The Changing Nature of American Power*. New York: Basic Books, 1990.

Olson, Mancur. *The Logic of Collective Action: Public Goods and the Theory of Groups*. Cambridge, MA: Harvard University Press, 1965.

Onuf, Nicholas. *World of Our Making: Rules and Rule in Social Theory and International Relations*. Columbia: University of South Carolina Press, 1989.

Oye, Kenneth, ed. *Cooperation under Anarchy.* Princeton, NJ: Princeton University Press, 1986.

Pilling, David. "Japan Urged to Cut Payments to UN." *Financial Times,* January 17, 2003.

Pollack, Mark A. *The Engines of European Integration: Delegation, Agency, and Agenda Setting in the EU.* New York: Oxford University Press, 2003.

Pollis, Adamantia. "Liberal, Socialist, and Third World Perspectives on Human Rights." In *Human Rights in the World Community,* edited by Richard Claude and Burns Weston. 2nd ed. Philadelphia: University of Pennsylvania Press, 1992.

"Privatization of INTELSAT." *American Journal of International Law* 95 (2001): 893–895.

Raustiala, Kal, and David Victor. "The Regime Complex for Plant Genetic Resources." *International Organization* 58 (2004): 277–309.

Rich, Bruce. *Mortgaging the Earth: The World Bank, Environmental Impoverishment, and the Crisis of Development.* Boston, MA: Beacon Press, 1994.

Risse, Thomas, Stephen Ropp, and Kathryn Sikkink, eds. *The Power of Human Rights: International Norms and Domestic Change.* Cambridge: Cambridge University Press, 1999.

Rohde, David. "Ted Turner Plans a $1 Billion Gift for U.N. Agencies." *New York Times,* September 19, 1997, A1.

Ruggie, John Gerard. "Multilateralism: The Anatomy of an Institution." *International Organization* 46 (1992): 561–598.

———, ed. *Multilateralism Matters: The Theory and Praxis of an Institutional Form.* New York: Columbia University Press, 1993.

Ryan, Stephen. *The United Nations and International Politics.* New York: St. Martin's Press, 2000.

Sampson, Gary P., and W. Bradnee Chambers, eds. *Trade, Environment, and the Millennium.* Tokyo: United Nations University Press, 1999.

Schmitter, Philippe. "Three Neo-Functionalist Hypotheses about International Integration." *International Organization* 23 (1969): 161–166.

Scholte, Jan Aart. *Globalisation: A Critical Introduction.* Houndmills, Hampshire: Palgrave, 2000.

Schultz, William F. *In Our Own Best Interest: How Defending Human Rights Benefits Us All.* Boston, MA: Beacon Press, 2001.

Secretary-General. *Renewing the United Nations: A Programme for Reform.* New York: United Nations General Assembly A/51/950, 1997.

———. *Strengthening the United Nations: An Agenda for Further Change.* New York: United Nations General Assembly A/57/387, 2002.

Shanks, Cheryl, Harold Jacobson, and Jeffrey Kaplan. "Inertia and Change in the Constellation of International Governmental Organizations, 1981–1992." *International Organization* 50 (1996): 593–628.

Simmons, Beth. "The International Politics of Harmonization: The Case of Capital Market Regulation." *International Organization* 55 (2001): 589–620.

Sinnar, Shirin. "Mixed Blessing: The Growing Influence of NGOs." *Harvard International Review* 18, no.1 (Winter 1995–96): 54–57.

Smith, Thomas W. "The New Law of War: Legitimizing Hi-Tech and Infrastructural Violence." *International Studies Quarterly* 46 (2002): 355–374.

Snidal, Duncan. "Coordination Versus Prisoners' Dilemma: Implications for International Cooperation and Regimes." *American Political Science Review* 79 (1985): 923–942.

Snyder, Glenn, and Paul Diesing. *Conflict among Nations: Bargaining, Decision Making, and System Structure in International Crises.* Princeton, NJ: Princeton University Press, 1977.

Stein, Eric. "International Integration and Democracy: No Love at First Sight." *American Journal of International Law* 95 (2001): 498–499.

Stiglitz, Joseph. *Globalization and Its Discontents.* New York: Norton, 2002.

Strange, Susan. "*Cave, Hic Dragones:* A Critique of Regime Analysis." *International Organization* 36 (1982): 479–496.

Susskind, Lawrence. *Environmental Diplomacy: Negotiating More Effective Global Agreements.* New York: Oxford University Press, 1994.

Thomas, Daniel C. *The Helsinki Effect: International Norms, Human Rights, and the Demise of Communism.* Princeton, NJ: Princeton University Press, 2001.

Thomson, Janice. "State Sovereignty in International Relations: Bridging the Gap between Theory and Empirical Research." *International Studies Quarterly* 39 (1995): 213–234.

Union of International Organizations. *Yearbook of International Organizations, 2004–2005,* vol. 5. Munich: K.G. Saur, 2004.

United Nations. "Convention (IV) Relative to the Protection of Civilian Persons in Time of War." *United Nations Treaty Series* No. 973, vol. 75. Geneva: UN, 1949.

———. *Charter of the United Nations.* New York: UN, 1965.

———. *International Convention on the Elimination of All Forms of Racial Discrimination,* 60 UNTS 195. New York: UN, 1966.

———. "Secretary-General's High-Level Panel on Threats, Challenges and Change." *A More Secure World: Our Shared Responsibility.* New York: UN, 2004.

———. "United Nations Peacekeeping Operations." United Nations Department of Public Information (DPI/1634/Rev. 39), August 2004.

United Nations Children's Fund. *2001 UNICEF Annual Report.* New York: UNICEF, 2001.

United Nations Development Assistance Framework. *UNDAF Guidelines.* New York: UN, 1999.

United Nations Development Programme. *Human Development Report 2002: Deepening Democracy in a Fragmented World.* New York: Oxford University Press, 2002.

———. "International Institutions Need Injection of Democracy." *Human Development Report 2002 News Release E-3,* July 24. Manila: UNDP, 2002.

———. *United Nations Development Programme Annual Report 2003: A World of Development Experience.* New York: UNDP, 2003.

United Nations Environment Programme. *UNEP Annual Report 1999.* Nairobi: UNEP, 2000.

United Nations General Assembly. *Convention Against Torture and Other Cruel, Inhuman or Degrading Treatment or Punishment.* UN General Assembly RES 39/46 Annex. New York: UN, 1984.

———. *Resolution 48/141: High Commissioner for the Promotion and Protection of All Human Rights.* New York: UN, 1994.

———. *Resolution 55/2: United Nations Millennium Declaration.* New York: UN, 2000.

———. *Resolution 55/5: Scale of Assessments for the Apportionment of the Expenses of the United Nations.* New York: UN, 2001.

———. *Resolution 60/1: 2005 World Summit Outcome.* New York: UN, 2005.

United Nations High Commission for Refugees. *Basic Information about the UNHCR.* Geneva: UNHCR, 2001.

———. *Helping Refugees: An Introduction to UNHCR.* Geneva: UNHCR, 2001.

———. *Revised UNHCR Financial Requirements for 2003, in USD, April 25, 2003.* Geneva: UNHCR, 2003.

United Nations Security Council. *Repertoire of the Practice of the Security Council.* Serial. New York: UN, 1946–present,

———. *Security Council Resolution 1031 on Implementation of the Peace Agreement for Bosnia and Herzegovina and the Transfer of Authority from the UN Protection Force to the Multinational Implementation Force (IFOR).* New York: UN, 1995.

————. *Security Council Resolution 1368.* New York: UN, 2001.

————. *Security Council Resolution 1373.* New York: UN, 2001.

————. *Security Council Resolution 1483.* New York: UN, 2003.

————. *Security Council Resolution 1593.* New York: UN, 2005.

Van Houtven, Leo. *Governance of the IMF: Decision-Making, Institutional Oversight, Transparency, and Accountability.* Pamphlet Series #53. Washington, DC: IMF, 2002.

Wapner, Paul. *Environmental Activism and World Civic Politics.* Albany: State University of New York Press, 1996.

Wendt, Alexander. *Social Theory of International Politics.* Cambridge: Cambridge University Press, 1999.

World Bank Group. *Making Sustainable Commitments: An Environment Strategy for the World Bank.* Washington, DC: World Bank, 2001.

————. *World Development Indicators 2001.* Washington, DC: World Bank, 2001.

————. *10 Things You Never Knew About the World Bank.* Washington, DC: World Bank, 2002.

————. *The World Bank Annual Report 2002.* Vol. 1, *Year in Review.* Washington, DC: World Bank, 2002.

World Conservation Union. *Membership Dues 2001–2005.* Gland, Switzerland: IUCN, 2001.

————. *Statutes and Regulations.* Gland, Switzerland: IUCN, 2002.

World Food Programme. *WFP in Statistics – 2001.* Rome: WFP, 2003.

World Health Organization. *Constitution of the World Health Organization.* Geneva: WHO, 1994.

————. *World Health Report 2001 – Mental Health: New Understanding, New Hope.* Geneva: WHO, 2001.

————. *Financial Report and Audited Financial Statements for the Period 1 January 2000–31 December 2001 and Report of the External Auditor to the World Health Assembly.* Geneva: WHO, 2002.

————. "Health Conditions of, and Assistance to, the Arab Population in the Occupied Arab Territories, Including Palestine." *Fifty-Fifth World Health Assembly.* Document WHA55/2002/REC/1. Geneva: WHO, 2002.

————. *Report of the Director-General, 2001.* Geneva: WHO, 2002.

World Intellectual Property Organization. *Annual Report 2001.* Geneva: WIPO, 2001.

World Trade Organization. *10 Common Misunderstandings about the WTO.* Geneva: WTO, 2002.

Young, Oran, ed. *The Effectiveness of International Environmental Agreements.* Cambridge, MA: MIT Press, 1999.

Film Source

Our Friends at the Bank. New York: First Run/Icarus Films, 1997.

Web Sources

Please note: All web sources are current as of May 12, 2005.

Annan, Kofi. "Secretary-General's Address to the General Assembly, New York, September 23, 2003." http://www.un.org/apps/sg/sgstats.asp?nid=517.

Asian Development Bank. "Members." http://www.adb.org/About/members.asp.

Bureau of Arms Control. *Fact Sheet: The Biological Weapons Convention.* Washington: U.S. Department of State, released on May 22, 2002. http://www.state.govt/ac/rls/fs/10401.htm.

Commission Centrale Pour la Navigation du Rhin. "Background History." http://www.ccr-zkr.org/.

Convention between the United States, Great Britain, Russia and Japan for the Preservation and Protection of Fur Seals (1911). http://fletcher.tufts.edu/multi/sealtreaty.html.

Convention Concerning the Protection of the World Cultural and Natural Heritage. http://whc.unesco.org/world_he.htm#debut.

Convention on the Marking of Plastic Explosives for the Purpose of Detection. http://untreaty.un.org/English/Terrorism/Conv10.pdf.

Council of Europe. *Convention for the Protection of Human Rights and Fundamental Freedoms.* http://conventions.coe.int/treaty/en/Treaties/html/005.htm.

European Court of Human Rights. "Subject Matter of Judgments Delivered by the Court." Strassbourg: Council of Europe, 1999–2004. http://www.echr.coe.int/Eng/Judgments.htm.

Group of 77. www.g77.org.

International Campaign to Ban Landmines. "Text of the Mine Ban Treaty." http://www.icbl.org/treaty/text.

International Civil Aviation Organization. "Facts About the ICAO." http://www.icao.org/cgi/goto.pl?icao/en/download.htm.

———. "How It Works." http://www.icao.org/cgi/goto_m.pl?/icao/en/howworks.htm.

———. "Legal Bureau." http://www.icao.int/icao/en/leb/.

———. "Technical Cooperation Bureau." http://www.icao.int/icao/en/tcb/.

International Court of Justice. "Declarations Recognizing as Compulsory the Jurisdiction of the Court." http://www.icj-cij.org/icjwww/ibasicdocuments/ibasictext/ibasicdeclarations.htm.

International Criminal Court. "Situations and Cases." http://www.icc-cpi.int/cases.html.

International Institute for Sustainable Development. *Earth Negotiation Bulletin.* http://www.iisd.ca.

International Monetary Fund. "About the IMF." http://www.imf.org/external/about.htm.

———. "The IMF at a Glance: A Factsheet – February 2005." http://www.imf.org/external/np/exr/facts/glance.htm.

———. "IMF Conditionality: A Factsheet – April 2005." http://www.imf.org/external/np/exr/facts/conditio.htm.

———. "IMF Members' Quotas and Voting Power, and IMF Board of Governors." http://www.imf.org/external/np/sec/memdir/members.htm.

———. "IMF Organization Chart (as of November 2003)." http://www.imf.org/external/np/obp/orgcht.htm.

———. "IMF Surveillance: A Factsheet – September 2004." http://www.imf.org/external/np/exr/facts/surv.htm.

International Organization for Standardization. "ISO Members." http://www.iso.org/iso/en/aboutiso/isomembers/index.html.

———. "Overview of the ISO System." http://www.iso.org/iso/en/aboutiso/introduction/index.html.

Interpol. "Fact Sheet: Interpol's International Notices System." http://www.interpol.int/Public/ICPO/FactSheets/FS200105.asp.

Mendez, Ruben. "United Nations Development Programme." http://www.yale.edu/unsy/UNDPhist.htm.

Office of the United Nations High Commissioner for Human Rights. "Commission on Human Rights." http://www.ohchr.org/english/bodies/chr/index.htm.

Rogoff, Kenneth. "An Open Letter to Joseph Stiglitz." http://www.imf.org/external/np/vc/2002/070202.htm#1.

South African Development Community. "Protocol on Politics, Defence and Security Co-operation to the Declaration and Treaty of SADC (2001)." http://www.sadc.int/index.php?action=a1001&page_id=protocols_politics.

United Nations. "Reform at the UN." http://www.un.org/reform/index.html.

United Nations Conference on Trade and Development. "Technical Cooperation." http://www.unctad.org.

United Nations Department of Peacekeeping Operations. "United Nations Peacekeeping." http://www.un.org/Depts/dpko/dpko/index.asp.

United Nations Department of Public Information. "Special and Personal Representatives and Envoys of the Secretary-General." http://www.un.org/News/ossg/srsg/.

———. "The United Nations System." http://www.un.org/aboutun/chart.html.

United Nations Development Programme. "About UNDP: A World of Development Experience." http://www.undp.org/about/.

United Nations Global Compact. "The Global Compact." http://www.unglobalcompact.org/.

United Nations High Commission for Refugees. "UNHCR Headquarters Structure." http://www.unhcr.ch/cgi-bin/texis/vtx/admin.

———. "Contributions to 2001 UNHCR Programs (in United States Dollars): Situation as at 31 December 2001." Geneva: UNHCR. www.unhcr.ch.

United Nations Office on Drugs and Crime. "About Us." http://www.unodc.org/unodc/about.html.

United States Department of State. "Fact Sheet: The International Criminal Court." Office of War Crimes Issues, Washington DC, May 6, 2002, http://www.state.gov/s/wci/fs/2002/9978.htm.

Universal Postal Union. "Universal Postal Union: Frequently Asked Questions." http://www.upu.int/news_centre/en/faq.html.

———. "UPU at a Glance." http://www.upu.int/about_us/en/glance.html.

World Conference against Racism. "Basic Information: The World Conference against Racism, Racial Discrimination, Xenophobia and Related Intolerance." http://www.un.org/WCAR/e-kit/backgrounder1.htm.

———. Durban Declaration and Programme of Action. http://www.unhchr.ch/html/racism/02-documents-cnt.html.

World Food Programme. "WFP Donors." http://www.wfp.org/appeals/Wfp_donors/index.asp?section=3&sub_section=4.

———. "Frequently Asked Questions." http://www.wfp.org/aboutwfp/faq/.

———. "WFP in 2003: A Quick Glance." Rome: WFP, 2003, http://www.wfp.org/aboutwfp/facts/2003/index.asp?section=1&sub_section=5.

World Trade Organization. "China to Join on 11 December, Chinese Taipei's Membership Also Approved." Doha WTO Ministerial 2001: Summary of 11 November 2001. http://www.wto.org/english/thewto_e/minist_e/min01_e/min01_11nov_e.htm.

———. "A Summary of the Final Act of the Uruguay Round." http://www.wto.org/english/docs_e/legal_e/ursum_e.htm.

———. "WTO Legal Texts." http://www.wto.org/english/docs_e/legal_e/legal_e.htm.

———. "WTO Organizational Chart." http://www.wto.org/english/thewto_e/whatis_e/tif_e/org2_e.htm.

Index

LINDA YUEH is an ...st, broadcaster, and author. She holds senior a... positions at Oxford University, London Busi... ...l, and the London School of Economics and ...cience. She was an anchor/correspondent at ... and Bloomberg TV. Linda is a widely published ...and serves as editor of a book series on econom... ...h and development.

Additional Praise for *What Would the Great Economists Do?*

"An extremely engaging survey of the lifetimes and ideas of the great thinkers of economic history, woven together with useful discussions of how their ideas still shape economic policy today. Yueh's book is reminiscent of Heilbroner's marvelous classic *The Worldly Philosophers*, but more focused on contemporary debates on inequality, trade, and productivity. Although targeted at readers interested in economic issues, this book would also make an excellent supplementary reading for undergraduate courses in economics, politics, and social studies."

—Kenneth Rogoff, Thomas D. Cabot Professor of Public Policy and Economics at Harvard University, former chief economist at the IMF, and the author of *The Curse of Cash*

"What would the great economists of the past make of today's problems? Linda Yueh takes on this ambitious task in this engaging book, introducing us to the work of each economist and conjecturing how they might have advised us. This book is a very readable introduction to the lives and thinking of the greats, and reminds us that policymakers continue to be, as Keynes wrote, 'slaves of some defunct economist.'"

—Raghuram Rajan, professor of economics at the University of Chicago, and author of *Fault Lines: How Hidden Fractures Still Threaten the World Economy*

"A timely and original guide to some of the key economic challenges facing society."   —Robert A. Cord, editor of *The Palgrave Companion to Cambridge Economics*

"Is economics a science in which each new generation's discoveries build on those of the old, or a humanistic study in which old ideas remain valid and relevant today? Linda Yueh's account of the thinking of the great economists demonstrates that both perspectives are true."

—John Kay, professor of economics at the London School of Economics, and author of *Other People's Money: The Real Business of Finance*

"A great way to learn in an easily readable manner about some of the greatest economic influences of the past, but also a good way to test your own a priori assumptions about some of the big challenges of our time."   —Jim O'Neill, former UK Treasury minister and chief economist at Goldman Sachs who coined the acronym "BRIC" to describe the emerging economies of Brazil, Russia, India, and China

"This well-written book provides more than an engaging discussion of how the 'Great Economists' changed the course of economic thinking and history. It links their insights to current economic challenges, assessing how their unique contributions can improve future well-being. It concludes by artfully bringing together the economists' individual insights to shed light on the backlash against globalization. Read it not only to learn about the world's great economists, but also to see how consequential thought innovations can be, and have been."   —Mohamed A. El-Erian, chief economic adviser at Allianz, and former CEO of PIMCO

"I certainly wish that it had been around when I started to study the subject."   —Dr. Matthew Partridge, *MoneyWeek*

"Readable, informative, and thought-provoking."
                                        —*Booklist* (starred review)

"A highly accessible and lively evaluation of the global financial crisis through the work of twelve top economists, from Adam Smith to John Maynard Keynes. Yueh . . . has a way of simplifying the arcane and ferreting out good news—of which we need a lot."
                    —*Newsweek*, "Best 50 Books of 2018 (so far)"

"To anyone with even a passing interest in the economic problems, large and small, affecting us today, *What Would the Great Economists Do?* comes at the right time: a highly accessible and acute guide to thinking and learning, from the men and woman whose work can inform and ultimately aid us in understanding the great national and global crises we're living through."
            —Nouriel Roubini, author of the *New York Times* bestselling *Crisis Economics: A Crash Course in the Future of Finance*

What Would the
Great Economists Do?

*How Twelve Brilliant Minds
Would Solve Today's Biggest Problems*

LINDA YUEH

Picador | New York

picadorusa.com • instagram.com/picador
twitter.com/picadorusa • facebook.com/picadorusa

Picador® is a U.S. registered trademark and is used by Macmillan
Publishing Group, LLC, under license from Pan Books Limited.

For book club information, please visit facebook.com/picadorbookclub
or email marketing@picadorusa.com.

The Library of Congress has cataloged the hardcover edition as follows:

Names: Yueh, Linda Y. (Linda Yi-Chuang), author.
Title: What would the great economists do? : how twelve brilliant minds would
solve today's biggest problems / Linda Yueh.
Description: First U.S Edition. | New York : Picador, 2018. | Includes
bibliographical references and index.
Identifiers: LCCN 2018001346 | ISBN 9781250180537 (hardcover) |
ISBN 9781250180551 (ebook)
Subjects: LCSH: Economists—History. | Economics—History. | Economics—
Philosophy. | Economic history.
Classification: LCC HB75 .Y85 2018 | DDC 330.15092/2—dc23
LC record available at https://lccn.loc.gov/2018001346

Picador Paperback ISBN 978-1-250-18054-4

Our books may be purchased in bulk for promotional, educational, or business
use. Please contact your local bookseller or the Macmillan Corporate
and Premium Sales Department at 1-800-221-7945, extension 5442,
or by email at MacmillanSpecialMarkets@macmillan.com.

Originally published in Great Britain as *The Great Economists* by Viking,
a part of Penguin Random House group of companies

First published in the United States by Picador

First Picador Paperback Edition: June 2019

D   10   9   8   7   6   5   4   3

To my family

Contents

Introduction: Great Economists on Our Economic Challenges

During times of fundamental change, economic expertise is in demand. Who better to help shape our economic future than the Great Economists? Their thinking transformed the modern economy into one characterized by unprecedented prosperity, relatively speaking, in even the poorest countries. Those ideas from the past can help guide us as we confront today's economic challenges.

Now is an ideal time to assess where the world economy is headed. Having come through the global financial crisis of 2008 and the Great Recession that followed it, the US, Britain, the European Union, Japan, China, and others are experiencing significant challenges to growing their economies and generating wealth. America, for long the leading economic engine of the world, faces the prospect of slowing growth as slow wage growth weighs on its future. In Britain, weak productivity growth and the historic referendum of June 2016 that resulted in a vote to leave the European Union will affect the country's economy for years to come. The EU, meanwhile, faces difficult questions about how to reform the euro area's economy to generate growth while sharing a single currency, the euro. Concerns over slow growth have long confronted Japan, which is at the forefront of a number of innovative economic policies to energize its sluggish economy, while China, too, faces structural challenges as it attempts to join the ranks of the world's rich countries. Emerging economies such as those in Asia, Africa, Latin America, and eastern Europe are also in the spotlight. After years of strong growth, they are slowing down, which raises the question whether these nations will have enough economic momentum left to eradicate poverty within their borders. Yet, we also live during a time of rapid technological change, much like the previous Industrial Revolutions that raised our living standards. We'll also consider what drives innovation and how to increase economic growth.

★

Who, then, were these Great Economists whose theories changed the world and whose ideas can help us with our challenges today? It was a difficult choice to make. Applying the criterion that their work must have direct implications for our current economic problems helped a little, but there remain many not on my list who might arguably have been included. Hyman Minsky, for example, who is discussed in the Irving Fisher chapter because the pair's combined thinking helps us better to understand the nature of financial crises. And Paul Samuelson's ideas on the distributional impact of international trade builds on the work of David Ricardo, so his thinking provides considerable insight into how those who have lost out in the globalization process discussed in the Epilogue might better manage their predicament.

This leads on to my second qualifier, which is that my selections also reflect the issues that I have chosen to focus on. Choices had to be made, so I have whittled a huge list down to one that is centred on economic growth – that is, the rate and the quality of development. How economies grow will be affected by the policy choices taken after the worst banking crash in a century and in the context of a globalized world. The 2008 financial crisis and the rise of emerging markets are among the fundamental factors in the past few decades that have transformed and will continue to reshape the world economy. The crisis showed that some of the old ways of growing an economy are unsustainable, while the fast growth of a number of developing countries suggests that it's time to examine how they did that and what it means for big global challenges such as eradicating poverty. Some countries have already confronted some of these issues, and therefore hold potential lessons for other nations. For instance, what can we learn from how the US and UK have been re-examining their growth drivers after the 2008 crisis, or how China has emerged as a major economy so rapidly? Other examples include how Europe is planning to increase investment to boost economic growth, and Japan's attempts to end decades of economic stagnation through massive government intervention. So, the quality and nature of economic growth will be central to this book.

You will note that I have largely chosen economists from an earlier vintage. The Greats, unsurprisingly, tend to focus on big general questions, such as growth, innovation and the nature of markets. Of course, there are eminent economists who are currently working on key problems. Many of the recent Nobel laureates are actively engaged in current policy debates, such as raising economic growth rates and assessing the role of government spending, but their research is rooted in the work of the originators of the general models that form the foundation of economics. This book reveals who those Great Economists were, where their ideas came from and how their insights have shaped economic thinking.

Unsurprisingly, my first subject is Adam Smith. It is almost a truism that all economists first turn to Smith when confronted with an economic question. I was reminded of it recently when I presented a BBC radio programme. I asked an academic why we tend to overlook the dominant services sector and instead focus on manufacturing, which comprises only around one-tenth of the British and American economies. He referred immediately to Adam Smith, who thought that the services sector was unproductive. Smith believed that the sector was comprised of 'buffoons, musicians, opera-singers',[1] whose output could not be traded and therefore did not add to national output in the same way as manufacturing. Smith was, naturally, a product of his times, which witnessed the advent of industrialization that led to an unprecedented increase in incomes and living standards. His 1776 *The Wealth of Nations* is the seminal work on the subject. Smith's legacy is evident in nearly every aspect of economics. We still view the economy through the lens he fashioned.

So, Adam Smith is the first Great Economist in the book. His idea of the 'invisible hand' of market forces – meaning the innate effects of supply and demand, rather than direct intervention by governments or other institutions – is the foundation of economic theory. As I explored in that Radio 4 programme, the British government is trying to rebalance the economy towards making things once again, after the 2008 crisis revealed the downsides of relying too much on financial services. So far they haven't succeeded. A decade later, the services sector has recovered to pre-recession levels, while manufacturing has not. And it's not just Britain. America, China and other major economies are also seeking to rebalance their economies so that they can grow in a more sustainable fashion. What would Adam Smith say about these attempts? How would he reconcile his affinity for manufacturing with an aversion to governments intervening in the workings of the 'invisible hand'?

An economist inspired by Adam Smith later became the father of international trade. In 1817 David Ricardo formalized the theory of comparative advantage that shows how every country benefits from free trade. This is true even if that country is worse than every other country in the world at producing everything. It should still focus on making what it was relatively less bad at, and specializing and trading would benefit it as well as the rest of the world. But, what if the result of trading on the basis of comparative advantage is that countries like America and Britain run persistent trade deficits, meaning that the value of the goods they import outstrips the value of their exports? What would Ricardo advise governments to do?

Karl Marx viewed the Industrial Revolution rather differently from Adam Smith. Although he too experienced the dramatic transformation of Western economies in the nineteenth century, Marx rejected market-driven outcomes and instead favoured collectivization over capitalism. He viewed the market economy as exploitative and unsustainable, and his views led the former Soviet Union and China, among others, to adopt a communist rather than capitalist system.

The collapse of the Soviet Union is generally viewed as an indictment of central planning. By adopting market-oriented reforms, China has emerged as the world's second largest economy. Still, China is undergoing perhaps the most challenging part of its marketization process. How would Marx judge the trail that the Chinese economy is blazing?

On the opposite side of the planning – market spectrum from Karl Marx was his near contemporary Alfred Marshall. Instead of the government running the economy, Marshall formalized how Smith's 'invisible hand' achieves an equilibrium for the economy through market forces. He showed how supply and demand determine the price and quantity of a good. Marshall's belief in a self-correcting market that moves towards an equilibrium means that we only need a *laissez-faire* state. There is no imperative for the government to intervene a great deal in the workings of the market economy, for instance, in the ups and downs of a business cycle. But, how about redistributing income in the face of rising inequality? How would Marshall have viewed inequalities that have burgeoned as the benefits of a growing economy disproportionately accrue to the top 1 per cent?

There's no doubt that inequality is high on the policy agenda, a reminder that we must consider the quality and not just the speed of economic growth. A best-selling book on the topic of inequality is by the French economist Thomas Piketty. Its popularity reflects a widespread concern that inequality is as high now in America as the Gilded Age of the late nineteenth century. A recent economics Nobel laureate, Joseph Stiglitz, has even pointed to inequality as one of the causes of the slow recovery after the Great Recession. So, how would Marshall view the worsening of income inequality which is often perceived as an indictment of capitalism? Are capitalist economies inevitably unequal?

Concerns over economic growth have certainly heated up since the 2008 global financial crisis, which was the worst economic downturn since the Great Depression of the 1930s. America was the epicentre, and Britain was deeply affected. Years later, there are still high levels of debt and less than robust economic growth. Irving Fisher, who lived through it, warned about the danger of the debt-deflation spiral after such crises. It's what Japan has experienced since its early 1990s real estate crash. As debt was repaid, output fell which led to falling prices or deflation and 'lost decades' of growth. What would Fisher advise in order to ensure that countries do not face 'lost decades' of growth? Are we at risk of repeating aspects of the 1930s, which was characterized by a second recession and stagnant income growth?

Arguably the economist who has been most discussed since the recent downturn, when unemployment returned as a worrying problem, is John Maynard Keynes. According to the think tank for the group of developed nations known as the Organisation for Economic Co-operation and Development (OECD), the long-term unemployment rate (a measure of those who have been out of work for more than one year) had increased by a staggering 77 per cent in the aftermath of the 2008 crisis. Youth unemployment reached double digits in some European countries such as Spain. It's less of an issue for the US and UK, but other forms of 'hidden' unemployment, such as underemployment and part-time work, are concerns. So, the role of government in promoting employment and reviving growth is front and centre in public policy.

It is well known that Keynes did not believe in the market's ability to self-correct, which was the dominant economic thinking at the time. Instead, he argued for government spending, and incurring a budget deficit if necessary, to bring the economy back to full employment. His views were shaped by the persistently high unemployment rates that followed the Great Depression, and Keynes's ideas made him an influential figure, even posthumously during the post-war period which saw the birth of large government programmes such as the welfare state.

In another parallel to today, the dominant economic debate since the Great Recession of 2009 has been over austerity – cutting government spending and raising taxes to reduce the budget deficit. One of the results of austerity measures is a huge drop in government/public/state investment, which hampers economic growth. Looking ahead, what would Keynes advise today's governments to do about public investment, an important driver of growth and full employment in the economy?

Another big economic debate is over how to make economies more productive. Recovery since the financial crisis has been slow by historical standards. Raising productivity, which has stagnated in many developed economies, is crucial if the economy is to grow; but it requires innovation. This may be the most important policy question for advanced economies, and the Great Economist best placed to address it is Keynes's contemporary and the advocate of 'creative destruction': Joseph Schumpeter. Schumpeter's theory placed entrepreneurs and innovators at the heart of not just the recovery but overall economic growth. So, what would he advise governments do today in order to raise productivity and innovation?

Another influential contributor to economic policy around that time was Friedrich Hayek. Hayek was the standard bearer for free-market economics. He was part of the Austrian School of economics, which rejected, among other theories, the standard explanations of business cycles. Hayek was diametrically opposed to the views of Keynes and believed in the supremacy of market forces. Hayek opposed the use of monetary policy, which is when the cost and quantity of money in the economy is adjusted to influence growth, as well as Keynes's fiscal activism, setting him at odds with much of the economics profession. Although Hayek found an intellectual home at the London School of Economics and Political Science, his theories are still not widely accepted in academia. With capitalism itself now under attack in the aftermath of the Great Recession by the Occupy movement and others, Hayek's ideas have come back into fashion as the search continues for arguments to defend the market system against growing scepticism. Those ideas can help us discern whether there are any lessons to be learned from the financial crisis.

Joan Robinson, another of the twentieth-century's leading lights, is the sole woman among the Greats in this book, which reflects the chronic dearth of women in economics. When I was an economics doctoral student at Oxford University, I found her theories on imperfectly competitive markets highly insightful. For instance, one of the most pressing economic challenges is low wages. The UK has the dubious distinction of being the only one of the G7 group of major economies where average annual wage growth failed to match inflation for much of the decade since the financial crisis. A general lack of growth in 'real wages' is a problem that goes beyond this last recession, and beyond UK shores. Japan and Germany have faced twenty years of stagnant wage growth for those workers earning the median wage, that is to say those whose earnings fall in the middle section of the pay distribution spectrum. Even worse, median wages in the United States have been stagnant for four decades. This is where Joan Robinson's work offers insights. In the two key factor markets, namely capital and labour, Robinson showed how deviations from the assumption of perfect competition, where all markets operate efficiently, can explain low wages and why pay does not reflect the output of workers. We'll ask what remedies Robinson might offer to address the challenge of stagnant wages plaguing major economies.

The next Great Economist certainly did not suffer from a lack of attention. Milton Friedman famously coined the phrase 'Inflation is always and everywhere a monetary phenomenon.' Friedman believed that the amount of money in the economy only affected prices, and therefore inflation, but not national output in the long run, which is the monetarist view of economics captured by his well-known quote. Throughout his long life Friedman remained an advocate of the free market and even initially considered the establishment of America's central bank, the Federal Reserve, to have been a mistake. Although he later accepted that the Fed was necessary to control the money supply, he insisted it should be confined to that role, and not be an activist institution. Unsurprisingly, he disagreed with the Keynesian view that fiscal policies have a lasting impact on the economy.

Part of the Chicago School of economics, in 1963 Friedman co-wrote with Anna Jacobson Schwartz one of the most influential books on monetary policy: *A Monetary History of the United States, 1867–1960*. They revisited the causes of the Great Depression to understand what happened and why it took so long to recover from the 1929 stock market crash. Their conclusion is that monetary policy was the culprit, specifically the Fed prematurely tightening the money supply, which they argued caused the crash and also led to a second economic downturn, known as a 'recession within the Depression', of 1937–38. So, what would Friedman say about the use of 'unconventional' monetary policy in the aftermath of the Great Recession with its parallels to the 1930s? Central banks have now deployed a dazzling array of policies, including quantitative easing (cash injections) and even negative interest rates (where commercial bank deposits at the central bank are being charged) to get more money into the economy. What would Friedman make of the activities of central banks which are largely operating in unknown territory?

The next pair of authors put forward contrasting views about the fundamental drivers of how an economy grows and develops. And both have heavily influenced current policies.

Douglass North deviated from many of his contemporaries in that he believed that institutions mattered for economic development. North's views have gained currency in recent years because standard growth theories haven't been able to explain fully why some countries become rich and others remain poor. Economists have turned to North's work following the Second World War on the role of institutions to understand why so few countries have become wealthy in the post-war period. As a result, institutions such as the rule of law have come to the forefront of development policies. We'll ask how North would reform institutions to promote economic development.

His contemporary Robert Solow holds a different perspective. Solow produced the seminal work on neoclassical economic growth that North deemed to be incomplete. The Solow model aims to explain growth by examining contributions of workers, the investment of firms in the productive capital of an economy and the role of technological progress. Unlike other recessions that saw a V-shaped output drop and quick recovery, the 2008 crisis has seen a sharp fall in national output or GDP (gross domestic product) but a sluggish recovery. Economists have become worried that this is our collective future. There's even a term revived by Harvard economist Lawrence Summers to describe a slow-growth world: 'secular stagnation'. This was a term used by Alvin Hansen in the 1930s after the last systemic banking crisis to describe the resultant slow growth due in part to ageing societies, among other issues.[2] Japan is the forerunner here, as the most aged economy. How would Solow judge the slow post-crisis recovery, and would he agree that we face a slow-growth future? This question is a pervasive one in the coming years for all developed economies.

Finally, the consensus around globalization is under challenge. After decades where opening up to the global economy was the priority for governments around the world, there is growing discontent with the uneven gains from trade. The economy as a whole benefits, but there are still winners and losers within a country. In the recent past, both the US and the UK have seen the public vote against the status quo, including a rejection of current trade arrangements. Would the Great Economists say that globalization is in trouble?

The rapid global economic growth of the post-war period was led in part by the expansion of international trade. So, prosperity is linked to globalization, particularly in the past few decades with the establishment in 1995 of the World Trade Organization (WTO), which has opened global markets. Globalization has linked all of us via the transmission of not just resources but also ideas from around the world. The concept of a bike-sharing programme in London can be picked up quickly around the world and become deployed by an app in Beijing, for instance. But, trade expansion is stalling and the multilateral system is becoming fragmented into an emerging system of regional and bilateral free trade agreements. Moreover, trade deals face voter backlash over the uneven benefits from globalization. What would the Great Economists say about what this means for trade as an engine of economic growth in the future? Most importantly, how should the backlash against globalization be addressed? Nobel laureate Paul Samuelson's work details the uneven effects of trade on workers in an economy. How should the distributional impact, where the entire economy benefits but some (for example manufacturing workers, farmers) lose, be addressed? Their ideas suggest ways to help even out the winners and losers from trade, and can point the way forward for the future of globalization.

This book will seek to uncover some of the answers to the big economic issues affecting all of us by drawing on the insights of the Great Economists. Their collective knowledge has already shaped the policies that governed the world economy during a period in which our living standards have significantly improved: from the Industrial Revolution through the Golden Age of economic growth after the Second World War to the current digital age. Perhaps their insights can help guide our economic future too.

I

Adam Smith: Should the Government Rebalance the Economy?

Widely viewed as the seminal figure in economics, Adam Smith witnessed the beginning of the Industrial Revolution, which fundamentally changed the Western world. During this time and in the decades that followed, Britain became the world's first industrialized economy. This extraordinary period formed the backdrop to one of the most influential books in economics.

Adam Smith's magnum opus, *An Inquiry into the Nature and Causes of the Wealth of Nations*, took a decade to write. It sets out the concept of the 'invisible hand', which refers to the unseen market forces that set prices by equating supply and demand. It has become the mantra for *laissez-faire* economics. Even though Smith himself never used that term in that specific way, his writings did envision a limited role for the state:

> The statesman, who should attempt to direct private people in what manner they ought to employ their capitals, would not only load himself with a most unnecessary attention, but assume an authority which could safely be trusted, not only to no single person, but to no council or senate whatever, and which would nowhere be so dangerous as in the hands of a man who had folly and presumption enough to fancy himself fit to exercise it.[1]

Smith was even more dubious when it came to taxation: 'There is no art which one government sooner learns of another than that of draining money from the pockets of the people.'[2]

Adam Smith would view a policymaker who intervened in the operation of market forces with scepticism. Yet, that's what post-industrial nations like Britain and the United States are attempting to do – roll back the deindustrialization process by encouraging manu-facturing and reducing the share of national output accounted for by services. This urge to rebalance the economy arose after the 2008 financial crisis which revealed the fragility of a large banking sector that brought the economy to its knees. It led the then-UK Chancel-lor George Osborne to start wearing hard hats and to promote the 'March of the Makers'. In the US, President Barack Obama invested in advanced or high-tech manufacturing. His successor, Donald Trump, explicitly extolled companies to bring factories back to America.

What would Adam Smith make of these efforts? Should govern-ment rebalance the economy towards making things once again? Is it possible to rebalance the economy in countries where the services sec-tor makes up more than three-quarters of national output, as it does in Britain and the US? The answer holds lessons for other economies that may follow those two nations as they embark on the typical eco-nomic path of industrialization followed by deindustrialization.

Industrialization, deindustrialization and reindustrialization

Great Britain became the first industrialized nation in the late eight-teenth and nineteenth centuries, followed by Germany and the United States. The period, which became known as the Industrial Revolution, saw the economy transformed from an agrarian society into one characterized by factories owned and run by merchants who traded their wares both at home and overseas.

In our own times, Britain and several other advanced economies, including the United States, have experienced yet another fundamen-tal structural change: deindustrialization. Since the 1980s Thatcher-era reforms that liberalized the financial sector – notably the 'Big Bang' of 1986, when markets were opened up to greater competition – Britain has seen industry give way to services. (Relatively speaking, that is. The UK is still the ninth biggest manufacturer in the world, and was in the top five until around 2004.) Similarly, although the US remains the second biggest manufacturer in the world (having been overtaken recently by China), its services economy accounts for the larger part of American national output. In the European Union the services sector makes up 70 per cent of the GDP or national output for the bloc, but the EU also counts among its ranks some of the biggest manufacturing nations in the world, for example Germany, France and Italy. Even the world's biggest manufacturer, China, which is only a middle-income country, has seen its services sector overtake industrial output in the economy.

When countries grow, they tend to industrialize, so they move out of agriculture and into manufacturing, which has higher productivity or output per worker and thus generates higher wages. Industrialization is how countries become middle class and prosper. Deindustrialization then follows. In advanced economies, manufacturing starts to become relatively less important as a share of output once they become richer and services in the business, retail and finance sectors start to dominate the economy while employment shifts from factories to offices or stores.

The 2008 crisis revealed the downside to having an economy with a large financial services sector. Banks had become complex and interconnected, and their business became harder to understand and to regulate. Their responsibility for causing the worst recession in a century prompted calls from the public to regulate the banks more tightly in the US and UK. The crash also led the American and British governments to want more manufacturing, thus they have sought to 'rebalance' the economy towards making things once again.

That's a big task. Manufacturing accounts for around only 11 per cent of Britain's value-added output, while, as noted, the dominant services sector accounts for over three-quarters of the economy. British manufacturing has declined from contributing a quarter of national output in 1980 to 20 per cent in the 1990s to just 12 per cent in the 2000s. It's a similar picture in the US. By contrast, manufacturing still makes up about 20 per cent of the German economy on the same value-added basis. At its peak, financial services alone made up some 8 per cent of UK national output, which is not that much smaller than all of Britain's manufacturing combined. This is the essence of deindustrialization, where industry has given way to a dominant services sector in the same way that agriculture was over-taken by manufacturing during Adam Smith's time.

The question is, can the US, and perhaps the UK, reverse deindustri-alization? It's a refrain heard frequently since the crisis. 'Made in America' and 'Made in Britain' are among the phrases uttered by governments and businesses after the worst recession in a century. But, reversing the process of deindustrialization is challenging in a globalized world economy.

Emerging economies like China can produce more cheaply while information and communications technology (ICT) has lowered the costs of logistics, so globalization makes it harder for rich nations to compete with lower-cost producers. In fact, Harvard economist Dani Rodrik even points to 'premature deindustrialization' in some devel-oping countries which are moving from agriculture directly to services due to the forces of globalization, which holds potentially worrying consequences for countries that have yet to gain a firm foothold in the middle-income stratum.

We are in unknown territory. The impetus for deindustrializa-tion is greater in Britain and America than in other nations. After suffering their worst financial crisis in a century, they are anxious for change.

That's not the sole consideration. Adam Smith may be the econo-mist who named the 'invisible hand' that allowed the market to dictate what was produced and how it was priced, but he did not think highly of the services sector. A product of his time, he did not believe that services could produce output that was as valuable as that from a fac-tory or a bakery. In fact, Smith didn't condone much of what makes up the modern economy, for example he wasn't in favour of joint-stock companies, which are the basis of modern-day corporations.

His legacy continues to affect attitudes today. Even the way that national statistics are collected breaks down manufacturing data in great detail while aggregating much of services output. That's prob-ably also because it's hard for statisticians to put a figure on what a consultant contributes while he sits at his computer or what a meeting adds to national output. We've all been in too many of those to know that they are not all productive!

So, should the government be trying to rebalance the economy? Can market forces driven by the 'invisible hand' be reshaped by the state? What would Adam Smith have to say about it all?

The life and times of Adam Smith

Adam Smith was born in 1723 in Kirkcaldy, a seaport near Edinburgh in Scotland. His deceased father was a Customs officer, and his well-to-do family was friendly with members of the Scottish Enlightenment. The Scottish movement paralleled the European Enlightenment, which counted among its ranks writers like Voltaire, and was characterized by a focus on science and rationality. This period has been called the Golden Age of Scotland, and Smith would figure prominently among its leading thinkers as the father of economic science.

Like many early economists, he wasn't taught the subject. Instead, he studied physics and mathematics at Glasgow University from 1737 to 1740. It was at this time that he also developed an interest in Stoic philosophy. Most early economists were also philosophers, among whom the likes of David Hume and John Stuart Mill were influential in shaping economic thinking.

Smith then studied at Balliol College, Oxford University until 1746. As he wasn't a member of the Church of England, he could not matriculate at that time, so was more like a visiting student. Suffice it to say he did not enjoy his time at Oxford: 'The discipline of colleges and universities is in general contrived, not for the benefit of the students, but for the interest, or more properly speaking, for the ease of the masters.'[3]

So, in the tradition of self-learning that has characterized a number of Oxford experiences, Smith spent his time there on the classics and immersed himself in modern languages. Since, in his view: 'In the university of Oxford, the greater part of the public professors have, for these many years, given up altogether even the pretence of teaching.'[4]

Afterwards, Smith returned to Scotland and gave a series of public lectures at Edinburgh University in 1748. It was there that he became friends with David Hume, a leading figure in the Scottish Enlightenment. That was when Smith's views on the 'invisible hand' started to form. He thought government intervention in the economy was a disruption of the 'natural course' of markets, a view which he later developed in *The Wealth of Nations*. His seminal work argued for a limited state that allowed markets to operate freely. As he stressed in one of his lectures: 'Little else is requisite to carry a state to the highest degree of opulence from the lowest barbarism, but peace, easy taxes, and a tolerable administration of justice.'[5]

Smith's successful lectures led to a professorship at his alma mater. From 1751 to 1764 he taught at the University of Glasgow. First, he took up the Chair in Logic, and was subsequently appointed Chair of Moral Philosophy. During this time he gained fame with the publication of his ethics lectures. In 1759 *The Theory of Moral Sentiments* was published, leading him to become a well-known figure in the European Enlightenment. He described his time as an academic as 'by far the most useful, and, therefore, as by far the happiest and most honourable' of his career.[6]

Nevertheless, in 1764 Smith was tempted to leave academia for a lucrative stint as private tutor to the third Duke of Buccleuch, who was the stepson of Charles Townshend, a politician. He accompanied the young duke for a two-year tour abroad, and spent 1764–6 in Paris, Toulouse and Geneva.

It was in France that he came across the Physiocrats, a prominent group of economists, who viewed agriculture, not manufacturing, as the source of wealth. For Smith, this jarred with the British experience of industrialization, and it is somewhat ironic that Smith's arguments in favour of manufacturing over services share some parallels with Physiocrat thinking.

Upon returning to Britain, Smith moved to London and spent 1766–7 researching public finances for Charles Townshend, who was now Chancellor of the Exchequer. He subsequently returned to Kirkcaldy to live with his mother, and focused for the next six years on writing *The Wealth of Nations*. From 1773–6, he returned to London to finish the book. Smith's publication aimed to influence British

MPs to support a peaceful resolution to the American colonies' War of Independence. In the final paragraph of *The Wealth of Nations*, Smith wrote that Britain should 'endeavour to accommodate her future views and designs to the real mediocrity of her circumstances'.[7] It was a sentence retained in all subsequent editions and reflected Smith's enduring belief that the market, and not the state, should dictate economic progress in all respects, including colonialism.

Adam Smith retired in 1776, the year that America declared independence, and he spent the next two years in Kirkcaldy writing another book, on the 'Imitative Arts', which covered painting, music and poetry. But, in 1778, he re-entered public life and became the Commissioner of Customs for Scotland, following in his father's footsteps. He moved to Edinburgh, where he lived again with his mother, Janet Douglas, a cousin who was also the housekeeper, and his heir, a cousin's son, David Douglas, who was to become Lord Reston, a distinguished jurist.

In 1784 he finished the third edition of *The Wealth of Nations*. A few years later, he also completed the sixth edition of *Moral Sentiments*, which included his thoughts on framing a constitution, which was highly topical at the time of the American Revolution as well as burgeoning revolutions on the Continent, notably in France.

Despite his path-breaking work, Adam Smith was highly self-critical of the slow pace of his writing. In 1785 he claimed the 'indolence of old age' and was uncertain that he could finish the 'Imitative Arts' or another book on the theory of jurisprudence. He had envisaged his major works as a trilogy: *Moral Sentiments*, *The Wealth of Nations* and a third book on Law and Jurisprudence, which was never written. Rather surprisingly, Smith expressed disappointment that he had not achieved more, and insisted that his manuscripts should be burned after his death.[8]

Why rebalance the economy?

Before we assess what Adam Smith would have made of the attempt, let's look at why there is a debate over rebalancing the economy. It's an issue that's at the forefront in Britain, a country that has one of the largest services sectors among advanced economies. As noted earlier, even though the US was at the epicentre of the 2008 financial crisis it remains the world's second biggest manufacturer while the UK has slid down the rankings. So Britain's experience in particular holds potential lessons for other countries.

Changing its economic growth drivers is indeed what Britain set out to do after the 2008 financial crisis. It was termed the 'March of the Makers' under the David Cameron government. The UK wants to rebalance its economy towards making things and selling more of its wares overseas. The two are related in the era of globalization, where much of manufacturing output consists of tradable goods. The British government wants to rely less on financial services, given the banking bust of a few years ago, but manufacturing accounts for only around a tenth of the economy, while the services sector accounts for the bulk of national output. Also, Britain, which until recently exported more to Ireland than to the emerging markets dubbed the BRICs (Brazil, Russia, India, China) combined, wants to reorient more towards developing economies and help its companies access the fastest growing markets in the world.

If it is to succeed in this endeavour, it clearly needs to be peddling the right stuff abroad. However, Britain's trade deficit – the difference between the value of imported and exported goods and services – widened precipitously and hit record highs in the years after 2008. That's not a great piece of evidence for the rebalancing efforts. The hope was that with sterling having lost about a quarter of its value at one point after the banking crash, a cheaper currency would boost exports in the same way that it did during the early 1990s when the pound left the exchange rate mechanism (ERM) that had tied it to the German Deutschmark. The last time that Britain had a trade surplus was towards the end of that decade in 1997, on the back of a depreciated pound.

Before then, Britain had run a deficit in its current account, the broadest measure of trade that includes financial flows, every year since 1984. Notably, the deficit in goods trade grew after the late 1990s with further deindustrialization. Recall that manufacturing's contribution to GDP has halved since 1980.

Offsetting part of the overall trade gap is the balance of trade in services, a figure that has been in surplus at least since 1966. Not only is it a long-standing surplus, it is also a large one, typically around 5 per cent of GDP. When the surplus in investment income earned from abroad is included, economic historian Nicholas Crafts points out that the total 'invisible' service trade balance has been in surplus for two centuries, since 1816.[9]

Britain is particularly good at providing services and ranks behind only the US in terms of total service-sector exports globally. These are not just financial services, but a range of business services including legal, accountancy, architecture, design, management consultancy, software and advertising. Also, the trade in services tends to be relatively high valued-added. As competitiveness is derived from quality rather than cost, margins tend to be larger. The fact that UK exports are increasingly represented by high-end manufactures and services might explain why the recent depreciation of sterling has failed to boost trade by as much as was hoped for. Prices still matter, but perhaps not as much as they used to.

One of Britain's problems is that the global trade in services, which it is particularly good at, has not opened up in the same way as manufacturing. Since the Second World War, the global trade in goods has boomed as multilateral organizations such as the World Trade Organization (WTO) and its predecessors have brought down tariffs and removed restrictive practices. The global trade in services, though, has not been liberalized to the same extent and this hurts Britain. By contrast, where the trade in services has opened up, Britain tends to do well. Higher education is a good example of a UK service industry that successfully serves overseas markets.

Thus, rebalancing the economy and reindustrialization are easier said than done. The recovery may have finally taken hold, but which of these businesses are driving it and which sectors have already recovered? The answers reveal that the recovery is not due to the economy's 'rebalancing'.

Manufacturing output as a whole has yet to recover its pre-recession level nearly a decade on. Past recessions have caused major shake-outs in British manufacturing. The industries that survived and prospered in the aftermath have tended to be in more specialized and higher technology niches.

There are pockets of activity which are doing well. The manufacture of alcoholic beverages is above 2008 levels. There are reports that Scottish whisky distillers, who account for a quarter of the UK's food and beverage exports, are even struggling to keep up with strong worldwide demand.

Britain's aerospace industry is also faring well. Rolls-Royce, with manufacturing plants in Derby and Bristol, is one of the world's largest producers of aircraft engines. Farnborough's BAE Systems is among the largest defence contractors in the world and is building new aircraft carriers.

Although the oil and gas industry is running down, operating expenditure in the oil industry has been growing strongly as it becomes more expensive to extract the remaining 'harder to get to' oil. Decommissioning expenditure is also on the rise. Furthermore, British expertise in maintaining extraction equipment, surveying and extracting hydrocarbons from difficult places is in high demand around the world.

Then there's the housing market. Like manufacturing, construction output has struggled even as the economy as a whole has recovered. Housebuilding is in the doldrums. The number of completed new dwellings has hovered around 150,000 per year; this is less than before the crash and far below the 250,000 per year that many experts argue is needed to meet long-term demand.

The services sector as a whole, however, regained and then exceeded its pre-recession level soon after the crash. But it is a large sector, consisting of a myriad of different activities, and its overall success conceals some internal difficulties. Two sectors to have done badly are, unsurprisingly, banking and government administration. In 2015, the latest year for which annual figures are available, financial services output remained depressed relative to its pre-crisis level despite improvements in the pension and insurance categories. In the public administration and defence sector, output had been falling steadily. The government's continuing squeeze on public spending is likely to push this lower.

Output in the telecommunications and information technology industries recovered quickly. The growing appetite for new technologies from households and businesses has continued unabated despite the depth of the recession.

Business and professional services, which includes a broad range of business-to-business services including legal, accountancy, management consultancy, architecture, scientific and technical research and consultancy, administrative and support services, human resources, public relations, and so on, contracted sharply during the recession. Compared to the first quarter of 2008, output was 15 per cent lower by the third quarter of 2009. The downturn was short lived, however, and the sector recovered strongly and now exceeds pre-recession levels.

It's clear, then, that Britain is a services-based economy. Its recovery from the global financial crisis underscores that fact. Although Britain might once have been correctly described as 'the workshop to the world' and 'a nation of shopkeepers', neither statement has been true for a while.

Manufacturing output and retail sales, once the mainstay of the economy, have been usurped by specialists advising the world how and where to invest, organizing their companies, proposing better product designs, writing contracts, preparing accounts and offering technical advice in the worlds of engineering, IT, architecture and finance. The output of these activities takes the form of blueprints, designs, specifications, recommendations, computer code, ideas, reports, databases and the like. Business activity increasingly consists of people sitting in front of computer screens and having meetings to appraise projects.

How hard is it to boost productivity and innovation in services? To what extent do policymakers misunderstand the importance of the services sector? What would it mean for economic growth if services were accurately measured?

It's harder to tailor policies for services than for manufacturing since services are intangible. But, for post-industrial economies, services comprise the bulk of output, so is there much of a choice? Could boosting innovation in services counteract the trend of declining productivity (and therefore stagnant wages) in advanced societies that we will investigate later in the book?

It's challenging to measure what can be produced in an hour by a professional service such as consultancy compared with the manufacture of a widget. For instance, a London consultancy firm doubled the price of the same report after the economy started to recover. As the price is determined by greater demand, the cost of the report rose even though what was supplied remained the same. It's hard to separate out the effects of a price increase or quality improvement. No wonder there are challenges in measuring the biggest part of the economy. Some companies are also doing both manufacturing and services. 'Manu-services' mean that we also underestimate the evolution of companies like Rolls-Royce, who make more money servicing and maintaining their engines than selling the engines themselves and yet continue to be viewed as a manufacturer rather than a supplier of services.

It's not only the output of services that's intangible; the investment is too. Economists are debating whether better measurement of intangible assets would increase GDP. When research and development (R&D) and other intangible investments were included, US GDP was increased by 3 per cent.[10] The OECD estimates that intangible investment, including that in human capital, such as education, and software, is as important as investment in tangible machinery and equipment in the UK.[11] Since 2014, investment in private R&D has been included in UK GDP. By this approach, UK GDP has been increased by around 1.5 per cent.

Intangible investment is what most firms in the services sector do. They invest in people. Most services companies invest in human capital since that's their main asset. Innovation comes from people who provide a service better. Even though the coffee machine is the same, we're aeons away from the tepid brewed coffee that used to be served in cafes as baristas now provide a wide range of espressos and cappuccinos. That intangible investment in their skills to produce a higher quality coffee is hardly measured. If it were, then the puzzle of Britain's slow productivity growth may be easier to solve if services output is actually higher than measured. Sir Martin Sorrell, the chief executive and founder of WPP, one of the world's largest advertising companies, says that his company invests twenty-five times more in human capital such as training programmes than physical capital in the UK. He believes that services such as those his firm offers are undervalued as contributors to growth.

The overall challenge is how to measure accurately the largely invisible output and input from companies in the services sector. That consultancy report that doubled in cost counts as doubled output of a service in official statistics. Does a price increase reflect an improved service or simply a higher bill? There are also meetings that could be done away with, but think about the ones where decisions are made and creative processes start flowing. Are meetings a drain on resources or profitable brainstorming sessions? Such imponderables are why it's difficult to know precisely how much of UK national output is mismeasured. It's certainly worth trying to do better since this invisible part of the economy generates the most employment.

Better measuring of services output would also affect the country's balance of payments. The UK has had a stubbornly high trade deficit despite the depreciation of sterling after the 2008 crisis. There is scope to boost exports of tradable services to help pay for the goods that are imported. Among the world's developing economies there is a growing market for services, including the highly skilled professional variety that Britain specializes in such as education and law. But those same economies also have burgeoning services sectors, so there is competition from those economies to consider if Britain's position as the world's second largest exporter of services is to be safeguarded.

Of course, effectively promoting the services sector abroad and supporting it at home depends on its clear quantification. Perhaps it is the difficulty of doing so that has contributed to policymakers focusing on promoting manufacturing. Whatever the reason, rebalancing the British economy hasn't exactly been successful: services have recovered to pre-crisis levels without too much help or attention from the government, but manufacturing has still to do so nearly a decade after the event.

So, should Britain continue its efforts to rebalance its economy? What would Adam Smith do?

Adam Smith on rebalancing the economy

Adam Smith's economic system is formulated around three pillars: the division of labour, the price mechanism and the medium of exchange (money). Both the price of goods or services and the wages of those who produce them are dictated by the price mechanism (dubbed by Smith as the 'invisible hand'). Money has a role set by the market to pay for goods/services, and its supply should not be distorted by the state, for example via mercantilist policies where the aim of trade is to run a surplus of exports over imports and to increase a country's store of gold and silver.

Let's delve into these concepts to discern how Smith would view the rebalancing debate.

It is clear that Smith was influenced by the rise of factories. He emphasized the efficiency of a division of labour that allowed for specialization within a production process that comprised several elements. Producing a woollen coat, for example, required wool to be gathered, spun, dyed, woven and tailored. Smith used pin-making to illustrate the benefits of specialization. He observed that ten workers each undertaking their specialized tasks could produce 48,000 pins a day whereas a single person undertaking every task might produce only ten, at most two hundred. In Smith's view, specialization led nations to become wealthy.

Smith also said that, because earnings could be exchanged for goods, the price of a good and the allocation of resources must be connected. He believed that every good had a 'natural' price, which was the cost of producing it. He drew a distinction between that price and the market price, the price consumers would be willing to pay for it. Supply and demand thus govern prices and the 'invisible hand' guides the market to an equilibrium.

But Smith was concerned about distortions that could cause the market price to deviate too far from the natural price. In his view, both the state and businesses could distort prices by interfering with market forces, the former by taxation, the latter by keeping prices artificially high. He concluded: 'Upon the whole . . . it is by far the best police [government policy] to leave things to their natural course.'[12]

This approach is known as *laissez-faire*, although Smith himself never used the term in such a specific way. The concept can be traced to English and Dutch thinkers of the seventeenth century who influenced French merchants during the reign of Louis XIV, a monarch who was keen on mercantilist policies and intervening in the economy. Reportedly, when a French minister asked a merchant what the government could do for him, the merchant replied: '*Laissez-nous faire, morbleu, laissez-nous faire!*' or 'Leave us be, dammit, leave us be!'

In terms of Smith's theories, an outcome of the market mechanism is that it allows self-interest to lead producers and customers to produce and purchase efficiently. As he famously observed: 'It is not from the benevolence of the butcher, the brewer, or the baker, that we expect our dinner, but from their regard to their own interest. We address ourselves, not to their humanity but to their self-love, and never talk to them of our own necessities but of their advantages.'[13]

Multiple producers seeking to sell their goods generate competition that moves prices toward an equilibrium. Revenues, in turn, are used to pay wages for workers (who are also consumers), so the economy benefits from every person in a society acting in their self-interest. Smith was not unaware of the ill consequences of self-interest, remarking that those with poor judgement were subject 'to anxiety, to fear, and to sorrow; to diseases, to danger, and to death'.[14] For the most part, though, an individual's ambition for '[p]ower and riches'[15] raised the economic welfare of the society:

> [E]very individual . . . neither intends to promote the public interest, nor knows how much he is promoting it . . . he intends only his own security; and by directing that industry in such a manner as its produce may be of the greatest value, he intends only his own gain, and he is in this, as in many other cases, led by an invisible hand to promote an end which was no part of his intention.[16]

That is the premise of Smith's economic system. His encounter with the French economic movement known as Physiocracy contributed to his views of what it meant for the structure of the economy. Although he disagreed with its emphasis, he built upon its ideas. The Physiocrats valued nature and agriculture, and did not think that manufacturing was productive. In their theories, farming was the sole source of wealth, while everyone else simply consumed what the farmers produced. For Smith, the context was different. Britain was undergoing an industrial revolution whereby manufacturing was increasing both productivity and incomes. Smith even witnessed a nascent consumer revolution as the middle classes began to buy mass-manufactured goods such as clothing.

Thus, Smith pushed these ideas further and crafted an economic system that valued the productive potential of manufacturing and merchants. In book III of *The Wealth of Nations*, 'Of the different Progress of Opulence in different Nations', he argued that, so long as there is no interference, capital will find its way to its most productive use.

After reviewing economic history, Smith argued that one path had led to prosperity: initially agriculture, followed by manufactures and finally foreign trade. Services weren't valued, as Smith could not have conceived of the technological revolution that would allow output from that sector to be traded as a commodity or a manufactured good on such a huge scale as it is today. For him, for example, a Mozart string quartet could be enjoyed only as a performance, not as a download or on a CD. Had Smith lived today, he might have changed his mind to support some services if they could be traded and had lasting value. That would add another reason as to why he would be concerned about the government rebalancing the economy. At its heart, Smith's views are centred on an undistorted market.

For his system to work effectively, there must be competition in the marketplace. But Smith also stipulated that such operations must be within the legislation and rules set by the government. The banking sector serves as a telling example. Smith believed that there should be competition among banks to reduce moral hazard, for example the possibility that banks might behave badly knowing they will be rescued. Government regulation could force banks to be more careful 'by not extending their currency beyond its due proportion to their cash'.[17] In other words, banks should depend on their cash and deposits for their lending operations and not get themselves in trouble by leveraging themselves in complicated ways.

More controversially, and reflecting his concern about banks, Smith supported setting a ceiling for interest rates, so that 'prodigals and projectors' could not take up the credit available and exclude the '[s]ober people' who would use the loans more productively.[18] (His fellow philosopher Jeremy Bentham considered this to be a betrayal of Smith's free-market principles!)

In this respect, Smith would agree with the need to reform financial services after a crisis. He would improve banking supervision and increase competition to ensure that credit flowed freely in the economy. Along these lines, Smith believed that some government intervention was warranted, but he was specific as to which areas. For instance, the state should maintain good transport facilities (roads, canals, navigable rivers), as that would break monopolies and encourage competition. His preference was to see such facilities regulated by local administration, or even deregulated if that lowered the cost of maintenance.[19]

Smith also advocated government spending on education. He worried about the impact of the division of labour on people, particularly of repetitive assembly work: '[The worker] naturally loses, therefore, the habit of such exertion, and generally becomes as stupid and ignorant as it is possible for a human creature to become.'[20] In his view, government had an obligation to counteract this effect with some provision of universal education. Smith also favoured public examinations to maintain educational standards, and focused on science, a feature of the Scottish Enlightenment: 'Science is the great antidote to the poison of enthusiasm and superstition; and where all the superior ranks of people were secured from it, the inferior ranks could not be much exposed to it.'[21]

But Smith also makes clear that there are areas where governments should not intervene, among them placing limits on the mobility of workers and capital, and enacting policies that hinder competition.

In particular, Smith believed that restraints on the freedom of trade and policies that favour some sectors of trade over others would force economic activity into unproductive channels. Government intervention to promote one sector against the market is bound to be less productive than if self-interested individuals were able to decide on merit which businesses to start or where to work or what to trade. Rebalancing the economy would fall foul of Smith's admonitions about governments believing themselves to be capable of choosing the most productive sectors.

The rebalancing argument cannot separate out the domestic sectors of the economy from a country's trade position since specialization within an economy is affected by globalization. When Britain specialized in manufacturing as the earliest industrial power, it imported agricultural goods. Smith certainly saw the interconnections between trade and the structure of the British economy.

In fact, Smith's beliefs about a circumscribed role for the state were influenced by his deep-seated opposition to the mercantilist policies of that time. He strongly objected to mercantilists distorting international trade by seeking to run a surplus.

In book IV of *The Wealth of Nations*, Smith criticizes the 'Mercantile System'. He explains why the policy that tries to improve the trade balance through imposing restrictions was inefficient. He was particularly against the regulation of the British trade in grain. He wasn't alone. It was a general preoccupation of Enlightenment economists to argue against protectionism. Smith viewed protectionist trade policies as diametrically opposed to an efficiently operating market. Smith reserved his severest criticism of mercantilist practices for the way that European merchants exerted their monopoly power in the American colonies, asserting that '[t]o prohibit a great people, however, from making all that they can of every part of their own produce, or from employing their stock and industry in the way that they judge most advantageous to themselves, is a manifest violation of the most sacred rights of mankind'.[22]

Although Smith equated free trade with the exercise of economic freedom, a theme throughout his work, he did make allowances for customs to generate government revenue if necessary:

From the above considerations it appears that Brittain [*sic*] should by all means be made a free port, that there should be no interruptions of any kind made to foreign trade, that if it were possible to defray the expences of government by any other method, all duties, customs, and excise should be abolished, and that free commerce and liberty of exchange should be allowed with all nations and for all things.[23]

Unlike many economists, Smith had the chance to put his theories into action. As the Commissioner of Customs for Scotland, he advocated the removal of all trade barriers, which was qualified only by the need to raise revenue for what he considered to be the proper purposes of governing a country. He supported levying duties on imports and exports at a moderate level, but not so high that smuggling would be profitable. True to his beliefs about government policies not distorting the market, he would set duties to be equal for different producers and importers, so that one group or one country would not have an advantage over another. For instance, he saw the inequity of exempting the product of private brewing and distilling (which was imbibed by the rich) from excise duty, while taxing the preferred tipples of the poor.

Having shown what the wealth of nations consists of, and how growth may be encouraged, or at least not discouraged, by governments, Smith in book V of *The Wealth of Nations* went on to discuss a necessary public expenditure: defence. But he was against the British going to war over its American colonies. He urged legislators to awaken from the 'golden dream' of empire and avoid 'a long, expensive and ruinous war'.[24] Smith had even advocated that colonists be given representation in Parliament. In correspondence with William Strahan MP (who was the publisher of both Smith and Hume) on 26 October 1775, Smith wrote that 'a forced and every day more precarious Monopoly of about 6 or 700,000 Pounds a year of Manufactures, was not worth contending for; [and] that we should preserve the greater part of this Trade even if the ports of America were open to all Nations'.[25]

Unsurprisingly, Smith stressed the economic gains from relinquishing the American colonies. In line with his view that markets operate efficiently, he saw the benefits of trading with America even if it was no longer a colony; indeed, he was willing to trade with anyone. Preferring one country over another was, after all, a product of government policy and distorted Smith's freely competitive markets.

In summary, then, Adam Smith would not have advocated that governments rebalance the economy if doing so meant introducing distortions into the operation of the market. He was particularly vehement when it came to trade, and he viewed such restrictive policies as not just inefficient for the market but also distortionary in terms of trading with other countries.

Neither Britain nor the United States has managed either to rebalance the economy towards manufacturing or to close their trade deficits after the 2008 global financial crisis. Instead, a dominant services sector and a persistent trade deficit continue to characterize these post-industrial economies. Smith wouldn't have been surprised. In his economic model, government cannot fundamentally change the economy; only add distortions to how the market functions.

Smith didn't suggest, however, that a nation's economic strengths could not be *shaped*. He did believe in government regulation and policies designed to improve market efficiency. Britain during his lifetime underwent a significant structural shift that was possible under the conditions set by the state. The advent of the Industrial Revolution itself is an example of how technological progress, which the state can influence, fundamentally altered the nature of an economy and a society. The digital revolution of the twenty-first century might even change the application of Smith's views on the unproductive services sector, since services output doesn't expire on use and we can now, for example, purchase and enjoy ad infinitum copies of our favourite musical performances.

Finally, as for the reshaping of a nation's advantage to be more competitive in a less than free trade system, Smith would certainly advocate for liberalization and opening up. But what if the global system failed to meet his standards? The next chapter explores how our second Great Economist, David Ricardo, would view the currently imperfect international trading regime and whether Britain and America should be worried about their large trade deficits under such a system.

A giant among economists

He may be the father of economics, but, like all economists, Smith was subject to criticism, and not just over advocating that colonists be given representation in Parliament! For instance, his friend and contemporary, David Hume, disputed Smith's claim that the rent of farms would make up a portion of the price of produce. Hume believed that rent would not factor into the price of a good traded in the market because the price is determined solely by quantity supplied and customer demand.

Nevertheless, Adam Smith was an influential if somewhat eccentric figure throughout his life. Among his known eccentricities was his banging his head against the wall while dictating *The Wealth of Nations* (he had to dictate because his handwriting was terrible). And although he had a designated heir, he gave away a great deal of his money, mostly in secret.

His greatest bequest is, of course, to economics. Smith is unquestionably the father of the field whose ideas of a freely competitive market still shape our thinking today. And he believed in human endeavour above all:

> The natural effort of every individual to better his own condition . . .
> is so powerful a principle, that it is alone, and without any assistance,
> not only capable of carrying on the society to wealth and prosperity,
> but of surmounting a hundred impertinent obstructions with which
> the folly of human laws too often incumbers its operations.'[26]

2

David Ricardo: Do Trade Deficits Matter?

Buying more from the rest of the world than a country sells – does it matter? It's a concern for a number of countries, but most notably for the advanced economies of the US and Britain, which have some of the largest persistent trade deficits. As discussed in the last chapter on Adam Smith, trade is related to being deindustrialized. So, this is a challenge that other economies may well confront as they develop. But, for the UK and US, it is a pressing issue now with potential lessons for other countries. What does a large trade deficit say about the health of the economy?

It's a long-standing issue, but one that has come into the spotlight as Britain's current account deficit, which is the broadest measure that includes trade and investment flows, rose to record highs after the 2008 financial crisis. There is no doubt that there are concerns about the UK's trade deficit. The Bank of England has warned about the consequences if foreigners stop investing in the UK after it leaves the EU, which would make the current account deficit harder to finance.

The United States also has a large trade deficit, but it enjoys the privilege of the US dollar being the world's reserve currency. That means foreigners more readily lend money to America to finance its deficit. But, the dollar's position has been questioned by the rise of currencies such as the Chinese renminbi (RMB).

The heart of the issue is this: does it matter if the US or Britain has a large trade deficit? It's been the case for decades. The geopolitical tensions may be higher, but has the economic sustainability of the deficit changed much?

The question of trade has garnered much analysis over centuries, particularly for the UK. International trade was one of the first topics tackled by economists in the late eighteenth century. The rejection of the protectionist Corn Laws in favour of opening up to the world economy marked the start of an era of globalization which contributed to Britain's prosperity.

It was at that time that the seminal work on international trade was penned by David Ricardo. Ricardo's *On the Principles of Political Economy and Taxation* is considered to be one of the classics in economics.

So, what would Ricardo make of the persistent trade deficits experienced by the UK as well as other deindustrialized nations such as the US? Ricardo's theory of comparative advantage, whereby countries gain from trade even if they are less efficient in all production than their trading partners, has transformed the thinking around international trade and showed why there are significant benefits from globalization. But to understand the context for Ricardo's economic theory, we must first take a look at his life.

The life and times of David Ricardo

Although one of the most influential economists of all time, one whose ideas still permeate the profession today, David Ricardo never went to university. Born in 1772, he was later to be disinherited by his Jewish family when he married a Quaker, Ricardo nevertheless used his father's connections at the London Stock Exchange to strike out on his own. He became one of the wealthiest men in Britain, as well as an economist, and late in life a parliamentarian.

Unlike most economists, Ricardo was a successful investor. He was really a stockbroker, dealing mainly in government bonds like his father. Similar to his near contemporary Nathan Mayer Rothschild, he was what was then known as a 'loan contractor', whereby he contracted to take on large chunks of government-issued debt and then sold them to the market at his own risk. During the Battle of Waterloo he bet against a French victory by investing in British securities. With that one call he became one of the richest men in England. At the time of his death, he was worth around £700,000.[1]

Another sign of his investment skills is that he was also a landlord. By the age of forty-three he had made £600,000 and purchased Gatcombe Park in Gloucestershire, which has been owned by Princess Anne since 1976. Ricardo's decision to buy land might have had to do with wanting to turn himself in a country gentleman. His investments gave him an annual income of some £28,000: £10,000 from his estates, £10,000 from mortgages elsewhere and £8,000 from French stocks. Translated into today's money, his estate was estimated to be worth £350–400 million, with an annual income of roughly £15 million. His wealth and standing contributed to his economic theories, which were based on three classes within a society.

Once Ricardo became wealthy, he focused less on his businesses. He began writing about economics by happenstance. His interest in economics, or what was known then as political economy, was triggered unexpectedly when he happened to pick up Adam Smith's *The Wealth of Nations* while visiting Bath in 1799. It wasn't until a decade later that he would write his first essay on economics. In his late thirties, Ricardo published a series of economic articles in the *Morning Chronicle*. His writings were published a year later as *The High Price of Bullion: A Proof of the Depreciation of Banknotes*. Due to the war with France, England's gold supply was under pressure so the Bank of England had stopped paying its notes in gold. Freed from this constraint, Ricardo argued that there was too much money printed by the central bank, which contributed to the high inflation of the time. This critique in his very first publication brought him to the attention of some of the leading thinkers of the time: Thomas Malthus, Jeremy Bentham and James Mill, father of the prominent philosopher John Stuart Mill.

An increase in tariffs on imported wheat in 1815 under the Corn Laws prompted his next major work, *Essay on the Influence of a Low Price of Corn on the Profits of Stock*. The argument against the protectionist Corn Laws formed the foundation for his future and seminal work that set out the basis for trade models in economics. In 1817, *On the Principles of Political Economy and Taxation* was published. Not only did Ricardo's arguments lead to the repeal of the Corn Laws, he also became a lawmaker.

By the time that he had published *Principles*, Ricardo was living both in Grosvenor Square in London and Gatcomb Park (the 'e' was added later). He was elected High Sheriff of Gloucestershire in 1818 and entered Parliament that year. He held his seat until his death a few years later.

In 1823, at the relatively young age of fifty-one, he died unexpectedly of an ear infection. He was survived by his wife, Priscilla, and seven of their eight children. Two sons followed him into Parliament. Ricardo's estate was divided among his family, and he also bequeathed some of his fortune to his friends Malthus and Mill.

Ricardo's career as an economist may have been brief but, during it, his theory of comparative advantage cemented his place in history as the father of international trade.

Like Adam Smith, Ricardo lived during a time of vast change. Undoubtedly, his views on trade were shaped by the protectionist debates over agriculture.

To give a sense as to how much the country had changed, less than one-fifth of the English population lived in the northern half of the country in 1751. By the early nineteenth century, that had risen to a quarter of the population owing to industrialization. A third of the population was urban, up from a quarter in 1751. England had become the most urbanized country in western Europe.

The Industrial Revolution caused Britain to become the richest country in Europe, too, but agricultural output grew less rapidly than the expanding population. As a result, there was heavy reliance on imports of food and raw materials. Those two categories made up almost all imports at a time when Britain was the largest trader in the world owing to its colonial empire.

Still, contrary to popular perception, early-nineteenth-century manufacturing remained dwarfed by the retail trade and crafts. The most popular occupations were those of baker, blacksmith, butcher, bricklayer, carpenter, mason, publican, shoemaker, tailor and, of course, shopkeeper. And, despite the country's prosperity, real wage growth, that is wage rises minus inflation, failed to keep pace with production per head from 1760–1850. Consumption per person was even stagnant between 1780 and 1820.[2]

But the fruits of the Industrial Revolution were accruing to some. Landlords were doing well and capital owners too, since they were investing in factories and machines. As a result, inequality increased. In 1810 the top 10 per cent of individuals owned around 85 per cent of the total wealth. This percentage rose to over 90 per cent by 1900. The top 1 per cent of households owned more than 50 per cent of the nation's wealth at the beginning of the nineteenth century, a figure that rose to nearly 70 per cent by the start of the twentieth century.[3] With his fortune of more than £600,000, Ricardo fell short of being counted as one of Britain's 179 millionaires, but was one of the 338 who had at least half a million pounds.

In Ricardo's day, more than one in two of the very wealthy men in Britain were landowners, a statistic all the more surprising because the Industrial Revolution had created fortunes for industrialists. Apart from land, the wealthy were in commerce and finance, for example bankers, brokers, merchants and ship owners. With his origins in the City of London, the financial centre of the world, and his huge country estates, Ricardo had a foot in both camps of the elite of his time. The bottom tier of society was the newly created class of wage earners. By the middle of the nineteenth century, the share of workers earning industrial wages had increased to around 80 per cent, more than doubling in a century.[4] Thus, a simplified three-tiered social structure formed the basis of Ricardo's economic models. For instance, *Principles* sets out a three-class capitalist economy in which the accumulation of capital depends on the profits made by the capitalists running Britain's industries.

Also, Ricardo believed Britain's economic prospects would be determined by the struggle between protectionist landlords and the rest of society. He observed: 'the interest of the landlord is always opposed to the interest of every other class in the community.'[5] Ricardo saw landlords pushing for protectionist laws like the Corn Laws that would help them but harm the economy.

Another important aspect of Ricardo's ideas was that he followed Jeremy Bentham's definition of utility for a society, which advocated the greatest happiness for the greatest number. Thus, he established a utilitarian basis for his argument in favour of free trade. As it was the most productive economic system, trade had the potential to fulfil Bentham's criterion.[6] In Ricardo's model of trade, because the economy as a whole benefits from international trade, the distributional consequences matter less.

His model of trade reflected his belief in the scientific nature of political economy. This was not a widely accepted view. When he entered Parliament, Ricardo was treated with great respect, but not after he proposed a tax on capital to pay off the national debt, something regarded as a 'wild sort of notion' even by his friends.[7] Practically every eighteenth-century economist thought the national debt was a bad idea and that some drastic measures were needed to pay it off. Ricardo's misfortune was that he was perhaps the most cogent.

Attitudes towards him changed after that. He came to be looked upon as a theorist, an epithet not intended as a compliment. Ricardo defended economic theory against those who relied on facts alone. Indeed, according to the economic historian Mark Blaug, 'the divorce between abstract theory and practical work was never more complete than in the heyday of Ricardian economics'.[8] That led to criticism of Ricardo by leading figures such as Walter Bagehot, editor of *The Economist*: 'To the end of his days, indeed, he never comprehended what he was doing. He dealt with abstractions without knowing that they were such; he thoroughly believed that he was dealing with real things.'[9]

The Austrian economist Joseph Schumpeter even coined the term 'Ricardian Vice', which highlighted Ricardo's alleged habit of making 'heroic assumptions'.[10] Schumpeter criticized Ricardo for introducing assumptions into a simplified representation of the economy in order to produce the desired results.[11]

Nevertheless, Ricardo's impact on economics is lasting, and not only in the area of international trade. Ricardo developed the theory of 'economic rent'. As more land is cultivated, farmers plough less productive land. But a bushel of corn sells for the same price, which does not depend on the productivity of the land. So, the farmers do not earn more if they have to work harder to produce a bushel of corn. Thus, only the landowners gain from higher land prices owing to scarcity. They have not exerted any effort to earn the higher rents charged to farmers. This is in line with his view of landowners, of course, that they were rent-seekers. Rent-seeking is one of the most widely used economic concepts today, for example, to explain why political corruption persists in some oil-rich countries, since there is an incentive to seek to hoard the 'rents' from selling oil and not share it with the country as a whole.

Ricardo's model of international trade

David Ricardo's approach to international trade was rooted in his background, while his interest in economics was stimulated by *The Wealth of Nations*, so it is unsurprising that he further developed Adam Smith's approach.

Smith wrote: 'If a foreign country can supply us with a commodity cheaper than we ourselves can make it, better buy it of them . . .'[12] Accordingly, Ricardo focused on what generated efficiency. His focus wasn't on achieving a trade surplus or avoiding a deficit, but on increasing trade which made a nation more productive. Ricardo and Smith both argued against the eighteenth-century mercantilist doctrine that a favourable balance of trade and money, including amassing gold and silver, led to economic growth. They exposed the fallacy that the way to grow was to aim for a trade surplus, instead of working efficiently and producing goods for the economy.

Ricardo's writings on trade were interlinked with his thoughts on the three great contemporary issues of his day: currency stability, national debt and protection of agriculture. International trade theory concerns more than simply looking at how the export or import sector is performing. Instead, he preferred to think of trade as domestic firms and their consumers selling and consuming across national borders. Hence his view that trade analysis ought to be linked to domestic economic policies. The event that shaped Ricardo's views was the parliamentary debate on the protectionist Corn Laws in June 1813, under which tariffs and restrictions were imposed on imported grain in order to keep domestic prices high. (Despite the name, 'corn' then referred to all farmed grains and not just corn.)

In Ricardo's theory, 'general profits must fall, unless there be improvements in agriculture, or corn can be imported at a cheaper price'.[13] Ricardo's model was based on what he had observed. The law of diminishing returns means there is a natural tendency for profit per marginal unit produced to decline, because the unit price will fall as supply increases. So, for Britain, the ability to trade abroad freely, especially in food, was important for economic growth. Ricardo saw a conflict between landowners, who were the proponents of the protectionist Corn Laws, and the rest: '[The landowner's] situation is never so prosperous, as when food is scarce and dear; whereas, all other persons are greatly benefited by procuring food cheap.'[14]

Ricardo and the Corn Laws

By the time of the Corn Laws there had already been a long history of government intervention in Britain. The state was heavily involved in the regulation and taxation of trade throughout the eighteenth and early nineteenth centuries. During the Industrial Revolution, Britain's trade policies were essentially mercantilist. The Corn Laws imposed significant tariffs on agricultural goods, while the Navigation Acts protected shipping by requiring all English trade to use English ships.

Since the reign of William and Mary, the British government had offered financial support to its prime constituency, namely landowners. British cereals were among the most expensive in Europe, yet until 1760 Britain was able to be a major grain exporter owing to government subsidies.[15] In the late eighteenth century there was a brief period of trade liberalization between Britain and France, but this ended with the Napoleonic Wars. This was followed by the reinstatement of the Corn Laws in 1815. Trade was not very free for much of the first half of the nineteenth century.

Adam Smith had excluded food in his defence of free trade. Ricardo, by contrast, was not too concerned about depending on foreign countries for food, noting that even during the Napoleonic Wars, France had continued to export corn to Britain after lobbying by French exporters. Ricardo also rejected the claim that free trade in corn would increase the volatility of food prices. He pointed to Holland, which depended almost wholly on foreign supply, and yet did not experience food price instability.[16]

Ricardo believed that trade brought about specialization, which would raise the efficiency of production. Free trade in corn would, in Ricardo's view, have 'a decided tendency to raise the real wages of labour . . . all capitalists whatever, whether they be farmers, manufacturers, or merchants, will have a great augmentation of profits'.[17] Although some might lose out,[18] the economic gains to the country as a whole were of far greater importance, or, as he put it: 'I shall greatly regret that considerations for any particular class, are allowed to check the progress of the wealth and population of the country.'[19]

Ricardo's campaign against trade restrictions played an important part in the eventual repeal of the Corn Laws in 1846, twenty-three years after his death. In addition, his arguments against the Bank of England issuing too much money led to the Bank Charter Act of 1844, also called the Peel Banking Act, which established a strict anti-inflationary monetary standard for the central bank.

After these two historic policy changes, Britain rapidly became the 'workshop of the world', exporting manufactured goods as befitting the world's first industrial nation. Great Britain became one of the most open major economies in the world, dominating international trade until the rise of the United States.

A tale of two trade deficits

Although Britain remains one of the most globally oriented economies, it has, since its nineteenth-century heyday, also acquired a large trade deficit. The broader concept was discussed in the previous chapter. Here, we look at the issue in depth.

Since the 2008 crisis, Britain's external deficit had hit a record high. The UK's current account deficit at 5.2 per cent of GDP in 2015 was the largest since at least 1948. The current account is a broad measure that includes traded goods and services as well as monies that flow into and out of the country. The deficit thus includes the cross-border movement of monies by large multinational companies, which isn't a source of concern. But the underlying structural trade deficit in goods and services, which excludes money flows, is 2 per cent or so of GDP. That is what warrants discussion. That's why we need to ask whether Britain should be concerned that it consistently buys more from abroad than it sells. Can the UK afford to keep doing this? Is that sizeable trade gap even measured accurately? That second question arises because most of the economy – more than three-quarters of national output – is comprised of services such as education and finance.

The two questions are related. If the biggest part of the British economy isn't accurately measured, then it follows that exports of services are also likely to be imprecisely accounted for. Therefore, it is possible that Britain's trade deficit in goods and services is not as large as it appears in the official statistics, which might make it somewhat less of a worry.

And the UK sells a lot of services overseas. In 2015, the export of services reached a record surplus of over 5 per cent of GDP. That certainly goes against the picture of a worsening overall trade deficit. Trailing only the United States, Britain is the second largest exporter of services in the world. By contrast, trade in goods recorded a record deficit of over 7 per cent of GDP, resulting in a net 2 per cent deficit.

Could the surplus in the services sector eventually push the trade deficit towards balance? That's not entirely unthinkable. Harvard economist Ricardo Hausmann and his co-author Federico Sturzenegger estimate that the large US trade deficit would actually be a surplus if assets that generate revenue but cannot be seen were properly accounted.[20] The same might well be true of the UK.

So, just how poorly is the dominant but not visible part of the UK economy, services, measured? Since the exports of services are called the invisible balance, it certainly increases the likelihood of mismeasurement. There are also 'manu-services', such as the output of firms in the engineering and software sectors that produce both goods and services, and these are easily misclassified by statisticians. If services were measured more accurately, perhaps we could worry a bit less about the trade deficit.

There is also huge scope for growth in the export of services. Unlike in manufacturing, post-war global trade liberalization has not progressed much in services. Nearly all of the global trade in goods is covered by a wide-reaching multilateral agreement overseen by the World Trade Organization (WTO). By contrast, services haven't seen the same degree of opening up of markets. Service-sector liberalization would help ameliorate Britain's and America's trade deficits since they are among the largest services economies. At present, Britain's service exporters face more trade barriers than their counterparts in manufacturing or resources, but if, for example, the Trade in Services Agreement (TiSA) currently being negotiated by some WTO members comes to fruition, then it would open up world markets for trade in services in a similar manner as manufactured goods and services would face far fewer obstacles to trade, which should reduce the UK's deficit.

Services trade is changing even without a new multilateral trade deal. As already noted, emerging markets are increasingly demanding the types of highly skilled professional services that Britain specializes in such as education and law. It may not be enough to overcome the traded goods deficit, but the demand for services is growing.

As in Britain, the majority of the US economy is made up of services like retail, creative industries and banking. Deindustrialization for the past half century has been associated with a loss of well-paid manual jobs and stagnant wages. It's partly related to globalization and the rise of offshoring, the phenomenon whereby nations with cheap labour costs have taken over the production of lower-end manufactured goods.

As in Britain, too, the trade deficit is a long-standing issue for America but there are signs of change. In the past decade, some factories have been returning to US shores. Is American manufacturing undergoing a renaissance? The 'advanced industries' are leading the US recovery, according to the Washington DC think tank, the Brookings Institution.[21] These are industries which invest a great deal in R&D and are more tech-focused. The revival of 'Made in America' was happening before President Donald Trump's 'America First' policy.

Rather unexpectedly, Tennessee is one of the states leading the revival of manufacturing. The largest car factory in North America, owned by Japanese firm Nissan, is located in the home of country music rather than Michigan. Nissan decided to site more of its car production in Tennessee in recent years, exporting to over sixty countries around the world, but the production lines of today are nothing that Henry Ford would recognize. Robotic arms assemble the cars while other robots drive supplies around a factory that is an astounding 5.3 million square feet. So, even as manufacturing expands, fewer workers are needed than before.

It's not only foreign companies that are coming to America. After decades during which production had been leaving the United States, American companies like Stanley Black & Decker, which were manufacturing in countries like China, have been returning. Stanley Black & Decker recently produced their first power tool in the US in over twenty-five years. The catalyst is an almost perfect storm of factors that have boosted American manufacturing. The extraction of oil from the country's shale has lowered energy costs and made the US competitive again. Rising wages in emerging markets such as China is another reason. Stanley Black & Decker calculates that it costs about the same to produce in America as it does in China, once logistics and transport costs are taken into account. Plus, the US has maintained its position as the technology leader, so productivity is high.

As for Tennessee, there is a long history of innovation in the state. Eastern Tennessee is where the atomic bomb was developed. Federal funding now fosters advanced industries, so those with a high proportion of R&D spending, and STEM (science, technology, engineering and mathematics) workers. For instance, the funding for Oak Ridge National Laboratory supports the development of 3D printing (also known as 'additive manufacturing'). This automated process requires only human programming for just one robotic arm to produce the husk of a car, secreting layer upon layer of plastic. The associated manufacturers who supply the parts and distribute the products also benefit. The company working with Oak Ridge to create the plastics that make the car body strong enough to withstand road stress is a reminder that manufacturing is still based in factories, as is clear from the smell of melting plastic and the loud whirling of machines that accompany this high-tech process.

For reshoring and reindustrialization to take hold, therefore, will require people to see industry in a new light. Will Americans really contemplate going back to work on the factory floor? A common concern of companies is the shortage of skilled workers. I conducted an informal survey of students at the University of Tennessee and found that most didn't see their future in manufacturing. Some wanted to finance those plants, while others said that they weren't good enough at mathematics to work in advanced industries. But they all agreed that manufacturing has an image problem: it might have provided suitable employment for their parents' generation, but it was not for them.

Still, the innovation side is flourishing. At Oak Ridge National Lab, a hundred students gather after school each day to compete to build the best robot. One of the signs that I saw said 'Made in America', but in Chinese characters. It's their way of signalling that the 'Made in China' labels in English on their clothes and electronics will soon face some serious competition. Stimulating competition and better economic output is what David Ricardo would have predicted when nations trade and spur each other on.

How advanced manufacturing is changing trade patterns

According to the Brookings Institution, advanced industries such as Nissan's automated factory discussed earlier have grown 30 per cent faster than US GDP since 1980. In an era of slow wage growth, advanced industries also report earnings growth that is five times faster than the average for the US. Since the start of the 2009 Great Recession, these industries have added around a million jobs.

However, the Information Technology and Innovation Foundation attributed the resurgence in manufacturing jobs to a rebound from the depths of recession. That opinion was echoed by the Center for Business and Economic Research at the University of Tennessee. They forecast that manufacturing jobs will decline once again and that industry will return to its long-term trend of winnowing employment in the face of both overseas competition and automation. That's consistent with the long-term trend where American industrial output has increased since 1950 in absolute terms, but has seen its share of GDP fall as services have grown more quickly.

It's a similar pattern in Britain. Like the US, British manufacturing has grown in absolute size over the past few decades. But, as a share of GDP, manufacturing now accounts for about one-tenth of national output. Despite the last recession, Britain is still among the top ten largest manufacturers in the world and the bulk of R&D spending, over 70 per cent, goes into the sector. Compared with its share of GDP, manufacturing makes an outsized contribution to exports, accounting for nearly half of what Britain sells abroad. But the UK still imports more manufactured goods than it exports, so there is a trade deficit. Again like America, the industries that sell overseas tend to be in advanced sectors, so technologically oriented firms with STEM workers constitute the new face of manufacturing too. But there hasn't been a rebound in manufacturing jobs in high-tech sectors like chemicals, pharmaceuticals or the motor industry. Only the aerospace industry has seen job growth nearly a decade after the recession. Also, labour productivity, that is output per worker, is low. Britain ranks above the world average, but lags behind other countries like the US as well as Germany. Could the UK also experience a reshoring of manufacturing? One issue is a scarcity of STEM workers, which is often mentioned as an impediment for UK employers in business surveys.

So, where does this leave advanced economies like Britain and America? Even if manufacturing output is reshored back to the US or the UK, manufacturing is unlikely to become the biggest part of the economy. Employment will also likely face pressure from robotics and automation. Still, the US experience with the reshoring of production holds lessons for Britain and others as to how to become more competitive in high-end manufacturing, which in turn has implications for what drives growth and also a nation's trade position.

In the previous chapter, we learned what Adam Smith would say about governments trying to rebalance their economies. But what about the related issue of setting trade policy? What would David Ricardo advise governments to do in the face of these trends and a large and persistent trade deficit?

Ricardo's theory of comparative advantage

David Ricardo's theory of comparative advantage states that each country should produce and trade what it is relatively least bad at. Even if China can produce everything more cheaply, America should still produce what it is relatively better at, and so should China. Thus, it is in the interests of every country to specialize in terms of what it produces and trade for what it no longer produces as much of. No nation is completely closed off to the world economy (even North Korea trades with China). That is known as 'autarky', where there is no trade. Thus, all countries choose to trade because international trade increases efficiency for an economy as well as consumption for its people.

Ricardo used the examples of English cloth and Portuguese wine to illustrate his theory. If it takes eighty Portuguese labourers to produce wine and ninety to produce cloth, then it should export wine and import cloth since it is more efficient at producing wine than cloth. Portugal should buy cloth from England even if it takes a hundred English workers to produce the cloth. That may seem surprising, but Portugal is more efficient at producing wine, so by specializing in wine, it can produce more and import what it is relatively less good at.

In England's case, it takes more labour to produce both cloth and wine than in Portugal, for example a hundred labourers to produce cloth and 120 to produce wine. So, England should specialize in cloth because it is relatively more efficient at weaving, though it is not an absolute advantage since Portugal can produce both cloth and wine with fewer workers. England would then import wine, which it is less efficient at producing.

By specializing and then trading, both countries can consume more than if they produced everything themselves. It's not an intuitive concept. Nobel laureate Paul Samuelson observed that this fundamental premise of international trade, comparative advantage, was the best example of an economic principle that is undeniably true yet not obvious to intelligent people.[22]

Does Ricardo's comparative advantage help us to understand whether we should be concerned about trade deficits? Firstly, there are criticisms of his theory to note. Ricardo has been accused of neglecting some of the most important issues in international trade, including presenting a static rather than a dynamic model. In Ricardo's model, countries cannot influence their comparative advantage – a country that is richly endowed with natural resources would specialize in agriculture, for example. But sometimes countries shape their comparative advantage in an attempt to influence what they specialize in, for example with government policies that promote certain sectors. This has become known as 'new trade theory'. This extension of Ricardo's model has been developed, notably by Paul Krugman who won the Nobel Prize for his work on a dynamic theory of trade. New trade theory implies for Britain that, even if it's not abundantly endowed with a large population, it can still promote high-tech manufacturing and need not be entirely squeezed out by lower-cost manufacturing nations.

Ricardo was also criticized for making unrealistic assumptions about the immobility of labour and capital. His theory of comparative advantage works because capital is not as freely mobile between countries as it is within a nation. If it were, English capital would move to Portugal and cloth as well as wine would be produced there too. The movement of labour is scarcely mentioned by Ricardo.

This leads to another problem as to whether or not Ricardo was assuming complete or incomplete international specialization. Countries don't usually entirely abandon a sector, so complete specialization is rare. But Ricardo doesn't examine the consequences of incomplete specialization, nor does he work out where prices of traded goods settle and just assumes it's at a mid-point between the prices of the two trading nations.

Perhaps more important than the technical objections is that Ricardo was thought to have ignored the question of the 'distributional' impact of trade as well as the politics of when nations trade. For instance, he assumes full employment and automatic adjustments of sectors of the economy to the introduction of international trade, neither of which is usually the case. Also, he doesn't address what happens to those who become redundant when their industries are abandoned or downsized following specialization. As ever, even though the country is better off, some will benefit more than others.

Ricardo has also been criticized for neglecting the unequal power relations between England and Portugal, the illustrative countries he used in *Principles*. The Cambridge economist Joan Robinson argued the Ricardian tradition would 'imply trade between countries of equal weight and at the same level of development. This rules out imperialism and the use of power to foster economic advantage.'[23] She added:

> in real life Portugal was dependent on British naval support, and it was for this reason that she was obliged to accept conditions of trade which wiped out her production of textiles and inhibited industrial development, so as to make her more dependent than ever.
>
> . . . When [capital] accumulation is brought into the story, it is evident that Portugal is not going to benefit from free trade. Investment in expanding manufactures leads to technical advance, learning by doing, specialization of industries and accelerating accumulation, while investment in wine runs up a blind alley into stagnation.[24]

It's worth pointing out that trade theory accounts for just one chapter in *Principles*. So, had Ricardo focused more on trade and less on the other economic theories in his seminal work, some of these criticisms might have been addressed.

Nevertheless, economists are agreed that Ricardo's theory helps to explain the basis of why and how nations trade. Economists recognize that the country as a whole gains from trade, but there will be losers in the industry in which the nation no longer specializes. They also see that, once politics is considered, less developed economies may struggle with negotiating the terms of trading with richer countries that provide them with aid.

For post-industrial economies like the United Kingdom's, cheaper manufactures from the developing world have made it harder for Britain to compete and hastened the move into services. So, globalization adds to the challenge of rebalancing the economy. Ricardo would see this as inevitable, but also as related issues to be addressed together.

David Ricardo wouldn't focus government policy on the current account deficit alone. The core of Ricardo's theory is that production and exchange were what determined economic prosperity, not the mercantilist policy deployed to foster a trade surplus in his day.[25] This is similar to Adam Smith, who believed that such efforts to promote a favourable balance of trade were 'absurd'.[26]

Like Smith, David Ricardo would instead urge policymakers to look at the health of the domestic economy and not focus solely on the trade position. How efficient a country is at producing goods and services will help determine its comparative advantage, and that leads to its trade balance. Aiming for a trade surplus without examining what needs to be done in the domestic economy to make exports more desirable to the rest of the world would have struck Ricardo as the wrong way to go about it.

Ricardo on whether trade deficits matter

There's no doubt that David Ricardo's theories held sway in his day as they do now. Trade barriers began to decline in the 1830s. In 1843, a weekly magazine titled *The Economist*, which supported the emergence of free trade and markets, was founded by James Wilson. It included work by Wilson's son-in-law Walter Bagehot. After the Corn Laws were repealed in 1846 and Britain became an industrial powerhouse, the rest of the world soon followed. When the United States was founded in the second half of the eighteenth century, tariffs represented nearly 100 per cent of the new government's revenues. By 1910 it was 50 per cent and it's since fallen to less than 2 per cent of the government budget.[27]

But, even as trade barriers persist in services and agriculture, the World Trade Organization's liberalization agenda has stalled in the twenty-first century.

So, in an imperfect global trade regime, America's and Britain's comparative advantage hasn't been able to deliver all of the benefits postulated by Ricardo. He would also be concerned about the lack of a level playing field in international trade. Ricardo would have pushed harder for the opening of global markets, particularly the relatively closed services sector. Services trade liberalization would help both America's and the UK's trade position and the global economy too, since over 70 per cent of world GDP consists of services.

With greater opening of trade and investment in services, Britain's deficit position may improve if its dominant sector can gain greater traction in world markets. In the meantime, Ricardo would not have been excessively concerned about Britain buying more from the rest of the world than it sells. He would have viewed the trade deficit of Britain as symptomatic of the structure of the economy. Specifically, the UK specializes in services, which, unlike manufactured goods, are partly non-tradeable. So, Britain imports goods that contribute to its trade deficit, while what it produces is in part consumed at home. In any case, he would have pushed for the UK to maintain the openness that it has had since the repeal of the Corn Laws. Finally, had Ricardo had the chance to expand his exposition of his trade model, given his recognition of the conflict among classes, he may well also have accepted measures to redistribute the gains from trade away from rent-seekers and more to those harmed. That would help those left behind when an economy begins to specialize in certain sectors and less in others.

The final chapter will tackle this issue and what Ricardo, and the other Great Economists, would say about how to help the losers from trade and what the backlash seen in various advanced economies means for the future of globalization.

3

Karl Marx: Can China Become Rich?

Karl Marx was one of the most influential, and also one of the most controversial, economists in history. Marx and his collaborator, Friedrich Engels, proclaimed in the opening sentence of the *Communist Manifesto*: 'The history of all hitherto existing society is the history of class struggles.'[1]

Marx was a man of contradictions. He advocated for the working class, but lived in genteel though poor circumstances. That was not uncommon for the time. Most nineteenth century European revolutionaries were middle-class intellectuals and not labourers. For instance, although Jenny Marx was the wife of a revolutionary, she continued to print stationery embossed with 'Baroness von Westphalen'.[2]

Despite Karl Marx's widespread influence, John Stuart Mill, one of the foremost thinkers of that time, had never heard of him,[3] perhaps because Marx published little in English during his lifetime. Marx's seminal book, *Capital*, was published in German. He was well known in German debates, but less so to an English audience.

Posthumously, Marx's theories of communism transformed the economies of some of the largest countries in the world. From Russia to China, communism took hold in some form as these nations sought an alternative to the US-led capitalist model at the start of the twentieth century. The notions of economic equality and communal effort were among the reasons Russia turned to Marx. Their communist revolution in 1917 led to the establishment of the Soviet Union, which vied with the capitalist United States as the economic model *du jour* during the Cold War which lasted from the end of the Second World War until the fall of the Berlin Wall in the late 1980s.

Marx's most notable success is communist China. The world's second largest economy and its most populous nation adopted communism after its 1949 revolution and has remained governed by the Chinese Communist Party ever since. But starting in 1979, when economic stagnation led its leader Deng Xiaoping to adopt reforms, China has moved away from a planned economy towards a more market-based one. These reforms generated remarkable economic growth, which propelled China from being one of the poorest economies in the world to challenger to the United States. But China's transition is ongoing and numerous difficulties remain, including how to sustain economic growth in a system that is still dominated by the communist state in certain sectors.

What would the father of communist ideology make of China's transition to a market economy and its reform challenges? Can a communist country like China grow rich?

The life and times of Karl Marx

Like David Ricardo, Karl Marx came of age during the Industrial Revolution, though in Germany, which it reached later than in Britain. Born in 1818, Marx grew up in Trier, an agrarian town which belatedly experienced industrialization. There was no industry there during his childhood, and not even a railway until 1860. As Marx commented of his hometown: 'there are simply no sources of earning a living on which we can count'.[4] Until the end of the eighteenth century the city was organized in a 'society of orders'. Rights pertained not to individuals but to groups based on birth or religion, and were even set out in legally binding charters. Under this system, Catholic clergy and petty nobles collected payments from peasants. It was far from fair or equitable, which are recurring themes in Marx's communist philosophy.

Marx is usually described as being descended from a long line of Trier rabbis. Marx's Jewish ancestors had to pay special taxes to their lords for the privilege of residing within their territory and were generally restricted in terms of their occupation to commerce and finance. There were often special restrictions on where Jews could dwell and even in their social relations with Christians. In Trier, some Jews paid 'protection money' and an annual 'New Year's Donation'.[5]

This social order came to a violent end after the French Revolution when, in 1797, Trier was annexed to the French Republic, which took the territory from the Holy Roman Empire. It then became a place in which all citizens were equal under the law. In 1812 the Prussian Chancellor Prince Karl August von Hardenberg issued an Edict of Emancipation for Jews, granting them freedom of residence and occupation, and the right to serve in the armed forces. For Heinrich Marx, Karl's father, the French Revolution offered an opportunity. He could become a lawyer, a profession which previously had been closed off to Jews.

But just a few years later, the government backtracked, deciding that Jewish attorneys would not be allowed to work in private practice. Heinrich decided to change his religion. He was not alone. Most of the leading families of the eighteenth-century German Jewish community had converted to Christianity by the 1830s. Most chose Catholicism, but Marx's father opted for Protestantism because he was an adherent of the Enlightenment whose library included works such as Thomas Paine's *Rights of Man*. He was among the Protestant intellectual middle class who wished to reconcile the rationalism of the Enlightenment with religious tenets.

Still, the Marx family were held in esteem. Typical of the German middle class, Heinrich Marx established his law practice with the dowry of his bride, Henriette Pressburg, who came from a well-to-do family. Karl Marx's mother was from the Netherlands and his aunt had married Lion Philips, whose grandsons were the founders of the eponymous Dutch electronics giant. Also, Heinrich Marx received from the Prussian government the title of *Justizrat*, or judicial councillor, which was a highly desired honorific for an attorney. Their family's social position led Karl's sister Louise to reveal later that she was 'extremely embarrassed' to have a communist leader for a brother.[6]

At a time when few were able to enrol in secondary education, Marx studied at the Trier Gymnasium. This preparatory school was at the pinnacle of the German educational system. He studied French instead of Hebrew for his third language after Latin and Greek, reflecting his father's wish that he pursue a legal rather than theological career. It led to French culture and history becoming an integral part of his ideas. He received high grades on his German and Latin exams, but, somewhat ironically, he did poorly in mathematics, an important element of modern economics.

After completing his secondary education, Marx enrolled at the University of Bonn. But, shortly thereafter, in 1836, he left for the University of Berlin and became engaged to Jenny von Westphalen back home in Trier. Her father, Johann Ludwig von Westphalen, was a senior Prussian bureaucrat and aristocrat. Following the suppression of the Revolution of 1848–49 against Prussian rule, her family lived as political refugees in London for a decade while her half-brother Ferdinand was the Prussian Minister of the Interior. But the social differences between the Westphalens and the Marxes were not great. Jenny's father's salary was less than that of Heinrich Marx. Thus, Jenny did not have a substantial dowry and Karl Marx was facing a decade without any income. In that light, his engagement could be considered an act of rebellion against nineteenth-century bourgeois society. There would be more to come.

Marx's PhD thesis was a comparison of the theories of nature found in the writings of Greek philosophers. It was slow going, and by the time Marx had finished it he had exceeded the statutory maximum of four years and had not applied for an extension. He submitted it instead to the University of Jena, the only German university that required neither a residence period nor a formal defence of the dissertation. It also boasted the lowest fees for granting a doctorate, which Marx received in April 1841.

Aged twenty-three, Marx returned to his native region to become a freelance writer after he had encountered the ideas of Georg Wilhelm Friedrich Hegel at university and joined a group known as the Young Hegelians. Formed by students after Hegel's death in 1831, they were a radical group who were disillusioned with the Prussian state and sought to undermine it with revolutionary ideas. Like other Young Hegelians, Marx abandoned any thoughts of an academic career. His father was not upset by his interests, though he believed his son was misguided. But he condemned his son for excessive spending. It led Marx to harbour a sense of grievance that he would not receive financial support during his parents' lifetimes: 'I have had . . . a falling out with my family, and, as long as my mother lives, I have no right to my fortune.'[7] He faced the prospect of no inheritance as well as no assets during a time when he also had little income.

A year later, Karl Marx found his first job. He became the informal editor for six months in 1842–43 of the *Rhineland News*, which introduced him to communist ideas. Marx enjoyed being a newspaper editor. For much of his life, journalism was the base for not only his livelihood but also his political activism. Marx wrote of the economic conditions: 'that Germany is poor in people who are economically independent, that 9/10 of educated young men must beg the state for bread for their future, that our rivers are neglected, that shipping is in wretched condition, that our once blossoming commercial cities are no longer flourishing.'[8]

In 1844 Marx began his lifelong collaboration with Friedrich Engels. Marx was residing then in Paris. He and his new wife had moved there a year earlier as he had few employment options in Germany and they decided to leave for more tolerant France. Engels and Marx had previously corresponded as they shared similar ideas. So, Engels stopped in Paris en route from England to Germany to meet Marx. What was supposed to be a brief encounter ended up lasting ten days.

While working diligently for the family firm in Manchester, Engels became increasingly sympathetic to communism. Manchester was the global symbol and centre of Britain's Industrial Revolution. Engels's mistress was an Irish immigrant named Mary Burns, who had been both a factory worker and a domestic servant. Through her and his work at his family's Ermen & Engels cotton plant, Engels observed that industrialization generated not only enormous wealth but also misery. There was a stark contrast between the suburban homes of the capitalists and the factory workers' slum neighbourhoods. In

1845 he published *The Condition of the Working Class in England* about his experiences, in which he described the exploitation of the industrial workers employed in factories and mills who produced the capitalists' wealth. So, Engels led a double life. He was a typical capitalist with a bourgeois family, but at the same time, he was a revolutionary who associated with and financed politically dangerous people, including Marx.

In January 1845 Karl Marx was expelled from France after the Prussian government protested against some of his commentary. There were standing orders to arrest him should he set foot in Prussian territory. Since he was given just ten days to leave the country, his pregnant wife was left behind to sort out their affairs. The Marx family moved to Belgium, where other German dissidents were residing, and stayed for three years.

By the middle of 1846 Marx had pawned all of their gold and silver due to his worsening financial situation. Engels was in equally difficult circumstances, having moved to Brussels to organize German workers with Marx, and was dependent on a monthly cheque from his father. Marx had to give up his apartment and move into furnished rooms at a hotel which meant employing fewer servants. Throughout his life, Marx's economic 'woes' were a very benign sort of genteel poverty. An additional expense was due to his being an aspiring political leader. Followers expected financial support and being accommodated as guests. Ironically, Marx's anti-bourgeois and communist beliefs made him reluctant to continue to depend on wealthier friends and supporters in Cologne who had previously sent him money. Marx tried to support himself as a freelance author, but press censorship in Germany made it almost impossible for him to get published.

It was at this time that he wrote his best-known work. Asked to do so by the Communist League, Marx penned the *Communist Manifesto* in collaboration with Engels. The pamphlet was published in February 1848 and it concludes: 'Let the ruling classes tremble at a Communistic revolution. The proletarians have nothing to lose but their chains. They have a world to win.'[9]

The final sentence proclaimed: 'Working Men of All Countries,

Unite!'[10] It is sometimes translated as: 'Workers of the World, Unite!' or 'Workers of All Lands, Unite'. This exhortation is engraved on Marx's gravestone.

In the *Manifesto*, Marx and Engels set out a ten-point guide for a future communist government, including the abolition of inheritance rights and the creation of a state bank with a monopoly on credit. Their version of communism stressed the revolutionary process of creating a new regime, which was radically different from competing forms of socialism. In fact, they denounced socialism as simply a merely reactionary critique of capitalism.

Marx expected capitalists to refuse to cooperate with such a communist government. It would result in an economic crisis that would enable the government to undertake more drastic measures. Marx believed that crisis led to revolution, which was what had happened with the overthrow of the monarchy and the proclamation of the First French Republic in 1792. (It was short-lived. In 1804, Napoleon Bonaparte declared himself Emperor of the First Empire of France, which collapsed in 1815.)

In a historical parallel, after the publication of the *Manifesto*, the 1848 Revolution which Marx supported led to the establishment of the Second French Republic. It was a new and radical form of government in Europe, which was welcomed by revolutionaries.

Marx did not have time to celebrate. In March 1848 he was exiled again, this time being given just twenty-four hours to leave Belgium. In fact, the police jailed him and his wife before then. Both were released the next day but had to leave the country immediately with their children, abandoning all their possessions.

Just a few weeks later, however, Marx and the other leading figures of the Communist League were in Paris at the invitation of the French Republic. Germany and Austria were also drawn into the revolutionary movement. It was then possible for exiled German radicals like Marx to return home, so he moved to Cologne and became the editor of the *New Rhineland News*. The post gave him a platform for his *Manifesto* ideas, including a call for a workers' revolution in Germany. It never happened. Instead, Marx stood trial for his insurgent activities and was expelled from Germany the following year.

Along with other activists of the 1848 Revolution, he moved in 1849 to London, which had a liberal policy on political refugees. Marx had fallen out with the Communist League by then. He was only thirty-one and intended to return to Germany and continue his revolutionary activities, but instead he remained in England until his death.

At the time, London had 2.4 million inhabitants, which made it the world's most populous city. The British capital was the centre of capitalism. Whatever happened at the Bank of England and the London Stock Exchange affected the world economy.

Marx spent time in the working-class neighbourhoods of London's East End, which was home to a large number of immigrant Germans. His family lived in Soho, which was then an immigrant, bohemian area of central London. He founded a journal similar to the one that he had edited in Cologne, *The New Rhineland News: Review of Political Economy*, which he sought to circulate in Germany. Meanwhile, the Marx family became increasingly impoverished, Jenny Marx observing: 'Conditions here are completely different from Germany. All six of us live in one room, with a little study attached, and pay more each week than for the largest house in Germany [in one month].'[11]

Although the Marx family struggled to pay for food, the children had a governess and a maid, which was not atypical for those living in genteel poverty. But they suffered tragedies. Three of the four children born in London died before reaching adulthood, while two of the three born in Brussels survived.

Professionally, there were also blows. In 1851 Louis-Napoléon Bonaparte came to power in France through a coup d'état. While serving as President of the French Republic, Napoleon Bonaparte's nephew titled himself Emperor Napoleon III. In reaction, Marx wrote a pamphlet, *The Eighteenth Brumaire of Louis Bonaparte*, which opens with the phrase that history repeats itself 'the first time as tragedy, the second time as farce'.[12] But it had minimal impact due to Marx's exile and the imprisonment of his followers in Cologne.

At least finances soon improved for the Marx family. From 1853 to 1862 Marx was a correspondent for a number of newspapers and was able to move the family to a new home in Kentish Town in north

London. His reporting on the Crimean War of 1853–56 and other foreign events raised his profile, as he wrote observations such as: 'Has [the bourgeoisie] ever affected a progress without dragging individuals and peoples through blood and dirt, through misery and degradation?'[13]

The war confirmed his belief that a revolution would be triggered by economic crisis – and the first global crisis finally occurred in 1857. A crash in railroad stocks in the US led to the Panic of 1857, which dragged down investors not only in America but globally. Banks in England, France and elsewhere in Europe were affected since financial markets had become interlinked. Jenny Marx observed how this crisis ended the long period of gloom for Marx that had lasted since the death of his eight-year-old son in 1855. Engels even told Marx he was concentrating on riding and shooting to prepare for a forthcoming revolution. But economic recovery started a year later in 1858 and the economic crisis did not lead to revolution. It did, however, lead Marx to become politically active once again.

The recession also caused his employer, the *New York Tribune*, to cut back on its European correspondents. As a sign of desperate times, in 1862 Marx even sought a position in business! After being turned down for a job at a London railway in his first foray into the business world, Marx was helped financially once again, and not for the last time, by Engels.

A year later, in November 1863, his mother passed away and Marx obtained his inheritance. Unexpectedly, a political ally, Wilhelm Wolff, also passed away in exile in Manchester and bequeathed to Marx the bulk of his assets. The family was able to move to a larger house, despite the fact that Marx still had no steady income. It was fortunate because Marx experienced a sudden deterioration of his health that year. He suffered from carbuncles, boils on the skin which were worsened by stress. It meant that he became an observer and not an active participant in the political upheavals in the next two years, which included the American Civil War and the Polish uprising against Russia.

Regardless, Marx's influence spread. He became involved with the International Working Men's Association (IWMA), known as the

First International, formed by an array of European workers' societies. It was followed by the 1889 Socialist or Second International, and the Third Communist International of 1919. The IWMA drew from Marx's theories, particularly the two books published in his lifetime: *A Contribution to the Critique of Political Economy* of 1859 and the first volume of *Capital: Critique of Political Economy*, published in 1867. Volumes 2 and 3 of *Capital* were edited by Engels posthumously.

Ironically, Marx's daughter Laura became involved with a radical French student living in exile who was a member of the International Working Men's Association. Marx had some trouble with this since his daughters had been prepared for bourgeois marriages. They eventually married, and Engels ended up supporting their family too.

Marxism

It was after the 1857 global crisis that Marx began writing his treatise on political economy, *A Contribution to the Critique of Political Economy*, which was published two years later. He analysed the ideas of the leading political economists of the day, particularly Adam Smith and his chief disciple, David Ricardo, as well as Thomas Malthus, Jean-Baptiste Say and James and John Stuart Mill, among others.

Somewhat surprisingly, Marx admired Ricardo, calling him 'the greatest economist of the nineteenth century'.[14] Even though Ricardo was a capitalist, Marx shared his belief in a conflictual course of capitalism. Recall from the previous chapter that Ricardo saw an inevitable conflict between the classes due to international trade. At the heart of Marxism was also a complex class society whose inherent inequalities provided the seeds of its self-destruction. Marx predicted that would lead to the end of capitalism; he believed that Ricardo just hadn't taken his analysis to its conclusion.

Marx's 'theory of surplus value' helps explain his involvement with trade unions and how the end of capitalism comes about. He argued that inputs such as machinery, fuel and raw materials made up a growing part of the cost of production relative to the wages paid to workers. Meanwhile, as production became more mechanized, demand for

labour would fall, creating unemployment. The unemployed constituted a 'reserve army', depressing wages for all workers since the
unemployed could be hired to replace any worker who demanded
higher pay. More expensive machinery also meant that factories
needed to run for longer hours to be profitable. By contrast, unions
advocated shorter working hours, which were beneficial for workers
but reduced the capitalists' profit. Marx believed that declining profits
and labour unrest would lead to the end of the capitalist system.

It was the lack of a revolution after the global crisis of 1857 that led
Marx to play down the importance of crises in bringing about the
end of capitalism. Marx had originally predicted the rise of a capitalist system, characterized by unrest and crisis, which would lead to its
destruction. Now he began to stress the importance of inequality,
particularly the misery of the working class. Marx documented the
many instances of exploitation and poverty that existed in stark contrast to the industrial output fuelling the growing wealth of the upper
classes, particularly in Great Britain from the mid-1840s to the mid-
1860s. He cited how, in 1863, a woman was reported to have worked
herself literally to death cleaning dresses for ladies preparing for
a royal ball.[15] (Though he omitted to mention his own financial
dependence on the capitalist Ermen & Engels textile mill and its
workers.)

Marx and Engels thought that revolution would come from the
most advanced economies because that is where the capitalist crisis
was most likely to occur. In their view, workers were unlikely to
attain power peacefully. A violent revolution would follow. Marx
saw a parallel with the Civil War in America, where Southern slave-
holders started a war when anti-slavery advocates came to power.

The end of the nineteenth century was when Marx finally saw his
communist theories in action. The last quarter of the 1800s saw frequent recessions coupled with deflation or falling prices. It has been
dubbed the Long Depression or the Great Depression of the nineteenth century. In the 1870s, economic crises plagued Europe and
North America. Stock market crashes led to deep recessions, which
generated high unemployment, labour unrest and strikes. During the
Long Depression, nineteen socialist and labour parties were founded

in Europe as well as trade federations. So, the downsides of industrialization paved the way for the workers' movement that appeared not
only in Europe but also elsewhere in the world.

That was also the period during which Marx's ideas took hold in
Russia. Russian was the first language into which *Capital* was translated. One reader was Vladimir Ilich Ulyanov. Although he had
never met Marx, Ulyanov helped organize Marxist groups to create
the 'St Petersburg League of Struggle for the Emancipation of the
Working Class' in 1895. After being jailed and exiled to Siberia for
several years, Ulyanov left for western Europe in 1900 to continue his
revolutionary efforts and adopted the pseudonym Lenin. In 1903
Lenin met other exiled Russian Marxists in London and established
the Bolshevik Party, which differed from socialist parties in that its
members advocated revolution to achieve their aims. When the Russian Revolution against Tsar Nicholas II erupted in 1905, Lenin
returned home. More than a decade of political unrest followed until
1917, when Lenin seized power. Russia then became the Soviet Union
or Union of Soviet Socialist Republics (USSR) in 1922 after Lenin
consolidated his position. The Soviet Union was the first Marxist
state in what Lenin intended to be a Marxist world.

Lenin's Soviet Union may have been the most prominent adopter
of Marxism, but Mao Zedong's China was the most populous. After
winning a civil war against the US-supported Kuomintang (the Chinese Nationalist Party led by Chiang Kai-shek), Mao's Soviet-backed
Communist Party adopted a communist system in 1949, more than
half a century after Marx's death. A falling out with the Soviet Union
in the 1950s, though, saw China split from Leninist thought and
adopt Maoist doctrines.

Although the Soviet Union had disintegrated by the early 1990s,
and Mao's extremist ideas are long gone, China is still run by the
Chinese Communist Party. To think about Marx in today's world,
we would most usefully look at China, which adapted Marxism into
its own form of communism that governs the world's second largest
economy.

But China's evolution towards becoming a market-based economy
is not what Marx would have envisaged. Unlike Russia, which

abandoned communism for democratization alongside the transition to a capitalist system, China retains elements of Marxist thought, including state ownership in key sectors, alongside significant marketization.

China's adoption of market-oriented reforms in 1979 was due to substantial challenges that arose in its centrally planned economy, which had followed communist principles. Economic decline led to the abandonment of a command economy after three decades. It was followed by nearly forty years of remarkable growth that propelled it to rank behind only the US in terms of the size of its economy. To sustain growth for the coming years, China has now embarked on another ambitious set of reforms to join the ranks of rich countries. Average income in China today is still only one-sixth of the US level.

What would Karl Marx make of it all? Is it possible for a communist state to become rich?

China's economic transformation

China has accomplished a remarkable feat in transforming itself from one of the poorest countries in the world into the second largest economy in under four decades. The economy has expanded at an average rate of over 9 per cent per year since market-oriented reforms began in 1979. Chinese statistics aren't the most reliable, but household surveys and others indicate that China has not only doubled its GDP or national output as well as national income every eight years or so, but also lifted hundreds of millions of its citizens out of abject poverty. In the world's most populous nation, with 1.3 billion people or one-fifth of humanity, the World Bank estimates that the country is on its way to ending extreme poverty, in which individuals live on less than $1.90 per day.

China is unusual in that, while it is transitioning from a planned economy that has dismantled many of its state-owned enterprises and banks, it is simultaneously a developing country in which half the population still live in rural areas. China is also an 'open economy' integrated with world markets.

China remains a communist state governed by the Chinese Communist Party. It's therefore unsurprising that the rule of law and other market-supporting institutions, such as private property protection, are weak, as there is no independent judiciary. This gives rise to the so-called 'China paradox', because the country has grown strongly despite not having a well-developed set of institutions. China's economic growth is, therefore, in many respects both impressive and puzzling. It is also, as with other fast-growing economies, not guaranteed in the long term.

An example of China's particular model of growth can be seen in the differences from other developing countries when it started to reform. Unlike them, China was industrialized early on, during the command economy period between 1949 and 1979. China followed Soviet-style industrialization plans in the 1950s and 60s that focused on transforming an agrarian society into an industrialized economy. China's centrally planned system established state-owned enterprises that created industries where none existed before. Since market-oriented reforms were introduced in the late 1970s, China has undergone a reindustrialization process of upgrading obsolete (state-owned) plants and premises into more advanced (largely privately owned) machines and factories. As Adam Smith well knew, industrialization propels faster growth, so China was able to grow faster than most developing nations struggling to industrialize over the past few decades. Industrialization is accompanied by investment in factories, R&D and so on, which gives a further strong boost to growth. Adding capital accumulated from years of investment has accounted for about half of China's economic growth since market-oriented reforms began. In other words, its success can be explained by the standard economic factors such as investment, but with additional features, notably the reindustrialization of what was then a lower-middle-income country, that are specific to its unusual context.

Another example of China's particular growth model is that productivity is also driven by 'factor reallocation', for example labour migrating from less efficient state-owned industries to the more productive private sector. The process of factor reallocation is contained within the industrial sector, so it is not captured by the urbanization and industrialization processes which usually explain how developing countries grow by moving workers from rural and agricultural sectors to urban and manufacturing work.

Moreover, China confounds any straightforward interpretation of the theories that link 'openness' to the global economy with economic growth. These explanations centre on the positive correlation between greater opening and faster development, as expounded by David Ricardo. Economies open to the global economy grow quickly because the experience of exporting and accessing global markets can lead to improvements in competitiveness. Domestic firms can also 'learn' from foreign investors with more advanced technology and managerial know-how. 'Openness' allows a developing country like China to 'catch up' in its growth rate if it can imitate the existing technology embodied in foreign capital and thus grow more quickly, and perhaps even eventually attain the standards of living of advanced economies.[16]

China is open to the global economy, but exercises elements of control that have prevented direct competition from foreign companies in its economy in a number of sectors. It utilizes a policy towards foreign direct investment (FDI) that furthers its own active industrial policies to develop domestic companies and launch them globally as Chinese multinational corporations. As such, the simple openness measures do not fully capture the nature of China's 'open door' policy that introduced market-oriented reforms in the external sector first in 1979, which then accelerated after 1992 and culminated in its joining the World Trade Organization in 2001.

Several metrics are needed to calibrate the influence on growth of opening up the economy to international trade. For instance, at the start of the reform period, when China was a poor country with a low rate of household saving that was only 10 per cent of GDP, foreign investment supplemented domestic investment, accounting for as much as one-third of the total. Since then, household savings have been as high as 50 per cent of GDP, which is arguably too high as the money has been used to fund investments that are not always productive, such as the 'ghost cities' where residential housing is built but not occupied. Foreign direct investment that established Chinese–foreign joint ventures and other foreign-invested enterprises were explicitly geared towards exports and prevented from selling into the domestic market, which protected Chinese industries from foreign competition. They were initially located in Special Economic Zones, which were created as export-processing zones similar to its East Asian neighbours. China thus became integrated with East Asia, as it joined regional and global production chains, and eventually became the world's largest trader. Undoubtedly, foreign investment and export-orientation benefited its economic growth, but China's policies defy easy categorization as they have always been uniquely tailored to the country's circumstances.

By the late 2000s China was contributing to the 'global macroeconomic imbalances', where the countries with significant trade surpluses (China, Asia and the Middle East oil exporters) saw their surpluses grow while the United States experienced larger trade deficits. The global imbalances and other aspects of the 'China effect' (or 'China price' whereby cheap Chinese labour has pushed down global prices for manufactured goods) point to the need to examine China as a large, open economy. In other words, it is similar to the United States in that what China does affects the world economy in a way that most countries do not. So openness has undoubtedly contributed to China's economic growth but in a nuanced manner.

The other part of technological progress needed for economic growth derives from domestic innovation, and not just reliance on foreign technology. Coming up with innovative technologies requires researchers and R&D investment. China has increased its focus on patents and investment in R&D since the mid-1990s in an effort to support economic growth. Although Chinese researchers and scientific personnel are numerous, the evidence regarding how advanced Chinese innovations are remains mixed. Yet this is the crucial area for sustaining China's growth and for it to become a rich nation. Protecting intellectual property is also a concern, exacerbated by China's lack of an effective rule of law, though the situation is improving.

Indeed, one of the most complex areas of Chinese growth is the role of legal institutions. The predominant view is that market-supporting institutions, such as those which protect property rights and provide contracting security, are important for growth. China has been considered paradoxical in having a weak legal system but strong economic growth. However, China as an 'outlier' requires a closer examination as to how markets were enabled, given the poor formal legal system. Specifically, the reliance on relational contracting, so transacting with those whom you trust, can help to reduce dependence on the judicial system which is being gradually improved as more Chinese firms clamour for better protection of their inventions. The institutional theories that deem a good legal system important for growth therefore apply to China, but there are again nuances to take into account.

The role of informal institutions such as social capital also cannot be overlooked. Entrepreneurs in China relied on social networks, known as *guanxi*, to overcome the lack of well-developed legal and financial systems. It is also the case that the cultural proclivity towards interpersonal relationships meant that social capital played a key part in facilitating the development of self-employment and the impressive emergence of the private sector. That China would allow entrepreneurs to emerge within a communist system is, perhaps, not something that Marx would have anticipated.

After reaching 'middle-income status' in the early 2000s, China found that it also needed to rebalance its economy to grow in a more sustainable manner. Its ability to overcome the 'middle-income country trap', whereby countries start to slow after reaching upper middle-income levels and never become rich, depends on it.[17] Poor countries tend to grow through exports and cheap manufacturing. Growth in a middle-income country is driven more by consumption by its own middle class, leading to a diversified economy that is not heavily reliant on exports to consumers in other countries. For China, rebalancing the economy away from old growth drivers will involve boosting domestic demand (consumption, investment in more productive sectors, government spending that provides social services) so that it grows more quickly than exports. China has also shifted towards services so that the 'factory of the world' now has a bigger services sector than manufacturing. China is still upgrading manufacturing, expanding overseas investment and opening up its financial sector further. China is also promoting the internationalization or global use of its currency, the renminbi or RMB. To achieve these aims will also require examining the institutional framework of the economy, including the role of state-owned enterprises and the legal system. The retention of large state-owned firms and the problematic lack of a 'level playing field' for both foreign and domestic private firms vis-à-vis state-controlled companies raise doubts as to the efficiency of China's markets and thus its ability to grow. So, for China to realize its economic potential will require a significant transformation of the structure of its economy.

There's also the issue of financial stability. An economic crisis, depending on the causes, could trigger a long-lasting downturn. Marx would view this as inevitable in a capitalist economy, of course. In China's case, a financial crisis linked to too much debt or some other issue in its banking system would not be surprising. All major economies experience crisis eventually. Estimates of total Chinese debt by the Bank for International Settlements and others place it around 260 per cent of GDP, which is similar to Europe and the United States. But a key difference is the large amount of corporate debt in China, which is more worrying than government debt if there is a risk of large-scale bankruptcies that could bring down the banking system. And part of that debt is owed to the shadow banking system, where lending is done outside of the formal banks. It's a murky sector which includes anyone who lends money without a banking licence, including loan sharks but also others. By definition, shadow banking debt isn't measured accurately, so the overall level of Chinese debt is a source of concern.

The growth of shadow banking is linked to the Chinese government not introducing sufficient competition into the state-owned banking system. A rapidly growing economy, powered increasingly by private entrepreneurs, requires credit. As private firms sought funds that the formal banking system, which predominantly lent to state-owned firms, were reluctant to provide, unlicensed lending grew. Shadow banking took off after the 2008 financial crisis in the

West. As Chinese exports were hit by recession in America and the EU, growth was affected and so the Chinese government encouraged private companies to grow. Some did that by borrowing from shadow banks. Local governments also tried to boost their economies by investing in infrastructure projects, so they too borrowed. They followed the dictates of the central government, which planned for a large fiscal stimulus that relied on localities to find the money and spend it. Because China doesn't have a well-established bond market where local governments can issue debt and borrow to fund their spending, some of them, too, turned to the shadow banking system.

Since the end of the 2009 Great Recession in the West, the Chinese government has been clamping down on shadow banking. China recognizes the dangers of a debt crisis, like the one experienced by Japan in the early 1990s, that could derail its growth for years. A similarity that China shares with Japan is that nearly all of its debt is domestically held. So, a financial crisis there wouldn't necessarily spread far beyond the Chinese border, though there would clearly be a significant impact if the world's second biggest economy were to suffer from a financial crisis severe enough to lead to economic stagnation.

In order to stop borrowers from turning to shadow banking, the government has tried to develop other instruments to allow companies and local governments to borrow, such as building up the bond markets (the market for corporate and government debt). As in other major economies, that would allow companies and local governments to issue bonds or debt and borrow from capital markets rather than shadow banks to fund their growth. Also, if the Chinese banking system was not predominately state-owned, and there was greater competition due to new bank entrants, this would provide another alternative to shadow banking. Reforming the state-owned banks that dominate China's financial system has been ongoing, but progress is slow owing to the powerful vested interests that benefit from running state-owned banks. This is an example where the communal property system hampers the growth of the increasingly marketized economy, and yet reform is difficult in a communist regime.

So, to sustain China's economic growth will require a series of reforms. Some of the challenges that the country faces are related to its communist political system and the retention of state ownership. Can they be overcome? Can a communist state become rich?

Marx and China

China's revolution seemed to fit Marx's paradigm. China's communist revolt in 1949 was led by rural peasants, which differed from the proletarian revolution in 1917 in the USSR. Even though he lived in the world's largest city after 1849, Marx became eventually convinced of the significance of agriculture in a capitalist economy and of the importance of social conflict in the countryside for revolution. In part, he gained these views from the French Physiocrats, David Ricardo and Thomas Malthus, all of whom considered the agricultural sector to be an essential part of the development process, and thus a source of capitalist conflict in Marx's view. In *Capital*, Marx wrote of the labourers, capitalists, and landowners. Yet in the *Communist Manifesto*, written nineteen years before, he focused on two classes in a capitalist society: the bourgeoisie and the proletariat.

Marx's three-class society characterized China better than Russia in this respect. The Soviet Union was formed from a proletariat uprising, while China's communists were people from the countryside who overthrew the landowners in the Chinese civil war. These were the peasant labourers who rose up, under Mao Zedong, against the capitalist and landowning classes. It was the type of revolution that Marx predicted: social conflict between the exploited labourers and the capitalist classes that would lead to the overthrow of the old system and the adoption of a communal or communist system of ownership.

Marx was opposed to private ownership of the means of production and described bankers as 'a class of parasites'.[18] In the *Communist Manifesto* there was a programme which would carve 'despotic inroads on the rights of property, and on the conditions of bourgeois production'.[19] It included:

1. Abolition of property in land and application of all rents of land to public purposes
2. A heavy progressive or graduated income tax
3. Abolition of all right of inheritance
4. Confiscation of the property of all emigrants and rebels
5. Centralization of credit in the hands of the state by means of a national bank with State capital and an exclusive monopoly
6. Centralization of the means of communication and transport in the hands of the State
7. Extension of factories and instruments of production owned by the State; the bringing into cultivation of wastelands and the improvement of the soil generally in accordance with a common plan
8. Equal liability of all to work; establishment of industrial armies, especially for agriculture
9. Combination of agriculture with manufacturing industries; gradual abolition of the distinction between town and country, by a more equitable distribution of the populace over the country
10. Free education for all children in public schools; abolition of child factory labour in its present form; combination of education with industrial production, etc.

During the command economy period that followed the Chinese revolution that spanned three decades from 1949–79, China adopted the Soviet communist model for a time. A Soviet style of central planning was undertaken in the first Five Year Plan in 1953. State-owned enterprises were created from formerly private firms, and centrally administered by about twenty ministries in the State Council, China's top policy body. The Chinese economy was 'Stalinist' in the sense of establishing urban industries, embarking on long-term planning and providing for scientific and technical education. But relations between China and the USSR broke down within a decade. Among their differences was that the Soviet premier Nikita Khrushchev and Mao Zedong differed on the interpretation of Marxism.

Khrushchev even accused China of misusing Soviet aid to fund its 'Great Leap Forward' in 1958, which he described as a 'harebrained' policy to try to industrialize the nation.[20] The disastrous Great Leap Forward, which lasted until 1962, saw tens of millions of Chinese starve as they followed Mao's dictate to smelt their pots in 'backyard furnaces' to create steel for industrial goods and neglected farming the land. They also fell out over relations with the West, for example Mao disagreed with Khrushchev's policy of co-existence with America. By the late 1960s China and the USSR had engaged in border clashes and even reoriented their nuclear missiles towards each other. As Maoist China went its own way after the split with the Soviet Union, Chinese economic policy also diverged from that of the USSR.

Still, China followed some of the principles set out in *The Communist Manifesto* and *Capital*, at least for a time. For instance, Marx believed that a worker's condition could only be improved by abolishing private property, so China created a state-owned sector comprising firms and banks. China ridding itself of private enterprises after 1949 meant state ownership of the means of production, so everyone was a worker as Marx espoused.

Marx also believed that in the initial stages of a communist society, workers would be paid not in money but in notes denoted by labour time. Pay would correspond to hours worked, after a deduction of a 'common fund' for investment and maintenance. These notes could be used to purchase goods, which were in turn priced according to how much labour time had been expended on their production. The system would be egalitarian and there would be no capitalists to exploit workers. China's post-1949 employment system was based on workers receiving work points per day that could be exchanged for goods, a system similar to what Marx had proposed.

Marx had also endorsed women's political participation. Under Chairman Mao, female labour force participation rivalled that of men's. Curiously, though, the same could not be said of wages, even though 'women hold up half the sky' in Maoist China. A woman earned eight work points for a day's labour as compared with ten for a man.[21]

One disadvantage was that no one did much work in a planned economy since work points were awarded every day by the state regardless of what was produced. That was not quite what Marx had predicted. He believed that more labour-time credits would be awarded for more intense work, so workers would be compensated equitably. Marx actually rejected a 'fair' distribution of income. Furthermore, in his system, workers would not receive the full value of their output. The surplus would go to the people collectively for communal services.[22]

But this collectively minded stage was never reached in any of the communist economies. For China and others such as Vietnam, the lack of incentive to work under central planning led to slow economic growth which in turn brought about the need for reforms. It's not what Marx had envisioned. State ownership of industries also led to inefficiencies and persistent shortages since no central planner could effectively set all quantities and prices as well as market supply and demand. China still retains communal ownership of property, at least nominally, since decades-long leases are permitted. The privatization of land in particular and also the reform of the remaining state-owned enterprises are hotly debated because they are sources of inefficiency that hamper economic growth.

One key concept that underpins Marx's analysis that may shed light on some of the reasons for the divergence between theory and reality is the assumption he makes regarding the rate of profit. It was Adam Smith who first asserted the tendency of the rate of profit to fall over time, which was later developed by David Ricardo and John Stuart Mill. A falling rate of profit leads to a 'stationary state' where the economy stops growing because profit has fallen so far that new investments are not profitable. They all saw it as culminating in the stagnation of a capitalist system, although Marx's version foresaw a workers' uprising that would follow thereafter and lead to the establishment of a communist regime.

For China and the USSR, profits fell as predicted. A lack of work incentive led to low productivity. But state-owned enterprises had to meet their production quotas. They tapped state-owned banks for investment funds, which led to increasingly unprofitable investments and a build-up of debt. A lack of profitability pointed to the need for market reforms. Economic stagnation became the trigger for abandoning Marxist principles. Ironically, the outcome predicted for capitalist economies was actually realized in communist ones.

China's transformation into a largely market-based economy, still ruled politically by a communist party, would not have been foreseen by Marx, for whom communism and capitalism could not coexist. Also, China had become very unequal; at one point during its heady growth rates in the early twenty-first century, communist China was more unequal than capitalist America. That was certainly not part of Marx's vision for a communist society. In China's current phase of reforms, as befits a middle-income country, it is seeking to rebalance its growth drivers and rely less on investment and more on consumption; less on exports and more on domestic demand; less on agriculture and lower-end manufacturing and more on high-tech manufacturing and services. This last aspect would have been particularly galling to Marx. His view on service sector workers was unequivocal: 'From the whore to the Pope, there is a mass of such scum.'[23] He shares that in common with Adam Smith. Marx did not see the value of priests or lawyers, since they did not produce anything of value. In his view, these were only exchanges of a service for money. The notion that intangible output can be as valuable as manufactured goods was simply not within the conception of Marx or the other Great Economists who preceded him. In this respect, Marx would not have approved of China's shift towards a service economy and, especially, away from communal production and farming.

Marx would not have recognized China today as an embodiment of his principles. So, it is unlikely that Marx would have condoned China's subsequent move to incorporate market forces into its economy. He might have been intrigued by the continuation of the communist political system governing an economy that shares challenges such as inequality in common with the most capitalistic of economies, the United States. If China overcomes its challenges and becomes rich under capitalism, then perhaps Marx might reconsider the role that his principles played in guiding communist China – because in Marx's theory, after capitalism takes hold, there is always scope for a worker rebellion and revolution in the future.

★

Marx did not live to see a world in which Marxism had taken hold across swathes of the globe, nor the concomitant Cold War which pitted the communist USSR against capitalist America, or China emerging as the world's second economic power. He died in 1883, just over a year after his wife, probably from tuberculosis, the disease that had killed his father and four of his siblings. Karl and Jenny Marx were both buried in Highgate Cemetery in north London.

The 2008 global financial crisis led some to become disillusioned with capitalism, and Marxism is somewhat back into fashion. A book published in the aftermath of the crisis was titled *How Karl Marx Can Save American Capitalism*.[24] That would have resonated with Marx. To varying degrees, the Great Economists were engaged with the policy debates of the day. Adam Smith and David Ricardo both served in government and actively reshaped economic policies, including the repeal of protectionist legislation. Marx, of course, was more revolutionary and would go further, having spent his life organizing workers to rise up against the capitalists. For him, it is evident that economics must move beyond philosophical principles that interpret and only attempt to influence policy. As he said: 'Philosophers have hitherto only interpreted the world; the point is to change it.'[25]

4

Alfred Marshall: Is Inequality Inevitable?

There's no doubt that inequality is high on the policy agenda. For instance, addressing income inequality is a refrain heard in Britain, whose current prime minister expressed concern for those who are 'just about managing' or, as her speechwriters dubbed them, 'JAMs'. How well people are faring relates to the quality of economic growth, and not just how fast an economy is expanding.

A somewhat surprising best-selling book is on the topic of inequality by the French economist Thomas Piketty. Who would have thought a 685-page book based on detailed economic research would end up on the *New York Times* best-seller list? Its popularity reflects a widespread concern that inequality is as extreme now in America as it was during the Gilded Age of the late nineteenth century. Economics Nobel laureate Joseph Stiglitz is among those who have pointed to inequality as one of the reasons for the slow recovery after the Great Recession of 2009 that followed the global financial crisis. Stiglitz has argued that highly unequal societies recover more slowly since growth mostly benefits the rich, who save more than they spend. And spending, not saving, fuels an economic recovery.[1] Are capitalist economies always unequal? What, if anything, can be done about it? Is it true that, as Winston Churchill observed in 1945 speaking in the House of Commons of the British Parliament: 'The inherent vice of capitalism is the unequal sharing of blessings; the inherent virtue of socialism is the equal sharing of miseries'?

Some time before Churchill's observation, Alfred Marshall

established neoclassical economics. He adapted the classical economics of Adam Smith, David Ricardo and others into a more analytical framework based on *laissez-faire* principles governing the market. Marshall transformed the way that we think about how different factors can change the prices and quantities of goods and services in the economy. This fundamental framework of economics was devised by this Cambridge economist. How would Marshall view the worsening of income inequality under capitalism?

The life and times of Alfred Marshall

Alfred Marshall was born in 1842 in Bermondsey, a lower-class London district, to a clerk at the Bank of England. He was the second of five children and attended a private school. With the help of a scholarship and financial assistance from an uncle, he then attended Cambridge University to study mathematics.

After graduation, he was elected a fellow in 1865 and then appointed in 1868 as Lecturer in the Moral Sciences at St John's College, Cambridge University. There he met his wife, Mary Paley, who had attended his lectures.[2] Her father and great-grandfather were both Cambridge dons (what fellows of Oxbridge – Oxford and Cambridge – colleges are called). She taught economics herself at Newnham, a women's college at Cambridge University. When they married, university regulations forced Marshall to resign his fellowship, and he took up the combined duties of Professor of Political Economy and Principal of Bristol University College, which had been established the previous year and later became the University of Bristol.

His *Economics of Industry* textbook, co-authored with his wife who became the first female lecturer in economics at Bristol and one of the first in Britain, was published in 1879. A couple of years later he resigned from Bristol and they spent a year on the European continent, which was when he began writing his seminal *Principles of Economics*. After their return to the UK, he resumed teaching at Bristol. But it was a brief return.

In 1883 he took up a tutorial fellowship at Balliol College, Oxford

University. Marshall was sceptical about his ability to attract students to study at the university since he did not believe that economics was treated as a serious subject.[3] PPE (philosophy, politics and economics) wasn't established as a formal degree until the 1920s. He was not there long, but, for a few terms at least, Balliol College counted both Marshall and Adam Smith among its fellows! To ease his departure, Marshall leant on John Neville Keynes, the father of John Maynard Keynes, to take his place. Keynes gave it a brief trial but decided that he preferred Cambridge. It is curious to consider whether history would have been different if he had stayed and his son been raised in Oxford.

In 1885, after the rules were changed to allow for marriage, Marshall returned to take up a professorship at Cambridge. This is where most of his career was spent, first as an undergraduate at St John's College from 1861–65, then as a fellow from 1865–77 and after his appointment as Professor of Political Economy in 1885, which he held until his retirement in 1908; he then remained an emeritus fellow until his death in 1924. It was in 1903 that he established what was to become the university's well-regarded economics undergraduate degree and thereby the Faculty of Economics and Politics.

Alfred Marshall was a late-Victorian intellectual. It was a time of political consensus on the major economic issues of the day. There was universal acceptance of free trade, for instance. Recall the abolition of the Corn Laws in 1846 discussed in the Ricardo chapter, which marked the start of an era of free trade. Marshall too defended free trade half a century later, when it was again under threat.

None of the leading economists of that time were supporters of the 'extreme *laissez-faire*' of the Manchester School of the 1830s and 1840s.[4] Those adherents were largely found on the Continent and in North America. Most economists were like Marshall in that they supported a system that included regulation of the workplace and other circumscribed roles for the government.

It wasn't until Marshall reached his forties that consensus on major economic issues began to break down. It was during the Long Depression in the 1880s when economics was being re-examined that Marshall made his seminal contributions. His theories formalized the building

blocks of a competitive market economy. Marshall incorporated rigorous analysis that led to more robust conclusions. He pioneered the use
of diagrams to illustrate the key concepts of modern economics such as
demand and supply, diagrams which are still taught and used today.[5]

By showing how production and consumption were determined
for the economy, Marshall's work sharpened debates over what constituted appropriate economic policy. In terms of production,
Marshall's diagrams depicted the effects of declining returns to additional units of capital and labour. When the point was reached at
which additional cost equalled additional return, he showed that was
the equilibrium where the additional or marginal unit should be produced. For instance, a firm will choose to produce a widget up to the
point where the cost does not exceed what it can be sold for. How to
reach equilibrium is now a basic concept underpinning economics.

As for consumption, his work on marginal utility analysis explains
how consumers behave. Each person decides to work or take leisure,
knowing the cost is an hour of effort that would have been compensated by wages. There is utility or enjoyment gained from leisure, but
that is balanced by the loss of earnings. Adding up every person's
utility offers a way of assessing the wellbeing of a society. This is one
of the reasons why Marshall once considered naming his subject
social economics rather than simply economics.

His textbook *Economics of Industry*, and his diagrams that showed
how optimal decisions are made by firms and people, propelled Marshall to rank among the leading English economists of his day. But
his seminal work was still to come. Marshall would soon transform
the field with his *Principles of Economics*. The first volume was published in July 1890, and it was even compared to Adam Smith's *The
Wealth of Nations*. On the centenary of Marshall's birth, *Principles* was
described as follows:

> Ideas of this sort might very likely have permeated English political
> economy in any case. They were in the air. But as a matter of plain
> historical fact their prevalence is due to Marshall. In its country of
> origin Alfred Marshall's *Principles* stands with Adam Smith's *Wealth
> of Nations* and Ricardo's *Principles* as one of the three great watersheds

in the development of economic ideas: with the usual qualifications, we may divide the history of English political economy into three distinct epochs – the Classical, the Ricardian and the Marshallian or reformed-Ricardian . . . it must be accounted as one of the foundation stones of modern American economics.[6]

Similar to Adam Smith with *The Wealth of Nations*, Marshall took a decade to write *Principles*. The planned second volume, though, was abandoned. Instead, Marshall made significant revisions up to and including to the eighth edition, published in 1920. There was a ninth edition, which showed all the amendments made in the previous eight, published posthumously by the Royal Economic Society in 1961 as Volume II. In all, Marshall spent around forty years on his book of diagrams, so around half his life was dedicated to his seminal work.

Not atypically for a late-Victorian, Alfred Marshall's interest in economics was inspired by an interest in welfare and equality of opportunities, which to him were the cornerstones of a prosperous society. It led Marshall to travel to Germany to learn German so that he could read the original writings of Immanuel Kant. He was then also able to read the works of Karl Marx and Ferdinand Lassalle. Marshall would later advise his students:

> We are told sometimes that everyone who strenuously endeavours to promote the social amelioration of the people is a Socialist – at all events, if he believes that much of this work can be better performed by the State than by individual effort. In this sense nearly every economist of the present generation is a Socialist. In this sense I was a Socialist before I knew anything of economics; and, indeed, it was my desire to know what was practicable in social reform by State and other agencies which led me to read Adam Smith and [John Stuart] Mill, Marx and Lassalle, forty years ago. I have since then been steadily growing a more convinced Socialist in this sense of the word . . .[7]

However, he did not accept all of their beliefs, such as communal property or revolution to effect change, as espoused by Karl Marx. Instead, Marshall believed in a prescribed set of roles for the government to improve welfare for the society and provide opportunities. For instance, he supported state provision of universal education so that even the poorest children could gain skills and compete for jobs in the economy. When it came to improving social conditions, Marshall, true to his life's work, believed in the market forces of supply and demand to raise wages for the poor: 'if the numbers of unskilled labourers were to diminish sufficiently, then those who did unskilled work would have to be paid good wages'.[8]

Although Marshall's work was based on utility theory, he didn't adhere to all of those tenets either. Jeremy Bentham's concept underpins utility theory: 'it is the greatest happiness of the greatest number that is the measure of right and wrong'.[9] In *Principles*, Marshall singled out Bentham's influence on the evolution of economics in the nineteenth century.

But Marshall's view was different from Bentham's, or from John Stuart Mill's idea of a utility-maximizing 'economic man'. Marshall was critical of the concept of seeking the greatest happiness for the greatest number. Instead, he argued that the whole might be larger than the sum of its parts. As we'll come to later, this adherence to utility maximization for society as a whole, which pays less attention to the distribution of that utility, may be why inequality has grown so rapidly in some capitalist economies.

For Marshall, interest in inequality and poverty permeated his work. To the Royal Commission on the Aged Poor in 1893 he declared: 'I have devoted myself for the last twenty-five years to the problem of poverty, and very little of my work has been devoted to any inquiry which does not bear upon that.'[10]

So, what would Alfred Marshall make of the growing inequality in the developed world that has seen as much inequality in early twenty-first century America as he witnessed during the Gilded Age?

Growing inequality

Some of the statistics on income inequality that have propelled it up the policy agenda are striking. For instance, the share of income going to the top has grown to the point where the richest 1 per cent of Americans account for a fifth of all the country's income. The richest 10 per cent of Americans account for half of all of the income in that wealthy country.

According to Thomas Piketty, it's slightly better in Europe. Still, in Britain, the top 10 per cent receive over 40 per cent of the income. In Germany and France, it's over one-third. All of these shares in Europe have risen since the 1970s, but not by so much as to rival the Gilded Age. It has in the US, though, which has led some to dub this era as the Second Gilded Age in America.

This phenomenon is not confined to the world's richest countries. Although developing countries have seen poverty fall dramatically, and a billion people have been lifted out of poverty since 1990, income inequality has remained largely unchanged since 1960.[11] Within countries, inequality on average has risen or not improved significantly, not just in the West but also in countries like China. This is while inequality between nations has fallen because of the relatively faster growth of emerging economies, which has narrowed the income gap between developed and developing countries.

Since the 2009 recession, inequality has been an issue particularly in America. During the economic boom of the 1950s in the United States, the top 1 per cent did only a little better than the rest, gaining some 5 per cent of the increased income. But since the Great Recession, the top 1 per cent have accounted for 95 per cent of the income gain, leaving the bottom 99 per cent with just 5 per cent of the gain between them. During recessionary periods, low interest rates make borrowing cheap and drive a recovery which typically boosts stocks. US markets have hit numerous record highs since the 2008 crisis, and such gains predominately go to the half of US households who own stocks. Of the richest 10 per cent of US households, 93 per cent own shares while it's just 11 per cent among the poorest quintile of households.

How much does inequality affect the recovery? The answer is by no means clear cut. Two Nobel Prize winners in economics, Paul Krugman and Joseph Stiglitz, disagree on whether inequality has played an important part in the slow recovery since the 2008 financial crisis.

Stiglitz argues that inequality impedes economic growth. The rich pay less tax than the poor as a share of their income, so growing inequality does not increase tax receipts as much as expected. Also, the poor consume more of their income than the rich. This lower 'marginal propensity to consume' of the rich was originally identified by John Maynard Keynes. In other words, poorer people have less disposable income and spend more of it on necessities like food. Richer people tend to spend proportionately less of their income since they have more money to spend. It implies that raising incomes for the poor would generate proportionately more consumption, which would drive economic growth.

Krugman, on the other hand, says that he hasn't seen evidence that the rich 'under-consume'. In one sense, the rich spend more than the poor. Someone spending 20 per cent of a £10,000 income would add £2,000 to the economy, while someone spending just 3 per cent of £100,000 would add £3,000. Krugman also points out that this comparison is a static one: you can measure how two people with two different levels of income act at any given point in time, but it's harder to predict how a person's spending would change if incomes were raised.

Stiglitz and Krugman may disagree over how much a role inequality plays in the slow recovery, but they agree that high levels of income inequality are a problem for economic as well as social reasons.

Income inequality has been problematic for a long time. Inequality fell after the Gilded Age and the Roaring Twenties, especially during the 1950s and 1960s when per capita GDP, which is a measure of average income, grew well during what's called the Golden Age of economic growth. But beginning in the 1970s, the income gap ceased narrowing, and then started expanding sharply after 1980, until now when America has become more unequal than ever before.

Is the land of opportunity really a society of haves and have-nots? Is the US economy now just enriching the rich? One theme is evident throughout this debate: the rich getting richer has squeezed the middle class. For the first time since at least the early 1970s, there are fewer people in the middle class than in the working and upper classes in the United States.[12] Indeed, within many nations around the world income inequality has increased, notably the gap between the richest 1 per cent and the rest of society. F. Scott Fitzgerald said that the very rich are different from you and me. But perhaps the rich are the same as each other around the world?

Anyone driving through the narrow streets of Shanghai's French concession will see immediately why the city was once called the Paris of the East. Ritzy shops like Prada share a block with older colonial-era houses – a rarity in China, where high-rise apartments dominate the city skyline. In the 1920s foreigners and Chinese mingled in what was considered to be the most cosmopolitan city in Asia. Now, with the rapid increase in wealth in China, it feels as though it has entered a Gilded Age.

Nanjing Road is one of its rare pedestrianized areas. It leads west from the Bund, an esplanade along the Huangpu River, and a crowded array of shops, hotels and cafes line both sides. Busy at all times of the day, the newly minted middle class in China is finally enjoying a lifestyle that the West takes for granted. But there are beggars crouched in the doorways of the designer shops. Communist China has become as unequal as capitalist America.

It's remarkable that China has more billionaires than the United States. Their number is also growing at a striking rate. A decade or so ago, there were just three dollar billionaires in China; there are now hundreds. That's a huge change in a country whose average income is the same as Costa Rica's.

The Chinese billionaires on the *Forbes* rich list are becoming ever-wealthier. The long-standing incumbent at or near the top of the list is Wang Jianlin, who made his money through the traditional routes of property and entertainment. Wealth was obliterated during the Cultural Revolution of the 1960s and 1970s, so the likes of Wang had to create their fortunes from scratch. He is now China's leading property tycoon and intends to build a global entertainment empire that will outshine Disney. His business took advantage of the opening of China's consumer market in the 1990s and the emergence of the new middle class. A remarkable number of people have been lifted out of poverty in a generation, and their demand for the offices, entertainment and cinemas Wang Jianlin provides has made him one of the richest men in the world and a celebrity in China. When he steps out of his Rolls-Royce, people stop to photograph him.

A new generation of entrepreneurs have also made their fortunes as a result of the digital revolution. Around a quarter of the newcomers to the *Forbes* rich list have been from China and many are young. They are predominately in the tech sphere, which has produced wealth for not only the younger cohort of businessmen but also those such as Alibaba's Jack Ma after his e-commerce firm's record-busting initial public offering (IPO), when shares issued for the first time to the public on the New York Stock Exchange raised $25 billion.

The entrepreneurs catering to the new middle class were unlike their predecessors, who made their money through real estate, a field requiring good contacts with the Chinese government since most property was state owned. But, like Wang Jianlin and others who took advantage of the privatization of real estate in China in the 1990s, this new generation is following the ongoing shift in the economy towards consumerism as the government seeks to make middle-class consumption the engine of growth rather than investment in property fuelled by corporate debt (see the chapter on Marx).

More than half of China's wealthy are entrepreneurs; the rest comprise investors and a small number of highly paid executives. The common factor is that, in the absence of inherited wealth owing to the Cultural Revolution, they are nearly all self-made men. (Like most of the super-rich around the world, China's billionaires are predominantly male.)

But the next generation is now coming of age; wealth is once again being passed on in China. The inheritors have been dubbed the *fuerdai*, which translates into the 'rich second generation'. The highest-profile cases of wealth inequality are among the children of the super-rich. It's not only the so-called princelings whose parents are Communist Party officials who are attracting attention. It's also those such as Wang Jianlin's son, Wang Sicong, who reveals his lifestyle on his microblog on Weibo, the Chinese version of Twitter. Whereas their parents tend to be frugal, the *fuerdai*, though they may work hard, play hard too. There is criticism in the media of their fast cars and extravagant spending. Their lavish lifestyles don't sit comfortably in a society that still propounds the virtues of socialism. Wang Jianlin told me when I interviewed him for my BBC TV programme that, as societies become middle class, their resentment against the rich grows. He cited Singapore and Hong Kong as societies in which such attitudes have emerged as their societies became better off.

His observation echoes studies that find that inequality and poverty are relative concepts. Indeed, it's not just the absolute difference between the incomes of the rich and the poor that matters for wellbeing. That's what is typically measured by indicators such as the Gini coefficient: an index that is zero if all individuals have the same income and one if one person has all the income in a country. But, as a society becomes increasingly dominated by a growing middle class, such comparisons are relative. In fact, in developed economies, it is income relative to the median income (the income of the middle person in the range of incomes) that defines poverty. By that gauge, nearly two million pensioners are poor in the UK when measured as those living on less than 60 per cent of the median income (measured as disposable income minus housing costs).

For China, the shifting societal perceptions of inequality follow from its own recent transformation into a middle-class society. It was as recently as 2001 that per capita annual income in China exceeded $1,000, the level that defines the world's poorest countries. It was only in 2010 that Chinese average incomes surpassed $4,000, the level that defines an upper-middle-income society. Even now, China occupies only a mid-table position in the league of countries ranked by average income.

But, of course, the average obscures the distribution of income, and despite its communist system, the past decade or so has seen China become an unequal society. The top 5 per cent of households account for about a quarter of all income. There is a large gap between urban and rural incomes, or urban households earning three times as much as rural ones. The coast also outpaces the interior in terms of wealth. But the pattern of inequality is moderating. Income inequality reached a peak in 2008 and has since declined. Nonetheless, China, like other emerging nations, is a society that has become very unequal in many respects within a short period of time.

Why has inequality risen over the past century?

One of the reasons for high inequality in countries like China is that, as countries industrialize and urbanize, they grow more quickly. Those who move into industry and cities earn more than those who don't, so income inequality tends to increase with economic development. But countries can reduce income inequality through redistributive policies. Without the social welfare system, inequality would be much higher in the US, the UK and much of the rest of Europe. The lack of such a well-established system is one of the factors contributing to China's high levels of inequality.

In developed countries, different forces are at work. First, globalization has pushed down median wages, and those who gain from international trade, namely the skilled workers and owners of capital, have earned more, while the middle- and lower-skilled have lost out in advanced economies. Another factor is something known as 'skill-biased technical change'. As the economy becomes more technologically driven, it's again the most skilled workers who reap the greatest rewards. The two are related, of course.

Thomas Piketty believes that inequality will rise when the returns to capital (r) exceed the growth rate of the economy (g). In this case, holders of capital (property, companies, stocks and so on) will see their incomes rise faster than average incomes in the long run.

Others think differently. In France and Britain, for example, the value of private capital as a share of income has skyrocketed to over 500 per cent since the 1970s, while for the US that ratio is a hefty 400 per cent. As this wealth is passed along, the gap between the rich and the rest grows, so inherited wealth is another explanation for inequality. Paul Krugman has pointed out that around half of the wealthiest ten Americans inherited their wealth.

Earned income is another driver of inequality. For instance, a CEO of America's largest listed (S&P 500) companies earns, on average, over 200 times that of an average worker in the same company. In the 1960s, it was twenty times as much. Why has this happened? Former US Labor Secretary Robert Reich gives decreased unionization weakening the bargaining power over wages of workers as one cause.[13]

It is likely that all these views have some merit, and that there are a number of factors that have contributed to growing inequality. Each of them suggests a different set of policy solutions. For instance, progressive taxes which tax the earnings of the rich at a higher rate than those of the poor would help to address some of the wage gap. If technological change is exacerbating inequality, then the fiscal system could be used to redistribute. That's what the chairman of former US President Obama's Council of Economic Advisers, Jason Furman, says they did. But others, including the founder of Bain Capital, Ed Conard, contend that raising taxes to reduce inequality is not a long-term solution and can harm companies.

And what about global forces at play that are outside government control? Piketty proposes a more radical solution: an internationally coordinated tax on wealth. But Angel Gurría, Secretary-General of the OECD, which is the think tank for advanced economies, disagrees. He says that national, not global, labour market and tax policies are needed to address inequality. Specifically, there should be a cut in taxes to encourage employment, offset by a rise in certain taxes, including green taxes.[14]

There is a divide between those who argue for redistribution through the tax system and those who are against government intervention. Those who favour more government action would also support policies to raise wages, including setting a higher minimum wage and promoting the creation of well-paid, middle-skilled jobs. Others might prefer policies designed to give every person the same opportunities to earn a living and reduce inequality through market forces, rather than taxing and redistributing after the fact. Their concern is that redistributive policies create the wrong incentives by taxing the successful and subsidizing the less well-off, thus discouraging both the rich and the poor to work. As the political joke goes: 'How can you tell the difference between a Republican and a Democrat? When a Republican sees someone drowning, he throws too short a rope and yells "the rest is up to you". A Democrat throws too long a rope and lets go of his end.'

Suffice it to say this is an unsettled debate. So, what would the father of neoclassical economics make of the rise in inequality, which has become such an issue that it has led some to question the validity of a capitalist system that permits it to happen?

Alfred Marshall's views on inequality

Alfred Marshall argued that the role of the state in addressing inequality should include the following considerations:

> Taking it for granted that a more equal distribution of wealth is to be desired, how far would this justify changes in the institutions of property, or limitations of free enterprise even when they would be likely to diminish the aggregate of wealth? In other words, how far should an increase in the income of the poorer classes and a diminution of their work be aimed at, even if it involved some lessening of national material wealth? How far could this be done without injustice, and without slackening the energies of the leaders of progress? How ought the burdens of taxation to be distributed among the different classes of society?[15]

That is the core of the debate. Marshall saw a trade-off between policies to more equally distribute income and the disincentives they create towards work. In his view:

> the chief dangers of socialism lie not in its tendency towards a more equal distribution of income for I can see no harm in that, but in its sterilizing influence on those mental activities which have gradually raised the world from barbarism.[16]

Marshall drew a distinction between production and redistribution, as did John Stuart Mill. Mill had argued in his *Principles of Political Economy* that economic laws governing production were not easy to alter, while redistributive policies were crafted by governments and changeable.[17] But Marshall initially did not support 'fiscal' redistribution through taxes. He viewed income taxes as inefficient because of their effects on work. But after the introduction of a graduated estate duty (higher rates on larger estates) in 1894, the forerunner to an inheritance tax, there was no disincentivizing effect on the willingness to work. That helped change Marshall's mind, since what he had proposed before, encouraging philanthropy, was not enough to reduce inequality.

So, during and after the First World War, Marshall came to believe in the benefits of progressive tax rates. He gradually accepted fiscal redistribution. What he did not support was equalizing income through extensive redistribution. It would at best achieve very limited results. Over the long run, such policies would hurt growth if people were disincentivized to work, and that would mean less money to redistribute. Redistributive programmes today do not go so far as to equalize incomes, in line with Marshall's concerns.

Progressive taxation is one of the standard tools used now to redistribute income. But the extent of redistribution differs across countries. For instance, there is less redistribution in America than in Europe, which has a larger welfare state. Bigger government, though, doesn't sit well with Marshall.

Marshall saw the government's role more as that of regulator than as provider of goods and services. Ensuring that businesses acted lawfully, that products were of good quality and fairly priced were the sorts of tasks that governments should undertake. And there shouldn't be a large number of bureaucrats: 'The function of Government is to govern as little as possible; but not to do as little as possible.'[18]

Marshall also favoured decentralization. He saw the benefits of experimentation and local competition. He strongly opposed local government as a delegated administrator of central government, though. In his view, education and town planning provided the greatest scope for local initiatives. However, larger tasks, such as the supply of water, electricity and gas, were to be undertaken by government only if they could not be undertaken efficiently by the private sector.

Where Marshall believed that government could help to reduce poverty was by improving the skill set of the poor to make them more competitive in the market. As mentioned earlier, he advocated education to make unskilled labour scarcer and thus better rewarded. He also proposed controlling migration to limit competition.

Like other Victorians, Marshall emphasized the impact on a person's character of any policies that sought to reduce poverty and inequality. Concern about being reliant on charity led to an inevitable emphasis on self-help and mutual assistance, which was a Victorian perspective. But Marshall recognized that factors such as insecure employment, unemployment, illness and old age were common among many of the 'deserving' poor.

His student and successor as Professor of Political Economy at Cambridge as well as literary executor, Arthur Cecil Pigou, believed that Marshall would have welcomed the government's efforts in promoting greater income equality after the Second World War. Marshall had become less concerned about the disincentive effects on work, except for a high tax on savings. So, he was more willing to accept socialist-type policies so long as they were not economically harmful. Still, Marshall worried about the negative effect on productivity 'from the deadening influence of bureaucratic methods'.[19] For instance, Marshall opposed nationalization on principle, except for natural monopolies, which are industries such as utilities where it is efficient to have one firm, and only accepted government involvement if it meant the task could be carried out more efficiently. This was in line with his opinion that economic prosperity depended on the forces of competition. So, he would not support socialist experiments in production, but came to accept fiscal policies designed to alleviate poverty. In this respect, a role for the state in the redistribution of income would be acceptable.

So, we might surmise that Marshall would weigh any tax purporting to reduce inequality carefully against the disincentivizing effects. The OECD recommendations of cutting taxes to encourage employment would be in line with Marshall's beliefs. Given his preference for evidence, he would be swayed by the studies of fiscal redistribution policies adopted since the creation of the welfare state after the Second World War. The International Monetary Fund (IMF) has looked at moderatively redistributive taxes and policies and concluded that they do no harm and might help to reduce income inequality.[20]

Marshall would recognize that the decision as to what level of inequality is acceptable would ultimately be a political one where economics merely provides the analytical tools to determine those benefits and costs to be considered. The US is less redistributive than Europe, which has a larger welfare state and some of the most egalitarian societies in the world, notably the Nordic countries. Americans have chosen to focus on promoting equality in opportunity, giving rise to the notion of an American Dream where everyone who works hard can have a house and a good job. China seems to be headed down the American path, with the phrase of the Chinese Dream used to promote similar ideas. But the dramatic rise in inequality in the United States over the past few decades suggests that the American approach is under challenge. Europe has a different problem in that its expensive welfare state, only some of which has to do with redistributive policies, is unaffordable, for example pension payments are increasing due to ageing societies. Thus, re-examining how to address inequality in capitalist economies has become a pressing issue for many countries.

Marshall's legacy

In May 1908, just before his sixty-sixth birthday, Marshall retired as a university professor in order to work on the second volume of his *Principles of Economics*, which he had announced nearly two decades earlier but was yet to complete. (He had wanted to retire earlier, in 1901, but could not afford to do so.) After retirement, though, he abandoned the second volume. In 1910 'Volume I' was removed from the sixth edition of *Principles*. Instead, he wrote three companions between 1919 and 1924.

One reason was, like many renowned economists, Marshall found himself very busy in retirement. In addition to revising *Principles*, he contributed to parliamentary commissions, engaged in correspondence and undertook other activities that took up his time. Mary Paley wrote that her husband said: 'I don't care for living except to work. He said that he was glad to have done all he could to help the world on.'[21] And he did just that. Marshall was active for nearly two decades after retirement. He died at home in 1924, a fortnight before his eighty-second birthday, due to cardiac failure.

The most important economist Marshall taught in his final decade at Cambridge was John Maynard Keynes, who, along with Pigou, became the major link in creating the Cambridge School who followed Marshallian thought. It is well known that Keynes had no formal qualifications in economics, like many Cambridge students at the time. They would formally study mathematics and pick up what they were really interested in along the way. Keynes's economics training consisted of attending Marshall's and Pigou's lectures and supervisions for a term or so, as well as reading Marshall's work. He probably got the best economics education on offer in England. The more specialist London School of Economics and Political Science was only founded in 1895. Thus, there are Marshallian foundations in Keynesian macroeconomics, particularly in terms of the need for economics to provide policy solutions.

This prompted Marshall and some of his contemporaries to alter the name of their subject from political economy to economics. He advocated for the change to avoid associating the subject with political considerations rather than with national objectives. It was not intended to narrow its scope.

As mentioned earlier, he had also considered calling it social economics. Marshall's economic theory was rooted firmly within the social sciences, where human responses to policies must be considered. So, fiscal measures to address inequality, within the context of rising social discontent that made such actions urgent, would have been consistent with his economic beliefs. A capitalist system that produced another Gilded Age, even more unequal than the original during his lifetime, is unlikely to have sat well with Marshall. And he would certainly have made his views known. His nephew, Claude Guillebaud, recalled the fear associated with an invitation to lunch for Marshall's students. They could never be certain when Marshall's intellect would crush them if they expressed an analysis or opinion that wasn't wholly rigorous.

Although Marshall is viewed as the economist who increased the rigour of economics, he taught his students to see economics as offering a set of tools and an analytical way of thinking but not to believe that the textbook reflected the real world. He described his approach as follows:

> a good mathematical theorem dealing with economic hypotheses was very unlikely to be good economics; and I went more and more on the rules –
>
> 1. Use mathematics as a shorthand language, rather than as an engine of inquiry.
> 2. Keep to them till you have done.
> 3. Translate into English.
> 4. Then illustrate by examples that are important in real life.
> 5. Burn the mathematics.
> 6. If you can't succeed in 4, burn 3. This last I did often.[22]

5

Irving Fisher: Are We at Risk of Repeating the 1930s?

In October 1929, shortly before the Great Crash, the American economist Irving Fisher infamously declared that stocks had reached a 'permanently high plateau'.[1] But just days later, on 24 October, commonly known as Black Thursday, the market dropped. This was just a precursor to a larger fall. The following week, on 29 October, what became known as Black Tuesday, the stock market crashed. Over those few days, the stock market lost a quarter of its value.

Fisher told the shell-shocked audience of the National Association of Credit Men that he believed nothing fundamental had happened, and they should ride out the temporary storm in the markets. He said: 'The trough was close and the ensuing rally will see the markets quickly return to previous highs.'[2] But, as we know, Fisher was wrong. The Great Crash became the Great Depression and the resulting plunge in the markets wiped out his own $10 million fortune. Ever the optimist, or just out of sheer desperation, he continued to predict a recovery in stock markets and the US economy. However, neither would happen until the end of the 1930s.

Fisher's loss was not just financial. His reputation suffered irreparable damage and he found himself marginalized by businessmen and politicians. Few were willing to take seriously somebody who had been so publicly and spectacularly proven wrong, and lost almost everything as a result. Fisher had marked himself out as a loser.

History, though, has been much kinder, and recognized Fisher's huge contribution to economics. The influential Austrian economist Joseph Schumpeter described him as potentially the greatest economist that America has produced.[3] Indeed, a great deal of modern day economics can be traced back to Fisher's work.

He was the first American economist of any standing. In the late nineteenth century, the US had comparatively few economic thinkers. This was largely because the US government intervened little in the economy, so economics had a limited role in policy. Fisher's work marked a turning point where the HQ of academic economics moved from Europe to the US and in doing so firmly aligned economics with mathematics and statistics. In 1930, he was the co-founder and first President of the Econometric Society, which developed the quantitative aspects of economics. Nearly every Nobel laureate in Economic Sciences has been a member.

Fisher viewed economics in the following way:

> The effort of the economist is to *see*, to picture the interplay of economic elements. The more clearly cut these elements appear in his vision, the better; the more elements he can grasp and hold in his mind at once, the better. The economic world is a misty region. The first explorers used unaided vision. Mathematics is the lantern by which what before was dimly visible now looms up in firm, bold outlines. The old phantasmagoria disappear. We see better. We also see further.[4]

It is remarkable just how much of modern economics, taught in university programmes today, was established by Irving Fisher. Yet he is seldom included in books such as this one, or considered by those studying the history of economic thought. This might have been because he never combined his ideas into a unified theory of economics, in comparison to, say, John Maynard Keynes's *General Theory*, which rather stole his limelight. He also had few disciples, working predominantly on his own and rarely supervising graduate students.

The Theory of Interest, published in 1930, is probably the nearest he came to a *General Theory* type of work. In many ways, it drew together previous research, and Fisher came close to anticipating much of the work of macroeconomic theorists of the late 1930s through to the 1950s. But he didn't carry it through. He was not interested in formulating a theory explaining the level of national income and its changes, as Keynes was to do a few years later.[5] By contrast, Fisher never really pushed his work, thinking of it as an academic project rather than of practical value.

His near death from tuberculosis early in his career led him to emphasize intellectual endeavours that he could accomplish in a short time, as he feared he might never complete long-term tasks.[6] Although he failed to meet his target of writing a book a year, he did manage to turn one out for every two years of his working life, along with scores of professional papers as well as hundreds of popular articles.

He was prolific despite being far from a full-time scholar. His academic work was often put to one side while he promoted his many crusades. He was a reasonably well-known public figure, but most non-economists would associate him with his views on public health, his advocacy for the League of Nations and his stance in favour of Prohibition. On top of this, he was also a businessman and director of companies, accumulating a large fortune before being wiped out by the Great Crash.

By almost all accounts, Fisher was a proud man and hated to be proved wrong. The events of the Great Depression were a chastening experience for him, and he sought to understand how and why his wealth had been lost and the economy and stock market failed to break out of the grip of depression. Between 1932 and 1937 he became an unpaid adviser to the US President, first Herbert Hoover and then Franklin D. Roosevelt. He was clearly motivated by a desire to fix the American economy and with it restore his own finances. It spurred his work on 'debt-deflation', the idea that economies can get trapped in a persistent deflationary spiral where prices fall as the economy stalls since people are not consuming and firms are not investing while they repay debt.

His work resonates in the post-2008 crisis period, where the fear of deflation has again returned to the radar of policymakers. Global growth rates have slowed and inflation rates have fallen persistently below the targets of central banks. Throughout history, episodes of deflation are very rare. However, Japan's 'lost decades' since the early 1990s have served as a warning of what might happen in the aftermath of a financial crisis.

Since 2008, advanced countries have struggled to recapture pre-crisis growth trends and inflation rates have slumped around the world, bringing many countries to the brink of deflation. The large build-up in public and private sector debt suggests the global economic situation is ripe for the debt-deflation that Fisher described as the cause of the Great Depression. So, are we at risk of repeating the experiences of the 1930s? And what might Irving Fisher suggest we do about it?

The life and times of Irving Fisher

George Whitefield Fisher, Irving Fisher's father, was a pastor in the New England Puritan Church. He and his wife, Ella, moved to the First Congregational Church in Saugerties-on-Hudson, New York, in 1865. Fisher was born there two years later.

In 1883 Irving Fisher's father was taken ill with tuberculosis. Back then this was almost always a death sentence and he was to succumb in June the following year, shortly after Fisher graduated high school. As a child, his skill in mathematics helped him to stand out and he was admitted to Yale University in 1884. This was to be the beginning of a lifelong affiliation with one of America's foremost universities.

However, he was now the breadwinner of his family. Apart from $500 his father had put aside for him, he knew he would have to both pay his own way at college and support his mother and younger brother, Herbert. As an undergraduate, he tutored mathematics and entered competitions, winning prize money in Latin, Greek and algebra.

His talent was quickly recognized at Yale. After graduating in 1888, he stayed on to do postgraduate study, but his horizons were much broader than mathematics. It is rumoured he had studied every natural and social science course available at Yale, and he began to think of a life in law or economics. Fisher revealed: 'How much there is I want to do! I always feel that I haven't time to accomplish what I wish. I want to read much . . . I want to write a great deal. I want to make money.'[7] In 1891 he decided to embark on a PhD in mathematical economics.

His doctoral thesis, titled 'Mathematical Investigations in the Theory of Value and Prices', took only one academic year to complete and was in some ways seminal. In it Fisher created a mechanism to compute the prices and quantities of goods in an economy. It was lauded by Nobel laureate Paul Samuelson as the 'greatest doctoral dissertation in economics ever written' and was a big step forward in the mathematical treatment of economics.[8]

The following year he was appointed to the Yale Mathematics Department. Shortly thereafter he married Margaret Hazard, or Margie as the family called her. Margie's father, Rowland, was a wealthy woollen manufacturer and the 'patriarch' of the small town of Peace Dale, Rhode Island. In the 1860s he had formed his own congregational church and invited George Whitefield Fisher to become its pastor. The Fisher family moved there in August 1868, and this is where Irving Fisher grew up, although he and Margie were not childhood friends.

At Yale, Fisher abstained from student frivolity due to his Puritan upbringing. But in the autumn of 1891, at twenty-four years of age, he was invited to a friend's home for dinner. Margie was there too and, for Fisher, it was love at first sight. Their engagement followed and their wedding took place in June 1893. They spent a fourteen-month honeymoon travelling and working around Europe, a period which also included the birth of the first of their three children.

Fisher returned to Yale in the autumn of 1894 to become an assistant professor in the Mathematics Department. A year later a permanent position arose in the newly established Economics Department and Fisher asked to be considered. After a brief inter-departmental tussle, Economics won out. Fisher was concerned about doing something of practical value, and saw mathematics as too abstract.

At that time, economic thought in US universities was strongly dominated by the German School. Their approach was historically based; theories were acceptable only from those able to demonstrate a thorough grasp of everything that had come before. Fisher, though, was at the vanguard of mathematical economics, which marked him out as a radical and was to ultimately set him apart from his own faculty.

It is perhaps ironic that having fought so hard to get him, the Economics Department was to then have a very marginal relationship with Fisher. He was not impressed with his fellow academics. He thought that they preferred to hide in the classroom rather than apply their subject matter to improving the human condition. Despite his long affiliation to Yale, he was rarely there, taught few classes and did not in general get on well with his colleagues.

In 1898 he was appointed professor and given lifetime tenure on $3,000 per year (about $85,000 in today's money). Things were looking up. His wife's family were wealthy, and money left in trust to Margie enabled them to lead a very comfortable life. Their house, at 460 Prospect Street in New Haven, had been a wedding gift from the Hazard family. It was large, fully kitted out and attended to by a number of servants. Fisher could also afford to hire his own secretaries to help him in his academic and campaign work.

But as Fisher was embarking on a successful and happy professional and family life, disaster struck. At the age of thirty he fell seriously ill with TB. He believed that his father had somehow passed on the disease to him and that it had remained dormant until then. It took him three years to beat the illness and recover his strength, but it was to be a life-changing event.

Fisher had revered his father and, although not overtly religious himself, he had inherited his strong moral and Puritan standards. Particularly after the trauma of years of illness, he became obsessed with diet and health. He did not smoke, or drink alcohol, coffee or tea; he never ate chocolate, and only rarely meat. He would arise at 7 a.m. each day and jog around the neighbourhood before a light breakfast. He exercised again around noon in his home gym or yard.

Often in the late afternoon he walked or jogged in a park. By 10.30 p.m., he was in bed after some calisthenics. He maintained his fitness regime when he travelled and insisted on his precise diet. On occasion he would even enter hotel kitchens to give specific instructions to the chefs.[9]

He was to become well known throughout America as a health guru. In 1915 he co-authored a book, *How to Live*, setting out basic rules of public hygiene. In total 400,000 copies were sold in the US and it was translated into ten languages. None of his economics writing was as successful. Fisher gave his royalties of $75,000 to the Life Extension Institute, an organization he co-founded two years earlier to promote healthy living and encourage frequent medical check-ups.

Some of his associations were controversial. He was president of the American Eugenics Society and the Eugenics Research Association. His belief in eugenics was based on the maintenance and improvement of the human race. However, he either did not seem to acknowledge or turned a blind eye to the links it had to racial supremacists.

One of his main crusades in life concerned Prohibition. The Eighteenth Amendment to the US Constitution, in effect from 1920, prohibited alcoholic beverages and was in place for thirteen years until it was repealed by the Twenty-First Amendment. He viewed alcohol as a poison that undermined productivity. Drinking alcohol was akin to self-harm. It was in the interest of the economy and society as a whole to abstain. His 1926 book *Prohibition at its Worst* argued that, even though Prohibition did not work perfectly – he was unhappy with the crime and bootlegging it generated – society was still better off than if alcohol were legalized. The problems were not with Prohibition per se, but because it had been introduced too quickly and before the public has been sufficiently educated in its merits. He tended to support presidential candidates in favour of the 18th Amendment outlawing alcohol and never reconciled himself to its repeal in 1933.[10]

His campaigns and activism in public affairs stemmed from his belief that economists should serve the public. And perhaps from a distrust of the political system:

> Our society will always remain an unstable and explosive compound as long as political power is vested in the masses and economic power in the classes. In the end one of these powers will rule. Either the plutocracy will buy up the democracy or the democracy will vote away the plutocracy. In the meantime the corrupt politician will thrive as a concealed broker between the two.[11]

Fisher was also aware of the foibles of economists:

> Academic economists, from their very openmindedness, are apt to be carried off, unawares, by the bias of the community in which they live.
>
> Economists whose social world is Wall Street are very apt to take the Wall Street point of view, while economists at state universities situated in farming districts are apt to be partisans of the agricultural interests.[12]

The Fisher family lived a comfortable life in New Haven. As a professor at Yale, Irving Fisher earned a salary which would have given him a better than middle-class income. In addition, his earnings were supplemented by his many other activities. But he also had expenses, particularly a growing number of staff and secretaries, to whom he would delegate a great deal. But the fact that he lived in a large house with many servants, and that his children were privately educated, was more of a reflection of the wealth he married into. It would not have escaped his notice that his wife's money was to a great extent maintaining his family's standard of living.

Fisher always thought that invention would be the key to making a personal fortune. He had tried many times, but his visible index card system was the breakthrough. It was a simple idea. He cut a notch at the bottom of an index card. These could be attached to a metal strip and mounted vertically, horizontally or even on a circular drum. It was a much more efficient way of finding records than flipping through boxes of cards. The concept had come to him in 1910, but he couldn't find anybody to manufacture the device. Eventually, in 1915, he decided to manufacture it himself, although he had no interest in the day-to-day running of the company, a task he delegated to managers and staff.

By 1919 the Index Visible Company was still struggling to turn a profit, despite a Fisher family investment of over $35,000. But his idea, which he had wisely patented, was practical as well as simple, and as the US economy grew quickly, and record-keeping became vital, it was adopted in companies across the country. As the Roaring Twenties gathered momentum, so did the Index Visible Company's profits. In the early 1920s he opened an office in New York, and even persuaded the state's telephone company to adopt the system.

In 1925, he sold his business to the company that was to later merge into Remington Rand. The company and patents were valued at $660,000, plus he received stock in the new company. At the age of fifty-eight, he had at last made a small fortune from his own endeavours. However, turning a small fortune into a large fortune required something extraordinary, and this came courtesy of a rampant bull market in stocks.

Fisher had invested heavily in the stock market, tending to favour start-up companies with innovative products. All proceeds and dividends were reinvested in the rapidly rising market. But he went further. He borrowed money to purchase stocks, a practice known as buying on margin that essentially allows an investor to leverage their portfolio. For example, suppose you buy $10,000 of stock, putting down only $1,000 of your own capital and borrowing the balance. If the market rises by 20 per cent, you are now getting a return of $2,000 (less interest on the $9,000 dollar loan) on your $1,000 investment. By leveraging yourself in this way, it is perfectly possible to generate a large paper fortune very quickly from a strongly rising market, and Fisher was estimated to have accumulated a staggering $10 million in this manner.

The downside to margin buying is revealed when the market falls, and assets become worth less than the amount of debt incurred in purchasing them. Borrowing to invest and being leveraged bring extraordinary gains in the good times, but result in potentially devastating losses should things go awry.

Fisher's behaviour in the late 1920s in many ways foreshadowed what would happen to the financial sector as a whole nearly a century later. Institutions that are highly leveraged and look sound can suddenly find themselves in a distressed position when the assets they hold become worthless. And in 1929, as the market crashed, Fisher was brought to financial ruin.

He had been a strong advocate of the rising bull market throughout the 1920s. At the end of 1928, he wrote a piece for the *New York Herald* predicting the continuance of the bull market through 1929. When, at the start of 1929, a growing minority voiced concern about a coming crash, Fisher remained steadfastly confident about the market. There is no doubt he was giving his honest opinion, but unfortunately it was catastrophically misguided. Ironically, he would later blame speculation by others about the value of stocks as the root cause of the Great Crash.

Another irony was that Fisher had pioneered the development of economic data. The Index Number Institute (INI) that he established in 1923 published weekly and monthly indicators of economic activity and prices. As such, Fisher should have been well placed to observe the vulnerabilities and imbalances afflicting the economy in agriculture, housing and manufacturing.

As history tells us, 29 October 1929 or Black Tuesday was not the worst of it. The market would continue to drop for a further three weeks. As the banks started to fail, crash would turn into depression. In 1929 there were 659 bank failures; this number would rise eightfold during the next three years.

The crash had a devastating impact on the Fisher family finances. His creditors came calling, but all he had to pay them with were stocks that were of little worth. On top of this the US tax authority, the Internal Revenue Service (IRS), was to pursue him over income he had not reported in the boom years.

Once again it was the Hazard family fortune that would provide the lifeline. Fisher's sister-in-law, Caroline, who was eleven years senior to Margie, had inherited the bulk of the family fortune. The crash had hit her extremely hard, but because her wealth was substantial she remained a rich woman. She lent Fisher stock to use as collateral for more loans to pay off his original creditors. Without this help in buttressing his financial position, it is likely the Fishers would have gone bankrupt in 1930. Over the course of the next decade, he would continuously turn to his sister-in-law to avoid bankruptcy, although Caroline's main concern was probably the welfare of her younger sister. As the requests for assistance came one after another, she grew tired of dealing with Fisher and even though he was family, she turned over her financial relations with him to her representatives.

In 1935, at the age of sixty-eight, Fisher reached Yale's compulsory retirement age. Now unable to pay the mortgage on 460 Prospect Street, he sold the house to the university, who allowed him and Margie to remain as life tenants. Eventually, even the rent became too much, and he was obliged to leave the house for the apartment in which he lived his final days.

Would it not have been better for Fisher to declare bankruptcy in 1930? In doing so, he would have lost both his house and his stock portfolio, neither of which was he eager to do. He never stopped believing the economy would turn upwards sooner rather than later, and with it the value of his stocks. He still saw an economic and financial recovery as the most likely solution to his financial troubles. His optimism was impressive. Unfortunately, every time he asserted that a turning point had been reached, things generally turned out to get even worse.

By 1941 Fisher had assets estimated at $244,000 but owed $1.1 million, including almost $1 million to his sister-in-law. This put his net worth in the red to the tune of $870,000. When Caroline Hazard died in March 1945, she forgave the debt in her will.

Irving Fisher's imprint on economics

In 1903, after returning to Yale upon his recovery from TB, Irving Fisher made some of his most valuable contributions to economics. He published two books of note: *The Nature of Capital and Income* in 1906 and *The Rate of Interest* in 1907. These books, which linked investment and the interest rate, formed the basis for his best-known work in economic theory, *The Theory of Interest*, published in 1930.

However, perhaps his most influential contribution concerned his Equation of Exchange, which sought to predict what might happen to prices when the money supply changed. It had been known for centuries that there existed a relationship between the amount of money in the economy and prices, commonly known as the Quantity Theory of Money. The long inflationary periods of the sixteenth and seventeenth centuries in Europe had coincided with the discoveries of Brazilian gold and Peruvian silver. Although the relationship had become part of conventional wisdom, until Fisher it had never been formalized or put to practical use.

The essence of the Equation of Exchange, written algebraically as $MV = PQ$, is that the total amount of money changing hands in the economy is equal to the total value of goods and services sold. On the left-hand side of the equation is the total money supply (M) multiplied by the velocity of circulation (V), a measure of how frequently money circulates in the economy. On the right-hand side is total spending on all the goods and services in the economy, given by the total quantity sold (Q) multiplied by the selling price (P). Although Fisher was not the first to formalize the relationship – $MV = PQ$ had already been written down by the Canadian-American astronomer and mathematician Simon Newcomb in his 1885 *Principles of Political Economy*[13] – it was he who both furnished the theory with a purpose and came up with the statistical methodology to validate it.

Fisher believed that, in the long run, the velocity of circulation is determined by institutional factors such as habits, business practices and systems of payment and credit. He also assumed that the output of the economy was determined by labour and capital; factors which are not related to prices or the money supply. So, if V and Q are fixed, and MV = PQ, there must be a direct association between changes in the money supply (M) and the price level (P). This was the essence of the Quantity Theory of Money. Changes in the money supply will, in the long run, have a direct and proportional impact on the price level. Although the theory imposed a strong prior assumption on the cause and effect, notably the direction of travel from money to prices, it became the central tenet of monetarism, an influential theory that argued that increasing the amount of money in the economy led only to inflation and not real economic growth. It was with this in mind that Milton Friedman was to later say: 'Inflation is always and everywhere a monetary phenomenon.'[14]

The assumption in the Quantity Theory of Money that the economy is in a long-run equilibrium is crucial. Most economists would argue that the economy is predominately in a state of transition. Furthermore, empirically the velocity of circulation tends not to look that stable. Therefore, if V and Q are changeable, there is not necessarily a direct and stable relationship between money and prices.

However, this theory gave Fisher scope to see how money and prices might affect national output, and how these short-run fluctuations influenced the business cycle. He believed it was possible for the public to confuse rising prices as being driven by increased demand from a growing economy rather than an increase in the amount of money in circulation. In this instance, a rising price level might temporarily stimulate purchases if consumers believed the economy was doing well, a misconception he called 'money illusion'. In order to test this proposition, he looked for short-term correlations between prices and output. He introduced the distributive lag model, where current output movements are modelled on seven monthly lags of price changes. He concluded that 90 per cent of short-term output movements were accounted for by recent changes in prices. His findings convinced him he had dealt a blow to all other business-cycle theories, as only around 10 per cent of cyclical movements were not explained by fluctuations in prices. However, Fisher himself had made strong assertions, in particular the assumed causality between prices and output rather than vice versa. Mainstream economists thought his work interesting, but were less than accepting of the conclusions.

Fisher had a long-standing concern with how prices are set in the economy. In 1911 he published a book called *The Purchasing Power of Money*. He wanted to educate the general public about the consequences of money supply and inflation as he felt that people were unable to connect the two, and therefore could not protect themselves from the consequences of inflation. He later noted the European hyperinflation after the First World War, for which many causes were cited, but not the one Fisher believed to be paramount: an uncontrolled expansion in the money supply. He also wanted to make people understand the costs of inflation and why its control should matter. Inflation redistributes wealth from savers to borrowers since inflation reduces the quantity of goods those savings can buy while borrowers benefit from a reduction in the real value of what they owe. Also, workers on fixed incomes saw their real wages decline while companies tied to contracts agreed under the false premise of stable prices also suffered.

Fisher's Quantity Theory of Money argued that a stable money supply was the key to stable prices. By stable money he meant money that held a constant purchasing power over goods and services available in the economy. He used terms such as the 'constant dollar', 'standardizing the dollar', 'unshrinkable dollar' or the 'commodity dollar' to describe a dollar that could buy a constant amount of goods and services. His 'commodity dollar' would encourage the public to think about the purchasing power of a dollar when it came to setting prices and writing contracts.

Fisher's idea was in direct contrast to the gold standard, the de facto economic policy of the day. The gold standard required the dollar to be exchangeable for a fixed quantity of gold, but it had not always been successful at achieving price stability. His concept of the commodity dollar required a dollar to be fixed in value against a group of commodities (goods), and its gold content adjusted to maintain its purchasing power.

He had observed that, between 1873 and 1896, the dollar's value increased as American prices fell. Fisher argued that this led to a prolonged depression as the supply of money was determined by the amount of gold, so the money supply was growing at a slower pace than was needed for the number of transactions necessary to maintain growth in the economy. The obvious solution would have been to reduce the amount of gold in the US dollar to lower its value. If that resulted in too much inflation then the amount of gold backing the dollar could be increased. Practically speaking, Fisher's idea required gold coins to be removed from circulation and replaced with 'gold certificates', which would circulate with gold bullion backing. This way, the amount of gold in a dollar being circulated can be disconnected from a fixed quantity of gold. The idea was to vary the amount of gold backing the dollar, in order to maintain its purchasing power. Or, as Fisher put it, the weight of gold behind the dollar would vary with prices.

The book was very well received around the world. Keynes described it as a better exposition of monetary theory than was available elsewhere. However, in calling for the abandonment of the gold standard, Fisher had placed himself at odds with the consensus of political and business opinion. Those who opposed Fisher's idea at least saw the logic, but did not believe it would be easy or practical to implement. They were also worried about undermining confidence in the operation of the gold standard, which already had been exposed as a fallible system of price stability. Tinkering with the gold standard was not a preferred option. Any admission that it was not perfect, or that the value of the dollar might require adjustment, was considered subversive and liable to undermine confidence in both the operation of the system and the value of the dollar.

After failing to convince President Woodrow Wilson of the merits of his plan, Fisher believed that he had to garner public opinion. He attempted to do so in 1914 by publishing a non-technical and popularized version of his 1911 work, which he called *Why is the Dollar Shrinking?* Fisher also gave the Hitchcock Lectures in 1917 on 'Stabilizing the Dollar', which later became a book of the same title. In 1927 he gave the Geneva Lectures focusing on the problem of money illusion. The lectures were turned into a short book written in large text and with the general public in mind. The first part of the book focused on how money illusion created economic cycles. The second part was the policy prescription, outlining what a monetary authority should do and how individuals could avoid money illusion to protect their real living standards. His effort was to be fruitless. Despite a succession of publications and numerous speeches between 1912 and 1934, he was unable to persuade policymakers to adopt the principle of the commodity dollar.

Although the commodity dollar idea never took off, similar schemes such as index-linked wages and pensions have become widely adopted. The development of price and quantity indices in economics was largely due to Fisher, who argued that wartime inflation had called for the indexation of wages to protect real take-home pay. He had already applied the concept to his own staff.

In 1922 he published one of his most technical works, *The Making of Index Numbers*. He described how indices of price and output movements could be constructed. A year later he established the Index Number Institute. This was a business to prepare and issue economic index numbers for publications. In 1926 he added an economic analysis section to the INI, and by 1929 some of his statistics were reaching over 5 million newspaper readers.

The idea of indexation can also be applied to debt so investors' returns are protected from inflation. While a director of Remington Rand, Fisher pioneered the first inflation-indexed bond, where investors earned a set real return regardless of what the inflation rate was. It didn't catch on, simply because most investors at the time did not understand what they were being sold. Today most debt issuance is still in nominal terms that do not take inflation into account, but inflation-protected bonds have become part of the debt issued by governments around the world.

Although indexation schemes are now fairly widespread, perhaps the country which has come closest to embracing Fisher is Chile. The UF, or Unidad de Fomento (Development Unit), was introduced in 1967. The UF is nominally the Chilean currency, but corrected for inflation. It remains in use today for wage contracts, for instance, so pay rises are awarded in real terms. The UF made indexing to inflation transparent, and Chile is the most inflation-indexed country in the world.

The Nobel Prize-winning economist Robert Shiller, in the spirit of Irving Fisher, has proposed that contracts in the US be expressed in terms of baskets reflecting the real value of a consumer's need, or in Fisher's terminology, a set of commodities they buy. He also suggested that governments could issue debt, so sell government bonds, denominated in terms of shares of nominal GDP and proposed calling these shares Trills. Each would pay a quarterly dividend equal to one trillionth of a country's national output, in which case the dividend would automatically correct for movements in inflation.

The intellectual pursuit that dominated Fisher's work stemmed from his experience in losing his fortune in the Great Depression. As events overwhelmed him, he sought out explanations. He did not like to be proven wrong, and needed to understand what was happening. He remained convinced the market and the economy would recover, but first he felt a strong need to explain the drama of the Great Crash.

In his 1930 book *The Stock Market Crash – and After*, Fisher identified why the market had been pumped up excessively in the years preceding the crash. First, overeager shoestring investors had driven the market up beyond its fundamental worth and were overextending themselves using credit. There was also the influence of margin buying in certain stocks. (This was, of course, exactly what Fisher himself had been doing.)

By 1932 the US economy was far from being in recovery mode and the quick rebound to the 1929 crash predicted by Fisher looked increasingly unlikely. Unemployment had hit 25 per cent compared to around 4 per cent in 1929. GDP had fallen by over 40 per cent. Nearly 6,000 banks had failed since the crash. Despite the terrible news, Fisher still believed the depression was bottoming out, and that the economy would quickly move away from depression in 1933. It didn't.

After his experience of the 1930s, Fisher produced a theory of business cycles different from the monetarist version of his earlier work.

This was the debt-deflation theory of depression, which he laid out in his 1932 book *Booms and Depressions*, and summarized a year later in his famous 1933 article in *Econometrica* entitled 'The Debt-Deflation Theory of Great Depressions'. Fisher identified all great depressions as starting from a point of overindebtedness:

> The public psychology of going into debt for gain passes through several more or less distinct phases:
>
> (a) the lure of big prospective dividends or gains in income in the remote future;
>
> (b) the hope of selling at a profit, and realizing a capital gain in the immediate future;
>
> (c) the vogue of reckless promotions, taking advantage of the habituation of the public to great expectations;
>
> (d) the development of downright fraud, imposing on a public which had grown credulous and gullible.[15]

In the case of the Great Depression, the overindebtedness originated in reckless borrowing by corporations who had been encouraged by high-pressure salesmanship of investment bankers. The collapse of the debt bubble then led to a self-perpetuating vicious circle of falling asset prices, which, as Fisher knew from experience, made it hard to repay one's debt. It led to further distressed selling, rising bankruptcies and even bank runs as loans went bad on banks' balance sheets.

He then described the process of debt-deflation, where attempts to liquidate assets in order to reduce debts become self-defeating, as the ensuing fall in prices raises the real value of debts even more. In other words, the real cost of borrowing is the nominal interest rate minus inflation, so deflation increases the cost of debt while inflation would reduce it. Fisher observed:

> Each dollar of debt still unpaid becomes a bigger dollar, and if the over-indebtedness with which we started was great enough, the liquidation of debts cannot keep up with the fall of prices which it causes. In that case, liquidation defeats itself. While it diminishes the number of dollars owed, it may not do so as fast as it increases the value of

each dollar owed. Then, *the very effort of individuals to lessen their burden of debts increases it, because of the mass effect of the stampede to liquidate is swelling each dollar owed.*[16]

For Fisher, the simple way out of the crisis was reflation of the price level, which would reduce the real value of debt. Although Fisher's work was to come back into vogue later, his prognosis was generally ignored in favour of John Maynard Keynes, who in 1936 published *The General Theory of Employment, Interest and Money*. Keynes identified excessive saving and a lack of aggregate demand as the cause of the ongoing depression, and urged the government to restore full employment through deficit-financed government spending.

Ben Bernanke and financial accelerators

One of the criticisms of Fisher's debt-deflation explanation is that price changes simply have a redistributive effect between debtors and creditors. Falling prices result in an increase in the real value of debts, and a transfer of wealth from debtors to creditors. Therefore, creditors gain while debtors lose, but the overall impact on society should be closer to zero.

Ben Bernanke, who served two terms as the chairman of the Federal Reserve between 2006 and 2014, and oversaw the US central bank's response to the 2008 global financial crisis, was previously an academic economist and scholar of the Great Depression. In an article published in 1983 he claimed to have rescued the Fisher debt-deflation hypothesis by adding the idea of the credit crunch.[17] This would be the missing link between deflation and dramatic declines in nominal incomes.

As prices fall, the real debt burden of debtors rises; but, far from benefiting, it actually hurts creditors because falling asset prices, rising loan impairments and bankruptcies lead to a fall in the value of assets on bank balance sheets. These collateral effects lessen the incentive for creditors to lend, resulting in a credit crunch, which then hits aggregate demand in the economy through a fall in consumption and investment.

This idea goes to the heart of the 'financial accelerator' concept, which describes how financial conditions tend to propagate business cycles. It is predominately based on the idea of asymmetric information. Those wishing to borrow to invest have a much better understanding of the projects than the creditor. Therefore, debt contracts often require the posting of collateral, which is an asset that is pledged by the borrower to the project. For instance, a borrower may pledge his home as collateral for a loan. So, the collateral comes down to the net worth of the debtor. Falling asset prices reduce this net worth. Therefore, an economic downturn can lead to a tightening of financial conditions and less credit availability.

The Great Depression and ensuing debt-deflation led to wide-scale distress among borrowers, lowering their ability to pledge collateral. But this also increased the risk to lenders as the average financial health of borrowers deteriorated, which impeded the flow of credit to the economy. The banking panics of the 1930s caused banks to shut their doors to avoid facing the risk of a run on their deposits. This, however, shut them off from their customers and increased the asymmetric information problems between borrowers and lenders, which further dampened normal lending activities to households and businesses.

Fast forward seventy years and it is clear that financial accelerator effects played a key role in the run-up to, and the aftermath of, the 2008 global financial crisis. As mortgage lending is secured on the value of houses, rising house prices tend to improve the financial conditions of lenders as default risks fall. This encourages further mortgage lending, which has the effect of raising prices further. This lending may also be directed at riskier parts of the mortgage market, that is sub-prime, or less than prime creditworthiness, lending. As homes are worth more, the loan-to-value ratios increase, which also gives homeowners the opportunity to refinance their mortgages at lower rates of interest.

It is possible that the way banks finance themselves today has increased the impact of the financial accelerator on lending activity.

Historically, banks have been viewed as institutions that intermediate between savers (their depositors) and borrowers (those who take out loans). Banks today, though, are less dependent on deposits for money creation. Global money markets are substantial and provide a large source of wholesale funding to financial institutions.

What this means is that banks themselves may not be dissimilar to other borrowers. Banks that are well capitalized are likely to be able to raise wholesale funds at lower interest rates than those that are poorly capitalized. For banks, it is typically expensive to raise new capital on the open market, so their balance sheets are primarily determined by earnings and asset values. In turn, the level of bank capital relative to regulatory levels can be an important determinant of a bank's cost of financing. But banks' capital positions also tend to be strongly pro-cyclical since assets tend to increase in value in a boom and fall in a recession. This further enhances the potential potency of the financial accelerator, observed in the large build-up of mortgage debt and high leverage of the financial sector in the run-up to the financial crisis.

It also means that in the aftermath of a financial crisis, where the banking system finds itself overleveraged, burdened with non-performing loans and insufficient capital, there can be a sharp drop in the flow of credit to the economy. This was seen in Japan when the financial problems of its banks and corporations contributed to lost decades of growth.

During the 1980s, the Japanese economy had performed spectacularly. Japan grew at an average rate of 4.5 per cent per year, and there was a widespread belief that it might even overtake the US as the largest economy in the world. However, the Japanese boom had been fuelled by a colossal run-up in property and equity markets. Japan has struggled to recover from the sharp correction in these that occurred in 1991, ushering in over two lost decades of stagnant growth and falling prices.

Since 1992, the Japanese economy has grown at an average rate of just 0.9 per cent per year, less than a quarter of its pre-1991 growth rate. In money terms, it was only in 2016 that Japanese national output surpassed its 1997 level. This is because its weak real growth had been accompanied by falling prices. Its benchmark stock index has also failed to recover since the early 1990s crash. The Nikkei 225, which peaked at over 38,000 at the start of 1990, had fallen to 14,000 in August 1992. After the recent financial crisis, the market fell to a low of under 9,000 before recovering to around 20,000. Despite its recent good performance, the Japanese stock market is still only valued at about half of what it was before the crash.

Japan's recovery is hampered by a rapidly ageing population and strong competition from its Asian neighbours. However, it is expectations of a stubbornly weak economy, where prices are falling, that have created a deflationary mind-set that is hard to break out off. This can become self-fulfilling where low expectations cause households and businesses to hold back spending, which then delivers the deflation they feared.

Escaping a deflationary trap

Irving Fisher's debt-deflation theory about depressions was based on a small sample of just three short periods of deflation, 1837–41, 1873–79 and the Great Depression of the 1930s. While it is not uncommon for prices to be falling in certain sectors or product markets, a sustained deflation in the general or average price level was actually a rare event until it occurred in Japan.

In such an event, Fisher's solution, as he recommended repeatedly in letters to President Roosevelt and colleagues, was basically reflation. He proposed that the central bank should simply increase the price level to near its 1926 level by expanding the money supply in line with his formulation of the Quantity Theory of Money. He also suggested stabilizing the financial system by providing a government guarantee of bank deposits to curb harmful and destructive bank runs. He believed that membership of the gold standard prevented the necessary monetary expansion since the dollars in circulation were constrained by the amount of gold. Dropping the gold standard would free the dollar and allow it to fall in value during a depression, which could boost exports and therefore the economy.

He also proposed a gift or loan to employers who increase their labour force. Otherwise, he had no enthusiasm for fiscal policy or public works programmes, which Fisher saw as simply the swapping of private sector debt for public sector debt. A fiscal stimulus might support output and employment over a short horizon (around two years), but would not address the underlying causes of the depression. As such, it was simply a painkiller rather than a cure.

The US did devalue its currency and leave the gold standard but by 1933 the economy still wasn't recovering. Fisher had believed that confidence would return the economy to prosperity immediately, but it did not.

Nearly a century later, as Japan's experience shows, it is clear that reflating an economy is not as easy as Fisher thought. Japan has undertaken a number of periods of aggressive monetary policies with the central bank injecting cash through quantitative easing (QE) programmes. It seems that the war against deflation cannot be won simply through robust action from the central bank.

Combating deflation requires a change in consumer attitudes and firms' behaviour, so it's a more complex process than it appears. In a 2002 speech, Ben Bernanke argued that Japan should consider a 'helicopter money drop'.[18] It would inject money directly into the economy; in essence, a free gift of money to citizens. As a permanent gift, it could have a strong impact on consumer and producer expectations of inflation.

So far no major central banks or Treasury departments have taken up Bernanke's suggestion. It would certainly be unconventional, but radical solutions may need to be considered in economies hamstrung by high levels of debt.

Japan indeed faces a number of barriers to economic growth besides deflation. First, it has a large overhang of public debt which has made governments reluctant to use fiscal policy. Second, structural changes in the economy and financial reforms are required. Bernanke argued in 2002 that political constraints rather than a lack of policy instruments were the reason Japanese deflation has been so long-lasting.

In considering whether the US could suffer a similar deflationary episode to Japan's following the collapse of the dotcom bubble between 2000 and 2002, Bernanke had correctly predicted it to be unlikely. His primary argument was the relative structural stability of the American economy compared to Japan's, and its stronger ability to absorb shocks and grow. In particular, he mentioned the younger workforce, flexible markets, entrepreneurial spirit and openness to technological change all contributing to this resilience – and, by implication, that these were some of the factors absent in Japan. Bernanke would soon face a test of his theories with the 2009 Great Recession that followed the global financial crisis, and the prospect of repeating the 1930s loomed again.

Minsky meltdowns

Irving Fisher's insights were revived in the 1990s by Hyman Minsky, who had incorporated ideas from Fisher as well as others in formulating his theory that private corporate debt, largely ignored in macroeconomic models, would lead to a financial crisis. He warned against speculative bubbles arising in inflated asset prices which had economy-wide implications.

The financial instability hypothesis developed by Minsky describes how credit bubbles form,[19] while Fisher's debt-deflation described how they collapse and drag the economy into recession and depression. Minsky believed that, after prolonged prosperity, capitalist economies tend to move from a financial structure dominated by stable finance to one that increasingly emphasizes speculative and Ponzi finance, which are unstable. He viewed such cycles as endemic to a capitalist system, their severity depending on the dynamics of such a financial system and the regulations that govern the economy.[20]

When he passed away in 1996 at the age of seventy-seven, Minsky hadn't seen that the 2008 sub-prime mortgage bubble would cause *The Economist* to dub it 'Minsky's Moment'.[21] During his lifetime, his work attracted little notice, but the global financial crisis would elevate Minsky and his ideas.

Former Fed chair Janet Yellen, while vice-chair to Ben Bernanke during the 2009 recession, gave a speech entitled: 'A Minsky Meltdown: Lessons for Central Bankers'. She pointed out: 'As Minsky's financial instability hypothesis suggests, when optimism is high and ample funds are available for investment, investors tend to migrate . . . to the risky speculative and Ponzi end.' She added: 'In retrospect, it's not surprising that these developments led to unsustainable increases in bond prices and house prices. Once those prices started to go down, we were quickly in the midst of a Minsky meltdown.'[22]

Much like Fisher, Minsky's prescription would have entailed recognizing the importance of debt in causing the boom. Yellen agrees: 'Regardless of one's views on using monetary policy to reduce bubbles, it seems plain that supervisory and regulatory policies could help prevent the kinds of problems we now face. Indeed, this was one of Minsky's major prescriptions for mitigating financial instability.'[23]

It seems that interest in both Fisher and Minsky has been revived by the recent global financial crisis. However, the debt-deflation stage of the financial instability hypothesis so far remains a threat rather than a reality.

The global financial crisis

Just as the Great Recession offers parallels to the Great Depression, debt has once again returned as an issue for major economies after the 2008 global financial crisis. At the end of 2015, government debt as a share of GDP was 243 per cent in Japan, 105 per cent in the US, 92 per cent in the euro area, and 90 per cent in the UK. Adding private sector debt would more than double these debt levels.

A comparison with the 1930s gives a different picture. Debt-to-GDP ratios shot up in the 1930s because of deflation, when falling prices increased the value of debt to be repaid. Now they are high because there has been so much borrowing in the recent past.

Large debts are, of course, a necessary condition for debt-deflation, but even though inflation rates have fallen below the 2 per cent target set by many major central banks, actual deflation is still the dog that hasn't yet barked. But does this mean we have escaped debt-deflation? Did policymakers learn the lessons from the 1930s? And what might they still need to do?

According to Irving Fisher, when inflation is low and the economy collapses, the central bank should act more aggressively than normal to avoid the onset of deflation. Central banks have, indeed, done just this, slashing interest rates to near zero per cent. However, this has created an additional problem of the 'zero lower bound' for interest rates.

As Bernanke says, a central bank that sees its policy rate driven down to zero is not out of ammunition. In this instance, deflationary episodes may require the central bank to think in terms of unconventional policies to avoid outright price declines à la Japan. It is possible for the central bank to set a negative interest rate, charging commercial banks for depositing money with it in the hope that they will lend the money instead. This is the type of unconventional monetary policy that has been adopted by the European Central Bank, the Bank of Japan and others.

Even if interest rates are close to zero, there should still be a policy response. Simply running the printing press is always an option. Money could be injected into the economy through asset purchases such as quantitative easing, or even more aggressively via the equivalent of a 'helicopter drop'. This could work through fiscal policy, say through a tax cut or an increase in government spending funded not by borrowing but through the central bank printing money. Fisher thought that it should always be possible to reflate the economy back to where it ought to be. To him, central banks have not exhausted their armoury should they need to fight against deflation.

Fisher had also in the 1930s called for monetary policy to act as a lender of last resort to stabilize the financial system in order to stop the debt-deflation process and reinstate the credit system. He had highlighted the connections between violent financial crises and fire sales of assets accompanied by a general decline in both aggregate demand and the price level. He, therefore, would have probably approved of the bailout of the investment bank Bear Stearns in March 2008, which meant that a series of defaults and asset price falls were not initiated as the bank went into liquidation. Would a bailout of Lehman Brothers just a few months later have helped to avoid the global financial crisis altogether? Ben Bernanke, Fed chairman at the time, didn't believe that Lehman posed the same systemic risk as Bear Stearns. Fisher would probably have asked whether rescuing this bank would have prevented a series of defaults which could have served as a trigger for the financial crisis. But would the global financial crisis have been triggered by something else instead?

Fisher would have agreed that a well-regulated financial system would guard against debt-deflation by avoiding large and unsustainable build-ups of debt in the first place. Well-designed regulatory and supervisory powers play a role in preventing deflation by maintaining financial stability. They can act to rein in exuberant financing from dangerous financial innovations, practices and attitudes. Regulations and reforms are also needed alongside lender of last resort facilities to curb potential moral hazard problems. In other words, if the central bank is always there to bail a bank out, then a bank has less of an incentive to act prudently. Regulation can reduce this risk. In this respect, he would have welcomed the new macroprudential regulatory powers given to central banks after the 2008 financial crisis to target financial stability alongside their existing mandate of price stability.

Fisher's final years

The years 1933 to 1939 saw a period of frantic effort by Fisher to solve the country's problems and his own financial doldrums. He failed at both. The country wasn't following his recommendations, his own assets would never recover their value and his debts would never go away.

By 1945, when his sister-in-law died and his debt to her of more than $1 million was forgiven, his life was winding down. Margie had died suddenly in 1940, the year he lost his house at 460 Prospect Street because he could no longer afford to pay the rent. On his own, and now seventy-three years of age, he lived in a modest apartment when he was not on the road.

His death was in many ways a sad affair and reflective of Fisher's character traits. In September 1945, he believed that a blockage in his bowels was due to a kink in the lower intestines, something he had experienced fifteen years earlier. It then had caused some discomfort but eventually cleared up by itself. He believed his diet and exercise would be sufficient to bring about good health, and did not seek a second or specialist medical opinion.

When in the autumn of 1946 his health began to deteriorate, X-rays found an inoperable tumour in his colon that had spread to his liver. Had he acted the year before, his cancer may have been treatable and he could have lived several more years. In 1947, he passed away, and was buried next to his wife and daughter in New Haven, Connecticut, the home of Yale University.

After his death, the net value of his estate was estimated at around $60,000. He would have been disappointed that it amounted to so little, and it was certainly not enough to fund an Irving Fisher Institute he hoped would cement his legacy to both economics and health. Nevertheless, what he did leave was considerable – in intellectual if not financial terms. Between 1891 and 1942 he wrote thirty books, with more than 150 English and foreign-language editions.

Pictures show Irving Fisher to have been straight-laced, and throughout his life he was disciplined in all matters. Because of his seriousness, crusades and sometimes controversial beliefs, many people, including his economics colleagues, had thought Fisher odd and humourless.[24] Despite growing recognition, he is still under-appreciated and not quite as lauded as a Great Economist as is warranted by his work. Fisher was at the vanguard of modern economics, essentially inspiring the leading central bankers who were at the helm when the entire banking system was on the brink of collapse. There is no doubt his thinking continues to remain relevant today.

6

John Maynard Keynes: To Invest or Not to Invest?

Few questions have been as prominent since the banking crash: should the British and European governments have cut public spending and adopted austere policies in the aftermath of the 2008 financial crisis?

In another parallel to the 1929 crash, this was also the question debated in Britain in the 1930s, which launched the Keynesian revolution in economics. John Maynard Keynes advocated government spending in a sharp break with neoclassical economics that eschewed the active use of fiscal policy in response to a downturn. Keynes gave an illustration:

> If the Treasury were to fill old bottles with banknotes, bury them at suitable depths in disused coalmines which are then filled up to the surface with town rubbish, and leave it to private enterprise on well-tried principles of *laissez-faire* to dig the notes up again . . . there need be no more unemployment and, with the help of the repercussions, the real income of the community, and its capital wealth also, would probably become a good deal greater than it actually is.[1]

Recognizing it's not ideal, but necessary, he adds: 'It would, indeed, be more sensible to build houses and the like; but if there are political and practical difficulties in the way of this, the above would be better than nothing.'[2]

Today the debate is again over the role of government spending while policymakers contend with high levels of public debt amidst a sluggish recovery in the aftermath of the worst financial crisis since the 1930s. Thus, Keynesian economics is back in the spotlight.

Keynes is not only influential because of his intellectual contributions. He was a compelling writer and known for his turns of phrase, including: '[Economics] should be a matter for specialists – like dentistry. If economists could manage to get themselves thought of as humble, competent people, on a level with dentists, that would be splendid!'[3] And: 'a speculator is one who runs risks of which he is aware and an investor is one who runs risks of which he is unaware'.[4]

John Maynard Keynes dominated British economics until the Second World War, but his influence extends globally. Across the Atlantic, America's first economics Nobel laureate, Paul Samuelson, was a standard bearer for Keynesian economics in the US. He helped to incorporate Keynesian thought into neoclassical economics, which became known as the 'neoclassical synthesis' – a term that he apparently coined – which underpins modern economics. Thus, without always being explicit, Keynes's ideas pervade the subject. They have certainly framed much of the fierce post-crisis debates over austerity and the best course of economic policy.

The life and times of John Maynard Keynes

Keynes was born in 1883, to the 'educated bourgeoisie', in his self-description of his social class.[5] As for his views of different social classes: 'Aristocrats were absurd; the proletariat was always "boorish". The good things in life sprang from the middle class.'[6]

He attended Eton College on a scholarship, followed by another scholarship to King's College, Cambridge. After working in the India Office of the British government, he returned to the University of Cambridge as a lecturer in 1909 and in 1911 was elected a fellow of King's, where he remained until his death in 1946.

His father was the Cambridge economist John Neville Keynes, which is why he is often referred to as Maynard Keynes. Describing John Neville Keynes, his son's noted biographer, Robert Skidelsky, wrote: 'the real barrier to a successful academic career was not lack of originality, but anxiety'.[7] Neville Keynes had turned down a professorship at the University of Chicago in 1894, perhaps reluctant to leave the familiarity of Cambridge, where he had a comfortable existence as Registry – the college's top and well-compensated administrator. He wrote two books in his career, the second of which accorded him a doctorate when he was thirty-eight. He lived another sixty years but rarely wrote again. Still, Alfred Marshall considered Neville Keynes his best student and asked him to edit the prestigious *Economic Journal*, founded in 1890. He declined, though his son Maynard Keynes took it on when he became a fellow at King's. Maynard Keynes exceeded his father's academic legacy in other respects too.

As his great-grandmother reminded him, 'You will be expected to be very clever, having lived always in Cambridge.' Maynard Keynes did not let her down, and excelled from a young age.[8] He has been described as standing 'head and shoulders above all the other boys' in his prep school, both physically and mentally.[9] At Eton, he won thirty-nine prizes, including the top awards for history and English, all of the main mathematical prizes, and even one in chemistry. He worked diligently and followed his father's habit of monitoring closely how his time was spent. In a letter to his parents he wrote: 'In a minute and a quarter my light has to be put out and I have many things to do before then.'[10]

After graduation, Keynes spent two years in the India Office as a civil servant. Keynes sat the civil service entrance exam and ironically did poorly in economics. He would have come top had it not been for the economics mark, but had to be content with second. This was important because the successful candidates could choose from the available posts in the different civil service departments in order of their rank in the exam. The Treasury was the plum job, but there was only one post available that year and the top candidate, a bright classicist from Oxford University called Otto Niemeyer, took it. Keynes, therefore, had to settle for the India Office. Had Keynes come top and got into the Treasury, he might have stayed. We might never have had the Keynesian revolution in economics.

Coming full circle, in the 1920s and 30s, when struggling to push his unorthodox policies arguing for government spending against the orthodox 'Treasury view', Keynes's principal opponent in the Treasury, and later in the Bank of England, was none other than Sir Otto Niemeyer, GBE, KCB. According to the *Oxford Dictionary of National Biography*, he was 'the outstanding Treasury official of the post-war years'. Keynes subsequently wrote in the Preface to his *General Theory*: 'The difficulty lies, not in the new ideas, but in escaping from the old ones, which ramify, for those brought up as most of us have been, into every corner of our minds.'[11]

During his time at the India Office, he did impress his immediate boss, Basil Blackett. Blackett later moved to the Treasury; and in the financial chaos of August 1914 remembered Keynes and called him in to help out temporarily. He ended up staying for the whole war. Thus, Keynes entered the Treasury in a rather more privileged and somewhat freelance position: he had a commanding role in the financing of the war, rubbed shoulders with all the top politicians and became the Treasury's chief representative at the Paris Peace Conference.

The aftermath of the First World War provided the context for some of Keynes's most lasting ideas. It led to *The Economic Consequences of the Peace*, and that conditioned the rest of his career. In the book, John Maynard Keynes argued that Germany could not afford the post-war reparations demanded in 1919. Sales broke records in England and the US; this book made Keynes's name.

Keynes found the work at the India Office easy but uninspiring, which is likely to have contributed to his decision to return to Cambridge after a short spell to become an academic. His time in government proved to be a valuable link, as he was to contribute actively to economic policy during both world wars.

He returned to Cambridge to take up a lectureship after being encouraged to do so by Alfred Marshall, with whom an earlier term of postgraduate work comprised Keynes's entire formal training in economics. Keynes had remarked at the time in a letter to his friend, the writer Lytton Strachey: 'Marshall is continually pestering me to turn professional Economist . . . Do you think there is anything in it? I doubt it.'[12]

Keynes had frequent occasion to return to London as he was part of the Bloomsbury Group, an intellectual collective who took their name from the district in London where many of them lived and whose membership included Strachey as well as Virginia Woolf and E. M. Forster. All enjoyed the arts, including ballet and after years of homosexual dalliances Keynes fell in love with the Russian ballerina Lydia Lopokova after watching her perform in 1921. They embarked on an affair and married four years later after she obtained a divorce from her husband, when Keynes was forty-two and she was thirty-three. It was a marriage that lasted for the rest of his life.

Rather unusually for an academic, Keynes – like Ricardo and Fisher before him – was also an investor. He made a fortune, but was nearly bankrupted several times. In 1936 he was worth over £500,000, or an eye-watering £27 million in today's money. Then he nearly lost it all in the 1937–38 recession when he was heavily leveraged, having borrowed to invest in the stock market. Still, at his death in 1946 he had an investment portfolio of £400,000 (£12 million today) and an art and book collection worth £80,000 (£2.5 million today).[13]

His experiences in the post-war boom and ensuing economic stagnation shaped his world-view. Unlike the classical economists, who believed that economies reacted quickly to shocks, Keynes believed the effect to be much more sluggish. For instance, savings were not used for investment, such as buying new equipment. Instead, Keynes saw at first hand that savings were used to fuel speculation. At that time investors had to deposit only 15 per cent when buying shares, and this high degree of leverage increased the speculative frenzy which prompted investors to keep betting.

This experience shaped his famous 'animal spirits' description of investment and the role of investors. He defined 'animal spirits' as 'a spontaneous urge to action rather than inaction, and not as the outcome of a weighted average of quantitative benefits multiplied by quantitative probabilities'.[14] It framed his view of investors:

professional investment may be likened to those newspaper competitions in which the competitors have to pick out the six prettiest faces from a hundred photographs, the prize being awarded to the

competitor whose choice most nearly corresponds to the average
preferences of the competitors as a whole, so that each competitor has
to pick, not those faces which he himself finds prettiest, but those
which he thinks likeliest to catch the fancy of the other competitors,
all of whom are looking at the problem from the same point of view.
It is not a case of choosing those which, in the best of one's judgment,
are really the prettiest, nor even those which average opinion genu-
inely thinks the prettiest. We have reached the third degree, where
we devote our intelligences to anticipating what average opinion
expects average opinion to be. And there are some, I believe, who
practise the fourth, fifth and higher degrees.[15]

As Keynes once wryly observed, 'Worldly wisdom teaches that it
is better for reputation to fail conventionally than to succeed
unconventionally.'[16]

The Keynesian revolution

It was the time of the Great Depression and a sluggish economic
recovery between the two world wars that saw the launch of the
Keynesian revolution. Keynes's seminal work grew out of the Depression. It wasn't the first time that unemployment was an issue. The
economic woes of the late nineteenth century during the Long
Depression led to the term 'unemployment' appearing for the first
time in the *Oxford English Dictionary* in 1888. But it was of a different
magnitude in the Great Depression. From 1929–33, the US unemployment rate rose from 3 per cent to 25 per cent. Income in 1933
was lower than in 1922. The UK also entered a prolonged depression
and saw unemployment double to 20 per cent.

Keynes was critical of the Treasury's classical view, which was
to await the recovery passively, since they believed that economies
self-corrected in the long run. The long run for classical economists
was long indeed. Modern economists are inclined to think that the
long run is the amount of time needed for fixed capital to adjust,
whereas the classical economists of that time thought that population

had to adjust, so birth and death were also part of the long-run adjustment.

Undoubtedly, Keynes's legacy was to switch the focus from the long run to the short run, where adjustments were sluggish and governments could thus play a role. He famously observed: 'But this *long run* is a misleading guide to current affairs. *In the long run* we are all dead. Economists set themselves too easy, too useless a task if in tempestuous seasons they can only tell us that when the storm is long past the ocean is flat again.'[17]

In *The General Theory of Employment, Interest and Money*, published in 1936, Keynes focused on the short run. He homed in on deficient demand, which included weak household consumption and low firm investment, as determinants of the Great Depression. He argued that, even in normal times, the incentive to invest is too weak and the propensity to hoard cash is too strong. Without the necessary investment, the economy tends to operate at less than full employment, where all labour is deployed productively. If there were also a 'shock' to investment demand, such as a stock market crash, output and employment would decline, resulting in economic slumps. So, Keynes proposed that governments should incur debt to move the economy back to full employment. He stressed that government borrowing to spend need not be inflationary if the economy was operating below its potential, and advocated deficit spending, where the government borrowed to spend during downturns and repaid debt during the good times: 'The boom not the slump is the right time for austerity.'[18] A practical economist, he proposed a board of public investment to plan to have a stock of projects ready for when other types of investments started to decline.

Keynes saw some of his ideas put into action, albeit not entirely to his liking. He believed President Franklin D. Roosevelt's US National Industrial Recovery Act of 1933, commonly known as the New Deal, would improve the banking system and transport infrastructure of America, but the amount of government spending or fiscal stimulus injected under FDR's plan was much smaller than the 11 per cent of GDP or national output Keynes believed was needed. Thus, he was critical of the legislation for putting reform before recovery. Britain was even worse in Keynes's view. The UK government balanced the budget. Despite the lack of government support, a combination of exchange depreciation and low interest rates brought about a recovery. But it was temporary. In 1937–38, both economies once again fell into sharp recession.

Like now, there was a heated debate over what more spending would mean for the budget deficit and high levels of government debt. A budget deficit arises if the government spends more than it receives in a given year. Government debt is the total accumulated deficit over time. Keynes criticized the UK Treasury for confusing capital spending with government 'deficit finance'. Keynes argued that public investment was a tool for correcting an economy that was operating below its full potential but which his critics thought would lead to even bigger budget deficits.

Keynes was also concerned about uncertainty dampening investment and disagreed with neoclassical economists over the role of the interest rate.[19] They viewed the interest rate as the price which balanced savings and investment. Keynes argued instead that savings rose and fell with income. Keynes believed that uncertainty was why people held on to money, even if it was not the most sensible investment decision: 'For it is a recognized characteristic of money as a store of wealth that it is barren; whereas practically every other form of storing wealth yields some interest or profit. Why should anyone outside a lunatic asylum wish to use money as a store of wealth?'[20]

He continues: 'Because, partly on reasonable and partly on instinctive grounds, our desire to hold Money as a store of wealth is a barometer of the degree of our distrust of our own calculations and conventions concerning the future.'[21]

The implication was that deficit spending would lead to higher levels of national income, which would generate more savings that would in turn pay for the greater amounts of accumulated government debt.

It wasn't Keynes's only involvement in government policy. During the Second World War Keynes became involved in the Beveridge Report that was published in 1942 and which was the foundation of the British welfare state, introducing a comprehensive social insurance system covering individuals 'from cradle to grave'. It fitted into his theories of how fiscal policy can influence the economy. In other words, unemployment benefits act as 'automatic stabilizers' that increase government spending during downturns without the government having to choose to act.

In sum, the Keynesian revolution altered the face of economics in proposing that economies were frequently not at full employment and output. As demand could fall short, and not all of what was produced would be bought, there was a role for government spending in righting the economy.

Keynesian economics held sway until the 1970s, which was a decade of high inflation, propelled by two oil price shocks that led to dramatic price rises. The British economy was in the doldrums but suffered from inflation and a weak currency, which raised import prices of oil and other goods. By the autumn of 1976, the UK required bailing out by the International Monetary Fund (IMF), which lent it $4 billion and demanded deep cuts in government spending to reduce Britain's indebtedness. The demonstrable end of the Keynesian era in the UK was when the British prime minister, James Callaghan, in 1976 remarked that the country could no longer spend its way out of recession and even added that it had only worked before by 'injecting bigger and bigger doses of inflation into the economy'.[22]

Unusually, the 1970s was also a period of high unemployment. This combination of high inflation and high unemployment, known as stagflation, contradicted the standard relationships. That era saw the rise of New Classicists and monetarists like Milton Friedman, whose theories explained stagflation and propelled him onto the stage. Keynes's ideas fell out of favour. There is a parallel in that Keynes's ideas were in vogue during the 1930s because they could explain the pressing issue of the time, which was unemployment.

By 1980, *laissez-faire* had become the dominant theory in the US with the election of President Ronald Reagan. When he was the Republican candidate for the presidency against the incumbent Democrat, Jimmy Carter, he quipped: 'Recession is when your neighbour loses his job. Depression is when you lose your job. Recovery is when Jimmy Carter loses his job.' Reagan won.

Still, that decade also saw the emergence of the New Keynesians, such as Nobel laureate Joseph Stiglitz, because unemployment was once again an issue in the aftermath of the economic revolutions that took place under both Reagan and Callaghan's Tory successor, Margaret Thatcher. New Keynesians justified limited government intervention since unemployment can remain high for a long time, but incorporated New Classical theories about how people behave to explain why it takes time for economies to return to equilibrium.

By the end of the twentieth century, the New Neoclassical Synthesis emerged, which was similar to the movement in the 1950s during which the Neoclassical Synthesis approach had appeared. The New Neoclassical Synthesis incorporated the New Keynesians, New Classicists and monetarists into one framework that incorporated parts of each theory to explain how the economy works.

The New Neoclassical Synthesis thus includes New Classical theories of how consumers make decisions across time periods as well as incorporating 'rational expectations' theory. Rational expectations posits that consumers know that a tax cut today will mean tax rises in the future, so they don't change their behaviour, thus a tax cut would not raise consumption and boost growth. Intriguingly, only a surprise government policy would work. The concept of rational expectations has been challenged owing to its assumption that consumers behave completely rationally and can process huge amounts of information. Indeed, government fiscal policies such as those advocated by Keynes which are not 'surprises' have impact, though the evidence is that consumers behave somewhat, though not completely, rationally in response to tax cuts.

At the start of the twenty-first century, Keynes was back in the spotlight as deficits and public spending re-emerged as contentious issues after the 2009 Great Recession.

Budget deficits and austerity

Britain's budget deficit may have been halved since the 2008 financial crisis, but it was still around 5 per cent of GDP at the end of the 2014/15 Parliament. It's worth recalling that, when Britain was rescued by the IMF in 1976, its budget deficit was 6.9 per cent of GDP. But the deficit wasn't as much a concern this time, or indeed in 1993 when its previous post-war high of 7.8 per cent was reached. That's because Britain was affected by the global financial crisis that had increased the level of government debt in the world's major economies.

Following the 2008 crash, Britain's debt had increased to around 90 per cent of GDP, substantially above the 60 per cent level obliged by the EU Maastricht Treaty. Two of the three major credit rating agencies didn't see that level of debt as compatible with the AAA top credit rating. After the EU referendum vote to leave the European Union in 2016, Britain was downgraded from its last remaining AAA rating.

The UK government has cut the rate of increase in government spending in order to reduce the yearly deficits and stabilize the overall debt level. Was austerity the right thing to do? The IMF had urged Britain to reconsider imposing austerity before the economy had fully recovered. And not just Britain. The initial years of the recovery saw governments from Europe to America cutting public expenditure while private demand was weak. In the UK, the recovery was tepid and output even contracted at times. In fact, 2012 saw two non-consecutive quarters of negative GDP growth, although that's not a recession since the formal definition requires two such consecutive quarters.

In Britain, the pace of austerity had slowed alongside the economy, but was such a policy necessary? Part of the rationale for cutting government spending was that investors would not want to lend to the UK if it did not show that it was reducing its budget deficit. Otherwise the government's debt might increase to unsustainable levels. This view was exacerbated by the context of the euro crisis that erupted in early 2010. Britain was, of course, not party to that crisis and may even have benefited as investors sought safer investments in non-euro countries. But that backdrop drove some of the thinking about deficits and austerity.

At the end of 2009, during the midst of the Great Recession, Greece needed a bailout after admitting that its government accounting was at best unreliable. Investors sold off Greek government bonds and eventually other euro area countries with high levels of government debt also saw their borrowing costs rise. As fewer investors were willing to lend Greece money, it became more expensive and ultimately impossible for the Greek government to borrow to finance its normal operations. Portugal faced a similar problem. It was a different picture for Ireland and Spain as well as Cyprus, all of which rescued their own banks. But in doing so, their budget deficits shot up and they ended up also needing help from the 'troika' that oversaw the rescue programmes for countries which shared the single currency: the EU, the European Central Bank (ECB) and the IMF.

European governments believed that fiscal discipline was needed to restore investor confidence, so pushed ahead with austerity. Before the crisis, Greece borrowed at the same advantageous rates as Germany since bond markets seemed to view the euro area as one entity. That contributed to too much borrowing by the Greek government. Though that scenario is unlikely to be repeated, euro area leaders came up with additional reforms to try to enforce fiscal restraint. They stressed the need for member countries to adopt fiscal discipline if they are to share a single currency and a common monetary policy.

There is a move to create a fiscal union which would go beyond the budget deficit rules that are centrally enforced by the European Commission, which can set penalties for countries that miss their targets. There is even discussion of establishing a European Treasury as the central fiscal authority for the euro area. It certainly adds a political dimension to the austerity debate and also raises questions over whether the EU is heading towards a federal system, with fiscal powers split between nations and supranational institutions.

After the acute phase of the euro crisis subsided, concerns over economic weakness prompted the ECB to do something it declined to do during the Great Recession. For the first time, in 2015, the ECB undertook quantitative easing (QE) and made large-scale cash injections into the economy by buying government debt. This increase in the amount of money available to lend had, via the simple mechanics of supply and demand, the effect of driving down borrowing costs, which have since remained cheap. This is in the context of low government bond yields around the world, which would be expected in a slow-growth environment.

The combination of slow growth and low borrowing costs has added a new dimension to the austerity debate. Should governments be taking greater advantage of cheap rates to invest? Should budget deficits and debt be a secondary consideration when economic growth remains sluggish?

Investment and low interest rates

This question is being asked in both Europe and the US. In America, there is a push for more infrastructure investment, although the Republicans in Congress remain concerned about adding to the fiscal deficit. Of course, Republicans traditionally follow a non-interventionist philosophy, and are suspicious about the role of government in both investment and the economy in general. As former Republican President Ronald Reagan observed of government intervention: 'government's view of the economy could be summed up in a few short phrases: If it moves, tax it. If it keeps moving, regulate it. If it doesn't move, subsidize it,'[23] and remarked on a separate occasion, 'The nine most terrifying words in the English language are: I'm from the Government and I'm here to help.'[24]

This explains why the US plan is counting on private investors to help finance its projects.

On the other side of the Atlantic, the debate over investment has found more political common ground. Britain has moved into the spotlight when it comes to this debate since the vote to leave the European Union in June 2016 led the Bank of England to restart QE, which helps sustain low borrowing costs. Yields on ten-year government debt, known as gilts, fell to record lows of around just 1 per cent after the Brexit vote. Record lows had also been reached for twenty- and thirty-year debt. It meant that, for the first time, the British government could sell debt by paying around 1 per cent interest for a decade. Even with interest rates being raised in 2017 for the first time since the banking crisis, borrowing costs remain fairly low. So, do low interest rates affect the question of whether governments should borrow to invest now?

Keynes pointed out that there is no 'crowding out' of private investment when the economy is operating below its potential. 'Crowding out' refers to how governments borrowing to invest would make it harder for private firms to do so because their demand for loans would push up the interest rate and make it more expensive for others to borrow. However, since the British economy lost over 6 per cent of its output during the 2008 recession, and interest rates for loans are low, 'crowding out' would be unlikely, because the economy has lost so much output that there is a lot of scope for the public and private sectors to invest before their demand for funds pushed up borrowing costs. Moreover, increasing public investment can help economic growth, as it can have a 'crowding in' effect. In other words, government investment can make private investment more efficient, for example a good telecoms infrastructure increases the returns to a pound invested by a private company by giving them the fibre network to deliver faster services.

In Britain, public investment has been slashed deeply. It is easier to cut capital expenditure on projects such as highway repairs than to reduce the current budget dominated by public sector services. During the height of austerity, between 2008 and 2011, public investment fell from 3.3 per cent of national output to 1.9 per cent, a staggering 40 per cent decline. Will that ground be made up and, more pertinently, will this trend of low investment be reversed? It would likely mean adopting Keynes's view that public investment should be separated out from what governments spend from day to day. Unlike such current spending, Keynes would argue that investment generates future returns and should not be lumped in with daily payments for civil servants in assessing the budget of a government.

Indeed, with the establishment of a National Infrastructure Commission in 2015, and given this context of low borrowing costs, the British government now aims to invest and reverse the years of cuts to public investment.

The European Union has also acted on a large scale. The EU changed its focus to take advantage of low rates in a way that should not lead to ballooning budget deficits.

European Commission President Jean-Claude Juncker's infrastructure investment fund, the European Fund for Strategic Investments (EFSI), commonly referred to as the Juncker Plan, was established in 2015. It sought to raise the considerable sum of €315 billion over three years by working with the European Investment Bank (EIB), which issues bonds to finance projects that develop digital, transport, energy and other infrastructure, as well as improve funding for small and medium-sized enterprises (SMEs). This is indeed a way to leverage a relatively small sum into an ambitious pool of money. The EU has itself invested €16 billion and there was a further €5 billion put in by the EIB. The top AAA-rated EIB can then issue bonds, taking advantage of low interest rates, to leverage the initial €21 billion into a fund large enough to make a difference in jump-starting European growth. The European Commission plans to increase the size and duration of the EFSI. Bolstered by its initial success, European policymakers are keen to rejuvenate infrastructure, which needs to be updated in many countries in order to keep up with the needs of businesses, particular in a fast-changing digital era.

The EFSI ambitiously seeks to encourage private companies to invest, thereby largely reducing the impact of the infrastructure spending on government fiscal positions. But that means a reliance on public-private partnerships, which have a mixed record when it comes to maintaining long-term infrastructure projects, such as railways.

Still, the focus of the fund on small and medium-sized enterprises, which are Europe's best job creators but have suffered most from the low amounts of bank lending while the banking system rebuilds itself after the financial crisis, is pertinent.

These SMEs would also benefit from updated infrastructure.

During the last recession, it was public investment that was slashed as a part of austerity programmes in the EU, just as it was in Britain, much to the detriment of spending on infrastructure. Investment in the euro area has been around 15 per cent below its pre-crisis level. Thus, the OECD and others have argued that increases in public investment would boost economic growth and thus even reduce government debt.

Why, then, has it been so difficult to increase investment since the crisis? One constraint has been the imposition of fiscal austerity by governments whose main focus is on the budget deficit, which for the most part includes capital investment. It's only in the very recent past that economic growth has regained priority. That largely explains the public side, but private investment has also dropped sharply since the recession.

German companies, for instance, have doubled their retained cash in the past decade, and others have as well. American multinationals have amassed record amounts of cash on their balance sheets. Resolving why these companies don't invest is key to understanding why one of the pillars of growth, investment, hasn't delivered during the recovery.

Government and consumer spending were hit hard and slow to recover, leaving deficient demand, both public and private, which is a disincentive for companies to invest since future sales don't look strong. The sharpness and the duration of the Great Recession also created uncertainty over whether or not to commit funds for investment stretching well into the future. Plus, the time it took for decimated banking systems in Europe and America to recover forced some companies to retain their earnings in case they needed cash during a time when bank lending remained constrained. For investors there were also other, more enticing, places to put cash. Stocks, for instance, were pushed to sky-high levels by low interest rates across major markets. But global stock markets have since been descending from their heady heights. And there's uncertainty from the US, which has begun to normalize (i.e. raise) interest rates earlier than the rest of the world. This means that investments with fixed returns, such as in infrastructure, can be relatively more attractive. Traditionally, investing in roads or energy doesn't achieve a high return, though it does tend to be stable. Yields from infrastructure such as utilities and toll roads are usually set by regulators and range from 3 to 4 per cent. In a low-rate environment, that's not a bad return. Of course, one of the challenges is still the slowness with which major public projects are granted approval. Still, there's no shortage of such projects being proposed by EU member states. In any case, growth in the world's largest economic entity would help the world economy.

The renewed focus on growth by not just the European Commission but also national governments offers more opportunities to reconsider the investment and growth nexus pointed out by Keynes. The debate over whether governments should themselves be borrowing more to invest, and whether such capital expenditure should be separately considered in budgets as Keynes proposed, is unsettled. So, what would Keynes make of the current austerity debate, which has shifted to become more about a debate over government investment?

Keynes on the government's role in the economy

Keynes argued for government spending as a means to counteract slow economic growth. Especially during a recovery from a recession or depression, private demand is deficient, so extra spending by government is needed to ensure that aggregate demand remains sufficient to maintain full employment. But what would Keynes have made of the debate over governments borrowing to invest in times outside acute crises or recession?

The cash hoarding that he predicted is evident in the post-crisis economy. Even though interest rates are very low, not enough firms are borrowing to invest, which has contributed to the slow-growth environment. For the reasons noted earlier, when investment doesn't respond to interest rates, unlike in normal times, monetary policy is no longer enough to boost the economy, which means that fiscal policy is also needed to increase investment and generate more growth.[25]

Investment is one of the components identified by Keynes that make up the level of aggregate demand in the economy. Consumption is generally viewed as being more stable than investment. When income increases, consumption tends to rise but not as much and also declines by less. Since some income is saved while the rest is consumed, the gap between consumption and production must be filled by investment if full employment is to be maintained.

Classical economists had assumed that savings automatically became investment. Keynes's insight was to treat savings distinctly. He discovered the 'paradox of thrift' that arises when, as more people try to save, the aggregate amount of savings in an economy actually *falls*. This happens because, as savings increase, consumption falls, which reduces total output, which in turn reduces the income from which savings are made. The problem gets worse the richer societies become since wealthier people tend to save a higher fraction of their income. This is why he advocated 'heavy death duties', which would redistribute wealth, especially unearned wealth, towards those more inclined to consume than save.[26] So, some redistribution of wealth from the rich would help investment, but Keynes worried that too much redistribution would hurt growth.

As Keynes believed that the normal tendency was for the marginal propensity to save to be stronger than the incentive to invest, he was supportive of governments borrowing to invest since he believed the economy usually operated below its potential and public investment should therefore supplement private investment. His idea was to use fiscal policy to maintain a high level of public or semi-public investment. Investment should encourage consumption by raising the overall level of output and thus income to consume out of. The more consumption there was, the higher the national income, and therefore the greater the savings of the society that could be used to finance investment. A permanently high level of publicly directed investment would offset fluctuations in private investment, and contribute to the economy remaining in a 'quasi-boom'.[27] Keynes viewed the state as an investor in line with its role in providing a social safety net discussed earlier, though he worried about the costs of Beveridge's welfare state.

Keynes proposed government action to accelerate or delay

investment projects as necessary: 'I expect to see the State . . . taking an ever greater responsibility for directly organizing investment . . . I conceive, therefore, that a somewhat comprehensive socialization of investment will prove the only means of securing an approximation to full employment.'[28]

Keynes urged the government to take on a greater role in investment as the need became clearer. His notion of 'socializing investment' may well encompass a government-backed infrastructure bank or fund to help get projects off the ground. He might not have viewed private sector participation as necessary, but might have been willing to include private investors who would pool their money with the government to build infrastructure. This is in line with the EU investment fund described earlier that leverages public funds to attract private financing.

Would this policy lead to persistent budget deficits? This was one of the criticisms of Keynes. It's why governments have been reluctant to borrow to invest. They fear bond investors will ask for higher returns to lend them money, increasing the borrowing costs for a country that could jeopardize its economic growth.

The verdict is far from settled. The Chicago School of monetarists say that Keynes's counter-cyclical policies are bound to fail since their effects will be anticipated, either immediately or after a short lag. Harvard economist Robert Barro argues that future tax rises to pay for government deficit spending are figured into long-term interest rates by investors and savers. That will lead to higher rates in the future and make government borrowing more expensive and the budget deficit less affordable. This view can be traced to David Ricardo. Under Ricardian equivalence, rational people know that the government debt will have to be repaid at some point in the form of higher taxes so they save in anticipation and do not increase current consumption that boosts growth. Still, the perceived need to increase investment and economic growth has shifted the public debate closer to what Keynes advocated even during non-crisis times. There is also a growing inclination to separate capital from current spending in government accounts, so investment doesn't count the same as day-to-day public spending. Given the debate over low investment, low borrowing costs and concerns over growth, Keynes's relatively lesser-known views on public investment could have a greater impact on the structure of an economy than his better-known arguments about government deficit spending.

Keynes's legacy

Keynes passed away in 1946 after helping to construct the post-Second World War Bretton Woods System, which included the formation of the sister institutions of the IMF and the World Bank. His memorial service was held at Westminster Abbey, close to Parliament, where he had latterly become a member of the House of Lords. He was survived by his widow, Lydia Lopokova, who continued his work with the Arts Council of Britain and lived another thirty-six years.

She died at the beginning of the Thatcher era, which saw the rollback of Keynesianism. But despite being in and out of favour, Keynes has had an enduring impact on economics. It's something that Keynes himself had predicted. The final passage of *The General Theory* reads:

> The ideas of economists and political philosophers, both when they are right and when they are wrong, are more powerful than is commonly understood. Indeed the world is ruled by little else. Practical men, who believe themselves to be quite exempt from any intellectual influence, are usually the slaves of some defunct economist. Madmen in authority, who hear voices in the air, are distilling their frenzy from some academic scribbler of a few years back. I am sure that the power of vested interests is vastly exaggerated compared with the gradual encroachment of ideas . . . soon or late, it is ideas, not vested interests, which are dangerous for good or evil.[29]

Keynes believed that there are no intractable economic problems, and that well-run economies would produce prosperity. Writing in 1930, he predicted: 'the *economic problem* may be solved, or be at least within sight of solution, within a hundred years. This means that the economic problem is not – if we look into the future – *the permanent problem of the human race.*'[30]

It means that we can look forward to a fifteen-hour working week, as 'three hours a day is quite enough'.[31] But, it would lead to an even greater challenge:

> [M]ankind will be deprived of its traditional purpose . . . Thus for the first time since his creation man will be faced with his real, his permanent problem – how to use his freedom from pressing economic cares, how to occupy the leisure, which science and compound interest will have won for him, to live wisely and agreeably and well.[32]

7

Joseph Schumpeter: What Drives Innovation?

Innovation is the engine of economic growth, or, as Joseph Schumpeter put it, innovation in a capitalist economy is the 'perennial gale of creative destruction'.[1] Schumpeter's view was that the economy undergoes long cycles as new technologies are adopted, while existing technologies become obsolescent. And those new technologies give a boost to economic growth.

Joseph Schumpeter was perhaps the first economist to define the 'capitalist engine', in his 1942 *Capitalism, Socialism and Democracy*, his most important work.[2] Contrary to popular belief, the term 'capitalism' was not devised by Adam Smith. It is thought to have first appeared in *The Newcomes*, an 1854 novel by the author of *Vanity Fair*, William Makepeace Thackeray. According to the *Oxford English Dictionary*, Thackeray used the term capitalist to denote an owner of capital. Of course, Karl Marx referred to capitalism in his 1867 *Capital*, after which it was often used as an antonym for Marxism.

According to Schumpeter, 'Creative Destruction is the essential fact about capitalism.'[3] He framed capitalism around his theories about how the capitalist engine powers the economy. The economy is in constant flux, affected by waves of technological innovation, which explains how countries become more productive and wealthier over time. In his view, 'Stabilized capitalism is a contradiction in terms.'[4]

For example the steam engine, electricity and, more recently, the computer have all transformed the way that we work. Such innovations raise productivity, which increases the growth potential of the economy. In contrast to Marx, Joseph Schumpeter aimed to be value-neutral and analytical, so that his research would not be affected by ideology. Instead of revolution, Schumpeter's work delved into the details of the businesses responsible for path-breaking inventions and then explored the relationships between those innovations and the manner in which the economy and our living standards were improved by them.

It helped that Schumpeter had experience in the business world as well as in economic policy. He was a lawyer and an academic in his twenties and Austria's finance minister in his thirties, then became a banker before returning to academia. Although he made a fortune, he lost it all in a stock-market crash, which perhaps was a blessing in disguise, since it forced his return to economics. He eventually became a professor at Harvard University, where he wrote some of the most influential texts in the field.

Based on his own career, Schumpeter saw bankruptcy and the obsolescence of some industries simply as part of the cycle of the economy whose growth had benefited millions of people. He observed on one occasion: 'Practically every enterprise [is] threatened and put on the defensive as soon as it comes into existence,'[5] and, on another: 'It is the cheap cloth, the cheap cotton and rayon fabric, boots, motorcars and so on that are the typical achievements of capitalist production . . . the capitalist process, not by coincidence but by virtue of its mechanism, progressively raises the standard of life of the masses.'[6]

But Schumpeter didn't take the capitalist system for granted. He believed capitalism required vibrant entrepreneurship and prudent regulation. It was indeed an engine in that sense. Like a physical engine, capitalism required fuel, or it could break down.

What would the creator of 'creative destruction' say about the innovation challenges that abound in the world's major economies today? What would Schumpeter make of the challenge of innovating in a predominantly services, and increasingly digital, economy? That is the state of the UK, the US and most post-industrial economies, including Germany and others that may have retained a larger manufacturing base but whose services sector is still the largest part of their economies. And what would he have made of China's innovation, which is an important factor in terms of whether it can join the ranks of prosperous nations?

The life and times of Joseph Schumpeter

Joseph Schumpeter was born in 1883 in Triesch, a small town to the south-east of Prague, in the Austro-Hungarian (or Habsburg) Empire. The empire was expansive, including today's Austria, Hungary, Czech Republic, Slovakia, Slovenia, Croatia and parts of Poland, Ukraine, Italy and Romania. Both Schumpeter's grandfather and great-grandfather were mayors as well as businessmen. In fact, the family textile business brought the first steam engine to the town.

Schumpeter grew up at a time when the engine of capitalism was transforming society. The electric motor and internal combustion engine were dramatically changing the economy, much as the steam engine had done before. Along with the telephone and railways, these inventions increased economic growth and rendered old businesses obsolete.

In 1901 the world's three largest industrial firms were United States Steel, American Tobacco and Standard Oil. German companies, such as Krupp and Thyssen in steel, Siemens in electrical equipment and chemical giants Bayer, Hoechst and BASF had all become industrial powerhouses. But, in the empire, most people still lived on farms, while small businesses were losing out to cheaper products from industrializing nations such as America, Germany and Britain.

German Austria's per capita income in 1913 was only about half that of Britain, though twice that of Hungary. Most people had no access to indoor plumbing, clean water or mass-produced shoes and clothing. Telephones and central heating were available only to the wealthy. Austrian bureaucrats still handwrote documents even though typewriters had been in use for twenty years.

Because Schumpeter had grown up during a time of vast change, his Harvard student and later economics Nobel laureate Paul

Samuelson described him as 'completely qualified to play the important sociological role of the alienated stranger'.[7]

After Schumpeter's father passed away when he was five, he moved with his mother to Graz, where one of the few universities in the Austro-Hungarian Empire was located. It was highly unusual for a young widow to move to another town. While there, she married a member of the Austrian nobility. He was a sixty-five-year-old retired general who was more than three decades her senior. The move to Graz and his mother's second marriage meant Schumpeter could attend the best schools. He became fluent in six languages, including Greek and Latin. The family later departed for Vienna, where Schumpeter eventually attended the city's prestigious university.

At that time, German-speaking universities were among the best in the world and the University of Vienna was among the top echelon for economics.[8] Like other European universities at the time, Vienna's economics professors were part of the Faculty of Law. Schumpeter's degree, received in 1906, was not in economics but in civil and Roman law, which gave him knowledge of history. Later on, he practised as an attorney, which provided exposure to the business world.

Unlike those economists who were interested in reforming public policy, the Austrian School strove to make economics more rigorous and move it away from politics altogether. This shaped Schumpeter's concept of the subject. He believed that economics should be 'neutral' and free from politics, which compromised objective analysis.

While studying, Schumpeter encountered the three leading approaches to economics. First, the Classical School, founded by Adam Smith and promulgated by David Ricardo and John Stuart Mill, among others. These largely English economists were actively involved with public policy. Schumpeter, though, criticized them for their lack of imagination: 'Those writers lived at the threshold of the most spectacular economic developments ever witnessed. Vast possibilities matured into realities under their very eyes. Nevertheless, they saw nothing but cramped economies, struggling with ever-decreasing success for their daily bread.'[9]

Despite his rejection of capitalism, and belonging to a school of thought of his own, Karl Marx was the only one who stressed the dynamics of a capitalist system, which left a mark on Schumpeter.

The German Historical School, which detailed histories of various industries and institutions, also affected Schumpeter. Centred in Berlin, its leading economist was Gustav von Schmoller and its well-known sociologist was Max Weber, who wrote *The Protestant Ethic and the Spirit of Capitalism*. Schumpeter believed their school didn't give enough credence to economic theory. But he admired Weber, who was willing to theorize as long as it was based on data, so they occasionally worked together despite the fact that the German and Austrian schools conflicted. Their common ground was the new doctrine of marginalism, investigating how individuals optimize their decisions to work and consume. In the final part of the nineteenth century, marginalism changed the foundations of economics, which ushered in an early version of the neoclassical revolution. W. Stanley Jevons, Carl Menger and Leon Walras are often quoted as the leading lights.

The rise of the Austrian School cannot be separated from the particular history of the Austro-Hungarian Empire. The empire was vast, conservative and aristocratic. Its economic policy was *dirigiste*. It had been, and still viewed itself as, the most powerful state in Europe. It controlled almost all of central Europe and most of the important industries were kept in state hands or under tight regulation.

The good side of this was that it had a large and meritocratic civil service, and key positions were held not by politicians but by professionals like Eugen Böhm von Bawerk in the Ministry of Finance, who rotated in and out of academia and the civil service. (Schumpeter was to follow in his footsteps, becoming finance minister in the post-war republic.) Such policies made the empire an important centre for economics. The society was very well organized and apparently quite stable.

But the bad side, of course, was that everything was slow and sclerotic as well as resistant to change. There was no real economic freedom for entrepreneurs so the economy was failing to adapt and invest, falling seriously behind other European nations, particularly the upstart Prussians. Underneath the surface, there were growing social strains until the shock of the First World War destroyed the system.

The Austrian School was a reaction to all this, hence their defining characteristics: entrepreneurship, anti-equilibrium and anti-planning. It was, as with all economic theories, rooted in its time. Just as Adam Smith reacted to the inefficiencies of eighteenth-century British government, the Austrian School reacted to the weaknesses of the nineteenth-century Austrian government.

The Austrian School was led by Schumpeter's professors. In 1905 Schumpeter enrolled in a seminar led by Menger's former student Böhm von Bawerk, who was a three-time finance minister of imperial Austria. His classmates included Ludwig von Mises, who became one of the leading free-market economists of the twentieth century through his own writings and those of his pupil Friedrich Hayek.

During his five years as an undergraduate Schumpeter published three articles. They appeared when he was just twenty-two. He wanted to pursue a career as both a professor and a public servant like his mentor, Böhm von Bawerk. But a lack of money and his middle-class background were impediments.

His circumstances changed with marriage. In 1907, at the age of twenty-four, he wed Gladys Ricarde Seaver, the thirty-six-year-old daughter of a Church of England official. Gladys was upper class and their marriage propelled Schumpeter into the aristocracy, much as his mother's second marriage had done for her.[10]

Schumpeter discovered that he could work as a lawyer in Cairo, which was then effectively a protectorate of Britain, with no experience. It was not possible in Vienna or London to do so. The newlyweds moved there, and in ten months Schumpeter had earned enough to finance his family for years.

They returned to Vienna, and in 1908 he published *The Nature and Content of Theoretical Economics*. The manuscript was his effort to reconcile the German Historical School with the Austrian marginalists in order to end the battle of Continental economics. It was similar to what Marshall had done when he synthesized the new marginalism with the old classical tradition of Smith and Ricardo.

Although it didn't sell well, the book contributed to his qualifications at the University of Vienna. Along with his examinations and delivery of the standard series of lectures, Schumpeter gained the certification to teach at any university in the Austro-Hungarian Empire.

He had wished to stay in Vienna, but ended up at the University of Czernowitz in present-day Ukraine. Schumpeter hadn't wanted to relocate to a remote city at the extreme eastern border of the empire, but he wasn't there long. At the age of twenty-eight, he left to become the youngest professor of political economy in the empire at the University of Graz, which was second in size only to the University of Vienna.

Schumpeter's *Theory of Economic Development* was published soon after, in 1911. This was the book that made his name and it was to become one of the classics in economics. An English edition was later published by Harvard University Press in 1934 with the subtitle: *An Inquiry into Profits, Capital, Credit, Interest and the Business Cycle*. The ideas in this very early work formed the core of Schumpeterian economics, which were later developed in *Business Cycles* (1939) and the most popular of his books, *Capitalism, Socialism and Democracy* (1942).

Schumpeter spent five months lecturing in America, which raised his profile, but soon after his return home the First World War broke out. Gladys had returned to England so was cut off from her husband. By 1920 he began to describe himself as unmarried, though the couple had not divorced.

By the age of thirty-two, Schumpeter had written three significant books and twenty articles. His profile was further heightened by a lecture entitled 'The Crisis of the Tax State'. In it, he criticized the tax regime, which he argued had reduced innovation by causing entrepreneurs 'to migrate to countries of lower taxation'.[11] He also highlighted how excessive demands for social services could weaken the capitalist system. It was after that lecture that he became Minister of Finance in Austria's First Republic. It was rather unusual for a political novice to become a senior government official and at the age of thirty-six, but they were exceptional times. The First World War turned Austria almost overnight from the most historic, biggest and a stable state in Europe into one with dire economic prospects and on the brink of revolution.

After leaving government in 1919, he wanted to stay in Vienna and live comfortably, so he became a banker and professional investor. He received a licence to operate the Biedermann Bank, which he viewed as compensation for his brief and challenging stint as finance minister.[12] He even eventually resigned from the University of Graz in 1921.

In his new occupation, Schumpeter gained insight into the role of banks in creating credit that could fund entrepreneurs. Between 1920 and the end of 1922 there was hyperinflation in Austria, despite which Schumpeter had managed to accumulated a significant fortune by the age of forty. But a year later, in 1924, Vienna's stock market crashed, losing a staggering three-quarters of its value. Schumpeter suffered similarly, because he was reluctant to unload his stocks as their value fell. He remained loyal to even failing firms, especially the entrepreneurial ones. It seems even the creator of 'creative destruction' found it hard to let firms fail.

Although he still had his position at the Biedermann Bank, Schumpeter fell into debt and was forced to resign. He ended up paying back the bank by borrowing from friends. It would take a decade before he was able to repay his debts. Having failed in both business and politics, Schumpeter himself epitomized the entrepreneurship that he would later write about.

Not everything was dire. While all this was going on he had fallen in love with Anna Josefina Reisinger, whom he had known since she was a child. Anna was the daughter of the concierge of the apartment building in Vienna where he had grown up, and more than twenty years younger than Schumpeter. Her parents objected but when she turned eighteen, they reluctantly allowed her to accept Schumpeter's proposal.[13]

Schumpeter joined the prestigious University of Bonn, which meant that he had a stable source of income and they could marry. Neither set of parents were supportive, Schumpeter's mother objecting to Anna's working-class background while Anna's parents were concerned about his age and his reputation as a womanizer. And then there was his marriage to Gladys, from whom he secured a civil waiver without her knowledge.

They finally married on 5 November 1925, when he was forty-two and she was twenty-two and without their parents' attendance. A year later, Anna died in childbirth, as did their baby son. His mother passed away around this time too. Schumpeter never escaped from the emotional stress of that year and buried himself in work.[14] During his seven years in Bonn, he was prolific and published sixty-five articles. He also made money through penning popular pieces and lecturing to business audiences to pay his debts and send money to Anna's parents, which he did for the rest of his life. True to his beliefs, he disliked prescribing policy remedies because it might compromise his objectivity. But, it was hard not to be involved during the 1930s. So, he wrote a series of articles as the world and Germany suffered from the Great Depression. He criticized bailouts of old or low-growth industries, but supported government intervention to help companies with strong growth potential. As a condition of public assistance, though, Schumpeter argued that they must adopt innovative practices.

Despite these challenging times, Schumpeter witnessed the impressive wholesale reinvention of business, which fed into his theory of 'creative destruction' where the innovators flourish. Small and medium-sized German businesses, mostly family owned, upgraded their operations and became known globally for their quality. Many of these *Mittelstand* companies are still around today, for example Hohner harmonicas, Krones labelling machines and the Jil Sander fashion label.

Big businesses also reinvented themselves. Five of Germany's ten largest firms manufactured steel at the time of his move to Bonn. By the time he left, several had merged to become Vereinigte Stahlwerke (United Steelworks), which was the biggest steel and mining company in Europe.

As his prolific research raised his profile, Schumpeter received numerous academic offers, including one from Harvard University. A good salary at an elite economics department led Schumpeter to accept a one-year visiting appointment from 1927–28 while maintaining his position at Bonn. As is common among those taking up visiting positions, Schumpeter found that he liked Harvard better and eventually accepted a permanent post in 1932. Given his stature, Schumpeter received the maximum salary for Harvard professors, which allowed him to send money regularly to friends and former students in Europe and pay his remaining debts in Vienna.

It was during this time that Schumpeter established the Econometric Society in 1930, along with the Norwegian economist and co-recipient of the first Economics Nobel Prize Ragnar Frisch and Yale's Irving Fisher. They wanted to promote the use of mathematical and statistical methods in economics, which Frisch named 'econometrics'. Schumpeter wrote the lead article for the society's first issue of *Econometrica*, which began publication in 1933 and remains a leading journal today.

Not all professors enjoy both teaching and research, and arguably few are great at both. Schumpeter was one of the rare exceptions. He organized several small discussion groups, including the Schumpeter Group of Seven Wise Men, who were rising stars. This group included the best of the Harvard Economics Department: Douglas V. Brown, Edward Chamberlin, Gottfried Haberler, Seymour Harris, Edward Mason, Overton H. Taylor and, his favourite, the future Russian Nobel laureate Wassily Leontief.[15] His students included stars such as America's first Nobel laureate in economics Paul Samuelson, who would correct Schumpeter's mathematical errors.

An engaging figure in public, Schumpeter was a popular teacher. But in private, he suffered from anxiety and despondency, and made his research the focal point of his days. As Schumpeter himself proclaimed: 'My work is my only interest in life.'[16] He even graded himself daily on his productivity, for example 0, 4/6, 0, 0, 1/3, 5/6, 1 for a weekly mark of just 50 per cent.[17]

But not all aspects of academic life suited Schumpeter. He disliked departmental meetings and referred to his colleagues as the 'fools' (a play on the German pronunciation of 'full' professors) and 'asses' (associate and assistant professors).[18]

After Adolf Hitler became Chancellor of Germany in 1933, Schumpeter became an active recruiter for American universities, working to secure places for German, particularly Jewish, economists. By the inter-war period many had left Vienna and the university's economics faculty was in decline.

Around that time, Schumpeter met Romaine Elizabeth Boody Firuski, a thirty-five-year-old graduate student in economics at Harvard who came from a prosperous old New England family. In 1920 she had received the first *summa cum laude* degree from Radcliffe College, the all-women sister college to Harvard. After an unhappy marriage had ended, she returned to Cambridge, Massachusetts, and worked as a research assistant for Schumpeter and others, and resumed writing her dissertation on English trade. He became her co-supervisor and she received her PhD from Radcliffe in 1934. Though he was fifty in 1933, and she was fifteen years younger, she was an intellectual partner and soon she became more. They married in New York in August 1937; his third marriage and one that lasted until his death in 1950.

Schumpeter's trio of major works was completed at Harvard: *Business Cycles: A Theoretical, Historical, and Statistical Analysis of the Capitalist Process* in 1939, *Capitalism, Socialism and Democracy* in 1942 and *History of Economic Analysis*, which was published posthumously in 1954.

Although he had laboured over *Business Cycles*, it did not receive widespread acclaim. This was a disappointment to Schumpeter, since he had spent seven years writing what he thought would be his seminal work. To make matters worse, at a Harvard seminar that his students organized to discuss it, they ended up talking about John Maynard Keynes's recent *The General Theory of Employment, Interest and Money*. Schumpeter's wordiness contrasted with Keynes's succinct prose, which may have also contributed to the students' choice. Several remarked that it was the only time they ever saw Schumpeter so angry.[19]

Ever since the 1936 publication of Keynes's magnum opus, the English economist had outshone Schumpeter. Keynes did not make much mention of the business cycle research of Schumpeter or other Continental European economists. In return, Schumpeter disputed even the title of the book, specifically the 'general' part, since he believed that Keynes's theory applied only narrowly to an economy in depression.[20]

What the *General Theory* did was offer a new explanation of the

Great Depression that outlined a way forward for the world economy. By contrast, Schumpeter did not believe in prescribing economic policy, consistent with his long-standing view that politics compromised objective economic analysis. In the Preface to *Business Cycles* Schumpeter wrote: 'I recommend no policy and propose no plan.'[21] That hurt the appeal of the book at a time when the public was seeking answers to the worst economic downturn in history.

Schumpeter had been active in European economic policy before, so he was not without opinion. Although he was not a fan of FDR's New Deal and he opposed Keynes's fiscal activism funded by deficit spending, Schumpeter believed that America needed public investment. In 1933 unemployment rose to a staggering 25 per cent. After falling with the introduction of the New Deal, it rose again to over 17 per cent in 1939, after the second recession of that decade. It was then that he started writing the book that would leave his mark on the subject. *Capitalism, Socialism and Democracy* began as a series of essays, which reacted to a time of turmoil. It encompassed the Great Depression, the rise of Marxism that challenged capitalism and the Second World War.

It was published in 1942, but due to the Second World War it wasn't until the second (1947) and third (1950) editions that *Capitalism, Socialism and Democracy* became prominent. The book struck a popular nerve since it captured the great debate of the period. At that time, 40 per cent of the global population was living under communism and another quarter or so in at least partly socialized economies.

Schumpeterian economics

Joseph Schumpeter's most influential work addressed fundamental questions about how an economy operates. Schumpeter wondered if capitalism was doomed to fail, as argued by Marx. If socialism replaced capitalism, would the economy prosper? The third part of the title refers to whether there would be democracy alongside either capitalism or socialism.

Schumpeter makes the case emphatically for capitalism. He argues that people's lives had improved tremendously because of 'creative destruction':

> The opening up of new markets, foreign or domestic, and the organizational development from the craft shop and factory to such concerns as US Steel illustrate the same process of industrial mutation – if I may use that biological term – that incessantly revolutionizes the economic structure *from within*, incessantly destroying the old one, incessantly creating a new one. This process of Creative Destruction is the essential fact about capitalism.[22]

Schumpeter's firms were not powerless to influence the economic environment, in stark contrast to standard economic models. In using the term 'business strategy', Schumpeter challenged the assumption of 'perfect competition', where all firms are identical, and sell homogeneous products, so have no strategic decisions to take. He viewed firms as making decisions about employment, production and investment, which all affected the growth of the economy. He also disagreed with economic models where transactions happened seamlessly without lawyers, accountants or the numerous other operational aspects of real businesses.

He also argued against the anti-big-business sentiment then prevalent in America. The US was home to about half of the world's biggest companies and yet had a strong entrepreneurial culture. Schumpeter argued that such 'trustified' capitalism did not stifle innovation or prevent the growth of new businesses. Alongside US multinationals, thousands of new companies emerged. Through the process of 'creative destruction', the most innovative survived. Schumpeter notes that from 1897 to 1904, 4,227 American companies merged into 257 large corporations, including such well-known names as Goodyear, Pepsico, Kellogg, Gillette, Monsanto, 3M and Texaco.

In Schumpeter's view, few monopolies survived in the long term, owing to 'creative destruction'. The successful innovator might reap monopoly profits for a while, but others in the same industry will soon try to imitate the product. The entrepreneur will preserve his profit for as long as possible through patents, further innovation and advertising, which are all acts of 'aggression directed against actual and would-be competitors'.[23] But every entrepreneur's profit is temporary because competitors will eventually copy the innovation, causing market prices to fall. This sequence, which Schumpeter calls 'competing down', is observable in all industries except those protected by government. It may take several years and can be hard to see, but it is inevitable. For Schumpeter, because high profits are possible, even if temporary, big business contributes positively towards innovation and therefore economic growth.[24] So why are monopolists frequently in the spotlight? In Schumpeter's view: 'Why then all this talk about monopoly? . . . Economists, government agents, journalists and politicians in this country obviously love the word because it . . . is sure to rouse the public's hostility.'[25]

Schumpeter also believed that capitalism was a fragile system. The rise of big business undercut smaller ones who commanded greater loyalty from workers and also tended to have more political influence in their communities. In addition, society was likely to resist major innovations because they tend to destroy the status quo. He observed: 'Entrepreneurs were not necessarily strangled', but 'they were not infrequently in danger of their lives'.[26] For instance, craft guilds in Britain invoked medieval laws and petitioned for regulations outlawing factories and mechanical devices. In the early 1830s rural labourers smashed the new threshing machines which were threatening their livelihoods. In fact, 'the history of capitalism is studded with violent bursts and catastrophes'.[27] Schumpeter also thought that people might act against their economic interests because of their beliefs: 'Socialist bread may well taste sweeter to them than capitalist bread simply because it is socialist bread, and it would do so even if they found mice in it.'[28]

Thus, Schumpeter warned: 'I felt it my duty . . . to inflict upon the reader . . . my paradoxical conclusion: capitalism is being killed by its achievements.'[29] So, political oversight was needed. Schumpeter believed that the upheaval caused by entrepreneurs could engender social turmoil which may even lead the capitalist engine to stall. Thus, economic growth required a stable government, specifically the rule of law and protection of private property. The system that he most admired was the British one with its constitutional monarchy and bicameral Parliament comprising Commons and Lords. He held in high regard Britain's apolitical civil service, which gave that stability to a capitalist system. It is only within such a system that Schumpeter's 'creative destruction' could flourish.

In Schumpeter's system: 'The introduction of new production methods, the opening up of new markets – indeed, the successful carrying through of new business combinations in general – all these imply risk, trial and error, the overcoming of resistance, factors lacking in the treadmill of routine.'[30] These disruptions to the routine explain why economies expand and go through periods of 'destruction'. Schumpeter argued that innovations in specific industries affected other parts of the economy, such as their suppliers, distributors and, eventually, customers. In the nineteenth and early twentieth centuries, economic growth was driven by a series of breakthroughs. Specifically, five industries led economic development: cotton textiles, railroads, steel, automobiles and electricity. Such industry-specific innovation 'does not follow, but creates expansion'.[31]

Rather than an economic concept of an equilibrium that an economy returns to, Schumpeter's view of innovation involves continuous disequilibrium that is led by entrepreneurs transforming an industry with economy-wide effects.

To enable such entrepreneurial innovators, Schumpeter stressed the importance of credit in a capitalist system. He believed capitalism to be the only system that enables people to become entrepreneurs before they have the funds to found an enterprise: 'it is leadership rather than ownership that matters'.[32] It was not only a bank credit line to keep a business operating that was necessary, but money for new ventures, which can be lost if the start-up fails without jeopardizing the entire economic system. In his career as a banker and investor, Schumpeter underwrote precisely such firms, even though it cost him his personal fortune.

That is also why he believed that the economy benefited from the rise of big business because they could afford to gamble on innovation. They also had access to capital markets, such as raising money by issuing debt on bond markets, as well as retained earnings, so were less reliant on more conservative bank loans. For instance, in the early twentieth century, firms such as American Telephone and Telegraph (AT&T), General Electric (GE), Eastman Kodak and DuPont set up research departments to develop new products. They made innovation an integral part of their business. Later in the century, large firms worldwide followed suit.

Perhaps the best examples of the Schumpeterian notion of innovation and economic growth are found in the East Asian economies, which underwent their 'growth miracle' during the mid-twentieth century, namely Japan, Korea, Taiwan and Singapore.[33] Schumpeter even lectured to great acclaim across Japan in early 1931. He generated extensive media coverage that is hard to picture today for economic lectures. Japanese policymakers notably adopted a Schumpeterian approach. They stressed saving and investment, and actively promoted a broad range of innovation across numerous industries. A slew of new Japanese multinational companies such as Sony, Sanyo and Honda eventually became globally competitive. During that period of the 1960s to the 1980s, Japan achieved the highest sustained growth rate for a major economy and became the world's second biggest economy. Japan's innovative companies led the nation to such growth that Japan even threatened America's standing.

Schumpeter's work established the crucial role that entrepreneurs play in capitalist economies, even though entrepreneurship itself can't be simply modelled mathematically. In his view, innovation is 'a feat not of intellect, but of will . . . a special case of the social phenomenon of leadership'.[34] In Schumpeter's definition, the entrepreneur is not a business executive or even the owner or chief executive of a successful firm. He is 'the modern type of "captain of industry" – obsessively seeking an innovative edge'.[35] It can even be hard to identify the entrepreneur: 'nobody ever is an entrepreneur all the time, and nobody can ever be only an entrepreneur'.[36] Particularly in large firms, the entrepreneur often not only innovates but also carries out management. In short, Schumpeter saw entrepreneurship as a key factor to start the engine of growth: 'Without innovation, no entrepreneurs; without entrepreneurial achievement, no capitalist returns and no capitalist propulsion.'[37]

For Schumpeter, 'Capitalist evolution spells disturbance. Capitalism is essentially a process of economic change.'[38] This change comes from innovative entrepreneurs. He outlined five types of innovation that derive from entrepreneurs:[39]

- The introduction of a new good, for example one with which consumers are not yet familiar, or of a new version of a good that is of better quality.
- The introduction of a new method of production.
- The opening of a new market.
- The conquest of a new source of raw materials or half-manufactured goods.
- The creation of a new organization of any industry, like the creation of a monopoly position (for example, through trustification) or the breaking up of a monopoly.

In summary, Schumpeter sees entrepreneurship as 'essentially one and the same thing' as technological progress that raises the growth of the economy.[40]

The challenge of staying on top as innovators

Nokia and BlackBerry

In the process of 'creative destruction', innovative products will displace old ones. In aggregate, the efforts of companies to improve the level of technological innovation hold the key to the success of the economy. The transition from old to new, though, is rarely seamless and includes the rise and fall of not just individual businesses but entire industries.

Nokia and BlackBerry phones are good illustrations of Schumpeter's 'creative destruction'. Nokia was once worth $150 billion but was eventually sold for just $7 billion. How did all of this market value disappear?

For Finland's Nokia it was the culmination of a rapid rise and fall. It introduced its first mobile phone in 1987 and by 1998 had overtaken Motorola to become the global market leader in handset sales. In

2005 it sold its billionth phone. Its peak was probably in 2007. By then its share of the global handset market had reached 40 per cent, including nearly half the smartphone market at the time, and its market capitalization hit $150 billion. Before its sale, its global market share had fallen to just 15 per cent, and this was mainly accounted for by its range of cheaper phones. Its share of the global smartphone market had plummeted to just 3 per cent.

A similar story of boom and bust describes the Canadian firm Research in Motion (RIM). Back in 2003 it launched the BlackBerry. By allowing people to email easily from their phones, its popularity grew quickly and its secure network was favoured by businesses and governments. The addictive nature of the phone led to it being nicknamed 'CrackBerry'. By the middle of 2008, the company was valued at around $70 billion.

The subsequent decline was steep and the landing hard. Just a decade after its founding, RIM reported losses of $1 billion that meant cutting 40 per cent of its global workforce. Haemorrhaging cash and sitting on a stockpile of unsold handsets valued at $930 million, it was bought out by a consortium led by Toronto-based private equity group Fairfax Financial in 2013. The price was just $4.9 billion. Together, Nokia and RIM have seen roughly $200 billion evaporate. How?

In 2007 Steve Jobs walked onto the stage at the Moscone Center in San Francisco, pulled an iPhone from his pocket and talked of a revolutionary product that was going to change everything. The rest, as they say, is history. Apple's take-off, along with Google's Android system, has mirrored the decline at Nokia and RIM.

So where did Nokia and RIM go wrong? Were they just the latest victims of 'creative destruction' in the digital age?

They weren't the first. In January 2012, after over 130 years of operations, Kodak filed for bankruptcy. The American company had once sold over 90 per cent of all film in the US and its little yellow boxes could be seen all around the world. Its death knell sounded simply because it was out-innovated in the very technology it had pioneered for over a century.

Ironically, Kodak had developed a prototype for the digital camera in 1975. But by the time it became apparent that it would be a game changer, it was too late. Japan's Canon and Fuji had already established a decisive lead in the digital camera market.

Kodak's is not an atypical story. A large incumbent company, successful for decades, finds it difficult to adapt to new technologies while it makes good profits in the traditional business areas. It is then left adrift once the whole industry has shifted for good. The lesson is, adapt or die.

Is this also true of Nokia and RIM? Nokia was innovative in hardware and was the dominant force at the outset of the smartphone market. However, Apple, and then Android, saw the value of software. Touch-screen technology changed the way people used their phones and both had app stores that were easy to use.

Perhaps Nokia showed a lack of urgency. In the early days of the iPhone era, the drop-off in global market share was gradual rather than abrupt, and Nokia was able to retain its position as the market leader. BlackBerry's problem was that it catered primarily for business users and was left stranded when, with the advent of social media, innovation in the mobile phones market became strongly consumer-led. RIM failed to respond to the consumerization of IT.

In today's high-technology era, consumers expect constant innovation and are quick to punish the products that fall behind. The pace of creative destruction has quickened and brands are no longer as resilient as they once were.

This is evident from the increase in stock market churn over the past few decades. In 1958 the average tenure of the companies listed on the S&P 500 was sixty-one years. By 1980, this had fallen to twenty-five years, and is now down to eighteen years. If the trend continues, three-quarters of the firms currently listed on the S&P 500 will be replaced by 2027.[41]

Apple and Samsung

What about the disrupter Apple? Could US technology giant Apple's empire fall? Apple has made bumper profits from international sales. In 2017, it was the most valuable traded company in the world in history. And what about Korea's Samsung, the market leader in the global smartphone market?

Japan's Sony is a cautionary tale. During the 1980s and early 1990s, Sony was the Apple of its day. The company was synonymous with quality in the electronics industry. In 1979 it launched the iconic Walkman. Even when cheaper personal stereos flooded the market, the demand for Walkmans remained high because people trusted the brand. During the 1990s it teamed up with the Dutch electronics giant Philips to perfect the compact disc media format, but that was probably its peak.

When Apple launched its iPod in October 2001, Sony was criticized for being slow off the mark in the MP3 market. Since then its fortunes have been all downhill. The stock of the company had been downgraded to junk status due to its severe challenges to improve sales and profitability, while its core businesses are subject to obsolescence and rapid changes in technology.

It is very premature to forecast the eventual decline of Apple, but Sony, Kodak, Nokia and RIM exemplify the potential force of creative destruction. It's been over a decade since the first iPhones started flying off the shelves. Apple, along with Samsung, has been at the vanguard of the smartphone revolution. The two companies dominate the global smartphone market. But there are signs that worldwide growth in smartphone sales is beginning to slow, and new competitors are emerging, notably from China. What might that mean for these two smartphone giants?

There are indications of market saturation in the world's developed markets, while stronger growth has been found in developing and emerging economies such as China. According to the International Data Company, half of smartphone sales around the world are below $100, excluding sales taxes. Prices have fallen as smartphone technology becomes standardized and a swathe of manufacturers target the budget end of the market. In developed markets, customers are becoming more price-sensitive and a bit less brand-orientated. Wiko, a French start-up that is majority owned by a Chinese firm, sells some of its phones for less than that $100 benchmark. It has quickly claimed a share of the French market and has set its sights on the rest of Europe.

Consumers are also benefiting from rapid improvements in stand-ard technology, so a cheap price does not necessarily mean low quality. In 2012 less than half of all smartphones priced at $80 or less had a processor faster than 1 gigahertz. A couple of years later, nine out of ten at this price did. Budget smartphones have also followed the trend of larger screen sizes.

Then there are the new competitors from China. After Samsung and Apple, the next three biggest smartphone makers are all from China. They are eating into Samsung's world market share, which has fallen from one-third to around one-fifth. For Apple, two-thirds of its sales are outside the US, and in those markets the iPhone is fa-cing considerable competition from cheaper brands.

And there are many of them. There are 6,000 handset manufactur-ers in Shenzhen alone. Once a fishing village close to Hong Kong, it's now a massive tech hub rivalling Silicon Valley in California. This area produces the majority of the mobile phones in the country, and China produces more than half of the 2.5 billion phones sold around the world annually.

In light of this competition, what might happen to the smartphone pioneers Apple and Samsung in the coming years and how might they adapt to the maturing market and growth in manufacturers of cheaper smartphones?

The iPhone generates the biggest portion of Apple's total revenues. It's an expensive product. With Google's Android operating system used in nearly three-quarters of all smartphones, the iPhone is look-ing increasingly like a luxury and niche brand. Apple has never been an out-and-out hardware company and might respond by developing its complementary software and services. iTunes has about a billion subscribers, and with its acquisition of Beats Music, Apple has made a foray into the video and music streaming business. It has also devel-oped a mobile wallet, working with MasterCard and Visa.

Samsung manufactures smartphones at a range of prices, but is coming under intense competition from manufacturers of cheap phones. It has started branching out into what it calls 'wearable tech' through a range of smartwatches. Apple too has launched a smart-watch. However, the uptake of wearables has been slow. It is perhaps too early to say whether smartclothing, smartglasses or smartwatches will come to challenge or even replace the smartphone.

There is also scope for smartphones to become even smarter. The recent trend to increase screen sizes could lead to flexible screens or built-in projectors. Augmented reality may encourage people to live their lives through their smartphone screens by allowing us to interact in real time with our surroundings.

Battery developments have so far failed to keep pace with the power demands of more sophisticated devices. It is ironic that as our mobile technology becomes more advanced, we need more regular access to a wall socket.

Figuring out the next innovation, though, will undoubtedly matter for these two, especially as there's immediate competition on their heels. The world's third largest mobile handset maker, Chinese firm Huawei, has launched a big screen smartphone, a phablet (phone + tablet), with an eye to challenging Samsung and Apple in the global smartphone market. In Schumpeter's theory, how these companies manage the 'creative destruction' process matters not just for them, but also for their home economies. Schumpeter viewed the rise and fall of companies as the source of economic growth. As entrepreneurs create new companies and innovative products, the economy prospers along with them. Whereas standard models of the economy assigned no role to individual firms except as homogeneous producers of widgets, Schumpeter gave entrepreneurs the biggest role in explaining how innovation comes about and boosts the growth of an economy.

China's innovation challenge

China is the major economy currently facing the considerable challenge of becoming an innovator. Is it possible for 'Made in China' to become 'Designed in China'? Japan made that transformation, but many more countries have failed than have succeeded.

In the 1980s movie *Back to the Future*, Michael J. Fox's character Marty McFly travelled back in time to the 1950s. He met a scientist who demanded proof that he was from the future. Even though Doc Brown scoffed at the idea of an actor (Ronald Reagan) as the US president, Marty managed to convince him. But Doc's incredulity was further stretched when Marty says that in the future Japan will make 'all the best stuff'. In Doc's time, 'Made in Japan' was synonymous with products that were cheap and of low quality.

In roughly thirty years, Japan came to rival the United States and was the world's second-largest economy. Japanese manufacturing was transformed from producing low-cost goods into launching world-beating companies such as Toyota. Now that China has overtaken Japan economically, could its companies become the next global competitors? Just as one company can overtake another, so one country can overtake another too.

Innovation, of course, takes many forms. But there's one thing in common: talent. It's what Joseph Schumpeter pointed out, which is that innovation comes from innovators. Can China produce the next Steve Jobs, for instance? Will there be innovators that transform the way that we live through their inventions and ingenuity? The answer to the question of Chinese innovativeness goes beyond manufacturing and into all areas of society, including the creative industries.

The Chinese government is actively investing in innovation. R&D spending has increased rapidly. China is predicted to surpass even US R&D spending in the coming years. Of course, it's not just what is spent or the number of patents filed that determines innovation. It's how useful these inventions are. And that data does not yet exist for China.

To complicate matters, much manufacturing now involves global supply chains. For instance, half of China's exports are made by foreign-invested enterprises, so it's multinational companies that are producing in China as well as domestic firms. Harvard economist Dani Rodrik estimated that the value of Chinese exports suggests that they come from a country with a much higher per capita income. Does that mean that China produces innovative exports or is it a place for global assembly?

A case study is Huawei. The giant telecoms equipment firm was founded in Shenzhen in 1987 by Ren Zhengfei. It imported telecoms equipment from nearby Hong Kong, just across the then Chinese border. It now makes the networks that power the internet and mobile phone networks around the world. Huawei products are used by companies such as Vodafone since they make the USB dongles that provide mobile internet connections. As mentioned above, it has also entered the smartphone market. Ren could be one of Schumpeter's entrepreneurs since he transformed his business from being just an importer of telecoms equipment into the world's largest telecommunications company, one that invests heavily in R&D and technological innovation.

Huawei faces specific challenges as telecoms and tech can engender suspicion of industrial espionage. Ren's stint in the Chinese army is a cause for concern in the US and other places such as Australia. It adds to suspicion that he works with the Chinese government. Huawei denies all the allegations made against the firm, but it is still banned from bidding for US government contracts.

Ren Zhengfei even based Huawei's sprawling campus on Silicon Valley. The green, open environment is designed to encourage innovation and collaboration, and there are on-site basketball courts and ping-pong tables, which is unusual in China. Graduates say that Huawei is a prestigious place to work. Ambitious young engineers want to be part of a global, innovative company and they even call themselves *Huawei-ren* or Huawei people, the Chinese version of Googlers.

However, there are numerous obstacles faced by Chinese non-state companies like Huawei. It was only in the late 1980s that consumer markets developed in China as the centrally planned economy was liberalized and private firms emerged. State-owned companies still dominate key sectors of the economy and bank credit. As a private firm, Huawei could not rely on government policy that promoted Chinese-foreign joint ventures to gain technology and know-how. Instead, the company innovated and undercut competitors to gain market share.

Another difference in the Chinese attitude towards innovation is that firms like Huawei innovate to serve a market need. In other words, they don't create something entirely new and then look for a market for it. For instance, Huawei developed an 'anechoic' chamber that eliminates echo so they can test for interference from their antennae or handsets. It's one of only a few such chambers in the world and it is designed to fill a need and where they have a competitive advantage from their massive amounts of data. As Huawei operates in 150 countries and over one-third of the world's population uses their products, they have a great deal of data with which to test and then fine-tune and improve their products.

But the next stage still needs to be invention, which is well recognized in China. Tech companies like Huawei spend around 10 per cent of their revenue on R&D, which is in the same league as the biggest global innovators. Half of Huawei's 150,000 employees work in R&D and it holds over 50,000 patents, making it one of the top five patent filers worldwide. Of course, spending on R&D doesn't necessarily translate into an innovative product. Around a quarter of Chinese patents are in product design, which is viewed as less innovative than a new product, but it is a category of innovation recognized by Schumpeter, who saw the value of improving the quality of an existing good. In the US, the figure is much lower, less than 10 per cent.

Huawei is also working on cutting-edge research. In competition with Silicon Valley, the company is developing a universal translator to enable people to converse in different languages using software that will translate context and not just words. Research is being undertaken on artificial intelligence that can even interpret jokes, which are among the hardest things to translate. For instance, how would the following joke be translated?

English: Why did the chicken cross the road? To get to the other side.

Chinese: How do you get an elephant into a refrigerator? You open the door, and put it in.

The Chinese elephant plays the same role as the chicken in the joke.

Huawei's next strategic move was to make its name known not just to industry insiders, but to the 7 billion people around the world. It became the first Chinese company to make it into Interbrand's top 100 global brands. Huawei believes it can take on the market leaders because its innovation is centred on customer needs. But can it get global customers to choose its smartphones over Samsung's and Apple's? If Huawei succeeds, that would point to whether China can make that difficult leap from imitator to innovator. And that could help China become a prosperous nation.

The thing about history is that it rarely repeats itself. One advantage that Chinese firms have over Japan is that their home market has more than a billion people, so they start with the advantage of scale. Scale gives Chinese companies a leg up because they have a billion consumers to sell to, so they can test new products and services without leaving Chinese borders and facing foreign competition. A downside, though, is that it is possible to become a very large Chinese firm without facing global competition. Although nothing is ever guaranteed, it is possible that China will be the source of the next global giants.

That is precisely the aim of the 'going global' policy. China's Alibaba Group is the world's largest online retailer. Few may have heard of it before its IPO on the New York Stock Exchange since the company operates predominantly in China. But, as with other Chinese companies that are coming of age, Alibaba has become a multinational company. If Alibaba truly breaks into overseas markets, that is precisely where China would like to see its firms succeed. If 'Made in China' continues to be viewed as low quality, then it will not sell well to consumers around the world. But if Chinese brands become synonymous with being the best in the world, that would also mark China's transition into a country that can produce innovation.

The correlation between the emergence of innovative companies and the growth prospects of their home countries fits Schumpeter's view of how innovation fuels the engine of economies. As a case study, China's experience exemplifies how even a fast-growing economy faces obstacles. For countries that do not benefit from Chinese growth rates, the challenge is even bigger.

Motivated to the end

What would Joseph Schumpeter think about how contemporary companies and countries should innovate?

Schumpeter's legacy is to show that capitalism depends on entrepreneurs who in turn require a supportive system. He rejected the simple assumptions made by economists about how producers and consumers operate.[42] He believed that what was needed was empirical analysis of actual businesses, such as the ones discussed earlier, to understand the innovative activities of entrepreneurs. With that understanding, we can then assess what propels the engine of economic growth.

The above companies largely rose and fell through competition over the past several decades. It's become evident that, in this digital era, start-up costs have dropped sharply, so in that sense entrepreneurship has become easier than before. The internet allows a business to be set up at virtually zero cost, which makes self-employment, particularly in the services sector, simpler and cheaper. Therefore, so long as countries were supportive of entrepreneurs in terms of providing a stable system with sources of funds for investment, Schumpeter would not see innovating in the services sector as harder than in manufacturing. So, in predominantly services economies like Britain, America and much of western Europe, Schumpeter would not view entrepreneurship as more challenging than when he witnessed the emergence of manufacturing powerhouses, which had much higher start-up costs, and yet succeeded.

As Schumpeter foresaw, innovative companies have helped to lead their home countries' economic growth. Apple's and Google's dominance mirrors America's reign at the top of the global economy. The challenger China's encroachment is reflected in the rise of its start-ups that are snapping at the established tech giants' positions. Unlike state-owned companies, a number of Chinese multinational firms, such as Alibaba and Huawei, have been founded by entrepreneurs. Such entrepreneurial innovators are those whom Schumpeter had in mind when he described companies shaping the growth of economies. So long as China continues to produce innovative companies, then he would expect the world's second biggest economy to transform itself into an innovative economy and 'Made in China' to be seen as a marker of quality.

Whether it's America or China or Japan, entrepreneurs will

determine the growth potential of the country, in Schumpeter's view. As described in *Capitalism*, entrepreneurial innovation is the dynamic element that drives how economies evolve through a process of 'creative destruction', which is as visible today as during his time.

But, due to the economy experiencing constant innovation and obsolescence as a result of entrepreneurship, the inventor of 'creative destruction' would be reluctant to predict how a capitalist system might evolve. Schumpeter would be unlikely to be found on a stage at a conference predicting the next technology to disrupt an established market!

He had ample opportunities to do so. By his mid-sixties, Joseph Schumpeter was one of the most famous economists in the world. There was no Nobel Prize in economics during his lifetime, but he was hugely acclaimed.

Schumpeter was elected as president of the American Economic Association in 1947, the most prestigious office in the country for an economist and one of the very few occasions in its history that a foreign-born economist had been chosen. In 1949 he was also selected as president of the new 5,300-member International Economic Association headquartered in Paris.

Acclaim only fuelled his work ambitions. During 1949 and the early part of 1950 he wrote twelve articles, the most in any comparable period since the 1920s. He died of a cerebral haemorrhage one month before his sixty-seventh birthday at the height of his fame. His final book, *History of Economic Analysis*, was published posthumously in 1954.

Motivated to the end, Schumpeter was similar to those he wrote about. He didn't believe that entrepreneurs, or indeed consumers, would ever be satisfied. He placed himself, with his penchant for reinvention during a varied career, among the ranks of those innovators, many of whom have changed the way that we live. Schumpeter believed that the innovator-entrepreneur had a 'will to conquer . . . Our type seeks out difficulties, changes in order to change, delights in ventures.'[43]

8

Friedrich Hayek: What Can We Learn from Financial Crises?

On 15 October 2011 members of the Occupy movement attempted to set up a protest camp in Paternoster Square, outside the London Stock Exchange. They were foiled, as the area was privately owned, so any protesters would have been trespassing and the police were able to seal off the entrance before any could enter. However, the group of around 3,000 people simply gathered instead outside nearby St Paul's Cathedral, where an indefinite camp was established. A month earlier a similar encampment had been set up in New York's Wall Street, and soon protests of different sizes emerged in cities around the world.

Occupy's slogan, 'We are the 99 per cent', referred to the high proportion of global wealth accounted for by the top 1 per cent of the distribution. They reflected the widespread public anger in the aftermath of the 2008 global financial crisis. The protesters called for financial reform, a fairer distribution of income and wealth and a rejection of austerity.

The Occupy movement reflected the modern version of a struggle that had been ongoing since the previous century. The twentieth century had witnessed an ideological battle between socialism and welfare state capitalism, culminating in the triumph of the latter with the fall of the Berlin Wall and the lifting of the Iron Curtain in 1989, which led to the break-up of the Soviet Union in 1991. Economics Nobel laureate Milton Friedman had observed:

There is no figure who had more of an influence on the intellectuals behind the Iron Curtain than Friedrich Hayek. His books were translated and published by the underground and black market editions, read widely, and undoubtedly influenced the climate of opinion that ultimately brought about the collapse of the Soviet Union.[1]

In the aftermath of the global financial crisis, the future of capitalism was once again up for debate. Had he been alive, free-market proponent Friedrich Hayek would have challenged the view that capitalism's time was up. He believed that the prosperity of society was driven by creativity, entrepreneurship and innovation, which were possible only in a society with free markets.

Hayek was a leading voice of the Austrian School. In the 1940s he disavowed the Keynesian revolution that was sweeping through the economics establishment. He attacked socialism when the welfare state was being formed in most major economies. In Hayek's view, socialism would invariably lead to central planning. When it comes to technological development, no progress can be made unless people are allowed to move into unexpected areas and learn from their mistakes. In *The Road to Serfdom*, Hayek describes how totalitarian regimes are not just unproductive but also suppress these freedoms. (The title of his best-known book comes from a phrase used by the French writer Alexis de Tocqueville, 'the road to servitude'.[2]) Instead, markets create the price signals and incentives to orientate the economy most efficiently.

To the wrath of the Occupy protesters, he would also have been less concerned about inequality, as he strongly believed societal progress was driven by the ideas of a few. When it came to financial markets, he would have said that they were already overregulated instead of not regulated enough. There is no doubt that Hayek would have been a controversial figure in the post-crisis world. Certainly, having spent most of the twentieth century fighting socialism, he would have much to say on the future of capitalism in the twenty-first.

The life and times of Friedrich Hayek

Friedrich August von Hayek was born in 1899 in Vienna. His father was a doctor employed by the Municipal Ministry of Health, and his mother came from a wealthy landowning family.

From a young age, Friedrich, or Fritz, as his mother called him, was determined to become a scholar. His father's true passion was botany and he had become a part-time lecturer at the University of Vienna, but above all wanted to become a university professor. This rubbed off on the young Friedrich. He helped his father with his botanical collections and came to believe that professorship was the highest accolade.

Despite this, and unlike many of the Great Economists featured in this book, he was not a first-class pupil. In fact, he showed little interest in studying at school and was actually rather rebellious. At the age of fourteen he failed Latin, Greek and mathematics and had to repeat the grade. Even so, he was still considered bright.

By the time Hayek turned fifteen, his attention was captured by the political excitement stoked up by the events that would lead to the First World War and the collapse of the Austro-Hungarian Empire. His focus turned to political philosophy, including ethics, morals, politics and economics.

Two years later, in March 1917, with the war still continuing, Hayek joined the army. He was still two months short of his eighteenth birthday, and after seven months of training was sent as an officer to the Italian front. He nearly did not survive the war. A piece of his skull was stripped by shrapnel. He nearly died when jumping from an observation balloon without first detaching his headphones, and he was nearly shot down in a dog fight. He had decided he wanted to join the diplomatic service, but before doing so he ended up joining the air force to prove he was not a coward.

However, the war was to end sooner than Hayek expected. In late 1918 he returned from Italy and enrolled at the University of Vienna. He studied law, but became interested in psychology, and eventually chose to become an economist: 'I was about equally interested in economics and psychology. I finally had to choose between the things I was interested in. Economics at least had a formal legitimation by a degree, while in psychology you had nothing. And since there was no opportunity for a job, I decided for economics.'[3]

Economics was part of the law faculty and offered, Hayek believed, the best vocational and financial prospects.

Life in Vienna, the capital city of the new Republic of Austria, was tough immediately after the war. Over a million young men from the Austro-Hungarian Empire had perished in the fighting. There were chronic shortages of food and fuel. Hyperinflation, or dramatic price increases, plagued the economy.

As with much of Europe, the conditions were ripe for communism and socialism to take over. There was a sudden acceptance and respect for Marxism, the welfare state and the planned economy. Hayek, though, was never enamoured of Marxism. He considered it very doctrinaire, and although reform and revolution were the sentiment of the day, he did not believe socialism to be the answer.

Economics at the University of Vienna was firmly established in the liberal free-market tradition, where Carl Menger was the architect of what came to be known as the Austrian School of economics. This school of thought contrasted with the collectivism of Marxism sweeping through much of Europe, emphasizing the importance of individuals and their free actions. Menger had described the concept of spontaneous order, wherein it is possible for a peaceful society to arise simply as a result of the rule of law creating the societal structure in which people flourish. The role of government then is not to direct the economy, but to establish and enforce the laws of property and those governing exchange that enable individuals to interact with each other in a mutually beneficial way. Liberty is a reflection of the supremacy of law, not its absence. Spontaneous order would be the centrepiece of much of Hayek's later thinking.

In 1921 he started working in the Austrian Office of Accounts (set up to settle international debt claims) for the economist Ludwig von Mises, who was well known as a monetary theorist and part of the Austrian School of economic thought at the University of Vienna. A couple of years later Hayek moved to New York in order to broaden his economics training. While he was working as a research assistant at New York University, his fellow Austrian Joseph Schumpeter wrote letters of introduction for him to meet a range of American economists.[4] It was there that he started work on a theory of business cycles. He also began, but did not complete, a doctoral thesis. The postwar hyperinflation in Austria had destroyed his family's wealth and he could not afford to live in any way other than poorly. After only one year, he returned to Austria.

Hayek was back in Vienna in 1924, once again in the Office of Accounts. But his marriage to Hella Fritsch soon thereafter led him to seek a more permanent job. Hayek had been close friends with von Mises, who helped to establish the Austrian Institute for Business Cycle Research based in Vienna, and in 1927 Hayek became its director. Initially, he had just two clerical assistants. It was later funded more generously by the Rockefeller Foundation. Hayek wrote prolifically during this period. His brief tour of the US led him to realize how new economic and statistical techniques could be introduced into economic research.

In the late 1920s Hayek wrote a number of articles in which he began to articulate business cycle theory. He opposed the US central banking system, the Federal Reserve, which had been set up in 1913. Hayek disapproved of the Fed's role in economic ups and downs.

It was not just monetary policy. Hayek also disputed the use of fiscal policy in moderating business cycles. His work was an early attack on John Maynard Keynes's hypothesis of excess saving or the paradox of thrift, discussed in Chapter 6. One of these articles, the 'Paradox of Saving', published in 1929, had caught the attention of Lionel Robbins, a young economist who had been recently appointed head of the Economics Department at the London School of Economics and Political Science (LSE). Hayek was the same age as Robbins.

Robbins wanted to bring British economics more fully into the twentieth century, so he sought a qualified theorist and one who was familiar with the other traditions. He sought to make the LSE a leading institution in the internationalization of British economics, and also to help him in his argument with Cambridge's John Maynard Keynes. In particular, Robbins opposed Keynes's ideas of increased spending on public works to battle the Great Depression. Robbins and Keynes had repeatedly clashed, and Robbins saw Hayek as an ally. So, Hayek arrived at the LSE in 1931 to deliver a series of four lectures, after which he was invited to join the faculty.

Hayek versus Keynes

It is fair to say that watching economics videos is not always the most exciting pastime. However, it is worth viewing *Fear the Boom and Bust*, launched on YouTube in 2010, where two proxies of Hayek and Keynes engage in a rap battle. Their argument is over the cause of the business cycle, and so far it has been viewed in excess of 6 million times. A sequel, where the two characters proclaim their responses to the Great Recession, is also available to watch should the mood take you. Their debate, although focused on the Great Depression of the 1930s, has been resuscitated by the recent global financial crisis. There is all of a sudden new interest in what Keynes and Hayek have to say about booms and busts.

Hayek was seen by many as Robbins's bulwark against Keynesian domination of economics and policy. It was not just Hayek versus Keynes, but also the LSE versus Cambridge. Despite this, the relationship between Hayek and Keynes was mutually respectful, even though they disagreed on most things and were rather being pitted against each other. In fact, Hayek and Keynes grew closer during the Second World War. Hayek became a British citizen in 1938, but his Austrian birth prevented him from serving in the war. When the London School of Economics relocated to Cambridge to avoid the Luftwaffe's Blitz on London, it was Keynes who had arranged rooms at his college, King's, to serve as Hayek's base.[5] The two purported rivals even spent a night together on the roof of the college chapel on the watch for German bombers.[6] In 1944 Keynes nominated Hayek to become a fellow of the prestigious British Academy instead of his disciple, Joan Robinson.[7] Upon Keynes's death in 1946, Hayek wrote to his widow that Keynes was 'the one really great man I ever knew, and for whom I had unbounded admiration'.[8] In contrast, Hayek never spoke with such personal admiration about Milton Friedman, even though they were both strongly connected with the Chicago School brand of liberalism in the 1950s and 1960s.

Hayek had been an early fan of Keynes, especially for his outspoken views on the Treaty of Versailles wherein he criticized the huge reparations demanded of Germany because he believed they would lead only to default. Keynes's 1923 *A Tract on Monetary Reform* was even lauded by Hayek. Keynes was also very generous in return. In the 1920s, Keynes was an influential economist, well known and highly regarded around the world, while Hayek was young, not a native English speaker, and far from established. Yet Keynes had responded graciously to Hayek's letters – so graciously that Hayek probably overestimated Keynes's professional opinion of him.

Perhaps at Robbins's behest, given the LSE–Cambridge rivalry, Hayek would later frequently criticize Keynes. In his review of Keynes's 1931 *A Treatise on Money* he had been very critical, even though Keynes had positively acknowledged the emerging German and Austrian Schools. But Keynes replied in kind. He was terribly rude about Hayek's *Prices and Production* of the same year, describing it as: 'one of the most frightful muddles I have ever read . . . It is an extraordinary example of how, starting with a mistake, a remorseless logician can end up in Bedlam.'[9] Throughout his life, and after Keynes's death, Hayek would give interviews in which he questioned Keynes's understanding of the most basic economic concepts. He tended to get annoyed by what he regarded as the inconsistencies in Keynes's work and his propensity to change his position on economic issues.

Hayek would say that he and Keynes differed on most aspects of economics. Keynes was a pragmatic English economist focused on the practicalities of the subject and had little time for the more systematic European modes of thought. Hayek was the exact opposite. So, on technical matters, they could hardly agree on the meaning of terms, let alone understand each other. Where the argument was most public was over the drivers of fluctuations in the economy or business cycles. Keynes believed that recessions were the consequence of weak aggregate demand. The economy was subject to bouts of optimism and pessimism known as 'animal spirits'. However, government policy could do much to offset the impact of these on national output and employment.

Hayek's model of the business cycle is far more nuanced and harder to understand. This may be one of the reasons it was not so widely accepted, both at the time and subsequently, by economists and policymakers. Hayek's model is as follows. First, there are many different stages of production in creating goods. Each final good reflects the processing of primary and intermediate goods. At each stage of production there is a requirement for businesses to install capital goods such as machines. These are not the same for different factories and cannot be easily transferred across sectors or stages of production. Therefore, once installed, the stock of capital can only be used to produce certain goods.

So, it is possible for capital to be allocated inefficiently in the economy if it is directed to areas where demand has been temporarily boosted and cannot be sustained. As capital investment is not reversible or transferable, capital is essentially stuck and abandoned if under-utilized. The savings that funded the investment have been wasted, and could have been more efficiently used elsewhere in the economy. Hayek believed this misallocation of capital could arise from monetary policy, specifically if interest rates had been held too low, as that leads to bad investments.

This, according to Hayek, accounted for the Great Depression. The US Federal Reserve had kept interest rates too low throughout the 1920s. As a result, much of the capital investment was inappropriate and unsustainable going into the 1930s. A recession ensued as this build-up in capital was abandoned.

In stark contrast to Keynes, Hayek believed the government should then resist the urge to interfere. He viewed recessions as a necessary evil, simply periods of liquidation resulting from the past overaccumulation of capital. This is similar to what Nobel laureate Paul Krugman calls the 'hangover theory' of recessions.[10] Any policy that stimulates the economy may relieve some short-term suffering, but would ultimately prevent recovery by helping to maintain inefficient capital stock levels. It is the economic equivalent of the 'hair of the dog'. After a hard night of excessive drinking, a shot of vodka might perk you up for an hour or so, but will eventually lead to an even worse hangover.

As a theory of business cycles, Hayek's approach in *Prices and Production* was largely rejected. A few years later, in 1936, Keynes's *General Theory* swept all before it on both sides of the Atlantic. Even the London School of Economics essentially became Keynesian. Later on, Milton Friedman and Anna Jacobson Schwartz, in their 1963 book *A Monetary History of the United States*, would provide a widely accepted explanation of the Great Depression linked with the tightening of the money supply as the banking system folded. By contrast, Hayek's views that low interest rates during the 1920s led to the depression received little credence.

Keynes was very much the showman, witty and articulate. Hayek, by contrast, lacked charisma and the power of communication. He spoke with a thick Austrian accent and was by several accounts a poor teacher. It is said that his students at the LSE asked him to lecture in German as it was more understandable. His writing was not always that easy to follow either. Milton Friedman was a staunch admirer of Hayek, but still described Hayek's 1941 *Pure Theory of Capital* as basically unreadable.[11]

Suffice it to say that Keynes was more interventionist in the economy than Hayek. He agreed with Hayek over the evils of communism and fascism, but believed the market economy was unable to always self-regulate efficiently. Keynes was not an advocate of government intervening in business activities, but thought it should provide the conditions under which such activities take place. But while Keynes was telling politicians they could make things better, Hayek was telling them they would just make things worse. It cannot be a total surprise that they were more readily drawn to the Keynesian view.

Hayek's path to fame

In the late 1930s Hayek simply became forgotten as an economist and his views were no longer a topic of academic discussion. Hayek himself also began to step away from technical economic theory and towards broader issues of social inquiry. He had not forgotten his background in the Austrian School, which was firmly at odds with social planning and excessive government intervention in the economy. His contemporary von Mises had questioned how it would be possible for any economic system, by which he meant communism, to exist without a price mechanism to allocate and incentivize economic activity. He believed that critics of capitalism, and, at the time of the inter-war years, there were many, failed to point out how a socialist system could be properly organized. Without prices, there would be no way for the baker to know how much to sell his bread for.

Collectivist Economic Planning, which Hayek edited in 1935, marked his transformation from economic theory to political philosophy. He argued that society is more efficient when rules or laws enable each individual to use their own knowledge and abilities for their own purpose rather than conform to the plan of a central authority. He was opposed to the idea that it was possible to manage a technologically advanced society from a central perch. The role of the government is to help individuals maximize their own talents, ideas and knowledge. Hayek's fundamental belief is that fragments of knowledge could not be brought together into a single brain. Given the complicated nature of technologies and production processes, it would require knowledge that no single person or a committee could possess. However, a pricing system with profit incentives could establish a market, provided it was backed with recognition of private property, contracts, laws, societal norms and the ability to exchange goods.

As the Second World War started to wind down, Hayek had become an increasingly obscure academic. However, that was to change abruptly with the publication of *The Road to Serfdom* in 1944. It would make him one of the world's best-known thinkers.

The Great Depression before the war had shaken belief in the capitalist system and people had become used to centrally planned wartime economies. Hayek wanted to warn the British public about the dangers resulting from government control of economic decision-making through continued central planning, whether communist or fascist. He argued that the abandonment of individualism led not only to a loss of freedom and the creation of an oppressive society but inevitably also to totalitarianism and effectively the serfdom of the individual. Centralized planning was undemocratic because the will of a small number was imposed on the people and the rule of law and individual freedoms were sacrificed.

The Road to Serfdom received positive reviews upon publication. The Second World War was not quite over, but by now it was simply a question of when, rather than if, the Axis powers would be defeated. Across Britain, the question 'what next?' was already being asked.

The book was to make Hayek famous, and not just in economic or academic circles. Keynes referred to it as a 'grand book',[12] and sales far exceeded Hayek's modest expectations for what he had earlier described to his publisher, Routledge, as a semi-popular work. The initial 2,000 print run sold out within days. Routledge ordered another 2,000 copies and over the next two years fought a generally losing battle to keep up with demand. Wartime rationing of paper did not help matters, and Hayek often referred to *The Road to Serfdom* as that 'unobtainable book'.[13]

However, it was in America where its success far exceeded expectations. The book was primarily written for a British audience and its academic tilt meant it wasn't expected to do well there. Furthermore, it was at odds with the post-war political climate of the day in America, and had already been rejected by a number of US publishers. However, the University of Chicago Press agreed to publish the book and the US edition was published in September, six months after the British version, again with an initial 2,000 print run.

It took off in a big way. A glowing review in *The New York Times* promoted interest, and soon the publishers realized they had a success on their hands. Another 5,000 copies were released and, just days later, 5,000 more. The book reached real prominence when *Reader's Digest*, which followed the *NYT* in describing it as 'one of the most important books of our generation', published a twenty-page precis. In those pre-TV days, its readership of 6 million could launch a blockbuster, and it made Hayek a household name in the US as people looked to life after war.

In Britain it did not quite have the political influence Hayek had hoped for. After the end of the Second World War, the welfare state was established in the UK. Conservative Prime Minister Winston Churchill had quoted and used Hayek's book heavily in the 1945 election campaign against Clement Attlee and the Labour Party as an anti-socialist text. It did not have much resonance with the British public, though, as Labour won a landslide victory. It is fair to say that Hayek was not a supporter of the new interventionist government.

Hayek preferred most activities to stay in private hands, but did see the need for a limited role of government in markets to perform the tasks that markets were not capable of. These included outlawing poisonous substances and preventing crime, but also providing a basic safety net. He wrote:

> there can be no doubt that some minimum of food, shelter, and clothing, sufficient to preserve health and the capacity to work, can be assured to everybody . . . Where, as in the case of sickness and accident, neither the desire to avoid such calamities nor the efforts to overcome their consequences are as a rule weakened by the provision of assistance, where, in short, we deal with genuinely insurable risks, the case for the state's helping to organize a comprehensive system of social insurance is very strong.[14]

In many ways Friedrich Hayek was at his peak in terms of celebrity and reputation after the publication of *The Road to Serfdom*. He had conceived the idea of setting up a society to bring German scholars back into mainstream classical thought after the Second World War, and a couple of years later, between 1 and 10 April 1947, the first Mont Pelerin Society conference took place in Switzerland. Hayek invited intellectuals who supported classical liberalism – in all, thirty-nine individuals from ten countries. Hayek was the first president and stayed in post until 1961. It continues today in the same liberal tradition, and eight Nobel Prize winners have been members.

Hayek had always been interested in psychology and after the success of *The Road to Serfdom* he indulged himself working on his next project, *The Sensory Order*. Published in 1952, the book set out a division of knowledge within societies where each person's share of knowledge was infinitesimally minuscule, which limited the knowledge attainable for any individual.

By this time, Hayek was drifting away from the London School of Economics. It is fair to say that he was no longer producing technical work. Keynes's death in 1946 had made it impossible to engage with him, thus removing one of Hayek's motivations. A messy divorce from his wife, Hella, also caused him to lose friends in London, among them his one-time biggest supporter, LSE's Lionel Robbins, who was appalled at Hayek's treatment of his ex-wife. Hayek had always believed he had married the wrong person,[15] admitting he had been on the rebound after discovering that his childhood sweetheart and distant cousin, Helene Bitterlich, had married another. He left Hella and their two children in 1949 and filed for divorce. In the face of Hella's objections, it was granted in 1950 via a court in Arkansas, where he was a visiting lecturer at the time and where the divorce laws were permissive. Helene was recently widowed, and a few weeks later the couple were married in Vienna. Hayek resigned from the LSE and the newlyweds moved stateside to start a new life in Chicago.

The Chicago School of economics was a school of thought based on free-market economics and a libertarian philosophy. It was not quite the same thing as the actual economics faculty within the university. Although the Chicago School was happy to identify with Hayek, given how well he fitted with their approach, he was not coveted by the Economics Department itself. *The Road to Serfdom* was recognized as an important book, but still mainly treated as a popular rather than a scholarly text. In the department's view, Hayek was now off the beaten track of economic research and no longer at the forefront of the technical work done at the university.

Furthermore, life in America in the 1950s was much different from the Great Depression years of the 1930s, and there was less interest in business-cycle theory, where Hayek's main research interests had been situated. In fairness, the lack of enthusiasm between Hayek and the Economics Department was probably mutual, since Hayek himself no longer considered himself solely an economist.

Instead, Hayek joined the university's John U. Nef Committee on Social Thought as Professor of Social and Moral Science. This multidisciplinary faculty consisted of a range of social and natural scientists, including the writer T. S. Eliot and the 1938 Nobel laureate in Physics, Enrico Fermi, allowing Hayek to study interests outside mainstream economic theory.

His next major work was *The Constitution of Liberty*. Hayek set out to show how liberty drove wealth and growth rather than the other way round. The more government is restricted, the more likely to arise are the individual spontaneity and creativity so vital to the advance of knowledge and civilization. He also reiterated previous arguments about the division of knowledge, and how it would be practically impossible for one human mind to comprehend and make efficient use of all the knowledge that guides society. The implication is of a very limited role for government in not just the economy, but also society.

In this book, he also laid out his thoughts on global inequality across nations. He did not think it was wholly a bad thing, in that it reflected the progress made by advanced Western countries, which would allow other countries to catch up faster than the centuries it took for Western countries to become advanced. On the same basis, he was also comfortable with inequality within societies, believing diversity to be necessary for society to prosper. There would be no mutual progress without inequality. According to Hayek, this was not an ethical consideration but historically observable: 'Recent European experience strongly confirms this. The rapidity with which rich societies here have become static, if not stagnant, societies through egalitarian policies, while impoverished but highly competitive countries have become very dynamic and progressive, has been one of the most conspicuous features of the post-war period.'[16]

In Hayek's view, society evolves so that the behaviour of successful individuals is adopted and imitated. The evolution of society is shaped by the new ideas of a comparative few. People with the better ideas determine developments; thus the market is an evolutionary mechanism where the economically talented prosper. Society can choose between equality and productivity. However, he did not agree with entrenched status quos, and the power, wealth and privilege they bestowed.

It took four years for Hayek to finish *The Constitution of Liberty*, completing the manuscript in 1959 to mark his sixtieth birthday. The book was published in February 1960 and intended for a general readership. Hayek considered it his best work, his magnum opus, and had suitably high expectations. *The Road to Serfdom* he described as a semi-popular book, but *The Constitution of Liberty* was, he hoped, to be *The Wealth of Nations* for the twentieth century.[17]

Unfortunately for Hayek, it would not come close to reaching the popularity of *The Road to Serfdom*. This time the book was not reviewed in *Time* or *Life*, and the *Reader's Digest* did not consider it suitable for a condensed version. Perhaps *The Constitution of Liberty* just did not capture the mood of the time in the way that *The Road to Serfdom* had as people looked beyond the Second World War. In 1962 Milton Friedman published *Capitalism and Freedom*, which he also felt was underappreciated.

Friedrich Hayek left Chicago and America in 1962, citing financial reasons. His divorce from Hella and frequent trips to Europe had put some pressure on his finances. He decided to re-enter the German-speaking world at the University of Freiburg in West Germany. He stayed there until 1969, when he spent a year as visiting professor at UCLA before he returned to Austria and the University of Salzburg. He would make one final move, returning with Helene to Freiburg in 1977, where he spent his remaining days.

During this time, his effort was predominately dedicated to

writing *Law, Legislation and Liberty*, the follow-up to *The Constitution of Liberty*. It is fair to say that *Law, Legislation and Liberty* was far more abstract than his earlier books. He made no effort this time to write for a general audience, assuming readers were familiar with his previous work.

The book was published in three volumes: *Rules and Order* (1973), *The Mirage of Social Justice* (1976) and *The Political Order of a Free People* (1979). One of the reasons it took so long to write is that between 1969 and 1974 his progress had been interrupted by ill health and depression. However, two events were to revitalize him.

The Nobel Prize in economics had been established in 1969. It was rumoured that the committee were keen to award the prize to Gunnar Myrdal, one of the pioneers of the Swedish welfare state, but it had been specified at inception that no Swede could win in the first five years. The sixth year was 1974, and Myrdal duly received the award that year. However, the prize was shared with Hayek. Both economists were reportedly surprised, Hayek because he had won; Myrdal because he had to share the award.[18]

Hayek had not considered himself a contender because his work in technical economics was too far in the past. Many American economists had forgotten him altogether; it was over ten years since he had left Chicago. The highest prize in economics rejuvenated him, and helped to restore both his health and motivation.

The 1970s had seen the major economies hit by stagflation (a combination of high inflation and high unemployment) in the aftermath of the 1973 oil price spike. In line with his previous theory of the business cycle forty years earlier, Hayek felt that the high inflation of the 1970s would lead to an economic crisis on the same scale as the Great Depression. Inflation had to be stopped in its tracks, even at the expense of short-run output and employment.

In 1976, a couple of years after he won the Nobel Prize, Hayek published *The Denationalization of Money*, where he ventured his idea that money should be issued by private firms rather than the government. His reckoning was that competition between money providers would favour the most stable of the currencies in circulation. The same competition would also enforce self-regulation. The work was widely derided. Milton Friedman pointed out that there was nothing in current law to prevent bilateral trade using any medium of exchange accepted by all parties. Curiously, the recent rise of crypto-currencies, such as Bitcoin, which are digital currencies that can be used to make purchases on the internet, are an example of non-governmental money.

Nevertheless, Hayek's body of work had made an impression on the politicians who would introduce free-market economics into the British and American economies in the 1980s. Hayek had been associated with a London-based think tank, the Institute of Economic Affairs (IEA) since its establishment in 1955. He had been contacted by the IEA's founder, the businessman Antony Fisher, after he had read *The Road to Serfdom*. The idea of the IEA was to promote free markets and the limitation of government intervention in the economy. The IEA had been closely associated with the Conservative Party leader Margaret Thatcher, who became the British prime minister in 1979. She was greatly influenced by Hayek's thinking and regularly quoted him in Cabinet and other meetings. On one occasion she interrupted a speaker who was urging the Conservatives to take a middle way on a variety of policy issues by pulling out a copy of *The Constitution of Liberty*, banging it on the table and proclaiming: 'This is what we believe!'[19] Thatcher had made Hayek relevant again. On her tenth anniversary as prime minister, she wrote to Hayek thanking him for his contribution to ideology and policy.

The Fatal Conceit was Hayek's last major work. Published in 1988, it pointed out the flaws and errors in socialism. In many ways, it was designed to be the crowning summary of his life's work and an epilogue to *Law, Legislation and Liberty*. The insight was that the price system is an instrument which enables millions of people to adjust their efforts to events and conditions of which they have no concrete, direct knowledge:

> It took me a long time to develop what is basically a simple idea . . . I gradually found that the basic function of economics was to explain the process of how human activity adapted itself to data about which it had no information. Thus the whole economic order rested on the

fact that by using prices as a guide, or as signals, we were led to serve the demands and enlist the powers and capacities of people of whom we knew nothing . . . Basically, the insight that prices were signals bringing about the unforeseen coordination of the efforts of thousands of individuals . . . became the leading idea behind my work.[20]

In essence, Hayek had built on Adam Smith's 'invisible hand' and specifically homed in on the role of prices in determining the value of goods and services in an economy. With a knowledge of prices, people can choose to produce certain goods or work in certain industries. The economy as a whole operates efficiently even though no one has coordinated their efforts. The book was seven years in the making, and not well received. It marked the end of his professional career.

A year later, it was tremendously fitting that Hayek would witness the fall of the Berlin Wall and the disintegration of the Soviet Union that followed it. He lived long enough to see the victory of capitalism over communism, but only just. In 1992 he died at the age of ninety-two.

Hayek and the global financial crisis

At the time of his passing, Hayek had seen the dominance of capitalism over communism at the end of the Cold War between the Soviet Union and the United States. Yet, just two decades later, the capitalist system would face another great challenge. The 2008 financial crisis led to disillusionment with capitalism's excesses.

What would Friedrich Hayek have made of the 2008 global financial crisis that incited the recent backlash against capitalism? Hayek had argued that the Federal Reserve played a role in precipitating the Great Depression by keeping interest rates too low through the 1920s so that bad investments culminated in the Great Crash of 1929. It is likely he would have made a similar argument about Fed policy in the run-up to the global financial crisis.

Hayek would have probably traced it back to the steep cuts in interest rates the Fed made when the US economy looked like it was faltering after the bursting of the dotcom bubble. Between 2000 and 2004, the US interest rate was cut from 6.5 per cent to just 1 per cent. Inflation was low and growth was weak, so the Fed acted to ease the economic slowdown by cutting interest rates to try to boost investment and consumption. But this led to too much and riskier borrowing in the housing market, which would lead to bigger problems in sub-prime mortgages just a few years later. Hayek would have objected to central banks believing that they can successfully intervene in the economic cycle.

What would Hayek have advised during the global financial crisis itself? Since, for him, recessions were not necessarily pleasant but better for long-term health, he would not have in principle opposed the liquidation of the investment banks Bear Stearns and Lehman Brothers, or the government-supported lenders Fannie Mae and Freddie Mac. In theory, his work through the years points to a ready acceptance that insolvent institutions, or those that lent badly, should be allowed to go bust. What is not clear is whether he would have felt the need to bail these institutions out in order to prevent the systemic failure of otherwise sound businesses that their collapse might instigate.

We can be more certain that Hayek would be strongly against the huge quantitative easing (QE) programmes whereby central banks injected large amounts of cash into the US, European and Japanese economies. In the 1970s, he favoured allowing the economy to right itself without government intervention, even at the cost of higher unemployment in the short run. He would have thought that QE was nothing more than a bailout of failed institutions, primarily used to shore up their balance sheets and provide liquidity to the banks that had acted irresponsibly before the crash. The flow of easy money would simply allow the liquidation and restructuring of bad investments to be prolonged. QE has been described by Stanford economist John Taylor as 'mondustrial policy' ('monetary-industrial policy') since it represents discretionary government involvement in the economy to support certain industries.[21]

Naturally, Hayek's starting position is that all of this should have been unnecessary in the first place. The pain of the recession could have been avoided had the boom in lending and vast credit expansion not occurred. The standard viewpoint as people survey the wreckage caused by financial markets was that they were not regulated enough. Followers of Hayek, though, would go the other way. It wasn't the case that financial markets were allowed too much freedom, but that they just were not free enough. Prior to the crisis, they would say there was an abundance of regulation already in place. Government regulations actually created a false expectation among investors that they were protected from risk and default. If financial markets were unregulated, Hayek would argue, they would naturally develop the institutions that ensure trust and their reputation.

This view has been aired in the annual Hayek Lecture hosted by the Institute of Economic Affairs since his death in 1992. For instance, the 2012 lecture, 'Why We Still Need to Read Hayek', was given by John Taylor, who reflected on the tumultuous events of the global financial crash and what Hayek might have made of the post-crisis problems in the US economy.

Taylor set out the free-market principles he believed that allowed America to prosper: 'people are free to decide what to produce, what to buy, where to work, how to help others'. These choices should be made 'within a predictable policy framework based on the rule of law, strong incentives from the market system and a limited role for government.'[22]

These principles have sometimes been abandoned, with unfortunate consequences. Leading up to the Great Depression, the Fed sharply reduced the growth of the money supply, the government raised tax rates and tariffs and went beyond market principles in the National Industrial Recovery Act. In the 1960s and 1970s there were short-term stimulus packages as well as wage and price controls. The financial crisis reflects the latest abandonment of Hayek's principles. Governments bailed out financial institutions and responded to the crisis with aggressive monetary policies.

Avoiding these interventions would allow economic growth, in Hayek's view, driven by the market and not by government policies, to resume. Once the foundations of a market economy were properly set, including appropriate regulation of the financial system, then economic prosperity would return. And that would mean that there was a chance of restoring faith in the capitalist system.

Hayek would probably have agreed with a paraphrased version that substituted 'capitalism' for 'democracy' in an observation by his supporter Winston Churchill: 'No one pretends that democracy is perfect or all-wise. Indeed, it has been said that democracy is the worst form of Government except all those other forms that have been tried from time to time.'[23]

Hayek's influence

In 1979 Friedrich Hayek remarked: 'I have arrived at the conviction that the neglect by economists to discuss seriously what is really the crucial problem of our time is due to a certain timidity about soiling their hands by going from purely scientific questions into value questions.'[24]

Hayek was not timid and robustly promoted the ideology of the capitalist system. This avid defender of capitalism would certainly stand up for the free market as being preferential to the alternatives. None other than former British prime minister Margaret Thatcher, whose ethos was based on free-market principles, was an admirer: 'Adam Smith, the greatest exponent of free enterprise economics till Hayek and Friedman . . .'[25] Thatcher also remarked: 'All the general propositions favouring freedom I had either imbibed at my father's knee or acquired by candle-end reading of [conservative politician Edmund] Burke and Hayek . . .'[26]

Friedrich Hayek, though, was concerned about the pedestal upon which economists can be placed. In his 1974 speech accepting the highest prize in economics, he said:

> I must confess that if I had been consulted whether to establish a Nobel Prize in economics, I should have decidedly advised against it . . . It is that the Nobel Prize confers on an individual an authority which in economics no man ought to possess . . . [T]he influence of the economist that mainly matters is an influence over laymen:

politicians, journalists, civil servants and the public generally. There is no reason why a man who has made a distinctive contribution to economic science should be omnicompetent on all problems of society – as the press tends to treat him till in the end he may himself be persuaded to believe. One is even made to feel it a public duty to pronounce on problems to which one may not have devoted special attention.[27]

Hayek was certainly influential, and whether he was comfortable with it or not, his influence remains evident today. Former US Treasury Secretary and Harvard economist Lawrence Summers said of Hayek: 'What's the single most important thing to learn from an economics course today? What I tried to leave my students with is the view that the invisible hand is more powerful than the [un]hidden hand. Things will happen in well-organized efforts without direction, controls, plans. That's the consensus among economists. That's the Hayek legacy.'[28]

9

Joan Robinson: Why Are Wages So Low?

It is one of the most pressing questions in American economic policy. Jason Furman, chairman of former US President Obama's Council of Economic Advisers, told me that the question he was asked most often by the president was: 'What's going on with wage growth? And what does that mean for the future of the economy?'[1]

The leader of the most powerful country in the world was asking this question. And it's not just a problem for America. It's a big issue for Britain and other major economies, ranging from Germany to Japan. Wages, after accounting for inflation, for the average worker in America have been stagnant for forty years. In the UK, there's been an unprecedented fall in real earnings since the 2008 global financial crisis. In Germany and Japan, median wages earned by people in the middle of the distribution have been stagnant for about two decades.

With the economic recovery underway in the United States and Britain, unemployment has come down dramatically to long-term levels of less than 5 per cent. So, it looks like employment has recovered from the recession. A healthier labour market usually means jobs and also better wages. Yet, puzzlingly, wages are not growing well.

It's not what models of perfectly competitive labour markets would predict. In those theories, workers are paid the value of their output so their wages would not be low if the economy was growing and more of what they produced was demanded. But as Joseph

Schumpeter said in Chapter 7, perfect competition is one of the unrealistic constructs of economics that helps with solving mathematical equations but isn't how the real world operates.

This is where the sole female among the Great Economists in this book made her seminal contribution. Joan Robinson rejected perfect competition and sought to explain how imperfections can lead to discrepancies in wages and employment that are actually observed in markets. Because of her path-breaking work, Joan Robinson is viewed as 'the most important woman in the history of economic thought'.[2] Her place among the Greats, particularly at a time when there were few female economists, is noteworthy. Even now, women are significantly under-represented in the economics profession. Of the over 50,000 academic economists in the world, less than one-fifth are women.

Robinson's first book, *The Economics of Imperfect Competition*, was published in 1933 and brought her international recognition. Her ground-breaking manuscript was finished just three years after she began her study of economic theory. It changed the way that we think about how prices and wages are determined. She analysed price determination under monopolistic conditions, where there is monopoly power and less than perfectly competitive markets. In other words, markets were not full of firms too weak to influence the industry, the prices of goods or the pay of workers. She argued that where there was imperfect competition, workers are paid less than the market value of their labour. Widely read on both sides of the Atlantic, the book quickly became a standard text in this new research field of imperfect competition. It was reprinted thirteen times between 1933 and 1965.

Robinson's work followed Keynesian thought, so it disputed the neoclassical economic notion of perfectly competitive markets. In other words, she sided with John Maynard Keynes against their Cambridge predecessor, Alfred Marshall. The year after Keynes's *The General Theory of Employment, Interest and Money* appeared in 1936, she published *Essays in the Theory of Employment*, which refined and extended Keynes's ideas specifically in the labour market. She followed that work with another book, *Introduction to the Theory of*

Employment, impressively in the same year. It was the first textbook that would ingrain Keynesian concepts into economics.

Although she had been a follower of Keynes, she later concluded that neither neoclassical nor Keynesian economics could account for long-term economic outcomes. But she thought that Keynesian economics had the best shot. So, her last major work attempted to explain how economies develop. Published in 1956, *The Accumulation of Capital* presented a theory of how capital accumulation in the economy, which consists of investment by firms and the government, changes over time in an attempt to better explain the long-run dynamics of growth.

Robinson was plied with honours throughout her long career. But she was also controversial. Although she was one of the most influential and prolific economists of the time, with a publication record stretching from 1932 to two years after her death in 1983, she was never awarded the highest prize in economics. Nobel laureate Paul Samuelson said: 'I was surprised that she never received the Nobel Prize.' He added: 'She has been a very contentious figure, but also a very important figure.'[3] Robinson was under consideration by the Swedish Academy in the mid-1970s and apparently short-listed but repeatedly passed over.

The possible reasons why she went from Keynes's inner circle to an outsider are varied. In addition to growing scepticism over Keynesian economics, Joan Robinson rejected even her own earlier work rooted in Keynesianism as she sought new answers to the long run. She also rejected the mathematical focus of economics that had gradually emerged, led by Irving Fisher and others discussed in earlier chapters. One of her favourite sayings was: 'I never learned mathematics, so I had to think.' When she was approached to serve on the board of the Econometric Society, she refused on the basis that she could not read the highly technical articles published by the leading in-house journal, *Econometrica*, which were about quantification and theory.[4]

Writing a book on Marxian economics as she moved beyond Keynesianism also contributed to her marginalization from mainstream economists. And her support of the communist regimes of

China and North Korea did not make her popular. She did not hide her beliefs; she even dressed up in Vietnamese peasant outfits to give lectures.[5] A part of it also probably reflected the challenges she faced in a male-dominated era and profession.

Yet Joan Robinson was a pioneer in introducing imperfect competition into economics, a concept that has fundamentally transformed the field. As Robinson once observed: 'The subject matter of economics is neither more nor less than its own technique.'[6] She has given economists the techniques and tools to help analyse the challenge of low pay, among others.

The life and times of Joan Robinson

Joan Robinson (née Maurice) was born into an elite family in Surrey in 1903. Her father was a baronet and a major general in the British army in the First World War. Her grandfather was a famous surgeon who taught at Cambridge University, where she studied and built her career.

She read economics at Girton College, graduating in 1925 without much distinction and with a Second Class degree. The following year she married Austin Robinson. He was to become a significant Cambridge economics professor and editor of the *Economic Journal*, but nevertheless was to be overshadowed by Joan. They moved to India for two years as he was to become the economics tutor to the young maharajah of the Indian state of Gwalior.

When her husband returned to Cambridge University, she began attending Piero Sraffa's lectures on the 'advanced theory of value', which was the standard term for what we would now describe as the theory of what determined prices in an economy. Sraffa's article in the *Economic Journal* in 1926 had radically abandoned the assumption of competitive markets and focused on monopolies. Before then, the theory of monopoly was used only to analyse firms with dominant market power, such as public utilities or railways. After his article, interest grew in analysing imperfectly competitive markets. His work stimulated research among Cambridge and other economists, including Robinson, who would go on to establish imperfect competition as a new branch of economics.

It wasn't an easy time for female economists. In 1881 students at Girton and Newnham, the two Cambridge colleges for women, received permission to sit for honours examinations and have their papers evaluated, which were the same as those set for men. But they would not receive degrees. Cambridge was the only British university where women were still excluded from lectureships and administrative positions. It wasn't until 1925, the year that Robinson graduated, that women could take up university posts. They remained excluded from college fellowships at men's colleges, which formed the core of Cambridge teaching and research.

In addition to the barriers faced by women at Cambridge, Robinson had earned less than a First Class degree. She had to publish research that would serve in place of a successful fellowship dissertation to establish herself as a serious economist. As an upper-middle-class woman, she had domestic help and thus she had research time. In the span of just a year and a half, between March 1931 and October 1932, she completed what would become a trail-blazing book, *The Economics of Imperfect Competition*.

In thinking about firms with monopoly power, Robinson recast the theory of what determines prices in less than perfectly competitive markets. In so doing, she was also able to reconcile the two sides of economics. On the one side were those who used diagrams to establish precise theoretical relationships, for example price and quantity. The other side were the empiricists who thought data trumped theory.[7] Robinson's diagrams were based on empirical observations about how markets actually operated, which was less than perfect, and resulted in wages that were lower than a worker's output warranted.

Another factor in Robinson's ascendancy to the core of Cambridge economics was her relationship with the Cambridge economist Richard Kahn. In 1930 they shared ideas. By 1931 they were having an affair. They were discovered by none other than John Maynard Keynes: 'Early in 1932 Keynes surprised them on the floor in Kahn's study, "though I expect", he told [his wife] Lydia, "the conversation was only on *The Pure Theory of Monopoly*".'[8]

Robinson's pregnancies in 1934 and 1937, which produced two daughters, did not seem to change their relationship. In 1938 Robinson suffered a psychiatric breakdown and she and her husband began leading separate lives.[9] In 1952 she suffered another breakdown, though less severe than the first one.

Richard Kahn could have been a potential competitor in developing a new theory of imperfect competition. Instead, he became a supporter. Kahn was a protégé of John Maynard Keynes. She joined him, her husband, Sraffa and James Meade in what was known as the 'circus'. In 1935 Robinson was one of these five economists Keynes entrusted for feedback on *The General Theory*.[10] This placed Joan Robinson at the centre of Cambridge economics. Keynes even wrote the Introduction to her *Introduction to the Theory of Employment*, which was the first textbook in Keynesian economics.

In 1934, Robinson had been appointed to a part-time probationary lectureship at Cambridge University. By 1937, she had a full-time probationary lectureship, which led to a permanent lectureship the following year. She was amidst some of the most influential economists of the time. In 1938 Cambridge economics was led by Keynes, Sraffa and Kahn. As well as those, there was J. R. Hicks and A. C. Pigou. John Hicks would later receive both a knighthood and, in 1972, the highest prize in economics. He shared the Nobel Prize with Kenneth J. Arrow for their work on introducing welfare concepts into economics, such as assessing how people's utility or happiness is affected by economic choices. Arthur Pigou more fully developed the idea of 'externalities', the costs or benefits to others that are not taken into account by, for example, a polluter or a person who plants trees. A Pigouvian tax is a tax that is imposed on the polluter to get them to internalize the social cost of their polluting activities.

Despite her distinguished perch, Joan Robinson faced competition in claiming to lead a new research field. Edward Chamberlin at Harvard University published *The Theory of Monopolistic Competition* three months before Robinson's *The Economics of Imperfect Competition*. But at a roundtable discussion held at the American Economic Association (AEA) meeting in December 1933 on the topic they adopted

Robinson's concept, and not Chamberlin's, to set the parameters of the new research area. She was helped by Kahn's visits to American universities, which broadened Robinson's references in her book as compared with Chamberlin's. Edward Chamberlin, though, would go on to develop the fruitful field of industrial organization, which researched questions such as oligopolistic interaction that analysed how a few companies can dominate an industry, for example the airline sector. Robinson would later develop her more theoretical approach in the field of labour economics rather than the theory of the firm. Curiously, one of the discussants of the papers presented was Chamberlin himself, and it was chaired by Joseph Schumpeter. Schumpeter would later recommend Robinson for honorary membership of the AEA: 'I know I shall be considered out of order if in this anti-feminist country, I suggest honoring a woman, but Mrs. Joan Robinson had a well-earned international success with her book *The Economics of Imperfect Competition* in 1933. By virtue of it she holds a leading position in one of the most popular lines of advance.'[11]

Robinson's next book complemented and extended Keynes's *General Theory*. In March 1936, only a month after Keynes's book appeared, she published an article titled 'The Long-Period Theory of Employment'. Since Keynes's assumptions focused on the short run, Robinson extended his work to analyse long-term conditions. In June of the same year, another article, 'Disguised Unemployment', appeared, which again extended Keynesian economics. Keynes argued that insufficient demand resulted in unemployed workers. Robinson posited that when workers are laid off, they take less productive jobs in order to survive even if they resort to selling matches on street corners. Although they are technically employed, such employment was really disguised unemployment, which meant the official unemployment rate was not telling the whole story. Robinson's *Essays in the Theory of Employment*, published in 1937, further explored the problems around employment that were raised in the *General Theory*.

Joan Robinson's emergence as a world-leading economist was impressively rapid. In 1930 she was the wife of a Cambridge faculty member. By the end of that decade she was an internationally respected economist at the heart of the Keynesian revolution. Yet she was only made a full professor at Cambridge University in 1965, the year her husband retired from his professorship.

Joan Robinson published her last major work in 1956. *The Accumulation of Capital* was a study of economic growth models that moved away from the standard Keynesian and neoclassical approaches to gain a deeper understanding as to why some countries prosper. Like her other research, this work is highly readable, especially as she makes her case using diagrams and figures rather than equations and complex mathematical models. Along these lines, her work in the 1960s increasingly moved towards economic development issues, especially in India, but also in China and North Korea.

That was not the sole new direction of research that she pursued. Robinson also examined the basis of economics, as in her 1962 book, *Economic Philosophy*, where she wryly observed: 'All along [economics] has been striving to escape from sentiment and to win for itself the status of a science.'[12] She added: 'lacking the experimental method, economists are not strictly enough compelled to reduce metaphysical concepts to falsifiable terms and cannot compel each other to agree as to what has been falsified. So economics limps along with one foot in untested hypotheses and the other in untestable slogans.'[13]

Still, Robinson saw the task of economists as 'sort[ing] out as best we may this mixture of ideology and science. We shall find no neat answers to the questions that it raises.'[14]

Robinson's imperfect markets

Joan Robinson's work on imperfect competition offers no neat answers but can help explain why wages have failed to keep pace with productivity, that is, output per worker, since markets are just not perfect in the real world. It might seem curious to many why it took so long to discover this! In fact, one would be hard pressed to give many examples of a perfectly competitive market. It goes to show how entrenched had become the idea that the market works perfectly efficiently, driven by the 'invisible hand'. It wasn't until

Keynes challenged the neoclassical view of quickly self-righting markets that the ground was laid for the work of Robinson and others to develop theories of imperfectly competitive markets.

Under perfect competition, a firm would choose to produce at the point where the volume it sells is warranted by the cost of producing it. Workers would be paid the value of the last unit of output they produced. Employers would not be able to pay less because exploitation (known as 'economic rents') would be eroded by competition, i.e., another firm would be able to pay a bit more until the point where the wage equalled what they could sell the last unit for. So, the last or 'marginal' unit reveals the value of what a worker has produced, which then sets the wage.

But Robinson points out that if markets are imperfectly competitive, then firms *can* earn economic rents because rents aren't entirely eroded by competition.[15] In that situation, firms have market power. This could be the result of accidents of history, in that some were first in the market, others held patents, and still others have influence over the market due to the entrepreneurship of their founders.

She developed a theory of 'monopsony' to refer to the market power that firms can wield in the labour market alongside the more familiar and established term, monopoly power, where firms have market power in the product market and can charge more for a good or service above their costs, earning them monopoly profits. Monopsony power allows employers to pay workers less than the value of their output, and keep more for themselves.

There has been an active debate over whether monopsony exists. Economists have been sceptical about firms being able to possess power over labour markets. The British National Health Service (NHS) is an example of an organization whose main employer, in this case the government, is pretty much the sole employer, so can set wages and employment conditions. Others include the local labour markets of many towns, which are often dominated by one or two major industries. (Robinson used coal mining as the most extreme example of her day.) Indeed, the classical economists made the somewhat surprising point that, almost by definition, there are always significantly fewer employers than workers. Employers are not usually worried about where their next pay cheque is coming from, unlike employees. Employers typically have a much stronger common interest than workers. The end result is that quasi-collusive cartels or monopsonies are not that uncommon, which is then somewhat balanced by workers unionizing.

These, though, are considered rarer than firms with monopoly power. Because workers can change industries, monopsonies are not as common as monopolies. Numerous examples of monopolistic industries come to mind. For instance, a few firms dominate the mobile phone market and a few search engines monopolize the internet. We've seen some of these firms become the subject of regulatory inquiries for anti-competitive practices due to their market power.

According to Robinson, if there are imperfections in the labour market that cause it to be less than perfectly competitive, then those imperfections can lead to different wage levels. This is plausible since workers are not homogeneous or perfectly interchangeable. For instance, workers have different willingness or ability to work, which is known as labour supply elasticity. Full-time versus part-time work is a good example of how much labour a worker wants to, or can, supply to the employment market. If a woman has childcare responsibilities, then she may only take on part-time work. It means that employers can offer different wages even to equally productive individuals. Employers 'exploit' these labour supply differences and earn 'rents' by offering wages that are less than the output produced. (Rents can also be gained in other contexts, such as when monopolists gain what would have gone to consumers.) If there are imperfections in both factor (labour) and product (for example rail) markets, then there are even greater potential 'rents'.

Wages also affect employment levels. If some groups have higher 'reservation wages', that is, a wage level that tips them into deciding to enter the labour force or not, and accept a job or not, then there will be different employment levels too. That is seen in the different labour force participation rates for men and women, which are usually lower for women, who may not choose to work if their wage barely covers their childcare or other familial costs such as taking care of elderly parents, for instance.

Robinson's theory shows that if there is not perfect competition, which is highly likely, then workers will receive lower wages than they should earn based on their productivity, and firms will earn 'rents'. Such 'exploitation' of workers will persist until the market structure changes so that competition leads firms to lose their market power. This market power is what enables firms to pay wages below what the workers produce.

Robinson's ideas paved the way for an examination of what determines wages. Her theories show how the problem of low pay goes beyond labour productivity and is related to the structure of markets.

The problem with pay

Low pay wasn't always a problem. After the Second World War in the 1950s and 1960s, wages grew strongly during what is known as the Golden Age of economic growth. Then, the oil crises of the 1970s struck. Wage growth slowed all over the world to some extent. In the United States in particular by the end of the 1970s, median wage growth – the wages of people in the middle of the income distribution – started to stagnate.

Still, the post-Second World War period saw wage growth of 4 per cent on average per annum even after the 1970s slowdown. But then the Great Recession hit in 2009 and there was a huge fall of economic output, as well as wages, after the financial crisis.

Some countries, mostly emerging economies, have done better, both before the crisis and afterwards. China in particular has done well. The growth of China since 1979 has led to double-digit annual increases in wages even after the crisis. India has also done relatively well. Many emerging economies are industrializing, so wage growth is less of a problem than in advanced economies.

By contrast, wages in the UK were affected badly. In Britain there was a more than 10 per cent fall in real wages (wages after adjusting for inflation) in the six years after 2008. Wages started picking up again around 2013, but that fall in real wages is unprecedented. The only other time this was seen was in the 1920s.

Since 2009 the pace of nominal wage growth in the UK has slowed to around 2 per cent. At 2 per cent, wage growth is about half the level it was 20–30 years before the Great Recession. When inflation is at 2 per cent, that means stagnant real wages since the pay increase is eroded by having to pay higher prices. Britain did experience real wage growth in 2014 for the first time since the crisis, but only due to negligible inflation. That lasted about two years until inflation started to pick up again in 2017, when real wages again declined.

The economy has recovered and unemployment has fallen back to below the long-term level of around 5 per cent in Britain and the US, but wage growth has lagged behind. It is peculiar because wages would usually improve along with the economy. Over the long run, the fundamental reason that wages grow is because of productivity growth driven by new technologies and ideas. It means that businesses can afford to pay workers higher wages.

But the International Labour Organization (ILO) finds that since the early 1980s, the productivity growth of workers exceeded that of their average wage growth in several large developed economies, including Germany, Japan and the United States. For France and Britain, productivity and wages grew at a similar pace. The UK suffers additionally from poor productivity growth (that is discussed in Chapter 12). So, productivity growth has outpaced wage growth in a number of advanced economies in recent decades.[16] Why has this relationship between what firms can afford to pay workers and what they do pay broken down?

Globalization is one explanation. There's no example of globalization that's closer to the West than the reunification of Germany in the early 1990s. Cheaper workers from East Germany, and less costly places to produce just a short distance away in eastern Europe, brought the challenge of globalization home. There was a vast wage differential between West and East Germany. With greater competition, workers in what had been West Germany experienced wage stagnation around the mid-1990s. That's when Germany gained the title 'the sick man of Europe'. Growth rates were between 0 and 1 per cent and economic prospects were looking poor. But Germany had a remarkable transformation just before the Great Recession hit.

At that time Germany was in a strong position because the export markets, in particular in Asia, but also in Europe, were buying Germany's manufactured products. China needed German capital goods to build its factories, in particular for the production of higher-end consumer goods to which China started to turn by the 2000s. So, when the recession hit, Germany was in a strong economic position.

This transformation was forced by globalization, specifically the accession of eastern European countries into the European Union in the early 2000s. There was the possibility that German industries could relocate production into these new EU countries, where wages were much lower, and German companies were threatening to do so unless unions or worker representatives agreed to wage restraint and became more flexible about employment terms.

In the face of the threat posed by globalization, the unions agreed. An important change was that wage negotiations were decentralized from the level of the industry and region down to the level of the firm. In that way, wage deals could reflect the needs of particular companies in a very competitive and fast-changing environment.

So, Germany gained competitiveness of output at the cost of wages, which, particularly at the lower end, started to fall. At the median, wage growth was essentially stagnant. And that's partly why German industry has become more competitive. Of course, there have also been improvements in productivity, but wage restraint has played a large role.

The flexible approach of both employers and unions helped to retain domestic production in many of Germany's core manufacturing sectors and kept employment in the country, albeit with workers earning less. This is in contrast to a number of its European neighbours such as France and Italy, who have seen some of their manufacturing leave the country. Germany was the first European country to come out of recession. Afterwards, it became something of an economic superstar, exporting a great deal not just to China and other developing countries but also to Europe and the US. As economic conditions improved, though, so did wage pressure, which led to a minimum wage being introduced for the first time in January 2015.

But global competition isn't the only reason wages in developed economies are low. Japan was successfully competing in the global economy while its workers had lifetime job security until it suffered a real estate bubble that burst in the early 1990s. Yet, now, it exemplifies another phenomenon that has contributed to low wages: the emergence of non-permanent or temporary workers.

Across rich countries, the proportion of temporary workers has increased. The OECD, which is a think tank centred on advanced economies, finds that the average wage of a temporary worker versus a permanent one is as much as 50 per cent lower in the worst case (Spain) and nearly 20 per cent lower even at the more equal end (Germany).

In Japan, the proportion of temporary workers in the labour force has doubled since 1999. A large portion of those on temporary contracts are women. Almost 40 per cent of the workforce has comprised casual and part-time employees, whose wages are often much less than half of those with permanent employment contracts. The lifetime employment system that was part of the Japanese miracle in the 1980s ended up with the collapse of that system a decade later.

After the crash, Japanese companies were looking for short-term profits so had to reduce labour costs. Replacing full-time with non-regular workers was one solution. These replacements are often *haken*, or temporary agency workers. Their employment lacks security, they earn less than half a regular worker's wage and, unlike permanent workers, receive no guaranteed wage increases.

Another factor keeping wages down is that it is difficult for Japanese workers to move to another company. The lifetime employment system created a labour market where few change employers after getting a permanent job. As a result, Japanese workers do not have a strong bargaining position. And competition from temporary workers restrains the wages of all workers.

This helps to explain why median wages in Japan have been stagnant for two decades and raising wages is a priority for a Japanese government desperate to get the economy going again through consumption growth fuelled by higher incomes. There are also social consequences that the government is keen to avoid. Men in temporary employment, for example, are less likely to settle down, because their earnings are not enough to support a family.

But it's not only Japan that's seen the rise of job insecurity, or only temporary workers that are a cause of low wages. There's another factor that's seen most acutely in the world's biggest economy: automation.

The number of robots used in manufacturing is increasing dramatically. It's most concentrated in sectors like automobile production, but it's spreading throughout the advanced economies. Over the last couple of decades in the US and across the industrialized countries, technology has improved in leaps and bounds. Computers have complemented and enhanced the skills of professionals, so jobs at the high end of the skill distribution are growing. But the same innovations have replaced the jobs of people in the middle of the skill spectrum, for example in automated factories. Jobs at the lower end of the skill distribution are less affected, since services jobs such as fast-food restaurants are still filled by people. So, jobs at either end of the skill distribution are growing, while those in the middle are declining.

The middle class (those earning between 50 per cent below and 50 per cent above the median income) has shrunk to less than half the US population for the first time since at least the early 1970s, according to the Pew Research Center. The data from the last recession show why: more than half of jobs created since 2010 are low wage. This process, which has been happening for over a quarter of a century, is known as the 'hollowing out' of the middle class.

So, technology has benefited some more than others. While technology helps to raise overall economic growth, it does not follow that the gains are shared equally by firms and workers, a development that would not surprise Joan Robinson. In 2015, the US produced around $18 trillion of GDP. About $10 trillion is paid to workers in wages and benefits, but the rest is largely company profits. Over the past few decades, the proportion of earnings that goes to workers in the form of wages has gone down, while the proportion going to businesses in the form of profits has gone up. This is another reason wages around the world are not rising as expected alongside productivity and economic growth. Thus, even if productivity increases, wages may not increase proportionately.

Trade union membership also plays a role. US data for the last hundred years show that when the proportion of workers in trade unions has dropped, the share of income going to the poorest Americans has also fallen. Trade union density is now less than 10 per cent and the share of income going to the bottom 90 per cent of households is also at a near century low.[17] In short, weaker worker bargaining power and technology have contributed to the shrinking middle class in America. Coupled with globalization and the growth of part-time jobs, these factors help explain low wages in the US and elsewhere.

Of course, wages in rich countries are not low in absolute terms. The level of wages even at the lower percentiles of the distribution in Germany is much higher than in many other European countries. Even so, wage growth is a problem, especially for those in the middle class who are experiencing earnings stagnation.

What would Joan Robinson make of the low-pay challenge?

Robinson's theory of wage determination

In Robinson's model of the labour market, firms determine how much labour to employ by comparing their output and cost. Taking into account how much revenue it produces, a firm sets its employment level at the point where the 'marginal product' of what is produced is just equal to the 'marginal cost' of employing the next unit of labour. This is regardless of whether the product or factor markets are perfect or imperfect. When markets are imperfect, then employers have market power and can 'exploit' workers by paying them less than what is earned from their output. Because such exploitation arises from the unequal bargaining strength of employers and employees, one way to reduce exploitation is to increase the bargaining power of workers, for example through trade unions or collective bargaining. Legislation to place workers on a more equal footing with employers is another avenue. Germany did that by giving workers statutory representation in the boardroom. The rights of non-unionized workers also require protection.

Bargaining strength is important in many cases, but raising wages through bargaining is not the sole solution to the problem of exploitation in Robinson's theory. That could result in unemployment and continued exploitation at the higher wage, since a firm with market power could demand a sub-optimal amount of labour. The remedy would be to remove the source of the market imperfection by increasing competition. This would erode a firm's monopoly or monopsony power. In a competitive market, a firm that exploited its workers would lose them to another firm that did not. Greater competition for workers would prevent their wages from falling too low. In Robinson's view, the remedy for low wages would be to fix the imperfections in the market itself by regulating to increase competition. That would provide a longer-lasting solution.

But Robinson also thought that greater competition might drive down wages, because prices fall as competition increases, and workers are paid the value of their marginal product; that might even be less than the former exploitative wage. She believed a minimum wage would help, and attached great importance to government intervention to improve exploitative outcomes as well as increasing competition in markets.

Accordingly, she would probably have been in favour of the OECD's recommendations to boost pay by reforming labour markets to make them more competitive. Regulating markets so there are fewer entry barriers increases competitiveness, and that has improved employment outcomes across advanced economies. Allowing the more productive firms to flourish means that they will attract workers away from less productive ones. This reallocation of jobs generates benefits for the economy as well as for the workers who have better job opportunities.

The OECD is also concerned about the growth of temporary contract workers. This would certainly worry Joan Robinson. The increase in temporary or part-time jobs would fall under her theory of 'hidden' or 'disguised' unemployment. The United States measures not only the number of people who are officially unemployed, but also those who want and are available for full-time employment but have had to accept part-time work. When this number is added to the official unemployment rate, along with those who are available for work but not seeking employment, the US unemployment picture looks less rosy. This U-6 unemployment rate, as it is known, has fallen alongside the official unemployment rate since the financial crisis, but it hovers around 9 per cent. The U-6 unemployment rate rose as high as 17 per cent during the Great Recession, more than doubling from around 8 per cent before the crash.

Disguised unemployment contributes to low wages, as discussed earlier when we examined the increase in part-time work in advanced economies, and is another example of how Robinson's ideas have shaped how we think about unemployment. Instead of being content to take the official unemployment figures at face value, recognizing underemployment as a form of unemployment helps to identify another pressure driving down earnings. In Robinson's view, when workers move from lower to higher productivity jobs, then those workers should earn higher wages, provided the market is competitive. By utilizing Robinson's definition of unemployment, the United States has a truer picture of its workforce with which to assess its economic policies. It's a practice that some other countries such as those in Europe are beginning to develop, which is unsurprising, given the increase in part-time work and the challenge of low pay in advanced economies.

Robinson believed that government policy can play a role in addressing low wages, so long as policymakers examine the deeper causes of pay. The exploitation of workers will continue so long as firms wield market power. But, similarly to Joseph Schumpeter, she believed that the monopoly power of firms would not survive. Any firm that was earning 'rents' would attract other firms to the same industry. Greater competition means that monopsonies will not last. Still, like her one-time mentor, John Maynard Keynes, Robinson believed that addressing the short-run issues that workers face during periods where there are monopolies exploiting them are more important than waiting for the market structure to sort itself out in the long run. Given how long the problem of low pay has persisted, and the continuing fall in the share of income going to workers versus that going to the owners of capital, Robinson would say this issue requires urgent action. Her theories do not address all of the causes of low pay, but they can help to identify some of the ways in which slow wage growth can be remedied.

A remarkable life

There is no doubt that Robinson's research has helped economists sort out some of the answers to questions such as why pay does not behave as predicted by perfectly competitive markets. But, as she also stresses, without scientific proof like in natural science, economic analysis cannot offer definitive answers. The best that we can strive for is to be guided by more realistic models of the labour market. Robinson thus points out one of the reasons why we should all study economics: 'The purpose of studying economics is not to acquire a set of ready-made answers to economic questions, but to learn how to avoid being deceived by economists.'[18]

Joan Robinson passed away in 1983 after a long and influential life. Her work opened up a whole new way of looking at markets by rejecting the standard economic views of wages and others based on an unrealistic belief in perfect competition. Those markets don't really exist, but low wages do.

The solution to the problem of pay, unsurprisingly, is complex, as would be expected in Robinson's complicated world of imperfect competition, worker exploitation and the resultant low wages. Still, for workers who are in work, it's a problem that can be solved. As Robinson remarked: 'The misery of being exploited by capitalists is nothing compared to the misery of not being exploited at all.'[19]

10

Milton Friedman: Are Central Banks Doing Too Much?

The 2008 financial crisis has introduced new economic terms into popular use, like central banks undertaking quantitative easing (QE or cash injections), forward guidance (central banks saying what they think interest rates might be in the future), negative interest rates (central banks charging commercial banks for depositing money with them) and macroprudential policy (central bank regulations aiming for financial stability), to name a few. These are in addition to using interest rates to target price stability or inflation, and are 'unconventional' or fairly new monetary policy tools.

All of which raises the question: Are central banks doing too much? And is what they are doing working to help the economy? It's untested ground. Bank of England Governor Mark Carney quipped that they're trying to get 'theory to catch up with practice', while former Fed Chairman Ben Bernanke reworked the classic economics joke: 'The problem with QE is that it works in practice, but it doesn't work in theory.'*

The main unconventional policy is QE. It has been restarted once again in Britain after the referendum vote in June 2016 to leave the European Union. QE is also being used by euro area countries and Japan even while the US central bank has ceased. Injecting cash to boost the economy because interest rates have been cut to zero or even into negative territory is one of the most controversial monetary policy tools in recent times. Cutting rates is one way of making

---

* The original was: 'It works in practice, but does it work in theory?'

lending cheaper, which can increase borrowing by households and firms who then respectively spend and invest and so aid the recovery. But because interest rates were at rock bottom, central banks needed another way to increase the amount of credit in the economy. QE was that policy. Simply put, central banks electronically 'printed' money and used it to buy bonds, which are government or corporate debt. This put money onto the balance sheets of companies that thus sold their bonds in exchange for cash, which central banks hoped would be invested and boost the recovery.

This represents a new era in monetary policy. The leading scholar in monetary economics is Milton Friedman. He made his name researching the causes of the Great Depression that followed the last systemic banking crash in 1929. His conclusion that the crisis was due to poor monetary policy fundamentally changed our understanding of that period and of post-crisis policies.

To this day Friedman remains a divisive figure in popular opinion, but that's largely a reflection of the very libertarian and pro free-market positions he was to take publicly later in life rather than the body of economic research that led to his 1976 Nobel Prize. He was viewed as one of the key influences behind the Reagan and Thatcher administrations in the 1980s, both of which were ideologically driven towards smaller government and more *laissez-faire* capitalism. Both leaders attracted criticism, some of which inevitably reflected on Friedman as a well-known conservative who was central to their economic thinking.

Like most academics, by the time he received his Nobel Prize he was really past the zenith of the research that propelled him to the award in the first place. This is generally true of grand prizes, but particularly true for the economics Nobel Prize in the years following its inception in 1969, when there was a lot of catching up to do to recognize the pioneers. Between the late 1930s and early 1960s, Friedman produced a remarkable body of work. His theories on monetary policy and other economic concepts, such as what drives people to consume, remain deeply engrained in the subject and in public policy today.

It was only in the 1960s that Friedman turned towards political writing. His involvement in public affairs then continued to the very end of his life in 2006. In 2003 he had publicly backed Hollywood actor Arnold Schwarzenegger for Governor of California. (The Terminator claimed, in fact, that Adam Smith and Friedman were among his influences.)

It's fair to say that Friedman had a career of two halves. The first as an academic economist; the second as a public figure and political influencer. To a certain extent, the second half has overshadowed the first and it has become increasingly necessary to recall just how large and long-standing his contribution to economics was.

Friedman's views on the Great Depression were game-changing. In the aftermath of the 2008 financial crisis, policymakers were at great pains to try to avoid the mistakes made in the 1930s, most of which had been identified by Friedman. Since the crisis, central banks around the world have thrown the kitchen sink at reviving their battered economies, keen to avoid accusations of repeating the mistakes pointed out by Friedman.

In 2005, one year before his death, he published an article in the *Journal of Economic Perspectives*. Here he reaffirmed his conjectures over the role of monetary policy in the Great Depression and the grave mistakes made by the Federal Reserve. Had he been alive, Friedman would undoubtedly have had a lot to say about the events that followed a few years later, the reaction of policymakers to them, and where we find ourselves today.

The life and times of Milton Friedman

Milton Friedman was born in 1912 in Brooklyn, his parents having emigrated separately to America in the late nineteenth century from Carpathian Ruthenia, part of the old Austro-Hungarian Empire located in Ukraine, Slovakia and Poland, leaving family and everything else behind. They met in New York's Jewish community. When Friedman was one year old they moved to the small commuter town of Rahway, New Jersey, twenty miles outside New York City. This is where he grew up with his three sisters. The family was not wealthy and lived modestly, running a shop from their home.

From an early age Friedman was marked out as an excellent student, and spent much of his free time in the local library. He entered the first grade a year early, skipping kindergarten altogether. In the middle of the sixth grade he was promoted into the seventh, making him two years younger than most of his peers. Although he was smaller than the other children, he was talkative and had a loud voice.[1]

Friedman graduated high school a month short of his sixteenth birthday in 1928. That same year he enrolled at Rutgers University in nearby New Brunswick, leaving the family home for the first time to live on campus. His strong exam performance and family circumstances saw him qualify for a scholarship.

He originally intended to major in mathematics. As a relatively young child, he had observed that 'individuals who have exceptional mathematical ability get early deferences and develop great confidence in their ability to solve problems'.[2] However, like many economists over the years, including several in this book, he was pulled away from the 'proper' sciences towards the social science of economics. One of the key influences on Friedman at this time was Arthur Burns, who was later to become America's central banker as chairman of the Federal Reserve. Friedman's father had died of a heart attack when he was fifteen and about to enter his final year of high school. Burns was Friedman's professor at Rutgers, and it was he who convinced the youngster that economics was a useful subject that could help end the depression in which America was then mired. Friedman described Burns as being like a 'surrogate father'.[3] He cited Burns and another Rutgers economics professor, Homer Jones, who would also become a central banker as senior vice-president of the regional Federal Reserve Bank of St Louis, as his reasons for becoming an economist.

When Friedman entered Rutgers, the Roaring Twenties were nearly over. By the time he graduated in 1932 with a Bachelor's degree in economics, achieving high but not exceptional honours, the Great Depression had set in. With a quarter of the workforce unemployed, the economy seemed to be the urgent problem.

Many people have gone through Friedman's life, looking for early influences in which his libertarian and monetarist thinking might be rooted. However, if there were any at this time, they were certainly well hidden. It appears that the Great Depression and the potential for economics to play a role in alleviating the crisis were as big a factor as any in piquing Friedman's interest.

After Rutgers, at the age of just twenty, Friedman headed to the University of Chicago, with which he was later to become so closely associated. The two big names at Chicago at this time were Jacob Viner and Frank Knight. Viner was a leading trade economist and economic historian, while Knight was renowned for his work on the impact of uncertainty on markets. During much of their time at Chicago, Viner and Knight jointly edited the *Journal of Political Economy*, published by the university's own press; it remains one of the leading economics journals to this day.

It was there that Friedman met his wife Rose (née Director). Both were postgraduate students and they sat next to each other in Viner's class. He arranged his students alphabetically, and there was no one between them. Friedman and Rose had much in common. She was born in Russia in 1911, and had moved to the US with her family in 1914 before the outbreak of the First World War. She was also Jewish, but her family was more strictly orthodox. (In fact, Friedman had effectively been agnostic since the age of thirteen.) Rose had completed her undergraduate studies at Chicago. Like Friedman she was good at mathematics and had graduated high school just after her sixteenth birthday, meaning she also skipped at least one year.

Their courtship was slow. Having started dating in 1932, they spent long periods apart as Friedman's career took him elsewhere. They were finally married in 1938, when they were both twenty-six years old. They had two children: Janet, born in 1943, and David, born two years later. One of the biggest upheavals once they started a family was that Friedman had to change his work habits. His preferred time to work in his youth was from midnight to 4 a.m.

He gained an intellectual partner in Rose, who played a significant role in Friedman's research, and they would later write books together. He recalls 'many a pleasant summer evening discussing consumption data and theory in front of a blazing fire'.[4]

★

After graduating in 1933 from Chicago with a Master's degree in economics, Friedman was to spend a year at Columbia University in New York before returning to Chicago. But as the academic year came to a close, he needed a job. America was in the midst of the Great Depression and President Franklin D. Roosevelt's New Deal programme had been attracting the brightest minds to Washington, DC. Friedman's friend from Chicago, Allen Wallis, had gone to work for the National Resources Committee. He followed. Between 1935 and 1937 he worked on developing a cost of living index. His work there contributed towards the PhD he earned from Columbia and was the basis for *A Theory of the Consumption Function*, which he would publish twenty years later while a professor at Chicago. Friedman considered this his most technical piece of research, for which he was to later win the Nobel Prize, along with his work on monetary economics and business cycles.[5]

After two years in Washington, Friedman moved back to New York to work at the National Bureau of Economic Research (NBER). One of his professors from Columbia, Wesley Mitchell, was director. He also taught part-time at Columbia and worked as a research assistant for Simon Kuznets, who was to go on and win the 1971 Nobel Prize in economics. He had encouraged Friedman to work with empirical data, which at the time was a field in its formative stage, and became an important part of Friedman's approach to economics.

In September 1939 war broke out in Europe, but with little immediate effect on either Friedman or America generally, which was not to enter the war for another two years. So life continued fairly normally for Friedman. During the 1940–41 academic year, he moved to the University of Wisconsin as a visiting professor. By now he was twenty-eight, and it was his first proper academic appointment. Although he was then offered a non-tenured position at the university, he turned it down in order to head back to Washington to work as an aide to Secretary of the Treasury Henry Morgenthau, who had played a key role in developing and financing the New Deal under Roosevelt.

In 1943 he relocated again to New York to join the Statistical Research Group at Columbia University. This was a prolific research period, during which he spent time developing techniques for improving the measurement of war materials. It was a formidable department run by his friend Allen Wallis. In May 1945 the war in Europe was winding down and Friedman returned to teaching. His good friend from Chicago, George Stigler, who would go on to win the 1982 Nobel Prize, was at the University of Minnesota teaching microeconomics and put in a good word for him. Friedman joined to teach macroeconomics and through the academic year 1945–46, they shared an office, becoming known as 'Mr Micro' and 'Mr Macro'.[6]

Towards the end of the academic year, an opportunity arose at the University of Chicago. Ironically, it was Stigler who was targeted, but he failed his interview with the president of the university. Chicago was the then home to the Cowles Commission for Research in Economics, which was a centre focused on linking economics to mathematics. Stigler was not deemed mathematical enough. He was in good company. Friedrich Hayek also claimed he was rejected on similar grounds. But this meant that opportunity knocked for Friedman. Stigler was generous, saying that his own rejection was to be a great service to Chicago.[7]

Friedman started teaching at the University of Chicago in 1946. It was then, and still is, one of the world's leading departments for economics. Its faculty was full of eminence: twenty-nine winners of the Nobel Prize in Economic Sciences since its inception in 1969 have had some connection with Chicago's Department of Economics. But things had changed significantly since Friedman attended as a student a decade earlier. Its two leading lights had faded. Viner had moved to Princeton University, and Knight's influence in economics had waned as he moved into political philosophy.

The department had been the home of the Cowles Commission since 1939. Friedman certainly acknowledged the scholarship Cowles brought to the university, but ultimately saw the world differently. His background at the National Resources Committee, the Statistical Research Group and the NBER steered him towards a statistical presentation of economic data rather than the formulaic presentation of theory favoured by the commission. Friedman believed strongly that economic theory should be subject to empirical corroboration to test its relevance to the real world. Prediction was the key factor;

theories and policies should be evaluated not on the basis of the realism of their assumptions but solely on the basis of the accuracy of their predictions. He considered Cowles as excessively formal and too concerned with tautological mathematics rather than explaining the world.

Friedman was able to push Cowles out of Chicago as his own power in the faculty grew. In 1951 he was awarded the third ever John Bates Clark Medal, the then-biennial (since 2009, annual) award for the best American economist under the age of forty, and probably the most prestigious prize in economics at the time since the Nobel Prize in economics didn't yet exist. He was now where Viner had been previously as the dominant figure in the department. In fact, he was teaching Viner's old course on price theory.

He was a popular teacher, but at the same time a tough grader who demanded high standards. It was not uncommon for him to award no 'A' grades in an entire academic year, and often he would only read and grade the first 500–1,000 words of his students' essays to encourage them to write more clearly and concisely. If a student were late to class, he would usually stop teaching until the student had taken his seat. Students had to present their work in order to participate at his workshops. Despite these pressures and the risk of low grades, students flocked to his classes because of his insight and his explanatory powers. Outside the classroom he was regarded as kind and generous. When he and Rose spent a year travelling the world in the early 1960s, they were hosted by many of his former students.

The notion of the 'Chicago School' has become associated with monetarism (a belief that the total amount of money in an economy could not permanently alter the economy) and *laissez-faire* capitalism. It coincided with Friedman's tenure at the university, which was to span three decades between 1946 and 1976. Perhaps it should really be referred to as the 'Friedman School'?

In 1976, Friedman was awarded the Nobel Prize in economics. At the time, the award was then only in its seventh year, but it was still a big deal and, without any doubt, the biggest prize available in economics. His award raised eyebrows due to his perceived closeness to the Chilean junta led by General Augusto Pinochet which was then in government.

It was a controversial topic, particularly in Scandinavia with its strong social democratic tradition and home to many Chilean refugees.

Since the 1950s, a number of students from Chile had studied economics at the University of Chicago. Friedman had little direct contact with them unless they had either taken his course or attended his workshops. Before the military coup that brought Pinochet to power in 1973, free-market policy ideas held little sway in Chile. In March 1975 Friedman had visited Chile as part of the Chicago–Chilean studies programme. He met Pinochet for forty-five minutes. This trip was seen by many in the context of the growing influence of the 'Chicago Boys' in Chilean economic policy. As a result, Friedman was perceived to be closely associated with the regime, *The New York Times* going so far as to identify him personally as the guiding light of the junta's economic policy. There were protests at the University of Chicago and for the next decade Friedman often entered public debates through side entrances. As he stood to make his laureate speech, a member of the audience shouted: 'Down with capitalism. Freedom for Chile.' Friedman is so far the only recipient of a Nobel Prize to be heckled at his acceptance presentation.

Although he was an advocate of the economic reforms introduced in Chile, he never publicly endorsed or supported the regime. In fact, as a libertarian, the suppression of freedoms would have run counter to his beliefs. He himself viewed the protests as hypocritical and baseless. In a speech in Chile, Friedman had criticized the regime as being too restrictive and argued that freedom was the best way of achieving prosperity for the country. He turned down honorary degrees from Chilean universities since he did not want acceptance to be conveyed as support for the regime politically.

It should be said that the majority of the media was supportive of his award, including the *Wall Street Journal*, *The Financial Times* and *Newsweek*. He had, after all, been awarded the prize for his contribution to economics rather than politics.

In terms of his political leanings, Milton Friedman is closely associated with strong libertarian views. He once wrote:

Fortunately, we are waking up. We are again recognizing the dangers of an overgoverned society, coming to understand that good objectives can be perverted by bad means ... Fortunately, also, we are as a people still free to choose which way we should go – whether to continue along the road we have been following to ever bigger government, or to call a halt and change direction.[8]

He also had some pithy sayings to encapsulate his views: 'If you put the federal government in charge of the Sahara Desert, in five years there'd be a shortage of sand.' And, in an echo of Adam Smith: 'With some notable exceptions, businessmen favor free enterprise in general but are opposed to it when it comes to themselves.'[9]

His views were set out in his best-selling *Capitalism and Freedom* (1962), which sold over a million copies. Despite its success, Friedman felt a little frustrated that it was not more widely acclaimed. Perhaps because Friedman was, as yet, little known outside economic and academic circles, it had largely been ignored by the main US publications. It was reviewed only by top-ranked economics journals such as the *American Economic Review*.

Capitalism and Freedom was largely collated from his Volker Lectures given between 1956 and 1961, organized by the William Volker Fund to promote libertarian views, and was strongly influenced by John Stuart Mill's *On Liberty*. The book argued for a limited role for government in a free society with more to be done by the market. He highlighted a number of unjustified activities of government. The list included unnecessary intervention in markets. Friedman opposed price support for agriculture, tariffs, rent control, minimum wages, maximum ceiling prices and fixed exchange rates. He also opposed direct government involvement in the economy, highlighting the detailed regulation of industry, the control of radio and television, toll roads, public housing and national parks, and the legal prohibition of carrying mail for profit as examples of taking government too far. Friedman was also in favour of the legalization of drugs, school vouchers, health saving accounts and an end to conscription in peacetime.

In short, Friedman advocated a limited role for government, countering objections with: 'Underlying most arguments against the free market is a lack of belief in freedom itself.'[10] For Friedman, each government policy needed to be carefully analysed for its impact on the economy. In his view: 'One of the great mistakes is to judge policies and programs by their intentions rather than their results.'[11]

He also argued for a negative income tax to replace the plethora of social security and welfare schemes and to guarantee a minimum income. This was first proposed in the 1950s, but became a serious policy prospect when in 1969 President Richard Nixon proposed the Family Assistance Program. It bears some resemblance to the universal basic income (UBI) now being debated, whereby the government gives a basic level of income to every citizen. Friedman's concept of a negative income tax would return income to those earning below a threshold. It is somewhat more complex than UBI, but would still have been simpler than the welfare system at the time. The original idea was to make sure that work paid more than state benefits. However, the work provision was eventually removed, much to the annoyance of Friedman. The idea dominated welfare reform discussions until failing in the Senate Finance Committee in 1970. Friedman also advocated a flat tax, which removed entirely any progressiveness in the tax system (when those with higher income levels pay a higher proportion of their earnings in tax). This was not just about incentivizing work but also about improving the simplicity of the system and lowering the high costs of compiling tax returns. In the end, he settled for a significant reduction in the top rate of tax from 70 per cent to 28 per cent, which President Ronald Reagan delivered in the 1980s.

A few years earlier, in 1977, Friedman had retired from the University of Chicago at the age of sixty-five. He took a role at the conservative Hoover Institution at Stanford University as a senior research fellow, where his wife also had an office. His intention was to do academic work at a more leisurely pace, and he and Rose collaborated on a number of papers, essays and books in the years that followed.

In 1980 the Friedmans published *Free to Choose*, which was the bestselling non-fiction title in the US that year, shifting some 400,000 copies. It was based on two principles. The first was the political freedom inherent in Thomas Jefferson's Declaration of Independence: the preservation of life, and liberty, and the pursuit of happiness. The second was Adam Smith's notion of economic freedom, where free exchange is to the benefit of the economy and was largely free from government intervention.

At the time, his old friend Allen Wallis had become chairman of the Corporation for Public Broadcasting (PBS) and had recommended Friedman for a programme. The Harvard economist John Kenneth Galbraith had recently filmed a series on the history of economic thought, and Friedman was thought to offer an ideological balance to Galbraith's more Keynesian views. So, $2.5 million was raised to film a documentary series consisting of ten episodes. Each show consisted of a half-hour presentation by Friedman on a specific topic followed by a discussion for the same period of time. *Free to Choose* earned Friedman more in royalties than all his other books combined, and the television series it accompanied made him a household name.

Friedman's political influence

After the publication of *A Monetary History* in 1963, Friedman stepped back from academic economics to pursue more political writing. In his early life, Friedman had never really exhibited any strong political leanings, but by then his teaching load had been much reduced and his academic endeavour was less intense than before. He felt the US was heading in a more libertarian direction, and compulsory conscription to fight in the Vietnam War had made his ideas popular among college graduates. It was also the time of libertarian thinkers such as Ayn Rand and Friedrich Hayek.

Milton Friedman was also becoming increasingly well known as a leading conservative economist. He became involved in Arizona Republican Senator Barry Goldwater's presidential campaign in 1964. A *Newsweek* article had suggested he could do for Goldwater what J. K. Galbraith had done for John F. Kennedy. Although Goldwater lost by a landslide to incumbent President Lyndon B. Johnson, the campaign gave Friedman exposure and a huge boost to his public profile. It led to a regular column in *Newsweek*, for which he wrote over 300 pieces between 1966 and 1984.

In the 1968 presidential race he was once again brought into the fray on the Republican side. His former mentor Arthur Burns, now a presidential counsellor and chairman-in-waiting of the Federal Reserve, had been asked to set up an advisory committee on the economy to provide recommendations to Richard Nixon, should he win. He did, and between 1970 and 1971 Friedman and the president met on several occasions, but the relationship was becoming fraught. Nixon had tried to persuade Friedman to use his relationship with Burns to put pressure on the Fed to lower interest rates but he refused. The 1971 wage and price controls introduced by Nixon were anathema to Friedman's free-market orthodoxy. In his memoirs, Friedman described this as the most damaging thing Nixon had done to the US, including the Watergate scandal that led to his resignation in 1974. His initial strong support for Nixon had become rather tepid as early as 1972.

In 1976 Friedman threw his support behind Ronald Reagan. He had first met Reagan in 1967 while he was a visiting professor at UCLA and Reagan had just been elected governor of California. They shared similar views on the funding of higher education. Reagan was ideologically close to Friedman. He had read some of the most free market of economists, including Ludwig von Mises and Friedrich Hayek. It was said he read *Capitalism and Freedom* while running for governor. In 1975 Reagan vacated that office, and a short while later Friedman indicated he would support his presidential campaign.

Reagan failed to win his party's nomination that year, but in 1980 became the Republican presidential candidate. Reagan made clear his economic convictions: control federal spending and rein back regulation, reduce personal income tax rates and introduce predictably sound and stable monetary policy. All of these could have come from Friedman. Reagan won a landslide victory over the Democratic incumbent, Jimmy Carter. Although Friedman did not serve in the Reagan administration, he was widely seen as the guru behind the scenes through the Economic Policy Advisory Board.

Despite his outspoken views, it was never thought that Friedman wanted a full-time political position. He turned down a seat on the

Council of Economic Advisers, the highest body advising the US president, on numerous occasions. He would almost certainly have accepted the post of Chairman of the Federal Reserve,[12] though it seems he was never offered it. He enjoyed, with Rose, a lifestyle that saw them spend various parts of the year in Chicago, Vermont, California and, of course, Washington, DC. Perhaps he also thought it would be better for his longer-term influence to not be hamstrung by having always to toe the party line as a government official.

Across the Atlantic, Friedman's thinking had found an additional home in the UK. Prime Minister Margaret Thatcher was ideologically similar to Reagan, and Britain was set for a radical change in direction. In the 1970s the economic policy debate in Britain was essentially Friedman versus Keynes. Friedman had even debated with well-known Keynesians on British TV, which revealed him to be an effective communicator. Friedman's style was to have a very simple, punchy message and stick to it. His opponents pointed to all the complexities and difficulties, and probably lost the audience as a result. After one such debate a journalist asked a Keynesian who would win if Friedman had debated Keynes himself. The answer was: Friedman would win, but Keynes would be right!

In addition, much of Friedman's thinking had been disseminated through the right-wing think tank, the Institute of Economic Affairs, where his views on the inadequacy of Keynesian stabilization policy and the benefits of a low-tax, low-regulation economy and monetary stability had enjoyed an enthusiastic audience. In Reagan and Thatcher, Milton Friedman had found two world leaders who were acolytes of the free-market capitalism and monetarist ideologies he had championed over the previous two decades.

Friedman's influence didn't end there. His seminal work in economics was no less influential in shaping how modern central banking still works today. *A Monetary History of the United States, 1867–1960* was perhaps Milton Friedman's magnum opus in terms of economic ideas. It was jointly authored with Anna Jacobson Schwartz, with whom he began work in 1948, but it wasn't until 1963 that their 884-page treatise was published. The work had initially been commissioned by the National Bureau of Economic Research. Arthur Burns had replaced Wesley Mitchell as director and he asked Friedman to study monetary factors in economic activity, especially in the business cycle.

The research was to question the Keynesian view of the Great Depression. Keynes had identified the weakness of aggregate demand stemming from an excess of saving and a dearth of investment in the aftermath of the stock market crash of 1929 as the main cause. This gave credence to the idea that the New Deal programmes of President Franklin D. Roosevelt helped to resolve the crisis. The Keynesian view gave little weight to monetary factors. With interest rates having fallen close to zero, an active monetary policy which sought to stimulate the economy through changing rates would be like 'pushing on a piece of string'. Just as pushing on a piece of string does nothing of substance, interest rates that low likewise cannot move the economy in any direction. So, the Keynesians concluded that the Fed had done everything it could and that monetary policy had simply run out of bite.

Friedman and Schwartz categorically disagreed and placed monetary forces at the heart of the crisis. The project was very data intensive, mainly because much of the necessary information on the stock of money had not yet been collected. Until Friedman and Schwartz developed the M1 and M2 metrics of measuring the money supply, the Federal Reserve had no way of gauging the amount of money in the economy. They were to conclude that, had the Federal Reserve been publishing these statistics between 1929 and 1933, the Great Crash may have never become the Great Depression, or at least the magnitude and persistence of the downturn would have been mitigated because the negative impact of monetary policy would have been evident.

In fact, they said the stock market crash of 1929 was partly the result of the Federal Reserve's actions in 1928. The stock market had risen sharply at the back end of the 1920s, causing the Fed to implement a deliberate tightening of policy in the spring of 1928 to curb speculation on Wall Street. The governor of the influential New York Fed, Benjamin Strong, had strong reservations about using monetary policy to constrain the boom, but died in October 1928. His death created a leadership vacuum at one of the twelve regional

banks that feed into the US central bank's decisions. Friedman and
Schwartz argued that, had it not been for the premature death of
Strong, many of the subsequent mistakes made by the Fed might
have been avoided. His successor, George Harrison, was more in line
with the rest of the thinking of the central bank in pushing for an
interest rate hike. Rates subsequently rose to 5 per cent, the highest
since 1921. This was sufficient to slow the growth of the US economy, which hit its cyclical peak in August 1929. The downturn in the
economy was a precursor to the stock market crash in October.

Friedman and Schwartz, though, did not see the Great Depression
as the inevitable conclusion of the crash of 1929. The stock market did
lose half its value between September and November, including a
big drop on Black Tuesday, 29 October. However, the market had
doubled in the previous eighteen months and stocks actually recovered 20 per cent in the six months after the crash. There had also been
plenty of other significant falls in the stock market in recent history
that had not resulted in depression. The US economy had experienced
bigger shocks that were not followed by a protracted downturn.

In the first year of the Great Depression, US GDP dropped by a
massive 12 per cent and unemployment increased to 9 per cent. However, falling prices or deflation in 1920–21 had seen a decline in
national output of some 7 per cent and a rise in unemployment to
between 9 and 12 per cent. Despite this, the rest of the 1920s had been
a rip-roaring time for the American economy.

One of the key findings in *A Monetary History* was what Friedman
and Schwartz described as the 'Great Contraction' between 1929 and
1933. They were referring not to a large drop in GDP or prices, but
to a decline in the amount of money available in the economy as a
consequence of widespread bank failures. In the year following the
crash, the US money supply fell by a relatively small 2.6 per cent as
the Federal Reserve cut interest rates and lent heavily to the banking
sector. Injecting a great deal of cash into banks gave them some
much-needed liquidity and prevented the stock market collapse from
precipitating an immediate banking crisis. However, the Fed believed
that further loosening of monetary policy might pump up the stock
market bubble and lead to inflation.

Between 1930 and 1933 the US money supply contracted by over a third, coinciding with a raft of bank failures. Between October 1930 and March 1933 there were four major bank runs. Most of these occurred between August 1931 and January 1932, when there were 1,860 bank failures and the money supply fell at an annual rate of 31 per cent. As deposits were withdrawn for fear of failure, banks had less money to lend, so the supply of credit to the economy evaporated, which led to downward pressure on output and prices.

It was not just fear of encouraging a further run-up in prices of assets such as stocks that had made the Federal Reserve reluctant to pump money into the economy, where it was especially needed by a banking sector which was haemorrhaging deposits. The US had maintained its membership of the gold standard, an international system of fixed exchange rates. In September 1931 a wave of speculative attacks on sterling had forced Great Britain out of the standard. Speculators thought the economy was weak, so the currency should weaken too, which was not possible since it was fixed to a set amount against gold. They sold off sterling, which meant the British government needed to use its gold reserves to maintain the value of the currency. That was considered too expensive, so Britain abandoned the gold standard. As speculators turned their attack towards the US, the Fed was forced to raise interest rates to make buying the dollar more attractive. They tightened monetary policy between August 1931 and January 1932 to stem the outflow of gold as international investors liquidated their dollar deposits.

Friedman was not an advocate of fixed exchange rates. Continued membership of the gold standard, he believed, had held the Fed back from a more convincing monetary stimulus. He observed that the best performing countries through the early 1930s were those that were not in the gold standard, those that had abandoned the system and those that were in the standard but had large gold reserves. In each of these three cases, the countries involved could exercise more flexibility in monetary policy in response to the economic depression.

Friedman and Schwartz argued that this might have prevented the Federal Reserve from being more active and forceful. To emphasize the point, they cited the events of April to August 1932, when the Fed, under pressure from Congress, made a $1 billion open-market purchase (a monetary injection equivalent to about 2 per cent of national income) which was successful in stemming the drop in the money supply and stimulating a small rise in GDP and industrial production. But when Congress broke for recess and the economy looked like it was on the turn, the loosening of policy ended. Friedman and Schwartz argued that, had it not done so, the economy may well have continued to improve.

The Fed was also a poor lender of last resort to the banking system. There was little coordination between the Federal Reserve Board of Governors based in Washington and the Regional Reserve Banks. There was also a stigma attached to accessing the Federal Reserve's discount window facilities, which allowed financial institutions access to emergency funding from the central bank in times of stress as banks did not want to advertise their vulnerability in case it might ignite a run on their deposits. In any case, access to the window was limited and only associated banks were eligible. The liquidity support for the banking system was severely flawed.

In November 1932, Franklin D. Roosevelt won a landslide victory against Herbert Hoover, with the Democrats also taking large majorities in both Houses of Congress. However, FDR didn't assume office until March 1933 and in the meantime, bank failures continued. It was widely believed that FDR would devalue the dollar or leave the gold standard altogether. It was costly to maintain a currency peg to gold, especially when the economy was in serious trouble. This encouraged the large-scale conversion of dollars into gold, putting further pressure on the banking system as dollar deposits were withdrawn.

One of FDR's first acts on taking office was a week-long banking holiday from which 5,000 banks never reopened their doors. However, this allowed the insolvent banks to be weeded out. The New Deal programme that significantly increased government spending to boost the economy was also in force, but Friedman and Schwartz pointed to the dollar devaluation of 60 per cent and its exit from the gold standard as the more important factors in halting the Great Contraction. It returned monetary freedom to US policymakers.

Between 1933 and 1936 there was a strong recovery and reflation in the US economy. The 1933 and 1935 Banking Acts introduced changes to the Federal Reserve System to enhance the ability of the Fed to stabilize the banking system. The measures included extending the ability of the Federal Reserve to more easily lend money based on receiving collateral, including to non-financial firms; the Glass–Steagall Act, resulting in the separation of commercial and investment banking functions; regulation of deposit interest rates; and strict limits on entry to the market. Also important was the creation of the Federal Deposit Insurance Corporation (FDIC) in 1933 to stem the problem of ruinous bank runs. The FDIC remains in place today and guarantees that depositors won't lose their money (currently up to $250,000) if a bank goes under.

The bottom line from *A Monetary History* was that the Fed caused the crisis, turning a stock market crash into a full-blown depression by failing to pump sufficient liquidity into the economy to support the banks. Instead, they allowed runs on bank deposits to proceed relatively unchecked, resulting in bank failures and a severe deflation in output and prices. In a speech given in 2002 to commemorate Milton Friedman's ninetieth birthday, then Fed chairman Ben Bernanke apologized on behalf of his organization. He said: 'You're right, we did it. We're very sorry. But thanks to you, we won't do it again.'[13]

Little did he know that soon, he would be given the opportunity to live up to these words.

Friedman and the 2008 financial crisis

The global financial crisis occurred in 2008 with repercussions across the world economy. Financial deregulation since the 1980s meant that financial markets and global linkages across national borders became much more diverse. Then, in 1999, the Gramm–Leach–Bliley Act repealed the Glass–Steagall Act of 1933 that had previously separated retail from investment banking. More of the risks undertaken by investment banks could be transmitted to retail (deposit-holding) banks. In the 2008 crisis, we were at the cusp of the first potential systemic banking failure since the 1929 crash that had led to the passage of Glass–Steagall in the first place.

European banks were exposed to US sub-prime mortgages and some had also borrowed from US wholesale money markets. It meant that European bank lending became less reliant on deposits since they could access the same cheap money as the Americans. When Northern Rock failed in 2007, it was the first bank run in Britain in more than a century. The UK is closely linked to US financial markets and also faced the prospect of a systemic banking collapse during the 2008 crisis.

So, did central banks act sufficiently to avoid repeating the mistakes of the 1929 crash? Have central banks learned the lessons from the Great Depression, including those set out by Milton Friedman, whose seminal research changed our view of the 1930s?

Ben Bernanke, like Friedman, was also a scholar of the Great Depression. Therefore, when the global financial crisis struck in 2008, he was well placed as Fed chair to prevent the same mistakes from happening again.

Like the Great Depression, the recent financial crisis was preceded by an asset price boom, but this time centred in the housing market rather than the stock exchange. According to the Case-Shiller repeat sales index, US house prices doubled between 1999 and 2007. This was largely due to a huge expansion in housing credit. The quasi-government enterprises Fannie Mae and Freddie Mac strongly supported government policy to extend home ownership to lower income households by effectively underwriting mortgages requiring smaller down payments and allowing higher price-to-income ratios. The result was an increase in mortgage lending to less financially secure households. NINJA (no income, no job, no assets) and NO-DOC (no documentations) were acronyms that became commonplace in the mortgage market. There was rapid growth in the two riskiest components of the market, sub-prime and Alt-A mortgages, which are both below 'prime' or the standard measure of creditworthiness.

Despite this, the banking sector had, or so it thought, found a way to mitigate the increased riskiness of lending. Riskier mortgages could be repackaged with others into mortgage-backed securities (MBS) and given the highest (AAA) credit ratings for the credit-worthiness of the debt, while still offering a higher rate of return than other safe assets such as Treasury bills. Credit default swaps (CDS) could be purchased to provide insurance against any losses should there be a default. Bankers created funds, such as special purpose vehicles (SPVs) and structured investment vehicles (SIVs), to hoover up these financially engineered securities offering better returns than safe assets like government debt, and sell the SPVs and SIVs to clients. These special funds often borrowed heavily in the money markets and, being based offshore, avoided the capital requirements and regulatory oversight of other financial institutions. Between 2001 and 2005 there was a lending boom in America like no other.

The collapse in house prices in 2007 triggered massive defaults in the US mortgage market. Homeowners with negative equity walked away from their properties. It meant that the originators of mortgages, or those that had bought mortgage-backed securities, found themselves with assets worth less than their liabilities. The banks were in trouble.

It is true that this financial crisis, though, differed from the Great Depression in several important ways, thus the lessons from the 1930s may not have carried over exactly, but it is still useful to compare the two. The Great Depression analysed by Friedman and Schwartz in *A Monetary History* was essentially a liquidity crisis. Banks facing runs on their deposits needed a forceful and competent lender of last resort to stem the flow. Here, the Federal Reserve failed.

In the global financial crisis, the biggest problem was solvency rather than liquidity. It became difficult to price complicated and opaque securities backed by a pool of assets where the value, quality and riskiness of each were difficult to ascertain. So the credit market could not determine which firms were solvent and which were not. Naturally, lenders were unwilling to extend loans without being able to determine the creditworthiness of the borrower. Most of these problems lay with the investment banks.

The Fed reacted quickly to the crisis. It cut interest rates sharply and extended discount window facilities. Learning the lessons from the previous crisis, the TAF (term auction facility) enabled banks to bid anonymously for funds from the Fed and avoid the stigma of being seen as an institution in trouble. Transparency in policymaking is usually considered preferable, but in crisis mode opacity might be the better option.

The Federal Reserve also made a number of large-scale asset purchases in a process known as quantitative easing (QE). Between November 2008 and June 2010 it purchased around $175 billion of long-term securities, thus injecting that amount of cash into the economy. In November 2010, as the economy wobbled, it made further purchases of long-term Treasury bonds amounting to $600 billion in its QEII programme. Finally, a third dose of QE was initiated in September 2012 when the Fed announced the purchase of $40 billion in mortgage-backed securities each month for an indefinite period. This was dubbed 'QE infinity' by investors. The final QE programme was raised to $85 billion in December, before being tapered back to $65 billion per month in June 2013. By the time QE was halted in October 2014, the three QE programmes had seen the Federal Reserve accumulate a staggering $4.5 trillion in assets.

As a result, the M2 measure of money supply, which had tanked during the Great Depression, had increased sharply in the global financial crisis following the large expansion of the Federal Reserve's balance sheet. A repeat of the bank panics and runs seen between 1930 and 1933 was also avoided.

Would Friedman have approved of the QE and other policies used in dealing with the 2008 crisis?

In terms of purchasing government debt such as Treasury bonds in order to drive down long-term interest rates and inject liquidity into the banking system, he would have been undoubtedly in favour. However, the purchase of mortgage-backed securities in his mind might have been conceived as a bailout of a troubled asset. His prescription for the Great Depression was for the Fed to provide liquidity, not bailouts.

The Fed's response to the crisis also involved the direct rescue of certain financial institutions deemed too systemically important to fail. The investment bank Bear Stearns was particularly exposed to the US mortgage market and in 2008 was rescued by JPMorgan in a move strongly backed by the Federal Reserve. This was justified by the risk posed by Bear, the collapse of which could have brought down the entire banking system. In July 2008 the US Treasury bailed out and part-nationalized the government-supported enterprises at the heart of the crisis, Fannie Mae and Freddie Mac.

However, a couple of months later, Lehman Brothers was allowed to go bust. The fallout was to turn a US mortgage market crisis into a global financial crisis. Bernanke was later to argue in a 2012 speech that because Lehman was insolvent and posed less of a systemic risk than Bear Stearns, the Federal Reserve had no legal standing to make a bailout using public funds. The next day, however, the giant insurance firm AIG was rescued as the Fed was concerned about the impact on the credit default swap market if it were allowed to fail.

In the global financial crisis, the Federal Reserve provided direct credit to specific markets and businesses in need of liquidity. Friedman's recommended approach in the Great Depression was simply to flood the economy with general liquidity and allow solvency issues to sort themselves out. He might have viewed the targeted interventions made by the Fed, i.e. to save Bear Stearns and AIG but allow Lehman Brothers to go under, as undermining its independence and credibility and getting involved in specific cases.

However, the world in 2008 was different from 1929. There were now players in the financial sector that were literally too big to fail, in the sense that they might bring down the entire system with them. This was not such a problem in the Great Depression, when the systemic risks of any specific bank failure were quite low. With this in mind, Friedman might have grudgingly accepted Bernanke's approach as the best way forward. Of course, he would have been against the involvement of government-supported enterprises in the US housing market in the first place, and would have viewed the crisis as largely a result of the government's unsuccessful intervention in the mortgage market.

There is no doubt that Friedman's scholarship changed perceptions of the Great Depression. By focusing on the role of monetary policy, it greatly aided the response to the more recent crisis. But what about the unconventional monetary policies used afterwards to support the recovery?

The effectiveness of QE still relies to some extent on an ill-functioning banking system. It's all very well to create money; but that money still has to get out into the economy so small firms in particular can borrow and invest. There has been some evidence of positive impact from these unconventional monetary policies along those lines, but some worry about the side effects of increasing the supply of money so dramatically, especially since some of the money has flowed into stock markets which had reached heady heights around the world. It's fair to say the jury is largely still out.

Milton Friedman, though, was generally supportive of QE, which he witnessed in action in Japan. Japan was the first country to adopt QE after its real-estate bubble burst in the early 1990s, so this policy was initially used nearly two decades before the global financial crisis. Friedman approved of what the Japanese central bank did, commenting on their policy: 'The surest road to a healthy economic recovery is to increase the rate of monetary growth.'[14] He argued that the Bank of Japan should undertake QE since interest rates had been cut to rock bottom and the economy was still in dire straits:

> Defenders of the Bank of Japan will say, 'How? The bank has already cut its discount rate to 0.5 per cent. What more can it do to increase the quantity of money?' The answer is straightforward: The Bank of Japan can buy government bonds on the open market, paying for them with either currency or deposits at the Bank of Japan, what economists call high-powered money. Most of the proceeds will end up in commercial banks, adding to their reserves and enabling them to expand their liabilities by loans and open market purchases. But whether they do so or not, the money supply will increase . . . There is no limit to the extent to which the Bank of Japan can increase the money supply if it wishes to do so.[15]

Since he supported QE in Japan, Friedman would have viewed the use of unconventional policies such as cash injections by the US, the UK, the euro area and elsewhere as just as necessary to get lending going in these economies. Central banks in Japan and Europe setting negative interest rates would fall under the same canopy of using a novel tool to try to increase the flow of money into the economy.

But Friedman would have viewed more cautiously the grant of macroprudential policy which gives central banks more direct power to regulate markets to further their monetary policy aims. However, the financial system is much more complex and global today, so Friedmanites may well support the notion that targeting credit and debt levels has become an important area for central banks to manage as part of keeping the monetary system stable. Working out how these policies of targeting inflation and financial stability should work together would surely have been up Friedman's street as economists are now devising a framework for a new monetary policy era.

Finally, for those who question the effectiveness of unconventional tools, particularly QE, Friedman would probably point to the successful winding down of this policy as the American economy has recovered. Even if these policies generated some adverse consequences such as pushing up stock prices, the priority would be to keep monetary policies supportive until the economy was on a sound footing.

Friedman would say that not acting to keep money flowing in the system was the reason why the Great Depression was 'Great'. In response to critics of Japan's loose money policy, Friedman wrote in the *Wall Street Journal*: 'After the US experience during the Great Depression, and after inflation and rising interest rates in the 1970s and disinflation and falling interest rates in the 1980s, I thought the fallacy of identifying tight money with high interest rates and easy money with low interest rates was dead. Apparently, old fallacies never die.'[16]

He warned that this mistake should not be repeated. After all, it was four years after the US economy was thought to have recovered in 1933 that the country was plunged back into recession in 1937. As policymakers contemplate potential parallels to the 1930s, Friedman would have urged them to heed this lesson and not rein back monetary policy prematurely.

Two Lucky People

Milton and Rose Friedman's long marriage and partnership extended beyond family life. They formed a prolific pair, especially in their later years at the Hoover Institution, when Friedman had stepped back from academic economics to focus on his popular writing. It was during this collaborative time that they co-authored the best-selling *Free to Choose* in 1980 as well as *Tyranny of the Status Quo*, published in 1984. They also co-wrote *Two Lucky People: Memoirs*, published in 1998.

Friedman himself regarded *Capitalism and Freedom*, published in 1962, to be 'a better book' than the very commercially successful *Free to Choose*, published two decades later.[17] He thought it was 'more philosophical and abstract, and hence more fundamental'.[18] In his view, the latter book complements the former. Friedman even named his Vermont hilltop home, situated in 120 acres, 'Capitaf' after *Capitalism and Freedom*.[19] However, most economists would regard his *A Monetary History of the United States, 1867–1960*, written with Anna Jacobson Schwartz, as his finest work.

Rose outlived Friedman by three years, passing away at the ripe age of ninety-eight in 2009. She would have witnessed her husband's work being invoked and applied to the first systemic banking crisis since the one of their formative years in the 1930s.

Milton Friedman would have relished that his widow saw his research being applied: 'The true test of any scholar's work is not what his contemporaries say, but what happens to his work in the next twenty-five or fifty years. And the thing that I will really be proud of is if some of the work I have done is still cited in the textbooks long after I am gone.'[20]

II

Douglass North: Why Are So Few
Countries Prosperous?

It's one of the enduring conundrums of our time: why so few countries are prosperous. But will it remain one? There has been tremendous progress, so much so that the World Bank has stopped categorizing countries as 'developed' or 'developing' and now uses regional classifications instead. Are we really about to witness the end of poverty and find the solution to the decades-old question of why so few countries are rich?

How few is few? Well, of the just under two hundred countries in the world that produce economic data, only about fifty are classified as high income. It is a difficult club to join. The World Bank estimates that of the 101 countries that were classified as middle-income in 1960, just a baker's dozen had become prosperous by 2008.[1] Those whose per capita GDP or average income have approached the level of the United States are: Equatorial Guinea, Greece, Hong Kong SAR (China), Ireland, Israel, Japan, Mauritius, Portugal, Puerto Rico, Singapore, South Korea, Spain and Taiwan.

The answer to why only thirteen countries have become rich in the past half-century should include an analysis of the types of institutions that underpin their economies. Possessing good institutions is what economists have come to focus on after standard economic factors, such as capital, labour (including human capital that accounts for education and skills) and technological progress specified in neoclassical growth models, have been unable to explain in full why some nations prosper while many do not.

The seminal research on institutions and economic development was pioneered by Douglass North. He, and those who followed him, systematically analysed how some countries adopted good institutions and what might be done to reform the bad ones. North observed:

> The evolution of government from its medieval, mafia-like character to that embodying modern legal institutions and instruments is a major part of the history of freedom. It is a part that tends to be obscured or ignored because of the myopic vision of many economists, who persist in modeling government as nothing more than a gigantic form of theft and income redistribution.[2]

In North's view, the existing models were unable to answer the essential question as to why economic growth varies across nations:

> What accounts for their widely disparate performance characteristics? This divergence is even more perplexing in terms of standard neoclassical and international trade theory, which implies that over time economies, as they traded goods, services, and productive factors, would gradually converge. Although we do observe some convergence among leading industrial nations that trade with each other, an overwhelming feature of the last ten millennia is that we have evolved into radically different religious, ethnic, cultural, political, and economic societies, and the gap between rich and poor nations, between developed and undeveloped nations, is as wide today as it ever was and perhaps a great deal wider than ever before.[3]

It seems hardly radical, but North took economics out of its comfort zone, which consisted of examining more easily measured inputs like labour and capital and instead brought in politics, sociology and history in order to understand why some countries succeed and others fail.

North won the Nobel Prize in economics in 1993. Along with his fellow laureates Ronald Coase (who won in 1991) and Oliver Williamson (who won more than a decade later in 2009), North founded the field of New Institutional Economics. This work was later expanded upon by MIT economist Daron Acemoglu and University of Chicago political scientist James Robinson, notably in their book *Why Nations Fail: The Origins of Power, Prosperity, and Poverty*, and by many others who have built on North's work on the role of institutions in economic development.

North spent his career trying to find the reasons behind economic disparity, which he formalized as: 'What accounts for societies experiencing long-run stagnation or an absolute decline in economic well-being?'[4] This is the question posed in this chapter, and is also, perhaps, the key economic challenge of our time.

The life and times of Douglass North

Douglass North was born in 1920 in Cambridge, Massachusetts. His father's job as an insurance executive meant that the family moved frequently during North's childhood. He lived in both Canada and Switzerland as well as in several US states. For his first degree, North pursued a triple major in philosophy, political science and economics at the University of California at Berkeley. His recollection of his studies will give many hope: 'My record at the University of California as an undergraduate was mediocre to say the best.'[5]

He became a navigator in the Merchant Marine in the Second World War after graduation. He had hoped to go to law school, but the war intervened and he ended up serving. North explained: 'I was a conscientious objector. I didn't want to kill anybody. I picked something where other people would shoot at me but I wouldn't shoot back.'[6]

It was during these three years, which North said gave him time to read, that led him to relinquish his plans for a career in law. Instead, he thought that he should become an economist or a photographer. They were certainly diverse choices. The former won out because, as he recalled: 'what I wanted to do with my life was to improve societies, and the way to do that was to find out what made economies work the way they did or fail to work'.[7]

Towards the end of the Second World War, North married for the first time and subsequently fathered three sons. His second marriage was in 1972, to Elisabeth Case. They met when she was an editor at Cambridge University Press, having previously worked at Michigan University Press. After their marriage, she was credited with editing some of his articles.

After the war, North returned to the University of California at Berkeley to earn a PhD in economics. His first academic job, which he took up in 1951, was at the University of Washington. He remained there for 32 years until he joined Washington University in St Louis, where he spent the rest of his career. He also held visiting professorships at Cambridge, Stanford and Rice Universities, though none of North's permanent appointments were at top-ranked universities. This illustrates not only that it is possible to succeed outside of the top universities, but also how difficult it is to gain acceptance from them for unorthodox ideas.

As noted, after four decades of research he won the highest prize in the discipline, receiving the Nobel Prize in economics in 1993 for his pioneering work on institutions and how they influence economic development. This was a question that interested North from the very start of his career. Even his PhD dissertation focused on explaining differential regional growth rates within the US, and was the basis of his first book, *The Economic Growth of the United States from 1790 to 1860*, published in 1961.

In 1966–67 came a change of focus as North decided to study European economies after he received a grant to live in Geneva for a year. It was an intellectual turning point:

> I quickly became convinced that the tools of neo-classical economic theory were not up to the task of explaining the kind of fundamental societal change that had characterized European economies from medieval times onward. We needed new tools, but they simply did not exist ... it was not possible to explain long-run poor economic performance in a neo-classical framework. So I began to explore what was wrong.[8]

It was a long road, and one that eventually led him to work with political scientists in the 1980s. That research culminated in his seminal work, *Institutions, Institutional Change and Economic Performance*, published in 1990. His research filled a gap in economics, offering an explanation of why so many countries remain poor:

> The disparity in the performance of economies and the persistence of disparate economies through time have not been satisfactorily explained by development economists, despite forty years of immense effort. The simple fact is that the theory employed is not up to the task.
>
> ... Put simply, what has been missing is an understanding of the nature of human coordination and cooperation. Now, that certainly should not surprise a disciple of Adam Smith. Smith was concerned not only with those forms of cooperation that produced collusive and monopolistic outcomes, but also with those forms of cooperation that would permit realization of the gains from trade.[9]

North created a new way of thinking about economics, which put human behaviour at the core. It led to a long career of not just research but also policy engagement. North was advising countries around the world on applying institutional analysis to their growth policies while in his eighties![10]

Douglass North believed that institutions are the key to understanding the development of an economy. In the Preface to *Institutions, Institutional Change and Economic Performance* he wrote: 'History matters. It matters not just because we can learn from the past, but because the present and the future are connected to the past by the continuity of a society's institutions.'[11]

He was not the first scholar to deploy history in economic argument, but he pioneered the incorporation of institutions into economic analysis. North defined institutions as: 'the rules of the game in a society . . . Institutions reduce uncertainty by providing a structure to everyday life.'[12] So, institutions can be formal, such as laws, or informal, such as those that police societal norms of behaviour. North believes both can evolve over time, which is why history matters a great deal in understanding how development occurs. His work rejected the separation of political and social institutions from the workings of the economy.

North argued: 'Institutions affect the performance of the economy by their effect on the costs of exchange and production.'[13] In other words, poor institutions are costly. At a minimum, excessive regulations are burdensome and add cost to doing business. At the extreme, economies cannot grow if there are unstable political institutions that lead to war or conflict.

Understanding this link between institutions and development points the way to the necessary reforms. For instance, North attributes the success of the United States to its institutions: 'US economic history has been characterized by a federal political system, checks and balances, and a basic structure of property rights that have encouraged the long-term contracting essential to the creation of capital markets and economic growth,' and contrasts that with its southern neighbours that have struggled to develop beyond middle-income status: 'Latin American economic history, in contrast, has perpetuated the centralized, bureaucratic traditions carried over from its Spanish/Portuguese heritage.'[14]

Through studying these economies, North concludes that the institutions that have been good for development include the rule of law as well as openness to globalization. Those institutions provide positive incentives for people to engage in business and productive activities, which generate economic growth. Specifically, he points to market-supporting institutions as important: 'the underlying institutional framework persistently reinforced incentives for organizations to engage in productive activity'.[15] In particular, North believed that institutions mattered for technological progress, a key element of economic growth. North found this was common among prosperous economies, such as the United Kingdom: 'The security of property rights and the development of the public and private capital market were instrumental factors not only in England's subsequent rapid economic development, but in its political hegemony and ultimate dominance of the world.'[16]

He believed that the lack of such good institutions is why some developing countries have lagged behind. In his view, many of their institutions do not provide the sort of positive incentives that exist in the US and UK: 'The opportunities for political and economic entrepreneurs are still a mixed bag, but they overwhelmingly favor activities that promote redistributive rather than productive activity, that create monopolies rather than competitive conditions, and that restrict opportunities rather than expand them. They seldom induce investment in education that increases productivity.'[17]

He also believed that institutions perpetuate themselves. This view that good and bad institutions tend to self-perpetuate implies there is 'path dependence' in economic development. Path dependence was used by North to explain vicious circles of poverty and virtuous circles of growth. In a virtuous circle, the government invested in education and technological improvements that reinforced the good institutions, which generated growth that helped such good institutions to persist. In other words, path dependence means that good or bad institutions lead to persistently good or bad institutions, which reinforce an economy's growth path – either positively or negatively. What comes next depends on what has come before.

For North, path dependence helps to explain differential long-run economic outcomes. It's also why he posited that it's hard to reform economies to change their course, which will require political and social change that can be slow to bring about: 'Reversal of paths (from stagnation to growth or vice versa) . . . will typically occur through changes in the polity.'[18]

Before we look at what North would say about how to address the current development challenge, let's first examine in more detail why so many countries remain poor.

The development challenge

One aspect of the development challenge may not exist for long. The United Nations, with the support of all countries around the world, and the World Bank have set an ambitious target of ending extreme poverty by 2030. It would mean that, for the first time, there would be no one who lives on less than $1.90 per day, adjusted for what a dollar buys in the country or 'purchasing power parity'. What would it take? Could we really see the end of poverty?

First, there has been a great deal of progress already. The poverty rate in the developing world has fallen dramatically since 1981. Back then, more than half (52 per cent) of the global population lived on less than $1.25 per day. That's dropped to around 10 per cent under the comparable measure of $1.90 per day.

One of the UN's Millennium Development Goals (MDGs) was to halve poverty by 2015 from 1990 levels. In fact, this was achieved five years early. In 1990, more than one-third (36 per cent) of the world's population lived in abject poverty. That was halved to 18 per cent in 2010, due largely to China's rapid economic growth, and progress in the East Asian region. Four out of five people lived in poverty in 1981 and that has fallen to 8 per cent. On current trends, the fastest growing region in the world could see the end of poverty within a generation.

Sub-Saharan Africa is the only region where the number of people living in extreme poverty has increased during the past three decades. Even though the percentage of the African population living in extreme poverty is slightly lower than in 1981, population growth means that there is a greater number of people living in poverty. They account for more than half of the extreme poor in the world, despite Africa making up only 11 per cent of the global population.

In all, over a billion people have been lifted out of poverty worldwide since 1990, which is an extraordinary achievement. For the first time in history, just one in ten people live in extreme poverty around the world, and both the United Nations and the World Bank believe we are moving towards the historic goal of ending extreme poverty by 2030, so achieving the first of the Sustainable Development Goals (SDGs) adopted in 2015.*

Could we really be the first generation in history to succeed in eradicating global poverty? What precisely does the end of poverty look like? It doesn't mean that no one lives on less than $1.90 per day.

---

* The other sixteen Sustainable Development Goals are: zero hunger; good health and well-being; quality education; gender equality; clean water and sanitation; affordable and clean energy; decent work and economic growth; industry, innovation and infrastructure; reduced inequalities; sustainable cities and communities; responsible consumption and production; climate change; life below water; life on land; peace, justice and strong institutions; partnerships for the goals.

The World Bank assumes that a 3 per cent poverty rate is equivalent to the end of poverty since there will be some who move into poverty only temporarily, perhaps when they lose their jobs. This is known as 'frictional' poverty.

To get to that point would take a heroic effort. The number of poor people will have to decrease by 50 million every year until 2030. That is the equivalent of a million people per week. That pace is daunting. If met, it would mean lifting all but a quarter of a billion people out of an estimated 8.6 billion people on the planet then out of abject poverty.

Which policies might get us to that outcome? A country that we can perhaps learn from is fast-growing China. It had a higher poverty rate in 1990 than Africa, yet it has accounted for the bulk of global poverty reduction in the past few decades. But growth alone is clearly not enough, since Africa, the second fastest growing region in the world after Asia, has failed to make similar progress.

Drawing lessons from one country or region to another always needs to be done carefully and the Chinese economy is in transition from central planning under the governance of a one-party state, as discussed in the Marx chapter. That means, for instance, that land is effectively owned by the government and leased from the state. It doesn't mean that some haven't become very wealthy developing land gained through government favour, but most people have been lifted out of poverty through self-employment and not by exploiting the land and its resources. This is in contrast to Africa, where, as Oxford economist Paul Collier points out, unlike China, income growth has been based on natural resources and the gains have not been widely shared.[19]

In China, policies were designed to raise the productivity of agriculture, which lifted hundreds of millions out of poverty in rural areas. The World Bank has proposed similar targeted growth policies, such as supporting agricultural productivity, in developing countries.

Unlike Africa, China did not rely much on overseas aid, a standard tool in poverty alleviation policies. This has contributed to the mixed evidence about the impact of aid on reducing poverty, which has led to a fiery debate. Still, the UK-based Overseas Development

Institute (ODI) believes that there is a role for aid, but that there needs to be an overhaul of the way it is used.

So, it is tricky to apply lessons drawn from the past to the remaining stubborn pockets of poverty. Around half of the extreme poor live in Africa and another third in South Asia. For instance, Tanzania, which has grown well and been devoid of conflict, has seen the number of poor increase from 9 million two decades ago to 15 million. South Asia also lags in terms of the progress made in East Asia despite its growth, so again it is not possible to count on growth alone to lift the remaining 767 million people out of poverty.

Doubtless, the circumstances of individual countries matter a great deal in terms of what works, as North would stress. But if the progress made in the past couple of decades can be replicated in some fashion and tailored to individual countries, then it's possible that the remaining poor could be lifted out of abject poverty. That would imply that the 36 per cent poverty rate in 1990, which had dropped to 18 per cent in 2010, would fall by a comparable magnitude by 2030. It would indeed mean the end of poverty in our lifetimes. As Nobel laureate Robert Lucas, Jr, remarked:

> Is there some action a government of India could take that would lead the Indian economy to grow like Indonesia's . . . ? If so, *what*, exactly? If not, what is it about the 'nature of India' that makes it so? The consequences for human welfare involved in questions like these are simply staggering: Once one starts to think about them, it is hard to think about anything else.[20]

There is also the prospect of a crisis derailing economic growth. That has been a feature of developing countries in the post-war period. Once prone to crisis, Douglass North's theory of path dependence would suggest that it is not surprising that it occurs time and again.

A history of crises

Even among emerging economies or emerging markets, which are alternative terms for developing countries that have a track record of economic reform and good growth prospects, the past few decades have been characterized by a series of financial crises that has prevented sustained growth spells. China may have had a four decade-long growth spell that has not been interrupted by crisis and it has nearly eradicated extreme poverty, but that is not the case for many other developing countries.

What is known as the first-generation currency crisis refers to the Latin American crisis of 1981–82. Countries such as Brazil, Mexico, Argentina and Chile had three traits that made them vulnerable: a large budget deficit, so their governments were borrowing to spend, a large trade or current account deficit, so they were importing more than they were exporting, and high inflation, so prices were rising fast. These traits put pressure on their fixed exchange rate against the US dollar, known collectively for those four countries as the *tablitas*. Large deficits and inflation in a country often cause investors to sell their holdings of its currency and buy others that are more stable, usually the dollar, which is what happened in Latin America. The 'twin deficits' (budget and trade) and high inflation are why emerging economies are viewed as vulnerable to growth-derailing crises.

The second-generation currency crisis refers to the collapse of the European exchange rate mechanism (ERM) in 1992. Even though that was a crisis involving developed economies, there are similar features to the Latin American episode. Many Britons still recall Black Wednesday, when sterling and other currencies, such as the Italian lira, left the peg to the Deutschmark (DM) that they had signed up to two years earlier. A loss of market confidence meant that to keep their currencies pegged would have meant raising interest rates to unacceptable levels if investors were to be persuaded to buy sterling and maintain the exchange-rate peg. UK interest rates had reached 15 per cent, and the impact on economic growth of staying in the ERM would simply have been too detrimental during a recession. High interest rates made borrowing more expensive and depressed investment, so worsening growth. Unlike the Latin American economies, the troubled European nations did fairly well after the crisis. Weaker currencies made what they sold abroad cheaper, so exports became more competitive and Britain, for instance, grew well during the 1990s. One difference between Latin America and Europe is that the latter had more stable institutions such as well-regarded central banks, which emerged from the debacle with their reputations more or less intact, whereas in Latin America the crisis led to a loss of confidence in their economic systems and investors pulled out for the long term. This is in line with North's theory that good institutions persist and breed prosperity even through crises.

The third-generation financial and currency crisis took place in Asia in 1997–98. What distinguishes the Asian financial crisis from the first two is that it was a financial crisis that led to a currency crisis. When foreign investors suddenly pulled their money from Thailand after years of capital inflows into the country, it led the Thai baht to collapse. There was a 'sudden stop' of cash inflows that had been lent to Thai businesses. The crisis spread to Malaysia, Indonesia, Hong Kong and South Korea. To try to retain the foreign money to which their businesses had grown accustomed, these economies had to raise interest rates, which hurt growth. (It was similar in that sense to the ERM crisis.) When money flowed out of these countries, their currencies collapsed as investors had no need to keep hold of them any longer. That is why it is known as a financial crisis first and foremost.

What was surprising about the third-generation crisis was that it affected Asian economies, which, unlike Latin America in the early 1980s, were viewed as growing well and did not have huge trade or fiscal deficits. Yet the five economies initially involved were mired in crises that hurt their growth for years. The other worrying trait of the third-generation crisis was contagion, the impact of the Asian financial crisis also being felt in emerging economies around the world. It affected Russia in 1998, Turkey in 1999 and Brazil and Argentina by the early 2000s. This was not because these economies traded much with or invested a great deal in the affected Asian nations, but probably because investors became indiscriminately wary of all developing markets, plunging those economies into crisis too. Argentina, on the other side of the world from where the crisis began, ended up with the largest sovereign default in modern times until Greece took that title a decade later.

This history highlights that the most vulnerable to crises are those emerging economies with the greatest exposure to foreigners owning their debt. When creditors no longer want to hold that debt, it is more expensive for countries to borrow on debt markets because they have to pay a higher interest rate to attract lenders. The reason foreign debt is in focus is because when their loans and other investments, dubbed 'hot money', leave the country, those investors will sell that nation's currency too. A weaker currency then makes it more expensive to repay debt that is denominated in US dollars, which worsens the debt problem. Borrowing in US dollars is referred to as the 'original sin' of developing countries for this reason. This is why there is so much focus on a country's foreign exchange reserves, so that vulnerable economies can show that they possess foreign currency sufficient to pay for their imports and debt and are less affected by currency and capital movements.

Such crises can derail economic growth for years. A currency or financial crisis can and has prevented emerging economies from becoming rich, since an extended period of growth is a necessary trait of the countries that have overcome the middle-income trap discussed earlier. South Korea and Taiwan both grew strongly for over two decades, for example. If developing countries can grow for sustained periods, not only would poverty end in those countries, but also they might even be propelled into the ranks of the rich.

When it comes to sustained high growth rates, there is another concern. Economic growth of emerging markets has slowed in the 2010s. Among the large emerging economies, the so-called BRIC economies owing to their initials, Brazil and Russia have struggled to grow while India and China continue to develop but at a more moderate pace. It's a trend mirrored in the smaller emerging economies. And that raises the question as to whether the emerging market growth story may be over before they have ended poverty and become prosperous.

But their slowing growth should not be unexpected since many of them have become middle-income countries in recent years after a couple of decades of strong growth. For the first time, emerging economies account for more than half of the world's GDP, but, as the rich countries know from experience, richer nations grow more slowly than poorer ones. It's not surprising that the fast-growth spell of emerging economies has slowed down.

After China, India and the former Soviet Union opened up in the early 1990s their economies immediately benefited from access to world markets. Their integration with the global economy helped launch an era of globalization where terms like offshoring came into vogue and globalization surged: exports of goods and services increased from 20 per cent of world GDP to around 30 per cent by the 2010s. Foreign investment poured into cheaper and fast-growing emerging economies as they opened up, which helped their companies to learn from more established multinationals and contributed to a growing new middle class in those countries.

As countries become richer, their pace of growth inevitably slows. Developing ones grow quickly because they are starting the process of industrializing and trading from scratch, so the gains are relatively larger and arrive quickly. Richer nations grow more slowly since they have to innovate and upgrade their industries in order to raise their productivity. For China, 4 per cent growth would be a cause for disappointment; for the USA it would be magnificent.

According to Douglass North, what determines how much an economy will slow down, and thus its long-term growth prospects, is the quality of its institutions. Vietnam and Myanmar, a pair of newly globalized economies, offer useful case studies. They both hold huge promise, but also face significant obstacles. South Africa is another notable case. Let's consider each in turn.

Vietnam's institutional challenge

In 1986 the Vietnamese government launched a series of market-oriented reforms known as *doi moi*. Since then the country has been in transition from central planning to a 'socialist market economy' with the Communist Party remaining in charge. Vietnam is a sizeable country, not quite China's 1.3 billion, but at over 90 million people its population is among the twenty largest in the world. So, Vietnam is a potentially significant economy, given its population. Like China, Vietnam instituted economic reforms in a lagging economy while retaining the communist political regime.

One leftover from the old system is that its state-owned companies dominate bank lending and account for more than half of the country's bad debt. Vietnam is sometimes viewed as the 'next China' owing to its stable transition and communist rule, but there are concerns about a looming debt crisis. The creation of market-oriented institutions and the dismantling of the centrally planned apparatus that had governed the market will attempt the challenging task of altering the path of the economy, the sort of difficult 'path dependence' described by Douglass North.

Among the hardest institutions to reform are state-owned enterprises. For Vietnam, the dominance of such firms, and their associated bad debt, remains a problem years after the launch of *doi moi*. In common with other nations, Vietnam created 'bad banks' or asset management companies to take the bad debts off the books of the state-owned banks. This is what China did in 1999, when it created four such companies to try to clean up the balance sheets of its big state-owned banks prior to opening up the sector when it joined the World Trade Organization in 2001. But the problem with bad debt is not just the stock, but the flow. In other words, the continued accumulation of debts from inefficient state-owned enterprises cannot be ignored.

China in the mid-1990s took a huge step forward in privatizing or restructuring most of the state-owned firms. The number of large state-owned enterprises dropped from about 10 million to less than 300,000 by the end of that decade. It still has a sizeable state-owned sector, but a notable attempt was made to cut the flow of bad debt by increasing the efficiency of the remaining state-owned firms. This was by partially privatizing or selling shares in even the largest state-owned firms, including banks. Of course, China created other problems for itself when it used the banking system to provide most of the finance behind its large fiscal stimulus to boost the economy during the 2008 global financial crisis, discussed in Chapter 3.

Vietnam has pledged to reform its state-owned enterprises, but it has progressed slowly. It wasn't until 2011 that Vietnam started to reduce the number of state-owned enterprises significantly, from 1,309 to 958 in the five years to 2015. And it has a lot more to privatize to get to its target of 190 by 2020. So, it has taken around three decades to reform state firms.

Again like China, Vietnam decided not to follow the 'shock therapy' route taken by the former Soviet Union when it quickly transitioned from a centrally planned economy during the early 1990s. Instead it gradually introduced market forces, including allowing non-state firms to operate, so that the government could slowly reform the state-owned sector.

Looking at the decade-long recession that the former Eastern Bloc nations experienced after their rapid transition, it probably isn't surprising that China and Vietnam seem to have done the smart thing. However, there is an important impediment to both of their reforms, namely that undertaking a more rapid transition removes the inefficient 'hand' of the state. Quickly dismantling the old system prevents the build-up of vested interests and the creation of new power bases in the marketized economy by those who benefit most from the ongoing reforms and can forestall further progress. (Of course, there were numerous problems with the transition of Russia and others, including the unrealistic expectation that a private economy could just fill the vacuum if the old state one was dismantled.)

China undertook what has been described as an 'easy-to-hard' reform sequence in that politically easier reforms like incentivizing agricultural output were done first, while leaving the harder reforms of the state-owned sector for later. As the theory predicted, those new power bases have made it more difficult to implement further reform. Similarly, Vietnam's reforms seem to be mired in the inability of those who run the state-owned firms to allow them to become at least partly if not wholly privatized. In other words, those who benefited from the reforms of the economy are now hanging on to their inefficient firms, which are a drag on the banking system.

There are consequences for the Vietnamese economy. Vietnam's government debt is half of GDP and, importantly, over one-third is owed to foreign creditors. When the debt of state-owned enterprises is added in, the figure doubles to a sizeable 100 per cent of GDP. When the total debt owed by the government is the same magnitude of a country's annual national output, concern over a potential debt crisis grows. To avert it would require cutting off the flow of bad debts from state-owned firms as well as pushing ahead with some degree of privatization. To achieve this will require overcoming a raft of vested interests.

The lesson for countries tackling reforms is, as North had warned, that the power of vested interests in keeping institutions unchanged must be considered as well as the efficiency of the proposed measures. For Vietnam, it is a warning worth heeding.

Myanmar's fast changing institutions

Myanmar, formerly known as Burma, has also recently opened up. It faces a different sort of challenge than Vietnam does, but is similarly reforming the very structure of its economy and its institutions in order to alter its economic path.

Investors call the country the 'final frontier'. The *Star Trek* reference aside, there is a sense of the yet to be explored about Myanmar. It is the last large Asian economy to become globally connected, and opened up only in 2011 after half a century of military rule and the release from house arrest of Nobel Peace laureate Aung San Suu Kyi.

The statistics tell the story: in 2011 just 6 per cent of the population had access to a mobile device and only about 10 per cent had a bank account. Decades of military rule have left Myanmar underdeveloped and one of the poorest countries in Asia. But that also means that, with the right sorts of institutional reforms, it has significant potential to grow quickly. It sits in the world's fastest-growing region with well-established global supply chains, which can help an economy industrialize and grow rapidly if it is part of the worldwide manufacturing network. Unlike many smaller countries in developing Asia, Myanmar, with a population similar in size to that of South Korea, can utilize a significant home market to promote growth as well as expand its exports. This explains the interest of many multinational corporations who eye an under-served market. Plus, it is well endowed with oil, gas and minerals. Thus, Myanmar is one of the countries that can attract foreign investment for all three reasons that typically motivate multinational companies: natural resources, lower costs and new markets.

Myanmar's potential has certainly caught the attention of the world's largest companies looking for the next double-digit growth economy. But opening up too quickly to investment flows has pitfalls, as seen in the numerous crises plaguing emerging economies outlined earlier. This was avoided by China, which has led to talk of the so-called Beijing Consensus serving as an alternative model for newly marketizing nations.

In vogue after the success of China's growth and the critiques levelled at the Washington Consensus, could the Chinese model be a model for Myanmar as it embarks on a historical opening to the global economy?

Of course, there may not even be a consensus about the Beijing Consensus, as the Chinese growth experience cannot be easily modelled. And there are many elements of China's marketization process that are similar to the Washington version. The Washington Consensus was a model of economic development promulgated during the 1980s and 1990s that stemmed from the IMF and US Treasury, both located in Washington, DC. The model was premised on privatization and financial and trade liberalization. As a number of developing countries failed to benefit from following these prescriptions, which was seen both in the decade-long recession of the former Soviet Union during the 1990s and in the 1980s Latin American crisis, the Washington Consensus fell out of favour and developing countries sought an alternative. Some turned to China, whose market-oriented reforms proceeded at a more gradual pace and with sequencing of key reforms. For instance, state-owned enterprises were slowly reformed and were not subject to mass privatization until a couple of decades into the reform process. China also established a non-state sector that absorbed the laid-off workers, so preventing persistent large-scale unemployment. But as discussed earlier, one consequence is that reforms are incomplete and state ownership persists.

China is not alone in growing rapidly in the region. South Korea, Taiwan, Singapore and Hong Kong did the same, serving as a partial model for China as it enacted targeted reforms to boost global integration into production and supply chains that allowed these economies to industrialize through plugging into worldwide manufacturing. State-directed credit also helped to avoid specialization in less desirable areas such as primary (agricultural, resource) products.

As a model of development, the Beijing Consensus in emphasizing gradual and managed opening to the world economy and slower reforms of the existing economic institutions could be more appealing than a more rapid marketization model. Key to the Beijing Consensus is industrialization, which in China's case involved reindustrialization as existing and new industrial firms were reformed and encouraged to enter into higher tech industries. For Myanmar, which is not a transition economy, so it does not have state-owned enterprises like China to restructure, the more standard Lewis model would apply. Crafted by the Nobel laureate Arthur Lewis, this model sees economic growth occurring when workers move out of low-productivity agriculture and into more productive factories and the services economy. Although with a different stress, the end result is the same: industrialization supports economic development. That shift to industry could launch Myanmar into the rapid-growth phase experienced by other Asian countries.

So, the Beijing Consensus perhaps offers a better set of guidelines for Myanmar than the Washington Consensus as it is derived from the experience of its East Asian neighbours. About 70 per cent of Myanmar's population are employed in the agriculture and resources sector, which accounts for over half of the country's economic output. It means that there is a lot of scope to industrialize, which can launch a country into fast growth as it 'catches up', as occurred in the East Asian 'miracle' economies of South Korea, Taiwan, Singapore and Hong Kong, which are among the few that have become rich in the post-war period.

However, as a latecomer and a richly endowed country, plugging into regional production chains will be key or else Myanmar risks specializing in resources and being crowded out by more competitive foreign firms. It is in the right region to exploit that potential, since about half of the world's consumer electronics are produced in Asia. It means Myanmar has the potential to grow in a diversified manner and could develop rapidly if it industrializes. But the bumpier road travelled by some of its Southeast Asian neighbours suggests that success cannot be taken for granted. And it will depend on government policies, also including in the crucial area of social stability. The East Asian 'tiger' economies of Hong Kong, Singapore, South Korea and Taiwan had also enacted land reform and other forms of redistribution that allowed their growth to be accompanied by greater equity. By contrast, China's lack of such policies contributes to it having levels of inequality that are causing social resentment. That is another lesson to note from the growth experience of its neighbours. Institutional reforms, such as adopting redistributive policies to promote income equality alongside industrialization, can allow Myanmar to develop economically without the high levels of income inequality seen in China. These are the very sorts of reforms that Douglass North would propose. Myanmar has already begun to alter the path of its economy and, if successful, then the once bright economy in Southeast Asia can re-emerge and take its place in the fastest growing region in the world.

Exemplified by Vietnam and Myanmar, Asia is progressing with institutional reforms and its growth has led to expectations that extreme global poverty might be eradicated. But Africa remains the big question mark, where so many of the world's poor still reside. Still, South Africa's transformation, led by another path-altering political change, offers a glimpse as to what is possible.

Africa's progress and challenges

When apartheid finally ended in South Africa in the early 1990s, the phrase 'Africa rising' was often heard. Over the past couple of decades, Africa was the second fastest growing region in the world after only Asia. This is a far cry from the years when the region's dominant issues were discussions about debt forgiveness. But poverty rates remain stubbornly high.

This is despite the fact that on the back of the extraordinary commodity boom of the 2000s, African nations have grown well, many quite rapidly, averaging 5 per cent a year in the past decade. This was the longest expansion of incomes in the region in thirty years.

Whether these countries can sustain that economic growth, and do more for poverty reduction, depends on a number of factors, including whether they have managed to industrialize and mechanize agriculture using the proceeds from the commodity boom. That would make growth more inclusive in that the benefits from it are widely shared, which would matter a great deal to poverty reduction. Whether they have done enough to adjust to the end of that extraordinary period will soon be evident in their economies.

For the dominant economy in the region, the transformation post-apartheid has been notable and serves as a case study of effective institutional change. At one stage, South Africa accounted for one-third of the entire output of the nearly fifty countries in sub-Saharan Africa. Its average income during the 1980s was less than $3,000 per capita, which ranked it as a lower middle-income country. By the 2010s, a couple of decades after the end of apartheid, incomes had doubled and propelled South Africa to become an upper-middle-income country. And it became part of the BRICS, the 'S' to Brazil, Russia, India and China. South Africa is one of the five large emerging economies highlighted by financial markets. Its popularity with investors seeking higher returns signalled its arrival as one of the new players in the global economy.

This is not to suggest that South Africa doesn't have challenges. To name just a few, income inequality and joblessness remain tough issues. The average income of black Africans in the country is one-tenth to one-fifth of that of whites. Work is another persistent problem. With the unemployment rate at over 25 per cent, the lack of jobs, particularly for the black population, is a recurrent concern. Some of these economic woes are legacies of apartheid, which was a system of racial segregation in place between 1948 and the early 1990s. It was ended after the release from prison in 1990 of Nelson Mandela, who was later elected president. Mandela had worked for decades to end the unfair system that designated the majority of the South African population second-class citizens. Even though official discrimination against blacks has ended, they remain less well off economically more than two decades later. It's an example of Douglass North's path dependence and why institutions are slow to change, even with the will to do so. And how it takes time for a disadvantaged group to advance even after the formal barriers have been removed since they start from a weaker economic position. It's one of the challenges holding back the country's growth potential decades after Nelson Mandela led the nation into a new era.

This jars with the perception that South Africa is an attractive destination for investors. This is why the country has been described as having a First World financial market within a Third World economic system. Further reform of its economic and political institutions is needed to close that gap, as South Africa has been a beacon for the sub-Saharan region but also epitomizes the development challenges the region still faces. For other African nations, South Africa demonstrates how far a country can advance when institutions are reformed to be more equitable. This is in line with the work of Douglass North: economic development that focuses a great deal on understanding the institutional impediments to growth. Every African nation has its own history and institutions to grapple with, but there is no question that their success will determine whether global poverty will be eradicated in the coming years.

Taking stock

So, what would Douglass North make of the development challenges in the years ahead? What would he say about why some nations remain poor while others have become rich? Is the sharp divide in the world's economies set to continue? After all, current trends point not only to the end of the need to distinguish between developed and developing countries, but also to a concern that the emerging economy growth story could be over before those countries have overcome poverty.

North would certainly recognize that economic growth does not necessarily mean poverty reduction. He believed that poor institutions can persist and enrich some without any resultant economic growth benefiting the country as a whole: 'Rulers devised property rights in their own interests.'[21] So, North believed that institutions can be corrupt, particularly when it comes to who owns such assets as natural resources and land, which have been a source of conflict in Africa.

But North would argue that countries can learn from successful cases such as those in Asia where institutions have worked to bolster economic development and reduce poverty: 'Clearly the existence of relatively productive institutions somewhere in the world and low-cost information about the resultant performance characteristics of those institutions is a powerful incentive to change for poorly performing economies.'[22]

Notably in East Asian nations such as South Korea and Singapore, good governance seems to have played a role in their growth. Their government policies were geared at promoting manufacturing and exporting. They also focused on expanding education to the entire society. These sorts of institutions are ones that North would describe as good for economic growth.

But good institutions are not easy to come by. Simply transplanting a well-crafted set of rules or even an entire legal system into a developing country doesn't work. That's evident from the countries of the former Soviet Union's unsuccessful attempt to adopt Western legal systems during its transition from communism to capitalism. After the collapse of the USSR in the early 1990s, those newly independent countries in eastern and central Europe adopted the Western rule of law and regulations. But decades later, legal protections and rights are still not effectively enforced in many of those nations. Laws that are imposed artificially rather than develop organically do not necessarily fit. The challenge for economies is how to build good institutions suitable to their domestic contexts. As North observed:

> Although formal rules may change overnight as the result of political or judicial decisions, informal constraints embodied in customs,

traditions, and codes of conduct are much more impervious to deliberate policies. These cultural constraints not only connect the past with the present and future, but provide us with a key to explaining the path of historical change.[23]

Thus, North would say that bolstering the rule of law will take time as culture changes gradually, but developing rules-based institutions that provide for good governance will eventually determine how such countries will develop down the line. Of course, political stability and a lack of conflict are also essential or good institutions will struggle to take hold. North was well aware of the challenges of developing beneficial institutions within often messy political and economic backdrops in the world's poorest countries. It's why he advocated paying attention to informal institutions, which includes doing business with those you trust while the legal system improves. Social networks or social capital help to explain how countries with poor legal systems do business as the moral pressure, often from their own communities, constrains bad behaviour; for instance, if your neighbour absconds with your money, then his family will be ostracized in the village. How societies interact is crucial in understanding how institutions evolve. North stressed: 'Informal constraints matter. We need to know much more about culturally derived norms of behavior and how they interact with formal rules to get better answers to such issues.'[24]

To get those answers about how norms of behaviour will influence the reform of formal institutions such as the rule of law will require economics to broaden its perspective to include the messier aspects of how societies operate. As North put it in one of his last contributions:

> My pet peeve all through the last twenty years or thirty years has been the narrowness of economists, in fact of all social scientists, in not opening up whole new areas . . . I think the biggest thing I want to leave with you is how we've got to study more about how the mind and brain work and how the structure is evolving over time as we get more information, more knowledge, and when it's going in directions that are creative.[25]

North's research has certainly opened up the subject. As a result of his path-breaking work and legacy, economists have considered institutions much more carefully as an essential part of understanding economic development. For instance, building on North's work, Daron Acemoglu and James Robinson, whose book was mentioned earlier as an exemplar of the current thinking in economics, examined in detail instances from around the world in which bad institutions led to dire outcomes. They concluded that the issue is when the institutions that underpin the economy are extractive and encourage exploitation rather than productive effort:

> Nations fail today because their extractive economic institutions do not create the incentives needed for people to save, invest, and innovate. Extractive political institutions support these economic institutions by cementing the power of those who benefit from the extraction. Extractive economic and political institutions, though their details vary under different circumstances, are always at the root of this failure ... The result is economic stagnation and – as the recent history of Angola, Cameroon, Chad, the Democratic Republic of Congo, Haiti, Liberia, Nepal, Sierra Leone, Sudan, and Zimbabwe illustrates – civil wars, mass displacements, famines, and epidemics, making many of these countries poorer today than they were in the 1960s.[26]

They agree with North that path dependence leads to a vicious circle of persistently poor development, and also that it is possible to break the cycle: 'The solution to the economic and political failure of nations today is to transform their extractive institutions toward inclusive ones. The vicious circle means that this is not easy. But it is not impossible.'[27]

Acemoglu and Robinson point to successes, including Botswana, China and the American South, which are 'vivid illustrations that history is not destiny'.[28] But it will require a broad-based political and social coalition to push for reforms, as proposed by North, and a bit of luck 'because history always unfolds in a contingent way'.[29]

There are more successes now than ever before. Research by the OECD estimates that by 2030, for the first time in history, more than half of the world's population will be considered middle class. That's 4.9 billion out of an estimated 8.6 billion people. In 2009 1.8 billion (out of around 7 billion) people earned between $10 and $100 per day, a measure of the income that defines the new global middle class. That's enough to buy a refrigerator, adjusted for what a dollar buys in their countries.

In 2030, nearly two-thirds of the middle class worldwide – 3 billion people – will be in Asia on current trends. The United Nations describes it as a historic shift not seen for 150 years. The European and North American middle class will fall from more than half of that class's world total to one-third.

Because of Douglass North's insights, we are closer than ever before to understanding how to end poverty. Following his precepts, a number of countries have developed successfully in the past few decades, leading to an unprecedented expansion of the middle class around the world. Even if economics doesn't have all of the solutions, looking more broadly at institutions holds the promise that one day we will learn why some nations are rich and others are poor, and, most importantly, why some nations fail and why some ultimately prosper.

North would agree: 'We are just beginning the serious study of institutions. The promise is there. We may never have definitive answers to all our questions. But we can do better.'[30]

12

Robert Solow: Do We Face a Slow-Growth Future?

Economic growth across major economies is slower today than before the 2008 global financial crisis, but not just as a result of the crash. Economies such as the United States, the euro area, Japan and the UK had been experiencing a marked slowdown in productivity growth since the mid 2000s.

Some economists are warning about permanently slower growth in advanced economies, in part because their ageing populations will be less productive. Could these economies be facing what the former US Treasury Secretary and Harvard economist Lawrence Summers describes as 'secular stagnation'? If so, then those countries face a worrying economic future. Fewer workers require fewer office buildings and less equipment, which also depresses investment and therefore the economic outlook. That point seems to be approaching: US labour force growth slowed to just 0.2 per cent in 2015, down from 2.1 per cent from the 1960s to 1980s; for the UK, the annual average rate of labour force growth is somewhat better, but it is still down to around 0.6 per cent.

An overwhelming concern is that the situation in Japan in the early 1990s will be repeated in the West. When the real estate bubble burst, the ensuing economic collapse revealed an underlying stagnation that had been masked by the crisis. Japan's problems have been compounded by a population that has been shrinking since 2010. A smaller workforce makes it harder to improve productivity and raise output growth. Slow productivity growth in particular is an issue for

Britain, which is facing its weakest recovery in modern memory. This is a lesson to heed, since national output has recovered to pre-crisis levels, but productivity continues to lag behind the overall recovery.

So, the new normal growth rate may be lower than before. Or, worse, be stagnant. How worried should we be?

The author of the workhorse of economic growth models, Robert Solow, might provide some answers. The Solow model shows that economic growth occurs when workers and capital are added to the economy, but that it is sustained only when there is also technological progress. Better technology improves labour productivity, which increases capital accumulation by slowing down the diminishing returns to capital. Diminishing returns happen when a worker is given more than, say, two computers; that worker won't produce as much with the third computer as compared with the first two unless there is better software that allows computing to be done without the person using it all the time. Technological progress allows the existing inputs of workers and capital to be used more efficiently. An increase in output due to technology is referred to as total factor productivity (TFP) in economic growth models. Physical capital as well as human capital – the skills and education of workers – are central to this model. It's especially pressing for rich countries, where the working-age population is ageing or even shrinking and having better-skilled workers is even more important. How to raise productivity lies at the heart of whether or not we're doomed to a stagnant future.

What would Robert Solow, whose pioneering work has helped us to understand what generates economic growth, make of the prospect of low productivity and a slow-growth future for major economies?

The life and times of Robert Solow

Robert Solow was born in 1924 in Brooklyn. The son of Jewish immigrants, his was the first generation of the family to go to college. He attributes his intellectual awakening to the New York City public school system, where a teacher got him interested in nineteenth-century French and Russian novelists. That wasn't the only trigger that Solow describes: 'Like many children of the Depression I was curious about what made society tick.'[1]

That curiosity led to him obtaining a scholarship to attend Harvard University in 1940. After serving in the US army from 1942 to 1945, he returned to Harvard and his fiancée, Barbara Lewis, known as Bobby. They had met before he was deployed and wrote to each other daily while he was serving in North Africa and Italy. After the end of the war, Bobby graduated from Radcliffe College, the all-women sister college to Harvard. In 1945 they married and both embarked on their doctoral studies in economics at Harvard. Bobby completed her dissertation after a thirteen-year interruption to raise their three children and later taught at Brandeis and Boston universities, where she focused on Irish and Caribbean economic history. They were married for nearly seventy years until her death in 2014 at the age of ninety.

Bobby may have been the reason that Solow became an economist. He asked his wife whether the economic courses that she had taken were worthwhile. Solow was persuaded and pursued economics, which brought him under the tutelage of Wassily Leontief and others.[2] Leontief was a Nobel laureate who won the top prize in economics in 1973 for his work on measuring inputs such as labour and capital and their relationship to national output, presented in 'input–output tables'. As his research assistant, Solow produced the first set of measurements of how much capital investments added to output in the American economy.

As Solow's interests turned to statistics and probabilistic models, he spent 1949–50 studying these subjects at Columbia University, which had more experienced teachers in that area. It helped him finish his doctoral dissertation, which modelled changes in wage distributions and unemployment. His thesis won the Wells Prize at Harvard, which offered not just publication as a book but also $500, which was a considerable sum in 1951. But upon rereading the thesis, Solow thought he could improve upon it, so it remains unpublished and the cheque is still uncashed.

After he received his PhD in economics that year, he joined the Massachusetts Institute of Technology, where he became a professor in 1958. Solow spent his academic career at this leading economics faculty, though he was also visiting professor at Cambridge and Oxford universities in the 1960s.

Solow was active in public policy from the start. After obtaining his PhD, he took on consulting assignments for the RAND Corporation in 1952. During his time working with the President's Council of Economic Advisers from 1962–68, Solow helped draft the Keynesian-influenced economic policies that were the hallmark of the John F. Kennedy and Lyndon B. Johnson administrations. In 1965–69, he served on President Johnson's Committee on Technology, Automation and Economic Progress, and then on President Richard Nixon's Commission on Income Maintenance from 1969–70. Solow even spent a spell as a central banker when he was director and later chairman of the board of the Federal Reserve Bank of Boston from 1975 to 1980. In recognition of his long public service, Solow was awarded the Presidential Medal of Freedom in 2014, the highest honour granted to civilians by the United States government.

Solow had received accolades from the start of his career. In 1961 he received the prestigious John Bates Clark Medal, awarded to the best US economist under the age of forty. It is now often viewed as a precursor to the Nobel Prize. He was well regarded throughout his career, which included serving as president of the American Economic Association in 1979. He is also a past president of the Econometric Society, member of the National Science Board, Fellow of the British Academy and recipient of the National Medal of Science. Perhaps unsurprisingly, Solow was awarded the highest prize in economics in 1987 for his work on economic growth. Before the award he had been mentioned regularly as a possible Nobel laureate, which led him to quip: 'My friends have been telling me that I would get it if I lived long enough.'[3]

Yet, economic growth was not his first interest. Solow had intended to focus on statistics and econometrics in his academic career. He attributes his switch to macroeconomics to chance. He was allocated an office next to Nobel laureate Paul Samuelson at MIT. In his 1987

Nobel Prize autobiography, he commented: 'Thus began what is now almost forty years of almost daily conversations about economics, politics, our children, cabbages and kings.'[4]

Solow retired in 1995 to make room for younger scholars, though he remains active in numerous scholarly projects, and still occupies an office that was next to Samuelson's until the latter's death in 2009.

The Solow growth model

In influential articles in 1956 and 1957,[5] Robert Solow laid the foundations for understanding economic growth. The Solow growth model is the standard neoclassical model that is taught in every textbook, including mine. The best-known result from growth models is the Solow residual. The Solow residual refers to the unexplained portion of economic growth which isn't attributed to adding inputs such as workers and capital. The residual captures technological progress, which generates more output from a set of inputs. Of course, it also captures anything else not related to inputs of labour and investment, so temporary rises in government spending and monetary easing also get included. It means that some, but not all, of what is captured in the Solow residual is the productivity advancing technology needed to sustain economic growth over the longer term. This is the TFP (total factor productivity) mentioned earlier.

Across countries, there is a clear association between periods of high output growth and significant technological progress. Developed nations all grew well between 1950 and 1973, and then slowed together during 1974–87. There seems to be a connection with the adoption of similar technologies. For instance, the strong period of growth in the 1950s and 60s is associated with post-war technological advances, such as widespread air travel and industrial robots.

Curiously, recent technological improvements, centred on computing, information and communication technologies (ICT) and the internet, do not seem to have raised productivity across the economy. Solow's 1987 observation that 'You can see the computer age everywhere but in the productivity statistics' is known as the Solow paradox.[6] He revisited this question decades later, but concluded that we still do not know, as the role of computing is still evolving. Solow points out that since our lives and work have been transformed by computers, this technology should have improved our productivity. But productivity growth was slow from around 1970 to 1995, which is the period when computing took off. In a shorter period, from 1995 to 2000, productivity growth was faster, which may be attributed to the lagging effects of adopting computing. Solow believes it takes time for businesses to learn to use computers productively, so the early years were not a good indicator. In a 2002 interview he doubted that productivity growth would revert to the fast pace seen previously because 'Comparing the computer with electricity or the internal combustion engine just doesn't seem to me to be justified yet.' Solow also revealed: 'I always thought that the main difference the computer made in my office was that before the computer my secretary used to work for me, and afterward I worked for my secretary.'[7]

Solow's scepticism reflects one view that the ICT revolution would not generate as much economy-wide productivity improvement as the earlier Industrial Revolution that introduced general purpose technologies such as the steam engine during Adam Smith's era, or the Second Industrial Revolution that saw the introduction of railways and electrification during the period lasting from the late nineteenth century until the First World War. Others disagree and expect that productivity will improve once these new ICT and digital technologies become truly embedded into work practices and businesses. A major challenge to Solow's view is related to technology. The developers of endogenous growth models from the 1960s onwards criticized Solow for not explaining where technology came from.

Endogenous growth models treat technology as determined within the model; in other words, 'endogenously' generated by the capital and labour within an economy. The neoclassical Solow model was alleged to treat technological progress as if it were 'manna from heaven'. By contrast, endogenous growth theories attempt to explain how technological advances come about, raising the productivity of an economy. Those models say that educated researchers and investment in R&D are what generates technological improvements, which in turn boosts economic growth.

Solow was unconvinced by some of the assumptions of endogenous growth, particularly in its simplest form, known as the AK model. (The 'A' in the title of the model refers to the economics shorthand for technology, while 'K' refers to capital.) This theory says that the rate of technical improvement in an economy is proportional to its growth rate; in other words, technology and the economy grow at the same rate. Solow thought that process seemed too neat to be plausible. Although they differ in terms of how growth comes about, these models follow the implications set out by the Solow model. Endogenous growth theories extend Solow's neoclassical model in spelling out how innovators produce technological progress.

Another criticism relates to the work of Douglass North discussed in the previous chapter. A difficulty of the Solow model is that it can account for differences in growth rates across countries only by appealing to technological progress. So, institutions such as those favoured by North play little role in explaining why some countries are wealthy while most are not.

On the other hand, the Solow model can explain why countries have different levels of per capita income, and indicate whether we are converging to a slow-growth future. Growth should speed up if an economy is operating below its steady state, or the level of output that it is capable of producing. So, if an economy is starting to develop and has low levels of capital stock, then it should realize higher returns to its capital than a country which is developed and has had a lot of capital accumulation. If these economies have the same levels of technology, investment rate and population growth, then the developing country will grow faster than the developed one because of diminishing returns to capital discussed earlier. The output per worker gap between these countries will narrow over time as both economies approach the steady state. This important prediction of the neoclassical model is known as the convergence hypothesis: developing countries will grow faster than developed countries if they have the same steady state until they converge to the same income level.

Does this bear out empirically? If there is convergence, then there should be an inverse relationship between a nation's starting level of income and subsequent growth. Japan, which started at a much lower level of development in the post-war period, grew more quickly than other more developed economies. From 1950 to 1990, Japan experienced growth that was on average much faster than that of the US. For rich countries there was an inverse relationship between their initial level of per capita income and growth rate between 1880 and 1973. However, there is no clear relationship in more recent periods for either rich countries or all countries in the world. So, there is limited evidence of convergence.

Some poorer and middle-income countries (particularly China) have grown faster, and begun to catch up with wealthier nations, which is what the model predicts. But there are many poor countries that have grown slowly. In terms of the world income distribution, instead of seeing convergence, there have been signs of polarization between rich and poor nations.

What about those nations that are developed and experiencing a slowdown in growth? What can be done to raise productivity in advanced economies? It is a question that other nations may also eventually face.

The productivity challenge

The Organisation for Economic Co-operation and Development (OECD) highlights the productivity challenge as one of the biggest issues since the 2008 banking crisis.[8]

Britain is among the worst affected. By any number of metrics, UK productivity (output per hour) is lower than it should be based on pre-crisis trends, which is a puzzle. In other words, productivity growth has slowed down considerably since the crash.

One way to think about the immediate post-crash period is that it has been a job-rich recession. Employment recovered a year earlier than output, and unemployment never hit the 3-million mark reached during the recessions of the early 1980s and 1990s. But output per worker was lower during this period since less output was demanded in a recession than in normal times. Since the 2008 crisis, output per worker grew at just 0.2 per cent per year, which is a fraction of the 2.1 per cent average growth rate between 1972 and 2007. Wage flexibility helped to maintain jobs during the latest recession, a decline in real wages making it possible to keep people in work.[9]

Employers hoarding workers instead of laying them off doesn't explain the entire productivity puzzle.[10] Part of the answer may be that the British economy has a large services sector in which it is difficult to measure either investment or output accurately.[11] But the US also has a large services sector and doesn't suffer from the productivity problem to the same extent, so mismeasurement is unlikely to be the whole story either.

The Bank of England has concluded that output per hour is around 16 per cent lower than expected.[12] Unlike previous recessions, productivity hadn't picked up during the recovery. This is the essence of the 'productivity puzzle'.

That said, productivity growth was already slowing down before the crisis. The OECD points to low investment as an explanation. As a share of GDP, UK investment began to trail that of the US, Canada, France and Switzerland in the 1990s. Investment fell from around a quarter of GDP in the late 1980s to just over 15 per cent. Low investment means there's less productive capital for employees to work with, and thus lower output per worker.

This was also one of the conclusions of the Bank of England. They can explain between half to three-quarters of the productivity puzzle. Mismeasurement accounts for around a quarter. They then looked at cyclical factors related to the business cycle and also at the possible structural reasons behind lagging productivity, i.e. how the economy is structured as opposed to cyclical variations. Some of the cyclical factors concern hoarding workers and doing work that doesn't immediately add to output. Structural reasons include low capital investment and inefficient resource allocation, where workers are not moving from low- to high-productivity sectors. That can happen when there are high firm survival rates resulting in so-called zombie firms that have survived only due to the extraordinarily low interest rate environment.

This is not just a UK problem, however. The term 'secular stagnation' has been revived as a concern for all developed economies and requires revisiting our models of growth. The slow recovery of the United States was what led Harvard economist Lawrence Summers to warn about a slow-growth future for advanced economies. At the forefront of this issue is Japan. Since its early 1990s crash it has experienced several 'lost decades' of growth, not helped by the survival of zombie firms in its initial recovery, which contributed to those unproductive years. Since then, Japan has launched the most aggressive economic policy in the world in an attempt to end decades of stagnation. As the rich economy with the most aged population, which is an important factor contributing to secular stagnation, how Japan fares will hold lessons for others.

Japan's 'lost decades'

Japan's growth since the early 1990s has hovered around 0–1 per cent and productivity growth has been poor. The three major economic policy 'arrows' introduced by Japanese prime minister Shinzo Abe at the end of 2012 with the aim of revitalizing the world's third largest economy have been dubbed 'Abenomics'.

The first arrow – aggressive expansion of the money supply in an attempt to end deflation or price declines – has failed to hit the target consistently. There have been positive signs, but the challenge of ending years of stagnant prices is immense. Stock markets have hit multi-year highs but the real economy hasn't benefited sufficiently. Higher market valuations alone have not been enough for firms to raise wages that are fundamental to sustaining price rises. They are instead looking for more output per worker in order to justify higher pay. Average real wages were hit by the 2008 crisis and are yet to recover fully.

The second arrow, fiscal policy, hasn't quite hit the mark either. In one instance, a 2014 government decision to raise the sales tax from 5 per cent to 8 per cent, the first such increase in seventeen years, squeezed spending and tipped the economy back into recession. In its immediate aftermath, GDP contracted at an annualized pace of 7.3 per cent in the April–June quarter, the worst contraction since the economy shrank by 15 per cent in the 2008 global financial crisis. This mirrored 1997, when a sales tax increase had sent the economy into recession, revealing an underlying weakness of demand. Raising taxes was intended to reduce Japan's indebtedness. It was always the case that any attempt to address the country's staggering debt, which at around 240 per cent of GDP is the highest in the world, would be an economic drag, but the scale of it is a reminder of the fragility of the revival of the Japanese economy.

The hardest arrow to score with was always going to be the third – the structural reforms that target the way that the economy is constituted and run. How can Japan raise productivity when its population and labour force are shrinking? Can firms be enticed to invest in a country where consumption demand is low after years of stagnation have taken their toll and people are concerned about taking on debt? Abe's structural reforms include over 240 initiatives to raise productivity. Such reforms take time, and ministers warn that it could take a decade for Abenomics to work. So it may be years before the positive impact of any structural reforms are felt. Abe is Japan's sixth prime minister in ten years. Time is seemingly a luxury for Japan's leaders, yet it's the very thing that they need to turn around an economy that's been struggling for decades, during which Japan has fallen from the world's second largest economy to its third.

The country that overtook it also faces slower growth and an ageing population. For a middle-income country, China has a demographic profile that is similar to rich nations. Its working-age population is shrinking, though it has ended its 'one child policy' to counter the ageing demography. Also, if Britain and America as well as Japan are counting on innovation to keep them rich, China needs to get there before its growth slows down, as discussed in previous chapters.

For Europe, the focus is also growth, and a lot is hanging on the governments' ability to deliver. German Chancellor Angela Merkel has said that the legitimacy of the European project depends on people becoming better off. So the European Union is also focused on raising growth through investment, as discussed in the chapter on John Maynard Keynes.

Raising growth and productivity to counteract a stagnant future is, then, a common challenge for major economies. And it is one that has been increasingly recognized by policymakers. Turning to Great Britain, the government has begun to focus on economic growth, particularly with respect to its particularly worrying low-productivity challenge.

The UK government's renewed focus on growth

During the 2008 banking crash, 'benign neglect' of the productivity issue by successive governments who were focused on the immediate crisis meant there was insufficient attention paid to economic growth. As the country worst affected by the global productivity slowdown, Britain has since placed this issue at the centre of its economic growth agenda. For one thing, following research by the Bank of England and others, the government has focused on raising investment.

For instance, it has established a National Infrastructure Commission. The UK needs investments in 'hard' infrastructure (such as transport links) as well as 'soft' (such as digital networks), which can be just as important to induce business investment. Britain's track record on this issue has been somewhat mixed. Development of the digital economy has been impressive in some respects. For instance, Silicon Roundabout in London has attracted more venture capital than other European cities. But there are also areas of the country where even getting a mobile phone signal is challenging. The other significant area where investment is needed is skills. Business surveys routinely point to a skills shortage cramping their growth. It seems that investment is needed in physical and also digital infrastructure as well as in human capital.

Greater devolution of taxation powers to local governments decentralizes decision-making authority, which can boost investment. It has worked in Germany and China, where local banks and authorities have better knowledge of their regions. But it can also create inefficient competition among localities and generate duplicative activities that are protected by local vested interests.

Increasing private investment is needed, so clarity about policies and transparent regulations matter. As one example, some companies are deterred from making sizeable infrastructure investments, which can otherwise be attractive owing to their fixed returns, by regulatory changes. Others worry about Brexit, which adds to uncertainty over Britain's future economic relationship with the European Union.

Increasing public investment can help to boost private investment, as government expenditure in infrastructure can have a 'crowding in' effect. In other words, government investment can make private investment more efficient, for example good telecoms infrastructure increases the returns to a pound invested by a private company. Yet, public investment since 1997 has averaged just 2.4 per cent of GDP, which is 1.1 percentage points below the average for the G7 advanced economies.

As mentioned before in the Keynes chapter, the debate concerns whether the government should take advantage of very low interest rates to borrow and increase public investment. Keynesians would support separating government investment from current budgetary spending because investing today will generate greater returns in the future.

It's not just government policy, of course, that matters for investment. The Bank of England also identified misallocation of capital as a related issue. To invest, businesses need financing. It's less of a problem for large firms, but the vast majority of the country's businesses are small. A financial system dominated by banks that have been focused more on repairing their balance sheets than on lending is an impediment. Turning to capital markets is less easy because of the small size of Britain's debt markets for companies. It's an issue that the US does not face since most lending comes not from banks but from bond or stock markets, where companies issue debt or shares to raise funds. It's also an issue for the EU, which is trying to reduce reliance on bank lending through the creation of a new Capital Markets Union that aims to promote a larger and more integrated debt market in the European Union.

There's no question that investment is important, and it's related to the structural issues that underpin the productivity puzzle in the UK. The topic of low wages was discussed in the Joan Robinson chapter. Lower pay means that some companies hire workers instead of installing more units of capital, which depresses investment.[13]

The OECD has looked at this issue and finds that weak output growth is a drag on productivity. That brings us full circle in that output per worker or machine can't increase strongly if overall economic growth remains subdued. Importantly, wages are related to productivity. The OECD says that, because labour productivity has been 'exceptionally weak' since the crisis, real wages and per capita GDP or average incomes have largely been flat. So it's not just the economy as a whole that suffers, but individuals too.

Even if concern about the recent decline in output per worker is less of one because jobs have been preserved, the longer-term trend is still a great source of worry since productivity matters for economic growth. For instance, the sustainable way for us all to enjoy higher incomes requires increasing productivity. The causes of low productivity are not entirely unknown, and the consequences affect our future standards of living. So, if the productivity puzzle has become more prominent on the policy agenda, then that helps the government to focus on what really matters for the long-term standard of living in the UK.

Solow on the slow-growth dilemma

What would Robert Solow have suggested as a solution to the slow-growth dilemma?

Ensuring that investment stays buoyant is particularly urgent after a financial crisis and recession. Solow has argued that long-run growth prospects can be affected by an economic downturn. This has been an issue for Europe for many years. He observed:

> as suggested for instance by the history of the large European econo-mies since 1979, it is impossible to believe that the equilibrium growth path itself is unaffected by the short- to medium-run experience. In particular the amount and directions of capital formation is bound to be affected by the business cycle, whether through gross investment in new equipment or through the accelerated scrapping of old equipment.[14]

Low investment tends to follow a financial crisis in which banks were not lending and firms were not keen to invest. This can have lasting effects on the growth potential of an economy. So, business cycles, which are considered to be short- or medium-run events, can alter the long-term prospects of an economy. This was seen in Japan after its early 1990s crash and is now a worry in the aftermath of the 2008 financial crisis for the US, UK, the euro area and other devel-oped economies.

Solow also points out that related high unemployment, which is an issue for the euro area after the 2010 crisis that erupted with a bailout for Greece, can have an impact on an economy's future as joblessness could cause it to be stuck on a lower growth path for a long time: 'I am also inclined to believe that the segmentation of the labor market by occupation, industry and region, with varying amounts of unem-ployment from one segment to another, will also react back on the equilibrium path.'[15]

This is the well-known concept of hysteresis, whereby long stints in unemployment render workers' skills obsolete. It impedes them from rejoining the labour market and thus reduces the number of productive workers, meaning that unemployment will remain higher than before the crisis and hurt the country's growth potential. The lingering high rates of unemployment in the euro area, particularly youth unemployment, which has been in double digits in some coun-tries for nearly a decade, highlight this concern of Solow's. Workers are crucially important in economic growth models, as they are not just the labourers but also the innovators.

Thus, Solow would most likely agree that more investment to boost growth is needed. In his model, technological progress, the crucial ingredient in economic growth, could be impeded through low investment: 'much technological progress, maybe most of it, could find its way into actual production only with the use of new and different capital equipment. Therefore the effectiveness of innovation in increasing output would be paced by the rate of gross investment.'[16]

Reversing the decline in investment, especially since the 2008 crisis, takes on a new urgency, since as Solow observed: 'the way remains open for a reasonable person to believe that the stimulation of investment will favor faster intermediate-run growth through its effect on the transfer of technology from laboratory to factory'.[17]

In short, whether we face a slow-growth future depends on increasing investment and decreasing unemployment, because both of these factors affect the innovation and technology improvements that underpin economic growth, as per Solow's model. Since technology determines the prospects of an economy, how much is invested in capital and people matters a great deal. Those productive factors determine how innovative an economy can be, and thus its economic future, or its new equilibrium path. In Solow's view:

> The new equilibrium path will depend on the amount of capital accumulation that has taken place during the period of disequilibrium, and probably also on the amount of unemployment, especially long-term unemployment, that has been experienced. Even the level of technology may be different, if technological change is endogenous [determined by the amount of capital and workers in the economy] rather than arbitrary [where innovations happen from time to time in a less deterministic way].[18]

The new path of economic growth, whether it is fast or slow, is within the control of the government and shaped by the decisions of firms and workers, so it is not just the inevitable outcome of an ageing society or other factors. Some of Japan's economic stagnation is thought to be related to its demographics since its population is the oldest and fastest ageing in the world. Its heavy investment in robot-ics is perhaps one way of using technology to supplement a shrinking workforce. Instead of workers producing output, they may be substi-tuted by robots producing that output. But that also raises the prospect that robots will lead to unemployment in certain sectors. Automated production of goods and services might just be used to replace retiring workers, but it could force some out of a job too.

Solow would view the possibility that we face a slow-growth future as depending on how investment and workers fare, since they determine the productivity growth of the economy. Investment by governments (which hinges on the austerity debate from the earlier chapter on Keynes) or private firms can help restore the capital stock that has plummeted since the crisis which would help to reduce the likelihood of a slow-growth future. Government can make it more attractive to invest by providing tax incentives to promote innova-tion or improve infrastructure. So long as investment can be increased, then Solow would not view a slow-growth future as inevitable. His model is based on growth deriving from capital accumulated through investment and productive workers, so policies to support both of those factors of production would generate more output.

It's challenging, as seen in Japan, and some factors like demograph-ics are difficult to alter, but the above suggestions can help and the advent of new technologies could be game changing. Solow would probably view the debate over whether the technologies of the digital era are as productive as the steam engine or electrification of the earl-ier industrial revolutions as being related to investment. If the computer age is to increase productivity and so lead to a stronger phase of economic growth, it will require investment in not just R&D but also people's skills and firms' practices to embed those technologies into how businesses operate.

The basic tenets of Robert Solow's model of economic growth point the way forward. As the saying goes, demography is not des-tiny. After all, as I write this, Solow is an active economist working well into his nineties.

★

Robert Solow is not only a scholar but also understands the importance of contributing to public discussions of economic issues. He once wrote an essay entitled 'How Economic Ideas Turn to Mush'. He observed that it was challenging to convey complicated ideas outside one's profession. Once an economic idea reaches the public, it has been changed in one way or another.[19] Solow offers this advice to economists:

> Try to formulate an economic problem in a very clear, focused way. Try to answer one question at a time, and insist on that. And above all – this is really what's difficult – at least I know that I tend to forget it: Don't omit qualifications. Never claim more than you actually believe or can justify. What makes that hard is that what people want – especially if they're being fed it in sound bites on a television program or in a two-sentence quotation in *The Wall Street Journal* – what they want is something very definite. They don't ever want those qualifications. And you must never let them off that hook. The interesting thing is that I think it's useful. An economist trying to talk to the general public gains respect by insisting on the qualifications, by not appearing as a pundit, as someone who knows all the answers.[20]

Solow may also be one of the few academics who appreciates the importance of work–life balance. Each summer he decamps to Martha's Vineyard, a popular seaside retreat for those living in Massachusetts, where he works on his research and also sails.[21] He had spent some of his million-dollar Nobel Prize money on a jib for his boat. Even in his leisurely pursuits, Solow sees parallels with the life of an economist:

> Apart from the activity itself, the main thing I like about sailing is that it teaches you that the water and the wind out there don't give a damn about you. They're doing whatever the laws of physics tell them to do and your problem is to adjust as best you can. And learning to adjust, to adapt, is not a bad thing for economists to learn either: Adapt to changes in the world . . . You've got to fit your model to the world, not the world to your model.[22]

Epilogue: The Future of Globalization

Economic prosperity has been linked to globalization. The rapid global economic growth of the post-war period was accompanied by the fast expansion of international trade and investment. As we buy goods and access information, often without regard to national borders, it's unlikely that globalization will be rolled back. But trade expansion and the opening up of markets are stalling. The global trade system covering nearly all nations' exports and imports under the World Trade Organization (WTO) is fragmenting into a set of accompanying regional and bilateral free trade agreements. This colossal challenge to the future of globalization and the growth of the world economy would benefit from the ideas of the Great Economists.

A couple of dramatic events in the past few years have highlighted a backlash against the uneven gains from globalization. Although there are numerous differences between Britain's decision to leave the European Union and the ascendancy of political outsider Donald Trump to the White House, the two events reveal a number of things about the electorate's discontent with the status quo, including globalization.

In a historic referendum in June 2016, Britain became the first sovereign nation to vote to leave the European Union. Some of the surveys of voters suggest that a backlash against globalization played a role in Brexit, alongside dominant themes such as sovereignty and immigration. The UK government has insisted that Britain will maintain its global outlook, which will constitute a different set of policies than its current trading relationships with EU and non-EU countries, and will certainly be important to future prosperity.

Across the Atlantic, in the closely fought 2016 US presidential election, Republican candidate Trump had identified international trade as one of the problems confronting America that he would fix in order to 'Make America Great Again'. In his inauguration speech, Trump made it clear that, in his administration, economic policy would be driven by the principle of 'America First'. He said it means there are two rules: 'Buy American, Hire American'. Of course, as in Britain, the disaffection of the US electorate is not just with trade. But the targeting of globalization in response to economic challenges reflects an underlying discontent with the uneven benefits from opening up to the global economy. Populism fuelling anti-establishment sentiment poses a challenge to current economic policies.

Trump's predecessor, Barack Obama, attributes some of the discontent to globalization:

> Globalization combined with technology combined with social media and constant information have disrupted people's lives in very concrete ways – a manufacturing plant closes and suddenly an entire town no longer has what was the primary source of employment – and people are less certain of their national identities or their place in the world . . . There is no doubt [this] has produced populist movements both from the left and the right in many countries in Europe . . . When you see a Donald Trump and a Bernie Sanders – very unconventional candidates who had considerable success – then obviously there is something there that is being tapped into: a suspicion of globalization, a desire to rein in its excesses, a suspicion of elites and governing institutions that people feel may not be responsive to their immediate needs.[1]

So, is globalization in trouble? What would the Great Economists make of this backlash against it? And, most importantly, what would they advise to best help the losers from it?

The changing face of free trade

There has been a shift away from multilateral trade deals that apply to all WTO members, which encompass the near totality of trading nations. There is still a push for free trade agreements that reduce tariffs, and to adopt other measures to ease trade and investment, but these are increasingly in the form of regional and bilateral trade agreements. Europe has trade and customs agreements either agreed or pending with some eighty countries, all but a handful of them with other WTO members, which reflects the importance of continued liberalization and opening up of overseas markets for trade beyond the current coverage of the WTO.

Let's remind ourselves what tariffs encompass and why they are economically inefficient. Tariffs are the charges that governments impose on imports and exports. They are effectively a tax, so can distort prices. Because tariffs add a cost, and thus reduce economic efficiency, they can be a drag on growth. Free trade agreements (FTAs) such as the EU's single market, aim to eliminate most of them. But, a number of governments use tariffs to protect their industries from competition from bigger global rivals until they are more mature. Labour groups also want protection for domestic jobs. So, tariffs are more than just an economic decision to impose a tax. There are often political motives behind their imposition.

There are also non-tariff barriers (NTBs) to add to the mix. These are the other ways to be protectionist without imposing tariffs, such as through insisting on standards for certain industries that can restrict imports. For instance, Thai prawn exporters found it hard to meet American standards for the type of net that allowed them to sell to the US. Regulations matter even more for the services sector, which is the biggest part of the British, American and most other major economies. This is the main reason for the push by the EU for an international agreement on services. The Trade in Services Agreement (TiSA) has the potential of opening up the biggest part of the global economy and becoming a major element of the next big round of multilateral trade liberalization under the WTO. TiSA was launched in 2013 and attempts to open up the services market, which comprises 70 per cent of global and EU GDP but only 25 per cent of world and EU exports. In other words, trade in goods may have been liberalized under the current WTO regime, but for major economies the biggest part of their national output, which is services, faces barriers in global markets.

Countries want to reduce trade barriers, and are increasingly seeking to do so via regional FTAs that are in addition to their WTO membership. Had President Trump not pulled the US out, the

Trans-Pacific Partnership (TPP) would have been the world's biggest free trade area, linking North America with Pacific Rim countries encompassing parts of Latin America and Asia. The US under the Obama administration had hoped to gain from this new trade agreement since 61 per cent of US goods exports and 75 per cent of US agricultural exports go to the Asia Pacific region. The European Union has also been pursuing an equally ambitious free trade agreement with America. The Transatlantic Trade and Investment Partnership (TTIP) would be a FTA that would link the US with the EU.

The pursuit of massive regional FTAs is a reaction to the World Trade Organization expansion stalling. It has been a long time since the last big WTO initiative, the Doha Round of 2001, where countries launched negotiations to open global markets up further. So, instead of trying to wrangle a deal with almost the entire world, regional trade agreements have sprung up and bilateral agreements have expanded, though it would be better for all countries to trade on the same terms with all others.

The problem with this approach is that if a country hasn't signed up to the rules of the new free trade areas (or hasn't even been invited to join), it's excluded and can't share the benefits. Being left out of TPP and the TTIP means China is striking its own deals. China is negotiating with ASEAN (Association of Southeast Asian Nations) and other Asian nations to form a regional free trade agreement, the Regional Comprehensive Economic Partnership (RCEP). China had also offered to set up a Free Trade Area of the Asia Pacific (FTAAP) as an alternative to the TPP.

These regional FTAs are not the best outcome relative to a multilateral agreement under the WTO, but perhaps they're better than not having any new trade deals at all. The creation of sizeable free trade areas where domestic companies can gain economies of scale by selling to a much larger customer base than would otherwise be possible is one of the motivations, especially for smaller economies.

That's why Southeast Asia is also pursuing an ambitious free trade area. The single market that ASEAN launched at the end of 2015, known as the ASEAN Economic Community (AEC), is comparable to the EU in terms of population. With over 600 million people, the

AEC links the ten nations of Southeast Asia ranging from rich Singapore to poor Laos into a bloc aiming for the removal of tariffs and sharing common standards. The AEC intends to rival the EU and perhaps even eventually overtake it, based on the 5 per cent plus economic growth rate of ASEAN as compared to the 1–2 per cent growth of the EU. The AEC is also considering a single visa regime, akin to an Asian version of Europe's Schengen Agreement.

ASEAN policymakers emphasize that the impetus behind the AEC is to compete with the sizeable markets of the EU and the US as well as neighbouring China and India. With twice the population of the United States and one that is similar to the scale of the EU, the AEC has the potential to become one of the largest economic entities in the world. If, like the EU, the AEC becomes a common reference point for the rest of the world and, like the US, a market that global businesses feel obliged to be in, then it will have succeeded. It seems that Southeast Asians certainly have that ambition.

The US is adding uncertainty by focusing on bilateral trade agreements, which is a significant change from its previous agenda of multilateral and regional free trade. For President Donald Trump, the reason is that he is putting 'America First'. With the shift in the world's biggest economy, the question of how to address the backlash against globalization will be even more important.

Trumpism

The rise of Donald Trump is perhaps the most striking example of how those who have lost out economically in the past few decades sought a political outlet to convey their frustrations. An exit poll of voters conducted by *The New York Times* revealed that his voters thought the economy was performing poorly and their families' financial situation was worse as compared to those who voted for Democratic candidate Hillary Clinton.[2] There are other causes of disaffection. But globalization is in Trump's sights. This has worrying ramifications.

As discussed in the Joan Robinson chapter, median wages have been stagnant in America for forty years. The picture hasn't improved with the 2009 Great Recession. Jobs occupied by those in the middle of the wage spectrum, earning roughly $13.83–21.13 per hour, made up about 60 per cent of those lost during the last recession, but just 27 per cent of those created in the recovery. And it's not just in this recession. I recall attending a lecture by then President Bill Clinton who spoke about how many jobs had been created in the recovery after the early 1990s recession. A woman raised her hand and said, 'Yes, Mr. President, I have three of those jobs and still can't make ends meet.'

Economists attribute the stagnation of living standards to two main factors: globalization and 'skill-biased technical change'. The latter refers to technological progress benefiting skilled workers. In the US and across the industrialized countries, innovations such as computerization and automation have complemented and enhanced the skills of professionals. But the same innovations have replaced jobs that used to be done by people in the middle of the skill spectrum. The growth of automation especially has dramatically changed manufacturing. The number of robots has been increasing and, although presently concentrated in sectors like automobile production, their use is spreading throughout the economy. Hence jobs at either end of the skill distribution are growing, while those in the middle are declining.

This is intertwined with globalization. As discussed in the Ricardo chapter, trade creates 'losers' when an economy imports what was previously made domestically. The 'winners' are those who work in the industries that are expanding because a country is specializing in that sector and exporting from it. As US imports of manufactured goods have increased, mid-skilled jobs in that sector have been disappearing. After growing from 13 million jobs in 1950 to peak at nearly 20 million in 1980, 2010 saw a drop to a historic low of about 11.5 million. A rebound since the recession has taken manufacturing employment up to around 12.3 million, although this is still lower than in 1950. It's a similar pattern in the UK. Around 2.6 million people work in manufacturing, a figure that has halved since the late 1970s. Manufacturing accounts for 8 per cent of all jobs, down from a quarter in 1978.

This combination of factors has resulted in a lack of improvement in living standards for many Americans in the middle of the income distribution, and it's a big part of the dissatisfaction with the status quo expressed in the last election.

I had my own experience of the rise of Trump when I presented a documentary for the BBC titled *Linda for Congress*. I went on the road to take the pulse of the electorate before the 2016 elections by embarking on a hypothetical campaign to run to become a United States congresswoman. We 'hired' a campaign manager, a pollster, a fundraiser, a speech writer, etc. – the whole set of political campaign staff. As an economist and broadcaster, I am familiar with politicians but it never occurred to me to want to become one.

In order to remain impartial, I ran as an Independent. That worsened my chances straight away because I didn't have the support, financial and otherwise, or the voter base of the Democratic or Republican party. John Whitbeck, the head of the Republican Party in Virginia, said that he would 'crush' me if I ran against his guy.

Jokingly, I hope, because that's where my hypothetical district was. We chose Virginia because it's one of the handful of super-swing states in the US presidential election. It's purple in complexion (a blend of Democrats and Republicans, so blue and red), and that was reflected in the fact that it had a Democratic governor but was represented by predominately Republican Congress members. We focused on the 5th District, since the incumbent was a Republican while the previous one had been a Democrat.

I travelled through the state to meet voters. I met a tobacco farmer in Keysville who ran a global business selling his crops, including soybeans, to Russia, Vietnam and Brazil, among others. I met him in his impressive house on ten acres of land with its own lake and horses. As an exporter, he was supportive of open global markets, but he did not think that globalization worked for Americans. For instance, he told me that he was opposed to President Obama's trade and immigration policies, which promoted greater openness. But, when I asked him about how he ran his farm, he told me that he wrote to his congressman to help get permission to employ his Mexican farmhands.

I experienced similar reactions at a Methodist church in Farmville and a Christmas Parade in Cumberland. The voters I met were a mix of Republicans and Democrats, among whom was a grandmother who was watching the parade on the back of a pick-up truck with her extended family. This housekeeper told me that it seemed wrong for a family of six to live on just $12 an hour. She, like most of the others I had met, were blue-collar workers whose livelihoods had been squeezed by globalization and technological change that has shrunk the number of mid-skilled, well-paid factory jobs.

And, like others, she was voting for Trump, though they were nice about my hypothetical campaign. What stuck with me was the support that Trump had, especially among those who believed that they had lost out in the past few decades. Now that Trump is president, his supporters want a bigger piece of the economic pie.

Helping the losers from globalization

The question is how best to do so. This challenge isn't just for America but for any nation where the benefits of globalization have not been shared fairly.

The impressive growth of emerging economies in the past few decades has led to less inequality between nations as more poor countries 'catch up' to rich ones during an era where markets around the world have become increasingly connected through trade and investment. Globalization has helped emerging economies to grow well since they have been able to export to America and Europe while benefiting from Western investment.

So, because of the relatively faster growth of emerging economies, inequality has fallen across nations as the income gap has narrowed between developed and developing countries. Yet, global income inequality has stayed largely unchanged. That's because *within* countries, inequality on average has either failed to improve significantly or, in some cases, even become worse.

Recall from the Alfred Marshall chapter how sharp the rise in inequality has been in America. Inequality in America has risen so much that the current era has been dubbed a Second Gilded Age.

Although not always so stark, inequality is a problem for many nations, including Britain, where economic disparity has contributed to a backlash against globalization and even against capitalism itself. The term 'inclusive growth', which refers to economic growth that benefits everyone in a society, has been touted in the United Kingdom. It's also been heard in America, which has suffered from a 'squeezed' middle class and stagnant wages.

Though the rise in income inequality can be partly traced to globalization, that does not suggest the remedy is to be found in trade policy alone. As detailed in the David Ricardo chapter, there are certainly distributional effects from trade – some groups will win, others will lose – even if the overall economy gains. But there are other factors at play too. It's difficult to disentangle the effects on inequality stemming from trade from those that arise due to technological change that rewards the highly skilled more than those workers in the middle of the skill spectrum; the latter has a larger impact. Even though there are measures that can be included in trade agreements to ensure that appropriate standards for labour and environment protection are met, domestic policy measures such as redistribution and government spending on skills are more likely to be able to address directly growing inequality.

An example of a fiscal policy that can aid redistribution and economic growth is government-backed investment in both hard and soft infrastructure, as noted in the Keynes chapter. With low borrowing costs after the financial crisis, the US, British, European, Japanese and other governments don't have to pay much to raise capital on bond markets, so it may be a good time to invest, as discussed in that chapter. Infrastructure investment could generate well-paid, middle-skilled jobs, since the sector spans manufacturing as well as the digital economy. Such targeted fiscal policy could raise incomes for certain segments of the population instead of general policies that redistribute income. Improving infrastructure and raising the income of the middle class who comprise the bulk of consumers are both likely to increase growth.

Helping the losers from globalization and addressing inequality should, then, be primarily a domestic rather than a trade issue for governments. Yet, the backlash against globalization focuses policymakers' attention on trade agreements, which means that further opening up is under strain. But the burst of foreign direct investment that accompanied the rapid growth of international trade since the early 1990s was one of the reasons developing countries grew so well that a billion people were lifted out of extreme poverty and reduced the gap between them and rich nations.

What would our Great Economists make of all of this? Would they say globalization is in trouble?

Great Economists on the backlash against globalization

For Adam Smith and David Ricardo, pursuing free trade would be at the top of their priorities. During the era of the classical economists, which included the repeal of the Corn Laws, being an open economy helped the UK punch above its weight in the world. They would undoubtedly urge countries to focus on the benefits of globalization.

For Karl Marx, the election of Trump may be read as a populist revolt against the capitalists who have gained from globalization while the working classes have lost out. Joan Robinson, who latterly supported communist regimes in China and North Korea, may well share that sentiment. Their aims would include wanting to see a radical change in institutions, particularly around employment, to address inequities.

Consistent with his policies to reduce inequality, Alfred Marshall would urge using moderate redistribution in terms of taxes and transfers to help the losers from globalization. Given his later conversion to redistributive policies, he would probably agree that the focus should be on domestic and not mainly trade policies to address the distributional impact from globalization.

Irving Fisher would be watching for signs of major economies turning inward, which would add to the risk of repeating the 1930s. That's when protectionist measures such as the Smoot–Hawley Act imposed high tariffs on imports into the United States, which worsened the Great Depression. Fisher would also be monitoring the impact of heightened economic uncertainty stemming from growing anti-globalization sentiment on international investors who buy government debt and determine the borrowing cost for all of us. The less well-off would be hit hardest as they are more likely to rely on loans to fund their homes, for instance.

For John Maynard Keynes, an active government which spent to help the losers from globalization would be an answer. He would advocate increasing public investment to create those middle-skilled jobs that have been hollowed out by the globalization process. He would certainly not shy away from deploying an array of domestic policies to address the backlash against globalization and boost economic growth at the same time.

His contemporary Joseph Schumpeter would concur with the need for all nations to maintain their global outlook. More open and competitive markets speed up the process of creative destruction, which is good for growth in the long run. He wrote during the depths of the Great Depression and subsequent world war, so unsurprisingly, he would value openness to the world and say that it was essential for strongly growing nations.

Friedrich Hayek and Milton Friedman would agree. They would advocate for free markets, in particular, ensuring that political events such as Trump's America First policy and Brexit did not mean that the US and Britain turned inward and compromised the operation of markets. Hayek viewed globalization as enabling path-breaking nations to move ahead, which then allowed other countries to benefit from catch-up growth by imitating successful nations. They would applaud both the openness of many markets around the world and the greater interconnectedness of nations that followed.

Douglass North would urge an examination of where the current trade deals have failed to address the concerns of losers and reform them where appropriate. He may also embody the most pertinent views as to how to manage Brexit in particular. Britain leaving the EU presents a circumstance entirely different from that of a country seeking a trade agreement afresh. North's work stresses how path dependence and history matter. For him, building on existing institutions would be vital to formulating a future relationship between the UK and the EU.

Robert Solow would stress that investment is key to stronger growth and better jobs. But international agreements on investments are few (the EU and China intend to agree one), so he would presumably support a push to set common standards on investment and liberalize or open up the services sector, for which rules and regulations are more important than tariffs.

Undoubtedly, most of the Great Economists would strongly advocate for a continuing process of liberalization and not a turn inward, given how important globalization has been for economic growth. The sentiment would be even stronger for their intellectual followers who have lived through the extraordinary period of globalization since the end of the Cold War in the early 1990s and incorporated such insights into their research. There are many who have benefited from the pioneering research of the Great Economists, but MIT's Paul Samuelson stands out. His theories embody the synthesis of Keynesian and neoclassical ideas that characterize economics today. Samuelson helped develop the 'neoclassical synthesis' approach, which is the basic framework for modern macroeconomics, discussed in the Keynes chapter.

In addition, Paul Samuelson's seminal work furthered David Ricardo's model and has become the standard set of theories for analysing the impact of international trade on the economies of trading nations. Samuelson's research explained how trade boosted growth, but at the same time unevenly affected workers. His work can help us think about the 'losers' from international trade. So, the ideas of this great economist can point to how to address the backlash against globalization.

Paul Samuelson, 'the last of the great general economists'

Paul Samuelson was born in 1915 and came of age in the 1930s, when the rise of protectionism worsened the US economy. Samuelson was the leading Keynesian in America after the Second World War, although he described himself as a 'cafeteria Keynesian' as he merely selected the parts that he liked.[3] He adopted Keynesianism after being taught by top neoclassical economists at the University of Chicago, where he enrolled at the age of sixteen, after which he obtained his PhD at Harvard University and joined MIT in 1940.

Regarding his approach to economics, Samuelson remarked: 'I did not throw out my education lightly, but what I was being taught was of no use in explaining what I saw around me. It was the Great Depression . . . Keynesianism really fitted what was going on pretty well.'[4]

But he changed his mind after 1967: 'I had distrust . . . of American Keynesianism. For better or worse, US Keynesianism was so far ahead of where it started.'[5]

Samuelson had by then joined together neoclassical economic thought with John Maynard Keynes's approach, a consensus view that had starting emerging in the post-war period, into a framework known as 'neoclassical synthesis'. Samuelson's textbook *Economics* helped to popularize this approach. It has been in continuous print since 1948. Later editions were revised by Yale economist William Nordhaus; the nineteenth edition was published in 2009, the year of his death. *Economics* was the best-selling economics textbook for decades; millions of copies were sold worldwide. Samuelson was quoted as saying: 'Let those who will, write the nation's laws if I can write its textbooks.'[6] As a sign of his stature, he was awarded the Nobel Prize in 1970, the first American to be recognized, in the second year of the annual award.

So, this great economist's work, including his ideas on trade, embodies the legacy of the dominant mainstream strands of economics that we have covered in this book. When he passed away at age ninety-four, *The Economist* described him as the 'last of the great general economists'.[7] Samuelson was a generalist who worked on a wide range of issues concerning the economy, such as trade and public finance. He didn't specialize in any one area, as later economists tended to do.

It's fitting that this final chapter includes what this 'last of the great general economists' would have made of the backlash against globalization. Paul Samuelson just missed the recovery from the global financial crisis that has heightened the debate over the impact of globalization. His work on the welfare effects of trade, building on the Ricardian model, can help assess how globalization policies can be reshaped, given the political discontent revealed by Brexit and Trumpism.

His research has helped to explain how people's livelihoods are affected by trade; specifically, he has shown how trade affects wages and incomes within a country. His factor price equalization theorem says that, when nations trade, prices of traded goods will converge, and so would the wages of those producing those products. That means that wages in America will decline and move towards those of its trading partner, for example China, over time in the traded sectors. It helps to explain the stagnant median wages of particularly blue-collar workers, especially in manufacturing.

Trade, therefore, has a direct impact on incomes and standards of living. Having helped to identify this effect, Samuelson, whose approximate lineage is Keynesian, would be likely to have looked to domestic fiscal policy to help the 'losers' from globalization. Based on his work on social welfare or welfare for a society, he would have recommended that all such redistributive policies be judged through the lens of an ethical observer to decide which policy was better than another. The challenging practicalities of implementing such an approach also helps explain why good policies are not always adopted.

But leaving the distributional consequences of globalization unaddressed would allow the negative attitudes against globalization to continue and doubts could even be raised over whether it is beneficial to trade. That is worrying for the future of global economic growth itself. The challenge would be getting leaders to act. An adviser to US presidents, Paul Samuelson once remarked: 'I can't think of a President who has been overburdened by a knowledge of economics.'[8]

At least the right questions are now being asked, even though the solutions are not straightforward. Samuelson would have approved. He once quipped: 'Good questions outrank easy answers.'[9]

The way forward

Brexit and Trumpism are among the most prominent political expressions of discontent with the status quo. Globalization's unequal impact, creating winners and losers, is part of that status quo. But there are other factors, such as robotics and automation, at play too.

Still, it can be easier to be unhappy with globalization because it is more discernible than the impact of encroaching technological change. If trade did not improve welfare and benefit a nation, then Samuelson believed that countries wouldn't engage in it and would revert to a state of 'autarky' in which there was no international trade.[10] Yet there has been trade among nations for centuries; it is a question of addressing where and why trade doesn't work for everyone.

That would be precisely the sort of challenge that the Great Economists would relish. For them, the chance to redefine how globalization is managed so that the benefits can be spread more widely would be viewed as an opportunity to rethink some fundamental concepts. They would surely embrace as intellectually stimulating the challenge of re-examining how to raise the quality of economic growth and not just its speed. Explaining how the economy optimally operates, and analysing what hasn't worked and how that can be improved, is how they made their collective mark on the world.

The Great Economists in this book set the foundations of economics and crafted the models that underpin the field to this day. They formulated the general models to explain how the economy works. From Adam Smith's 'invisible hand' to the Solow model of economic growth, we have, respectively, the general model of how an efficient market operates and what generates prosperity. The Great Economists also shared a propensity to push the boundaries of economics to come up with models that better explained the real world; for example Joan Robinson was not content with the assumption that markets operated perfectly all the time so she developed a theory of imperfect competition.

And the Great Economists were all drawn to the most pressing economic issues of the day, for which they offered analyses and ways forward. Recall that David Ricardo's theory of international trade contributed to the repeal of the protectionist Corn Laws, while John Maynard Keynes played a part in the recovery after the 1930s Great Depression. Milton Friedman tackled the cause of that depression, which helped the central bankers in charge of the 2009 Great Recession to avoid repeating the mistakes of the last systemic banking crisis. Thus, the insights of the Great Economists, which have been gleaned from over two centuries of studying the world's economic problems, can help us shape the future of globalization and confront today's challenges.

Although they were very different characters, and sometimes disagreed fiercely about how the economy works, the Great Economists were similar in a number of respects. The key one is that they formulated general models to tackle the biggest economic challenges. That is why their thinking remains relevant today. The legacy of their lives and work demonstrates that ideas have always had a lasting impact on society – both then and now.

Acknowledgements

I am hugely indebted to Graeme Chamberlin for his steadfast support of this project. His many contributions to the book, including numerous insightful additions, based on his impressive economic knowledge, were invaluable.

I am also extremely grateful to Martin Slater. His encyclopaedic knowledge of economics, and of economists, added so much to the book. He injected colour and helpful historical context, which were greatly appreciated.

This book would not have been possible without the support and encouragement of my brilliant publisher, Daniel Crewe, at Viking. His insightful edits and keen interest have improved the text and he has been a delight to work with throughout. I feel lucky that he came up with the idea for this book that suits my interests so well.

Another key person is my agent, Will Francis, of Janklow and Nesbit UK. He is, simply put, terrific in every respect. I am very fortunate to have him in my corner as a long-standing supporter.

I would like to thank my US publisher, Pronoy Sarkar, at Picador, an imprint of Macmillan. His enthusiasm for this book is infectious! I feel fortunate to have his support and encouragement.

I would also like to acknowledge the many wonderful journalists with whom I have worked over the years. Their dedication to telling stories of relevance to people's lives made it possible for me to present a wide variety of TV and radio programmes that cover some of the most important economic and business issues of our time. I am delighted to include some of those adventures here.

A special thanks goes to Hannah Ludbrook for her enthusiastic promotion of my book, and to Connor Brown for all of his help throughout the enjoyable process. I also appreciate all of the work of Sarah Scarlett at Penguin Random House, who has looked after the international rights so well. And I thank Trevor Horwood for his diligent copy-editing of the manuscript, as well as Dave Cradduck for his thoughtful compilation of the index. Indeed, a huge thanks goes out to the helpful Ellie Smith and the entire team at Viking/ Penguin Random House for their energetic support of this book.

The contributions of my students, colleagues and members of the public are also evident throughout this work, since they have helped me identify the economic issues that matter most. Our interactions in the classroom, at conferences and in public forums have left an indelible imprint on me as to how economics affects our lives. I am immensely grateful to have had so many opportunities to hear and discuss the impact of economic policies.

Finally, I would like to thank all of you – the readers of this book – for being interested in the big economic challenges of our time. It is only through your engagement that we can go about crafting a better economic future for us all.

Glossary

BRIC economies The acronym stands for Brazil, Russia, India and China, a term coined by investment bank Goldman Sachs to identify the large emerging markets with good growth potential.

current account deficit/surplus The difference between the value of traded goods and services, and portfolio capital, flowing into and out of the country.

first-generation currency crisis The Latin American crisis of 1981–82.

forward guidance Central banks giving guidance as to where interest rates might be in the future.

G7 A group comprising seven of the world's major economies – Canada, France, Germany, Italy, Japan, the United Kingdom and the United States – formed with the intention of shaping global economic policy.

global financial crisis The failure of many of the world's leading financial institutions precipitated in 2008 by the collapse of the US sub-prime mortgage market.

gold standard Exchange rate system operational in the nineteenth and early twentieth centuries in which participating countries fixed their currencies to be exchanged for a specified amount of gold.

Great Crash The collapse of the US stock market in October 1929. Also known as the Wall Street Crash.

Great Depression The worldwide economic downturn that followed the *Great Crash* and lasted for most of the 1930s.

Great Recession The recession that followed the *global financial crisis* in 2009.

IMF (International Monetary Fund) A Bretton Woods institution focused on global economic stability.

inclusive growth Economic growth that benefits everyone in a society.

laissez-faire Literally 'let (people) do'. Used to describe a policy of non-intervention by the state or government.

Long Depression The global recession that occurred during the last quarter of the nineteenth century.

macroprudential policy Central bank regulations aiming for financial stability.

median income The level of income of the person at the midpoint of the distribution.

monopoly A firm that has market power in the product market.

monopsony A firm that has market power in the labour market.

OECD (Organisation for Economic Co-operation and Development) A think-tank for advanced economies, based in Paris.

negative interest rates Central banks charging commercial banks for depositing money with them.

purchasing power parity (PPP) A theory of exchange rate determination, which argues that the exchange rate will change so that the price of a particular good or service will be the same regardless of where you buy it.

quantitative easing (QE) Cash injections into the economy by a central bank.

Ricardian equivalence David Ricardo's theory that rational people know that the government debt will have to be repaid at some point in the form of higher taxes so they save in anticipation and do not increase current consumption that boosts growth.

second-generation currency crisis The collapse of the European exchange rate mechanism (ERM) in 1992.

STEM Science, technology, engineering and mathematics.

third-generation financial and currency crisis The Asian financial crisis of 1997–98.

Wall Street Crash See *Great Crash*.

World Bank A Bretton Woods institution focused on alleviating poverty.

WTO (World Trade Organization) An intergovernmental organization formed in 1995 that regulates international trade, which was preceded by the General Agreement on Tariffs and Trade (GATT), in force since 1947.

Bibliography

Acemoglu, Daron and James A. Robinson, 2012, *Why Nations Fail: The Origins of Power, Prosperity, and Poverty*, London: Profile Books

Agénor, Pierre-Richard, Otaviano Canuto and Michael Jelenic, 2012, 'Avoiding Middle-Income Growth Traps', *Economic Premise*, 98, World Bank, Washington, DC

Allen, Robert Loring, 1993, *Irving Fisher: A Biography*, Cambridge, MA and Oxford: Blackwell

Aslanbeigui, Nahid and Guy Oakes, 2009, *The Provocative Joan Robinson: The Making of a Cambridge Economist*, Durham, NC: Duke University Press

Bagehot, Walter, 1895, 'Ricardo', in Walter Bagehot, *Economic Studies*, ed. Richard Holt Hutton, London: Longmans, Green & Co., pp. 197–208

Barnett, Alina, Sandra Batten, Adrian Chiu, Jeremy Franklin and María Sebastiá-Barriel, 2014, 'The UK Productivity Puzzle', *Bank of England Quarterly Bulletin*, Q2, pp. 114–28

Behrens, Kristian, Giordano Mion, Yasusada Murata and Jens Südekum, 2014, 'Trade, Wages, and Productivity', *International Economic Review*, 55(4), pp. 1305–48

Bernanke, Ben, 1983, 'Nonmonetary Effects of the Financial Crisis in the Propagation of the Great Depression', *American Economic Review*, 73(3), pp. 257–76

———, 2002, 'Deflation: Making Sure "It" Doesn't Happen Here', remarks by Governor Ben S. Bernanke before the National Economists Club, Washington, DC, 21 November; www.federalreserve.gov/boarddocs/speeches/2002/20021121/

Blaug, Mark, 1956, 'The Empirical Content of Ricardian Economics', *Journal of Political Economy*, 64(1), pp. 41–58

———, 1985, *Economic Theory in Retrospect*, Cambridge: Cambridge University Press

Buchholz, Todd, 2007, *New Ideas from Dead Economists: An Introduction to Modern Economic Thought*, New York: Penguin

Burns, J. H. and H. L. A. Hart, eds., 1977, *A Comment on the Commentaries and A Fragment on Government*, The Collected Works of Jeremy Bentham, Oxford: Clarendon Press

Cairncross, Alec, 1993, *Austin Robinson: The Life of an Economic Adviser*, Basingstoke: Palgrave Macmillan

Caldwell, Bruce, 1998, 'Why Didn't Hayek Review Keynes's *General Theory*?', *History of Political Economy*, 30(4), pp. 545–69

———, 2004, *Hayek's Challenge: An Intellectual Biography of F. A. Hayek*, Chicago: University of Chicago Press

Campbell, John, 2008, *Margaret Thatcher*, vol. II: *The Iron Lady*. London: Vintage

Chamberlin, Graeme and Linda Yueh, 2006, *Macroeconomics*, London: Cengage

Churchill, Winston, 1974, 'Speech, House of Commons, November 11, 1947', in *Winston S. Churchill: His Complete Speeches, 1897–1963*, ed. Robert Rhodes James, vol. VII, London: R. R. Bowker, p. 7566

Clement, Douglas, 2002, 'Interview with Robert Solow', *The Region*, Federal Reserve Bank of Minneapolis, 1 September; www.minneapolisfed.org/publications/the-region/interview-with-robert-solow

Colander, David C. and Harry Landreth, 1996, *The Coming of Keynesianism to America: Conversations with the Founders of Keynesian Economics*, Cheltenham: Edward Elgar

Collier, Paul, 2007, *The Bottom Billion: Why the Poorest Countries are Failing and What Can Be Done About It*, Oxford: Oxford University Press

Cooper, Douglas P., 1973, 'Dr. Paul Samuelson', *The Douglas P. Cooper Distinguished Contemporaries Collection*, 1 September; www.wnyc.org/story/paul-samuelson/

Crafts, Nicholas, 2005, 'The First Industrial Revolution: Resolving the Slow Growth/Rapid Industrialization Paradox', *Journal of the European Economic Association*, 3(2/3), pp. 525–34

David, Paul A., 1990, 'The Dynamo and the Computer: A Historical Perspective on the Modern Productivity Paradox', *American Economic Review*, 80(2), pp. 355–61

De Vecchi, Nicolò, 2006, 'Hayek and the *General Theory*', *European Journal of the History of Economic Thought*, 13(2), pp. 233–58

Dworkin, Ronald W., 2015, *How Karl Marx Can Save American Capitalism*, Lanham, MD: Lexington Books

Ebenstein, Alan, 2001, *Friedrich Hayek: A Biography*, New York: St. Martin's Press

Ebenstein, Lanny, 2007, *Milton Friedman: A Biography*, New York: Palgrave Macmillan

Fisher, Irving, 1892, 'Mathematical Investigations in the Theory of Value and Prices', *Transactions of the Connecticut Academy*, 9, p. 119

———, 1919, 'Economists in Public Service: Annual Address of the President', *American Economic Review*, 9(1), Supplement: Papers and Proceedings of the

Thirty-First Annual Meeting of the American Economic Association, pp. 5–21

———, 1930, *The Stock Market Crash – and After*, New York: The Macmillan Company

———, 1933, 'The Debt-Deflation Theory of Great Depressions', *Econometrica*, 1(4), pp. 337–57

———, 1997, *The Works of Irving Fisher*, 14 volumes, ed. William J. Barber, assisted by Robert W. Dimand and Kevin Foster, London: Pickering & Chatto

Fisher, Irving and H. Bruce Brougham, 1928, *Prohibition Still at its Worst*, New York: Alcohol Information Committee

Fisher, Irving Norton, 1956, *My Father: Irving Fisher*, New York: Comet Press Books

Fitzgibbons, Athol, 1988, *Keynes's Vision: A New Political Economy*, Oxford: Oxford University Press

Flatau, Paul, 2001, 'Some Reflections on the "Pigou-Robinson" Theory of Exploitation', *History of Economics Review*, 33, pp. 1–16

Foster, Richard, 2012, 'Creative Destruction Whips Through Corporate America', *Innosight Executive Briefing*; www.innosight.com/wp-content/uploads/2016/08/creative-destruction-whips-through-corporate-america-final2015.pdf

Friedman, Milton, 1963, *Inflation: Causes and Consequences*, Bombay: Asia Publishing House

———, 1991, 'Economic Freedom, Human Freedom, Political Freedom', address by Milton Friedman, The Smith Center, Seattle Central College, 1 November; http://seattlecentral.edu/faculty/jhubert/friedmanspeech.html

———, 1999, 'Transcript for: Friedrich Hayek', Think Tank with Ben Wattenberg, pbs.org; www.pbs.org/thinktank/transcript726.html

———, 2002 [1962], *Capitalism and Freedom: Fortieth Anniversary Edition*, Chicago: University of Chicago Press

———, 2012, 'Milton Friedman in His Own Words', Becker Friedman Institute for Research in Economics, University of Chicago; https://bfi.uchicago.edu/news/post/milton-friedman-his-own-words

Friedman, Milton and Rose Friedman, 1980, *Free to Choose*, San Diego: Harcourt

———, 1998, *Two Lucky People: Memoirs*, Chicago: University of Chicago Press

Friedman, Milton and Anna Jacobson Schwartz, 1971 [1963], *A Monetary History of the United States, 1867–1960*, Princeton: Princeton University Press

Goodridge, Peter, Jonathan Haskel and Gavin Wallis, 2013, 'Can Intangible Investment Explain the UK Productivity Puzzle?', *National Institute Economic Review*, 224, pp. R48–R58

Groenewegen, Peter, 1995, *A Soaring Eagle: Alfred Marshall 1842–1924*, Aldershot: Edward Elgar

Hansen, Alvin H., 1939, 'Economic Progress and Declining Population Growth', *American Economic Review*, 29(1), pt I, pp. 1–15

Hausmann, Ricardo and Federico Sturzenegger, 2007, 'The Missing Dark Matter in the *Wealth of Nations* and Its Implications for Global Imbalances', *Economic Policy*, 22(51), pp. 470–518

Hayek, Friedrich A., 1979, *A Conversation with Friedrich A. von Hayek: Science and Socialism,* Washington, DC: American Enterprise Institute for Public Policy Research

———, 1986, 'The Moral Imperative of the Market', in *The Unfinished Agenda: Essays on the Political Economy of Government Policy in Honour of Arthur Seldon*, London: Institute of Economic Affairs

———, 1994, *Hayek on Hayek: An Autobiographical Dialogue*, ed. Stephen Kresge and Leif Wenar, Chicago: University of Chicago Press

———, 2001 [1944], *The Road to Serfdom*, London and New York: Routledge Classics

———, 2006 [1960], *The Constitution of Liberty*, London and New York: Routledge

International Labour Organization, 2014, *Global Wage Report 2014/15*, Geneva: International Labour Office

———, 2016, *Global Wage Report 2016/17*, Geneva: International Labour Office

International Labour Organization and Organisation for Economic Co-operation and Development, with contributions from the International Monetary Fund and World Bank Group, 2015, 'The Labour Share in G20 Economies', report prepared for the G20 Employment Working Group, Antalya, Turkey, 26–27 February

Jörberg, Lennart, 1997, 'Robert W. Fogel and Douglass C. North', in *Nobel Lectures in Economic Sciences, 1991–1995*, ed. Torsten Persson, Singapore: World Scientific, pp. 61–126

Keynes, John Maynard, 1924, 'Alfred Marshall, 1842–1924', *Economic Journal*, 34(135), pp. 311–72

———, 1931, 'The Pure Theory of Money: A Reply to Dr Hayek', *Economica*, 34, pp. 387–97

———, 1936, *The General Theory of Employment, Interest and Money*, London: Palgrave Macmillan

———, 1937, 'The General Theory of Employment', *Quarterly Journal of Economics*, 51(2), pp. 209–23

———, 1963 [1931], 'Economic Possibilities for Our Grandchildren', in *Essays in Persuasion*, New York: W. W. Norton

———, 1971–89, *The Collected Writings of John Maynard Keynes*, 30 vols., ed. Elizabeth Johnson and Donald Moggridge, Cambridge: Cambridge University Press

King, John E., 2013, *David Ricardo*, Basingstoke: Palgrave Macmillan

Krugman, Paul, 1998, 'The Hangover Theory', *Slate*, 4 December; www. slate.com/articles/business/the_dismal_science/1998/12/the_hangover_ theory.html

Lucas, Robert E., Jr., 1988, 'On the Mechanics of Economic Development', *Journal of Monetary Economics*, 22(1), pp. 3–42

Marshall, Alfred, 1890, *Principles of Economics*, vol. I, London: Macmillan

———, 1961, *Principles of Economics*, vol. II, London: Macmillan for the Royal Economic Society

Marx, Karl, 1978 [1853], 'The Future Results of British Rule in India', *New York Daily Tribune*, 8 August 1853, in Robert Tucker, ed., 1978, *The Marx-Engels Reader*, 2nd revised edn, New York: W. W. Norton

———, 1990–92 [1881–83], *Capital*, ed. Frederick Engels, trans. Ben Fowkes (vol. I) and David Fernbach (vols. II and III), London: Penguin Classics

———, 2008 [1852], *The Eighteenth Brumaire of Louis Bonaparte*, Rockville, MD: Wildside Press

Marx, Karl and Friedrich Engels, 2015 [1848], *The Communist Manifesto*, London: Penguin Classics

McCraw, Thomas K., 2007, *Prophet of Innovation: Joseph Schumpeter and Creative Destruction*, Cambridge, MA: Harvard University Press

McCulla, Stephanie H., Alyssa E. Holdren and Shelly Smith, 2013, 'Improved Estimates of the National Income and Product Accounts: Results of the 2013 Comprehensive Revision', US Bureau of Economic Analysis, Washington, DC

Milanovic, Branko, 2016, *Global Inequality: A New Approach for the Age of Globalization*, Cambridge, MA: Harvard University Press

Milgate, Murray and Shannon Stimson, 1991, *Ricardian Politics*, Princeton: Princeton University Press

Mill, John Stuart, 1848, *Principles of Political Economy*, London: John W. Parker

Minsky, Hyman P., 1992, 'The Financial Instability Hypothesis', The Jerome Levy Economics Institute of Bard College, Working Paper No. 74

Mitchell, Brian R., 1988, *Abstract of British Historical Statistics*, Cambridge: Cambridge University Press

Muro, Mark, Jonathan Rothwell, Scott Andes, Kenan Fikri and Siddharth Kulkarni, 2015, 'America's Advanced Industries', Brookings Institution,

Washington, DC; www.brookings.edu/wp-content/uploads/2015/02/AdvancedIndustry_FinalFeb2lores-1.pdf

Nasar, Sylvia, 2011, *Grand Pursuit: The Story of the People Who Made Modern Economics*, New York: Simon & Schuster

Newcomb, Simon, 1885, *Principles of Political Economy*, New York: Harper

Nobelprize.org, 1974, 'Friedrich August von Hayek – Banquet Speech', Nobel Media AB 2014; www.nobelprize.org/nobel_prizes/economic-sciences/laureates/1974/hayek-speech.html

———, 1987, 'Robert M. Solow – Biographical', Nobel Media AB 2014; www.nobelprize.org/nobel_prizes/economic-sciences/laureates/1987/solow-bio.html

———, 1987, 'Robert M. Solow – Prize Lecture: Growth Theory and After', Nobel Media AB 2014; www.nobelprize.org/nobel_prizes/economic-sciences/laureates/1987/solow-lecture.html

———, 1993, 'Douglass C. North – Biographical', Nobel Media AB 2014; www.nobelprize.org/nobel_prizes/economic-sciences/laureates/1993/north-bio.html

North, Douglass C., 1988, 'Institutions, Economic Growth and Freedom', in *Freedom, Democracy, and Economic Welfare: Proceedings of an International Symposium*, ed. Michael A. Walker, Vancouver: Fraser Institute

———, 1990, *Institutions, Institutional Change and Economic Performance*, Cambridge: Cambridge University Press

North, Douglass C., Gardner Brown and Dean Lueck, 2015, 'A Conversation with Douglass North', *Annual Review of Resource Economics*, 7, pp. 1–10

OECD, 2012, 'Income Inequality and Growth: The Role of Taxes and Transfers', OECD Economics Department Policy Notes, No. 9

———, 2013, 'New Sources of Growth: Intangible Assets', Paris: OECD; www.oecd.org/sti/inno/46349020.pdf

———, 2015, *Economic Surveys: United Kingdom*, Paris: OECD

Ostry, Jonathan D., Andrew Berg and Charalambos G. Tsangarides, 2014, 'Redistribution, Inequality, and Growth', International Monetary Fund Staff Discussion Note SDN/14/02; www.imf.org/external/pubs/ft/sdn/2014/sdn1402.pdf

Parsons, Talcott, 1931, 'Wants and Activities in Marshall', *Quarterly Journal of Economics*, 46(1), pp. 101–40

Pessoa, João Paulo and John Van Reenen, 2013, 'Decoupling of Wage Growth and Productivity Growth? Myth and Reality', Centre for Economic Performance, London School of Economics and Political Science Discussion Paper No. 1246; http://cep.lse.ac.uk/pubs/download/dp1246.pdf

Pigou, A. C., 1953, *Alfred Marshall and Current Thought*, London: Macmillan

Pigou, A. C., ed., 1925, *Memorials of Alfred Marshall*, London: Macmillan

Piketty, Thomas, 2014, *Capital in the Twenty-First Century*, Cambridge, MA: Harvard University Press

Ranelagh, John, 1991, *Thatcher's People: An Insider's Account of the Politics, the Power and the Personalities*, London: HarperCollins

Reagan, Ronald, 1986, 'The President's News Conference', 12 August; www.presidency.ucsb.edu/ws/?pid=37733

———, 1986, 'Remarks to State Chairpersons of the National White House Conference on Small Business', 15 August; www.reaganlibrary.gov/archives/speeches/1986/081586e.html

Reich, Robert, 2012, *Beyond Outrage: What Has Gone Wrong with Our Economy and Our Democracy, and How to Fix It*, New York: Vintage Books

Ricardo, David, 2011 [1817], *On the Principles of Political Economy and Taxation*, London: John Murray

Robinson, Joan, 1932, *Economics is a Serious Subject: The Apologia of an Economist to the Mathematician, the Scientist and the Plain Man*, Cambridge: Heffer

———, 1962, *Economic Philosophy*, Harmondsworth: Pelican Books

———, 1969 [1933], *The Economics of Imperfect Competition*, London: Palgrave Macmillan

———, 1974, *Reflections on the Theory of International Trade: Lectures Given in the University of Manchester*, Manchester: Manchester University Press

———, 1980, 'Marx, Marshall, and Keynes', *Collected Economic Papers*, vols. II–V, Cambridge, MA: MIT Press

Ross, Ian Simpson, 2010, *The Life of Adam Smith*, 2nd edn, Oxford: Oxford University Press

Samuelson, Paul A., 1969, 'The Way of an Economist', in *International Economic Relations*, ed. Paul A. Samuelson, International Economic Association Series, London: Macmillan, pp. 1–11

———, 1977, 'Joseph A. Schumpeter', *Dictionary of American Biography*, New York: Scribner

———, 1986, 'Gold and Common Stocks', in *The Collected Scientific Papers of Paul Samuelson*, vol. V, ed. Kate Crowley, Cambridge, MA: MIT Press

———, 2005, *On Being an Economist*, New York: Jorge Pinto Books Inc.

Schumpeter, Joseph, 1928, 'The Instability of Capitalism', *Economic Journal*, 38, pp. 361–86

———, 1934, *The Theory of Economic Development*, Cambridge, MA: Harvard University Press

———, 1939, *Business Cycles: A Theoretical, Historical and Statistical Analysis of the Capitalist Process*, 2 vols., New York: McGraw-Hill

———, 1942, *Capitalism, Socialism and Democracy*, New York: Harper & Brothers

————, 1951, *Ten Great Economists from Marx to Keynes*, New York and Oxford: Oxford University Press

————, 1954, *History of Economic Analysis*, New York: Oxford University Press

————, 1955, 'Social Classes in an Ethnically Homogeneous Environment', trans. Heinz Norden, in *Imperialism, Social Classes: Two Essays by Joseph Schumpeter*, New York: Meridian Books

————, 1991 [1918], 'The Crisis of the Tax State', in *The Economics and Sociology of Capitalism*, ed. Richard Swedberg, Princeton: Princeton University Press

————, 1997 [1954], *History of Economic Analysis*, London: Routledge

Shove, Gerald F., 1942, 'The Place of Marshall's *Principles* in the Development of Economic Theory', *Economic Journal*, 52(208), pp. 294–329

Skidelsky, Robert, 1995, *John Maynard Keynes*, vol. II: *The Economist as Saviour, 1920–1937*, London: Penguin

————, 2003, *John Maynard Keynes 1883–1946: Economist, Philosopher, Statesman*, New York: Penguin

————, 2010, *Keynes: The Return of the Master*, London: Penguin

Skousen, Mark, 2001, *The Making of Modern Economics*, Armonk, NY and London: M. E. Sharpe

Smith, Adam, 1759, *The Theory of Moral Sentiments*, London: A. Millar; Edinburgh: A. Kincaid & J. Bell

————, 1978 [1763], *Lectures on Jurisprudence* (alternative title for the *Lectures on Justice, Police, Revenue and Arms*), ed. Ronald E. Meek, David D. Raphael and Peter G. Stein, Oxford: Clarendon Press

————, 1979 [1776], *An Inquiry into the Nature and Causes of the Wealth of Nations by Adam Smith*, eds. R. H. Campbell, A. S. Skinner and W. B. Todd, Oxford: Clarendon Press

Solow, Robert, 1956, 'A Contribution to the Theory of Economic Growth', *Quarterly Journal of Economics*, 70(1), pp. 65–94

————, 1957, 'Technical Change and the Aggregate Production Function', *Review of Economics and Statistics*, 39(3), pp. 312–20

Sperber, Jonathan, 2013, *Karl Marx: A Nineteenth-Century Life*, New York: Liveright

Stewart, Dugald, 1793, 'Account of the Life and Writings of Adam Smith', read to the Royal Society of Edinburgh and published in Adam Smith's posthumous *Essays on Philosophical Subjects* of 1795, London and Edinburgh: T. Cadell Jun and W. Davies

Stiglitz, Joseph, 2012, *The Price of Inequality: How Today's Divided Society Endangers Our Future*, New York: W. W. Norton

Sutter, Robert G., 2013, *Foreign Relations of the PRC: The Legacies and Constraints of China's International Politics Since 1949*, Lanham, MD: Rowman & Littlefield

Taylor, John B., 1993, 'Discretion Versus Policy Rules in Practice', *Carnegie-Rochester Conference Series on Public Policy*, 39, pp. 195–214

———, 1999, 'A Historical Analysis of Monetary Policy Rules', in *Monetary Policy Rules*, ed. John B. Taylor, Chicago: University of Chicago Press, pp. 319–48

———, 2009, 'The Need to Return to a Monetary Framework', *Business Economics*, 44(2), pp. 63–72

———, 2012, 'Why We Still Need to Read Hayek', The Hayek Lecture, The Manhattan Institute for Policy Research, New York City; www. hoover.org/sites/default/files/hayek-lecture.pdf

Thatcher, Margaret, 1993, *The Downing Street Years*, London: HarperPress

Thompson, Derek, 2009, 'An Interview with Paul Samuelson, Part One', *The Atlantic*, 17 June; www.theatlantic.com/business/archive/2009/06/an-interview-with-paul-samuelson-part-one/19586/

Turner, Michael J., 1994, 'Before the Manchester School: Economic Theory in Early Nineteenth-Century Manchester', *History*, 79(256), pp. 216–41

Wapshott, Nicholas, 2011, *Keynes Hayek: The Clash That Defined Modern Economics*, New York: W. W. Norton

Wood, John Cunningham, ed., 1993, *Alfred Marshall: Critical Assessments, Volume IV*, London: Routledge

World Bank, 1993, *The East Asian Miracle: Economic Growth and Public Policy*, Washington, DC: World Bank

World Bank and Development Research Center of the State Council of China, 2013, 'China 2030: Building a Modern, Harmonious, and Creative Society', Washington, DC; http://documents.worldbank.org/curated/en/781101468239669951/China-2030-building-a-modern-harmonious-and-creative-society

Yellen, Janet, 2009, 'A Minsky Meltdown: Lessons for Central Bankers', presentation to the 18th Annual Hyman P. Minsky Conference on the State of the US and World Economies – 'Meeting the Challenges of the Financial Crisis'; www.frbsf.org/our-district/press/presidents-speeches/yellen-speeches/2009/april/yellen-minsky-meltdown-central-bankers/

Yergin, Daniel and Joseph Stanislaw, 1998, *The Commanding Heights: The Battle Between Government and the Marketplace that is Remaking the Modern World*, New York: Free Press

Yueh, Linda, 2010, *The Economy of China*, Cheltenham: Edward Elgar

———, 2011, *Enterprising China: Business, Economic, and Legal Developments Since 1979*, Oxford: Oxford University Press

———, 2013, *China's Economic Growth: The Making of an Economic Superpower*, Oxford: Oxford University Press

Notes

Introduction: Great Economists on Our Economic Challenges

1. Adam Smith, 1979 [1776], *An Inquiry into the Nature and Causes of the Wealth of Nations*, eds. R. H. Campbell, A. S. Skinner and W. B. Todd, Oxford: Clarendon Press, bk II, ch. 3, para 2.
2. Alvin H. Hansen, 1939, 'Economic Progress and Declining Population Growth', *American Economic Review*, 29(1), pt I, pp. 1–15.

1 – Adam Smith: Should the Government Rebalance the Economy?

1. Adam Smith, 1979 [1776], *An Inquiry into the Nature and Causes of the Wealth of Nations*, ed. R. H. Campbell, A. S. Skinner and W. B. Todd, Oxford: Clarendon Press, bk IV, ch. 2, para. 10.
2. Ibid., bk V, ch. 2, pt II, appendix to arts. I & II, para. 12.
3. Ibid., bk V, ch. 1, pt III, art. II, para. 15.
4. Ibid., bk V, ch. 1, pt III, art. II, para. 8.
5. Dugald Stewart, 1793, 'Account of the Life and Writings of Adam Smith, LL. D.', read to the Royal Society of Edinburgh and published in Adam Smith's posthumous *Essays on Philosophical Subjects* of 1795, London and Edinburgh: T. Cadell Jun and W. Davies, pp. lxxx, lxxxi.
6. Ian Simpson Ross, 2010, *The Life of Adam Smith*, 2nd edn, Oxford: Oxford University Press, p. xxxi.
7. Smith, *Wealth of Nations*, bk V, ch. 3, para. 92.
8. Ross, *Life of Adam Smith*, p. xxxi.
9. Brian R. Mitchell, 1988, *Abstract of British Historical Statistics*, Cambridge: Cambridge University Press, pp. 869–73.

10. Stephanie H. McCulla, Alyssa E. Holdren and Shelly Smith, 2013, 'Improved Estimates of the National Income and Product Accounts: Results of the 2013 Comprehensive Revision', US Bureau of Economic Analysis, Washington, DC

11. OECD, 2013, 'New Sources of Growth: Intangible Assets', Paris: OECD; www.oecd.org/sti/inno/46349020.pdf

12. Adam Smith, 1978 [1763], *Lectures on Jurisprudence* (alternative title for the *Lectures on Justice, Police, Revenue and Arms*), ed. Ronald E. Meek, David D. Raphael and Peter G. Stein, Oxford: Clarendon Press, p. 499.

13. Smith, *Wealth of Nations*, bk I, ch. 2, para. 12.

14. Adam Smith, 1759, *The Theory of Moral Sentiments*, London: A. Millar; Edinburgh: A. Kincaid and J. Bell, pt IV, s. 1, para. 10.

15. Ibid.

16. Smith, *Wealth of Nations*, bk IV, ch. 2, para. 9.

17. Ibid., bk II, ch. 2, para. 106.

18. Ibid., bk II, ch. 4, paras. 14–15.

19. Ibid., bk I, ch. 11, pt 1, para. 5.

20. Ibid., bk V, ch. 1, pt 3, art. II, para. 50.

21. Ibid., bk V, ch. 1, pt 3, art. III, para. 14.

22. Ibid., bk IV, ch. 7, pt 2, para. 44.

23. Smith, *Lectures on Jurisprudence*, p. 514.

24. Ibid., bk V, ch. 3, para. 92.; Ross, *Life of Adam Smith*, p. 315.

25. Ross, *Life of Adam Smith*, p. 302.

26. Smith, *Wealth of Nations*, bk IV, ch. 5, Digression concerning the Corn Trade and Corn Laws, para. 43.

2 – David Ricardo: Do Trade Deficits Matter?

1. John E. King, 2013, *David Ricardo*, Basingstoke: Macmillan, p. 5.

2. Ibid., pp. 15–16.

3. Thomas Piketty, 2014, *Capital in the Twenty-First Century*, Cambridge, MA: Harvard University Press, pp. 314–15.

4. Nicholas Crafts, 2005, 'The First Industrial Revolution: Resolving the Slow Growth/Rapid Industrialization Paradox', *Journal of the European Economic Association*, 3(2/3), pp. 525–34.

5. David Ricardo, 2011 [1817], *The Works and Correspondence of David Ricardo*, vol. IV, ed. Piero Sraffa, Cambridge: Cambridge University Press, p. 21.

6. Murray Milgate and Shannon Stimson, 1991, *Ricardian Politics*, Princeton: Princeton University Press, p. 144.

7. King, *David Ricardo*, p. 36.

8. Mark Blaug, 1956, 'The Empirical Content of Ricardian Economics', *Journal of Political Economy*, 64(1), pp. 41–58.

9. Walter Bagehot, 1895, 'Ricardo', in Walter Bagehot, *Economic Studies*, ed. Richard Holt Hutton, London: Longman, Green & Co., pp. 197–208.

10. Mark Blaug, 1985, *Economic Theory in Retrospect*, Cambridge: Cambridge University Press, p. 136.

11. Joseph Schumpeter, 1997 [1954], *History of Economic Analysis*, London: Routledge, pp. 472–3.

12. Adam Smith, 1979 [1776], *An Inquiry into the Nature and Causes of the Wealth of Nations*, eds. R. H. Campbell, A. S. Skinner and W. B. Todd, Oxford: Clarendon Press, bk IV, ch. 2, para 12.

13. Ricardo, *Works and Correspondence*, IV, p. 23.

14. Ibid., p. 21.

15. King, *David Ricardo*, p. 88.

16. Ricardo, *Works and Correspondence*, IV, pp. 28, 32.

17. Ibid., p. 35.

18. Ibid., p. 33.

19. Ibid., p. 41.

20. Ricardo Hausmann and Federico Sturzenegger, 2007, 'The Missing Dark Matter in the *Wealth of Nations* and Its Implications for Global Imbalances', *Economic Policy*, 22(51), pp. 470–518.

21. Mark Muro, Jonathan Rothwell, Scott Andes, Kenan Fikri and Siddharth Kulkarni, 2015, 'America's Advanced Industries', Brookings Institution, Washington, DC; www.brookings.edu/wp-content/uploads/2015/02/AdvancedIndustry_FinalFeb2lores-1.pdf

22. Paul A. Samuelson, 1969, 'The Way of an Economist', in *International Economic Relations*, ed. Paul A. Samuelson, International Economic Association Series, London: Macmillan, pp. 1–11, at p. 9.

23. Joan Robinson, 1974, *Reflections on the Theory of International Trade: Lectures Given in the University of Manchester*, Manchester: Manchester University Press, p. 1.

24. Ibid., pp. 1, 6.

25. Mark Skousen, 2001, *The Making of Modern Economics*, Armonk, NY and London: M. E. Sharpe, p. 18.

26. Smith, *Wealth of Nations*, bk IV, ch. 2, para 43.

27. Skousen, *The Making of Modern Economics*, p. 103.

3 – Karl Marx: Can China Become Rich?

1. Karl Marx and Friedrich Engels, 2015 [1848], *The Communist Manifesto*, London: Penguin Classics, p. 9.

2. Todd Buchholz, 2007, *New Ideas from Dead Economists: An Introduction to Modern Economic Thought*, New York: Penguin, p. 129.

3. Ibid., p. 116.

4. Jonathan Sperber, 2013, *Karl Marx: A Nineteenth-Century Life*, New York: Liveright, p. 4.

5. Ibid., p. 5.

6. Ibid., p. 24.

7. Ibid., p. 72.

8. Ibid., p. 99.

9. Marx and Engels, *Communist Manifesto*, p. 39.

10. Ibid.

11. Sperber, *Karl Marx*, p. 255.

12. Karl Marx, 2008 [1852], *The Eighteenth Brumaire of Louis Bonaparte*, Rockville, MD: Wildside Press, p. 1.

13. Karl Marx, 1978 [1853], 'The Future Results of British Rule in India', *New York Daily Tribune*, 8 August 1853, in Robert Tucker, ed., 1978, *The Marx-Engels Reader*, 2nd revised edn, New York: W. W. Norton, p. 662.

14. Sperber, *Karl Marx*, p. 450.

15. Ibid., p. 431.

16. Linda Yueh, 2013, *China's Growth: The Making of an Economic Super-power*, Oxford: Oxford University Press, chapter 5.

17. World Bank and Development Research Center of the State Council of China, 2013, 'China 2030: Building a Modern, Harmonious, and Creative Society', Washington, DC; http://documents.worldbank.

org/curated/en/781101468239669951/China-2030-building-a-modern-harmonious-and-creative-society

18. Karl Marx, 1991 [1883], *Capital: Volume III*, ed. Frederick Engels, trans. David Fernbach, London: Penguin Classics, p. 678.

19. Marx and Engels, *Communist Manifesto*, p. 27.

20. Robert G. Sutter, 2013, *Foreign Relations of the PRC: The Legacies and Constraints of China's International Politics Since 1949*, Lanham, MD: Rowman & Littlefield, p. 23.

21. Linda Yueh, 2010, *The Economy of China*, Cheltenham: Edward Elgar, chapter 4.

22. Buchholz, *New Ideas from Dead Economists*, p. 136.

23. Ronald W. Dworkin, 2015, *How Karl Marx Can Save American Capitalism*, Lanham, MD: Lexington Books, p. 72.

24. Ibid.

25. Sperber, *Karl Marx*, p. 65.

4 – Alfred Marshall: Is Inequality Inevitable?

1. Joseph Stiglitz, 2012, *The Price of Inequality: How Today's Divided Society Endangers Our Future*, New York: W. W. Norton.

2. Peter Groenewegen, 1995, *A Soaring Eagle: Alfred Marshall 1842–1924*, Aldershot: Edward Elgar, p. 227.

3. Ibid., p. 294.

4. Michael J. Turner, 1994, 'Before the Manchester School: Economic Theory in Early Nineteenth-Century Manchester', *History*, 79(256), pp. 216–41.

5. John Maynard Keynes, 1924, 'Alfred Marshall, 1842–1924', *Economic Journal*, 34(135), pp. 311–72.

6. Gerald F. Shove, 1942, 'The Place of Marshall's *Principles* in the Development of Economic Theory', *Economic Journal*, 52(208), pp. 294–329.

7. A. C. Pigou, ed., 1925, *Memorials of Alfred Marshall*, London: Macmillan, p. 334.

8. Alfred Marshall, 1961, *Principles of Economics*, vol. II, London: Macmillan for the Royal Economic Society, pp. 598–614.

9. J. H. Burns and H. L. A. Hart, eds., 1977, *A Comment on the Commentaries and A Fragment on Government*, *The Collected Works of Jeremy Bentham*, Oxford: Clarendon Press, p. 393.

10. John Cunningham Wood, ed., 1993, *Alfred Marshall: Critical Assessments, Volume IV*, London: Routledge, p. 290.

11. Branko Milanovic, 2016, *Global Inequality: A New Approach for the Age of Globalization*, Cambridge, MA: Harvard University Press, p. 166.

12. Pew Research Center, 2015, 'The American Middle Class is Losing Ground: No Longer the Majority and Falling Behind Financially', 9 December; www.pewsocialtrends.org/2015/12/09/the-american-middle-class-is-losing-ground/

13. Robert Reich, 2012, *Beyond Outrage: What Has Gone Wrong with Our Economy and Our Democracy, and How to Fix It*, New York: Vintage Books, p. 142.

14. OECD, 2012, 'Income Inequality and Growth: The Role of Taxes and Transfers', OECD Economics Department Policy Notes, No. 9, Paris: OECD.

15. Alfred Marshall, 1890, *Principles of Economics*, vol. I, London: Macmillan, pp. 96–7.

16. Talcott Parsons, 1931, 'Wants and Activities in Marshall', *Quarterly Journal of Economics*, 46(1), pp. 101–40, at p. 128, n. 7, citing Alfred Marshall's letter to the editor of *The Times*, 'The Post Office and Private Enterprise', 24 March 1891.

17. John Stuart Mill, 1848, *Principles of Political Economy*, London: John W. Parker, pp. 13–14.

18. Pigou, *Memorials of Alfred Marshall*, p. 363.

19. A. C. Pigou, 1953, *Alfred Marshall and Current Thought*, London: Macmillan, p. 56.

20. Jonathan D. Ostry, Andrew Berg and Charalambos G. Tsangarides, 2014, 'Redistribution, Inequality, and Growth', International Monetary Fund Staff Discussion Note SDN/14/02; www.imf.org/external/pubs/ft/sdn/2014/sdn1402.pdf

21. Groenewegen, *A Soaring Eagle*, p. 737.

22. Pigou, ed., *Memorials of Alfred Marshall*, p. 427.

5 – *Irving Fisher: Are We at Risk of Repeating the 1930s?*

1. 'Fisher Sees Stocks Permanently High', *The New York Times*, 16 October 1929, p. 8.
2. Ibid.
3. Joseph Schumpeter, 1951, *Ten Great Economists from Marx to Keynes*, New York and Oxford: Oxford University Press, p. 223.
4. Irving Fisher, 1892, 'Mathematical Investigations in the Theory of Value and Prices', *Transactions of the Connecticut Academy*, 9, p. 119.
5. Robert Loring Allen, 1993, *Irving Fisher: A Biography*, Cambridge, MA and Oxford: Blackwell, p. 229.
6. Ibid., p. 17.
7. Irving Norton Fisher, 1956, *My Father: Irving Fisher*, New York: Comet Press Books, p. 26.
8. Irving Fisher, 1997, *The Works of Irving Fisher*, 14 vols., ed. William J. Barber, assisted by Robert W. Dimand and Kevin Foster, London: Pickering & Chatto, vol. I, p. 4.
9. Allen, *Irving Fisher*, pp. 147–8.
10. Irving Fisher and H. Bruce Brougham, 1928, *Prohibition Still at its Worst*, New York: Alcohol Information Committee.
11. Irving Fisher, 1919, 'Economists in Public Service: Annual Address of the President', *American Economic Review*, 9(1), Supplement: Papers and Proceedings of the Thirty-First Annual Meeting of the American Economic Association, pp. 5–21, at p. 16.
12. Ibid., p. 10.
13. Simon Newcomb, 1885, *Principles of Political Economy*, New York: Harper, p. 346.
14. Milton Friedman, 1963, *Inflation: Causes and Consequences*, Bombay: Asia Publishing House, p. 17.
15. Irving Fisher, 1933, 'The Debt-Deflation Theory of Great Depressions', *Econometrica*, 1(4), pp. 337–57, at p. 349.
16. Ibid., p. 344.

17. Ben Bernanke, 1983, 'Nonmonetary Effects of the Financial Crisis in the Propagation of the Great Depression', *American Economic Review*, 73(3), pp. 257–76.

18. Ben Bernanke, 2002, 'Deflation: Making Sure "It" Doesn't Happen Here', remarks by Governor Ben S. Bernanke before the National Economists Club, Washington, DC, 21 November; www.federal-reserve.gov/boarddocs/speeches/2002/20021121/

19. Hyman P. Minsky, 1992, 'The Financial Instability Hypothesis', The Jerome Levy Economics Institute of Bard College, Working Paper No. 74.

20. Ibid.

21. 'Minsky's Moment', *The Economist*, 30 July 2016; www.economist.com/news/economics-brief/21702740-second-article-our-series-seminal-eco nomic-ideas-looks-hyman-minskys

22. Janet Yellen, 2009, 'A Minsky Meltdown: Lessons for Central Bankers', presentation to the 18th Annual Hyman P. Minsky Conference on the State of the US and World Economies – 'Meeting the Challenges of the Financial Crisis'; www.frbsf.org/our-district/press/presidents-speeches/yellen-speeches/2009/april/yellen-minsky-meltdown-central-bankers/

23. Ibid.

24. Allen, *Irving Fisher*, p. 9.

6 – *John Maynard Keynes: To Invest or Not to Invest?*

1. John Maynard Keynes, 1936, *The General Theory of Employment, Interest and Money*, London: Palgrave Macmillan, p. 129.

2. Ibid.

3. John Maynard Keynes, 1963 [1931], 'Economic Possibilities for Our Grandchildren', in *Essays in Persuasion*, New York: W. W. Norton, p. 373.

4. John Maynard Keynes, 1971–89, *The Collected Writings of John Maynard Keynes*, 30 vols., ed. Elizabeth Johnson and Donald Moggridge, vol. XII, *Economic Articles and Correspondence: Investment and Editorial*, Cambridge: Cambridge University Press, p. 109.

5. Robert Skidelsky, 2003, *John Maynard Keynes 1883–1946: Economist, Philosopher, Statesman*, New York: Penguin, p. 53.

6. Ibid., p. 53.

7. Ibid., p. 36.

8. Ibid., p. 43.

9. Ibid., p. 45.

10. Ibid., p. 60.

11. Keynes, *General Theory*, p. 5.

12. Todd G. Buchholz, 2007, *New Ideas from Dead Economists: An Introduction to Modern Economic Thought*, New York: Penguin, p. 210.

13. Robert Skidelsky, 2010, *Keynes: The Return of the Master*, London: Penguin, p. 62.

14. Keynes, *General Theory*, p. 103.

15. Ibid., p. 158.

16. Ibid.

17. Keynes, *Collected Writings*, vol. IV: *A Tract on Monetary Reform*, p. 65.

18. Keynes, *Collected Writings*, vol. XXI: *Activities 1931–1939: World Crises and Policies in Britain and America*, p. 390.

19. John Maynard Keynes, 1937, 'The General Theory of Employment', *Quarterly Journal of Economics*, 51(2), pp. 209–23.

20. Ibid., pp. 215–16.

21. Ibid., p. 216.

22. Skidelsky, *Keynes: The Return of the Master*, p. 107.

23. Ronald Reagan, 1986, 'Remarks to State Chairpersons of the National White House Conference on Small Business', 15 August; www.reaganlibrary.archives.gov/archives/speeches/1986/081586e.html

24. Ronald Reagan, 1986, 'The President's News Conference', 12 August; www.presidency.ucsb.edu/ws/?pid=37733

25. Graeme Chamberlin and Linda Yueh, 2006, *Macroeconomics*, London: Cengage, ch. 4.

26. Keynes, *General Theory*, p. 373.

27. Ibid., p. 322.

28. Ibid., pp. 164, 378.

29. Ibid., pp. 383–4.

30. Keynes, *Essays in Persuasion*, p. 366.

31. Ibid., p. 369.

32. Ibid., p. 366.

7 – *Joseph Schumpeter: What Drives Innovation?*

1. Joseph Schumpeter, 1942, *Capitalism, Socialism and Democracy*, New York: Harper & Brothers, p. 84.

2. Thomas K. McCraw, 2007, *Prophet of Innovation: Joseph Schumpeter and Creative Destruction*, Cambridge, MA: Harvard University Press, p. x.

3. Schumpeter, *Capitalism*, p. 83.

4. Joseph Schumpeter, 1939, *Business Cycles: A Theoretical, Historical and Statistical Analysis of the Capitalist Process*, vol. II, New York: McGraw-Hill, p. 1033.

5. Schumpeter, *Business Cycles*, vol. I, p. 107.

6. Schumpeter, *Capitalism*, pp. 67–8.

7. Paul A. Samuelson, 1977, 'Joseph A. Schumpeter', *Dictionary of American Biography*, New York: Scribner, Supplement Four, p. 722.

8. McCraw, *Prophet of Innovation*, p. 40.

9. Joseph Schumpeter, 1954, *History of Economic Analysis*, New York: Oxford University Press, p. 571.

10. McCraw, *Prophet of Innovation*, p. 60.

11. Joseph Schumpeter, 1991 [1918], 'The Crisis of the Tax State', in *The Economics and Sociology of Capitalism*, ed. Richard Swedberg, Princeton: Princeton University Press, pp. 114–16.

12. McCraw, *Prophet of Innovation*, pp. 104–5.

13. Ibid., pp. 117–19.

14. Ibid., p. 165.

15. Ibid., p. 213.

16. Ibid., p. 223.

17. Ibid, p. 225.

18. Ibid.

19. Ibid., p. 271.

20. Nicolò De Vecchi, 2006, 'Hayek and the *General Theory*', *European Journal of the History of Economic Thought*, 13(2), pp. 233–58.

21. Schumpeter, *Business Cycles*, vol. I, p. vi.

22. Schumpeter, *Capitalism*, p. 83.

23. Schumpeter, *Business Cycles*, vol. I, pp. 104–7.

24. Schumpeter, *Capitalism*, pp. 93, 99–100.

25. Ibid., pp. 99–100.
26. Schumpeter, *Business Cycles*, vol. I, pp. 243–4.
27. Ibid., pp. 100–102.
28. Schumpeter, *Capitalism*, pp. 167, 170, 190–91.
29. Ibid., p. xiv.
30. Joseph Schumpeter, 1955, 'Social Classes in an Ethnically Homogeneous Environment', trans. Heinz Norden, in *Imperialism, Social Classes: Two Essays by Joseph Schumpeter*, New York: Meridian Books, pp. 120–22.
31. Joseph Schumpeter, 1928, 'The Instability of Capitalism', *Economic Journal*, 38, pp. 361–86.
32. Schumpeter, *Business Cycles*, vol. I, pp. 103–4.
33. World Bank, 1993, *The East Asian Miracle: Economic Growth and Public Policy*, Washington, DC: World Bank.
34. Schumpeter, 'The Instability of Capitalism', pp. 364–6.
35. Joseph Schumpeter, 1934, *The Theory of Economic Development*, Cambridge, MA: Harvard University Press, pp. 75–8.
36. Schumpeter, *Business Cycles*, vol. I, pp. 102–3.
37. Schumpeter, *Business Cycles*, vol. II, pp. 907–1033.
38. Schumpeter, *Economic Development*, pp. 75–8.
39. Ibid., p. 66.
40. Schumpeter, *Capitalism*, pp. 101–2, 110.
41. Richard Foster, 2012, 'Creative Destruction Whips Through Corporate America', *Innosight Executive Briefing*; https://www.innosight.com/wp-content/uploads/2016/08/creative-destruction-whips-through-corporate-america_final2015.pdf
42. Schumpeter, *History of Economic Analysis*, pp. 19, 27.
43. McCraw, *Prophet of Innovation*, p. 500.

8 – Friedrich Hayek: What Can We Learn from Financial Crises?

1. Milton Friedman, 1999, 'Transcript for: Friedrich Hayek', Think Tank with Ben Wattenberg, pbs.org; www.pbs.org/thinktank/transcript726.html
2. Bruce Caldwell, 2004, *Hayek's Challenge: An Intellectual Biography of F. A. Hayek*, Chicago: University of Chicago Press, p. 2.

3. Friedrich A. Hayek, 1994, *Hayek on Hayek: An Autobiographical Dialogue*, ed. Stephen Kresge and Leif Wenar, Chicago: University of Chicago Press, p. 40.

4. Caldwell, *Hayek's Challenge*, p. 150.

5. Bruce Caldwell, 1998, 'Why Didn't Hayek Review Keynes's *General Theory?*', *History of Political Economy*, 30(4), pp. 545–69, at p. 556.

6. Nicholas Wapshott, 2011, *Keynes Hayek: The Clash That Defined Modern Economics*, New York: W. W. Norton, p. xi.

7. Sylvia Nasar, 2011, *Grand Pursuit: The Story of the People Who Made Modern Economics*, New York: Simon & Schuster, p. 402.

8. Ibid.

9. John Maynard Keynes, 1931, 'The Pure Theory of Money: A Reply to Dr Hayek', *Economica*, 34, pp. 387–97, at p. 394.

10. Paul Krugman, 1998, 'The Hangover Theory', *Slate*, 4 December; www.slate.com/articles/business/the_dismal_science/1998/12/the_hangover_theory.html

11. Alan Ebenstein, 2001, *Friedrich Hayek: A Biography*, New York: St. Martin's Press, p. 81.

12. Athol Fitzgibbons, 1988, *Keynes's Vision: A New Political Economy*, Oxford: Oxford University Press, p. 178.

13. Ebenstein, *Friedrich Hayek*, p. 128.

14. Friedrich A. Hayek, 2001 [1944], *The Road to Serfdom*, London and New York: Routledge Classics, pp. 124–5.

15. Caldwell, *Hayek's Challenge*, p. 133.

16. Friedrich A. Hayek, 2006 [1960], *The Constitution of Liberty*, London and New York: Routledge, p. 44.

17. Ebenstein, *Friedrich Hayek*, pp. 196, 238.

18. Ibid., p. 261.

19. John Ranelagh, 1991, *Thatcher's People: An Insider's Account of the Politics, the Power and the Personalities*, London: HarperCollins, p. ix.

20. Friedrich A. Hayek, 1986, 'The Moral Imperative of the Market', in *The Unfinished Agenda: Essays on the Political Economy of Government Policy in Honour of Arthur Seldon*, London: Institute of Economic Affairs.

21. John B. Taylor, 2009, 'The Need to Return to a Monetary Framework', *Business Economics*, 44(2), pp. 63–72.

22. John B. Taylor, 2012, 'Why We Still Need to Read Hayek', The Hayek Lecture, The Manhattan Institute for Policy Research, New York City, 31 May; www.hoover.org/sites/default/files/hayek-lecture.pdf

23. Winston Churchill, 1974, 'Speech, House of Commons, November 11, 1947', in *Winston S. Churchill: His Complete Speeches, 1897–1963*, ed. Robert Rhodes James, London: R. R. Bowker, vol. VII, p. 7566.

24. Friedrich A. Hayek, 1979, *A Conversation with Friedrich A. von Hayek: Science and Socialism*, Washington, DC: American Enterprise Institute for Public Policy Research, p. 6.

25. Margaret Thatcher, 1993, *The Downing Street Years*, London: Harper-Press, p. 618.

26. John Campbell, 2008, *Margaret Thatcher*, vol. II: *The Iron Lady*, London: Vintage, p. 628.

27. Nobelprize.org, 1974, 'Friedrich August von Hayek – Banquet Speech', Nobel Media AB 2014; www.nobelprize.org/nobel_prizes/economic-sciences/laureates/1974/hayek-speech.html

28. Daniel Yergin and Joseph Stanislaw, 1998, *The Commanding Heights: The Battle Between Government and the Marketplace that is Remaking the Modern World*, New York: Free Press, p. 150.

9 – Joan Robinson: Why Are Wages So Low?

1. 'The Inquiry', presented by Linda Yueh, BBC World Service, 8 March 2016.

2. Nahid Aslanbeigui and Guy Oakes, 2009, *The Provocative Joan Robinson: The Making of a Cambridge Economist*, Durham, NC: Duke University Press, p. 1.

3. 'Prof. Joan Robinson Dies at 79; Cambridge', *The New York Times*, 11 August 1983.

4. Paul Flatau, 2001, 'Some Reflections on the "Pigou-Robinson" Theory of Exploitation', *History of Economics Review*, 33, pp. 1–16.

5. Aslanbeigui and Oakes, *The Provocative Joan Robinson*, pp. 2–3.

6. Joan Robinson, 1932, *Economics is a Serious Subject: The Apologia of an Economist to the Mathematician, the Scientist and the Plain Man*, Cambridge: Heffer, p. 4.

7. Aslanbeigui and Oakes, *The Provocative Joan Robinson*, pp. 48–9.

8. Robert Skidelsky, 1995, *John Maynard Keynes*, vol. II: *The Economist as Saviour, 1920–1937*, London: Penguin, pp. 448–9.

9. Alec Cairncross, 1993, *Austin Robinson: The Life of an Economic Adviser*, Basingstoke: Macmillan, p. 172.

10. Aslanbeigui and Oakes, *The Provocative Joan Robinson*, p. 9.

11. Ibid., p. 133.

12. Joan Robinson, 1962, *Economic Philosophy*, Harmondsworth: Pelican Books, p. 25.

13. Ibid., p. 28.

14. Ibid.

15. Joan Robinson, 1969 [1933], *The Economics of Imperfect Competition*, 2nd edn, London: Macmillan, ch. 18 on monopsony.

16. International Labour Organization, 2014, *Global Wage Report 2014/15*, Geneva: International Labour Office, p. 10.

17. International Labour Organization and Organisation for Economic Co-operation and Development, with contributions from the International Monetary Fund and World Bank Group, 2015, 'The Labour Share in G20 Economies', report prepared for the G20 Employment Working Group, Antalya, Turkey, 26–27 February.

18. Joan Robinson, 1980, 'Marx, Marshall and Keynes', *Collected Economic Papers*, vol. II, Cambridge, MA: MIT Press, p. 17.

19. Robinson, *Economic Philosophy*, p. 45.

10 – Milton Friedman: Are Central Banks Doing Too Much?

1. Milton and Rose Friedman, 1998, *Two Lucky People: Memoirs*, Chicago: University of Chicago Press, p. 22.

2. Ibid., p. 262.

3. Ibid., p. xi.

4. Ibid., p. 165.

5. Lanny Ebenstein, 2007, *Milton Friedman: A Biography*, New York: Palgrave Macmillan, p. 100.

6. Ibid., p. 47.

7. Ibid., p. 52.

8. Milton and Rose Friedman, 1980, *Free to Choose*, San Diego: Harcourt, p. 310.

9. 'Milton Friedman in His Own Words', 2012, Becker Friedman Institute for Research in Economics, University of Chicago; https://bfi. uchicago.edu/news/post/milton-friedman-his-own-words.

10. Ibid.

11. Ibid.

12. Ebenstein, *Milton Friedman*, p. 187.

13. Ben Bernanke, 2002, 'On Milton Friedman's Ninetieth Birthday', Remarks by Governor Ben S. Bernanke: At the Conference to Honor Milton Friedman, University of Chicago, 8 November; www.federalreserve.gov/boarddocs/speeches/2002/20021108/default. htm

14. Milton Friedman, 1997, 'Rx for Japan: Back to the Future', *Wall Street Journal*, 17 December.

15. Ibid.

16. Ibid.

17. Milton Friedman, 1991, 'Economic Freedom, Human Freedom, Political Freedom', address by Milton Friedman, The Smith Center, Seattle Central College, 1 November; http://seattlecentral.edu/faculty/jhubert/friedmanspeech.html

18. Milton Friedman, 2002 [1962], *Capitalism and Freedom: Fortieth Anniversary Edition*, Chicago: University of Chicago Press, p. xii.

19. Ebenstein, *Milton Friedman*, p. 182.

20. 'Milton Friedman in His Own Words'.

11 – Douglass North: Why Are So Few Countries Prosperous?

1. Pierre-Richard Agénor, Otaviano Canuto and Michael Jelenic, 2012, 'Avoiding Middle-Income Growth Traps', *Economic Premise*, 98, Washington, DC, World Bank, p. 1.

2. Douglass C. North, 1988, 'Institutions, Economic Growth and Freedom', in *Freedom, Democracy and Economic Welfare: Proceedings of an*

International Symposium, ed. Michael A. Walker, Vancouver: Fraser Institute, p. 7.

3. Douglass C. North, 1990, *Institutions, Institutional Change and Economic Performance*, Cambridge: Cambridge University Press, p. 6.

4. Ibid., p. 7.

5. Lennart Jörberg, 1997, 'Robert W. Fogel and Douglass C. North', in *Nobel Lectures in Economic Sciences, 1991–1995*, ed. Torsten Persson, Singapore: World Scientific, pp. 107-8.

6. Douglass C. North, Gardner Brown and Dean Lueck, 2015, 'A Conversation with Douglass North', *Annual Review of Resource Economics*, 7, pp. 1–10, at p. 6.

7. Nobelprize.org, 1993, 'Douglass C. North – Biographical', Nobel Media AB 2014; www.nobelprize.org/nobel_prizes/economic-sciences/laureates/1993/north-bio.html

8. Ibid.

9. North, *Institutions, Institutional Change and Economic Performance*, pp. 11, 12.

10. Nobelprize.org, 'Douglass C. North – Biographical'.

11. North, *Institutions, Institutional Change and Economic Performance*, p. vii.

12. Ibid., p. 3.

13. Ibid., p. 5.

14. Ibid., p. 116.

15. Ibid., p. 9.

16. Ibid., p. 139.

17. Ibid., p. 9.

18. Ibid., p. 112.

19. Paul Collier, 2007, *The Bottom Billion: Why the Poorest Countries are Failing and What Can Be Done About It*, Oxford: Oxford University Press.

20. Robert E. Lucas, Jr., 1988, 'On the Mechanics of Economic Development', *Journal of Monetary Economics*, 22(1), pp. 3–42, at p. 5.

21. North, *Institutions, Institutional Change and Economic Performance*, p. 7.

22. Ibid., p. 137.

23. Ibid., p. 6.

24. Ibid., p. 140.

25. North, Brown and Lueck, 'A Conversation with Douglass North', pp. 8, 9.

26. Daron Acemoglu and James A. Robinson, 2012, *Why Nations Fail*, London: Profile Books, pp. 372–3.

27. Ibid., p. 402.

28. Ibid., p. 426.

29. Ibid., p. 427.

30. North, *Institutions, Institutional Change and Economic Performance*, p. 140.

12 – *Robert Solow: Do We Face a Slow-Growth Future?*

1. Nobelprize.org, 1987, 'Robert M. Solow – Biographical', Nobel Media AB 2014; www.nobelprize.org/nobel_prizes/economic-sciences/laureates/1987/solow-bio.html

2. Barnaby J. Feder, 1987, 'Man in the News: Robert Merton Solow; Tackling Everyday Economic Problems', *The New York Times*, 22 October.

3. Ibid.

4. Nobelprize.org, 'Robert M. Solow – Biographical'.

5. Robert Solow, 1956, 'A Contribution to the Theory of Economic Growth', *Quarterly Journal of Economics*, 70(1), pp. 65–94; Robert Solow, 1957, 'Technical Change and the Aggregate Production Function', *Review of Economics and Statistics*, 39(3), pp. 312–20.

6. Paul A. David, 1990, 'The Dynamo and the Computer: A Historical Perspective on the Modern Productivity Paradox', *American Economic Review*, 80(2), pp. 355–61.

7. Douglas Clement, 2002, 'Interview with Robert Solow', *The Region*, Federal Reserve Bank of Minneapolis, 1 September; www.minneapolisfed.org/publications/the-region/interview-with-robert-solow

8. OECD, 2015, *Economic Surveys: United Kingdom*, Paris: OECD.

9. João Paulo Pessoa and John Van Reenen, 2013, 'Decoupling of Wage Growth and Productivity Growth? Myth and Reality', Centre for Economic Performance, London School of Economics and Political Science, Discussion Paper No. 1246; http://cep.lse.ac.uk/pubs/download/dp1246.pdf

10. Alina Barnett, Sandra Batten, Adrian Chiu, Jeremy Franklin and María Sebastiá-Barriel, 2014, 'The UK Productivity Puzzle', *Bank of England Quarterly Bulletin*, Q2, pp. 114–28.

11. Peter Goodridge, Jonathan Haskel and Gavin Wallis, 2013, 'Can Intangible Investment Explain the UK Productivity Puzzle?', *National Institute Economic Review*, 224, pp. R48–R58.

12. Barnett et al., 'The UK Productivity Puzzle'.

13. Kristian Behrens, Giordano Mion, Yasusada Murata and Jens Südekum, 2014, 'Trade, Wages, and Productivity', *International Economic Review*, 55(4), pp. 1305–49.

14. Nobelprize.org, 1987, 'Robert M. Solow – Prize Lecture: Growth Theory and After', Nobel Media AB 2014; www.nobelprize.org/nobel_prizes/economic-sciences/laureates/1987/solow-lecture.html

15. Ibid.

16. Ibid.

17. Ibid.

18. Ibid.

19. Robert Solow, 1989, 'How Economic Ideas Turn to Mush', in *The Spread of Economic Ideas*, eds. David Colander and A. W. Coats, Cambridge: Cambridge University Press, pp. 75–84.

20. Clement, 'Interview with Robert Solow'.

21. Feder, 'Man in the News'.

22. Clement, 'Interview with Robert Solow'.

Epilogue: The Future of Globalization

1. 'Globalization and Rapid Change Sparked Backlash, Says Obama', *Financial Times*, 15 November 2016.

2. Jon Huang, Samuel Jacoby, Michael Strickland and K. K. Rebecca Lai, 2016, 'Election 2016: Exit Polls', *The New York Times*, 8 November; www.nytimes.com/interactive/2016/11/08/us/politics/election-exit-polls.html

3. Derek Thompson, 2009, 'An Interview with Paul Samuelson, Part One', *The Atlantic*, 17 June; www.theatlantic.com/business/archive/2009/06/an-interview-with-paul-samuelson-part-one/19586/

4. John Cassidy, 2009, 'Postscript: Paul Samuelson', *The New Yorker*, 14 December.

5. Thompson, 'An Interview with Paul Samuelson'.

6. David C. Colander and Harry Landreth, 1996, *The Coming of Keynesianism to America: Conversations with the Founders of Keynesian Economics*, Cheltenham: Edward Elgar, p. 28.

7. 'Paul A. Samuelson obituary', *The Economist*, 17 December 2009; www.economist.com/node/15127616

8. Douglas P. Cooper, 1973, The Douglas P. Cooper Distinguished Contemporaries Collection, 1 September; www.wnyc.org/story/paul-samuelson/

9. Paul A. Samuelson, 1986, 'Gold and Common Stocks', in *The Collected Scientific Papers of Paul Samuelson*, vol. V, ed. Kate Crowley, Cambridge, MA: MIT Press, p. 561.

10. Paul A. Samuelson, 2005, *On Being an Economist*, New York: Jorge Pinto Books Inc.

Index

Page references in **bold** refer to a complete chapter devoted to an economist.